Crislayne Alfagali
Blacksmiths of Ilamba

Work in Global and Historical Perspective

Edited by
Andreas Eckert, Sidney Chalhoub, Mahua Sarkar,
Dmitri van den Bersselaar, Christian G. De Vito

Work in Global and Historical Perspective is an interdisciplinary series that welcomes scholarship on work/labor that engages a historical perspective in and from any part of the world. The series advocates a definition of work/labor that is broad, and specially encourages contributions that explore interconnections across political and geographic frontiers, time frames, disciplinary boundaries, as well as conceptual divisions among various forms of commodified work, and between work and 'non-work.'

Volume 15

Crislayne Alfagali

Blacksmiths of Ilamba

A Social History of Labor at the Nova Oeiras
Iron Foundry (Angola, 18th Century)

DE GRUYTER
OLDENBOURG

FAPESP/ Processo: 2022/09295-2

The opinions, hypotheses and conclusions or recommendations expressed in this material are those of the author and do not necessarily reflect the views of FAPESP.

ISBN 978-3-11-162483-9
e-ISBN (PDF) 978-3-11-078815-0
e-ISBN (EPUB) 978-3-11-078828-0
ISSN 2509-8861

Library of Congress Control Number: 2023930402

Bibliographic information published by the Deutsche Nationalbibliothek
The Deutsche Nationalbibliothek lists this publication in the Deutsche Nationalbibliografie; detailed bibliographic data are available on the internet at http://dnb.dnb.de.

© 2024 Walter de Gruyter GmbH, Berlin/Boston
This volume is text- and page-identical with the hardback published in 2023.
First published as: Crislayne Gloss Marão Alfagali. Ferreiros e fundidores da Ilamba. Uma história social da fabricação de ferro e da Real Fábrica de Nova Oeiras (Angola, segunda metade do século XVIII) Luanda: Fundação Dr. Antón, 2018.

Cover image: Notícia da Fábrica do Ferro de Nova Oeiras do Reino de Angola, 1797. Arquivo Histórico do Tribunal de Contas [Portugal] – Erário Régio, 4196, fl. [8].

www.degruyter.com

To Tereza and Edemar,
my parents

To Silvia Lara,
my professor

Acknowledgments

This is one of the hardest parts to write, for there is no space to thank all of those who helped me during these years. The first person I would like to thank is my advisor, Silvia Lara, for her boundless support, her attentive reading, her patience to correct over and over, and her incitement to reflect with shrewd questions. For all of that and more, I owe the merits of this study to Professor Silva.

In all of the institutions I visited, I counted on the generous support of historians and archivists. In Lisbon, I am grateful for the attentive and caring guidance of Professor Luis Frederico Dias Antunes. At the Instituto de Investigação Científica Tropical and at the Arquivo Histórico Ultramarino, I am indebted to all the researchers and employees who taught me how to read the catalogues and patiently searched the many boxes I requested. I am deeply grateful to Carlos Almeida, Carlos Teixeira, Branca, Rosinha, and Mário for the attentiveness with which they received me. At the National Library, I am particularly grateful for Ms. Natália's kindness and Mafalda's and Conceição's friendliness, always offering me hot coffee to keep me warm and awake during the long, cold evenings. The same happened in many other archives and libraries, whether Portuguese or Spanish; at the Center for African Studies in Leiden, Holland; and at the library of the Royal Museum for Central Africa in Tervuren, Belgium. I would like to thank each employee and librarian, for without their work and dedication, there would be no story to tell.

I am enormously grateful to Alexandra Aparício, director of the Arquivo Histórico de Angola, in Angola, and the other researchers and employees of that institution, Dr. Honoré Mbunga e Cariato, Lutete, Luci, and Paula. Special thanks to Mr. Januário, with whom I shared the study room and who promptly searched for the documents I requested. Every morning I was met with a wide smile and eager enthusiasm for one more day of work.

My visit to Luanda would have been entirely different without the help of Professor Maria Conceição Neto. I have no way to thank her for everything she did for me. Likewise, I cannot express what it meant for me to spend a weekend in Dondo with the Galho family, Andelson André, Ms. Suzelma, and Ms. Micalina, and all the friends I made there. They kindly took me to see the ruins of Nova Oeiras and those of other historical sites in the region. It would have been impossible for me to undertake that voyage without those people's generosity. "I found out that Luanda is big, *mama auê*," as Mathias Damásio sings. On that other margin of this "river called the Atlantic," in many ways I felt as if I was on this margin. I therefore thank all of those who welcomed me, like my landlord, Mr. Anselmo, and my housemate, Professor Linda.

I met people who became very important for the development of this project in congresses and scientific meetings. I am grateful to Mariana Candido for her intellectual generosity, providing me with sources, bibliography, and participating in my qualifying exams and my dissertation defense. I am also grateful to Mariza Soares and Flávia Carvalho for her comments on the research and their encouragement.

In Rio de Janeiro, I would like to thank Professor Regina Wanderley, who helped me in the research at IHGB, and Professor Roberto Guedes.

I thank the architect Katia Sartorelli Verissimo and her team for the elaboration of the models for this research.

I thank Professors Roquinaldo, Lucilene, and Bob for their valuable observations, suggestions, and critiques during the dissertation defense.

To my friends and professors at IFCH in Unicamp, who motivated me since my Master's, I am thankful for their support. Thank you, Flávia, for your readiness to help. To dear Day, Raquel, Andréa, Leca, and Dani, who made these years much lighter and enjoyable, thank you! I am also grateful for the many cups of coffee, conversations, and support from Manu, Alisson, Rodrigo, Deivison, and Tati.

To my sister Débora and my beloved Guga, thank you for the *mineirinho* cheerfulness and love with which you filled my life. I also thank Rogéria and Mari for their friendship and encouragement.

To the quartet of which, even from afar, I am still a member: Gi, Tati, and Kelly, thank you for your friendship. I also thank the support of other friends from the times at Ufop, Professor Carlão, Fabiano, Fabrício, Dani, and Denise.

I thank my family for their patience, understanding, love, and lasting company. I especially thank my mother, Teresa, and my father, Edemar.

I thank Fundação de Amparo à Pesquisa of the State of São Paulo for the research fellowships. Without the structure provided by the Foundation, it would have been impossible to develop this project. I am also grateful to Fundação Dr. António Agostinho Neto (FAAN) and De Gruyter, for the opportunity to publish this book.

I dedicate this book to all of those who somehow collaborated to its development and conclusion.

Contents

List of Figures and Maps —— XI

List of Tables and Graph —— XIII

List of Abbreviations and Acronyms —— XV

Preliminary Notes —— 1

Introduction —— 3

Chapter 1 A Discontinuous Triangle: The Kingdom of Angola in the Eighteenth Century —— 20
1.1   The Ambundus in the Kingdom of Angola —— 20
1.2   Efforts toward Colonial Expansion to the Interior —— 30
1.3   Angola's Population —— 45
1.4   Vassalage and Tribute —— 56

Chapter 2 From Ilamba to Nova Oeiras —— 74
2.1   Mines and Land: Uses and Meanings —— 74
2.2   Iron and Steel, in Bars and Products —— 94
2.3   Nova Oeiras, a "Machine" Conceived in the *Sertão* —— 109
2.4   Civilian Settlements —— 133

Chapter 3 Work and Workers in Nova Oeiras —— 142
3.1   Labor Regulations —— 142
3.2   Disputes, Resistance, and Violence in the Sertão —— 169
3.3   Dominion, Dependence, and Work Relations —— 184
3.4   "All Those Who Have Some Notion of Ironwork" —— 192

Chapter 4 Blacksmiths and Smelters —— 205
4.1   Jingangula, Pulungus and Bellows Operators —— 205
4.2   From Biscay —— 231
4.3   Figueiró dos Vinhos —— 242
4.4   Knowledge Mismatch —— 245

Chapter 5 Successes and Failures —— 253
5.1   "Dry Thunderstorms": The Factory after Sousa Coutinho —— 253

5.2	Other Landscapes, Same Issues — **263**
5.3	Administration and Science — **275**
5.4	An Inside-Out Project — **293**

Final Words — 304

Attachments — 317

Sources and Bibliography — 357

Glossary — 381

Index — 385

List of Figures and Maps

Figure 1:	Iron objects
Figure 2:	Power insignias in Angola
Figure 3:	Iron for the trade of enslaved people
Figure 4:	The walls planned to dam the river, 1770 c.a.
Figure 5:	Map of the town of Nova Oeiras, 1770 c.a.
Figure 6:	Front view of the iron foundry of the Nova Oeiras Factory, 1855
Figures 7 and 8:	Blueprints of the iron foundry in Oeiras, 1855
Figure 9:	Schematic layout of the iron factory's building
Figures 10 and 11:	Interior of the machine room, hydraulic forge, and storeroom. Representation of the weir, 1770
Figure 12:	View of the iron factory in Oeiras, 1855
Figures 13 and 14:	Iron smelting in Nova Oeiras, 1797
Figure 15:	Interior of a hydraulic ironworks
Figure 16:	Details of the interior of the foundry building
Figure 17:	Water wheels that propelled the hammer (left) and the bellows (right)
Figure 18:	Blueprint of the Figueiró ironworks (circa 1624)
Figure 19:	Plaque identifying the architectural ensemble of the iron factory, 1973
Figure 20:	Plaque identifying the architectural ensemble of the iron factory (?)
Map 1:	Map of the Kingdoms of Loango, Kongo, Angola, and Benguela, 1764
Map 2:	Detail of the interior of the Kingdom of Angola, 1791
Map 3:	The Ilamba region, 1790
Map 4:	Topographic map of the province where Nova Oeiras was located, 1769 c.a.

List of Tables and Graph

Table 1: Residents of the Kingdom of Angola, 1777
Table 2: Enslaved laborers who worked at Nova Oeiras, 1768–1772
Graph 1: Factory expenses (1766–1772)

List of Abbreviations and Acronyms

ACL	Academia das Ciências de Lisboa
AHU	Arquivo Histórico Ultramarino (Lisbon)
AHA	Arquivo Histórico Nacional de Angola (Luanda)
AHM	Arquivo Histórico Militar (Lisbon)
AHTC	Arquivo Histórico do Tribunal de Contas (Lisbon)
AN	Arquivo Nacional (Rio de Janeiro)
ANTT	Arquivo Nacional Torre do Tombo (Lisbon)
BMP	Biblioteca Municipal do Porto
BNP	Biblioteca Nacional de Portugal
IEB	Instituto de Estudos Brasileiros da Universidade de São Paulo
IHGB	Instituto Histórico e Geográfico Brasileiro (Rio de Janeiro)
GEAEM	Gabinete de Estudos Arqueológicos de Engenharia Militar (Lisbon)
SGL	Sociedade de Geografia de Lisboa

Preliminary Notes

In this book, Bantu words that appear in Portuguese form in the sources are spelled according to the documentation, except for noble titles, rivers, and other toponyms, which are written according to the Kimbundu or Kikongo spelling.¹

It was impossible to rigorously transcribe a number of eighteenth-century political titles, positions, or functions that use Kimbundu words, because I do not speak that language. Whenever I was able to recognize political titles already translated in other historiographical works, I transcribe the name as cited in the document, and I indicate the closest translation in brackets, such as the Cabanga Cambango chiefdom (probably Kabanga kya Mbangu, identified as *soba* of Ilamba in *Livro dos Baculamentos*).²

All words in languages other than Portuguese that are neither toponyms, ethnonyms, nor noble titles are written in italics. Some words whose meaning is important for the analysis are further explained in the glossary at the end of the book. They are written with an asterisk, for example, *kimbari**.

Unfortunately, it is impossible to determine beyond doubt how Central Africans from the region that became known as the Kingdom of Angola called themselves in the eighteenth century. The Ambundu identity is a colonial construction that encompassed people from different origins and political affiliations. The term does not reflect that diversity. According to Virgílio Coelho, it would be more appropriate to use Tumundongo, which designates the native populations of the ancient kingdom of Ndongo. The author prefers that term over Mbundu, which has been widely employed in historiography, because the latter, even though it has been used since the sixteenth century in the Portuguese form Ambundu, does not "correspond in any context to that suggested by those populations' self-awareness." Ambundu (plural of Mbundu) means "Negroes," and it is presumably an elaboration of an ethnic

---

1 The current spelling of the Kimbundu language is based on its alphabet and the respective transcription rules contained in Resolution n. 3787 of May 23, 1987, of the Council of Ministers of the Republic of Angola. The Kimbundu alphabet is made up of the following characters: a, b, c, d, e, f, h, i, j, k, l, m, n, o, p, s, t, u, v, w, x, y, z. Transcription rules apply the following phonemes: mb, mp, mv, mf, nd, ng, nj, nz, ny. "According to Lepsus, both C and Q correspond to K; GE and GI correspond to a guttural sound (ge, gee); the atonic syllable at the end of words must be represented by U; S is phonetically equivalent to se/si, never to Z." José Delgado. In Antonio de Oliveira Cadornega, *História das Guerras Angolanas (1680)*, annotated and revised by José Matias Delgado (Lisbon: Agência-geral do Ultramar, 1972, v. III), 611; Aida Freudenthal and Selma Pantoja, eds., *Livro dos Baculamentos: que os sobas deste Reino de Angola pagam a Sua Majestade (1630)* (Luanda: Ministério da Cultura and Arquivo Nacional de Angola, 2013), 27.
2 Aida Freudenthal and Selma Pantoja, eds., *Livro dos Baculamentos*, 50.

group or a people "created by the Portuguese to designate a broad set of populations that speak the same language, i.e. Kimbundu." The author also believes that Kamundongo (similar to Tumundongo) acquired a pejorative connotation in Angola. Coelho employs Kimbundu as a substitute for Mbundu and uses that term to indicate community, culture, language, twinship in the cultural space, peoples, system. He does so because, "to designate the notion of people or community, these populations commonly use the term *akwa.*" Such is the case with Akwakimbundu, the Kimbundu, "populations—or a community—that speak the Kimbundu language." [3]

I assume that Ambundu is not a better term to refer to Central Africans from the ancient Kingdom of Angola, since it undoubtedly entails a colonial perspective. It therefore reflects all the consequences of Europeans' views of Africans at the time, making it a biased term employed to sneer at those populations. On the other hand, employing a current-day ethnonym would be an anachronism, since we cannot assume that a present-day ethno-linguistic identity was the same as that assumed by Central Africans centuries ago. Therefore, considering that identities are historical constructions that change over time, I prefer to employ the term Ambundu, because it is what historical records use. In Bantu languages, the plural is usually indicated by a prefix (e.g. *kilamba,* plural of *ilamba*). In the case of Ambundu, since it is the Portuguese form of Mbundu, and since I want to emphasize the fact that it is a colonial construction, I will employ the Portuguese standard for the plural (Ambundus).

Nonetheless, I understand that the issue is controversial and can cause many problems. I therefore beg the reader, when encountering the term Ambundu in this text, not to relate it to Mbundu and its translation as "Negroes" or "//," [4] because that is in no way the meaning I attribute to it. When reading Ambundu, I hope that it is clear that our historical knowledge of the many and diverse inhabitants of that region in the eighteenth century, which we encompass under deficient and very generic terms, such as "Central Africans," is still quite limited, and we do not know how they called themselves. Having made this caveat, I hope to be able to unveil, throughout the text, the viewpoint of Central Africans regarding the history I am attempting to tell, even if I employ an ethnonym created by colonial agents.

---

3 Virgílio Coelho, *Em busca de Kàbàsà. Uma tentativa de explicação da estrutura político-administrativa do reino de Ndòngò* (Luanda: Kilombelombe, 2010), 203 and 204, note 1, 364.
4 Throughout the book, I use the term "enslaved" or "enslaved person/people" instead of "slave," except in citations and sources and texts by other authors, because the former "denounces the process of violence" underlying the process of enslavement, denaturalizing the condition of "slave" and "unveiling a content of historical and social nature concerning the struggle for power of people over people." Elizabeth Harkot-De-La-Taille and Adriano Rodrigues dos Santos, "Sobre Escravos e Escravizados: Percursos Discursivos da Conquista da Liberdade," in *III Simpósio Nacional Discurso, Identidade e Sociedade (III SIDIS)* (Campinas: Unicamp, IEL, 2012), 8 and 9.

Introduction

Pedro Manuel was an Ambundu smelter from the Angolan interior in the eighteenth century. His trade was complex and strenuous, and he therefore employed assistants and trainees and was always accompanied by two "bellows operators." The assistants mined the hills in search of iron ore, which was broken into smaller pieces for better smelting. That was only the beginning of the work: it was necessary to cut firewood, prepare the coal, build the furnace, gather sheaves of papyrus, and meticulously control the bellows, among other tasks. Employing specific methods that mixed practical knowledge with secret wisdom from the invisible world, acquired by their ancestors and perfected throughout many generations, Pedro manufactured iron of excellent quality.[1]

What was his secret? That was the question asked by many foreigners traveling in Angola, and Governor Francisco Inocêncio de Sousa Coutinho (1764–1772) was particularly determined to answer it. Pedro Manoel was not a unique smelter in the region; on the contrary, there were many smelters and blacksmiths spread out over an area rich in iron ore near Luanda, called Ilamba. Following the guidelines established by the Pombaline Reforms and aware of the high cost of European iron, Coutinho envisioned an alternative to supply not only Angola, but also Brazil and Portugal, with that valuable metal, and perhaps even to conquer new markets: building an iron factory. The enterprise was not to be modest; he conceived a factory to produce all the artillery necessary for the whole empire, not only of iron, but also of bronze. In honor of the great source of inspiration for his projects, the Count of Oeiras, and the important Portuguese geographical toponym, the factory was called Nova Oeiras.

What did the smelter Pedro Manoel think of this? It is difficult to find the answer to that question in the sources, since his name and trade are practically all we know about him. However, as a group of artisans—blacksmiths and smelters—, he and his colleagues left some impressions regarding the iron factory, which can be read between the lines of official documents. It was those tracks I attempted to follow.

At the iron factory, many blacksmiths and smelters were dependents of African chiefdoms in the region. Those chiefdoms' viewpoint is more clearly expressed in the sources. African chiefdoms were high up in the hierarchical structure of the Kingdom of Angola and controlled the iron mines and their dependents' labor force.

---

[1] Certidão de José Francisco Pacheco, inspetor das obras da fábrica, sobre o estado da fábrica de ferro. São Paulo de Assunção de Luanda, March 13, 1773. AHU_CU_001, Cx. 52, D. 28.

In general, the dependence of the governor, who wanted to build the factory, on the *sobas* who sent the workers is one of the main conflicts and issues for debate examined in this book. Under what terms did this partnership occur and what were its consequences for both the chiefs and their subjects? These are questions that guide the present text. The point of the inquiry is to understand that history from the standpoint of the Ambundus—of people like Pedro Manuel, the blacksmiths and smelters of Ilamba and the African chiefdoms—in their attempt to deal with projects and actions imposed on them by colonial agents.

In April 1765, the governor of Angola, Francisco de Sousa Coutinho, started researching iron mining in the Kingdom of Angola, which lead to the construction of the Royal Iron Factory of Nova Oeiras. Originally, the idea was to build two factories, and to that end, two civilian settlements would be created to sustain them with food production and labor force. The factory in Ilamba (a region located between the Kwanza and Mbengu Rivers) would exploit "earth iron"—i.e. it would be necessary to dig underground galleries to extract the ore. It would be established in the town of Novo Belém and would be named after it, by the Nzenza River, which allowed transporting the metal to the city of Luanda. The other factory would exploit the mountains containing "stone iron," located at the confluence of the Lukala and Luinha Rivers (affluents of the Kwanza River), in the Massangano jurisdiction, next to the town of Nova Oeiras.[2]

The documentation regarding the Novo Belém Factory is not as extensive as that on the Nova Oeiras Factory, but it indicates that iron was produced there under the supervision of intendant João Baines from 1765 to 1768. Since it was impossible to exploit earth iron—i.e. "tearing the ground"—in 1768 the governor ordered both factories to be united in Nova Oeiras, sending all the iron produced in Novo Belém and all its workers to that location.[3]

Academic works on eighteenth-century Angola at some point examine the history of the formidable iron factory, whose ruins are impressive even today. In particular, those works that research the government of Francisco de Sousa Coutinho,

---

[2] The Lukala River is the largest tributary of the Kwanza River and traverses the provinces of Uige, Malanje, and Kwanza Norte. The Luinha River connects the municipalities of Cazengo and Golungo Alto. We decided to maintain the term "factory" because it is what we found in eighteenth-century documentation. Its meaning is restricted to this historical period, and is close to Bluteau's definition of a "factory" as "a house or workshop where certain goods are manufactured." Therefore, it should not be associated with the large industries of the Manufacturing System. Raphael Bluteau, *Vocabulário portuguez e latino*, 10 v. (Lisbon / Coimbra: Colégio da Companhia de Jesus, 1712–1728), entry "fábrica."

[3] Gastão de Sousa Dias, *D. Francisco Inocêncio de Sousa Coutinho. Administração Pombalina em Angola* (Lisbon: Editorial Cosmos, 1936), 39.

known as the "philosopher administrator," analyze the Factory as a symbol of the projects of the Portuguese conquest of Angola and its hinterland. Gastão de Sousa Dias, Ralph Delgado, Jofre Amaral, and Antonio da Silva Rego authored works that exalt Sousa Coutinho; to them, the iron factory was an example of his government's genius and the possibilities of Portuguese colonialism. Written during the Estado Novo, these works reveal their commitment to the colonial perspective, justifying the actions of colonial agents and the conquest and exploitation of Angola.[4]

Historiography has renovated the interpretations of the government of Sousa Coutinho and the iron factory, criticizing the approach of the aforementioned authors. In the master's theses of Ana Madalena Trigo e Sousa and Mônica Tovo Machado, and in the PhD dissertation of Flávia de Carvalho, we find documental references and studies devoted to the African viewpoint of that history.[5] Reading those works was very important in the development of this analysis, even though they only cursorily examined the history of Nova Oeiras.

The works of Catarina Madeira Santos are also indispensable. She understands the construction of Nova Oeiras as part of a project of a "polite government"

---

4 Gastão de Sousa Dias, *D. Francisco Inocêncio de Sousa Coutinho, Administração Pombalina em Angola*; Jofre Amaral Nogueira, *Angola na época pombalina. O governo de Sousa Coutinho* (Lisboa: n.p., 1960); Antonio da Silva Rego, "A Academia Portuguesa da História e o II centenário da fábrica de Ferro em Nova Oeiras, Angola," in *Coletânea de Estudos em honra do prof. Dr. Damião Peres* (Lisbon: Academia Portuguesa da História, 1974), 385–398; Ralph Delgado, "O Governo de Sousa Coutinho em Angola," *Stvdia*, no. 6 (1960): 19–56, no. 7 (1961): 49–86, no. 10 (1962). See also: Maria Teresa Amado Neves, "D. Francisco Inocêncio de Sousa Coutinho: Aspecto moral da sua acção em Angola," in *I Congresso de História da Expansão Portuguesa no Mundo* (Lisbon: Sociedade Nacional de Tipografia, 1938), 120–150; A. Fuentes, "Dom Francisco Inocêncio de Souza Coutinho. Esboço de uma obra que se perdeu," *Boletim do Instituto de Angola*, no. 4 (1954): 35–40; Marques do Funchal, *O Conde Linhares* (Lisbon: n.p., 1950).
5 Ana Madalena Trigo de Sousa, *D. Francisco de Sousa Coutinho em Angola: Reinterpretação de um Governo 1764–1772*, thesis, Master's in History (Funchal / Lisbon: Universidade de Nova Lisboa, 1996). The work undertakes an in-depth analysis that has not been revisited by historiography as it deserves; Mônica Tovo Soares Machado, *Angola no Período Pombalino: O Governo de Dom Francisco Inocêncio de Sousa Coutinho – 1764–1772*, thesis, Master's (Faculty of Philosophy, Letters, and Human Sciences of the University of São Paulo, 1998); Maria Adelina de Figueiredo Batista Amorim, "A Real Fábrica de Ferro de Nova Oeiras. Angola, Séc. XVIII," *Clio*, Revista do Centro de História da Universidade de Lisboa, v. 9, 2003, 189–216; Patrícia Bertolini Gonçalves, "Iluminismo e administração colonial. Angola vista por brasileiros no século XVIII," *VIª Jornada Setecentista; conferências e comunicações* (Curitiba: Aos Quatro Ventos, 2006), 481–490; Ana Madalena Trigo de Sousa, "Uma tentativa de fomento industrial na Angola setecentista: a "Fábrica do Ferro" de Nova Oeiras (1766–1772)," *Africana Studia* no. 10 (2007): 291–308; Flávia Maria de Carvalho, *Sobas e homens do rei: interiorização dos portugueses em Angola (séculos XVII e XVIII)* (Maceió: Edufal, 2015). See also: José Gentil Silva, "En Afrique portugaise: L'Angola au XVIIIe siècle," *Annales. Histoire, Sciences Sociales*, 14ème Année, no. 3 (1959): 571–580.

for Angola, a notion directly related to the history of the ideas of the Enlightenment, which involved an effort to turn Angola into a colony of civilian settlements, rather than merely a colonial outpost. The author interprets the creation of the Nova Oeiras Factory as a "government device"—in other words, "a heterogeneous ensemble that encompasses discourses, institutions, architectural arrangements, regulatory decisions, laws, administrative measures, scientific statements, and philosophical and moral proposals." At the end of her account of the conditions that enabled the establishment of a polite government in Angola, the factory emerges as a quintessential symbol of that enlightened effort.[6]

This book cites in a number of places that historiography, whose purpose was to understand the colonial projects, institutions, and government mechanisms of the Portuguese administration of the Kingdom of Angola in the eighteenth century. It is important to note that in that work we observe an interest in understanding how African populations dealt with those external impositions in their everyday practice. However, our proposal follows a different route—its interest is to invert the viewpoint of the analysis and approach the issue of the iron factory from the standpoint of local determinations, of the choices made by African leaders, and thus analyze the social and political tensions involved in the establishment of a project of this magnitude in the *sertões* (backcountry) close to Luanda.

In other words, by analyzing new sources or documents already known, but examined with a different perspective and in the light of the current historiographical debate, our point of departure is not the Portuguese state, the government, enlightened culture, or the Scientism of the Enlightenment; rather, we are interested in the social relations of the local actors—the *sobas*, their subjects, the *ilamba*, the *imbari*, the factory workers, Central Africans, Europeans, Luso-Africans, foreigners and their relations with royal officers, tradesmen, *sertanejos* (people from the *sertões* or hinterlands). If on one hand there is a vast bibliography on the experiences of the administration elite, on the other hand there is still much to be done to better understand how Central Africans thought, acted, resisted, negotiated, adapted, and reflected on what was happening to them and their world.

By focusing on the Ambundu viewpoint and analyzing the internal dynamics in Angola, this book necessarily dialogues with Africanist bibliography. In order to understand the social and political structure of Ndongo, the main Ambundu kingdom, we resort to classical works that productively analyze the characteristics of

---

[6] Catarina Madeira Santos, *Um Governo "polido" para Angola: reconfigurar dispositivos de domínio (1750–c.1800)*, 21.

the first contacts between Portuguese and Africans, the local resistances, and their repercussions during colonial occupation.

Jan Vansina and David Birmingham were pioneers in shifting the viewpoint of analyses on the history of Angola; the emphasis is no longer on missionary actions and the "peaceful" Portuguese expansion, but rather on the sociopolitical context of the Ambundus and the impact of the European presence on a wide variety of aspects of Africans' lives.[7] John Thornton is a heir of those studies. In his research on the political configuration of the Kingdom of Kongo from the fifteenth to the mid-eighteenth century, he emphasized that that kingdom's internal transformations were more decisive of its fate than the external pressures of colonization of the traffic of enslaved people.[8] Along the same lines, but based on the Mbangala oral tradition, Joseph Miller traced the history of "Mbundu states," whose structure was based on the concentration of power on specific matrilineal lineages and their continuity through time.[9] Beatrix Heintze is the author who has most examined the history of Angola in the sixteenth and seventeenth centuries, with special emphasis on the Ndongo political and social formation and its contacts with the Portuguese during the colonial expansion.[10] Finally, in *Em Busca de Kábàsà* (In Search of Kábàsà), Virgílio Coelho focuses on the debate on "Kimbundu" lifestyles, worldview, and ethnic, linguistic and symbolic traits.[11]

Since the iron factory was built in the heart of Ilamba, a region with a long history of contact with the Portuguese, we became interested in knowing the history of the micropolitics of African chiefdoms and their alliances with colonial powers. In this respect, the writings of Jill Dias and Isabel de Castro Henrique were essential, which examine the history of the political and social microcosms in the African hinterlands and the formation of new ambiguous identities that

---

[7] Among other texts: Jan Vansina, *Kingdoms of the Savanna* (Madison: Wisconsin University Press, 1966); David Birmingham, *Trade and Conflict in Angola: The Mbundu and their neighbours under the influence of the Portuguese, 1483–1790* (Oxford: Clarendon Press, 19660; Jan Vansina, *How Societies are Born: Governance in West Central Africa before 1600* (Charlottesville: University of Virginia Press, 2004).

[8] John Thornton, *The Kingdom of Kongo: Civil War and Transition 1641–1718* (Madison: University of Wisconsin Press, 1983). Cf. also: Linda M. Heywood, John K. Thornton, *Central Africans, Atlantic Creoles, and the Foundations of the Americas, 1585–1660* (New York: Cambridge University Press, 2007).

[9] Joseph C. Miller, *Poder político e parentesco: os antigos Estados Mbundu em Angola*, trans. Maria da Conceição Neto (Luanda: Arquivo Histórico Nacional de Angola, 19950.

[10] Beatriz Heintze, *Angola nos séculos XVI e XVII. Estudos sobre Fontes, Métodos e História* (Luanda: Kilombelombe, 2007).

[11] Virgílio Coelho, *Em busca de Kábàsà: Uma tentativa de explicação da estrutura político-administrativa do reino de Ndòngò* (Luanda: Kilombelombe, 2010).

at times collaborate and negotiate with colonial powers and at other times resist and reject the colonial presence. Based on these authors, we were able to advance in the reconstruction of aspects of the trajectory of political titles and lineage leaders, especially in that region, which in the eighteenth century made up the *sertão*[12] near the city of Luanda.[13]

Another important point of the book is its analysis of the mechanisms of local exploitation of African workforce. To that end, it was necessary to understand the changes in labor relations over time and how the colonial initiative regulated the provision of services of the dependents of lineage chiefs. We assume as a point of departure that the ways of establishing colonial domination are necessarily related to the forms of control of the African workforce. This topic is not examined by the historiography that deals with the relations established by vassalage treaties between the Portuguese and the Africans,[14] and is another contribution of this book.

A unique study on Central African labor, which reflects on labor legislations, is Elaine Ribeiro dos Santos's master's thesis on the workers in Henrique Dias de Carvalho's expedition (1884–1888). The author reconstructed the experience of porters, guides, and interpreters based on the work of the Portuguese military officer, outlining their everyday practices and strategies of resistance before the expedition's commander and African authorities.[15]

The academic production on African labor in Africa, whether free, obligatory, compulsory, or penal, focuses on the second half of the nineteenth century and the twentieth century.[16] At the same time, the historiography on Angolan society in

---

[12] *Sertão* is a word associated with the hinterland.
[13] Among others: Jill Dias, "Changing Patterns on Power in the Luanda Hinterland, the Impact of Trade and Colonization on the Mbundu ca. 1845–1920," *Paudema* 32 (1986): 285–318; Jill Dias, "O Kabuku Kambilu (c. 1850–1900). Uma identidade política ambígua," in *Actas do Seminário Encontro de povos e culturas em Angola*. Lisboa: Comissão Nacional para as Comemorações dos Descobrimentos Portugueses (1997), 15–52; Isabel de Castro Henriques, *Percursos da Modernidade em Angola: dinâmicas comerciais e transformações sociais no século XIX* (Lisbon: Instituto de Investigação Científica Tropical, 1997).
[14] Beatriz Heintze, *Angola nos séculos XVI e XVII*, 2007; Catarina Madeira Santos, "'Escrever o poder.' Os autos de vassalagem e a vulgarização da escrita entre os africanos: o caso dos Ndembu em Angola (séculos XVII–XX)," *International Symposium Angola on the Move: Transport Routes, Communication, and History*, Berlin, September 24–26, 2003; Flávia Maria de Carvalho, *Sobas e homens do rei* (2015).
[15] Elaine Ribeiro dos Santos, *Barganhando sobrevivências: os trabalhadores centro-africanos na expedição de Henrique de Carvalho (1884–1888)*, thesis, Master's in History (São Paulo: Universidade de São Paulo, 2010).
[16] Among others: Adriano Parreira and Dale T. Graden, "África em debate: uma herança identitária – o trabalho forçado," *Africana Studia*, no. 5 (2010): 135–168; Jeremy Ball, "Relatos de investigação sobre o trabalho forçado em Angola na era colonial," in *Actas do II Encontro Internacional*

previous periods mostly focuses on analyzing the trade of enslaved people. While we believe that that trade is a central element in the history of Angola, this study is a contribution to the social history of African labor in the eighteenth century. Obviously, there are many connections with the trade of enslaved people, but the purpose here is to discuss how the borders between the different modalities of labor that coexisted in the Central African *sertão* developed, especially in the Nova Oeiras Factory.

A key historiographical debate centers on the impact of the transatlantic trade of enslaved people on African societies. Some historians propose that neither the trade nor its end had profound repercussions in the continent's history. David Eltis, for example, assumes that standpoint especially in regards to the demographic impact of the trade, stating that, for Ashanti, from the standpoint of demographic estimates, the trade was probably never important. According to Thornton, it is a mistake to imagine that Europeans imposed the trade on African merchants and political leaders, since they "did not personally suffer large-scale losses and were able to continue trading." These and other authors were combatting the idea of an eternal Africa, of societies that only experienced significant changes due to external stimuli.[17]

Other scholars went beyond demographic research and analyzed the impact of the Atlantic economy on the changes in internal slavery within the continent itself.[18] In regards to Angola, many authors relate the transatlantic trade to changes in war, colonial expansion, the debt networks created by the trade of enslaved people, transformations in the Ambundu political structure, among other factors.[19] In

---

de História de Angola. v. II (Luanda: Arquivo Nacional de Angola; Ministério da Cultura, 2015), 79–110.

[17] David Eltis, *Economic Growth and the Ending of the Transatlantic Slave Trade* (New York: Oxford University Press, 1987), 77; John Thornton, *A África e os Africanos na formação do mundo atlântico, 1400–1800*, 122–125, 152. Among others, see also: J. D. Fage, "Slavery and the Slave Trade in the Context of West African History," *The Journal of African History* 10, no. 3 (1969): 393–404; Philip Curtin, *Economic Change in Precolonial Africa: Senegambia in the Era of Slave Trade* (Madison: University of Wisconsin Press, 2 vol., 1975).

[18] Paul Lovejoy, *Transformations in Slavery: A History of Slavery in Africa* [1983], second ed. (Cambridge: Cambridge University Press, 2000); Patrick Manning, "Contours of Slavery and Social Change in Africa," *The American Historical Review* 88, no. 4 (1983): 835–857; Frederick Cooper, *Plantation Slavery on the East Coast of Africa* (Portsmouth: Heinemann, 1997). For an earlier debate discussing demographic and social issues, see: Walter Rodney, *How Europe Underdeveloped Africa* (London: Bogle-L'Ouverture Publications, 1972); Joseph Inikori, *Forced Migrations: The Impact of the Export Slave Trade on African Societies* (London: Holmes and Meier, 1982).

[19] Among other studies: Jill Dias, "Changing Patterns on Power in the Luanda Hinterland: The Impact of Trade and Colonization on the Mbundu ca. 1845–1920" (1986); Isabel de Castro Henriques, *Percursos da Modernidade em Angola* (1997); Beatrix. *Angola nos séculos XVI e XVII. Estudos sobre*

this book, we understand the trade as a structuring factor of the societies involved in the construction of Nova Oeiras. In addition, we analyze the eighteenth century, the heyday of the trade of enslaved people, when contacts with Europeans and the trade of captives had been going on for a long time, especially in the Atlantic Zone, in Luanda's hinterland.

Regarding the trade's circuits and the history of relations between dealings in Africa and their links to the transatlantic trade, *Way of Death* is an indispensable reference.[20] Among the studies focusing on the social history of the Kingdom of Angola, I highlight the recent works of Roquinaldo Ferreira on the connections between Angola and Brazil, and that of Mariana Candido, the first in-depth study on the history of Benguela, with an emphasis on African culture and society. The trade of enslaved people continues to be a central issue in these studies, but they differ from other approaches because their authors attempt to contribute with a qualitative analysis, tracing the life trajectories of those involved in the trade and trying to understand the mechanisms of enslavement, the forms of resistance, and the consequences of the trade according to the experiences of Africans and their descendants. As heirs of prior studies, they highlight the role of the "people who built these places [Benguela and Luanda] and inserted them in the global economy."[21]

---

fontes, métodos e história (Luanda: Kilombelombe, 2007); José Curto, "Un buttin illégitime: razias d'esclaves et relations luso-africaines das la région des fleuves Kwanza et Kwango en 1850," In Isabel de Castro Henriques, Louis Sala-Mollins (ed.), *Déraison, Esclavage, et Droit: les fondements idéologiques et juridiques de la Traite Négrière et de l'Esclavage* (Paris: Unesco, 2002); Roquinaldo Ferreira, *Transforming Atlantic Slaving. Trade, Warfare and Territorial Control in Angola, 1650–1800*, dissertation (PhD) (Los Angeles: University of California, 2003); Beatriz Heintze, *Angola nos séculos XVI e XVII* (2007).

20 Joseph C. Miller, *Way of Death. Merchant Capitalism and the Angolan Slave Trade, 1730–1830* (Madison: University of Wisconsin Press, 1988).

21 Roquinaldo Ferreira, *Cross-Cultural Exchange in the Atlantic World. Angola and Brazil during the Era of the Slave Trade* (New York: Cambridge University Press, 2012); Mariana P. Candido, *An African Slaving Port and the Atlantic World. Benguela and Its Hinterland* (Nova York: Cambridge University Press, 2013), 24; in Brazil, graduate programs have encouraged (especially after law n. 10.639 made the teaching of Afro-Brazilian History and Culture mandatory in the educational system's official curriculum) the study of African culture and societies. The topic of eighteenth-century Angola has been revisited and important contributions have emerged recently, such as Flávia Maria de Carvalho's *Sobas e Homens do Rei: relações de poder e escravidão em Angola (séculos XVII e XVIII)* (Maceió: EDUFAL, 2015); and Ingrid de Oliveira's dissertation, *Textos militares e mercês numa Angola que se pretendia reformada: Um estudo de caso dos autores Elias Alexandre da Silva Correa e Paulo Martins Pinheiro de Lacerda*, dissertation (PhD in History) (Niterói: Instituto de Ciências Humanas e Filosofia, Universidade Federal Fluminense, 2015).

This book dialogues more closely with that historiography with a perspective of social history, inscribed in the English expression, "the history from below." History "seen from below" has brought together historians who have pushed back the discipline's limits by examining the history of the experiences of men and women from subaltern classes. It is an approach that examines historical processes neglected in classical narratives that privilege large events and illustrious people or that were not considered in structuralist analyses by Marxist historians. This historiographical movement, whose main representatives are Edward Thompson and Eric Hobsbawm, is a heir of the pioneering study by George Rudé, *The Crowd in History* (1961), on popular movements in France and England (1730–1848), specifically strikes, mutinies, rebellions, insurrections, and revolutions.[22]

Following that theoretical tradition, Thompson analyzed the history of labor beyond the topics of institutions, unions, and great leaderships, focusing especially on workers' culture, customs, values, lifestyles, and experiences. For Thompson, the concept of experience "is indispensable to the historian, since it comprises the mental and emotional response, whether of an individual or a social group, to many inter-related events or to many repetitions of the same kind of event." Stated more clearly, according to the author, "experience arises spontaneously within the social being, but it does not arise without thought; it arises because men and women (and not only philosophers) are rational, and they think about what is happening to themselves and their world."[23] Since our focus is on labor history, this is a fundamental theoretical delimitation, which has also been employed by Africanists who reconstruct the trajectories of African workers in the nineteenth and twentieth centuries.[24]

In addition, this book shares an Afrocentric perspective, in the sense that it brings the role of Africans in history to the forefront of the narrative, while attempting to be more than an alternative to Eurocentric versions of the history of Africa and Africans. As the historian Ki-Zerbo noted, the purpose is not "to build a revenge-history that relaunches colonialist history like a boomerang

---

22 George Rudé, *A multidão na história: estudo dos movimentos populares na França e Inglaterra, 1730–1748*, trans. Waltensir Dutra (Rio de Janeiro: Campus, 1991).
23 E. P. Thompson, *A miséria da teoria ou um planetário de erros. Uma crítica ao pensamento de Althusser*, trans. Waltensir Dutra (Rio de Janeiro: Zahar, 1981), 15 and 16. In Jim Sharpe's words: "Thompson thus identified not only the general problem of reconstructing the experience of ordinary people. He also emphasized the need to try to understand people in the past, as far as it is possible for the modern historian, in the light of their own experiences and their own reactions to that experience." Jim Sharpe, "History from Below," in Peter Burke (ed.), *New Perspectives on Historical Writing* (The Pennsylvania State University Press, 1992), 26.
24 Frederick Cooper, "Work, Class and Empire: An African Historian's Retrospective on E. P. Thompson," *Social History* 20, no. 2 (1995): 235–241.

against its authors, but to shift perspectives and resuscitate forgotten or lost images."[25] For that reason, we intend to highlight the agency of the Ambundus and their descendants, because we understand that it is only by analyzing the networks of sociability they established with the Portuguese, with other Europeans, and with other Africans that we will be able to apprehend their experiences, their worldview, and their choices.

It is a history of the tensions between the interests of many characters who circulated in the Angolan *sertões* in the eighteenth century, identifying relations of domination and strategies of resistance, adaptation, and negotiation. For that reason, it is necessary to leave aside binary constructions such as "colonizer/colonized," "West/non-West," and "domination/resistance." Even if we consider that those dualities can be "useful mechanisms to begin studying issues of power," they end up limiting "research regarding the exact way in which power spreads and the way in which that power is dealt with, confronted, deflected, and appropriated."[26]

Finally, the purpose of delving into our particular interest in the history of the iron factory is not to write a monographic history. Rather, we believe that playing between the scales of analysis as proposed by the methodology known as microhistory is important. Endowed with the possibility of varying the scale, and thus constructing the macro through the micro, we consider reconstituting the elements of the histories of the *sobas*, the workers, and the royal officers who coexisted in Nova Oeiras as a fundamental methodological resource to reach our objectives.[27] This will enable us to make new interpretations of the social history of the Ambundus.

In order to accomplish those theoretical objectives, it was necessary to read the sources from a different standpoint and to face a difficulty that is common to all researchers who want to identify, through colonial administrative documents, the voices of those who were deemed subjugated. Achille Mbembe discusses

---

25 Joseph Ki-Zerbo, *Introdução*, in Joseph Ki-Zerbo (ed.), *História geral da África I: metodologia e pré-história da África*, second revised edition (Brasilia: UNESCO, 2010), XXXV. On the Afro-centric perspective, see: Paulo Fernando Moraes de Faria, "Afrocentrismo: entre uma contranarrativa histórica universalista e o relativismo cultural," *Afro-Ásia*, no. 29/30 (2003): 340; Mohamed Mbodj, "Le point de vue de Mohamed Mbodj," *Politique Africaine*, no. 79 (2000/3): 167 and 168; Steven Feierman, "African Histories and the Dissolution of World History," in R. H Bates, V. Y. Mudimbe, and J. O'Barr (eds.), *Africa and the Disciplines: The Contributions of Research in Africa to the Social Sciences and Humanities* (Chicago: University of Chicago Press, 1993), 186.
26 Frederick Cooper, "Conflito e conexão: repensando a História Colonial da África," *Anos 90* 15, no. 27 (2008): 23.
27 Paul-André Rosental, "Construir o 'macro' pelo 'micro': Fredrik Barth e a 'microstoria'", in Jacques Revel (org.). *Jogos de escalas* (1998): 151–172.

the distribution of the gaze in a colonial context, describing the European that observes the African:

> a certain manner of distributing the gaze ends up creating its object, fixing it, or destroying it, or returns it to the world under the sign of disfiguration or at least of 'another me,' a me that is an object, a marginal being. A certain form of the gaze has, in effect, the power to block the appearance of the 'third-being' and his inclusion in the sphere of the human.[28]

In this excerpt, Achille Mbembe dialogues directly with Frantz Fanon's text and ideas, discussing the modes of colonial representation. Even though we are examining a period that was much earlier than Fanon's experiences, we believe that the forms of European domination and conquest were already present through an "imperial gaze." This expression was used by Mary Louise Pratt when referring to naturalist voyages after the mid-eighteenth century and the way they produced new views on the colonial "other" and their cultures, elaborating "an Eurocentric form of global consciousness" or, as the author calls it planetary consciousness.[29]

Going back to Mbembe, the author reflects that, in the mid-eighteenth century, the first classifications of non-European human groups arose as if they were "a lesser form of being [...] the impoverished reflection of the ideal man, separated from him by an insurmountable temporal divide,"[30] a discourse that legitimated European expansion and domination over the world.

Therefore, generally speaking, we can assert that the perspective of the Portuguese authorities who wrote most of the documents we selected did not describe the participation of the "third-being," the African other, as a historical subject with the same complexity as Europeans, and for that reason endowed with an equally multifaceted worldview, knowledge, culture, and language. Nonetheless, that is by no means the only view that existed of the Ambundus. On the contrary, Africans resisted the single Eurocentric narrative, constructing alternative readings—an alternative history. Blacksmiths and smelters, for example, demonstrated their industriousness and courage in their own communities, and especially before authorities and royal officers, tradesmen, missionaries, etc.[31]

---

28 Achille Mbembe, *A crítica da razão negra*, trans. Marta Lança (Lisbon: Antígona, 2014), 191.
29 Mary Louise Pratt, *Imperial Eyes: Travel Writing and Transculturation* (New York: Routledge, 2008), 4.
30 Achille Mbembe, *A crítica da razão negra*, 38–40. However, it is important to remember that only in the nineteenth century did race become an essential concept backed by biology. This book examines an earlier period (one century before) to that of the theoreticians that became known as "racial Darwinists."
31 One must also remember Chimamanda Ngozi Adichie in her shrewd lecture on the dangers of a single history. "Begin a history with the arrows of Native Americans, not with the arrival of the

Hence, even though African voices are not protagonists at the moment of production of the sources examined here, we believe that we can find in them certain aspects of their experiences. Their voices are present even as dispersed traces—phrases, minor observations, summaries of their ideas and words. By collecting these traces and systematically cross-referencing them with the documentation, we can understand the African perspective in this history.

Carlo Ginzburg comments on this dialogic nature of the sources when examining inquisitorial trials. If the dialogue responds to the premise that, in documents, the "various characters are seen as conflicting forces," it is not always easy to detect the different voices expressed in historic sources. Sometimes the historian is tempted to watch "over the inquisitor's shoulder," "following his footsteps," assuming the perception of a judge. It is important to remember that that is only one of the various contradictory voices in the trial.[32] Therefore, as we analyze our sources, we must resist the interpretation of the European conquest of Africans, value judgments, and the filters established by Portuguese authorities, and attempt to understand the African viewpoint inscribed in them.

Stuart Schwartz further develops this reflection by recalling that the narratives constructed by conquerors and the conquered are a two-way avenue. For the author, all colonial knowledge was based on cultural encounters, on implicit ethnographies. What Schwartz means by this is that, on both sides of commercial, military, and/or fully colonial encounters, the "members of each society maintained often unspoken ideas of themselves and the 'others,' and the things that gave them those identities," a knowledge that did not need to be expressed, but that permeated the ways in which people thought and acted. Generally speaking, in the contact zones between different cultures, transformations continuously occurred in those forms of perception of themselves and the others, in a "dynamic tension between prior understandings and expectations and new observations and experiences."[33]

British, and you have a totally different history," says Adichie. That is the challenge we face, to tell the history of Nova Oeiras putting the *sobas*, the *ilamba*, the blacksmiths, and the smelters at the center of the narrative. Chimamanda Ngozi Adichie, *O perigo de uma história única*, lecture at the Technology, Entertainment and Design (TED) event in 2009, available at: https://youtu.be/qDovHZVdyVQ, accessed August 19, 2017.

32 Carlo Ginzburg, "O inquisidor como antropólogo," *Revista Brasileira de História* 1, no. 21 (1991): 6–10.

33 Stuart Schwartz, *Implicit Understandings: Observing, Reporting and Reflecting on the Encounters between Europeans and Other Peoples in the Early Modern Era* (Cambridge: Cambridge University Press, 1995): 2 and 3.

These tacit knowledges were disseminated in treaties, chronicles, memoirs, instructions, letters, laws… in short, a diverse typology of documents that (mutually) reflect the assumptions of one culture regarding another one, sometimes reinforcing stereotypes, at other times reaffirming instruments of domination and resistance. When analyzing the sources, we believe that it is important to examine the various voices that constitute them, thus analyzing the viewpoints and strategies of the various subjects of the Portuguese Crown and of Africans that were not under its dominion, in the context of colonization.

These brief theoretical/methodological observations are sufficient to identify one of the important analytical procedures adopted in the research that underlies this book, since we make use of documentation that is essentially official. Apparently, the different series of official fragments offer only a metropolitan perspective, or that of its agents of military conquest and exploitation of natural and human resources. However, if we refrain from looking over the shoulder of those who produced those documents, undertaking a careful reading of its elements, as the bibliography informs us, it is possible to observe many aspects regarding how Central Africans resisted the project of Nova Oeiras. Thus, in addition to the views of the metropolis and Portuguese authorities on the iron factory, its workers, and iron foundry knowledge, a reading against the grain[34] allows us to perceive many aspects of the African labor world and experiences in that specific context.

Most of the sources employed here are part of the correspondence between Luanda's government and overseas Portuguese authorities, more precisely letters and official documents exchanged between the government of the Kingdom of Angola, Francisco Inocêncio de Sousa Coutinho, and the Secretaries of the Navy and Overseas Affairs, Francisco Xavier de Mendonça Furtado (1760–1769) and Martinho de Mello e Castro (1770–1795). This documentation is scattered in archives in Brazil, Portugal, and Angola.[35] A complementary and essential part of this set of

---

34 "Brushing history against the grain" is one of Walter Benjamin's most emblematic ideas. In short, this expression speaks of the need to refrain from conceiving history as an ideal of "progress" of the dominant classes, of the big names, of the nineteenth-century colonial narrative that, based on a presumed European supremacy, justified colonialism. Walter Benjamin, "Sobre o conceito de História," in *Obras Escolhidas*, vol. I (São Paulo: Brasiliense, 1985).

35 These documents were first selected in Brazilian archives: Instituto de Estudos Brasileiros/USP, Instituto Histórico e Geográfico Brasileiro, especially in PADAB (Projeto Acervo Digital Angola–Brasil), Arquivo Nacional, and Fundação Biblioteca Nacional. In a second stage, in Portugal, we sought these sources and specialized bibliography in Arquivo Histórico Ultramarino, Biblioteca Nacional de Portugal, Arquivo Nacional da Torre do Tombo, Sociedade de Geografia de Lisboa, Academia das Ciências de Lisboa, Arquivo Histórico do Tribunal de Contas, Arquivo Histórico Militar, Museu Nacional de História Natural e da Ciência, Gabinete de Estudos Arqueológicos de Engenharia Militar,

documents is the correspondence, public announcements, and ordinances of the government of Angola—exchanged between the governor, the *capitão-mor*[36], and the royal iron factory intendants in the Angolan interior. This second set of sources was collected during a visit to the National Historical Archive of Angola, and it was essential to obtain more local and specific information on the everyday organization of labor in Luanda's hinterland. A significant part of that documentation is already known to historians, but the purpose of reconstructing the history of the iron factory "from below" required us to ask new questions to those sources. After all, as Hobsbawm says, "there is no material until our questions reveal it."[37]

In addition to the work with these textual sources, it is important to take into account visual records, blueprints, drawings, and maps of the region, the town of Nova Oeiras, the iron factory, and the modes of production and transformation of the metal. These images—some of them previously unknown—reveal how the town developed, the dimensions of the factory building, and provide detailed descriptions of work areas and tools in the notes of naturalist José Álvares Maciel in the late-eighteenth century.

The text is divided into five chapters: the first two present the general characteristics of Angola in the eighteenth century, and the other three examine what we believe are the most relevant issues. The first chapter provides a geographical and demographic overview in the eighteenth century of a part of the ancient Kingdom of Ndongo, which was called Kingdom of Angola, and its conquest by the Portuguese. The chapter aims at presenting the tensions between Central African authorities and colonial agents in the second half of the eighteenth century, when there was an effort to colonize the hinterlands—manifested in the iron factory project. This is followed by an analysis of the vassalage agreements established between the Portuguese and the *sobas* over time, from the standpoint of labor relations.

Chapter 2 describes and problematizes how the region of the Ambundu iron mines became Sousa Coutinho's Nova Oeiras. I first analyze Africans' relations with the iron mines as part of a sacred territory of their ancestors, since they had particular ways of exploiting the ores. I then demonstrate how the search

---

Biblioteca da Ajuda, Museu Nacional de Arqueologia, Museu Nacional de Etnologia, Biblioteca Municipal do Porto, and the Archives of the University of Coimbra. Since Biscayan masters were hired to work in Nova Oeiras, we visited some archives in Spain, especially in search of more information on iron smelting and forging techniques: Biblioteca Nacional de España, Archivo Nacional de España, and Archivo General de Indias.

36 *Capitão-mor* was a position of commander of the Portuguese outpost of Angola.

37 Eric Hobsbawm, "A história de baixo para cima," in *Sobre história: ensaios* (São Paulo: Companhia das Letras, 1998), 215–232.

for metals was an important characteristic of Portuguese colonization, which therefore spared no efforts to control the mines and exploit them. They are two different ways of perceiving the same natural resource, and, as we shall see, this led to conflicts and compromises. There was a long conflict over the lands where the factories were built. We examine the interests of the different individuals who participated in that conflict, attempting to identify the mechanisms they employed to legitimize their possession of the lands. In that section, I also examine the colonial project, the creation of the town of Nova Oeiras, the various factories that served as experiments to reach the final project, and finally the construction of the factory building.

In Chapter 3, I research the history of labor and laborers in Nova Oeiras—Africans, Biscayans, Portuguese, French, Brazilians. The emphasis is on the practices to recruit African workers for the iron foundries. I thus delimited overlays and discrepancies between the various forms of employment of this labor force, since in the factory coexisted enslaved, free, compulsory, and penal labor. When researching what was established in formal agreements between African chiefdoms and the Portuguese, I examine the process that became a presumably local tradition to legitimize political alliances—sending workers to a monarch as tribute—, which was a recurrent practice under the colonial administration.

At a narrower scale of analysis, I focus on aspects of everyday life in the factory and of the division and process of labor. This objectively allows us to demonstrate the complexity of the matter—the social fabric in detail—and to reveal the strategies employed by African rulers to maintain a millenary activity—iron foundry and commerce—under their dominion. It is a chapter on the tensions between various subjects, at a moment when labor relations were more deeply rooted—the governor, settlers, *capitães-mores*, *sobas*, *ilamba*, and *imbari* often come in conflict over the dominion and control of the labor of vassal Ambundus. Here, my dialogue with the historiography of social history focused on specific contexts is more incisive, especially in regards to the precariousness that the colonial situation imposed on Ambundu vassals, who were the main targets of illegal capture, kidnapping, and enslaving.

In addition, in Chapter 4, I examine the iron smelting and forging techniques employed by the Ambundus in Nova Oeiras. I highlight the meanings of the blacksmith trade for Central Africans—for whom this occupation had a magical/religious connotation. To that end, I resort to the memoirs that the former revolutionary from the *Inconfidência Mineira*, José Álvares Maciel, exiled in Angola, elaborated from 1795 to 1797, where he describes in detail his experiences with iron smelting in that region. In addition, I include the history of the techniques employed by other blacksmiths who worked there, especially Portuguese and Biscayans. It is a chapter about how workers, beyond providing their workforce to build

Nova Oeiras, produced knowledge that was indispensable to the development of metallurgy.

In the fifth and last chapter, I compare the different versions of the history of the factory and of iron production in Angola. I examine the reasons for the failure of Nova Oeiras, especially its technical inadequacy, since the different patterns of knowledge (European, African, Luso-American) were unable to adapt to Angola's hinterland in the eighteenth century, or rather, were unable to create a form of production that maximized natural and human resources. The connections between Portuguese conquests in Portuguese America and in the Kingdom of Angola were intense, especially in the eighteenth century. This is evident in the interaction between "subjects" on both sides of the Atlantic, and, in the case of the elaboration and planning of iron factories in those places, in the correspondence between Francisco de Sousa Coutinho and the governor of São Paulo, the Morgado of Mateus. Considering these issues, I compare two experiences of iron exploitation: the Nova Oeiras Factory and the factory that was the predecessor of what in the nineteenth century became the Ipanema Iron Factory, on the Araçoiaba hill in São Paulo.

Finally, I examine the unavoidable issue of the failure of the Nova Oeiras Factory. If there is any consensus in the historiography, it is that the initiative failed—and there are many explanations for that: that the change in governor interrupted Sousa Coutinho's enlightened project; that the iron mines were not sufficiently productive for large-scale manufacturing; that the *sertão*'s climate led to the death of European masters sent there, which left the factory without specialized workers, among other reasons.

However, the failure is a version of history told from the standpoint of colonial plans. If we invert the viewpoint, as we propose here, and tell the African version, the conclusion might be different. Iron production in Nova Oeiras by African blacksmiths, smelters, and bellows operators, using small bellows and furnaces, was constant in the eighteenth century, even after the Sousa Coutinho government. In addition, from the late-eighteenth century to at least the mid-nineteenth century, local workers sold their iron bars to the Royal Treasury. Therefore, we can conclude that Central Africans successfully continued to mine iron their own way and did not subject themselves to colonial plans and knowledge.

Through worker escapes, their refusal to learn foreign techniques, and the strategies employed by the *sobas* to sometimes collaborate and sometimes boycott the colonial project, Africans were able to preserve their dominion over iron exploitation over time. For that reason, we believe that Sousa Coutinho's plans for the iron factory failed mainly because they did not elicit permanent collaboration from African elites and workers; the Luanda government failed to convince them of the undertaking's success. We do not mean by this that the factory's construction and recruitment of labor force did not have a profound impact on the *sobas* around it. On the contrary, what we are saying is that the exhaustion of the factory's workforce, the ill treatment and "beatings" received by its workers, and the political and social breakup of African villages due to the constant desertion of men and women who did not want to be sent to work in the factory were not enough to contain the resistances to colonial domination.

Chapter 1
A Discontinuous Triangle: The Kingdom of Angola in the Eighteenth Century

1.1 The Ambundus in the Kingdom of Angola

Today's Republic of Angola is very different from what in the eighteenth century the Portuguese called the "Kingdom of Angola and its conquests," the "conquest of Angola," or simply "Angola." In the last quarter of the eighteenth century, it was an area delimited by the Portuguese presence in West Central Africa, which was located, according to Governor Francisco de Sousa Coutinho (1764–1772), on latitude 8°48', which corresponds to one of the current geographical coordinates of the city of Luanda—a town (*vila*) founded in 1576, promoted to the status of city in 1605.

> Angola is located at 8 degrees and 48 minutes; and since, either because of the interest of people of the past in the *sertão* or because of the greater difficulty of the Coasts, it was at first too far from the Coast, almost as the vertex of a triangle whose edges are the country's hinterlands; for that reason five leagues to the north of the Coast and ten to the south are lands that do not recognize The King Our Lord.[1]

This citation refers to the limited dominion of the African territory by the Portuguese. The domain's limits composed the form of a discontinuous triangle: its distant vertex on the Coast represented the port, the fort, and the city of Luanda; its

---

[1] Francisco Inocêncio de Sousa Coutinho (FISC), "Memórias do Reino de Angola e suas conquistas, escritas em Lisboa nos anos de 1773 e 1775," BMP, Codex 437, document 10. Antonio Parreira provides the following measures: 1 French league = 3 miles; 1 league (1641) = 1 Spanish mile; 1 Italian league = 3 miles = about 1,250 m. According to Joaquim Monteiro, in "Uma viagem redonda da carreira da Índia (1597–1598)," one Portuguese league corresponded to 5,920 m. If we take this value as reference, it means that the sovereignty of the King of Portugal was not recognized at approximately 29 km to the north and 59 km to the south of the Coast of Luanda. This demonstrates the limited geographical extension of Portuguese influence. However, we must pay attention to the "differences in the values given for the same distance, which when calculated in travel days, is dependent on the walking speed, atmospheric conditions, road conditions, the weight carried, and in many cases could result from calculation errors or writing inaccuracies. (...) The Africans of Congo determined land distances not with miles or space as such, but as days traveled by men with or without a load." Adriano Parreira, *Economia e sociedade em Angola na época da Rainha Jinga (século XVII)* (Lisbon: Editorial Estampa, 1997), 23 and 24. Joaquim Rebelo Vaz Monteiro, *Uma viagem redonda da carreira da Índia (1597–1598)* (Coimbra: Gráfica de Coimbra, 1985), 463.

https://doi.org/10.1515/9783110788150-008

sides were "the country's interior," and other vertexes were probably the fortress of Engoge in the north and Pungo-Andongo in the south. Thus, the conquest of Angola was a small part of West-Central Africa that recognized the dominion of the King of Portugal, surrounded by other domains that were not subjected to Portuguese jurisdiction. This is so because, to the north and south, African kingdoms resisted European conquest. They were usually called "potentates" in Portuguese sources, and over time, they established political agreements to mediate commercial relations with the foreigners, especially in regards to the trade of enslaved people.[2]

However, resistance to colonial occupation was not only felt in the discontinuous edges of this triangle; on the contrary, the interior of the Kingdom of Angola contained some Portuguese administrative units surrounded by *banzas*, *sobados*, i.e. politically autonomous African units, which had signed vassalage agreements with the King of Portugal. The toponymy of Luanda's *sertões* was entirely African, except for the town and the factory of Nova Oeiras. This geopolitical tension is one of the most expressive symptoms of the territorial and political fragility of the European presence in the region.

For Sousa Coutinho, the limited geographical extension of the Kingdom of Angola was the cause of the flights of enslaved people from the city of Luanda, who, in order to free themselves from slavery, did not miss the opportunity to flee to the province of Kisama, immediately to the south of that city, since that region was only subjugated by Portugal in the nineteenth century.[3] To the north, in addition to potentates, there was competition with English, French, Dutch, and Danish merchants, who were not intimidated by the fragility of the Portuguese dominion: "as early as 1680, Dutch trading posts were respected in the lands of the prince of Sonho," said Sousa Coutinho. The *mani* Sonho, or Count of Sonho, as he was

---

2 Sousa Coutinho does not cite the Kingdom of Benguela, south of the Kwanza River, as a vertex of this triangle, because this kingdom was declared independent with its own governor since 1612. However, after the Dutch were expelled in 1648, Benguela was governed by a *capitão-mor* appointed by the governor of Angola. Only in 1779 were governors appointed again. It should be emphasized that they were not separate kingdoms; on the contrary, commercial and political relations between these kingdoms became even stronger in the eighteenth century. About the Kingdom of Benguela, see Mariana P. Candido, *An African Slaving Port and the Atlantic World. Benguela and its Hinterland* (New York: Cambridge University Press, 2013).

3 Since the seventeenth century, Kisama became a destination for runaway enslaved people. B. Heintze recalls that oftentimes this reference to escapes to the region in the governors' texts was actually a way of justifying military expeditions before the chiefs to obtain enslaved workers. Beatriz Heintze, *Angola nos séculos XVI e XVII. Estudos sobre Fontes, Métodos e História* (Luanda: Kilombelombe, 2007), 524. Joseph C. Miller, *Way of Death. Merchant Capitalism and the Angolan Slave Trade, 1730–1830* (Madison: University of Wisconsin Press, 1988), 385.

known among the Portuguese, was the governor of a province of the Kingdom of Kongo with a privileged location for the trade of enslaved people, and often traded with other Europeans, undermining the Portuguese plans to monopolize it.[4]

Generally speaking, in the eighteenth century, the Kingdom of Angola was circumscribed by the province of Kisama to the south of the Kwanza River and by the Lunda Empire to the east of the Kwango River. To the west of the Kwanza River, there were the potentates of Kasanje, Holo, and Njinga-Matamba. To the north of the Ndande River, the Kingdom of Kongo, the Ndembu,[5] and the potentates of Musulu, Sonho, by the Mbrije River. In the region of the Kingdom of Loango, there were Mubire or Vili societies.[6] In Map 1, these divisions are clearer. It was published in Paris in 1764, and was drawn by Jacques Nicolas Bellin, an important cartographer from the French Navy.

In this map, the rivers that cut through the territory are highlighted: the Zaire River as a natural border between the Kingdom of Loango and the Kingdom of Kongo; the Kwanza River, the main waterway of the Kingdom of Angola; the Kunene River in Benguela, which until the late-eighteenth century marked the limits of the territory to the south of Angola known to the Portuguese—the lands beyond the Kunene River were unexplored territory.

Given the precarious nature of the Portuguese presence in African territory, many historians consider that it is erroneous to call the Kingdom of Angola a colony, or even to call colonial times the period of Portuguese occupation from the fifteenth to the nineteenth centuries. The first endeavors of Portuguese expansion are seen by these authors as attempts at colonial administration, especially after the appointment of the Governor General Francisco d'Almeida in 1592. For

---

[4] FISC, "Memórias do Reino de Angola e suas conquistas." The *mani* Sonho, head of the government of the Kingdom of Kongo, was one of the first commercial partners of the Portuguese. He was the main authority of Mpinda, a province in the northwest of the Kingdom of Kongo, on the south bank of the Zaire River. In an official letter dated 1766, Sousa Coutinho cites other potentates who, like Sonho, became a hindrance to the Portuguese conquest and the development of the trade of enslaved people: the *mani* Musulo and the *ndembu* Manicembo. They are described as "haughty potentates, the strongest and most assisted with gunpowder and bullets of the neighboring ports in which foreigners trade (...) almost all the wars we had with them were unsuccessful," Ofício do governador FISC. São Paulo de Assunção de Luanda, March 30, 1766. AHU_CU_001, Cx. 50, D. 7.
[5] "Southward from the Dande River to the Gengo (or Zenza) River was, and still is, the territory of the Dembo (Ndembu), a Kimbundu-speaking people with strong affinities to Kongo, who largely corresponded to the 'Ambundu' of older sources. Originally, Ndembu was not an ethnic designation, but a title of the great local chiefs. They formed a buffer zone between Kongo and Ndongo, and were largely independent, though with a distinct bias in favor of Kongo, whose sovereignty they recognized at certain times," Beatriz Heintze, *Angola nos séculos XVI e XVII*, 183.
[6] Joseph C. Miller, *Way of Death*, 30–33.

1.1 The Ambundus in the Kingdom of Angola — 23

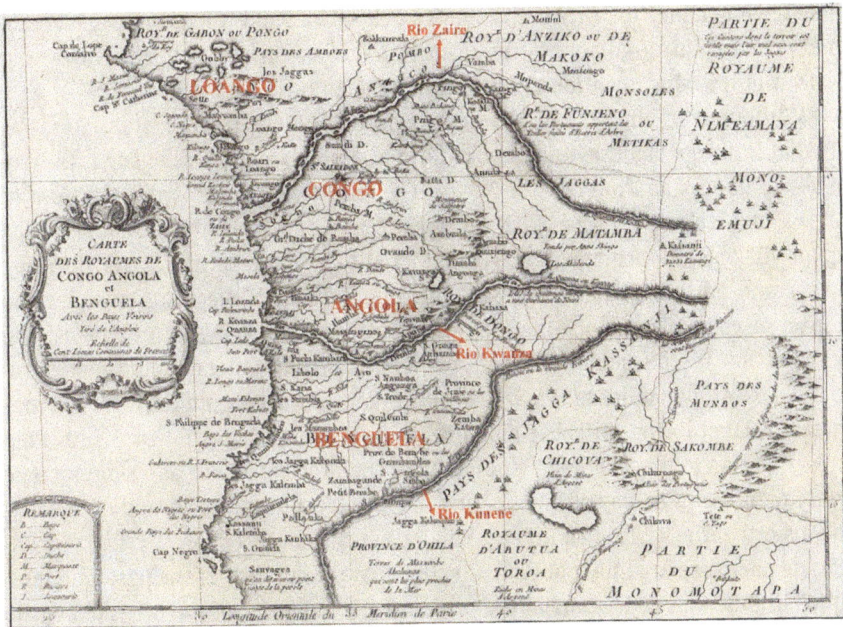

Map 1: Map of the Kingdoms of Loango, Kongo, Angola, and Benguela, 1764.
Source: Jacques Nicolas Bellin, "Carte des Royaumes de Congo, Angola et Benguela avec les pays Voisins, Tire de l'Anglois," 1764, *National Maritime Museum*, Paris, available at http://www.davidrumsey.com/luna/servlet/detail/RUMSEY~8~1~233286~5509680:Carte-des-Royaumes-de-Congo,-Angola?sort=Pub_List_No_InitialSort%2CPub_Date%2CPub_List_No%2CSeries_No?&qvq=q:angola;sort:Pub_List_No_InitialSort%2CPub_Date%2CPub_List_No%2CSeries_No;lc:RUMSEY~8~1&mi=16&trs=25, accessed July 1, 2016.

some, it was only after 1915, with a population of 20,000 white people, that a colonial administration was possible, with a fiscal administration only in place in the 1950s.[7] Another relevant issue is the expansion of slavery in Africa after the so-called legitimate trade, when enslaved Africans were no longer sent to America, but remained in the continent, working in various economic areas in order to

---

7 Honoré Mbunga, "A problemática da periodização da História de Angola: o período colonial," in *Actas do II Encontro Internacional de História de Angola* (Luanda: Arquivo Histórico Nacional de Angola / Ministério da Cultura, 2014), 149–171. The historian John Fage considers that the region "of the coastal states of the Gold Coast, Congo, Angola, the Zambezi Valley, and the cities of the peoples of tropical Africa continued to be very similar to what they were before the century of Henry the Navigator and Vasco da Gama." These authors argue that, before the Berlin Conference, and even some time after 1885, the Portuguese were mainly interested in the trade of enslaved people, and not in colonizing Angola. John D. Fage, *História da África* (Lisbon: Edições 70, 1997), 259.

meet new demands for African products, such as wax and ivory. Another element in support of this argument is the predominance of African political power and African elites, which continued up to the nineteenth century.

Without examining the merits of the chronology of Angolan history, in terms of what interests us here, it is important to note that we do not believe it is erroneous to understand the area of Portuguese influence known as the Kingdom of Angola as a colony. First, as Richard Reid reflected, the term "precolonial" ends up privileging the "colonial" and "attributes to a later period a transforming power and an inordinate meaning." With this, we do not mean to downplay the impact of colonialism since the late-nineteenth century in African societies. The point is that the division sometimes prevents us from understanding more profound African dynamics and political, social and economic conflicts that are intimately related to the different moments of European occupation in Africa. Reid calls attention to the decline in studies about the precolonial era as a symptomatic consequence of that way of interpreting the historical frameworks and of dividing the history of the African continent. Finally, in terms of this book, it is worth mentioning one more argument of Reid: the idea that the conflicts of the past (and multiple pasts) are an active part of the present—the memoirs and writings about the Nova Oeiras Factory demonstrate this decisively, as we shall see in the last chapter.[8]

Another aspect that is worth considering is that, in different territories of the Portuguese Empire, colonization occurred as in the formation of the Kingdom of Angola: at first, without an effective and continuous occupation of the territory and a political and administrative centralization that was limited to a few urban centers, in addition to the conflicts with the local populations. The process of occupation of Brazilian lands is an example of this. The governor of Maranhão said in the seventeenth century, "We are not lords of anything other than the coasts, and in the *sertões*, as I mentioned above, is everything that is useful."[9] For Ângela Domingues, the colonial territories in America were superimposed on preexisting territories, with which they coexisted.[10] This was also the way in which the Portuguese established themselves in Africa and that allowed them to

---

[8] Richard Reid, "Past and Presentism: The 'Precolonial' and the Foreshortening of African History," *Journal of African History* 52 (2011): 135–155.
[9] Carta de Francisco Coelho de Carvalho para Dom João IV. São Luís, May 20, 1647. *Apud*, Rafael Chambouleyron, Monique da Silva Bonifácio, Vanice Siqueira de Melo. "Pelos sertões 'estão todas as utilidades': Trocas e conflitos no sertão amazônico (século XVII)," *Revista de História*, no. 162 (2010): 18. Available at http://www.revistas.usp.br/revhistoria/article/view/19150, accessed April 25, 2016, p. 49. Emphasis added.
[10] Ângela Domingues, *Quando os índios eram vassalos. Colonização e relações de poder no norte do Brasil na segunda metade do século XVIII* (Lisbon: CNCDP, 2000), 215.

maintain the Kingdom of Angola—coexisting with African sovereignties that, by ruling over large populations, also controlled lands, natural resources, and the workforce to exploit them.[11]

For our studies, it is important to note that, after the second half of the eighteenth century, there was a change in Portugal's colonization efforts; in view of the Marquis of Pombal's projects of pragmatic Enlightenment,[12] Governor Sousa Coutinho developed a plan to reform the Kingdom of Angola, transforming it, from a trading post and colony permeated by forts (signs of conquest), to a colony of civilian settlements. As we know, Angola was not "reformed" as Pombal expected, for the trade of enslaved people remained as its main economic activity. Still, there was a colonial project to make an inventory of natural resources, lands, people, dominions, knowledge, and techniques; in other words, a project to map the space, which was put into practice and resulted in significant transformations in the region's societies. The establishment of Nova Oeiras in lands with a long history of contact with the Portuguese revealed the tensions that permeated that process.[13]

The Kingdom of Ndongo was the main kingdom in the region, and it was with its king, or *ngola* for the Ambundus, that the Portuguese made the first contact and

---

[11] In Brazilian and Portuguese historiography, there are heated debates about colonization of the overseas territories. Historians have discussed the dichotomies metropolis/colony and center/periphery, and some have emphasized the relevance of local powers and their ability to negotiate with the center. Given the scope of our study, it is necessary to point out that the term "colonies" already appears in the early-eighteenth century. Nuno Monteiro and João Fragoso use Father Raphael Bluteau's dictionary to explain that at first the term referred to the meaning it had in classical antiquity. However, they point out that in the last quarter of that century, due to the influence of political economy, there were more references to the "duality metropolis/colony." Therefore, our study covers precisely this period, which remains mostly undefined in historiography, in which the opposition between metropolis and colony presumably arose. All the more reason, after this caveat, to employ the term "colony." João Fragoso, Nuno Gonçalo Monteiro (org.), *Um reino e suas repúblicas no atlântico. Comunicações políticas entre Portugal, Brasil e Angola nos séculos XVII e XVIII* (Rio de Janeiro: Civilização Brasileira, 2017).

[12] Sebastião José de Carvalho e Melo received the noble title of Count of Oeiras in 1759, and ten years later that of Marquis of Pombal. The title of Count of Oeiras passed to the heirs of the House of Pombal. Since the period covered in this book encompasses both titles, we will employ both without categorically respecting their chronology.

[13] It should be noted that it has been repeatedly claimed that, in Angola, this colonization effort did not significantly expand the Crown's administrative network. However, in this book, we argue that the factory itself was a way of expanding the royal administration, as well as other commercial enterprises such as the search for gold mines, in addition to religious and cultural influences. Above all, we are interested in stressing that the exploitation of natural and human resources was massive and led to profound transformation in the local dynamics of Luso-African and Ambundu societies.

with whom they engaged in successive wars throughout the seventeenth century. According to Joseph Miller, the *ngola*'s power emanated from an insignia—made of iron, an ax or a knife that was a symbol of authority and access to the supernatural world—introduced by the Samba among the Ambundus, who became keepers of a sophisticated technology of iron smelting and forging.[14] In a corruption of the title *ngola*, the Portuguese called their new conquest the Kingdom of Angola, or, in many sources, simply Angola. In 1671, after successive armed conflicts, the Portuguese defeated the Ngola Ari and subjected to their authority the chiefdoms that had political titles among the Ambundus, who were formerly under the dominion of this Ndongo king, the *sobas** and, beyond that dominion, the *ndembu**.

Hence, the Portuguese occupation expanded on lands of that ancient kingdom and beyond, by subjecting the *sobados*, at first in the region near the Coast called Ilamba, between the Mbengu and Kwanza Rivers, and with time in the region that circumscribes the Kwanza corridor, passing through the mouth of the Lukala River, its main affluent, up to the limits of the Kingdom of Matamba. In the eighteenth century, the Portuguese administration of this territory was delimited on the north by the Ndande River, on the south by the Kwanza River, on the east by the Lukala River, and on the west by the Atlantic Ocean. In addition, since the early-seventeenth century, the captaincy of Benguela was established to the south of the territory. The potentate of Kisama, between Angola and Benguela, remained independent until the nineteenth century.

The Ambundus were mostly in the regions around the Kwanza River, an ethnolinguistic subgroup of those denominated by historiography as Mbundu. As Thornton says, Africa had well-developed industries that produced many commodities, even those that were imported from Europe, such as textiles, iron, copper, and alcoholic beverages.[15] Such was the case with the Ambundus, who grew rice, yam, palm oil, sorghum, among other products, and were great hunters. In addition, they exploited salt mines, metal works (iron and copper), and weaving. They raised cattle in areas where the tsetse fly was not a threat. According to Silva Correa, in the *sertões* it was customary for women to cultivate the land and thus engage in the "hard work of hoe and ax," "while the fathers, husbands, or relatives wove *en*-

---

[14] Joseph C. Miller, *Poder político e parentesco: os antigos Estados Mbundu em Angola*, trans. Maria da Conceição Neto (Luanda: Arquivo Histórico Nacional de Angola, 1995), 67.
[15] John Thornton, *A África e os africanos na formação do mundo atlântico, 1400–1800* (Rio de Janeiro: Campus, 2004), 89.

tangas (sic), [went] to war, or hunted bests."¹⁶ Silva Correa describes the skill of "black weavers":

> unaware of European looms, they weave between two sticks leaning against a wall, making cloths measuring two and a half palms wide and eight or ten palms long: one *entanga* is made up of three cloths joined lengthwise. (...) They make excellent blankets for cold countries; the rest is used for fishing nets and wax wicks.¹⁷

The polygamous husband was the basis of the social structure, because the more women a chief had, the more plantations (*arimos*) and more food he had access to, as well as a greater chance of obtaining more dependents and riches, since the chief's power was based on the number of subjects under his dominion. The Ambundus mainly followed matrilineal kinship relations of succession, whereby the chiefs had control over the land and his "offspring" (*filhos*)—a notion that referred to his subjects, whether free or enslaved. They placed a very high value on their lineages, and in a way they were able to preserve their social and political structure throughout the centuries, in spite of the transformations that took place as a result of the colonial influence. The elders, the lineage's "uncles," were called *makota** (*kota* in singular), and were the guardians and councilors of those who held Ambundu titles, such as the *ngola*; they were in charge of approving new leaders.¹⁸

As Flávia Carvalho demonstrates, in the Kingdom of Ndongo, it was not the *ngola*, but the *sobas*, who were the main protagonists of the alliances with the Portuguese, since they determined who could traverse their territories and established commercial agreements, serving as intermediaries in the relations between the foreigners and the local powers. Thus,

> in practice, the *ngola* was one more *soba*; he was attributed supernatural powers and his position contrasted in theory with the sovereignty that the Portuguese intended to legitimate before the Mbundu, and which they finally succeeded in doing in 1671, with the dethronement of the last *ngola* who was opposed to Portuguese interests.¹⁹

---

16 Elias Alexandre da Silva Correa, *História de Angola* (Lisbon: Clássicos da Expansão Portuguesa no Mundo. Império Africano, 1937), v. I, 113 and 156. In modern Kikongo, there is the form *ntánga*, "a thick fabric; dark red fabric." K. Laman, *Dictionnaire kikongo-français. Avec une étude phonétique décrivant les dialectes les plus importants de la langue dite kikongo* (Brussels: [n.p.], 1936), 787.
17 Elias Alexandre da Silva Correa, *História de Angola*, v. I, 156. Colleen Kriger has thoroughly studied the production of textiles in the Nigeria region, a craft that requires a large investment of time, skill, knowledge, and effort. Colleen E. Kriger, *Cloth in West African History*. The African Archaeology Series (Lanham, Maryland: Altamira Press, 2006).
18 Joseph Miller, *Poder político e parentesco*, 35 and ff.
19 Flávia Maria de Carvalho, *Sobas e homens do rei: interiorização dos portugueses em Angola (séculos XVII e XVIII)* (Maceió: Edufal, 2015), 125.

Hence, in the eighteenth century, the Ambundu *sobas* who were subjected as vassals to the Portuguese were members of the aristocracy of the then extinct Kingdom of Ndongo. In these societies with a complex political structure, the *soba* was the main representative. According to Jill Dias, throughout the Portuguese occupation, the *sobas* developed an "ambiguous identity," i.e. they adapted "politically and culturally to the Atlantic world, taking advantage of the new commercial opportunities and adapting to the colonial Portuguese presence, but without relinquishing their African identity and sociability or their political autonomy."[20]

Other Ambundu authorities appear in the Portuguese sources as subordinated or associated to the *sobas:* the aforementioned councilor, the *kota* or *sobeta* (lesser *sobas* under the jurisdiction of a more powerful *soba*), the *tandala**, the *ngolambole**, the *kimbanda**, the *kitombe**.

There was also the *kilamba**, described by Virgílio Coelho as a priest "in charge of appeasing the fury of nature's genies," although apparently this title's meaning changed with time due to the Portuguese influence, because it became characterized by its strong ties to the colonizers. The *imbari** (from the Kimbundu, *kimbari*, plural *imbari*, overseer, steward, housekeeper) were in a subaltern position; they were African warriors who occupied various positions serving the Portuguese in auxiliary troops, in the Black War. *Ilamba* and *imbari* were characterized by their involvement in the trade of enslaved people in the *sertões*.[21]

According to the chronicles of the missionary João Antônio Cavazzi de Montecúccolo, in the Kingdom of Ndongo, the first "chief of the country" was chosen because the *ngola-mussuri*, which means "blacksmith-king," was "sharper than the rest," for he knew "the way to prepare iron" and used this knowledge "shrewdly and assisted everyone in their public needs, earning the peoples' love and praise."[22] The founder of the Kingdom of Luba, to the east of Kongo, Kalala Ilunga, was associated to iron smelting, and royal rituals reproduced the blacksmith's work at the forge.[23] In many foundational myths of African societies, the associa-

---

[20] Jill Dias, "O Kabuku Kambilu (c. 1850–1900). Uma identidade política ambígua," in *Actas do Seminário Encontro de povos e culturas em Angola* (Lisbon: Comissão Nacional para as Comemorações dos Descobrimentos Portugueses, 1997), 15.

[21] In addition to these titles of nobility, the blacksmiths also had a privileged position among the elite of the Ambundu state due to their technical abilities, which also had a magical/religious function, explicitly revealed in the very history of the foundation of the Kingdom of Ndongo, through the myth of the blacksmith-king.

[22] Antonio Cavazzi de Montecúccolo, *Descrição histórica dos três Reinos do Congo, Matamba e Angola* (Lisbon: Junta de investigações do Ultramar, 1965), 164–166.

[23] Jan Vansina, *Kingdoms of the Savanna* (1966); Thomas Q. Reefe, *The Rainbow and the Kings: A History of the Luba Empire to 1891* (Berkeley: University of California Press, 1981).

tion between the control of metallurgy and iron mines and a sovereign's power was common.

Joseph Miller pointed out the importance of the myth of the blacksmith as the founder of what he calls Mbundu states, highlighting the need to understand the ideological reasons that led kings and chiefs to perpetuate those traditions. Beyond technological issues, there are other motives for the chiefs to attribute a foreign origin to the conqueror and founder of the kingdoms, for "alien origins of the ubiquitous civilizing hero endowed him and his successors with a legitimacy not granted to simple residents of the country, who seemed to be destined to be prophets without honor among their peers."[24]

According to Miller, the reasons for the formation of Mbundu states are related to the influence of "great men and women." Among the reasons cited, was the control of scarce and valuable resources, such as the salt mines of Baixa Kasanje, Kisama, and Libolo, and the iron deposits in the valley of the Nzongeji River and the climb to the Benguela plateau. Another reason were the institutional innovations that took place with time (as they associated with other groups), which attracted people to those states, as in the case of the Mbangala, warriors who associated with each other independently of lineages of belonging.[25] Ideological innovations also contributed to the Ambundus' consolidation, since having a title depended on the persuasion ability of the holder, who had the right to govern because he had access to "supernatural methods" to prove the claimed powers. Alliances with external allies was another essential factor in the development of these states.[26]

In this book, I employ the expression Kingdom of Angola to refer to the area of Portuguese influence from Luanda and its hinterland. I assume two premises: the first is the need to maintain the terms that appear in contemporary sources regarding the existence of this and other kingdoms. My interest in analyzing this specific historical circumstance also refers to the relations between the Kingdom of Kongo and the Kingdom of Portugal. Among the many similarities between both kingdoms, John Thornton highlights the fact that both were monarchies governed

---

24 Other Mbundu states, in addition to Ndongo, Mbondo, Libolo, Pende, Holo, Songo. Joseph Miller, *Poder político e parentesco*, 9 and 40.
25 The Mbangala composed "an association of males open to anyone without regard to their lineage, whose members subjected themselves to impressive initiation rituals that removed them from the protective bosom of their native filial group and simultaneously created strong bonds among the initiates, like warriors in a regiment of supermen, rendered invulnerable to their enemies' weapons," idem, ibidem, 160.
26 In view of the political agreements established between the Mbangala and the Portuguese, which were essential for the maintenance of both political powers. Idem, ibidem, 271.

by kings and nobility classes, whereby relations of "royalty, patronage, and influence dominated the political system."²⁷

The second premise has to do with the fact that Ambundu political elites began using this terminology as a symbol of social distinction before other authorities of the region. When describing the characteristics of the Ndongo royalty after their contact with the Portuguese monarchy, Linda Heywood analyzes the case of Njinga Mbandi. In 1624, she was called the "Lady of Ndongo," and a few months after the death of her brother, she became known as the "Queen of Ndongo." She not only "promoted herself as a ruler through her words and actions, but also paved the way for the continuity of the Ndongo royalty after herself," since the Portuguese recognized her as "Lady the Queen" and "Madam Ana," and called her "Your Honor."²⁸ Hence, by employing the concept of "kingdom," we are not imposing a notion that was foreign to eighteenth-century Ambundu societies. After more than two hundred years of contact with the Portuguese, African authorities appropriated the notion of royalty as a strategy to create and reinforce social hierarchies in their own societies, such as the case of the Njinga queen in the early-seventeenth century.²⁹

1.2 Efforts toward Colonial Expansion to the Interior

Since the seventeenth century, there was a continuous policy of expansion to the interior of the Kingdom of Angola—the Portuguese advanced toward the *sertões*, "establishing villas along the Kwanza [River] and, to the north, along the Mbengu and Ndande [Rivers]." The kingdoms of Matamba and Kasanje were stuck to the

---

27 John Thornton, "Early Kongo-Portuguese Relations: A New Interpretation," *History in Africa* 8 (1981): 183–204. Available at http://www.jstor.org/stable/3171515, accessed June 30, 2016.
28 Linda Heywood, "Descoberta de memória, construção de histórias: o rei do Kongo e a rainha Njinga em Angola e no Brasil," in Actas do II Encontro Internacional de História de Angola (Luanda: Arquivo Histórico Nacional de Angola/ Ministério da Cultura, 2014), 559 and 560. See also: Selma Pantoja, *Nzinga Mbandi: mulher, guerra e escravidão* (Brasilia: Editora Thesaurus, 2000); Marina de Mello e Souza, *Além do Visível. Poder, catolicismo e comércio no Congo e Angola, séculos XVI e XVII* (São Paulo: Edusp, 2018); Linda M. Heywood, *Njinga of Angola. Africa's Warrior Queen* (Cambridge: Harvard University Press, 2017).
29 Roquinaldo Ferreira comments on how Africans borrowed European elements in his book: "(...) Africans incorporated elements of European culture to reinforce social hierarchies among them." Roquinaldo Ferreira, *Cross-Cultural Exchange in the Atlantic World. Angola and Brazil during the Era of the Slave Trade* (New York: Cambridge University Press, 2012), 12; Roquinaldo Ferreira, "'Ilhas crioulas': o significado plural da mestiçagem cultural na África Atlântica," *Revista de História* 155 (2006): 17–41.

commercial logic of the trade of enslaved people dominated by the Portuguese, who sent agents to mediate negotiations in those locations.[30]

There is no doubt that the Portuguese expansion to the continent's interior was motivated by their interest in enslaving a larger number of people, to meet the demands of the transatlantic trade. Joseph Miller coined the term "slaving frontier" to characterize the advancements of the wars and raids in search of people to enslave toward the east, in the hinterlands of West Central Africa, from the sixteenth century to the 1870s and 1880s, when the frontier reached the region of the great lakes. The new areas subdued became slaveholding societies, i.e. they entered the commercial logic of foreign commodities in exchange for enslaved people who fed the transatlantic trade. Miller points out that the enslaving frontier advanced like a demographic wave that left political, social, economic, and even ecological instability in its wake, since African political elites became indebted with the traders and fell in the trap of the trade.[31] Later studies, such as those by Mariana Candido, demonstrate that the enslaved did not mostly come from the deep interior of the *sertões*, as Miller alleged; rather, they were recruited in the Portuguese area of influence. The enslaved were vassals of the King of Portugal, baptized, and fluent in Portuguese and European culture.[32]

In spite of the undeniable importance of the trade of enslaved people in Portugal's expansion, it was not the only factor that led to the territory's occupation. In addition to firmly establishing the frontiers of the conquest, which were fragile and constantly threatened by other Europeans or the various African potentates, the Portuguese searched for precious metals (gold and silver) or valuable ones

---

30 Elikia M'Bokolo, *África negra. História e Civilizações até ao século XVIII*, second ed. (Lisbon: Edições Colibri, 2012), 408 and 461.

31 "The slaving frontier zone thus washed inland in the 16th century and surged east like a demographic wave bearing the sea-borne goods of the Europeans on its crest." Joseph C. Miller, *Way of Death*, 149. One example of the frontier's expansion to the interior and its consequences were the wars between the Portuguese and, in particular, the *ngola* of Ndongo in the seventeenth century. After the so-called "Angolan wars," there was a period of drought in the region and political decomposition in the Kingdom of Ndongo.

32 See: Mariana P. Candido, *An African Slaving Port and the Atlantic World. Benguela and its Hinterland* (2013); Roquinaldo Ferreira, *Cross-Cultural Exchange in the Atlantic World* (2012); John Thornton, "As guerras civis no Congo e o tráfico de escravizados: a história e a demografia de 1718 a 1844 revisitadas," *Estudos Afro-Asiáticos*, no. 32 (1997): 55–74; Linda Heywood, "Slavery and its Transformation in the Kingdom of Kongo: 1491–1800," *The Journal of African History* 50, no. 1 (2009): 1–22. Linda Heywood and John Thornton mapped the wars in the hinterlands and their relation to the supply of enslaved people, seen in *Central Africans, Atlantic Creoles, and the Foundation of the Americas, 1585–1660* (New York: Cambridge University Press, 2007).

(copper and iron), while they also intended to undertake a spiritual conquest—the people's conversion to the Catholic faith.[33]

In the sixteenth and seventeenth centuries, the military campaigns and incursions by missionaries, colonial officers, and private individuals, such as merchants or *sertanejos*, allowed them to become acquainted with Luanda's *sertões*.[34]

Since the seventeenth century, the issue of territorialization of the Portuguese Empire became essential in overseas political communications. Controlling the sea and political and commercial networks based on alliances with the local populations became insufficient. The territorially discontinuous empire described by Luís Felipe Thomaz gave way to a new paradigm founded on territorialization. Occupying land and delimiting the territory thus became central elements of Portuguese colonization.[35]

In the second half of the eighteenth century, the space of Portuguese colonies was reassessed, in the context of Marquis of Pombal's reformist plans. The purpose of the incentives granted to civilian occupation and for the construction of new settlements was to order and control the space, in the context of a program of reforms that aimed at increasing royal authority in the colonies' interior, taking advantage of the "potential of the territories formerly unexplored" or little explored.[36] In general, there was an effort to unify the space in order to consolidate Portuguese sovereignty through political occupation and an "orderly urban layout," which also promoted presumably superior European values among the Crown's subjects, the "naturals of the land." These colonial plans were met with various forms of resistance to those attempts at ruling over the *sertões* and their people. It was no different in the Kingdom of Angola. The programs to remodel the interior, inspired in what was taking place in Portuguese America, were confronted by the local logics of territorial occupation, conflicts that were present

---

[33] Jill Dias, "As primeiras penetrações portuguesas em África," in Luis Albuquerque (dir.), *Portugal no Mundo* (Lisbon: Alfa, 1989), v. I, 281–298; Marina de Mello e Souza, *Além do Visível. Poder, catolicismo e comércio no Congo e Angola, séculos XVI e XVII*, thesis (Universidade de São Paulo, 2012).

[34] The accounts by Giovanni Antonio Cavazzi are an indispensable source for the history of the Kingdoms of Kongo and Angola until the seventeenth century. Cf.: Giovanni Antonio Cavazzi de Montecúccolo. *Descrição histórica dos três reinos do Congo, Matamba e Angola*, translation, notes, and index by Father Graciano Maria de Leguzzano (Lisbon: Junta de Investigações do Ultramar, 1965). 2 v.

[35] Luís Filipe Thomaz, *De Ceuta a Timor* (Lisbon: Difel, 1994), 207–243; Antonio Manuel Hespanha and Catarina Madeira Santos, "Os poderes num império oceânico," in José Mattoso (dir.), *O Antigo Regime (1620–1807)*, vol. IV de *História de Portugal* (Lisbon: C. Leitores, 1993), 395–413.

[36] Roberta Marx Delson, *Novas Vilas para o Brasil colônia. Planejamento espacial e social no século XVIII* (Brasilia: Edições Alva, 1997), 140.

even in the establishment of the town of Nova Oeiras, founded to contain the buildings of the homonymous iron foundry.

It was in this context of the promotion of greater control over the territory and its natural resources that European naturalists set out to inventory the nature and the peoples under colonial domination.[37] In Portugal, under the guidance of Domingos Vandelli (1735–1816), professor at the University of Coimbra, naturalists organized expeditions to Brazil, Cape Verde, India, Mozambique, and Angola.[38]

Cartographic representation, simultaneously the result of and a motivation for those expeditions, was one of the instruments employed to elaborate projects to explore the African interior. In addition, since the first decades of the eighteenth century, European diplomats devoted their efforts to legitimize the political appropriation of overseas territories through the use of geographical maps.[39] It was in this context that Governor Antonio Álvares da Cunha (1753–1758), the first to receive enlightened directives from then Minister Sebastião José Carvalho de Melo, emphasized the fundamental importance of cartography for the Kingdom of Angola, "for it is not possible to understand the vastness of these domains without someone making the effort to clearly show it in a geographical map."[40]

The 1790 map elaborated by the colonel and engineer Luis Cordeiro Pinheiro Furtado reveals the existing tensions in the complex geopolitics of the Kingdom of Angola. Based on his own travels through the *sertões* and on those sponsored by the Baron of Moçamedes (1779–1782), Pinheiro Furtado's map presents open frontiers and the Portuguese presence is represented by forts, fortress, districts, and markets. In the caption, the engineer explained that his map portrayed

> the current state of the Kingdoms of Angola and Benguela, with all the Portuguese establishments spread along the Coast and the interior of those *sertões*: it includes all black settlements in the country, whether vassals, allies, or enemies of the Portuguese Domain, up to the most distant corners known that provide objects for national export.[41]

---

37 Ronald Raminelli, *Viagens Ultramarinas: Monarcas, vassalos e governo a distância* (São Paulo: Alameda, 2008), 97.
38 William Joel Simon, *Scientific Expeditions in the Portuguese Overseas Territories (1783–1808)* (Lisbon: Instituto de Investigação Científica Tropical, 1983), 9.
39 Iris Kantor, "Cartografia e diplomacia: usos geopolíticos da informação toponímica (1750–1850)," *Anais do Museu Paulista* 17, no. 2 (Jul–Dec 2009).
40 Carta do governador Antonio Alvares da Cunha a Diogo de Mendonça Corte Real. São Paulo de Assunção de Luanda, August 8, 1753. AHU_CU_001, Cx. 38, D. 82. *Apud* Catarina Madeira Santos. *Um governo "polido" para Angola*, 101.
41 "Geographical map comprising the West Coast of Africa between the latitudes of 5 and 19 degrees south, and on the continent, the current state of the Kingdoms of Angola and Benguela, with all Portuguese establishments scattered along the Coast and the interior of those *sertões*. Identifying all the black settlements in the country, whose inhabitants are vassals, allies, and enemies of

34 —— Chapter 1 The kingdom of Angola (18th century)

In Cordeiro's explanation, we see a categorization of space: there is the Coast and the *sertões*—the close interior, as is commonly called in the bibliography, Luanda and its hinterland; the distant interior of the *sertões*, governed by potentates that were not vassals of the Portuguese Crown, which provided commodities and enslaved people "for national export." The term *sertão* has multiple meanings and similar connotations in the various localities of the Portuguese Empire. The *sertões* of the Kingdom of Angola are described in the sources as "uncultured," "dilated," "evil," "ill," "deserts," "devoid of resources," "closed," "subject to abuses," "violent," "brushwood," "rebellious," etc. In short, a region "where there is no police, charity, fear of God, fidelity, or the use of natural law."[42]

This last phrase by Silva Correa stands out because, in addition to expressing isolation and geographical ignorance of the *sertões*, it relates to a region that was not under Portuguese dominion and resisted the advancement of the Crown's subjects. It was therefore a territory under other domains that did not consider themselves vassals of the King of Portugal and everything that subjection implied, such as the Catholic faith. Examples of this were the potentates who kept the Portuguese from advancing into the deep *sertão* (Kasanje, Matamba) and who controlled the trade of enslaved people.

Returning to Pinheiro Furtado's letter, the phrase "little known lands" can be associated to the *sertão* as a distant vastness. What this map demonstrates is therefore that, at the turn of the eighteenth to the nineteenth century, Portuguese

---

the Portuguese domain, to the furthest known confines that provide goods for national export. The positions and spelling of prior and arbitrary maps were corrected with the observations of Field Marshal and Commander General of the National and Royal Corps of engineers, Luis Candido Cordeiro Pinheiro Furtado, then Lieutenant Colonel of the same Corps, who for the 10-year period in which he was in that Kingdom, he traveled in various expeditions directed and commanded by him through the entire Coast between Molembo and Cabo Negro, and the entire country, resorting to astronomical calculations and local knowledge from the best and most intelligent practitioners of the country's topography. Elaborated in the year 1790. Scale of 30 leagues. Drawn by the Engineer Captain Lourenço Homem da Cunha Eça." There is also a caption for the characters that indicate "Banza or black settlement. The chief called Souva" and for the "Presidio, or Portuguese Fort where there is a garrison." GEAEM, 1207-2 A-24 A-111. See Map 1 in the appendices.

42 Elias Alexandre da Silva Correa, *História de Angola*, vol. I, 31. These expressions are found in the following documents: Portaria sobre os jornais dos povos vassalos. São Paulo de Assunção de Luanda, December 7, 1770. AHU_CU_001, Cx. 55, D. 6 e 7. Carta de Luís Cantofer para FISC. São Paulo de Assunção de Luanda, August 18, 1770.C. 8744, fl, 6443, fl, 7. FISC, "Memórias do Reino de Angola e suas conquistas." As in the Kingdom of Angola, in the sixteenth-century Amazon, *sertão* acquired various meanings for the Portuguese administration: "vastness, distance, opposition to the coast, anarchy, refuge, violence, conversion," among others. Rafael Chambouleyron, Monique da Silva Bonifácio, and Vanice Siqueira de Melo, "Pelos sertões 'estão todas as utilidades': Trocas e conflitos no sertão amazônico (Século XVII)," 2010.

knowledge and appropriation of the African territory were minimal. In the case of the Kingdom of Angola, the vast *sertão* indicates that Portugal's political power was quite precarious in the territory, which allowed many African sovereignties to survive until the nineteenth century.

The space occupied by the Kingdom of Angola was divided in the map into settlements of "Negroes of the country"; note that there is no mention of white settlements. This reveals who actually populated the *sertões*. Among these population centers, there were some that were subjected to the Portuguese through the force of arms, as was the case with the ancient Kingdom of Ndongo. There were also allied communities that established political and commercial agreements with the Portuguese, especially in relation to the trade of enslaved people, such as the potentate of Holo or of Mbangala Kasanje. Finally, there were enemy societies that engaged in constant revolts against Portuguese domination, such as Kisama, which is identified as an "indomitable" province.[43]

In contrast with the *sertões*, the city of Luanda was organized in a similar way as other cities and capitals of the Empire. The political, military, administrative, and religious center of Luanda was in the Upper City, at the parish of Sé, whose headquarters was the church of Nossa Senhora da Conceição. The governor's palace, the main barracks of the guard corps, and the Municipal Council were also in that neighborhood. In the second half of the eighteenth century, in order to decentralize the administration, public buildings were built in the Lower City, or parish of Nossa Senhora dos Remédios, where the commercial center was located. Among them, stand out the Customs building, the Royal Treasury, the arsenal, the Ribeira das Naus waterfront, the Terreiro Público building (where food was collected and distributed), and the public walkway. In the neighborhoods further into the plateau, such as Rosário and Santa Efigênia do Carmo, there were orchards where maize and millet was usually grown, as well as camps of enslaved people awaiting shipment. The islands—Cazanga, Desterro, and Luanda—were reserved for apple orchards, fish drying, and leisure for rich residents.[44]

The description of Cordeiro's map also tells us that Portuguese occupation took place in the form of "scattered establishments," i.e. forts, commercial establish-

---

43 Regarding the constant rebellions of the *sobas* of Kisama, see: Aurora da Fonseca Ferreira, *A Kisama em Angola do século XVI ao início do século XX: autonomia, ocupação e resistência* (Luanda, Republic of Angola: Kilombelombe, 2012); Flávia Maria de Carvalho, "Sobas rebeldes de Angola," *Impressões Rebeldes* (Rio de Janeiro: UFF, 2016), available at http://www.historia.uff.br/impressoesrebeldes/?temas=sobas-rebeldes-nos-sertoes-do-ndongo-seculo-xvi, accessed September 20, 2016.
44 José Carlos Venâncio, *A economia de Luanda e hinterland no século XVIII. Um estudo de sociologia histórica* (Lisbon: Editorial Estampa, 1996), 35–40.

ments, fortress, and jurisdictions or districts. This way of dividing and classifying the territory under Portuguese dominion also appears in the work of the military officer Elias Alexandre da Silva Correa.[45] In his memoirs, he divided the territory of Angola into the "seashore," where there was the Port of Angola, the Fort of São Miguel, the Fort of Penedo, the Forts of Conceição and Necessidades, and the *"sertões"* or "the continent's interior," where the Portuguese built fortress and jurisdictions.[46]

The main function of fortress was to house the military troops, under the command of a *capitão-mor* or regent. Below him were three officers: a lieutenant, an *alferes*, and an assistant. These low-rank officers became key players in the circuits of the trade of enslaved people in the African interior. In order to develop this trade, there was a market next to every fortress—"where goods were displayed for sale, to allow for easy access to the captives."[47] The fortress built over time, following the corridor of the Kwanza River, were those of Massangano (1538), Muxima (1599), Cambambe (1604), Ambaca (1614), and Pedras de Pungo Andongo (1671), the north of the river. South of the Kwanza were the fortress of São Filipe de Benguela (1617) and Caconda, first founded in 1682 and transferred to the Katala region in the mid-eighteenth century because it was safer there. In the eighteenth century, two more fortress were founded: that of São José de Encoge in 1759, located in the Ndembu region, an important trading post for foreign goods from Loango and Cabinda, which were taken to Angola's interior; and the fortress of Novo Redondo, built in 1769 on the mouth of the Ngunza River in the Kingdom of Benguela, in

---

[45] The biography of the military officer Elias Alexandre da Silva Correa is practically unknown; we know that he came from Portuguese America—"born an American Portuguese." According to Ingrid de Oliveira, the main motivation of the military officer when writing *História de Angola* was to obtain privileges: "After serving the Marquis of Lavradio (1749–1753), he was transferred to Santa Catarina, at the time a captaincy attached to that of Rio de Janeiro. In 1778, he went to Lisbon to continue his studies. His objective was to build a successful military career: 'to gain, in the royal service, access to high positions and the esteem of medaled and well-born men.' With this purpose, according to Magnus Pereira, Elias Alexandre went as a volunteer to Angola. In August 1782, he was appointed Assistant of the Infantry Regiment of São Paulo de Luanda, with the rank of Captain." Ingrid Silva de Oliveira, *Textos militares e mercês numa Angola que se pretendia "reformada": um estudo de caso dos autores Elias Alexandre da Silva Correa e Paulo Martins Pinheiro de Lacerda*, thesis (Master's in History) (Rio de Janeiro: UFF, 2015), 210. Magnus Pereira, "Rede de mercês e carreira: o 'desterro d'Angola' de um militar luso-brasileira (1782–1789)," *História: Questões & Debates*, no. 45 (2006): 97–127.
[46] Elias Alexandre da Silva Correa, *História de Angola*, v. I, 19–24.
[47] Idem, 25.

an attempt to thwart the contraband of enslaved people by other European nations.[48]

Correa da Silva also cites the creation of jurisdictions or districts governed by a *capitão-mor* for a period of three years.[49] He highlights three districts near the Kwanza River: Icolo, Dande, and Golungo, the most important in the second half of the eighteenth century. There were also districts that developed around the fortress, such as Ambaca, Massangano, and Cambambe, and also jurisdictions without a direct relation to the fortress, such as Bengo, by the Mbengu River, and Libongo, north of the Ndande River, on the margins of the Lifune River.[50]

As we can see, in general the districts and fortress were located along rivers that guided the process of colonizing the interior. Whether to maintain *arimos*[51] or to occupy the territory, but especially as routes for the trade of enslaved people, rivers were essential to explore the lands of the Kingdom of Angola.

Ilídio do Amaral conducted a detailed study of the Kwanza River. While at first the river constituted an obstacle, since it was impossible to sail through its mouth, after the Portuguese settled on the coast, the river became essential to conquer Ndongo and establish the Kingdom of Angola. By the river was Massangano, a fort and town founded by Paulo Dias de Novais, which symbolized the entrance to the *sertão*, i.e. "the conquest of lands to the east (in Ngola territory), to the

---

48 Carlos Couto, *Os capitães-mores em Angola no século XVIII. Subsídio para o estudo da sua actuação* (Luanda: Instituto de Investigação Científica de Angola, 1972), 104 and 105.
49 Elias Alexandre da Silva Côrrea, *História de Angola*, v. I, 25.
50 Regarding this river and region north of the Ndande River: "At the mouth of the Ndande River to the North, at a distance of three leagues, the Lifune River flows out, a small and unnavigable river that nonetheless has the best water available in Portuguese dominions in this Coast of Africa. The sources of this and the Ndande River are said to be in the states of the two *Ndembu*, Dambi and Quitoxe. East of the state of Ambuila (powerful Dembo, and vassal of His Majesty, but evil and cunning) above the mouth of this Lifune River, one league inland, is the village of Libongo, vassals of His Majesty, where the mineral pitch comes from." Paulo Martins Pinheiro de Lacerda, "Notícias das regiões e povos de Quisama e do Mussulo – 1798," in *Annaes Marítimos e Coloniaes* 6, no. 4 (1846): 119–133. Transcribed by Arlindo Correa. Available at http://arlindo-correia.com/080109.html, accessed April 30, 2016.
51 "Lands on the outskirts of Luanda, along the Kwanza, Dongo, and Nande Rivers; the region came to be known as 'the city's breadbasket.' They were agricultural properties that over time were associated with traditional African forms of cultivation and leasing with larger capital investments." Selma Pantoja, "Donas de arimos: um negócio feminino no abastecimento de gênero alimentício em Luanda nos séculos XVIII e XIX," in Selma Pantoja (org.), *Entre Áfricas e Brasis* (Brasilia: Paralelo 15, 2001), 24.

north (in Ndembu territory), and to the south (in Kisama territory)."[52] The fort was located on a rocky hill at the confluence of the Lukala and Kwanza Rivers—a strategic location both to defend the territory and to obtain and ship enslaved people. Later, the forts built along the Kwanza River also served to protect that important commercial route—a communication route and source of supplies, since there were *sobado* plantations and vassal villages along the river.

The Catholic Church, which was an essential element of colonization ideals, was also present. Elias Alexandre describes the churches, brotherhoods, and convents that existed in the city of Luanda and that constituted a cohesive "ecclesiastical state," developed through the work of priests and religious orders. The situation of churches in the districts of the *sertão* was very different from that of those in the city; there were temples throughout the entire conquered territory, but many of them had no "priests to administer the sacraments," and even the city of Benguela suffered from that spiritual "sterility."[53] The complaints were not limited to the scarcity of priests; the character of the few priests available was also questioned. Sousa Coutinho complained of father Rodrigo Pereira Jaques and his involvement in the trade of enslaved people; Jaques was the vicar of the town of Nova Oeiras, and "because of his scandalous life and public commerce [he] was incapable of ministering a *sertão* of heathens and corrupted men"—an "evil man" who was also unprepared to congregate "people with different dispositions, customs, and languages."[54]

It is worth recalling that, in the district of Golungo, in the *soba* towns of Bango Aquitamba [Mbangu kya Tambwa], there was a mission of the Discalced Carmelites.[55] The order arrived in Luanda in 1659 with the mission of founding a convent

---

[52] Ilídio do Amaral, *O Rio Cuanza (Angola), da Barra a Kambambe: reconstituição de aspectos geográficos e acontecimentos históricos dos séculos XVI e XVII* (Lisbon: Ministério da Ciência e da Tecnologia / Instituto de Investigação Científica Tropical, 2000), 14 and 15.

[53] Elias Alexandre da Silva Côrrea, *História de Angola*, v. I, 106.

[54] Carta de FISC para o Cabido da Sé de Luanda. São Paulo de Assunção de Luanda, October 1767. PADAB, IHGB 126, DVD10, directory 22, image DSC00047.

[55] Friar Belchior de Sousa was born in Mondim de Basto in the late-sixteenth century. He studied grammar in Lamego. He served in the military in Alentejo. He professed as a Discalced Carmelite in the Convent of Nossa Senhora dos Remédios in Lisbon. He left for Angola in 1676, in the company of the governor and captain general of that kingdom, Aires de Saldanha, where he built a church and carried out missionary work in the lands of the *Soba* Bango Aquitamba [Mbangu kya Tambwa]." Entry "Belchior de Sousa," in Barroso da Fonte (coord.), *Dicionário dos mais ilustres Trasmontanos e Alto Durienses* (Guimarães: Editora Cidade Berço, 2001), available at http://www.do douropress.pt/index.asp?idedicao=66&idseccao=571&id=4137&action=noticia, accessed April 23, 2016. Cadonerga mentions that the "sons of the unparalleled Saint Theresa of Jesus, Discalced Carmelites," entered the provinces of Ilamba and Lumbu, "and have their residence in the lands and domains of the *soba* Bango a Kitamba, where they have done much service to God for the good of

for Saint Teresa there. In Mbangu kya Tambwa, the order also had a hospice.[56] Even in this mission, the priests appear not to have observed the precepts of religious life. There are news that, in 1754, a Discalced Carmelite priest, Friar Lourenço de Jesus Maria, had been living there for fourteen years "in the wilderness, without a religious life or a frock."[57]

The efforts to build civilian towns in the *sertão* like Nova Oeiras is another relevant aspect of the African territory in the second half of the eighteenth century. The Marquis of Pombal, in an opinion written in 1760, analyzed the conditions of foreign occupation of Africa's West Coast, in an attempt to justify the ban on the arms trade in the *sertão*. According to him, "the English, Dutch, and Danish establishments from Cabo Branco to Loango [were] miserable forts, without any form of colony or settlement, and most of them had no soldiers." Those nations' goal was merely to engage in the trade of enslaved people, and for that reason they traded in weapons without fear, since they had no intention of creating colonies there "that could annoy their black neighbors."[58] The Kingdom of Angola should be the opposite of that, just as Portuguese interests in its occupation were different. It was in the context of this comparative exercise that Pombal stated, "Angola is not a trading post, it has been different since the beginning. We have there a large city and many colonies, even in the interior, far from the sea."[59]

Considering all this information about the fragility of Portugal's dominion, Pombal's reading of the occupation of the Kingdom of Angola can only be considered excessive, even though the advancements of Portuguese colonization were quite unlike those of other European nations, which restricted their domains to the coastal areas.

---

those gentiles." Antonio de Oliveira de Cadornega, *História Geral das Guerras Angolanas*, annotated and revised by José Matias Delgado (Lisbon: Agência-geral do Ultramar, 1972), v. I, 239. Written approximately between 1670 and 1681, Cadornega's *História Geral das Guerras Angolas* has been an indispensable source to write the history of Angola. Cf.: G. Childs, "The Peoples of Angola in the Seventeenth Century According to Cadornega," *The Journal of African History* 1, no. 2 (1960): 271–279; B. Heintze, "Written Sources, Oral Traditions and Oral Traditions as Written Sources: The Steep and Thorny Way to Early Angolan History," *Paideuma* 33 (1987): 263–287.

56 Consulta ao conselho Ultramarino, November 27, 1665. *Monumenta Missionária Africana*, v. 12, doc. 243, p. 592. Consulta ao conselho Ultramarino, November 27, 1665. Carta régia à Câmara de Luanda, January 17, 1662. *Monumenta Missionária Africana*, v. 12, doc. 171, p. 425. *Apud* Alexandre Almeida Marcussi. *Cativeiro e cura. Experiências religiosas da escravidão atlântica nos calundus de Luiza Pinta, séculos XVII-XVIII*, dissertation (PhD) (Universidade de São Paulo, 2015), 237.

57 Parecer do governador Antonio Álvares da Cunha sobre as minas de ouro do rio Lombige. Belém, October 29, 1754. AHU, Códice 574, fl. 4 and 4v.

58 Parecer do Conde de Oeiras. Palácio de Nossa Senhora da Ajuda, November 20, 1760. AHU, Cód. 555, fl. 59 and 59v.

59 Idem, Ibidem.

However, Angola as a colony of white settlements was more of an intention of Pombal-oriented governments than a reality in 1760. Perhaps in an attempt to adapt reality to the intentions, after the second half of the eighteenth century, metropolitan policies promoted a new way of occupying the *sertão* in the Kingdom of Angola—civilian settlements. According to Catarina Madeira Santos, the towns would be added to the administration network composed of fortress, trading posts, districts, and markets, and should be separate from the *sobados:* "each new settlement was endowed with a judge, a *capitão-mor*, and a priest with a church and a parish."[60] During Sousa Coutinho's government, settlements were created in the Kingdom of Benguela and Luanda's hinterland.

Thus, the colonial presence in the Kingdom of Angola was sustained by the fortress, trading posts, markets, and civilian settlements, on one hand, and by the vassal *sobados* allied to the Portuguese, on the other. The ironworks established in Luanda's hinterland were also conceived as depots of the colonial administration of the *sertão*. The iron factories' superintendent often had to solve issues related to the fortress and districts close to the factory, which were mostly of a military nature. In November 1767, Sousa Coutinho ordered the superintendent of the factories, Antonio Anselmo Duarte de Siqueira, to march to the fortress of Ambaca and Pedras de Pungo Andongo with a cavalry that had arrived at the port of Luanda, to ensure the security of those fortress.[61] When Mbangala Kasanje requested assistance from Luanda's government in the war he was facing in its territories, Duarte de Siquiera was ordered to go to the market of enslaved people in those lands to protect the merchants present there at the service of the Portuguese Crown.[62]

At first, the ironworks were located in Ilamba, but the Nova Oeiras buildings were constructed between the Lukala and Luinha Rivers, a region also known as Lumbu (or Ilamba Alta), as we can see in Map 2. It is a part of a copy of the 1790 map by Pinheiro Furtado, dated 1791. This copy contains more detailed information than the 1790 map, but maintains the captions and explanations of the earlier map. These additions allow us to visualize Luanda and its hinterland on the northern bank of the Kwanza River in detail.

Most of the places we have described here are represented in the map; rivers, markets, districts, the town of Nova Oeiras, the iron factories (circled in red), the *arimos* where food was grown, the Mission of the Discalced Carmelites in the town

---

60 Catarina Madeira Santos, *Um governo polido para Angola*, 150.
61 Carta de FISC para Antonio Anselmo Duarte de Siqueira, coronel e intendente geral das reais fábricas do ferro. São Paulo de Assunção de Luanda, November 25, 1767. BNP, C. 8742, F. 6364, fl. 148.
62 Carta de FISC para Antonio Anselmo Duarte de Siqueira, coronel e intendente geral das reais fábricas do ferro. São Paulo de Assunção de Luanda, March 7, 1768. IEB/ USP, AL-083–027.

of the *soba* Mbangu kya Tambwa, the Cacuaco salt mines (sources of sea salt from the homonymous lakes), and the region's *sobados*.

Among the symbols employed by Pinheiro Furtado to refer to the various occupations, there is the cathedral, the church of Nossa Senhora da Conceição, which represents the city of Luanda. The church, the Municipal Council, and the governor's palace were the symbols of power of the orderly layout of the urban space in colonial cities. Fortress in turn provided the image of a fortress, signaling its main function, which was as a military garrison to defend the territory. Both the markets and the iron factory are indicated with a pink square, identifying places that were not controlled by local chiefs—a colonial establishment different from fortress. The map also demonstrates the importance of the salt mines, which are highlighted with their own symbol.

The many *banzas* (villages) of African chiefdoms and their subjects' *cubatas**, indicated with pink circles, described as "black settlements," are present throughout the entire territory. The *banza* of the *soba* Mbangu kya Tambwa is marked with the same pink circle, but with a cross added to indicate that there was a mission there, that of the Discalced Carmelites. In contrast with previous drawings, the Ambundu settlements represented here are out of tune with the ideal of a regular layout according to the European imaginary of spatial organization of the time—they are points with no defined form.

Cartographic language was also used to portray these contrasts between a world with planned buildings, which were actually made of adobe and clay, and a different world that they wished to subdue, whose organizational logics were not understood by Europeans or were seen with contempt. This is evident in the image's caption, "straw huts"—which is how royal authorities perceived African dwellings. It is not surprising that Governor Sousa Coutinho is remembered in the "Catalog of governors" as he who made repairs to fortresses, built settlements, "added to the palace of the [governor's] residence an excellent terrace overlooking the ocean."[63]

At this point, it is interesting to compare the fortress with the *quipacas** (from the Kimbundu *ekipaka*), which were veritable African forts—impenetrable stone trenches. In Angola's *sertão*, being acquainted and knowing how to use stone fortresses, resistant trees, etc., from the natural environment was a much more advantageous architectural strategy than adobe, stone, and lime.

---

[63] "Catálogo dos governadores do Reino de Angola. Com uma prévia notícia dos princípios de sua conquista e do que nela obraram os governadores dignos de memória," in *Coleção de notícias para a História das nações ultramarinas que vivem nos domínios portugueses ou lhe são vizinhas* (Academia Real das Ciências de Lisboa. Lisbon: Tip. da Academia Real das Ciências de Lisboa, 1826), 421.

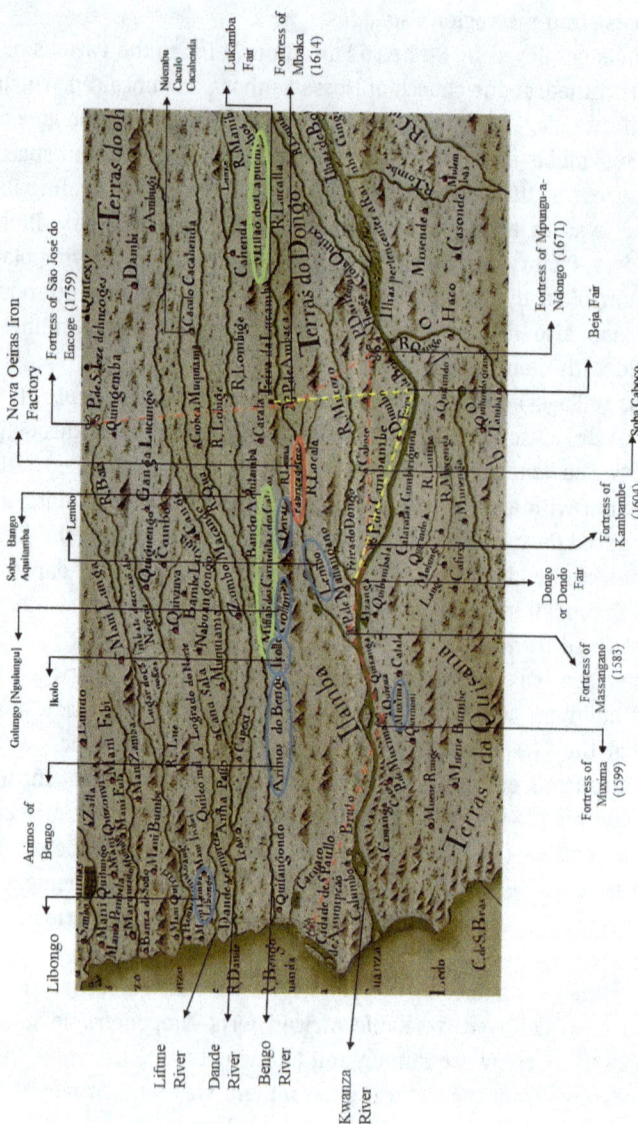

Map 2: Detail of the interior of the Kingdom of Angola, 1791.

Source: Part of "Mapa geográfico compreendendo a Costa Ocidental d'África entre 5 e 16 graus e 40 minutos de latitude Sul, representando no continente o estado atual dos Reinos d'Angola e Benguela (...)," by Luis Candido Cordeiro Pinheiro Furtado. Drawn by Lieutenant Colonel Candido Cordeiro Furtado and copied by the third-year student of the Royal Academy of Fortification, Artillery, and Design, Pedro José Botelho de Gouvea, Cadet of the Cavalry Regiment of Meklemburg." Lisbon, 1792. Municipal Library of Porto, BPMP_C-M&A-Pasta 24(17). The markings are ours.

The red line on the map shows the administrative and military network composed by the fortress during Portugal's occupation, especially along the Kwanza River. Next to it is a yellow line that points to a different network, a commercial one, composed of a few markets present in the territory—Lukamba (the great market of Ambaca), Beja, and Dongo. It is worth recalling that the main market of enslaved people was beyond the Kingdom of Angola, outside of Portugal's administration, in Kasanje, which was controlled by Mbangala.

These markings allow us to imagine the triangle of which Governor Sousa Coutinho wrote in his memoirs, which represented the area that was under Portugal's influence for the longest time. In addition to this nearby interior, the Portuguese presence penetrated the distant *sertões* in an even more precarious manner, by making alliances with local chiefdoms. One example of this is the important political player *ndembu* Kakulu Kakahenda, whose territory was outside the lines of the alleged triangle, and who became a vassal of the Portuguese Crown in 1615 and, from that time on, established alliances and partnerships with the Portuguese.

The blue circles shown on the map are districts, such as Golungo, Icolo, and Dande, or population centers, such as Libongo and Muxima, next to the homonymous fortress, Lembo, Bengo (near the Mbengu River), and Nova Oeiras. These more or less populated centers housed residents of many origins and were often associated to plantations, as was the case with the Mbengu *arimos*. Finally, Catholic missions are shown in green, which were another important form of colonial influence, considering their role in the colonization of the *sertões* by means of religion.

The map demonstrates how discontinuous that triangle was, not only in terms of its borders, but also of its interior, where Portuguese political units coexisted with politically autonomous African units, whose chiefs attempted to maintain as much independence as possible by establishing alliances with the Crown.

In the eighteenth century, there was an attempt to implement a series of reforms in the *sertões* in response to the fragility of agriculture and the moral decadence of *sertão* commerce, but also to the colonial desire to occupy that territory in a different manner. The names of the fortress and population centers are an example of this. Up to that point, they were toponyms related to the conquest of large *sobados*—Muxima, Cambambe, Golungo—, a way of signaling the victory of colonial forces in the territory. Settlements with names of European towns were meant to foster a different type of colonization—to promote industry, white occupation, and agriculture.

Apparently, the Portuguese developed a vast knowledge of the African territory. Although this profusion of maps is evidence of their efforts to colonize the interior, it is important to remember that a map is a system of symbols: in the case of Africa, European cartography was immersed in the objectives of the conquest, and maps were elaborated to reaffirm Portugal's occupation of the territory. The geographic portrayal of "black settlements"—as the engineer Pinheiro Furtado calls the *banzas*—, for example, is erroneous if we consider this space from the African standpoint. The Ambundus' relationship to the territory was related to "complex supernatural ties [that] connected each kindred group to their lands and encompassed the people and the territory in a single collectivity."[64] Land possession was collective; as the harvests exhausted the soil, new fields were created in a system of itinerant farming. In addition, the Ambundus had their own ways of mediating between the world of the living and the world of the dead. Their political chiefs, such as the *ngola* cited above, wore insignias of authority that allowed them to gain access to spiritual forces in order to guide their subjects.

The movement of *sobados* according to supernatural directives and/or in search of better lands for farming is not reflected by the fixed layout of Portuguese cartography; after all, they were two different conceptions of territorial occupation. For that reason, in 1797, Governor Miguel Antonio de Melo pointed out errors in Pinheiro's map:

> Because, since the black *banzas* or villages are made of straw and they change location almost every day to places that are always distant whenever they feel like it or are led to do so by their omens and superstitions, what is shown on the map today as populated, tomorrow will be deserted and full of vegetation inhabited by beasts.[65]

Also regarding their ties to the territory, African rulers did not relate their power to territorial expansion; rather, what was crucial for them was to expand their dominion over people. What gave power to an Ambundu ruler of a certain lineage was the number of dependents—also called *filhos* (offspring) in Portuguese documentation—under his control.[66] However, even indirectly, one thing led to another, since their dominion over people was at first determined by large plantations. As the Portuguese presence advanced to the interior, and with the local exploitation of

---

[64] Hence, for example, the spirits of the ancestors of a lineage could only rest if the bodies of the dead were buried in the lineage's lands. Joseph C. Miller, *Poder político e parentesco*, 239.

[65] Carta de Miguel Antonio de Melo, governador de Angola, para Rodrigo de Sousa Coutinho, secretário de Estado da Marinha e Ultramar. São Paulo de Assunção de Luanda, December 3, 1797. AHU_CU_001, Cx. 86, D. 66. *Apud* Catarina Madeira Santos, *Um governo polido para Angola*.

[66] According to Thornton, this would explain why African states did not usually encompass large territorial extensions, since "the state and its citizens could increase their fortune acquiring enslaved people and did not need to purchase land, unless they were short of space in their countries (which was not the case)." John Thornton, *A África e os africanos na formação do mundo atlântico (1400–1800)*, 162. According to the author, in Central Africa, "Kongo was the largest state, with 130,000 square kilometers; other states, such as Ndongo, were smaller, but still in that range." Idem.

natural resources, not only did agriculture lose many arms to the trade of enslaved people, but the relationship with a lineage-based possession of land underwent important changes, as we shall see in Chapter 2.⁶⁷

In any case, Portuguese expansion depended on alliances with local elites, whether as allies or vassals. As early as the first Portuguese initiatives to contact the ruler of Kongo in 1483, what ensured foreigners' permanence, displacement, and commerce were the relations they were able to establish with local chiefdoms. Our purpose here is not to discuss the historical process of relations of domination between the Portuguese and Africans, but to note that, without the acquiescence of the local states, foreign permanence would have been impossible. As the historian M'Bokolo recalls in a passage cited above, in spite of the precariousness of Portuguese domination, maintaining Angola was possible due to the trade of enslaved people, foreign commodities, and merchants, and it led to profound local transformations. The trade of captives was the most important and long-lasting relation of interdependence established with African elites, since it was consolidated through time as the foundational economy of the region, especially due to the demand for labor force in Portuguese America.

1.3 Angola's Population

Who were the residents of that territory? As the sources analyzed so far demonstrate, the Kingdom of Angola was mainly populated by Central Africans. Given the frequent migrations caused by the trade of enslaved people, they could be of different origins, languages, cultures, and political affiliations.⁶⁸

A good way to answer the question is to resort to population censuses by colonial administrators. Since the reign of Dom José I (1750–1777), metropolitan authorities were increasingly concerned with obtaining greater institutional control over the populations of their overseas dominions. Together with their intention to establish civilian settlements that took European ideas and values to the inhabi-

---

67 Eva Sebestyèn, "Legitimation through Landcharters in Ambundu Villages, Angola," in Thomas Bearth, Wilhelm J.G. Möhlig, Beat Sottas, and Edgar Suter (eds.), *Perspektiven afrikanistischer Forschung. Beiträge zur Linguistik, Ethnologie, Geschichte, Philosophie und Literatur. X. Afrikanistentag* (1993), 363–378. According to Mariana Candido, one of the great transformations in African societies caused by the transatlantic trade was an increase in the demand for cereals, which favored the accumulation of wealth in the hands of producers. Mariana Candido, *An African Slaving Port and the Atlantic World*, 84.
68 Daniel Domingues da Silva, *Crossroads Slave Frontiers of Angola, c. 1780–1867*, dissertation (PhD) (Emory University, 2011), 90–100.

tants spread out throughout the *sertões*, the governors of overseas conquests were forced to undertake periodical censuses of the populations. These censuses produced lists of names of inhabitants that, when arranged in a table, result in "population maps."[69]

The first population estimate was commissioned by the Secretary of State of the Navy and Overseas Affairs, Martinho de Melo e Castro, in 1776. Two years later, the map of "all residents and inhabitants of the Kingdom of Angola and their conquests elaborated at the end of year 1777, which includes vassal *ndembu*, potentates, and *sobas*" was published, coordinated by Governor Antonio de Lencastre.[70] Royal officers consulted the *sobas*, the parish priests in the interior, and the *capitães-mores*. Given the instability of the Church network in the *sertões*, the *capitães-mores* were in charge of collecting the information.

This source contains many inconsistencies related to the precariousness of the administrative and religious network, since the number of royal officials and clerics was insufficient to control the entire *sertão*. However, the biggest obstacle for a greater control by the metropolis over the territory and the population of the Kingdom of Angola came from the local leaderships. In Benguela, for example, the *sobas* feared that this list would benefit efforts to enslave people under their dominion, so they refrained from providing the correct data requested by royal authorities. As Antonio de Lencastre explained to the then Secretary of State of the Navy and Overseas Affairs:

> the size of these *sertões* and the mistrust that this novelty caused in the gentiles has delayed for so long the execution of the said order, and I can ensure Your Excellency that it was very

---

[69] The lists were to contain: "1) number of inhabitants; 2) occupations; 3) births, marriages, and deaths; 4) volume of imports; 5) volume of exports; 6) production, consumption, and exports; 7) prices; 8) entry and exit of ships." Mariana P. Candido, *An African Slaving Port and the Atlantic World. Benguela and its Hinterland*, 140–143. The purpose of this data survey was to know the number and quality of the residents, their occupations, and the taxes collected for the Royal Treasury. These sets of documents, which were part of a Pombaline policy of settlement and "civilization of the naturals" for the entire Portuguese Empire, also exist, as would be expected, for Portuguese America—Paraíba, Piauí, and São Paulo. They were conceived according to the principles set forth in *Political Arithmetick* by William Petty, an important thinker of English mercantilism with whom Pombal made contact. Sebastião José de Carvalho e Melo considered "the need to perform an 'examination of the number of inhabitants of the country at issue,' a survey of tillable land and its production, the amount with which they can be taxed, trade (what is sold and what is bought), income, and salaries," in view of the profits that the state could obtain. Antonio Cesar de Almeida Santos, "O 'mecanismo político' pombalino e o povoamento da América portuguesa na segunda metade do século XVIII," *Revista de História Regional* 15, no. 1 (2010): 103.
[70] Antonio de Lencastre. "Mapa de todos os moradores...." Luanda, July 15, 1778. AHU_CU_001_Cx. 61, D. 81.

difficult for the chiefs and the said gentiles to provide the list of all their offspring and subjects of their Lands, since there was no parish priest among them that could inform their number, and fearful that this novelty was designed to take from them the said offspring according to their number, which forced me to assure them many times that it was not for this purpose and that no harm would come to them, and with those assurances they provided the number of inhabitants of the said Lands to the officers I sent to them (...).[71]

The governor expressed, "I do not hold myself responsible for the uncertainty of the number of Negroes in the *sertão* because, for the reasons mentioned, I cannot justify or certify its truth." Moreover, this is a localized record, elaborated from a survey during a limited period of time. Having made the relevant caveats regarding the limitations of this source and having described its inaccuracies, we can now analyze its data.

Table 1: Residents of the Kingdom of Angola, 1777.

Gender/ Color	Children of white parents	Children of free brown parents	Children of enslaved brown parents	Children of free black parents	Children of enslaved black parents	Total
Men	1,031	1,762	244	191,816	17,643	212,496
Women	550	1,784	253	234,337	24,697	261,621
Total	1,581	3,546	497	426,153	42,340	474,117

Source: "Mapa de todos os moradores e habitantes do reino de Angola e suas conquistas tirado no fim do ano de 1777 em que entram os *Ndembu*, Potentados, e *sobas* vassalos." São Paulo de Assunção de Luanda, Luanda, 15 July 1778. AHU_CU_001_ Cx. 61, Doc. 81. The data summarized here was tabulated by Catarina Madeira Santos in the appendices to her dissertation. Cf: Catarina Madeira Santos, *Um governo "polido" para Angola*, 184.

In this survey, most of the men and women were adults (men were between the ages of 15 and 60, and women between the ages 14 and 40) and most (89.88%) were children of "free black parents," i.e. the African population. The term "free" (*forro*) when related to "black" (*preto*) in this document, is used to designate those who were not enslaved by Europeans; we also believe, as does Joseph Miller, that the term is equivalent to being free as opposed to being enslaved—and not to having been freed, since the people formerly enslaved were not counted.[72] Howev-

---

[71] Antonio de Lencastre. "Mapa de todos os moradores...." Luanda, July 15, 1778. AHU_CU_001_ Cx. 61, D. 81.
[72] "A category that includes almost the entire African population, 'free' in the sense that they are not directly the property of an European of the Portuguese colony, but not necessarily of someone of local birth (and therefore 'free' in African terms). This category, which makes up 89.3% of the

er, we do not know how many of these were free by birth, i.e. how many were never enslaved by the Portuguese at some point in their lives; and we also do not know if they were enslaved under the jurisdiction of vassal *sobas*, because this information was not taken into account. Out of these 474,117 people, only 0.33 % were white, and the number of white women is almost half that of men. The intermediate layers were made up of enslaved people (9.03 %) and brown people (0.75 %). Once again, we see that the percentage of whites was very small compared to the vast majority of *pretos forros* (free blacks).

Historians who have analyzed the demography of the Kingdom of Angola over time have sought to interpret those results in the context of the transatlantic trade. Among these assessments, John Thorton highlights especially a large number of women among the African population, which was disproportionate to the number of men in the same group. The cause for this imbalance was presumably the trade of enslaved people's demand for adult men.[73] Patrick Manning complicates this argument, differentiating the dynamics of the trade on the coast from those in the interior. He compared the late-eighteenth century censuses with data from the export of captives, and supported his findings with studies of the prices of enslaved people. He concluded that the men destined for the transatlantic trade were mostly from the interior, while women were mostly from the coastal region. To compensate, the coast retained most of the women who came from the interior. The central issue for Manning was to demonstrate that the inland populations of West Central Africa suffered demographic depopulation throughout the history of the trade of enslaved people.[74]

It is not our intention to delve into issues regarding demographic dynamics, but rather to present, within the limitations of the documentation, a general picture of the population of the Kingdom of Angola. José Curto explains that, for the city of Luanda, at least 30 censuses were conducted between 1773 and 1844, but the counts after 1798 are more reliable because the demographic categories of the censuses became more uniform.[75]

---

total, reflected the effects of the import of dependents by the African population of the conquest." Joseph Miller, *Way of Death*, 160.

[73] John Thornton, "The Slave Trade in Eighteenth Century Angola," *Canadian Journal of African Studies* 14, no. 3 (1980): 417–427.

[74] Patrick Manning, "The Enslavement of Africans: A Demographic Model," *Canadian Journal of African Studies* 15 (1981): 499–536. See also: José C. Curto, "Demografia histórica e efeitos do tráfico de escravizados em África: uma análise dos principais estudos quantitativos," *Revista Internacional de Estudos Africanos* 14–15 (1991): 268.

[75] From 1798 onward, the censuses presented the following: "civilian numbers concerned single and married persons and widows, births, marriages, and deaths, emigrants and immigrants, classified according to color, gender, and social condition, while the data on administrative personnel

The reality of the fortress in the interior is even more unequal in terms of the number of white people. At the Cambambe fortress, according to a 1798 survey, there were 19 white men (15 of them older than 25 years of age), 77 "blacks," and 42 mulattos. In Muxima, there were only two whites, 65 mulattos, and 468 "blacks." In the district of Dante, no white people were counted; in Encoge, there were only four, and in Pedras de Pungo Andongo, five.[76]

There were therefore very few white people in Angola, especially in the *sertões* that were further away from the Coast. Governor Sousa Coutinho often sent soldiers and workers from the kingdom, the islands, and Brazil to the town of Nova Oeiras.[77] The mortality caused by Angola's "evil climate" was part of the whole iron factory's history in that town. In 1773, Captain José Francisco Pacheco, one of the people responsible for administering the work at the iron factory, recorded the deaths of 77 white people during the three years he worked there: 43 mechanical workers (carpenters, blacksmiths, masons, miners), 29 exiled convicts, and five women.[78]

Something important observed by Curto is that, until the mid-nineteenth century, color status was defined by the association of birth and economic criteria.[79] Joseph Miller supposes that the white women identified in the population census of the city of Luanda in 1773 were actually daughters of influential Luso-African families, whose wealth and social prestige "whitened their appearances," just as in Brazil, where "money whitened people."[80] Brazilian historiography has analyzed the polysemy of the terms that appear in eighteenth-century sources, which sometimes determined skin color and, sometimes, social condition. It is important to understand how the terminology developed in specific historical situations. In this

---

concerned bureaucrats, government troops, and the clergy, usually with a reference to their marital status. Last but not least, all of these censuses contained separate boxes with quantitative information on households and the occupational distribution of part of the civilian population." José Curto and Raymond Gervais, "A dinâmica demográfica de Luanda no contexto do tráfico de escravizados do Atlântico Sul, 1781–1844," *Topoi* (2002): 92.
76 Maps of the fortresses from 1798. AHU_CU_001, Cx. 89, Doc. 88. This information regarding the men who worked in the interior were consulted in Catarina Madeira Santos, *Um governo polido para Angola*, 119 and ff.
77 In 1767, the governor sent nine soldiers and workers to Nova Oeiras; two of them were "very wealthy great farmers." Carta a Antonio Anselmo Duarte de Siqueira, São Paulo de Assunção de Luanda, September 27, 1769. PADAB, IHGB 126, DVD10,22 DSC00044.
78 Certidão de Francisco José Pacheco, inspetor de obras da fábrica de Nova Oeiras. São Paulo de Assunção de Luanda, March 13, 1773. AHU_CU_001, Cx. 57, Doc. 28.
79 José Curto and Raymond Gervais, "A dinâmica demográfica de Luanda no contexto do tráfico de escravizados do Atlântico Sul, 1781–1844," 95.
80 Joseph Miller, *Way of Death*, 293.

regard, Silvia Lara considers that the association between skin color and social condition "(...) was not direct, but rather transversal, passing through zones in which both aspects were either confused or distanced, and in which disparate criteria of social identification were superimposed."[81] Holding an administrative, military, or religious position, skin color, wealth, political and/or family insertion, among other factors, are categories that could work together to determine social hierarchies and/or skin color.

So far, we have examined data from population maps and censuses organized in Lisbon and conducted in the overseas possessions with general color designations such as "black" (*preto*), "white" (*branco*), "brown" (*pardo*), and "mulatto" (*mulato*). There are other documents, commissioned by the government of Luanda and elaborated by royal officials in the hinterland of the city and the fortress, which provide more detailed information on the types of residents of the Kingdom of Angola. We are referring to the sources of the fortress, where, when referring to the mestizo population, they employ a wider range of terms: "brown" (*pardo*), "mulatto" (*mulato*), "darkish" (*fusco*), "half darkish" (*meio fusco*), and even "honest color" (*cor honesta*). Thus, while in the population maps there is a more generic classification, in the "news from fortress" from the inland *sertões*, the designations are varied and change from one place to another. This type of source provides lists of the names of residents as well as their skin color, occupation, position, military rank of the heads of household, and ownership of cattle and enslaved people. Roberto Guedes considers that the greater variety of terms to designate color in the "news" relative to those found in the "maps" is indicative of an attempt by fortress authorities to create local hierarchies, which qualified "the color of the people/families, as well as their status or social positions," in a society marked by the trade of enslaved people and slavery in Africa.[82]

---

81 Silvia Hunold Lara, *Fragmentos setecentistas, escravidão, cultura e poder na América portuguesa* (São Paulo: Companhia das Letras, 2007), 131. It is important to note how these associations between color and birth and social hierarchies took place in other parts of the Portuguese colonial empire. For example, Larissa Viana, when studying brotherhoods in colonial Rio de Janeiro, examined the scope and limits of the idea of the formation of a *"pardo* (brown) identity" among brotherhood members. Considering that identities "are relative and changeable, products of social negotiations or impositions," the author warns that, for *pardos*, "the reference was not only the mestizos, but also more subtle forms of identification typical of the slave society, since *pardo* indicated a certain distance from the African condition." Larissa Moreira Viana, *O Idioma da Mestiçagem: as irmandades de pardos na América Portuguesa* (Campinas, SP: Editora da UNICAMP, 2007), 159.
82 Roberto Guedes, "Branco africano: notas de pesquisa sobre escravidão, tráfico de cativos e qualidades de cor no Reino de Angola (Ambaca e Novo Redondo, finais do século XVIII)," in Roberto

There is therefore a significant difference when we reduce the scale of analysis and study the fortress population. In a list of the residents of the Massangano fortress, 87 of them were identified: 33 of "honest color," 22 "darkish," 18 "brown," five "white," two "half darkish," one "brown or half brown," five "blacks," and one "darky" (*escuro*). This is an example of the diversity of terms employed to designate the mestizo population of the *sertão*, which was the one that occupied public positions—the Crown's subjects. Ariane Carvalho notes that "darkish" and "honest colored" people held important positions and occupations in this fortress. Only "blacks," "darkies," and "half darkish" people did not own enslaved people.[83] One hypothesis is that, as in Portuguese America, the intermediate categories between whites, alluding to freedom, and blacks, referring to enslaved people, arose as a way of removing the stigma of slavery.

Resuming the intention of sketching a general landscape of the demographic situation in eighteenth-century Angola even if we cannot attribute numerical and estimative rigor for the reasons outlined above, the assessment based on late-eighteenth-century censuses—a little more than a century after the defeat of the king of Ndongo—demonstrates that white settlement of the Kingdom of Angola was a metropolitan directive whose implementation met many obstacles.

In his memoirs, Governor Francisco Inocêncio de Sousa Coutinho also reiterated the "scarcity of people." He divided the Europeans sent to the kingdom into three classes: "merchants or clerks, who soon become first-class people or die; corrupted convicts full of vices and diseases; and islanders brought by the governor." The islanders were mistreated during the voyage, and those who arrived in Luanda died soon. Marriage between them and "ordinary women" was rare; "very few are able to contribute to the colony's advancement," and even new couples were unable to survive one year in the *sertão*, when they did not "perish from misery" on the beaches of Luanda. Among those sentenced to exile, he distinguished the "clean" from the "miserable and worthless from the jails"; the former were interested in jobs and trades, even though they refused to marry, and the latter were the "corrupted and desperate," such as "prostituted women" who, according to the governor's depreciative view, only served as a "scandal to justice, in bad and

---

Guedes (org.), *Dinâmica Imperial no Antigo Regime Português: escravidão, governos, fronteiras, poderes, legados. Séculos XVII–XIX* (Rio de Janeiro: Mauad X, 2011), 55.

83 Ariane Carvalho da Cruz, "Cor e hierarquia social no reino de Angola: os casos de Novo Redondo e Massangano (finais do século XVIII)," *XIV Encontro Regional ANPUH–Rio de Janeiro* (2010), available at http://www.encontro2010.rj.anpuh.org/resources/anais/8/1276742727_ARQUIVO_ArtigoAnpuhAriane.pdf, accessed May 27, 2016.

excessive taverns." For Sousa Coutinho, the two centuries of efforts at colonization by sending exiled convicts were leading the kingdom to ruin.[84]

From the second half of the seventeenth century and throughout the entire eighteenth century, there was a large flow of convicts exiled to Angola. Many of them accompanied the governors every three years and were sent to make up the colonial troops. In 1759, only a year after the arrival of the new governor Antonio de Vasconcelos (1758–1764), out of the 250 soldiers that went with him, only 142 survived, among convicts (102) and islanders (40). Natives of Lisbon were presumably more suitable for the military reinforcement of the colony, while the islanders, more able to adapt to the climate, were to foster the settlement and reforms of the colony. However, these plans never came to fruition. Desertion was constant, against which the authorities could do little. Militia wages were paid with common products from the trade of enslaved people, such as textiles and *jeribita*.[85] The soldiers, ill prepared for military confrontations and poorly paid, inserted themselves in the commercial networks, purchasing supplies and enslaved people.[86] In 1760, the Count of Oeiras had 60 couples sent from the Madeira Islands

---

[84] FISC, "Memórias do Reino de Angola e suas conquistas," fl. 5 and ff.

[85] Sugarcane spirits. Regarding the broad use of *jeribita* as currency in the trade of enslaved people, see: José C. Curto, *Alcohol and Slaves: The Luso-Brazilian Alcohol Commerce at Mpinda, Luanda, and Benguela during the Atlantic Slave Trade c. 1480–1830 and its impact on the societies of West Central Africa*, Dissertation (PhD) (Los Angeles: University of California, 1996). Regarding the textile trade in West Central Africa, see: Telma Gonçalves Santos, *Comércio de tecidos europeus e asiáticos na África Centro-Ocidental: fraudes e contrabando no terceiro quartel do século XVIII*, Thesis (Master's) (Universidade de Lisboa, 2014).

[86] Roquinaldo Ferreira, *Transforming Atlantic Slaving. Trade, Warfare and Territorial Control in Angola, 1650–1800*, Dissertation (PhD) (Los Angeles: University of California, 2003), 145–153. FISC, "Memórias do Reino de Angola e suas conquistas," fl. 5 and ff. About the white population in the Kingdom of Angola, the Count of Oeiras said: "The whites that were sent to that kingdom are almost extinct; some died of hunger and misery in the city and its surroundings, while others in the *sertões* as fugitives and vagabonds; and blacks have come to prevail to such an extent that the few whites that remain look upon the women of Europe with astonishment, as extraordinary creatures, most of them preferring to consort with black women." Parecer que o Conde de Oeiras apresentou a Sua Majestade sobre o que ainda falta para se restituir a Agricultura, Navegação, e o Comércio de Angola contra os monopólios vexações e desordens que fizeram os objetos das leis de 11 e 25 de janeiro de 1758. Lisbon, November 20, 1760. AHU, Cód. 555, fl. 56–57. In this period, Angola and Mozambique became the main destinations for those sentenced to temporary or perpetual exile. A large number of infractions received this punishment: crimes of lèse-majesté (against the state), forgery of coins, and crimes against citizens—theft or housebreaking, for example. In addition, the penalty was also widely used by the Court of the Holy Office, especially in sentences against Judaizers. The threat of being banished to the Portuguese territories in Africa was an important weapon used by the Portuguese administration. Angola in particular was seen as the "residence of death" because of its "evil climate, unknown diseases, hostile natives." On the penalty of

to the Kingdom of Angola, in a new attempt to promote the establishment of colonies in the *sertões* near Luanda.

Our contribution consists of highlighting how the Crown used deportation to send specialized workers, mechanical and technical experts, to Angola. After all, this was also a compulsory mode of labor.

In addition, in the eighteenth century, Gypsy families were also sent to Angola; in some cases, more than one generation was deported. In Portugal, since the Manueline Ordinances (1514–1521), discriminatory policies against Gypsies were promoted—they could not hold public and religious positions or receive honors. The restrictive measures intensified, leading to their expulsion from the metropolis in 1526, and those who failed to meet the deadlines to leave the kingdom were sentenced to compulsory labor in exile. While at first their destination was Brazil, in the eighteenth century, as we have seen, the port of arrival became Luanda. In 1720, the Senate of Luanda published a series or ordinances forbidding Gypsies to wear their "mantles," their black shawls, and other garments that were considered unseemly.[87]

Those white people who survived established relations with the local populations, giving rise to the Luso-Africans. Historiography has noted that, over time, especially in Angola, an elite was formed by families of Luso-Africans. They were independent from the *sobados* and, by controlling channels related to the transatlantic trade, they established strong ties with the Brazilian elites, constituting a group that was "very heterogeneous and hard to delimit, which included mostly black Africans (many of them formerly enslaved) and 'mestizos,' but also some whites," as described by B. Heintze.[88] Luso-Africans established family ties that sought to articulate the municipal and colonial elite, thus benefiting from the "accumulation of local administration positions with positions in the central administration of fortress; the exercise of military functions and especially their participation in acts of Conquest." Another characteristic of this mestizo elite

---

banishment, see: Timothy J. Coates, *Degredados e órfãs: colonização dirigida pela Coroa no Império português, 1550–1755* (Lisbon: Comissão Nacional para as Comemorações dos Descobrimentos Portugueses, 1998); Tânia Macedo, *Angola e Brasil: estudos comparados* (São Paulo: Arte & Ciência, 2002), 22 and ff.

87 Selma Pantoja, "Inquisição, degredo e mestiçagem em Angola no século XVIII," *Revista Lusófona De Ciência Das Religiões*, no. 5 and 6 (2004): 120.

88 Beatrix Heintze, "A lusofonia no interior da África Central na era pré-colonial. Um contributo para a sua história e compreensão na atualidade," *Cadernos de Estudos Africanos*, no. 7 and 8 (2005): 12.

was "the fact that these men were large landowners, whose produce supplied Luanda, and that they were thus also large owners of enslaved people."[89]

Many enslaved and freed people engaged in mechanical trades (masons, carpenters, blacksmiths) or became priests or *ngangas**, bleeders, barbers, street vendors, or fishmongers, while owning or working in taverns.[90] These trades were routine in Luanda.

Considering the magnitude of the trade of enslaved people in eighteenth-century Angola, the characters who worked as itinerant merchants in the *sertões* are fundamental to understand the social hierarchies that developed in this context. The *sertanejos* were mostly exiled convicts, former sailors from Brazil and Portugal, and *filhos da terra* (offspring of the land), as the locally born were called, including women. When they worked at the local markets, they were also called *feirantes* (market vendors), and they supervised the transport and sale of imported goods (Indian cloth, weapons, *jeribita*) to Angola's interior. Trade in the *sertões* was sponsored by merchants from Luanda and Benguela who provided those products to the *sertanejos*, who in turn sold them to the Africans in the *sertões* or traded them for enslaved people. The success of their endeavor depended on their association with the *capitães-mores* and *sobas*.[91] Many *sertanejos* became wealthy and traded for their own benefit, neglecting the debts incurred on the Coast, as denounced by Silva Correa: "the *sertanejo loaded with debts* and devoid of virtues considers himself in a better state than his predecessor (...). He excuses himself from his obligations as debtor, keeping only appearances, while he employs his commercial gains to his own advantage."[92]

Moral disapproval of *sertanejos*' attitudes and incompetence, considered quite far from European standards, are found in other eighteenth-century sources. When Governor Sousa Coutinho appointed Antonio Anselmo Duarte as superintendent of the iron factory, he justified his choice because he was a *sertanejo*: "it is true that, since we need someone that can perform the job skillfully, we can only expect it of a European, but for now I have an old *sertanejo* serving as intendant, who does what he is able to understand." The governor warned that the *sertanejo* should "re-

---

[89] Catarina Madeira Santos, "De 'antigos conquistadores' a 'angolenses,'" *Cultura* 24 (2007): 5.
[90] Suely Creusa Cordeiro de Almeida. "O feminino ao leste do Atlântico. Vendeiras, regateiras, peixeiras e quitandeiras: mulheres e trabalho nas ruas de Lisboa e Luanda (séculos XVI–XVIII)," in Roberto Guedes (org.), *África. Brasileiros e portugueses, século XVI–XIX* (Rio de Janeiro: Mauad X, 2013), 207–227; Roquinaldo Ferreira, *Cross-Cultural Exchange in the Atlantic World*, Chap. 4.
[91] Joseph Miller, *Way of Death*, 271–272; Roquinaldo Ferreira, *Cross-Cultural Exchange in the Atlantic World*, 32–34.
[92] Elias Alexandre da Silva Correa, *História de Angola*, v. I, 35.

ceive sufficient wages to keep him from trading," since that would distract him from the factory work.[93]

Roquinaldo Ferreira cites other categories of free and enslaved people who worked in the itinerant trade of captives, such as the *quissongos* ("free blacks who work for white men and escort enslaved Africans from the interior to the Coast").[94] The *pumbeiros** were the main agents of the trade. The name derives from the term that the Portuguese used in Angola to denominate the markets of the Kingdom of Kongo. In 1798, Governor Miguel Antonio de Melo explained in a letter to the secretary of the Overseas Council that "*pumbeiros* is the name employed in both languages [Benguela and Ambundu] to designate black people who take textiles and commodities obtained in the *sertão* from the hands of white market traders to sell to other black people in their lands." According to the governor, these agents were "more thieves than traveling envoys, and cause great damage to commerce in general by the thefts they commit and by those they facilitate to market vendors."[95]

They were also known as *funadores*, from the verb *funar*, which in the local languages meant "to negotiate by purchasing and selling."[96] These characters shared cultural and social aspects with their victims, and therefore "the success of their endeavor" depended on manipulating those symbols to differentiate themselves from the enslaved. One such symbol was the use of footwear; in this case, the traders were called "shod blacks" and were considered white. Many took advantage of their new social position to free themselves from their obligations to the Portuguese as their vassals, refusing, for example, to serve as porters carrying the merchandise of the market vendors.[97] These characters are an example of how

---

[93] Carta de FISC a Francisco Xavier de Mendonça Furtado, secretário de estado da marinha e ultramar, informando sobre o estabelecimento da real fábrica do ferro. São Paulo de Assunção de Luanda. December 29, 1766. PADAB, IHGB 126, DVD10,20 DSC00396. Antonio Duarte de Siqueira had distinguished himself commanding military expeditions against the "Ambuíla, Muçosos, and Manungos" potentates. "Catálogo dos governadores do Reino de Angola," 417.

[94] Roquinaldo Ferreira, *Cross-Cultural Exchange in the Atlantic World*, 59; Joseph Miller, *Way of Death*, 189–190, 271–272. In 1798, the governor of the Kingdom of Angola defined *quissongos* as those called "Benguelas in their language, blacks who, exempted from captivity, serve white men and rule over other enslaved blacks." Carta do governador Miguel Antonio de Melo para Rodrigo de Sousa Coutinho. São Paulo de Assunção de Luanda, April 30, 1798. *Arquivos de Angola* I, no. 6 (1936): 325.

[95] Carta do governador Miguel Antonio de Melo para Rodrigo de Sousa Coutinho. São Paulo de Assunção de Luanda, April 30, 1798. *Arquivos de Angola* I, no. 6 (March 1936): 325.

[96] Carta do governador Miguel Antonio de Melo para Rodrigo de Sousa Coutinho. São Paulo de Assunção de Luanda, April 30, 1798. *Arquivos de Angola* I, no. 6 (March 1936): 325.

[97] Roquinaldo Ferreira, *Cross-Cultural Exchange in the Atlantic World*, 61–63.

color was related to other conditions beyond skin tone and, on the other hand, how Africans and their descendants were at constant risk of enslavement.

1.4 Vassalage and Tribute

According to Vansina, the centralization of the Kingdom of Ndongo occurred gradually around the authority of the *ngola* through the conquest of the region's *sobados*, a process that often depended on the use of force while ensuring great political autonomy to local leaders in their own lands.[98] According to documents of the Society of Jesus from 1582 to 1610 studied by Heywood and Thornton, 736 *sobados* were under the sovereignty of the *ngola*'s insignia in the seventeenth century.[99] Therefore, the *sobas*, before the dominion of the King of Portugal, paid homage to the *ngola*, whose political power was demonstrated by the tributes paid to him by the provinces under his rule. In return for the *sobas*' loyalty, the sovereign guaranteed protection against invasion by enemies and foreigners and, through his supernatural powers, the fertility of the land, since he controlled the rains. The tributes owed to the *ngola* by the lineage chiefs were known as *luanda**, *futa**, and *vestir**, paid in the form of goods, especially enslaved people, cereals, animals, honey, and oil.[100]

At the time of the Portuguese conquest, the *capitão donatário* Paulo Dias Novais received, through a Grant Letter, the right to donate lands (*sesmarias*), with the condition that they be cultivated. The beneficiaries of the Society of Jesus were the most favored in the division of the donated lands. These parts of the territory of the former Kingdom of Ndongo encompassed "entire chiefdoms with their own borders and included all their inhabitants and respective goods,"[101] including rivers that were used for various purposes: irrigation, mills, among others. Since the fortunes of the Portuguese increasingly depended on the trade of enslaved people, the donation came to be known as "donation of *sobas*" or "distribution of *sobas*." Dom-

---

[98] Jan Vansina, *How Societies are Born: Governance in West Central Africa before 1600* (Charlottesville: University of Virginia Press, 2004), 200 and ff.
[99] Linda Heywood, John Thornton, *Central Africans, Atlantic Creoles, and the Foundation of the Americas, 1585–1660*, 73
[100] Aida Freudenthal and Selma Pantoja (eds.), *Livro dos Baculamentos: que os sobas deste Reino de Angola pagam a Sua Majestade (1630)* (Luanda: Ministério da Cultura e Arquivo Nacional de Angola, 2013), 1–23.
[101] Beatrix Heintze, *Angola nos séculos XVI e XVII*, 251. The author examines the issue of land at various moments; see especially 250–273. See also: Ilídio do Amaral. *O consulado de Paulo Dias de Novais: Angola no último quartel do século XVI e primeiro do século XVII* (Lisbon: Ministério da Ciência e da Tecnologia/ Instituto de Investigação Científica Tropical, 2000).

ination shifted from the land to the people, for it was more profitable to sell the subjects of the *sobas* who were gradually subjugated than to employ them in agriculture, for example. In short, this is how the "system of masters" developed, as religious or secular people who became owners of the lands and the people who lived in them were called.[102]

In the face of exploitation by the colonists, who were more interested in the trade of enslaved people than in the fruits of the land, the *sobas* in turn lost prestige among their dependents. In order to pay the tributes demanded by the master, the chiefs were constantly forced to carry out raids in neighboring villages, to invent crimes punishable with slavery, or to expel groups of offenders in order to enslave them later—which caused insecurity and fragility within the *sobados*. The masters, whether secular or Jesuit, offered nothing in return; they offered neither instruction nor protection to the chiefs under their tutelage, as specified by the law and the Jesuits' religious precepts.

For some authors, the institution of the masters was an old Ambundu tradition and represented the establishment of intermediaries between foreigners and the community, helping "the newcomer to adapt to the new environment," as well as preventing him from "acting incorrectly or in a way that offended local customs."[103] B. Heintze, however, believes that this interpretation is erroneous, since, in the sources that elucidate the relations between masters and *sobas*, it is clear that it was one of the justifications employed by the Jesuits to exert their dominion over the *sobados* and collect taxes.[104] It is very important to take into account that there was probably no African reference to the existence of masters, but was instead an institution created by the agents of the Crown, whether Jesuits or private individuals. This way of legitimizing a mechanism of exploitation

---

[102] Beatrix Heintze, *Angola nos séculos XVI e XVII*, 255.

[103] Alberto da Costa e Silva, *A manilha e o libambo. A África e a escravidão, de 1500 a 1700* (2nd ed.) (Rio de Janeiro: Nova Fronteira, 2011), 417 and ff. Catarina Madeira Santos, *Um governo "polido" para Angola*. "Those who controlled the *sobados* collected tribute from the African chiefs, either in the form of enslaved people, goods, or services. From the African standpoint, their acceptance of this subordination seems to derive from a similar institution in the Kingdom of Ngola, where the *sobas* had an 'elder' in the court who was their protector or 'master.' The role of the conquerors who settled together with Dias de Novais was probably initially associated with this Ambundu protector residing at the court of Ngola," Idem, 116.

[104] Beatrix Heintze, *Angola nos séculos XVI e XVII*, 262. The Jesuits "referred to the existence of a corresponding African organization, stating that the masters' institution had been copied from the traditional Mbundu intermediaries: a thesis that has been much quoted until recent times, but which became untenable—even if these intermediaries had existed in an institutionalized form —in the light of our present knowledge."

and domination based on internal characteristics of the Ambundu societies was recurrent over time, as we shall see further in this work.

After the death of Paulo Dias de Novais, who left no heirs, the Crown sent the lawyer Domingos de Abreu Brito to Angola, who was responsible for assessing the economic situation of the conquest. Abreu Brito decided that the occupation and administration of the territory should occur through a general government, which was created in 1591. One of the reasons for this change was the fact that the Society of Jesus and the private conquerors were growing rich and increasing their political prestige, which did not result in greater collections for the Royal Treasury and went against the centrality of the king as source of order in a corporate society. Flávia Carvalho considers that, in fact, "the extinction of the masters system and the implementation of the vassalage ceremony represented a nationalization, conducted by the Portuguese Crown, of the [masters'] power exercised over the *sobas*." The need for greater fiscal control over transactions in the interior was also an important factor in making the *sobas* direct vassals of the king of Portugal.[105]

Vassalage treaties have been constantly revisited by historiography. Beatrix Heintze was a pioneer in the exhaustive study of this phenomenon and the types of documents it generated. According to her, the term "vassal" was introduced by the Portuguese overseas as an instrument of power, which permitted lineage chiefs to become "vassals of the king of Portugal through a documented and recognized legal procedure established in the presence of witnesses," configuring a "type of interstate dependence." The vanquished had to promise to comply with all the conditions imposed and to swear an oath of fidelity and obedience. On the other hand, the victors had to "promise protection and investiture." The author further differentiates between "voluntary vassalage," when the chiefs, for political or economic reasons, voluntarily sought alliances with the Portuguese, and vassalage imposed by the force of arms. However, she notes that the former was less frequent. The vassal condition was normally imposed on local leaders, and the Portuguese established the terms of the contract.[106] At the top of the list of duties was military service; without it, it would have been impossible to maintain the Portuguese presence in Angola. In addition, vassals could not "carry out wars or acts of conquest, nor allow others to do so, against any vassal of the Crown, but, on the contrary, should support them until further notice from the government."[107]

---

[105] Flávia Maria de Carvalho, *Sobas e homens do rei*, 81 and 82.
[106] Beatrix Heintze. *Angola nos séculos XVI e XVII*, 395 and ff.
[107] Vassal agreement of Dona Isabel, regent of Ambuíla. São Paulo de Assunção de Luanda, July 1, 1664. *Monumenta Missionária Africana* (CD) – SI – V12_d203.

The right to free and unrestricted passage was also obligatory; the vassal *soba* was required to "allow free and unrestricted entry into his lands and domains to every Portuguese and their *pumbeiros*,"¹⁰⁸ as well as to missionaries. Another item referred to the surrender of all runaway slaves of the Portuguese who sought refuge in their territories. This demonstrates the strong mercantile nature of this relation of dependency, marked by the interests of the trade of enslaved people.

In short, the *soba* sealed his vassalage before a representative of the king—the governor or, more often, the *capitão-mor* of the fortress—to whom he was then "bound" or "annexed," in the sense of being subordinated. The contract was then signed at the nearest fortress. There was a symbolic procedure that marked the conclusion of the process, a celebration that incorporated Ambundu rituals for the enthronement of a new ruler—the *undamento*.

In the ceremony performed by the Portuguese, to *undar* a new vassal meant "pouring flour (or white clay) on the shoulders of the African chief, who rubbed it on his chest and arms." The successors of the vassal *soba*'s lineage had to submit to the investiture once chosen by the *makota*; otherwise, they were considered rebels and therefore punishable.¹⁰⁹ Thus, instead of being merely one part of the ceremony, the *undamento* became a synonym of vassalage itself.

How did the *sobas* perceive vassalage relations? According to Flávia Carvalho, the *sobas*, as far as they were able, used vassalage "as a strategy of defense and the establishment of military alliances against common enemies."¹¹⁰ The Old Regime's society was based on the concept of social inequality, the same way that Ambundu hierarchies themselves were not based on a concept of social equality. Thus, submission to the king of Portugal, even assuming an asymmetric reciprocity, permitted some room for action, based as it was on the idea of interdependence.¹¹¹

Catarina Madeira Santos believes that the treaties maintained more or less the same written formulas from the seventeenth century to the 1920s, and "this textual and institutional continuity demanded an intense exercise of the culture of vassalage and contributed decisively to popularize the legal-political vocabulary of feu-

---

108 Beatrix Heintze. *Angola nos séculos XVI e XVII*, 398.
109 Ibidem.
110 Flávia Maria de Carvalho, *Sobas e homens do rei*, 23.
111 While examining the grant letters conferred to the *sobas* and to other Africans and Luso-Africans, Ariane Cruz shows a different way of including these people in the Portuguese administration, emphasizing that violence was not the only way in which the relationship with the colonial power took place. There were "negotiations, appropriations, recognition, and legitimation." Ariane Carvalho Cruz, *Militares e militarização no Reino de Angola: patentes, guerra, comércio e vassalagem (segunda metade do século XVIII)*, Thesis (Master's) (Universidade Federal Rural do Rio de Janeiro, 2014), 83.

dal-vassalage roots."¹¹² However, in the eighteenth century, these agreements became more or less common, resuming with greater intensity in the second half of the century, which in itself represents a significant change.¹¹³ According to Madeira Santos, it is important to consider that, in the second half of the eighteenth century, with the new ordinances established by the Count of Oeiras and put into practice in Angola mainly by Francisco Inocêncio de Sousa Coutinho, vassalage treaties went from "legal instruments to promote peace to instruments of civilization."¹¹⁴

Another aspect of this change was the need to control the *sobados*' movements. The efforts to sedentarize African populations were related to the wars of conquest. In the second half of the eighteenth century, treaties began to determine that, after their defeat and submission, the *sobas* should return to their lands —which tied the *sobados* to the jurisdiction of a fortress, reinforcing the policy of settlement and territorialization. This was a strategic measure with well-defined goals: peacekeeping and occupation of the territory favored the trade of enslaved people and held back forays by other European nations into the territory.¹¹⁵

Flávia Carvalho sees the Portuguese policy of advancing to the interior in the *sertões* from a different standpoint. Attentive to local determinations, the author considers that their penetration was only possible through alliances with the *sobas*, because the chronology of vassalage agreements reflects the advance of colonial occupation.¹¹⁶

In the context of this book, these documents contribute to understand how the compulsory provision of services by the subjects of the vassal *sobas* was instituted over the centuries. This is a topic dear to our study, which focuses on the labor of the dependents of vassal *sobas*. Carlos Couto and Catarina Santos call attention to the issue¹¹⁷; however, in general, the bibliography on the subject does not dwell on the forms of regulation of the subjects' labor described in the agreements.

The publication of *Livro dos Baculamentos* allows us to understand the tributes owed by the *sobas* to the king of Portugal in the early-seventeenth century,

---

112 Catarina Madeira Santos, "'Escrever o poder.' Os autos de vassalagem e a vulgarização da escrita entre os africanos: o caso dos Ndembu em Angola (séculos XVII–XX)," *International symposium Angola on the Move: Transport Routes, Communication, and History*, Berlin, 24–26, 2003, p. 3.
113 Flávia Maria de Carvalho, *Sobas e homens do rei* (2015), and Beatrix Heintze, *Angola nos séculos XVI e XVII* (2007).
114 Catarina Madeira Santos, *Um governo "polido" para Angola*, 128.
115 *Idem*, 123 and 136.
116 Flávia Maria de Carvalho, *Sobas e homens do rei*, 23.
117 Carlos Couto, *Os capitães-mores em Angola no século XVIII. Subsídio para o estudo da sua actuação* (Luanda: Instituto de Investigação Científica de Angola, 1972), 245–252; Catarina M. Santos, *Um governo "polido" para Angola*, 123, note 314 and p. 129.

since the first known act of *undamento* dates back to 1664.¹¹⁸ The term *baculamento* (from the Kimbundu *bakula*, to pay tribute) was incorporated by the Portuguese and became the Portuguese word *bacular*. Royal officials established the location, the month, and the amounts collected, and committed themselves to provide receipts for the amounts collected, not to commit extortion, and to assist the *sobas* in case of war. The *baculamento* records were the basis for subjecting African chiefdoms to a new fiscal system.¹¹⁹

In the *baculamentos*, the vassal *sobas* signed a document before African and Portuguese witnesses attesting that the tribute they delivered corresponded to what they had previously paid to the *ngola*. For example, in July 1619, in the province known as Museke (near the Coast), the *soba* Kambambe "obliged himself and all his successors to pay tribute and *baculamento*" every year to El-Rei, "whose vassalage he has sworn in the presence of the lord governor in the manner of the land." Kambambe delivered "ten Indian pieces and twenty castrated [goats] and ten *enseques* of *massa* [sacks of *massambala* or sorghum], which is the same tribute and *baculamento* that his predecessors used to pay to the King of Angola."¹²⁰ The act was signed in the Muximba fortress by the chief, the interpreter (*tandala*)—since Kambambe did not speak Portuguese—, the fortress's *capitão-mor*, and other royal officials.

The *soba* Kambambe was defeated by the Portuguese in the early-seventeenth century in a battle over the silver mines that Kambambe presumably guarded. At the end of the century, the *soba* was described by Cadornega as the "head" (*nkanda*) of other *sobas*, "who they call Ganga." Kambambe was able to maintain his power, for he ruled over them with great prestige, with a "staff insignia."¹²¹ The amount and nature of the tributes are indicative of the *sobas*' political and eco-

---

118 Auto de vassalagem ao rei de Portugal de Dona Isabel, regente de Ambuíla. São Paulo de Assunção de Luanda, July 1, 1664. *Monumenta Missionária Africana* (CD) – SI – V12_d203.
119 Aida Freudenthal and Selma Pantoja (eds.), *Livro dos Baculamentos*, 15–23. See also: Aida Freudenthal, "*Sobas*, conquistadores e 'peças d'Índias,' 1619–1630," in Selma Pantoja and Estevam C. Thompson (orgs.), *Em torno de Angola: narrativas, identidades e as conexões atlânticas* (São Paulo: Intermeios, 2014), 69–87.
120 "Auto que mandou fazer o ilustríssimo senhor governador Luís Mendes de Vasconcelos do tributo e baculamento que se obriga a dar a cada um ano para a fazenda de Sua Majestade (…)," Presídio de Nossa Senhora da Assunção [Muxima], July 29, 1619. *Livro dos Baculamentos*, 87.
121 Antonio de Oliveira Cadornega, *História das Guerras Angolanas (1680)*, v. III, 242. Kambambe was not among the *sobas* of the homonymous presidio who served the iron factories in the eighteenth century. Given the importance of this chiefdom, one can imagine that, if it had still existed later in the eighteenth century, the colonial authorities would have requested the assistance of its dependents; this chiefdom is an example of the political dissolution that followed the conquest and the collection of tributes.

nomic power: Kambambe owed "ten India pieces" (healthy adult males, "those who are worth more than others"),[122] one of the largest payments recorded among Museke tribute payers. Of course, it was nowhere near the amount of 100 pieces that Ngola Hari, the ruler of Ndongo, was obligated to hand over when he became a vassal of the Crown in 1626.[123] There is no reference in Ngola's act of vassalage to the systematic dispatch of his subjects to work for the Portuguese.

Other smaller chiefdoms paid only a few bags of sorghum, such as the *soba* Kakombe ka Katwa from Ilamba.[124] The document that determines this leader's obligations is somewhat different from the previous one. In this case, the "captain and receiver," Bento Rebelo, went to the *banza* of another *soba*, Kyambata, who was probably already a vassal, and called Kakombe, who diligently attended to him, and there the vassalage was sealed. The captain noted, "the *soba* was very poor and small and could not offer anything else."

The document's editors warn that there was resistance to the enforcement of these tributes and that control of collections was often precarious. They cite, for example, the flight of many *sobas* to more powerful rulers or away from the routes known to the Portuguese, into the bush; in these cases, the collectors recorded, "this *soba* cannot be found." There were *sobas* like Kitexi, who committed himself to only one "piece of India" because "he had gone through war and the land was devastated and his people fled to Matamba and other parts."[125] In other cases, the *soba* rebelled and was no longer under Portuguese rule; for that reason, the collector indicated, "he has rebelled and does not pay."[126]

---

122 At the time, most of the enslaved ended up in the sugar plantations in Brazil. Until the Dutch occupation (1630–1654), the prices varied from 9$000 to 20$000 réis. Joseph Miller, "Slave Prices in the Portuguese South Atlantic, 1600–1830," in Paul Lovejoy (ed.), *Africans in Bondage: Studies in Slavery and the Slave Trade* (Madison: University of Wisconsin, 1986), 48. The price of the "pieces from India" varied from 22$000 réis in 1696 to 44$000 réis in 1701 (due to the discovery of gold in Minas Gerais in 1695). Roquinaldo Ferreira, *Transforming Atlantic Slaving* (2003).

123 Aida Freudenthal and Selma Pantoja (eds.), *Livro dos Baculamentos*, 186–190.

124 Termo de baculamento do *soba* Kakombe ka Katwa. Banza de Kyambata. Banza de Kyambata, June 11, 1621. Idem, 114.

125 Idem, 193.

126 Idem, 20. These tributes were abolished in January 1650 by Salvador Correia de Sá, who believed that abusive tributes were one of the causes of the *sobas*' rebellion against the Portuguese when the Dutch arrived. Beatrix Heintze, "Luso-African Feudalism in Angola? The Vassal Treaties of the 16th to the 18th Century," offprint of *Revista Portuguesa de História*, v. 18 (1980), 123. However, there are references to them in documents from the early-eighteenth century, which demonstrates that there was a difference between what the Court determined and what the administration practiced in Angola's *sertão*. Carta [provedor da Fazenda Real de Angola], Rodrigo da Costa Almeida, ao rei [D. Pedro II] remetendo uma relação do dinheiro enviado ao provedor-mor da Baía, Francisco Lamberto, desde 1702, por conta da moeda de cobre, dos *baculamentos*, dos direitos dos oficiais e da

For the purposes of this book, it is not necessary to provide other examples from *Livro dos Baculamentos*; for now, suffice it to say that no document mentions any obligation to provide service to royal officials or residents of the fortress, regardless of whether the *sobas* were powerful, "small," or the *Ngola* himself. Therefore, the dispatch of dependents of the *sobas* to work for the representatives of the Portuguese Crown does not appear in the *undamentos*, nor in the *baculamentos* owed to the representatives of the Crown. Another point to be highlighted is that the *capitães-mores* and the "recipients" of the tributes played a key role both at the time of elaborating and signing the agreements and in the collection of the goods.

The vassalage agreements of Dona Isabel, regent of Ambuíla (in the Ndembu region), and of the Duke of Wandu (north of the Ndembu region) do not specify labor relations.[127] In the former, dated 1664, Dona Isabel's obligations were basically not to allow emissaries from Kongo or Njinga, or other representatives from Ndembu, to go through her lands (probably to trade or to establish diplomatic relations). The second document, dated 1666, is more descriptive—the Duke of Wando promised to hand over the mines present in his lands, to allow passage through his territory, to assist the fortress and forts "with his person and arms," "to encamp his armies if necessary." In return, the King of Portugal guaranteed military protection and promised to treat the Duke "and all his vassals" with justice, and to recognize the vassal's "forums, privileges, honors, and statutes."

What is interesting about the second act is that the conditions for vassalage included not only conversion to the Catholic faith, but also for the Duke to seek "a captain [*capitão-mor*] for whatever might be of service to El-rei." Once again, the *capitão-mor* is a central figure. Even in the case of the potentate of Wandu, which had a longer list of obligations, there is no mention of a specific obligation to assist with labor.

In 1654, the "king of Ndongo" wrote to the king of Portugal complaining that he "lacked vassals" because his had been "usurped" and employed by the Portuguese and the settlers without his consent. The abuse generated significant apprehension among the other vassals of the *ngola*, who lived "with great discredit and risk," fearing the same fate. The Portuguese king ordered that the vassals be returned, and those who had died be compensated. He added that "the services" rendered should be paid for. Finally, he made a recommendation to the governor:

---

piparia que vieram com o governador Bernardino de Távora, bem como dos quintos e direitos das aguardentes. São Paulo de Assunção de Luanda, January 2, 1704. AHU_CU_001, Cx. 19, D. 1977.
127 Auto de vassalagem de Dona Isabel, regente de Ambuíla. São Paulo de Assunção de Luanda, July 1, 1764. *Monumenta Missionária Africana* (CD) – SI – V12_d203. Auto de vassalagem do duque de Wandu, n.p., January 11, 1666. *Monumenta Missionária Africana* (CD) – SI – V13_d001.

you should by no means allow my vassals to employ those of the said king in any way, without paying them for their labor and services, whether as porters or providing supplies, at fair prices and without exerting violence on them.[128]

Therefore, the Portuguese Crown did not recognize as a right of conquest the free labor of the subjects of the African authorities, nor did it consent to them being forced to work or be treated with "violence." On the other hand, the royal directive allows us to assume that it was common for fortress settlers and royal officials to co-opt the labor of the *sobados*' dependents, who were free Africans, since the beginning of the conquest.

Governor Sousa Coutinho wanted to know whether the free labor of the "offspring" (subjects) of the vassal *sobas* was an obligation established in the vassalage agreements—the governor wanted to know the "terms and acts of *undamento* that justified the services provided by the *sobas*." He resorted to the *capitães-mores* and asked them to look for the agreements among the fortress's documents. This was done, "inventorying all obligations such as providing workers for royal service, repairing churches, delivering letters, providing oil for the guard corps, and whatever else that truly appears in the records in this regard." The inventory created in 1770 provides information on 39 chiefdoms.[129]

In general, the *capitães-mores* responded with summaries of the *undamentos*. Some claimed that the papers had been lost and that the only copy was in the hands of the vassal *soba*, which demonstrates that these agreements were not usually reviewed by the *capitães-mores*. In Icolo, for example, the regent noted, "upon reviewing the record book, he found no agreements in it, nor acts of *undamento* of *sobas*."

The regent of the Kwanza district replied, "all services performed by his [the district's] *sobas* are paid to the letter, and they are not *undados* (subjugated as vassals) like those of the fortress, nor is there any evidence to justify private obliga-

---

128 Carta de El-Rei de Portugal ao governador geral de Angola. Lisbon, August 17, 1654. *Monumenta Missionária Africana* (CD) -SI-V11_d132. This document is analyzed by José Curto in: José C. Curto, "A restituição de 10.000 súditos Ndongo 'roubados' na Angola de meados do século XVII: uma análise preliminar," in Isabel Castro Henriques (ed.), *Escravatura e transformações culturais. África – Brasil – Caraíbas* (Lisbon: Editora Vulgata, 2002), 185–208. About the services provided by porters, Alfredo Margarido emphasizes that already in the first regulations enacted by the governors in 1666 their gratuitous employment was forbidden. Alfredo Margarido, "Les Porteurs : forme de domination et agents de changement en Angola (XVIIe–XIXe siècles)," in *Revue française d'histoire d'outre-mer,* tome 65, n. 240 (3ème trimestre 1978), 377–400.
129 Carta que Sua Excelência [FISC] escreveu aos capitães-mores de todos os presídios e distritos sobre o undamento dos *sobas, ilamba* e mais potentados. São Paulo de Assunção, October 3, 1770. AHU_CU_001, Cx. 55, D. 6 and 7.

tions." The administrative network of Luanda's hinterland included the fortresses —the fortress where the *sobas* swore their allegiance—and several districts. The regent suggests that there were *sobas* who were not *undado* in the area under Portuguese influence, and that they established other alliances with colonial agents, dividing the *sobas* into those of the districts and those of the fortress. This may be an inaccuracy by the regent or an indication that relations with the *sobados* were more complex than what appears in the vassalage documents.

If we follow the chronology of the conquest and the construction of the fortresses, we can see how the obligation requirements changed over time. The order is: Massangano (1583), Muxima (1599), Cambambe (1604), Ambaca (1614), and Pedras de Pungo Andongo (1671). Most of the *sobas*, *ilamba*, and *imbari* are from Massangano (24). The *capitão-mor* claimed that 11 of them were under the obligation "to provide offspring for all royal services required and to serve this town." Two *sobas* were to provide oil "to provide light for the guard corps and the prisoners." Four *ilamba* were to provide firewood, charcoal, and serve the *capitão-mor:* "for the private service of *capitães-mores*." The others were to provide "all royal services ordered" and "they currently serve with their offspring at the Royal Factory of Nova Oeiras." The *capitão-mor* specified that, in the agreements, the clause was the general designation of "royal service"; however, at that moment, since the factory required it, the chiefs were to serve there.

An emblematic case is that of Domingos Acaulo, about whom the official wrote that his name "does not appear in the books, but he has the obligation to provide offspring for royal service." The *capitão-mor* might have been referring to a practice governed by custom; it was known that the *sobas* provided "offspring for royal service," even if this was not established in the books.

In the cases of Muxima, Cambambe, Ambaca, and Massangano, there is nothing specifying that they should provide people for work. As in the previous vassalage agreements, fidelity and obedience to the king and his closest representative, the *capitão-mor*, are emphasized.

The district of Dante (near the river of the same name) is the only place where an official said that the *sobas* provided "punctual" assistance: "for the service of the capital city's fortifications and all other royal works, repairing churches, assisting missionaries and soldiers who are in the service of His Majesty."[130]

Therefore, the earliest agreements included the generic obligation to "provide offspring" for royal service. The expression is ambiguous and there is no indication that whatever fell under royal service was to be provided free of charge. On the contrary, the Portuguese king asserted in the mid-seventeenth century that all vas-

---

130 Ibidem.

sals of the *ngola* should always be remunerated. With time, more specific obligations arose, such as working in the iron factories of Nova Oeiras. Apparently, the provision of labor was added to the obligations of African authorities when the demand arose. However, it was not only demands that could be categorized as "royal service"; services rendered privately to the *capitães-mores* were also listed.

Can we rely on this source produced as a response to the governor, a higher authority than the *capitães-mores*, to whom they were subordinate and who could punish them? There is reason to believe so. The written formulas are reproduced in documents from different locations, as well as the required obligations. Moreover, in cases where they deviate from the norm, the officials themselves provide clues that allow us to perceive that what they did was unfair, that they caused harm, through the exaggerations with which they attempted to distance themselves from that practice. We can see, for example, that, in order to justify the employment of labor from the *sobados*, the regent of Dande emphasized that it was a matter of "punctual" assistance. In the Kwanza district, the official guaranteed that all services were "paid to the letter."

Reading the documentation confirms what Governor Sousa Coutinho suspected: the gratuitous and unrestricted employment of the services of the "offspring" of the *sobas*, the *ilamba*, and the *imbari* was not established as an obligation in the first vassalage agreements. Therefore, after concluding that it was an unfair procedure, as a good royal official aware of his duty to look after the common good, the governor determined that, from then on (October 1770),

> all aforementioned *sobas*, *imbari*, and *ilamba* were exempt from the obligations they had as a result of His Excellency's new orders, and only the *sobas* Kimbi and Kixingango had the obligation to provide oil every month for the guard and jail corps, and all other *sobas* only provided offspring for royal service and assistance to missionaries and military officers.[131]

Thus, the highest royal authority of the Kingdom of Angola acknowledged 200 years of local exploitation of the gratuitous labor of the *soba*'s dependents, who were free people, at least according to Portuguese social codes: "such contribution of labor being imposed without His Majesty's order, has been declared vicious by his royal clemency."[132] And he intended to change such impositions. How did the local chiefs, the *capitães-mores*, and the governors perceive that situation? How often were the "offspring" required to work? These are essential questions, which we will answer in due time in Chapter 3.

---

131 Ibidem.
132 Ibidem.

For now, we are interested in knowing the normative aspect of labor relations, the regulations, which are crucial because they reflect a policy of domination over the "offspring," the dependents of the *sobados*, the labor force of the Kingdom of Angola, which in turn is directly related to the way colonization was established. What was vassalage, if not a way to try to dominate the "people" of Angola's *sertões*? The *sobas*' power was based on their dominion over their "people," the "foundation" without which there was no possibility of agreement with the Portuguese. Colonial control over the *sobados*' subjects was indirect, mediated by local chiefs, and there was not enough military force to control the many forms of resistance (armed uprisings, flights, maroon communities). How, then, could they get these "people" to work? Apparently, the answer was the invention of a custom, a tradition, with the justification that the practice was established as an obligation in the *undamentos*.

When correcting this misconduct, Governor Sousa Coutinho determined what seemed fair to him: that some *sobas* should continue to provide oil to supply the militias and that all *sobas* should provide "offspring" only for royal service and to assist missionaries and military officers.[133] On the other hand, the government resolution and the documentation as a whole indicate that, until then, the gratuitous employment of labor from free Africans was the norm.

How many and who were the *sobas* subjected as vassals to the Portuguese in the mid-eighteenth century? Since these were important questions for the Portuguese Crown, the king ordered every new governor to know all the *sobas* who were subjected to his "obedience and peace, and those who were and now are not, and what was the reason for them to rise up and who gave it to them."[134] Having "risen up" (*levantado*) was a sign of rebellion, i.e. it was used to designate *sobas* who no longer recognized Portuguese rule.

These records did not always survive time or were accessible for historical analysis. Since the end of the sixteenth century, the Kwanza corridor was marked by intense military conflicts between the *sobas* and European invaders. As we have already mentioned, Aida Freudenthal and Selma Pantoja edited the book *Livro dos Baculamentos*, an indispensable source to understand power relations between them, as well as the system of tributes and the commercial network that existed

---

133 In an ordinance from 1770, the governor defines what is meant by royal service, assistance to missionaries, and aid to private individuals. Everything became remunerated. Portaria em que se estabelecem os jornais dos "pretos trabalhadores," assinada por FISC. São Paulo de Assunção de Luanda, December 7, 1770. AHU_CU_001, Cx. 55, doc. 6 and 7.
134 Regimento do Governo do Reino de Angola dado em Lisboa, February 12, 1676. AHU, Códice 544, fl. 3.

in the Kingdom of Ndongo in the early-seventeenth century.[135] The editors identified the *sobas* who were the subject of taxation by the Portuguese Crown between 1619 and 1639, from Hairi, along the northern bank of the Kwanza River, and "Beyond the Mbengu [River]," all the way to Cambambe (a Portuguese fort founded in 1604). In that region, there were 202 vassals and contributors. The vast majority were located in the region where the Nova Oeiras factory was built in the eighteenth century, in Ilamba and Lumbu, where 79 vassal *sobas* were under the obligation to pay tribute. The analysis of the aforementioned *baculamentos* allows us to have an idea of the local hierarchies among African leaders, with strong *sobas* protecting less powerful chiefs. This information, compared to that from other sources, provides an overview of relations among African powers and between them and the Portuguese.

Years later, the military officer Cadornega recorded the differences in the correlation of forces among African leaders: there were the *canda* (from the Kimbundu *nkanda, nhundu*), who, "with a staff insignia," were "heads and governors of the others," "powerful *sobas*," *sobetas* (minor authorities), *ilamba*, and *imbari*. [136]

In the late-seventeenth century, when the Portuguese conquest advanced further into the *sertões*, Cadornega counted an average of 250 vassal *sobas* from the city of Luanda to the fortress of Pedras de Pungo Andongo, founded after the conquest of the Kingdom of Ndongo, and authorities of Kisama, Libolo, in Ndongo lands, the vast majority of them located around the fortress of Ambaca (57) and Pedras de Pungo Andongo (36).

Only 21 of the *sobas* listed by Cadornega appear in the list of *baculamentos* at the beginning of the century.[137] The military officer also recorded many *ilamba* as important political leaders, most of them in Ambaca—something that the *baculamento* lists do not include.[138] This is another indication of how, by creating alliances with the Portuguese, even in the Black War, and establishing themselves

---

135 Aida Freudenthal and Selma Pantoja (ed.), *Livro dos Baculamentos* (2013), 15–23.
136 Antonio de Oliveira Cadornega, *História das Guerras Angolanas (1680)*, v. III, 237 and ff.
137 The *sobas* retain their political titles, which allows us to follow the history of these titles for generations. For example, when we find the *soba* Bango Aquitamba [Mbangu kya Tambwa] in the documentation from the seventeenth to the nineteenth century, we know that it is not the same person, but the many successors of this political title, who for a number of reasons manage to maintain their *sobado* over time. The work of editing *Livro dos Baculamentos* itself included notes indicating whether the title of the *soba* or *kilamba* is repeated in Cadornega's list. Our count derives from the list checked by the editors.
138 Antonio de Oliveira Cadornega, *História das Guerras Angolanas (1680)*, v. III, 244. In *Livro dos Baculamentos*, the *ilamba* appear as tax collectors from the *sobas*. Kilamba kya Phange is the only *kilamba* who appears as a payer of tributes, *undado*, and therefore a vassal. Aida Freudenthal, Selma Pantoja (ed.), *Livro dos Baculamentos*, fl. 28.

as important traders, the *ilamba* became important chiefs in the eighteenth century, controlling a considerable number of people.

The discrepancy may be explained by a number of factors. For example, Cadornega did not always name the *sobetas* or minor authorities, and this may have left out many leaders that were already subjects of the Crown—therefore, his list tends to be incomplete. Nevertheless, a comparative reading of these sources allows us to have an idea of the level of political dismantlement that affected the region in the first century of the Portuguese conquest. Regarding the area where Nova Oeiras was built, Cadornega noted, "Some of the *sobas* of Ilamba and Lumbu are diminished by the calamity of time."[139] This information is indicative of the political and economic enfeeblement and the poverty resulting from many years of war, pillage, and trade of enslaved people.

As we mentioned above, in 1770, in order to inventory the types of services provided by local authorities to the Portuguese and regulate the forms of labor supply, including for the iron factories, Governor Sousa Coutinho ordered the *capitães-mores* of the fortress and districts to send the vassalage terms and agreements through which the *sobas* were obligated to serve the conquerors. It was a way to know more about the African population and to control their relations with the authorities dispersed throughout the *sertão*. The *capitães-mores* of Muxima, Massangano, Cambambe, Pedras de Pungo Andongo, Ambaca, the District of Kwanza, Dande, Icolo, Golungo, and Bengo responded. However, as we saw, not all the clerks were able to find the required documents, sometimes justifying that they did not have them because they had handed them over to the vassal *sobas* themselves (as in the case of Golungo), sometimes that in the districts the *sobas* were not *undados*, but only in the fortress (such as in the district of Kwanza). Despite the many flaws in the list, there are names of 33 local vassal authorities divided as follows: six in Muxima, 24 in Massangano, one in Cambambe, two in Pedras de Pungo Andongo.[140]

---

[139] Idem, 236. Cadornega also records the Benguela chiefdoms, which we omit here given the geographical scope of our study. For that region, Mariana Candido demonstrates that the "collapse and emergence of new states inland of Benguela, such as Kakonda and Viye, can only be understood in a context of expanding Portuguese colonialism and the trans-Atlantic slave trade." Mariana Candido, *An African Slaving Port and the Atlantic world*, 6 and Chap II.

[140] Six other local leaders are mentioned, but their names are not cited. Carta de FISC aos capitães-mores de todos os presídios e distritos sobre o *undamento* dos *sobas* e mais potentados. São Paulo de Assunção de Luanda, October 3, 1770. AHU_CU_001, Cx. 55, D. 6 e 7. In this regard, there is a series of documents on the regulation of services provided by *sobas*, elaborated by FISC in 1770.

Cambambe is the only place where a woman is recorded as a *soba*—"Dona Ana *Soba*" was obliged "for herself" and for "all her *sobetas*," "the people," and the *imbari* to serve the king of Portugal. It is interesting to note that normally the *soba* title is presented before the authority's name (e.g. *Soba* Zombo Ndala Alexandre Francisco), which is not the case with Ana. Dona Ana was not the first female *soba* listed near Cambambe as having been "assigned" to the fortress—i.e. that she was under the jurisdiction of that fortress's *capitão-mor*. In the seventeenth century, Cadornega cited *Soba* Dona Joana Quioza as a chief attached to that fortress.[141]

In the case of the leader Ana, we only know her Christian name and two different titles of distinction (*soba* and *dona*), which join Portuguese and Ambundu criteria of social differentiation and hierarchization. In the case of Joana, on the other hand, despite being baptized, there is an indication that she belonged to a lineage, since she bears an African name—Quioza—, which is very close to the name of a *sobado* near the Muxima fortress in the eighteenth century—Quizua.[142] Was lineage what favored women's succession? The title *dona* was indicative of a prominent social and economic status in the Portuguese world, including Angola.

This brings to mind another woman who was a leader among the Ambundus, another Ana, the Portuguese name for Queen Njinga, whose fame as a strategist turned her into a unique historical character. In a recent book about Njinga, Linda Heywood examines the issue of the importance of women in the kingdom's political life. In European sources, as early as the sixteenth century, the women of the royalty of the Kingdom of Ndongo did not go unnoticed by foreigners. Their names were noted and their prominence highlighted in the most varied spheres: they participated in the *ngola*'s court, conceived actions to guarantee the succession to the throne, and were important religious leaders, among others.[143] Hence, *Soba Dona* Joana Quioza and *Dona* Ana *Soba* were not exceptions among the *sobas* in Angola. In addition, there were women *sobas* without the title of

---

[141] B. Heintze had already observed the preponderance of female leaders in this locality. Beatriz Heintze, *Angola nos séculos XVI e XVII*, 221. However, the author does not cite *Soba* Joana Quioza; for that reason, she imagines that only in the nineteenth century were women appointed as *sobas*. Cadornega's records indicate that there were female chiefs in Cambambe as early as the seventeenth century.

[142] "Mapa geográfico compreendendo a Costa Ocidental d'África (...)," 1790. GEAEM, 1207–2 A-24 A-111. See Map 2.

[143] Linda M. Heywood, *Njinga of Angola. Africa's Warrior Queen*, 2017, 15–17; on Queen Nzinga, see also: Marina de Mello e Souza, "A rainha Jinga de Matamba e o catolicismo – África central, século XVI," in *Congreso Internacional Las relaciones discretas entre las monarquías hispana y portuguesa: Las casas de las reinas (siglos XV–XIX)* (2007).

dona or a Catholic name, such as *Soba* Axila ya Bangi.¹⁴⁴ Understanding the differences between these leaders with more or less contact with the colonial universe is a central exercise to have a better understanding the role of African and Luso-African women as political leaders and diplomats.

It is also important to highlight that those women known as *donas* were essential players in the social and economic structure of the Kingdom of Angola, especially due to the new social arrangements resulting from the dynamics of the trade of enslaved people, which targeted men. Historians have been following the trajectories of some *donas* and have demonstrated that the network of the transatlantic trade of enslaved people represented an opportunity for local women. As a result of their involvement with the Portuguese and Brazilians, African women acquired wealth and social status, becoming partners in the trade of captives. They became known as *donas* and they controlled a large number of dependents in the many plantations and taverns they owned, which led them to become involved in commercial networks. Mariana Candido shows that, in the 1770s, many *donas* in Angola married up to four times, demonstrating that involvement with foreigners was used by Ambundu women as a strategy for economic and social upward mobility. However, it is important to remember that those women known as *donas*, studied by Candido, did not have the political and military power of Queen Njinga.¹⁴⁵

---

144 Roquinaldo Ferreira, *Cross-Cultural Exchange in the Atlantic World*, 78.
145 About the *donas*, see: Mariana P. Candido, *An African Slaving Port and the Atlantic World. Benguela and its Hinterland*, 318 and 319. Among other texts: Selma Pantoja, "Donas de arimos: um negócio feminino no abastecimento de gênero alimentício em Luanda nos séculos XVIII e XIX," in *Entre Áfricas e Brasis* (Brasília: Paralelo 15, 2001); Selma Pantoja, "Gênero e comércio: as traficantes de escravizados na região de Angola," *Travessias*, no. 4–5 (2004): 79–97; Selma Pantoja, "As fontes escritas do século XVII e o estudo da representação do feminino em Luanda," in *Construindo o passado angolano: as fontes e a sua interpretação. Actas do II Seminário internacional sobre história de Angola* (Lisbon: Comissão Nacional para as comemorações dos Descobrimentos Portugueses, 2000), 583–596; Selma Pantoja, "Women's Work in the Fairs and Markets of Luanda," in Clara Sarmento (ed.), *Women in the Portuguese Colonial Empire: The Theater of Shadows* (Newcastle-upon-Tyne: Cambridge Scholars Publishing, 2008), 81–93; Mariana Candido, "Dona Aguida Gonçalves marchange à Benguela à la fin du XVIII siècle," *Brésil(s). Sciences humaines et sociales* 1 (2012): 33–54; Mariana Candido, "Marriage, Concubinage and Slavery in Benguela, ca. 1750–1850," in Nadine Hunt and Olatunji Ojo (eds.), *Slavery in Africa and the Caribbean: A History of Enslavement and Identity since the 18th Century* (London/New York: I. B. Tauris, 2012), 66–84; Mariana Candido, Eugenia Rodrigues, "African Women's Access and Rights to Property in the Portuguese Empire," *African Economic History* 43 (2015): 1–16; Vanessa de Oliveira, "Gender, Foodstuff Production and Trade in Late-Eighteenth Century Luanda," *African Economic History* 43 (2015): 57–61; Vanessa de Oliveira, "Mulher e comércio: a participação feminina nas redes comerciais em Luanda (século XIX)," in Selma Pantoja, Edvaldo A. Bergamo, and Ana Claudia da Silva (orgs.), *Angola e as angolanas. Memória, sociedade e cultura* (São Paulo: Intermeios, 2016), 134–152.

We conclude here this brief, yet unavoidable and important parenthesis on female participation in Ambundu politics. In an "inventory of the *sobas, ilamba,* and *imbari* bound to the service [of the] Nova Oeiras iron factory,"[146] Dona Ana Soba is not listed among the vassals of Cambambe, only the Soba Dom André Fernandes Caboco Cambilo [Kabuku Kambilu],[147] who is recognized as one of the main African authorities north of the Kwanza River.

In another "inventory of the *sobas, ilamba,* and *imbari* of the district of Golungo who serve in the iron factories of Novo Belém and Nova Oeiras (...),"[148] there is a total of 67 vassal authorities listed for the region, most of them in the district of Golungo (65), and only two *sobas* from Ambaca. Most of the chiefdoms listed in these records are from the regions surrounding the factory; the fortress of Ambaca was at a greater distance, which explains why so few chieftains are listed from that region. In fact, Ambaca, described by Cadornega as very "dilated," was the largest area of the Kingdom of Angola and the most important for the trade of enslaved people, had a considerable cotton production, and had an average of 80 vassal *sobados* and *ilamba*.[149]

These sources show the gaps in the 1770 survey, since it was precisely the clerk of the Golungo district who claimed not to have found the vassalage agreements, since these documents had been kept by the *sobas* after the ceremony, and the clerk of Ambaca did not cite the names of local leaders in that list. In addition, the names are not repeated in the two lists, which may indicate that they are complementary. If we consider the possibility of adding up the data from these documents, taking into account that there is no repetition of names, we arrive at the

---

146 "Inventário dos *sobas, ilamba* e *imbari* anexos ao serviço dessa fábrica do ferro da Nova Oeiras respectivo aos Dízimos que pagavam antes da isenção que lhes concedeu o Exmo. Sr. e pelo que regularam de próximo, número de filhos que cada um tem, e os que são dão por mês para o serviço da mesma fábrica." Carta de D. Francisco Inocêncio de Sousa Coutinho para Antônio Anselmo Duarte de Siqueira, intendente geral das reais fábricas do ferro. Anexo: Inventário dos *sobas, ilamba* e *imbari*. São Paulo de Assunção de Luanda, December 29, 1768. IHGB 126, PADAB DVD10,22 DSC00303.
147 Jill Dias reconstructed the history of the *sobado* Kabuku Kambilu in the last decades of the nineteenth century. Jill Dias, "O Kabuku Kambilu (c. 1850–1900). Uma identidade política ambígua."
148 "Inventário dos *sobas, ilamba* e *imbari* do distrito de Golungo, que trabalhavam nas fábricas de ferro de Novo Belém e Nova Oeiras, sobre os dízimos que pagavam antes de serem isentos, o número de filhos capazes que cada um tem e que dão em dinheiro por mês (cópia posterior)." N.p., n.d.; PADAB, IHGB DL81, 02. Probably elaborated between 1768 and 1770.
149 The estimate is Vansina's, who cross-referenced several lists of vassal *sobas* over time. Jan Vansina, "Ambaca Society and the Slave Trade c. 1760–1845," *The Journal of African History* 46, no. 1 (2005): 23, note 88; Antonio de Oliveira Cadornega, *História das Guerras Angolanas (1680)*, v. III, 244. See also: Roquinaldo Ferreira, "O Brasil e a arte da guerra em Angola," *Revista Estudos Históricos*, no. 39 (2007): 3–23.

estimate that there were at least 100 local vassal leaders bound to the fortress and jurisdictions of Massangano, Muxima, Cambambe, Ambaca, Golungo, and Pedras de Pungo Andongo, by the second half of the eighteenth century.

Cross-referencing the lists from *Livro dos Baculamentos* and Cadornega with those of the eighteenth century, especially the list of the *sobas* who served in the factories, we find that among the 100 *sobas*, 44 were successors of leaders already identified in the seventeenth century, mostly from Ilamba, Lumbu, and Golungo. Therefore, the chiefs of that region, where the settlements of Novo Belém and Nova Oeiras were created, had a long history of relationship with the Portuguese. This permanence is a good example of how those chiefs established alliances with the colonizers in order to maintain their autonomy.

It is important to remember that this permanence does not mean that the *sobas* were vassals that entire time, because local nobles constantly rebelled against foreign domination, both because of the absence of an effective conquest and colonization, and because the settlers and royal officers had as their main activities the trade of enslaved people and war, relegating the settlement and occupation of the territory to a secondary place.

The point here is not to reproduce the colonial gesture and its eagerness to count and record, present since the conquest and so abundant during the Pombaline administration, which attempted to portray an image of control and domination.[150] The numbers obtained by cross-referencing the sources are not very representative and by no means account for the totality of African chiefdoms at the time, whether vassal or not. However, they allow us to conceive the dimension of the iron factory project in those *sertões* and the extent to which it mobilized various chiefdoms and their people. Furthermore, cross-referencing the data allows us to perceive how the correlation of forces between Africans and Portuguese changed over time during the Portuguese occupation—some chiefdoms survived, many others succumbed, while new ones emerged.

---

150 For Arjun Appadurai, in the colonial context, the profusion of numerical information, statistics, censuses, "gradually became more importantly part of the illusion of bureaucratic control and a key to a colonial *imaginaire* in which countable abstractions, both of people and resources, at every imaginable level and for every conceivable purpose, created the sense of a controllable indigenous reality." Arjun Appadurai, "Number in the Colonial Imagination," in Carol A. Breckenridge and Peter van der Veer, *Orientalism and the Postcolonial Predicament. Perspectives on South Asia* (Philadelphia: University of Pennsylvania Press, 1993), 317.

Chapter 2
From Ilamba to Nova Oeiras

2.1 Mines and Land: Uses and Meanings

The Ilamba region had valuable resources for the Ambundus, which was important for economic reasons, but not only. Ilamba Baixa was delimited by the Ndande River on the north and by the Luinha and Lukala Rivers to the east; on the west it extended up to about 40 km east of Luanda and the Kilunda Lagoon (located on the left bank of the Mbengu River), i.e. almost to the Atlantic Coast. This province, which appears in written sources in 1584, was the first to be conquered by the Portuguese, who called it "our Ilamba." Its most important leader was Mubanga, from the Ndongo lineage.[1]

Ilamba Alta or Lumbu, a region between the Luinha and the Ndande Rivers, according to Cavazzi, had many iron mines; part of Lumbu belonged to the *ngola*'s kingdom. Under Portuguese administration, part of the province of Ilamba Baixa and Lumbu were added to the district of Golungo.[2] The map below, dated 1790, shows five hills in Nova Oeiras, which were the iron reservoirs identified during the prospection to establish the factory. Note that Ilamba and Golungo were identified, but no *banzas* or *sobados* or any other type of settlement or occupation are marked. In this chapter, we will see that this absence does not occur in the information gathered by royal officials. Perhaps the absence was a way to attest a misappropriation of these lands and mines.

Joseph Miller points out that Keta, and ancient kingdom of the region, based its power on its control of the iron deposits in that locality. In the seventeenth century, this kingdom was already subordinated to the *ngola*. Controlling the salt and iron mines is identified by Miller as one of the causes for the creation of the

---

[1] Beatrix Heintze, *Angola nos séculos XVI e XVII. Estudos sobre Fontes, Métodos e História* (Luanda: Kilombelombe, 2007), 192 and 193; Aida Freudenthal and Selma Pantoja (eds.), *Livro dos Baculamentos: que os sobas deste Reino de Angola pagam a Sua Majestade (1630)* (Luanda: Ministério da Cultura e Arquivo Nacional de Angola, 2013), 47; Giovanni Antonio Cavazzi de Montecúccolo, *Descrição histórica dos três reinos do Congo, Matamba e Angola*, translation, notes, and indexes by Father Graciano Maria de Leguzzano (Lisbon: Junta de Investigações do Ultramar, 1965), v. I, p. 33; Alec Ichiro Ito, *Uma "tão pesada cruz": o governo da Angola portuguesa nos séculos XVI e XVII na perspectiva de Fernão de Sousa (1624–1630)*, Thesis (Master's) (USP, 2016), 81.

[2] Aida Freudenthal and Selma Pantoja (ed.), *Livro dos Baculamentos*, 50. The very word *Golungo*, the name of an ancient chiefdom in the region, may indicate that iron was exploited there. The suffix *-lungu* in Bantu languages is related to the smelting furnace.

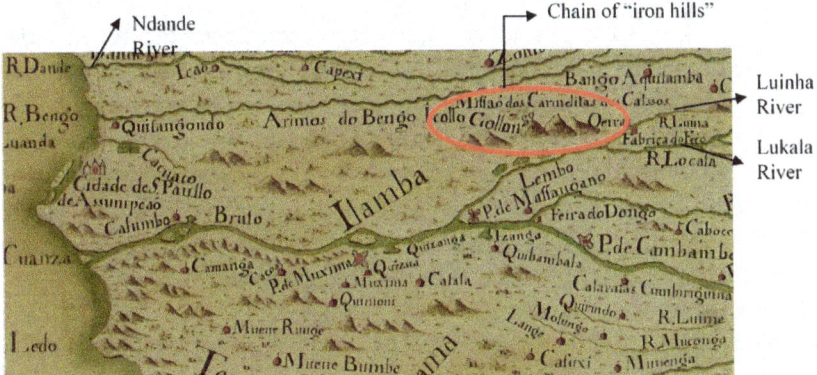

Map 3: The Ilamba region, 1790.
Source: Detail of "Mapa geográfico compreendendo a Costa Ocidental d'África entre 5 e 16 graus e 40 minutos de latitude Sul, representando no continente o estado atual dos Reinos d'Angola e Benguela (...)," by Luis Candido Cordeiro Pinheiro Furtado. Drawn by Lieutenant Colonel Luís Candido Cordeiro Furtado; and copied by the third-year student of the Royal Academy of Fortification, Artillery and Design, Pedro José Botelho de Gouvea Cadete, of the Meklemburg Cavalry Regiment. Lisbon, 1791. Municipal Library of Porto, BPMP_C-M&A-Pasta 24(17).

"Mbundu states," since these rare and necessary resources attracted "unrelated people from a vast area in search of the desired product." When the authorities of this market garnered sufficient prestige and wealth, "ambitious local rulers" transformed "their economic capital into political authority, creating a state that claimed jurisdiction over adjacent and even more distant lineages, as well as over the natural resources themselves." [3]

---

[3] Joseph C. Miller, *Poder político e parentesco: os antigos Estados Mbundu em Angola*, trans. Maria da Conceição Neto (Luanda: Arquivo Histórico Nacional de Angola, 1995), 267. The region was so important that, for Miller, the *ngola a kiluanje* established their capitals there and later "tenaciously resisted Portuguese advances into that area," idem, 77 and 86. This information is difficult to confirm because the capitals of Ndongo were not fixed. According to Beatriz Heintze, Kabasa (Cabaça in Portuguese documents), the residential city and capital of the Ndongo kings, may have been located in the province of Quituxila, near Ambaca. In the second half of the seventeenth century, "it was located somewhere between the Lukala and the Lutete Rivers, in the Ndongo province. It changed location several times. (...) The king of Ndongo appointed by the Portuguese in 1626 no longer resided in Cabaça, but in the natural fortress of Pungo Andongo, in the vicinity of which were 32 villages, one of them on the plain and others in the mountains. Its conquest by the Portuguese in 1671 marked the end of what remained of the Ndongo state." Beatrix Heintze, *Angola nos séculos XVI e XVII*, 229.

In Ilamba and Lumbu, the chiefdoms were mining iron long before the Portuguese initiatives to exploit this mineral, and not by chance were the iron factories of Nova Oeiras and Novo Belém established there (in the mid-1760s). Cavazzi's references and the oral tradition collected by Miler about the iron mines in this region, as well as the sources about the control of the technology to forge the metal, indicate that the mineral had been exploited there by the Ambundus for a long time. Access to this resource, as well as to the salt mines, increased the value of the land, which was the subject of disputes among the *sobas* themselves and also between them and other subjects of the Portuguese Crown.

During the wars of conquest, the chiefdoms closest to Luanda were gradually subjected as vassals, and as early as 1650, a large part of the region's population "had been resettled in lands north and east of Ambaca."[4] Therefore, as we showed in Chapter 1, the chiefdoms present there in the eighteenth century and that survived wars, enslavement raids, and high taxes by making alliances with the conquerors, had had a long relationship with royal agents.

The news that reached the Portuguese informed them that there were large iron deposits in the jurisdictions of Golungo (Ilamba and Lumbu), Ambaca, Cambambe, Caconda (region and fortress in the Kingdom of Benguela), and other very distant locations where the lack of rivers made it impossible to transport the metal.[5] In 1759, there were reports of the existence of two mines of "ferruginous earth," Kituxe and Kalombo,[6] located on the lands of the *soba* Kabanga kya Mbangu (LB)[7] in Ilamba. These mines were exploited by digging "deep pits" that were "very dangerous and deadly to the blacks" due to the frequent collapses caused by humidity.[8]

---

[4] Jan Vansina, "Ambaca Society and the Slave Trade c. 1760–1845," *The Journal of African History* 46, no. 1 (2005): 10.

[5] Carta de Antonio de Vasconcelos, governador de Angola, para Francisco Xavier de Mendonça Furtado, Secretário de Estado da Marinha e do Ultramar. São Paulo de Assunção de Luanda, May 9, 1762. BNP, C. 8553, F. 6362, fl. 2 and 3.

[6] About this Calombo mine, there is information about a place called Kambulu, which was presumably "the place of the old conc. of Golungo Alto, circ. civ. of Cazengo, distr. and prov. of Luanda, where it was believed there were gold and iron mines." They might be the same toponyms. Antonio de Assis Júnior, *Dicionário kimbundu–português, linguístico, botânico, histórico e corográfico. Seguido de um índice alfabético dos nomes próprios* (Luanda: Argente, Santos e Comp. Lda. [n.d.]), entry "Kambulu," 91.

[7] LB means that these titles paid tribute to the Portuguese Crown, in *Livro dos Baculamentos*, elaborated in the early-seventeenth century.

[8] Carta de Antonio de Vasconcelos, governador de Angola, para Francisco Xavier de Mendonça Furtado, Secretário de Estado da Marinha e do Ultramar. São Paulo de Assunção de Luanda, May 9, 1762. BNP, C. 8553, F. 6362, fl. 2 and 3. Antonio de Vasconcelos says that the mines collapsed because the workers had no "industry" to support the underground galleries. This is obviously a

Iron ore was also found in the place called Samba-Quiobe (or Sambaquiba), belonging to the *soba* Nguengue a Kimbemba in the jurisdiction of Massangano, "bordering that of Ilamba, district of Golungo." It was on this *soba*'s land that Sousa Coutinho built Nova Oeiras, where iron ore was found in ironstone on the earth's surface.[9] In "Notícias do Presídio de Massangano do Reino de Angola," dated 1797, the regent of the fortress informed the governor that, on the hillsides of the land of this important *soba*, "iron was extracted to make the hoes with which the people of this country till the land."[10] From there, he sent 19 ironstones as a sample to Luanda. The iron hills of Samba-Quibe in 1800 were famous for having "their surfaces covered with very rich ironstone"[11] and for the "advantage of having the stone of its metal on the surface."[12] The evidence shows that, in these localities, there was an iron mining technology under the control of local chiefdoms and, in the case of Nguengue a Kimbemba, under the dominion of the same lineage over time. The word *nguengue* means a very influential person, which leads us to think that it was a political title of considerable importance in the region, which perhaps based its sovereignty on the control of the iron mines.[13]

We found many blacksmiths in Ambaca, where the *sobas* Lunge Riaquitambe, Ndala ya Huyi (LB), Ndala Tandu (LB), and Ndambi a Kiza had many dependents who specialized in iron work, not only blacksmiths, but also smelters. Many of these specialized laborers who worked in this jurisdiction were native of Ilamba

---

prejudiced reading that assumes that Africans were "ignorant." For that reason, my claim is that they did have a technology to exploit mines, even if it was not sufficiently safe for the workers.

9 Carta de Antonio de Vasconcelos, governador de Angola, para Francisco Xavier de Mendonça Furtado, Secretário de Estado da Marinha e do Ultramar. São Paulo de Assunção de Luanda, May 9, 1762. BNP, C. 8553, F. 6362, fl. 2 and 3. "The ironstone is inexhaustible and just under the topsoil, so it is never necessary to dig to extract it; plenty is the firewood, with the advantage that in the year after they are cut they are renewed, and likewise many are the workers satisfied with the most modest wages, the means of transportation for my use are most comfortable; in short, everything concurs to the greatest progress." Carta de FISC para Francisco Xavier de Mendonça Furtado, secretário de Estado da Marinha e Ultramar. Luanda, February 17, 1767. RJIHGB 126, PADAB DVD10,20 DSC00410.

10 "Notícias do Presídio de Massangano do Reino de Angola, de 1797." IHGB, DL 31.07.

11 Carta de José Álvares Maciel para Miguel Antonio de Melo, governador de Angola. São Paulo de Assunção de Luanda, March 31, 1800. AA, v. IV, v. 52 to 53, 1939, p. 302.

12 Carta de Antonio Salines de Benevides, sargento-mor e ajudante das ordens do governo para Miguel Antonio de Melo, governador de Angola. São Paulo de Assunção de Luanda, November 15, 1800. AA, v. IV, v. 52 to 53, 1939, 327.

13 Antonio de Assis Júnior, *Dicionário Kimbundu-português, linguístico, botânico, histórico e corográfico. Seguido de um índice alfabético dos nomes próprios*, entry "nguengue."

and had moved there fleeing from hunger in their native land.[14] This fact confirms once again that there was an iron mining tradition in Ilamba. These documents also show that these mines, exploited by the *sobas*, were active during the establishment of the iron factory.

In light of this information, we begin to understand that Sousa Coutinho's colonial enterprise was actually an attempt to seize from the *sobas* an already consolidated industry that functioned quite well without outside interference.

Other important chiefdoms related to mines near Luanda are those of the *sobas* Mbangu kya Tambwa[15] (LB), Gongue Anamboa [Ngombeya Nambwa] (LB), and Cariata [Kariata Kakavingi]. There was gold and "crystalline stones" (diamonds) in their lands along the Lombige River in the vicinity of Lumbu.[16] In Cambambe, in the seventeenth century, there was lead mining. Copper mining was also routine; the Portuguese knew of mines in Kasanje and Ambaca.[17] In Novo Redondo, south of the Kwanza River, a copper mine was discovered on the land of the *soba* Hevo.[18] We do not know what chiefdoms controlled the trade of this metal in the Kingdom of Angola, on which the Portuguese obtained no further information: "since blacks consider it gold, they take great care to hide it."[19] Jill Dias explains the reason for this secrecy: "copper being much rarer, and therefore more valuable than iron, it was much sought after (…) to produce special artifacts—ornaments, ceremonial and ritual vessels."[20] What the Portuguese did not know was that those who smelted iron knew the techniques to smelt other ores

---

14 "Likewise, I know for a fact that many blacksmiths and smelters from Ilamba, who left their land because of famines, are present throughout this jurisdiction." Carta de FISC para Francisco Matoso de Andrade, *capitão-mor* de Ambaca. São Paulo de Assunção de Luanda, January 4, 1767. BNP, C – 8742, F – 6364. As we shall see, these blacksmiths actually fled to the interior because they started being captured.
15 The holder of the title Mbangu kya Tambwa appears as the "head" of 18 *sobas* in the late-seventeenth century. Antonio de Oliveira Cadornega, *História das Guerras Angolanas (1680)*. Annotated and revised by José Matias Delgado (Lisbon: Agência-geral do Ultramar, 1972), v. III, 237.
16 Carta de Martinho de Melo e Casto, secretário dos Negócios da Marinha e dos Domínios Ultramarinos, para Antonio de Lencastre, governador de Angola. Palácio Nossa Senhora da Ajuda, July 10, 1772. AHU, Códice 472, fl. 21v–26v.
17 Carta de Antonio de Vasconcelos, governador de Angola, para Francisco Xavier de Mendonça Furtado, São Paulo de Assunção de Luanda, June 28, 1762. AHU_CU_001, Cx. 45, D. 58. Carta de Fernão de Sousa ao rei de Portugal, August 13, 1625. *Monumenta Missionária Africana* (CD) SI – V07_d117.
18 Carta de FISC para Francisco Nunes de Morais, capitão regente do Novo Redondo. São Paulo de Assunção de Luanda, August 27, 1772. AHA, Códice 80, fl. 116.
19 Carta de Antonio de Vasconcelos, governador de Angola, para Francisco Xavier de Mendonça Furtado, São Paulo de Assunção de Luanda, June 28, 1762. AHU_CU_001, Cx. 45, D. 58.
20 Jill Dias, *Nas vésperas do mundo moderno: África* (Lisbon: Comissão Nacional para as Comemorações dos Descobrimentos Portugueses, 1992), 145.

and metals. One hypothesis is that the routine and well-known handling of iron concealed the production of other precious metals and objects.

Although the copper mines were the most guarded, in general Central Africans resisted revealing the location of their ores; all information regarding the mines was guarded with great secrecy. In the incursions in search of gold along the Lombige River, Governor Antonio Álvares da Cunha had the aforementioned *soba* Mbangu kya Tambwa, who was an old ally of the Portuguese, arrested, but the prisoner refused to cooperate in this matter. In the governor's words: "the only virtue of the blacks of these *sertões* is that they do not reveal secrets even if they believe that for that reason their life will be taken."[21] The *soba* remained in prison for three years. Álvares da Cunha's successor had him released because he learned that there was no gold in his lands, only gravel with a few sparks of gold.[22] However, in 1798, expeditions were again sent to the lands of Mbangu kya Tambwa in search of gold mines. The silence of the *sobado* leaders and the colonial persistence in undertaking new expeditions point to the existence of mines there under the control of the local chieftains, who would do anything not to lose them.[23] One ex-

---

21 Carta do governador Antonio Álvares da Cunha para o rei. São Paulo de Assunção de Luanda, February 28, 1756. AHU_CU_001, Cx. 43, D. 4027. This is another example of malachite mining in Serra do Bende ("in the dominions of a rebellious vassal of the King of Kongo"), also called green stones. The government of Luanda ordered that the quality of the ores therein be ascertained, and during the inspection "all that was contained in the said mountains, which the blacks hold in such esteem," was to be "discretely observed." The Portuguese troops were unable to enter the lands of Mani Kongo. Carta de FISC a Francisco Xavier de Mendonça Furtado AHU_CU_001, Cx. 54, D. 113 and 115.
22 Carta do governador Antonio de Vasconcelos para Tomé Joaquim da Costa Corte Real, secretário e Estado da Marinha e dos Domínios Ultramarinos. São Paulo de Assunção de Luanda, January 6, 1759. *Arquivo das colônias*, v. V, n. 30, 148.
23 Carta do governador Miguel Antonio de Melo ao *capitão-mor* do Golungo. São Paulo de Assunção de Luanda, January 22, 1798. AHA, Códice 322, fl. 13v. The same happened to military officer Antonio Candido Gamito, who visited other *Bantu* people, the *Maravi*, in the African East Coast, on the north bank of the Zambezi River, in 1831 and 1832. He was interested in observing gold mining in that place, carried out exclusively by women, but was warned "that [there was] a superstition that this work should only be seen by those who perform it, because the metal flees if someone else sees it." Viagem que seguiu do rio Tete ao Zambeze, liderada pelo major Monteiro. The travel diary was written by Gamito. Antonio Candido Pereira Gamito, *O Muata Cazembe e os Povos Maraves, Chevas, Muizas, Muenbas, Lundas e outros da África Austral* (Lisbon: Agência Geral das Colônias, 1937), v. I, 38. Carta de Antonio de Vasconcelos, governador de Angola, para Tomé Joaquim da Costa Corte Real. São Paulo de Assunção, January 6, 1759. SGL, *Arquivo das colônias*, v. V, no. 30 (1930), 148. Carta do governador Miguel Antonio de Melo ao *capitão-mor* do Golungo. São Paulo de Assunção de Luanda, January 22, 1798. AHA, Códice 322, fl. 13v. Instrução para Antonio de Lencastre governador do Reino de Angola. Palácio de Nossa Senhora da Ajuda, July 10,

ample provided by Jill Dias, although from a later period, makes the issue more evident; she cites that in the mid-nineteenth century, a *soba* from Golungo Alto (Lumbu) threatened with the death penalty anyone who divulged the location of his iron mines to white men.[24]

Gold seems to have become important to the African chiefs; otherwise, why so much secrecy? Gold and diamonds were undoubtedly valuable to Europeans. So much so that the first mine explorers were two private individuals: a Discalced Carmelite missionary, Friar Lourenço de Jesus Maria, who "lived in the bush," taking advantage of the mission on lands belonging to Mbangu kya Tambwa, and the miner Caetano Álvares, an expert in mining techniques. The Crown only learned of the undertaking because the friar denounced Caetano. The *sobas* probably made a deal with the friar and the miner to obtain some sort of commercial advantage.[25]

The secrecy regarding the mines had an immediate purpose: to protect an economic resource. However, in that society, that factor was inseparable from other reasons related of African cosmogony. Hampatê Bá recalls that, in the savannah tradition, minerals are the "children of the bosom of the earth," beings that have a language that is "incomprehensible to ordinary mortals." Blacksmith-smelters, as Hampatê Bá calls iron miners, must have a perfect knowledge of mineralogy, the forest, the plants, since they are expected to "know the plant species that cover the land containing a certain metal and detect a vein of gold simply by examining the plants and pebbles." It was thus man's responsibility to preserve the balance between the forces of nature, "for everything is connected, everything resonates with everything else, every action makes the forces of life vibrate and sets in motion a chain of consequences whose effects are felt by man."[26] One can imagine that specialized knowledge of minerals would not be easily revealed to the Portuguese, and that disturbing the earth on which the ancestors rested could not be a trivial matter, assigned to any unskilled mortal.

1772. AHU, Códice 472, fl. 21v -26v. These mines actually existed and were exploited in the twentieth century by the Lombige Mining Society (SOMIL) and the Angola Diamond Company (DIAMANG).
24 Jill Dias, "Relações econômicas e de poder no interior de Luanda ca. 1850–1875," in *I Reunião Internacional de História de África* (Lisbon: Instituto de Investigação Científica, 1989), 249. *Apud* Juliana Ribeiro da Silva, *Homens de ferro. Os ferreiros na África Central no século XIX*, 59.
25 Carta do governador Antonio de Vasconcelos para Tomé Joaquim da Costa Corte Real, secretário da marinha e dos domínios ultramarinos. São Paulo de Assunção de Luanda, January 6, 1759. *Arquivo das colônias*, v. V, no. 30, 148. Later, in 1754, the governor decided that the mines should be exclusively exploited by the Royal Treasury; the friar seems to have managed to escape (he was never found), but Caetano was imprisoned for four years, after which he was deported to Minas Gerais ("where, being well-known, his experiences can do no harm").
26 Amadou Hampatê Bá, "A tradição viva," in Joseph Ki-Zerbo (org.), *História Geral da África I. Metodologia e pré-história da África* (São Paulo: Ed. Ática/UNESCO, 1980), 195–199.

Perhaps the *soba*'s reaction regarding the iron mines in the nineteenth century was more forceful as a consequence of colonial actions in the eighteenth century; as far as they were able to scrutinize, "there was no river or stream left untouched (...) they explored the hills, hillsides, and plains."[27] There were many attempts to gain more control over the territory and exploit the local wealth. But the colonial interest in the mines was not new—it is worth recalling that, although the trade of enslaved people was the determining factor in the Portuguese conquest of Ndongo, since its beginnings, colonization and territorial occupation was related to the search for minerals, including the aforementioned salt mines, but especially precious metals.[28] The existence of the Cambambe silver mines remained in Portuguese imagination for centuries. Regarding the iron mines, besides the fact that Portugal had no tradition manufacturing the metal, it is fundamental to recognize that we are dealing with an administrative policy of mineral exploration, motivated at first by mercantilist objectives.[29] In the second half of the eighteenth century, the Iberian kingdom was undergoing a serious financial crisis, and the exploration of the iron mines within a more general context of economic reforms was one of the ways to overcome it.

There is evidence that the mining experience in Portuguese America determined some of the mining plans in Angola. In relation to gold, for example, the idea was to follow the demarcation of lands, imposing a capitation tax, as was done in the mines of Serro Frio. This is no doubt directly associated to the Diamantina Demarcation, which began in 1734 and gave rise to the Diamantina District. In Portuguese America, the immediate suspension of mining in the area was followed

---

27 Carta de Antonio de Vasconcelos, governador de Angola, para Tomé Joaquim da Costa Corte Real. São Paulo de Assunção, January 6, 1759. SGL, *Arquivo das colônias*, v. V, no. 30 (1930), 148.

28 Marina de Mello e Souza, *Além do Visível. Poder, catolicismo e comércio no Congo e Angola, séculos XVI e XVII*, thesis (Universidade de São Paulo, 2012), 63 and ff; Beatrix Heintze, *Angola nos séculos XVI e XVII*, 244.

29 For Birmingham, the salt mines were one of the main factors that attracted the Portuguese to Angola. David Birmingham, "Early African Trade in Angola and its Hinterland," in Richard Gray and David Birmingham (eds.), *Pre-colonial African Trade. Essays on Trade in Central and Eastern Africa before 1900* (London, New York, Nairobi: Oxford University Press, 1970). In her book, Juliana Ribeiro da Silva provides a history of Portuguese mineral exploitation overseas. Since the first Portuguese contacts with West Central Africa, they had an interest in minerals. The Ambundus lost many of their salt mines to the Portuguese, which must have implied irreparable damage, since salt was indispensable in the region and became an important currency of the land. In general, "the Portuguese in fact wanted to believe that there was inexhaustible wealth in Africa." Juliana Ribeiro da Silva, *Homens de ferro. Os ferreiros na África Central no século XIX* (São Paulo: Alameda, 2011), 36.

by the demarcation of the entire extractive area, a strategy to maintain control over future discoveries. Arraial do Tejuco, on the other shore of the Atlantic, depended on a broad administrative, military, and fiscal network, and still it was difficult to control smuggling. [30]

It was to be expected that these intentions were hindered by the tight control of the mines by African political elites, who by no means wanted their lands demarcated or burdened with further taxes. On the other hand, given the local conditions of the Portuguese militias and the fragility of the fiscal system in the Kingdom of Angola, it was impossible to replicate the system of the Diamantina District in Africa. Once again, the Portuguese depended on partnerships with the *sobas*, but in the case of the gold mines, they were unable to impose their will or establish alliances. Mbangu kya Tambwa's silence during his three years in prison is exemplary of this conflict. The *sobas* continued to resist the loss of control over this natural resource.

How was control over the mines enforced? With weapons, since the friar who explored the mines had many "armed Negroes" at his disposal, and Mbangu kya Tambwa was known for his support of the Portuguese in the so-called Black War, i.e. the African troops of the Portuguese army.[31]

The issue of mines therefore generated many tensions. When the government of Luanda decided to establish iron factories in Ilamba, the conflicts at first took the form of disputes over land ownership. Obviously, the government of Luanda needed some of the mines in the region, which were controlled by the local chiefs. In addition to the mines, Sousa Coutinho intended that part of the lands where he founded Nova Oeiras be used to create vegetable gardens to feed the factory workers and auxiliary service providers.[32] If we recall the centrality of the founding myths of the iron-king in Central Africa, iron ore alone entailed social, religious, and economic factors. For that reason, since the beginning of the enlightened plan for iron mining in the region, from the choice of the land to the establishment of the factories, the *sobas* claimed ownership of the land.

---

30 On mining in Comarca do Serro Frio, see: Júnia Ferreira Furtado, *O livro da capa verde: o regimento diamantino de 1771 e a vida no Distrito Diamantino no período da Real Extração* (São Paulo: Annablume, 1996).

31 In a battle, Elias Correa said that the Portuguese were only victorious thanks to the help of a "brave black captain of Mbangu kya Tambwa." Elias Alexandre da Silva Correa, *História de Angola* (Lisbon: Clássicos da Expansão Portuguesa no Mundo. Império Africano. Series E, vol. I), 227.

32 The governor said of the lands of the region: "Since I am told that from the Luinha River, where Nova Oeiras will be established, to the market of Zundo, there are admirable lands, settlements and seedbeds shall be created throughout, since those lands are unoccupied." "Instrução secretíssima para Antonio Anselmo Duarte de Siqueira," intendente geral da fábrica do ferro. (FISC). São Paulo de Assunção de Luanda, January 12, 1767. AHU_CU_001, Cx. 52, D. 73.

We were able to identify the lands of some *sobas* in the immediate vicinity of the factories: Nguengue a Kimbemba, owner of iron mines, cited above, "a *soba* bordering the other one," Kyambata kya Ngoto (LB). "And if one travels a distance of only ten or twelve leagues (approximately 50 km), the following *sobas* are found": Itombe ya KaNdongo (LB), Nzambi a Keta, Ngola a Kiato, Ngolome (LB), Kabuku Kambilu (LB), Kisala kya Kabuku (LB), Nzamba Nsungui, Kabuto and Kilamba Pedro Ambaxi. This list was elaborated by Captain Joaquim de Sousa Lobo in a mission commissioned by the governor, who requested "exact inventories" of the region where the factory would be established: "all the woods and firewood suitable for charcoal, within an appropriate distance to serve the said factory, as well as their amounts, quality, and thickness, and the number of *libatas* and *sobas* who can perform this service."[33] Lands and people were catalogued.

The description demonstrates that the official was aware of the borders between the lands of the various chiefdoms. The governor and his subordinates knew that those lands had an owner. Sousa Coutinho even stated this in official letters in January 1767, when he said that the factory that was established in Luinha was on the *terreno* (plot of land) of the *soba* Nguengue a Kimbemba. The factory at Novo Belém, in the heart of Ilamba Baixa, was on the land of Kilamba Ngongue a Kamukala.[34] In other words, the factories were established in areas that belonged, in both a political and an economic sense, to those *sobas* and *ilamba*.

A document dated February 1767, two years after the construction of the factories began, reports that the *sobas* bound to the Muxima fortress claimed ownership of the lands in the region. That year, the fortress's major sergeant wrote about conflicts between Muxima settlers and *sobas* regarding the "ownership of the lands where the factory stands." The settlers claimed to have purchased the land from the *sobas*, who in turn accused them of stealing it. The governor at the time ordered the superintendent of the iron factories to disregard those conflicts and listen only to those who presented documents proving ownership. He requested the sale papers because he was not sure whether "the *sobas* could sell the lands of their state."[35] This is the first mention, in the context of the factory's construction, of the idea that Ambundu land was not negotiable. There were other rules, not unknown to the Portuguese, that governed the relationship of Central Africans to their territory.

---

33 Instrução que levou o capitão Joaquim de Sousa Lobo. São Paulo de Assunção de Luanda, July 18, 1768. IEB/ USP, AL-083–099.
34 "Instrução que deve guardar Antonio Anselmo Duarte de Siqueira (...)". São Paulo de Assunção de Luanda, January 12, 1767. AHU_CU_001, Cx. 52, Doc. 73.
35 Carta de FISC para Antonio Anselmo Duarte de Siqueira, intendente geral das fábricas de ferro. São Paulo de Assunção de Luanda, February 18, 1767. BNP, C 8742, F6364, fl. 148.

This event was not the end of the matter. In April 1767, the factories' superintendent wrote to the governor suggesting that the town of Nova Oeiras be established near the *banza* of the *soba* Muxixi, on the banks of the Lukala River. The answer was that this would be disadvantageous, thus disapproving of the official's idea.[36] It is not surprising that, one year later, the *soba* Muxixi claimed "the lands of Luinha."[37] Most likely, the superintendent continued to occupy the land, reaching the *soba*'s territory, even without the Luanda government's approval.

Other *sobas* in the region joined the conflict. As happened in Muxima, in the Massangano fortress there was also a disagreement between *sobas* and settlers over the factory's lands. And once again, the governor distrusted the settlers, reflecting that no *soba* could have negotiated that because "usually *sobas* cannot sell their lands, since they are a sort of *morgado*[38]." The order from Luanda determined that land classified as "unused" could be occupied until the presumed owners presented "ownership deeds" that proved a "good or bad sale," i.e. the legitimacy of the deal.[39] If the unused lands had an owner, they were under obligation to cultivate them under "penalty of being taken from them if they did not do so soon."[40] Therefore, the superintendent was not authorized to occupy productive lands.[41]

The *sobas* in fact claimed ownership of lands and not only in the context of the iron factory. In 1759, when the Jesuits were expelled from the Kingdom of Angola, their possessions were seized by the Royal Treasury.[42] Among the many Jesuit pos-

---

36 Carta de FISC para Antonio Anselmo Duarte de Siqueira, intendente geral das fábricas de ferro. São Paulo de Assunção de Luanda, April 10, 1767. BNP, C 8742, F 6364, fl. 167.
37 Carta de FISC para o coronel Antônio Anselmo Duarte de Siqueira, intendente geral da fábrica do ferro. São Paulo de Assunção de Luanda, February 3, 1768. IEB/USP, AL-083–003.
38 A land ownership system that arose in Portugal in the thirteenth century whereby lands were bound to the seigneurial family and could only be transmitted to a single descendant after the owner's death. (T.N.)
39 Ibidem.
40 "Instrução que deve guardar Antonio Anselmo Duarte de Siqueira servindo o emprego de intendente geral da Fábrica do Ferro e que executaram também os capitães mores como intendentes particulares na parte que lhes é respectiva." São Paulo de Assunção de Luanda, January 12, 1767. AHU_CU_001, Cx. 52, Doc. 73
41 There is no mention of a specific type of crop that should be cultivated.
42 "Among the many enemies of the Society of Jesus in the first three centuries of its existence in Portugal, the Marquis of Pombal was the most implacable, to the point of achieving its expulsion, first from Portuguese territories in 1759, and then from all of Christendom in 1773, by order of Pope Clement XIV." Célio Juvenal Costa, "O Marquês de Pombal e a Companhia de Jesus," in S. L. Menezes, L. A Pereira, and C. M. M. Mendes (orgs.), *A expansão e consolidação da colonização portuguesa na América* (Maringá: EDUEM, 2011), 69. Regarding the Jesuits in the Kingdom of Angola, according to Catarina Madeira Santos, "the missionary assistance of the Society of Jesus in the Angolan *sertão*

sessions, houses, lands, *arimos*, and haciendas—the properties with the highest food production in Luanda and its hinterland—were listed. Ownership of these lands was claimed both by the residents of Luanda and the nearby *sertões* and by the *sobas*. The governor said that these disputes led to "eternal claims" that went unresolved, and about the *sobas* he stated the following: "there are some *sobas* who demand their right over a significant part of them because they have always claimed that [the Jesuits] held them illegitimately and had usurped them from their ancestors with the subtleties and deception that characterized them."[43]

Beyond the legal aspect, it should be noted that the disputes were between residents of areas under Portuguese administration—where representatives of the Luso-African elite predominated (as we saw in Chapter 1)—and the *sobas*, vassals of the Portuguese Crown, who administered their villages independently.

One of the main issues for the government of Luanda at the time was the promotion of agriculture to combat food shortages and poor water distribution. In a 1768 announcement, the governor requested a survey of all unused lands ("deserted *arimos*") along the Nzenza, Ndande, and Kwanza Rivers. The document allows us to understand how colonial policies themselves created conflicts over land. The governor promised to grant abandoned properties to those who denounced their unproductive state and made a commitment to cultivate them. If, in order to gain access to land, it sufficed to denounce its misuse, it was to be expected that there would be plenty of denunciations. The document also informs us that the lands in the kingdom were either "of a *sesmaria* nature" or "unduly purchased from the *sobas*."[44]

The governors' regulations determined that "all lands given, who gave them and what power they had to do so, and who possesses them" should be known, because there were reports that lands that had been granted were not being cultivat-

---

in the eighteenth century was minimal. Since the restoration in 1648, the Jesuits gradually abandoned the missions in the interior and concerned themselves mostly with the college in Luanda (whose construction began in 1607) and the *arimos* (plantations or agricultural properties) owned by them in various places, especially in the region of the Bengo River." *Um governo "polido" para Angola*, 129.

43 Carta de Antonio de Vasconcelos, governador de Angola, para o Conde de Oeiras. São Paulo de Assunção de Luanda, May 14, 1760. AHU_CU_001, Cx. 46, D. 4261. "Besides the *sobas*, there are also some settlers who, with eternal demands, disputed their right over them; and also the [Santa Casa da] Misericórdia in that city, which has fought with them for over fifty years over an inheritance left to that institution to by a man of whom they were heirs, and who died 137 years ago, with the said inheritance worth 400,000 cruzados, which they all kept to themselves; and they never satisfied the inheritance, even after the Misericórdia obtained sentences against them."

44 Bando sobre os *arimos* desertos. São Paulo de Assunção de Luanda, August 1768. IEB/ USP, AL-083–92.

ed. In light of this, lands without an owner were to be apportioned to those who committed themselves to cultivate them within a period of five years. If the private owners did not do so, they could be granted to someone else. This excerpt refers to what was established in the 1375 "law of *sesmarias*," complied in the Afonsine, Manueline, and Philippine Ordinances, with some wording changes. [45]

Regarding the "undue purchases to the *sobas*," or the "wrongful possession" in the case of the Jesuits, how to discover the legitimate owners? The first hypothesis is expropriation by force, for example, in a context of war. Vansina says that the *sobas* dispossessed during the conquest, having no other recourse, negotiated their lands with the settlers.[46] In the Portuguese occupation of the East African coast, for African chieftains, especially the Maraves, land was collective property —no chief could sell or alienate it, which was also the case among the Ambundus. In *Portugueses e africanos nos rios de Sena*, Eugénia Rodrigues provides a detailed inventory of the *prazos* in the Zambezi Valley region. In the Indian Ocean, a different legal framework was instituted for land distribution. The *prazos* were "emphyteutic concessions whereby the Crown maintained the direct domain and yielded the useful domain in exchange for the payment of an annual fee."[47] The lease initially lasted three generations and could be renewed. Like the *sobas*, the chieftains of the Sena Rivers came in conflict with the colonists, who claimed to have purchased their lands. At this point, this book can help us elucidate the origins of this type of confusion—after all, did settlers purchase land from the African elite or not? In the case of Mozambique, the Portuguese presence in African territory was sealed by offering textiles. In the transaction, "apparently, the African chief remained the lord of the land, even though the river merchants believed that they had purchased it or that it had been donated to them." Rodrigues observes that, in order to understand the conflict, we must distinguish between

---

[45] Instituted during the reign of Ferdinand I, the *sesmarias* were intended to combat the decline in Portugal's rural population. *Código Filipino, ou, Ordenações e Leis do Reino de Portugal: recompiladas por mandado d'el-Rei D. Filipe I*, facsimile edition of the fourteenth edition of 1821 by Cândido Mendes de Almeida (Brasilia: Senado Federal, Conselho Editorial, 2004), Livro IV, 43. In Portuguese America, *sesmarias* were also the main norm for land division at the time. In this regard, see Márcia M. M. Motta, *Direito à Terra no Brasil. A gestação do conflito (1795/1824)* (São Paulo: Alameda, 2009). On the land tenure regime in the Portuguese Atlantic, see: Antonio de Vasconcelos Saldanha, *As capitanias. O regime senhorial na expansão ultramarina portuguesa* (Funchal: Centro de Estudos de História do Atlântico, 1992), 190. On the East Coast, the Marquis of Pombal attempted to "sesmarize" the terms, but the system lasted until the early-nineteenth century.
[46] Jan Vansina, "Ambaca Society and the Slave Trade c. 1760–1845," 22.
[47] Eugénia Rodrigues, *Portugueses e Africanos nos rios de Sena. Os prazos da Coroa em Moçambique nos séculos XVII e XVIII* (Lisbon: Imprensa Nacional–Casa da Moeda, 2013), 25.

the "European concepts of donation and purchase" and "the acquisition of new subjects by African chiefs."[48]

It is plausible that a similar confusion may have caused the disagreements between the *sobas* and the fortress settlers, since the relations between them were based on offers of goods such as textiles, for example, considered a common object-currency in West Central Africa.[49] A gesture, a negotiation, a simple exchange of gifts had different meanings for those involved; we can imagine that what for the first settlers was a land purchase transaction, for the Ambundus represented an offer to authorize passage through their territory or to make an alliance, for example.

The settlers started to send their "deeds." Sousa Coutinho even received a list of those who claimed to own some of the lands that had been set aside to build the factory. The order was to compensate those who had part of their property wrongfully annexed to the factory.[50] The same cannot be said about the *sobas*. We have not found sources in which they proved their ownership of the land. However, there were two ways of dealing with land in Angola: the *sesmaria*, which established how settlers acquired land, and a "sort of *morgado*," which regulated African possession of their land. How to resolve the issue when both systems overlapped, when the same land was claimed by African chiefs and settlers? Which law was valid, that of the *sobas* or the Ordinances? Furthermore, what were the African rules for access to land and what was the African "*morgado*"?

According to historian Isabel de Castro Henriques, "African land is comprehensive, it encompasses all African territories: land is the cosmos," and therefore integrates the sacred space, since "for Africans the land is not an exchange value, since it belongs to the group only thanks to the mediation of spirits." Hence, in the African territory are found some of the "fundamental pillars of African identity"[51] —kinship and religion. Sacred trees, rivers, plants that provided the pigments of the sacred colors, the drums that took messages from one *cubata* to the next, the graves of the ancestors or the founding heroes are all important markers of

---

48 Idem, 357. Rodrigues also observes that merchants obtained land through military and matrimonial alliances in the territories of the Karanga states, which emerged from the Monomotapa Empire.
49 The term object-currency was coined by Paul Lovejoy in *A escravidão na África. Uma história de suas transformações* (Rio de Janeiro: Civilização Brasileira, 2002), 169–170.
50 Carta de FISC para Antonio Anselmo Duarte de Siqueira, intendente geral da fábrica de ferro. São Paulo de Assunção de Luanda, April 7, 1769. IEB/ USP, AL-083–223.
51 Isabel de Castro Henriques, "A materialidade do simbólico: marcadores territoriais, marcadores identitários angolanos (1880–1950)," *Textos de História* 12, no. 1/2 (2004): 40.

this territory.⁵² For example, in 1809, the *capitão-mor* of the Pedras de Pungo Andongo fortress commanded some vassal *sobas* to go live on one of the Kwanza islands. The chiefs did not accept because this went against "their rites," translated by colonial agents as "gentile laws."⁵³

When Sousa Coutinho referred to the *morgado*, the closest idea that the royal official could formulate to understand the *sobas*' relation to the lands of Ilamba was to relate the notion of kinship and the transmission of nobility titles among Africans, to European rights of inheritance and succession. According to Father Raphael Bluteau's dictionary, a *morgado* or "*morgado* property" was "property bound so that without being able to alienate or divide it, the successor justly possesses it in the same form and order as the institutor has declared."⁵⁴ The Philippine Ordinances established how the transfer of inheritance should occur, first privileging the first-born son, and "in the case that the first-born son should die during his father's lifetime, or that of the *morgado*'s holder, if that first-born son has a son, or a grandson, or legitimate descendants, those descendants in order shall have precedence over the second son."⁵⁵ The *morgado* also had to be confirmed by the possession of a document by the heirs. In making this analogy, the governor understood that land ownership was governed by kinship rules.

Even though there is a relevant historiography for other parts of the Portuguese Empire, especially for Portuguese America, India, and East Africa, the bibliography on land conflicts in the Kingdom of Angola and West Central Africa in general is scarce and focuses mainly on the nineteenth and twentieth centuries. For these authors, the rules of access to Ambundu land suffered a significant change after the decline of the trade of enslaved people, when Portuguese colonialism turned significantly to agricultural activities, the production of cassava, maize, and indigo, in addition to exploiting heather, ivory, and gum. Only then,

---

52 Regarding the multiple meanings of land for Africans, Holly Hanson presented an interesting example. Hanson studied how a system of social relations based on "reciprocal obligations" was the basis for the development of the Ganda state. The obligations revolved around land ownership (which was the payment of the obligation), and were imbued with affective meanings that determined social and political hierarchies. Holly Hanson, *Landed Obligation: The Practice of Power in Buganda* (Portsmouth: Heinemann, 2003).
53 Carta do *capitão-mor* de Pedras de Pungo Andongo, Matias Joaquim de Brito para o Governador Saldanha da Gama, AHA, Cód. 3018, s.fl., February 19, 1809. *Apud*, Catarina Madeira Santos, Um governo "polido," 129.
54 Raphael Bluteau, *Vocabulário portuguez e latino*, 10 v. (Lisbon/Coimbra: Colégio da Cia. de Jesus, 1712–1728), entry "morgado."
55 *Código Filipino, ou, Ordenações e Leis do Reino de Portugal: recompiladas por mandado d'el-Rei D. Filipe I*, Livro IV, Título 100, "Por que ordem se sucederá nos Morgados e bens vinculados."

in response to the expansion of agriculture, did the Portuguese resort to local exploitation of Central African labor.[56]

The sources consulted point in the opposite direction. As Mariana Candido emphasized, since the sixteenth century, in accordance with the logic of the rights of conquest and in the name of a just war, the Portuguese occupation influenced local policies of land distribution and control.[57] Over time, the expansion to Luanda's hinterland intensified, as the power of the Africans weakened. With the decline of the transatlantic trade, land tenure, which had always been an issue for colonialism, became central.

For the regions north of the Kwanza River, the most revealing studies on land tenure are those of Eva Sebestyén on the transmission of land tenure in the Ndembu, in N' Dalatando, and in the Samba Cajú *sobado*, in the region of Ambaca.[58] It is

---

[56] Cf.: Jill Dias, "Changing Patterns of Power in the Luanda Hinterland. The Impact of Trade and Colonization on the Mbundu ca. 1845–1920," *Paideuma* 32 (1986): 285–318; José Carlos Venâncio, *A economia de Luanda e Hinterland. No Século XVIII. Um estudo de Sociologia Histórica* (Portugal: Estampa,1996); Selma Pantoja, "Donas de '*arimos*': um negócio feminino no abastecimento de gêneros alimentícios em Luanda (séculos XVIII e XIX)," in Selma Pantoja (ed.), *Entre Áfricas e Brasis* (Brasilia: Paralelo, 2001), 35–49; Aida Freudenthal, *Arimos e fazendas: a transição agrária em Angola, 1850–1880* (Luanda: Chá de Caxinde, 2005); Aurora da Fonseca Ferreira, "A questão das terras na política colonial portuguesa em Angola nos anos de 1880: o caso de um conflito em torno da Kisanga," in Maria Emília Madeira Santos (dir.)m *A África e a instalação do sistema colonial – c. 1885–c. 1930* (Lisbon: Centro de estudos de História e cartografia antiga, 2001)< 261–272. On the Portuguese Empire in America, see: Tamar Herzog, *Frontiers of Possession: Spain and Portugal in Europe and the Americas* (Cambridge, Massachusetts: Harvard University Press, 2015); Maria Sarita Mota, "Apropriação econômica da natureza em uma fronteira do império atlântico português: o Rio de Janeiro (século XVII)," in José Vicente Serrão, Bárbara Direito, Eugénia Rodrigues, and Susana Münch Miranda (orgs.), *Property Rights, Land and Territory in the European Overseas Empires* (Lisbon: CEHC, ISCTE-IUL, 2015), 43–53; on East Africa, see: Eugénia Rodrigues, *Portugueses e Africanos nos rios de Sen* (2013); Maria Paula Pereira Bastião, *Entre a Ilha e a Terra. Processos de construção do continente fronteiro à Ilha de Moçambique (1763–c. 1802)*, thesis (Master's) (Universidade Nova de Lisboa, 2013); Albert Farré, "Regime de terras e cultivo de algodão em dois contextos coloniais: Uganda e Moçambique (1895–1930)," in José Vicente Serrão, Bárbara Direito, Eugénia Rodrigues, and Susana Münch Miranda (org.), *Property Rights, Land and Territory in the European Overseas Empire* (Lisbon: CEHC, ISCTE-IUL, 2015), 245–254.

[57] Mariana Candido, "Conquest, Occupation, Colonialism and Exclusion: Land Disputes in Angola," in José Vicente Serrão, Bárbara Direito, Eugénia Rodrigues, and Susana Münch Miranda (orgs.), *Property Rights, Land and Territory in the European Overseas Empires* (Lisbon: CEHC, ISCTE-IUL, 2015), 230.

[58] The author found 234 documents among "wills, lists of *sobas*, demarcations, inspections, purchase and sale of land, lawsuits by the *sobas* over land and power, correspondence with the Portuguese administration and family members, vassal agreements." Eva Sebestyén, "Legitimation through Landcharters in Ambundu Villages, Angola." *Perspektiven Afrikanistischer Forschung. BeiträgezurLinguistik, Ethnologie, Geschichte, Philosophieund Literatur. X. Afrikanistentag* (1993), 363–

therefore a region very close to Nova Oeiras. The author found documents kept by the *sobas* of the region about land disputes and purchase deeds from the seventeenth to the twentieth century. They are written records of the oral tradition used to legitimize land tenure, which maintain the narrative protocols of Portuguese wills, but with different contents. The testator does not list the property and the respective heirs; rather, he leaves a record of important information for his lineage, including information aimed at protecting his heirs from enslavement: "mainly a statement validating their kinship and a record of inspections that establish the boundaries of the lineage's property [land]."[59] Another important piece of information is that the documents of the *sobas* in the jurisdiction of the Ambaca fortress were only recognized as authentic if the fortress's official clerk recorded them. Therefore, the colonial administration recognized the lands of the lineages as long as they were attested by its officials. Once again, we can see the dependence of the African chiefs on fortress officials, since it was they who recorded and authenticated their "wills."

According to Sebestyén, these titles served two purposes: they met the "Portuguese requirements, since they reported in detail the *sobado*'s limits and the names of neighboring *sobados*"[60]; at the same time, the records served to safeguard the lineage's history: its origin, its migrations, its first settlement, local wars, and alliances. Whenever a new chief was elected, the *sobado*'s boundaries were reconfirmed through an inspection of its borders.

Land boundaries were determined differently among the Ambundus—they had a spiritual connotation. In the 1782 will of Dom Miguel Soba Caxinda Candala, the *soba* described the reasons for his people's migration: "seeing that my people were too many and had no space for farming." He also specified the alliances he made with other *sobas* to occupy new lands; the streams and rivers that served as land markers; as well as other particular markings—"establishing their markings."[61] According to Sebestyén, the border marks used were specific trees, which the author discovered had medicinal properties—"trees in the shape of a

---

379; Eva Sebestyèn, "Os 'arquivos' de *sobas* Ambundu: um caso transcultural dos testamentos em Angola," in *Actas do IV Curso de Verão da Ericeira. População: encontros e desencontros no espaço português* (2003), 51–74; Eva Sebestyèn, "O contexto cultural dos marcos de terrenos nas aldeias Ambundu/ Angola," *Africana Studia*, no. 24 (2015): 91–106.
59 Eva Sebestyèn, "Legitimation through Landcharters in Ambundu Villages, Angola," 364.
60 Idem, 365.
61 I would like to thank Roquinaldo Ferreira for sharing this document with the researchers at Cecult/Unicamp. Testamento de Dom Miguel *Soba* Caxinda Candala, May 15, 1782, s.l. AHA, Caixa 3465 (Avulsos) – Ambaca.

cross, pieces of clay, pieces of iron, stones," clay pots, among others.[62] In annual rituals related to the land, the *sobas* resorted to the support of their ancestors and water entities, "on the banks of the border rivers in order to have a good harvest, through offerings to the mermaids, *quiximbi* owners of the rivers, protectors of the land."[63]

If we take into account that these are not the first writings kept by lineage holders of this region that came to our knowledge, [64] it is likely that the *sobas* of the former Ilamba province also had titles to prove lineage ownership of their lands and that they presented them to the governor.[65] Perhaps due to his acquaintance with the documents kept by the *sobas*, Sousa Coutinho employed the analogy to the *morgado*, which could not be more appropriate. In the "Portuguese" *morgado*, inheritance followed the paternal line: sons, grandsons, etc. The Ambundus have a matrilineal tradition; therefore, in theory, it was not the father's family which was preferred in the succession, but the mother's. However, this is not what Sebestyèn observed: the transmission of titles occurred patrilineally—the *soba*'s son or daughter became the heir, the protector of the land and the lineage. In a practical sense, it was truly a *morgado*. The author considers the hypothesis that coexistence with the Portuguese may have introduced that change in the transmission and access to land.

The dispute over land was not only between royal officials, settlers, and traditional Central African authorities. Land tenure was also an issue that generated conflicts among the *sobas* themselves and between the *sobas* and the *ilamba* and the *imbari*. This is especially true with regard to the lands of Ilamba Alta, with its rich iron mines.

The *ilamba*, officers of the Black War, according to Beatrix Heintze, were rewarded "for their loyal service with land in the regions of the vassals [the

---

62 Eva Sebestyén, "Legitimation through Landcharters in Ambundu Villages, Angola," 365.
63 Eva Sebestyén, "O contexto cultural dos marcos de terrenos nas aldeias Ambundu / Angola," 93.
64 There is also, at least, the "Arquivo de Estado do Ndembu Kakulu Kakaenda," composed of 210 documents exchanged between the *ndembu* and the colonial administration, dating from the eighteenth to the twentieth century. Ana Paula Tavares e Catarina Madeira Santos (ed.), *Africae Monumenta. A Apropriação da escrita pelos africanos* (Lisbon: Instituto de Investigação Científica e Tropical, 2002), v. I.
65 It is interesting to note that already in the nineteenth century, in 1860, the *soba* Quipola, from Môssamedes, who claimed ownership of lands that were occupied by white people for the development of agriculture, requested that the governor give him the "land title" to prove that he was the rightful owner. This request deploys the argument that lineage ownership should be confirmed by the colonial authorities. Mariana Candido, "Conquest, Occupation, Colonialism and Exclusion: Land Disputes in Angola," 224.

sobas]."⁶⁶ The land where the Novo Belém factory was founded belonged to Kilamba Ngongue a Kamukala. Around Nova Oeiras, there were lands belonging to Kilamba Pedro Ambaxi, and the *soba* Muxixi, who claimed lands in Luinha, appears in other documents as *kilamba*.⁶⁷ Heintze and Vansina also suggest that the *ilamba* could become *sobas* over time. However, there seems to be a consensus in the sources that the *kilamba* occupied part of the *sobas'* lands, which also served to better spy on them, but did not possess their own land.⁶⁸

The cases presented here suggest that at least some of them did have land. There were probably *ilamba*, especially the first ones to associate with the Portuguese, who became lords of land, natural resources, and people, and who perhaps even became part of the political mechanisms of kinship, becoming *sobas*. Others were not so successful, remaining on the *sobas'* lands, as were many minor *sobas*, or *sobetas*, who congregated on the lands of a more powerful *soba*.⁶⁹ However, it is important to remember that the *ilamba* were not well regarded ("hated") by the *sobas* because of their espionage practices and alliances with the Portuguese,⁷⁰ since many subjects may have been subjugated to colonial rule thanks to the actions of the *ilamba*, the captains of the Black War.

The disputes over land were "eternal conflicts," as cited in a previous document. The clash over the land at Ilamba unfolded and another character appeared to claim the land—a "shod Negro," whose name was not mentioned in February 1768.⁷¹ This man is likely to be João Correia, who presented a petition with the "title of lord of the lands where Nova Oeiras was founded" to the Royal Treasury

---

66 Beatrix Heintze, *Angola nos séculos XVI e XVII*, 451; Jan Vansina, "Ambaca Society and the Slave Trade c. 1760–1845," 7 and 8. Although the plural of *kilamba* corresponds exactly to the name of this region (Ilamba), we do not know the reasons for this coincidence. We know that the *ilamba* were given land in return for their participation in the Black War. But was all that land donated to the *ilmaba*? It is a question to which we have no answer, because we have no further elements for analysis.

67 Carta de FISC aos capitães-mores de todos os presídios e distritos sobre o *undamento* dos *sobas* e mais potentados. São Paulo de Assunção de Luanda, October 3, 1770. AHU_CU_001, Cx. 55, D. 6 and 7.

68 See glossary.

69 Jan Vansina, "Ambaca Society and the Slave Trade c. 1760–1845," 2005, 8.

70 The feeling of hatred recorded by Cadornega was so evident that, in the documents found by Sebestyén, one phrase shows up repeatedly: "we are vassals of His Majesty, we want no subjection of services to *quilamba* and *quimbar*." The *sobas* apparently did not want their identity associated with that of the *ilamba* and *imbari*. Eva Sebestyén, "O contexto cultural dos marcos de terrenos nas aldeias Ambundu / Angola," 92.

71 Carta de FISC para Antonio Anselmo Duarte de Siqueira Intendente Geral das Reais Fábricas de Ferro. São Paulo de Assunção de Luanda, February 10, 1768. IEB/USP AL-083–009.

a year later, in February 1769. In this document, he claimed to own a tobacco plantation in that locality, as that he profited from the passage of the Luinha and Lukala Rivers by renting his canoes so that merchants and travelers could cross the rivers. With the settlement and the beginning of the construction of the factory, he lost his business and incurred great losses. The orders from Luanda once again required that "the property deeds on which the said lordship was based" be presented, that witnesses "true and free from all suspicion" be questioned to ascertain whether the lands were cultivated and how much they yielded, and also the bases that justified the right of passage of the rivers.[72]

Therefore, we have few clues in the documentation on the lands of Ilamba about how the conflicts involving land tenure between the local chiefs and other subjects of the Portuguese Crown were resolved. The documentation is fragmentary, full of contradictions and conflicts. In his June 1769 instructions to the superintendents of the iron factories, Sousa Coutinho provided guidelines on how they should regulate "uncertainties regarding the lands." The purpose of the instructions was to keep the factory from being founded with "violence," leading to revolts among Africans, settlers, and merchants (a complete failure, as we have seen). To that end, the governor reiterated that the rightful owner should present "his deeds." If someone did so, he would be compensated with other unoccupied lands. If there was no "free land" available, whoever occupied someone else's land had to pay tribute to the owner.[73]

In any case, the legitimate ownership of those lands in Ilamba does not appear to have been proven by anyone. What we observed is that all those people employed whatever resources they had available to prove their ownership. The conflicts reveal that, by building the factory, the government of Luanda managed to displease both the Africans and the settlers of the fortress. Since the issue does not appear again in the correspondence about the construction of the Nova Oeiras settlement and factory, it can be surmised that neither the *sobas*, nor the residents, nor João Correia were able to prove that their deeds were legitimate, which allowed the region to be occupied according to the plans of the Royal Treasury of the government of Angola. Another possibility is that they did have the deeds, but there were no witnesses to certify the ownership. Or that the royal officials

---

72 Carta de FISC para Antonio Anselmo Duarte de Siqueira, intendente geral das fábricas de ferro. São Paulo de Assunção de Luanda, February 27, 1769. IEB/USP, AL-083–223.

73 "Instrução porque se hão de governar o Intendente geral Antonio Anselmo Duarte de Siqueira na diligência que agora faz para a Nova Oeiras com os Capitães Manoel Antonio Tavares, Antonio de Bessa Teixeira e Joaquim de Bessa Teixeira a qual deve cada um guardar na parte que lhe é respectiva e por ela responder." São Paulo de Assunção de Luanda, June 2, 1769. IEB-USP, Al-083–254.

resorted to legal maneuvers, such as classifying the lands as unused or requesting the presence of witnesses that were not found or were not "true and free from all suspicion," through a series of resolutions, in order to expropriate the lands of the settlers, the *sobas*, the *ilamba*, João Correia, Misericórdia, and probably the *donas*,[74] who were large owners of *arimos*.

Despite the significant differences between the Portuguese overseas possessions, in all of them, the royal administration, "unable to maintain large contingents of soldiers and officials on the ground,"[75] resorted to private individuals to safeguard and administer the territories. In Angola, the vassalage of the African chiefdoms allowed the Portuguese to control the territory through an intermediary, minimizing the costs of a European administration of lands, including those that were unknown to them.[76] This ensured successful conquest and occupation, but generated conflicts between all the players described here. Generally speaking, in the eighteenth century, in the name of the Reason of State, the Crown and the government of Luanda attempted to take back a power they had shared with their subjects. In the process of appropriating the lands and mines of Ilamba, relations of interdependence between those players emerged, which allows us to observe the many nuances of the exercise of dominion.

2.2 Iron and Steel, in Bars and Products

Iron products from Europe, such as swords in various shapes, caught the attention of Africans because they were different from local products, and therefore ended up being valued as prestigious objects. For example, the Queen of Portugal once sent a sword to Hambo a Huila (south of Kwanza) as a present; these exchanges of "gallantries" were a common practice, part of the diplomacy between European

---

[74] Local women became major owners of *arimos* in Luanda's hinterland when they inherited them from old masters or from the death of their husband—a wealthy European or Luso-European. Those properties together with others, such as enslaved people, houses, stores, or taverns, made them wealthy and people started calling them *donas*. Selma Pantoja, "Donas de *arimos:* um negócio feminino no abastecimento de gêneros alimentício em Luanda (séculos XVIII e XIX)." In Selma Pantoja (org.), *Entre Áfricas e Brasis* (Brasilia: Paralelo Editores, 2001), 35–49.
[75] Eugénia Rodrigues, *Portugueses e Africanos nos rios de Sena*, 27.
[76] Mariana Candido, "Conquest, Occupation, Colonialism and Exclusion: Land Disputes in Angola," 224.

and African kingdoms to seal alliances and as a form of recognition of prestige and sovereignty.[77]

However, foreign objects were part of a complementary trade, which did not replace the locally made ones. Iron ore is one of the most abundant minerals on the continent and easily accessible, being found on the surface in many areas, not only in Ilamba, in the Kingdom of Angola. The clay required to build the furnaces and other equipment is also easily found, as is the wood for charcoal—a natural resource that was exhausted in some localities over time. Moreover, it can be said that this is the continent where ironworking was most widespread.[78] Therefore, all the conditions existed for the production and circulation of iron in bars and products.[79]

---

[77] Carta para o capitão de Moçâmedes do secretário do governo de Angola. Moçâmedes, May 22, 1849. AHA, Códice – 326, fl. 78v. See: Mariza de Carvalho Soares, "Trocando Galanteria: A diplomacia do comércio de escravizados, Brasil-Daomé, 1810–1812," Afro-Ásia 49 (2014): 229–271.

[78] Research demonstrates that, in Sub-Saharan Africa, iron smelting occurred independently, i. e. it was not imported to the region from other places. Another important finding has to do with the notion that, since iron reduction is very complex, it must have derived from experiments with copper, as a consequence of a "pyro-metallurgical" tradition. Archeologists find this issue controversial, but after reviewing new evidence, they have concluded that there is no pyro-metallurgical tradition in Africa that gave rise to iron smelting. Manfred K. H. Eggert, "Early Iron in West and Central Africa," in Peter Breunig (ed.), Nok. African Sculpture in Archaeological Context (Frankfurt: Africa Magna Verlag, 2014), 50–59. There are many studies on the origin and development of iron mining in Africa. I highlight here some anthologies and articles: P. R. Schmidt (ed.), The Culture and Technology of African Iron Production (Gainesville: University Press of Florida, 1996); Hamady Bocoum (ed.), The Origins of Iron Metallurgy in Africa. New Light on its Antiquity. West and Central Africa (Barcelona: UNESCO, 2004); J. O. Vogel (ed.), Ancient African Metallurgy: The Sociocultural Context (Walnut Creek: Aka Mira Press, 2000); S. B. Alpern. "Did They or Didn't They Invent It? Iron in Sub-Saharan Africa," History in Africa 32 (2005) : 41–94; B. Clist, "Vers une réduction des préjugés et la fonte des antagonismes: Un bilan de l'expansion de la métallurgie du fer en Afrique subsaharienne," Journal of African Archaeology 10, no. 1 (2012): 71–84. A classical historical study is Walter Cline's Mining and Metallurgy in Negro Africa (Menasha: George Banta Publishing Company Agent, 1937).

[79] In some places, Africans worked in furnaces with pre-heated air, a technique known in Great Britain only in 1828, which resulted in iron with a higher carbon content, more specifically, steel. The Englishman Nielsen was responsible for this technical improvement in Europe: heating the air blown into the furnace reduced the need for coal. Candice L. Goucher, "Iron is Iron 'Til it is Rust: Trade and Ecology in the Decline of West African Iron-Smelting," The Journal of African History 22, no. 2 (1981): 181; S. T. Childs and E. Herbert, "Metallurgy and its Consequences," in A. Stahl (ed.), African Archaeology: A Critical Introduction (London: Blackwell, 2005), 276–301; John Thornton, A África e os africanos na formação do mundo atlântico, 1400–1800, 90–93. On iron metallurgy in West Africa, see: Walter Rodney, History of the Upper Guinea Coast, 1545–1800 (New York: Oxford University Press, 1970), 186 and ff; P. de Barros, "Societal Repercussions of the Rise of Tradi-

In her book on blacksmiths in Central Africa, Colleen Kriger traced the entire history of metal mining in the region. Archeological studies have revealed a large number of metal tools. Despite the similarity of functions, the objects varied greatly. This is indicative of a wide variety of iron forging techniques in their many workshops and demonstrates that there was a large market for iron and copper products.[80] The iron bars produced at Ilamba could be processed or transformed at the forge of Central African blacksmiths into objects intended for various purposes, which fed a thriving network of commodities.

Iron was the raw material used to make tools for agriculture, fishing, hunting, weapons for war, ornamental objects (bracelets, necklaces), implements for the trade of enslaved people, and sacred objects—spears, cleavers, hatchets, hoes, *catanas* (a type of sword), chains, fetters. The metal was also an important currency on the African continent for the trade of enslaved people; the local elites demanded payment in the form of cowry shells, iron and copper bars, *manilhas*,[81] instruments of war, and metal parts. The iron and steel produced in many parts of Africa were of equal or superior quality to the bars supplied by Europeans. Controlling this technology allowed improved agriculture, which resulted in a greater production of food and attracted a larger population. This therefore gave more power to the rulers, since what legitimized the power of the local elites was their control over large numbers of dependents.

In the Kingdom of Ndongo, the blacksmiths of Ilamba produced a series of iron products, "musical instruments, ornaments, and weapons."[82] According to Beatrix Heintze, as early as the first half of the sixteenth century, Ndongo had a well-or-

---

tional Iron Production: A West African Example," *African Archaeological Review*, no. 6 (1988): 91–115.

80 Colleen E. Kriger, *Pride of Men: Ironworking in 19th Century, West Central Africa* (Portsmouth: N. H: Heinemann, 1999), 29–44. For Central Africa, it is important to note that archaeologists, ethnographers, and historians no longer maintain that the Bantu expansion was due to the mastery of iron metallurgy. Groups speaking other languages were equally important to the evolution of iron smelting technology. D. L. Schoenbrun, *A Green Place, A Good Place: Agrarian Change, Gender, and Social Identity in the Great Lakes Region to the 15th Century* (Portsmouth: Heinemann, 1998), 71; Eugenia W. Herbert, "African Metallurgy: The Historian's Dilemma," *Mediterranean Archaeology* 14 (1999): 41–48.

81 The *manilha* was a metal bracelet, "usually made of copper or brass, whose circumference does not close entirely, as if it were a 'C.' It was used as an ornament on arms or ankles and especially, perhaps as early as before the arrival of the Portuguese to the African coasts, as currency." Alberto da Costa e Silva, *A manilha e o libambo. A África e a escravidão de 1500 a 1700* (Rio de Janeiro: Nova Fronteira, 2002), 9.

82 Carta de Miguel Antonio de Melo, governador de Angola, para Rodrigo de Sousa Coutinho, secretário de Estado da Marinha e do Ultramar. São Paulo de Luanda, December 19, 1797. In: *Arquivos de Angola* IV, no. 52 to 54 (1939): 259–262.

ganized internal trade: "not only salt, but also copper, iron products, ivory, palm oil, as well as large and small cattle played an important role."[83] In addition to feathers, snail shells, imported beads, fake coral, elephant tails (*xinga*, Kimbundu: *muxinga*), and body paintings, metal rings (Kimbundu: *dilunga*, pl. *malunga*) and earrings were highly priced adornments among the Ambundus.[84]

Bells were also important because they were used for communication, since a bell, despite being a very small instrument, could be heard over a great distance."[85] Among the Ambundus and the Mbangala, the double bell without a clapper was a military instrument and a ritual object, and could be anointed with sacrificial blood, bringing success in combat. When it started being used by agents of Portugal's Black War, the double bell lost much of its sacred value.[86]

Coleen Kriger points to the use of different metals, such as iron alloys and copper, to make certain objects. She also mentions uses that eighteenth-century sources do not, such as the payment of dowries with iron bars, copper alloys, arrows, spears, knives, and other weapons, in addition to enslaved people, goats, sheep, and dogs. As the author explains, dowry was a way to concentrate fortunes in the hands of men; in addition, it was a way for wealth to circulate and be redistributed and an opportunity for individuals to play different roles in the social hierarchy.[87]

Isabel de Castro Henriques is another author who made a careful survey of the uses of iron in Angola. Among them, she highlights musical instruments that could not be made without a blacksmith, remembering that drums also served for communication between the *sobados*, the *cubatas*:

> drums of all sorts, especially big wooden drums made of hollowed logs, set the axes in motion, the *serpetes* [a cutting tool with a curved blade and handle], and any other tool capable of

---

83 Beatrix Heintze, *Angola nos séculos XVI e XVII*, 232.
84 Idem, 592.
85 Idem, 605.
86 Idem, 609.
87 Colleen E. Kriger, *Pride of Men: Ironworking in 19th Century West Central Africa*, 198. Among the collections of iron objects from Central Africa, that of the Belgian Congo in the Royal Museum for Central Africa in Tervuren, Belgium, stands out. I was in Tervuren, but was unable to visit the museum because it was undergoing a major renovation that would continue until 2018. The same happened in Luanda—the National Museum of Anthropology is also closed to reformulate the collection. Although Mr. Antonio kindly showed me part of the collection, the entire part dedicated to blacksmithing was inaccessible.

cutting down trees and creating these immense resonance boxes, which also serve for long-range communication.[88]

Iron was also needed to make tools for agriculture, hunting, and fishing. In addition to these products, iron bars were also bought and sold, since not all communities that produced iron objects in the Kingdom of Angola mastered the techniques to smelt the ore. In the land of the *soba* Mbangu kya Tambwa, for example, contrary to what was believed in the early-eighteenth century, no iron mines seem to have been exploited. It is true that there were many blacksmiths there who manufactured various products, but the iron they used came from "hatchets, hoes, and other old iron [implements]" that they bought or received when work was commissioned.[89] This leads us to believe that iron bars may have become important objects of exchange for commerce in the region. The images below depict the importance of iron for everyday activities.

Other metal objects were also made in the course of specific ceremonies blessed by priests. In both the Kingdom of Ndongo and the Kingdom of Kongo, iron insignias were related to royalty, such as ritual hatchets—the lineage emblem *ngola*. Joseph Miller explains that the *ngola* could be a hoe, a bell, an axe, a knife, small iron objects that allowed Ambundus greater mobility. The keeper of the *ngola* could gain access to the world of the dead and had essential spiritual forces at his disposal to solve his community's problems and disputes. Hence, material elements of culture with a seemingly trivial function, such as those cited above, could be imbued with spiritual meanings that were central to the social and political order.[90]

Writing about the role of blacksmiths in Central African religions in the nineteenth century, Juliana Ribeiro da Silva summarizes the main studies on the topic and provides new elements to rethink the issue. When analyzing the presence of iron objects and tools related to the blacksmith's trade, such as the anvil and the hammer, in enthronement ceremonies of new rulers, the author reminds us that these elements served "to cause a visual impact and also to remind the subjects of the king's [or ruler's] connection to a founding hero, the holder of extreme-

---

[88] Isabel de Castro Henriques, *Percursos da modernidade em Angola. Dinâmicas e transformações sociais no século XIX* (Lisbon: Instituto de Investigação Científica Tropical; Instituto da Cooperação Portuguesa, 1997), 323.

[89] Carta de Antonio de Vasconcelos, governador de Angola, a Francisco Xavier de Mendonça Furtado, Secretário de Estado da Marinha e Ultramar. São Paulo de Assunção de Luanda, May 9, 1762. BNP, C. 8553, F. 6362, fl. 2 and 3.

[90] Joseph C. Miller, *Poder político e parentesco*, 66–67.

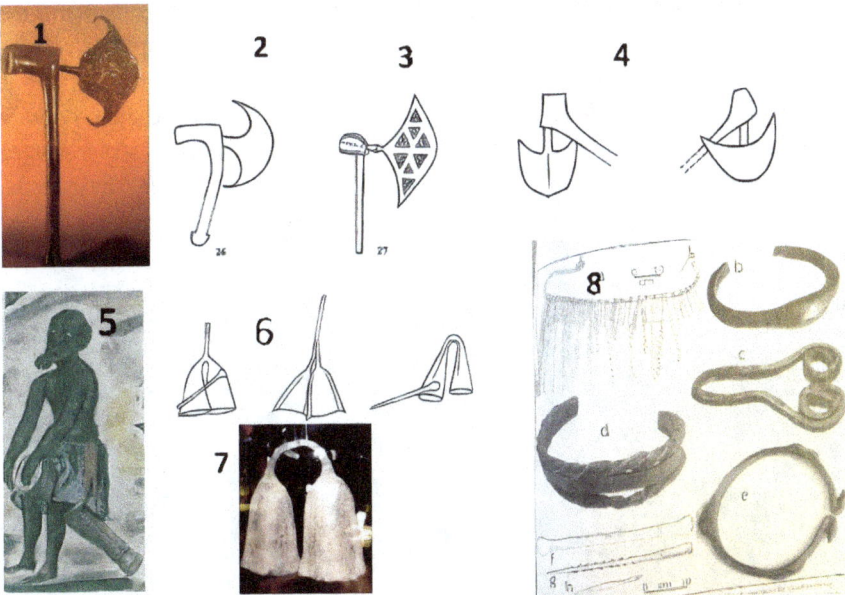

Figure 1: Iron objects.
Sources: **1** – Ax – an emblem of authority. Iron. Tervuren, Musée Royal de l'Afrique Centrale. In Jill Dias, *Nas vésperas do mundo moderno: África*, 140; **2** – Mbangala war hatchet; **3** – Ovimbundu hatchet (South of Kwanza); **4** – Hatchet or hoe that Njinga wore in her belt in the previous image; **5** – Drum used in Njinga's court. Giovanni Antonio Cavazzi de Montecúccolo. *Descrição histórica dos três reinos do Congo, Matamba e Angola*; **6** – Double bells; the first is Mbangala, the second is Ovimbundu, and the third was taken from the drawing of a Njinga warrior; **7** – Double bells. Museu Nacional de Etnologia (Portugal), AU.457, Angola; **8** – Ornaments for a bride, Nigeria, some of them with medicinal properties. Walter E. A. van Beek, "The Iron Bride: Blacksmith, Iron and Femininity among the Kapsiki/Higi," in Nicholas David, *Metals in Mandara Mountains Society and Culture* (New Jersey: Africa World Press, 2012).
Note: Numbers 2, 3, 4, and 6 were copied from Beatrix Heintze, *Angola nos séculos XVI e XVII*, p. 599 and ss.

ly important technological knowledge to ensure the population's welfare."[91] This observation reinforces what we have said about the social-political functions of iron utensils, a metal used to exercise dominion and legitimize the actions of the holder of the *ngola*. As Cadornega reveals, the *soba* Kambambe ruled over other lesser *sobas* with a staff insignia.[92] In the figures below, we can see the ritual

---

[91] Juliana Ribeiro da Silva, *Homens de ferro. Os ferreiros na África Central no século XIX*, 84.
[92] Antonio de Oliveira Cadornega, *História das Guerras Angolanas (1680)*, v. III, 241.

use of metal objects and their importance as symbols of lineage: Njinga and the kings of Angola carrying a hatchet, a spear, and a *zagaia* (short spear), wearing fine cloths or a leopard skin, a sign of power and wealth, in Figures 1, 2, and 3. In Figure 4, Ndembu Kakulu Kakenda is shown with two caps and adorned with all his other insignias. One wonders whether the objects themselves represented hierarchical gradations: bows and arrows were used by the *ngola*; the *ndembu* used two caps; and the *sobas* used staffs.

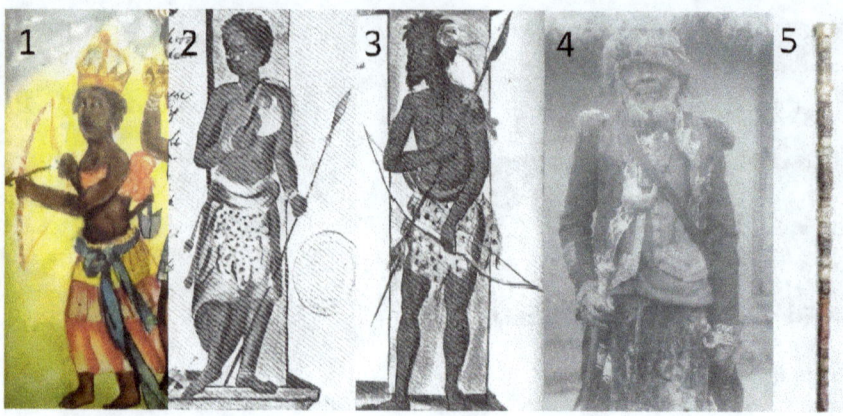

Figure 2: Power insignias in Angola.
Sources: **1** – Queen Njinga with a bow and arrow and an ax (the crown she wears is Cavazzi's addition to the image he had of symbols of royalty), Giovanni Antonio Cavazzi de Montecúccolo. *Descrição histórica dos três reinos do Congo, Matamba e Angola*; **2** and **3** – Depiction of the kings of Angola, arms, bow, *zagaia* (small spear), axe, and spear. Antonio de Oliveira Cadornega, *História das Guerras Angolanas (1680)*, v. III; **4** – Ndembu Kakulu Kakaenda "with all his insignias: cap, military coat with insignias; embroidered vest; leather bag on a shoulder strap; two staffs"; **5** – Staff belonging to Ndembu Kakulu Kakaenda, Museu da Sociedade de Geografia de Lisboa. Figures 4 and 5 were copied from Ana Paula Tavares and Catarina Madeira Santos (ed.), *Africae Monumenta. A Apropriação da escrita pelos africanos*, 454 and 457.

As with the double bells, which took on a more profane function, it was to be expected that in the eighteenth century, the Portuguese presence should have caused some transformations in the way Ambundus dealt with metal instruments. The *malunga* are one such example. The military officer Silva Correa mentioned the *malunga* in the context of the trade of enslaved people, described by him as "iron rings that fasten the hands to a long chain."[93] Cecile Fromont described an-

---

93 Elias Alexandre da Silva Correa, *História de Angola*, Clássicos da Expansão Portuguesa no Mundo. Império Africano Série E, vol. I, 96.

other use for the *malunga* in the Kingdom of Kongo—a bracelet used in succession ceremonies, and therefore related to royalty.[94] Among the Ambundus, the *lunga* (singular of *malunga*) was a sacred relic like the *ngola*, which gave its holder control over the fertility of the land and the rains.[95] There is also a hint of the idea of a bracelet, its use as an ornament. According to B. Heintze, upon her conversion, Queen Njinga threw to the fire all of her *malunga* (more than two thousand), obeying the Capuchin priest. The insignia were a means to contact the ancestors and the protective spirits. After her conversion, the queen was allowed to wear them, but ironically only those anointed by the missionaries.[96]

The passage in which the military officer Silva Correa describes the use of *malunga* exemplifies the value of these iron objects for the traffickers. The event has to do with an anonymous commander who received "a group of enslaved people" as spoils of war. One of the "black women bound in the irons of captivity" was so ill that she was unable to accompany the procession of enslaved people. In light of this, the commander had her shot and her arm cut off, "to keep from losing the *malunga*." [97]

To this day, *malunga* are used in the region as a ritual instrument,[98] as are staffs and caps as insignias of political power. It is therefore likely that these objects, as well as the double bell, lost much of their sacred aspect, but depending on who uses them, recover their supernatural functions.

In any case, the texts by the military officer Elias Correa show that iron was important because, in addition to providing indispensable products for agriculture, it made it possible to produce shackles employed in the trade of enslaved people—

---

[94] Cecile Fromont believes that the *malunga* bracelet grants the king a series of attributes derived from a network of semantic and visual associations related to its linguistic root, the material (iron) and its shape (a ring). Examining only one of these aspects, the word *malunga* belongs to a large lexical group in Bantu languages that brings together the ideas of divinity, infinitude, perfection in the sense of achievement, as well as notions of power and moral force. Cecile Fromont, *The Art of Conversion: Christian Visual Cutlture in the Kingdom of Kongo* (Chapel Hill: University of North Carolina Press, 2014), 40. A meaning close to the idea of ritual, of sacredness, appears in Assis Júnior's *Dicionário Kimbundu-português, linguístico, botânico, histórico e corográfico. Seguido de um índice alfabético dos nomes próprios*, entry "malunga," 276.
[95] Joseph C. Miller, *Poder político e parentesco*, 62.
[96] Beatrix Heintze, *Angola nos séculos XVI e XVII*, 594.
[97] Elias Alexandre da Silva Correa, *História de Angola*, vol. I, 96. *Malunga* may also refer only to an ornamental ring.
[98] Sebestyèn said that the *ndembu* who kept their "land titles" as sacred documents used the *malunga* emblem of power. Eve Sebestyèn, "Legitimation through Landcharters in Ambundu Villages, Angola," 363.

"cuffs and *libambos*."⁹⁹ Regarding this aspect, the documents on Nova Oeiras emphatically refer to the losses that would multiply if there were a shortage of metal instruments employed to capture people for enslavement. The importance of maintaining the production of *libambos*, an iron chain used to bind a retinue of 30 to 100 enslaved people by the neck, is one such example.¹⁰⁰ This instrument of capture, widely used not only in the Kingdom of Angola, but also in Portuguese America, was efficient to avoid frequent escapes (the very need for them is an indication that escapes were quite common), and also as an instrument of torture.¹⁰¹

Miller explained how the agents of the trade acted in the caravans, leaving the enslaved exhausted, with little food and drink, and suffering constant physical punishment, for fear that they would run away, rebel, or cast some spell against them or even free themselves from the chains. The instruments to inflict torture were *zagaias*, spears, shackles, and the *libambo* itself. The practice of branding captives with hot iron was also a long-standing practice to keep from getting them mixed up with other "pieces" of lesser value.¹⁰² Who manufactured these objects? To what extent did the trade of enslaved people lead to the emergence of a market of iron products not only in the Kingdom of Angola, but in the entire Atlantic world? These are questions that help us conceive the magnitude of the work of smelters and blacksmiths in Angola's interior. The objects below were used routinely in slaveholding societies on both sides of the Atlantic; the material elements of culture are fundamental to understand metalwork.

---

99 "Instrução que deve guardar Antonio Anselmo Duarte de Siqueira servindo o emprego de intendente geral da Fábrica do Ferro e que executaram também os capitães mores como intendentes particulares na parte que lhes é respectiva." São Paulo de Assunção de Luanda, January 12, 1767. AHU_CU_001, Cx. 52, Doc. 73. Carta de FISC para Francisco Matoso de Andrade, *capitão-mor* de Ambaca. São Paulo de Assunção de Luanda, May 25, 1767. BNP, C – 8742, F – 6364, fl. 182v. "(...) should Your Mercy find blacksmiths or smelters from Ilamba, send them to the said intendant, but those of this province should only be employed during the months of the *cacimbo* [drought] making iron so that the people can build their hoes, neck shackles, and other instruments for agriculture and trade, with the understanding that this all extends the trade of people."
100 In Kimbundu, *lubambu* means a chain or fetter, and was so common that it became synonymous of the caravan of enslaved people. The word became known in Alberto da Costa e Silva's classic *A manilha e o libambo*, which contains a more precise description: "the neck of a victim was placed in it, facing forward, and the fork was closed with a strongly attached piece of wood. Another wretch would see the fork rest on the back of his neck and then closed around his throat." Alberto da Costa e Silva, *A manilha e o libambo. A África e a escravidão de 1500 a 1700*, 9.
101 According to Silvia Lara, "an instrument of capture easily becomes a means of torture or has a morally demeaning effect." Silvia Hunold Lara, *Campos da Violência. Escravizados e senhores na Capitania do Rio de Janeiro (1750–1808)* (Rio de Janeiro: Paz e Terra, 1988), 73–74.
102 Joseph Miller, *Way of Death*, 193–195.

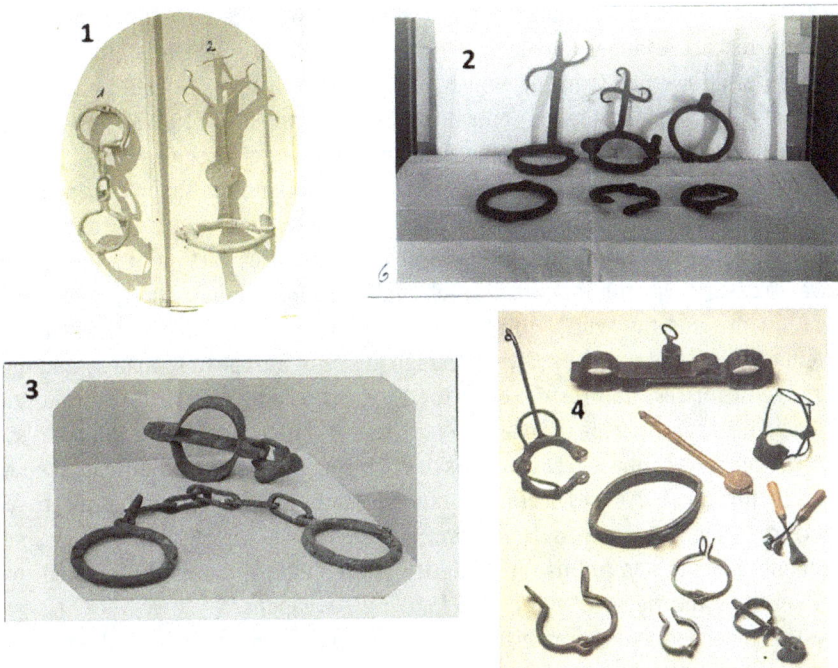

Figure 3: Iron for the trade of enslaved people.
Sources: **1** – Shackles and *libambo*. Museu Municipal Francisco Manoel Franco (Itaúna, MG); **2** – *Libambos* and *gonilhas*. Biblioteca Nacional (RJ), Arthur Ramos Collection; **3** – Shackles. Instituto Histórico e Geográfico de Alagoas. **4** – Set of instruments used to punish, immobilize, and brand enslaved people in Brazil: *viramundo*, *libambo*, iron belt, palmer, muzzle, neck shackles, handcuffs with lock, and branding irons. Museu Histórico Nacional (RJ).

African weapons in the Kingdom of Angola were meticulously observed by colonial agents, who recorded how they were made, used, and traded, probably with the purpose of better coordinating strategies to dominate these peoples. The very emblems of power of the authorities in Angola were related to hunting and warfare: bow and arrow and spears. In addition, spears and darts were also common weapons, as well as a knife called *nbili* (*mbili*, Kikongo: *mebele*, dagger knife), measuring 60 cm long and dabbed with poison.[103] In 1759, Governor Antonio de Vasconcelos added *zagaias* and hatchets to this list.[104] The hatchet was appropriated from con-

---

103 Beatrix Heintze, *Angola nos séculos XVI e XVII*, 601.
104 Carta de Antonio de Vasconcelos, governador de Angola, para Francisco Xavier de Mendonça Furtado, Secretário de Estado da Marinha e do Ultramar. São Paulo de Assunção de Luanda, January 18, 1759. BNP, C. 8553, F. 6362, fl. 1 and 2.

tacts with the Mbangala, who used it as a weapon of war. The sergeant major of the Ndande district, Manoel Correa Leitão, also cites *rodelas* (shields) and *catanas* (swords) used by the Mbangala, which were apparently appropriated by the Ambundus.[105] The high quality of Central African weapons is attested by Portuguese Crown officials. The materials they were made of were recognized as superior to those employed in Europe; the quality of the metal and the shape of the object were the result of the technical knowledge of local smelters and blacksmiths.

One of the governor's intentions in promoting the extraction of iron by the Royal Treasury was the manufacture of "bullets, bombs, and grenades to supply the (…) ships and the army"[106] to help the militias, which consistently lacked sufficient supplies and weapons. Given the high prices of European weaponry and the shortage of fortress and fortresses in the Kingdom of Angola, Sousa Coutinho invented a new specific type of spear, the *partazana*,[107] to "arm Negroes and fortresses." The purpose of those weapons was to empower the Black War, African armies fighting for the Portuguese, essential to maintain the colonization project. As Thornton stated, Europeans were forced to recognize African war tactics and weapons. I would add to this the dexterity of the labor of those who smelted the iron and the knowledge of those who forged the weapons.[108]

The governor sent a drawing of this special *partazana* ("I conceived a quality of *partazana* that, incorporating everything that has been seen and written about similar implements, will make this a formidable and safe weapon") in order to have 700 pieces manufactured in Rio de Janeiro, which would return to Luanda as ballast of the ships on route to the port of that city. There was a note specifying that they should be made with the 15 *quintais*[109] of iron cast in the Kingdom of Angola, and not with any other kind of metal, because he preferred "this over any-

---

[105] Manuel Correa Leitão, "Uma viagem a Cassange nos meados do século XVIII [1755]," edited by Gatão de Sousa Dias. Boletim da Sociedade de Geografia de Lisboa, série 56, no. 1 and 2 (1938), 20.
[106] Carta de Francisco Xavier de Mendonça Furtado, Conselheiro de Estado, Ministro e Secretário dos Negócios da Marinha e dos Domínios Ultramarinos, para FISC, governador de Angola. Palácio de Nossa Senhora da Ajuda, April 30, 1768. AHU, Códice 472, fl. 153–155.
[107] Bluteau defines *partasana* (spelled with an "s") as a "sort of halberd, but with a longer and wider iron. A halberd is an "offensive and defensive weapon used by archers of the guard of princes and by ensigns in battles. It is said to have been invented in Albania, from whence it took its name." Raphael Bluteau, *Vocabulário portuguez e latino*, entries "partasana" and "albarda."
[108] John Thornton, "Art of War in Angola, 1575–1686," *Comparative Studies in Society and History* 30, no. 2 (1988): 361. As Roquinaldo Ferreira demonstrated, the Brazilian troops sent to Angola and the use of horses were also important in strengthening Portugal's military presence in Angola. *Transforming Atlantic Slaving. Trade, Warfare and Territorial Control in Angola, 1650–1800*, dissertation (PhD) (Los Angeles: University of California, 2003), 159–171.
[109] Old unit of measurement that, in Portugal, was equivalent to approximately 60 kg. (T.N.)

thing else to make cutting instruments." Blacksmiths in Rio de Janeiro were therefore not to be deceived by the rustic appearance of the iron and steel, "imperfectly cast into small bars." They were also instructed to coat their weapons with steel, because this "mixture" was what the Ambundu technicians employed, and the result was so good that their instruments resisted long "durations" and the various uses (*empréstimos*) given to them.[110] This idea of the governor seems to have been carried out, because in 1773 he comments, "in Rio de Janeiro, many *partazanas* of my invention were made, for which I sent iron to the Count [of] Azambuja."[111] This is an evident record of the appropriation of an African technology, both in relation to the use of iron and to the manufacture of cutting instruments.

News about the excellent quality of iron from Ilamba are recurrent in the documentation. Although we take into account the observations of Antonio de Vasconcelos and other governors, such as Sousa Coutinho, who stated in his memoirs that the Ambundus "never purchased any iron from Europe,"[112] we cannot rely on

---

[110] FISC sends the iron (15 quintals—1 quintal is equivalent to approximately 60 kg, i.e. 900 kg of iron) through a merchant, Francisco Ferreira Guimarães, and orders the Count of Azambuja, Antônio Rolim de Moura Tavares, then viceroy of the State of Brazil, to supervise, together with Francisco Guimarães, the manufacture of the *partazanas*. Carta de FISC para Francisco Ferreira Guimarães. São Paulo de Assunção de Luanda, February 13, 1768. AHA, Códice 79, Fl. 78v – 80. Carta de FISC para o Conde da Cunha, António Álvares da Cunha, vice-rei do Estado do Brasil [the name of addressee is probably mistaken; in 1768, the viceroy of the State of Brazil was already the successor of the Count of Cunha, the Count of Azambuja]. São Paulo de Assunção de Luanda, February 15, 1768. AHA, Códice 79, fl. 80. Carta de FISC para Francisco Ferreira Guimarães. São Paulo de Assunção de Luanda, January 16, 1762. AHA, Códice 79, 192v.

[111] Carta de FISC sem destinatário. Lisbon, September 16, 1773. BNP, C 8553, F6362.

[112] Memórias do Reino de Angola e suas conquistas escritas por D. Francisco Inocêncio de Sousa Coutinho, governador e capitão general do Reino de Angola, escritas entre 1773 a 1775. Torre do Tombo, Condes de Linhares, mç. 44, doc. 2, fl. 42. We have little data on the import of this metal to Luanda. In 1756, the commanders of Galera de São José e Nossa Senhora do Rosário presented a shipment from the city of Lisbon to Luanda. Among the items listed, we found "12 quintals of iron from Biscay," "two arratels of steel," "three devices with three Flemish knives." In "Livro de receita e despesa da Fazenda Real do Reino de Angola do ano de 1765," expenses with iron totaling 352$000 réis were recorded, which purchased approximately 1 ton and 100 kg of the metal (159 quintals, 10 arrobas, and 111 pounds). The origin of these imported materials was not always noted, although shipment from Rio de Janeiro is often cited. In the case of tools—hoes, iron shovels, picks, large levers, sledgehammers—, they are recorded as imported from Rio de Janeiro and are intended to assist in the construction of the royal works. A total of 143$915 réis was spent in 1765 on these instruments. By 1781, a total of 607$274 réis was spent on costs and expenses of wood and ironwork also to be employed in the royal works. Terceiro livro da receita e despesa da Tesouraria Geral [da Junta da Administração da Fazenda Real] deste Reino de Angola. Palácio de São Paulo de Assunção de Luanda. January 8, 1780. AHTC, Erário Régio, 4191. Although the clerk's signature on

them to assert that, in the region of Ilamba and surroundings, no iron was imported from Europe, which we know existed, and even from other parts of West Central Africa. The internal trade controlled by Africans also occurred with other metals that could enter "inland" into the Kingdom of Angola, as cited by Vasconcelos, through internal trade networks. In 1801, the merchant Joaquim Correa Pinto, a "black man" native of the Kingdom of Angola, who dressed "in the European manner," provides information about copper traded at the Kasanje Market. According to Correa Pinto, the copper bars were manufactured in the Mulua nation (also called "Mwaant Yaav," which became known as the Luanda Empire) and latter purchased by the vassals of Jaga Kasanje.[113] This potentate in turn traded the metal in a market on the border of his territory, but did not allow merchants who were vassals of the Crown of Portugal to negotiate directly with the Mulua or to go to the lands they inhabited.[114] Thus, in addition to controlling the trade of enslaved people in the region, the potentate Mbangala Kasanje also controlled the access to important commodities, such as copper in bars or already transformed into instruments.

---

the book's cover is dated 1780, the book was also used to record the year 1781, so the data cited by us refers to that year.

[113] According to Isabel de Castro, the copper found in Luanda may have been produced in Kazembe, which paid tribute to Mwaant Yaav. Isabel de Castro Henriques, *Percursos da modernidade em Angola. Dinâmicas e transformações sociais no século XIX*, 313.

[114] Carta de Miguel Antonio de Melo, governador de Angola, para Rodrigo de Sousa Coutinho, secretário de estado da marinha e do ultramar. São Paulo de Assunção de Luanda, October 21, 1801. AHU_CU_001, Cx. 102, D. 26. In 1755, Manoel Correa Leitão described the Mulua as "very powerful, and from his domains, captains are sent by him to the west, to the north, to the south, and other parts, with very large troops, to conquer enslaved people, who they sell close to where they capture them, such as Benguela and other parts where they are sent to Kasanje, to Holo, and even to the kingdoms of Kongo, So. Sos (*sic*), Quiiacas, Quilubas, Ungus, all of which they have subdued with the sword, being so brave and feared for the damage they have done in all dominions, that the mere mention of their name is enough for them to win; so much so that today they even sell people to those neighboring the *Ndembu* Ambuela and Mutemos; great men indeed, and so famous among the nations in these vast forests, that no one speaks of anything else; it is a fact that, if it were not for them, we would not have so many enslaved people, because they, with their ambition and fame of victory, like land eagles, run through lands so remote from their homeland only to become masters of other people." Manuel Correa Leitão, "Uma viagem a Cassange nos meados do século XVIII." "At its height, the Lunda empire of Mwaant Yaav— as it is commonly referred to in literature— stretched from the Kwango River on the west (Kasongo-Lunda) to the Luapula River on the east, and its expansion affected the history of this vast area of Central Africa until the early- or mid-nineteenth century." Manuela Palmerim, "Identidade e heróis civilizadores: 'l'Empire lunda' e os aruwund do Congo," in *1ª Jornada de Antropologia intitulada "Modernidades, etnicidades, identidades"* (Universidade do Minho, 1998), available at http://repositorium.sdum.uminho.pt/bitstream/1822/5319/3/Identidade%20e%20heróis.pdf, accessed on August 2, 2016.

During his "voyage to Rios de Senna in Angola"[115] in 1802, Pedro João Baptista claimed to have found iron in the Luanda-Kazembe region (of the Mulua, mentioned above). He discovered that iron bars were being manufactured, to be delivered as tribute to the Quiburi (Kazembe chief of the homologous salt mine), who would in turn deliver them to Mwaant Yaav. This may be yet another use of iron—to serve as tribute delivered to the local chieftains, such as the great Mwaant Yaav. The traveler also noted that the blacksmiths traded their bars for flour and other supplies, which also shows a complementarity of Central Africa's complex internal market.[116]

In a voyage to the territory of the potentate Kasange in 1755, Manoel Correa Leitão recognized that the "great Kasanje" was the obstacle on the east that kept the Portuguese from advancing to the interior of the *sertões* near the Kwango River. He claimed that there was much iron, copper, and brass in that territory, and described in detail the weapons they used: iron and wooden arrows, "a sword five inches wide and three palms long," "five or six short lancets with an iron *choupa* [long and sharp tip]," knives, shields, spears.[117] Although he does not describe the exploitation of minerals in this locality in detail, this document provides evidence that iron, in addition to copper, was a commodity controlled by the potentate of Kasanje, or even that it was produced by specialized workers in that locality.

These excerpts show that there were metal trading circuits controlled by the elites of the great African potentates about which we know little, but which undoubtedly grew with the trade of enslaved people. In the coastal region, for example, in addition to the ports of Luanda and Benguela, taking advantage of the slave

---

115 Pedro João Baptista, "Viagem de Angola para Rios de Senna," "Explorações dos portugueses no interior d'África meridional (...) Documentos relativos à." Anais Marítimos e Coloniais, Lisbon, III, 5, 1843. *Apud* Isabel de Castro Henriques, *Percursos da modernidade em Angola. Dinâmicas e transformações sociais no século XIX*, 312.
116 Isabel de Castro Henriques, *Percursos da modernidade em Angola. Dinâmicas e transformações sociais no século XIX*, 312–315.
117 Manuel Correa Leitão, "Uma viagem a Cassange nos meados do século XVIII," 20. The attentive observations of Sergeant-Major Manuel Correa, a native of the city of Luanda, "a practical and intelligent person in the knowledge and languages of these *sertões*," are the result of the gaze of a military officer sent to those lands to cross the Kwango River and discover all the details regarding the people who inhabited the north, and whatever trade they might carry out on the other side of the sea. The Portuguese Overseas Council and the government of Luanda had long intended to reach the African East Coast.

routes south of Kongo, new trade networks led to other points in the North—Loango, Cabinda, Molembo—controlled by the French, the Dutch, and the English.[118]

Analyzing the documentation in light of the bibliography allows us to affirm that the Ambundus exploited their iron mines of ferruginous mud and ironstone, sometimes even by means of underground mines. When the Portuguese found Central Africans smelting steel, they believed that there were steel mines; the governor at the time even congratulated the official for the "discovery of steel." By controlling the amount of air blown into the furnaces, smelters from Ilamba could produce iron with a higher carbon content—i.e. steel.[119] The objects they produced were sold or exchanged for other goods in the regions surrounding the mines or blacksmiths' workshops, but they could also circulate through the *sertões* of the interior. The commercial circuits of iron and other metals formed complex "inland" networks about which we know little.

To conclude this discussion on the meanings and uses of iron in the Kingdom of Angola, especially in the second half of the eighteenth century, we must reaffirm the ease of access to iron in the region and, therefore, to knives and spears. Historians agree that this period is a time of great insecurity and intense enslavement, with strong social conflicts and tensions,[120] and that knives were an important currency of exchange in the region.[121] Therefore, control over the circulation of weapons was one of the colonial administration's concerns. In the Kingdom of Angola, a 1747 law determined that any enslaved person caught with a weapon could be deported to Brazil. However, carrying weapons was so routine that, in 1801, physical punishment was added as a penalty in an attempt to curb the practice.[122]

---

118 Joseph Miller, *Way of Death*, 209–215; Jan Vansina, "Long-Distance Trade-Routes in Central Africa," *The Journal of African History* 3, no. 3 (1962): 375–390.
119 Only archeological research can confirm this hypothesis; for now, we base our analysis on the written sources that, even when they do not mention "steel," mention the malleability of the iron produced there. Carta de FISC para João Baines, *capitão-mor* do Golungo. São Paulo de Assunção de Luanda, August 24, 1767. BNP, C 8742, F 6364.
120 Mariana Candido, *An African Slaving Port and the Atlantic World* (New York: Cambridge University Press, 2013), 233; Roquinaldo Ferreira, *Cross-Cultural Exchange in the Atlantic World. Angola and Brazil during the Era of the Slave Trade* (New York: Cambridge University Press, 2012).
121 Jill Dias says that knives often served as currency in the region. One such example was the throwing knife. Jill Dias, *Nas vésperas do mundo moderno: África*, 139.
122 Roquinaldo Ferreira, *Cross-Cultural Exchange in the Atlantic World*, 150 and 151.

Firearms were repaired by Ambundu iron artisans, including in the iron factories.[123] If we add to this the search for lead, saltpeter, and iron, we can understand Nova Oeiras's commitment to supply weapons to the Portuguese Empire.

The use of iron was common both in the distant *sertões* of Angola and in urban contexts. The attention paid by colonial agents to the mines, the workers, and the trade circuits is not gratuitous. Iron was profitable and dangerous—depending on whose hands it fell on—, but it was, above all, fundamental to the advancement of colonization: in agriculture, in dealing with enslaved people, in war, and in the maintenance of slavery. On one hand, gaining control over the technology to smelt and forge the metal became a colonial objective; on the other hand, resisting this appropriation became an important goal of the Ambundu political and economic elite.

However, the disputes over those lands, resources, and trade cannot be reduced into this simple binary opposition. Other agents participated in these conflicts: other African kingdoms (as in the case of Mbangala Kasanje), residents of colonial settlements, merchants in the *sertões*, royal officials. Still, Central Africans and colonial agents had different ways of perceiving the same natural resource. For the Ambundus, the economic dimension of mineral exploitation and land tenure was not unrelated to religious and political aspects, as is characteristic of their cosmogony, in which, as the historian Hampatê Bá reminds us, "everything is connected, everything resonates in everything."[124]

2.3 Nova Oeiras, a "Machine" Conceived in the *Sertão*

The historiography on the government of Sousa Coutinho provides little information about the history we have told so far, the mines exploited by the *sobas* Nguengue a Kimbemba, Nguengue a Kamukala, Lunge Riaquitamba, Huiadala, Ndala Tandu and Ndambi a Kiza, the ironworks controlled by Mbangu kya Tambwa. Nonetheless, the iron industry in and around Ilamba was old and well established in the roots of commerce in the region, administered by the local elites, for whom the mines were valuable and profitable. Without this foray into Ilamba, it is impossible to understand why and how the town and the factory of Nova Oeiras were established there, which is generally the point of departure of academic studies that analyze its history in the context of projects of the colonial administration

---

[123] In a 1768 order, the intendant was charged with repairing the weapons of three fortresses in the region. Carta de FISC para Antonio Anselmo Duarte de Siqueira. São Paulo de Assunção de Luanda, June 10, 1768. IEB/USP, AL-083–084.
[124] Amadou Hampatê Bá, "A tradição viva," 202.

in the eighteenth century. Although historiography is silent on these aspects, they were taken into account by Sousa Coutinho.

In the eighteenth century, dictionaries defined factory as a "house or workshop where some goods are manufactured," as described by Bluteau, but also as the building, the officers, and the materials, "the people, service animals, machines, supplies for some work," as Moraes Silva added. The terms *loja* (store), *oficina* (workshop), and *fábrica* (factory) are presented as synonyms, also related to the meaning of "manufacture," which was "the factory, the mechanics, and the artifact workshop" as well as "the work performed in them," and "industry," which referred to the "mechanical works" and the "art and skill of earning a living" with the craft.[125] Therefore, the Nova Oeiras factory was also intended to be a workshop, where knowledges of different origins intertwined in the search for the "secrets" of metallurgy.

It was also common to use the word *fábrica* in the sense of manufacture, as, for example, *fábrica do engenho*, sugar manufacturing. In the documentation, the expression *fábrica do ferro* (iron manufacturing) is recurrent. In 1633, Father Antonio Vieira considered the sugar mill an "incredible machine and factory." The capacity to concentrate a large number of workers under an intense work regime impressed anyone familiar with the mills.[126]

Edgar de Decca calls attention to the historical process of the development of the "putting-out system" in Europe, the mode of organization of work that gave rise to the factory system. Concomitant to this process, starting in the sixteenth century,

> in the colonial areas, the concentration of workers deprived of the means of production and expropriated of any technical knowledge appeared as the most efficient organization of labor to carry out the interests of capitalist profit, and there the role of the entrepreneur also became indispensable to the production process.[127]

The author argues that the labor process in the sugar mills in Portuguese America was a result of this new social organization of labor created to control, discipline, and hierarchize, with a single purpose: ensuring the profits of the mill owner. The construction of the Nova Oeiras factory should be understood from this perspective: the construction of a space of confinement, controlled and supervised to guarantee the greatest exploitation of labor. In a way, attempts were made to concen-

---

[125] Raphael Bluteau, op. cit., entries "fábrica," "oficina," "indústria." Antonio Moraes Silva, *Diccionario da língua portugueza*, entries "fábrica," "manufatura," "indústria."
[126] Edgar Salvadori de Decca, *O nascimento das fábricas* (São Paulo: Editora Brasiliense, 1982), 49.
[127] Idem, 43 and ff.

trate the workers, to seize their technical knowledge, and to deprive them of the means of production.

The idea of building an iron factory in Angola first appeared in the writings of Governor Antonio de Vasconcelos (1758–1764). It was he who collected ore samples, made the first smelting experiments, and sent specialized Central African workers to Lisbon so that the Kingdom's specialists could ascertain their metallurgical skills and knowledge.[128] Vasconcelos's plans were carried out by his successor. When Francisco de Sousa Coutinho received the orders from the Count of Oeiras to foster the exploitation of iron, an indispensable metal for the development of any industry at the time, he was informed of a historical knowledge of minerals that the subjects of the Crown had gathered over centuries of Portuguese occupation. In 1765, this governor decided to begin a major undertaking, whose construction lasted the eight years of his government and resulted in the buildings of the Nova Oeiras iron factory:

> In 1765, as I was building the great Fortress of the Sea, which was like the apprenticeship of my fatigues, having no iron for the works, and purchasing the little I could at 12$800 réis[129] per *quintal*, I decided to obtain it from the very plentiful mines of this Kingdom.[130]

The iron imported from Biscay, Sweden, or England was extremely expensive, and Portugal, which had no mines or large iron industries, nor techniques to exploit and refine it, depended on imports to supply the Kingdom and its overseas possessions. [131]

---

128 Carta de Antonio de Vasconcelos, governador de Angola, para Tomas Joaquim da Costa Corte Real, secretário de Estado da Marinha e do Ultramar. São Paulo de Assunção de Luanda, January 18, 1769. AHU_CU_001, Cx. 45, Doc. 4189.
129 12$800 is twelve thousand eight hundred réis. Réis was the Portuguese currency at the time.
130 Correspondência de Francisco Inocêncio de Sousa Coutinho, governador de Angola, dirigida ao morgado de Mateus, governador da capitania de São Paulo. São Paulo de Assunção de Luanda, August 12, 1769. BN (RJ), Coleção Morgado de Mateus Microfilme 12, fl. 31.
131 In Portugal, in the late-seventeenth century, during the Ministry of the Count of Ericeiras, Father Rafael Bluteau was in charge of hiring Italian technicians to produce iron in the municipality of Figueiró dos Vinhos. One of the royal units established in the region was denominated Engenho da Machuca, which "at the end of the seventeenth century had a smelting furnace, a refining furnace, and a boring mill; its production was mainly iron in the form of bars and rebars." But that factory was short-lived. Heitor Goes, *Monografia do concelho de Figueiró dos Vinhos*, Figueiró dos Vinhos (Portugal): Câmara Municipal, 2004, 90. In the face of a shortage of weapons, in 1764, Sousa Coutinho suggested that bronze and iron artillery be "all cast in Angola or Rio de Janeiro." He even mentioned the name of an entrepreneur who was willing to promote this trade, João Álvares Ferreira. Carta de FISC para Francisco Xavier de Mendonça Furtado. São Paulo de Assunção de Luanda, June 4, 1764. IHGB – PADAB, DVD10, 20 DSC00213.

In terms of economic policies of the Portuguese Empire, in the second half of the eighteenth century, the search for iron was part of what Fernando Novais called "enlightened mercantilism," because, in the measures adopted by the Pombaline cabinet, mercantilist ideas still predominated. Therefore, the iron industry was perceived as extremely important by the metropolis, which in turn did not produce enough for its own supply. The factories in colonial spaces would liberate the "metropolis from imports, contributing to the more general objective of the program of enlightened mercantilism, which was to better position itself in the international trade relative to other nations."[132] It is important to remember that one of the main concerns of the expansion and maintenance of the Portuguese empire was arms manufacturing. An iron factory in Angola that promised the returns of the hydraulic ironworks in northern Spain, using the skilled and inexpensive labor of Central Africans, seemed like the ideal solution:

> it occurred to His Majesty that, if an iron factory were to be established now within the limits of this city, considering that there is such an abundance of that metal, it would be possible to forge there not only all the pieces of artillery necessary for the forts of this Kingdom [of Angola], but also a large amount for the ships and the forts of America and this Kingdom, and likewise bullets, bombs, and grenades to supply the ships and the army.[133]

In the following pages, we will analyze the creation of the village of Nova Oeiras and the construction of the factory building. Although the factory is an unavoidable subject of historiography, the details of the stages of its planning and construction have not yet been studied. An iron factory requires many natural and human resources, and creating a building in the *sertões* near Luanda (approximately 200 km from the city), intended to overcome the iron shortage in the Kingdom of Portugal, the Kingdom of Angola, and Portuguese America, mobilized an incalculable amount of material, technological, and human investments.[134] It is possible

---

[132] Fernando A. Novais, *Portugal e Brasil na Crise do Antigo Sistema Colonial* (1777–1808) (São Paulo: Hucitec, 1995), 285.
[133] Carta de Francisco Xavier de Mendonça Furtado, Conselheiro de Estado, Ministro e Secretário dos Negócios da Marinha e dos Domínios Ultramarinos, para FISC, governador de Angola. Palácio de Nossa Senhora da Ajuda, April 30, 1768. AHU, Códice 472, fl. 153–155.
[134] When FISC wrote to the Overseas Council about the convenience of building this factory in Angola, he stated: "It is true that the said factories are more useful here than in Portugal (if there were any) because the workers and the wood are absolutely useless to His Majesty and the people if they are not thus employed; they are most valuable there, and not at all here; transportation to Lisbon and to Brazil is quite easy and swift, and since this work employs all the wealth of a plentiful mine, it provides all the utility of a manufacture and increases trade among the Kingdom's plantations, since the expenses with iron are paid with those goods. I am convinced that the profits from this metal for the Royal Treasury will be very close to those of gold in America's mines

to measure these efforts and sacrifices both through the writings of Sousa Coutinho, who produced a large amount of documents and memoirs extolling his achievements, and through sources written in later periods.

In the correspondence of Antonio de Lencastre, Sousa Coutinho's successor, harsh criticism was made of the manufacturing enterprise, described as a chimera of "horrendous expense." There we find an attempt to record the financial and human sacrifices that made possible the construction of Nova Oeiras—"accounts of the expenses incurred with the construction of the Nova Oeiras Iron Factory from the first of January 1766, in which year it began, until March 24, 1773."[135] It should be noted that there is documentation about the factory from April 1765, and not 1766, as the governor mistakenly informed. In any case, according to this calculation, more than 70 *contos de réis* were spent mainly in wages, but also in construction material, canoes to transport the iron bars, medicines, paper for the administration, and even paint for the paintings for the church next to the village. With this money, "all the public buildings" were built, such as the "administration houses, smithies, the treasury, prisons, and the residences of the masters of all trades and engineers," as well as a church with "three altars."[136]

The architect Fernando Batalha, who visited the ruins of the factory in the 1970s, was impressed by the building complex. He stated, "One can still see two extensive sections of the weir that dammed the river, the aqueduct that took water to power the mills, a large compartment for the hydraulic wheels, a smelting furnace, a large blacksmith shop with three warehouses, and a canal to drain the water."[137] Today, a considerable part of the buildings has been overcome by vegetation, so that we can barely see the weir wall.

In addition to the large human investment that led many families from nearby villages to migrate and left many *sobados* unpopulated, the factory required many of the natural resources of the region. To locate the factory between the rivers, it

---

if it is attended with the care I suggest and that it deserves." Carta de FISC para Francisco Xavier de Mendonça Furtado, secretário de estado da marinha e ultramar. São Paulo de Assunção de Luanda, February 17, 1767. AHU_CU_001, Cx. 53, D. 73.

135 Certidão de José Francisco Pacheco, inspetor das obras da fábrica, sobre o estado da fábrica de ferro. São Paulo de Assunção de Luanda, March 13, 1773. AHU_CU_001, Cx. 52, D. 28.

136 Carta de FISC para Francisco Xavier de Mendonça Furtado, secretário de estado da marinha e ultramar. São Paulo de Assunção de Luanda, September 6, 1769. IEB/USP, Al – 082–175. Parecer do capitão José Francisco Pacheco, inspetor das obras da fábrica, do engenheiro Antonio de Bessa Teixeira, "que também assistiu por algum tempo as mesmas obras," e do mestre de obras, Antonio Ribeiro Cardoso. ANTT, Condes de Linhares mç. 51, doc. 1, fl. 198. São Paulo de Assunção de Luanda, November 17, 1770.

137 Fernando Batalha, *Povoações históricas de Angola* (Lisbon: Livros Horizonte, 2008), 101.

was necessary to break through "a mountain range that stood between the ironworks and the Luinha and Lukala Rivers." Otherwise, it was impossible to transport both the ironstone and the bars easily. Creating that connection therefore enabled transporting all goods, "because now, textiles and supplies travel from Portugal all the way to the factory's door, and from there comes the iron straight to this city's warehouses."[138] The great undertaking also led to the discovery of new sources of firewood. Although there are few studies on the environmental devastation caused by the colonial presence in this region,[139] one can imagine the impact of destroying an entire mountain range. Located on the banks of the Lukala River, Nova Oeiras did not change its location again.

To foster the exploitation of nature, the site where Nova Oeiras was located was studied in detail during the years of its construction. From these analyses remained many drawings and blueprints. One of these documents is "Carta Topográfica da província que fornece águas, lenhas, e serventes à fábrica do ferro da Nova Oeiras," dated 1769, elaborated by Manuel Antonio Tavares, a military engineer trained at the Geometry and Fortification Course in Luanda in 1767, who worked for a long time with Sousa Coutinho on the factory project.[140] This map was stud-

---

[138] Carta de FISC para Francisco Xavier de Mendonça Furtado, secretário de estado da marinha e do ultramar. São Paulo de Assunção de Luanda, March 12, 1768. AHU_CU_001, Cx. 52, D. 6 and 73.

[139] It is important to highlight the studies on ivory trafficking, which had a great environmental impact in the region. From 1796 to 1825, 56,992 ivory tips were traded from West Central Africa. João Baptista Gime Luís, *O comércio do marfim e o poder nos territórios do Kongo, Kakongo, Ngoyo e Loango: 1796–1825*, thesis (Master's) (Universidade de Lisboa, 2016). On the organization and social effects of the ivory trade in Angola, see: Jill Dias, "Changing Patterns of Power in the Luanda Hinterland. The Impact of Trade and Colonization on the Mbundu ca. 1845–1920." On the impact of the changes in hunting patterns, see: Marcos Vinícuis Santos Dias Coelho, *Maphisa & Sportsmen. A caça e os caçadores no sul de Moçambique sob domínio do colonialismo c. 1895–c. 1930*, dissertation (PhD) (Universidade Estadual de Campinas, 2015). On the topic of Africa, see: William Beinart, "African History and Environmental History," *African Affairs* 99, no. 395 (2000): 269–302. Emmanuel Kreike studied northern Namibia in the twentieth century and showed how colonial rule, the capitalist market, and population growth contributed to dramatic environmental changes in the region. Emmanuel Kreike, *Deforestation and Reforestation in Namibia: The Global Consequences of Local Contradictions* (Leiden: Brill, 2010). The changes in land tenure patterns instituted during colonization were also decisive. Clover and Eriksen analyze this process for Botswana, Mozambique, South Africa, and Zimbabwe. J. Clover, S. Eriksen, "The Effects of Land Tenure Change on Sustainability: Human Security and Environmental Change in Southern African Savannas," *Environmental Science & Policy* 12 (2009): 53–70.

[140] The Geometry and Fortification Course of Luanda was founded in 1666, but was soon canceled for lack of teachers. Governor FISC resumed its operation in 1764 for members of the military, including soldiers. In a 1768 letter, there is a detailed description of Manuel Antonio Tavares's career. "he has served as Professor in the Geometry and Fortification Course since April 15, 1768: he worked with others and elaborated maps of all the coasts of the Kingdom of Angola; he went to

ied by Sara Ventura da Cruz, who reminds us that the cartographic profusion in the second half of the eighteenth century was related to a Pombaline political project, which aimed to "move from a politically plural and territorially discontinuous empire" to "active integration in and of the empire." In general, population centers and cartography are integrated in this project, which "sought the territorialization of the state and the colonization of intermediate spaces, by establishing population centers that would guarantee a more permanent dominion, rather than the advances and retreats inherent to military conquest."[141]

The map is structured by the representation of the Kwanza, Lukala, and Luinha Rivers—the former was essential to transport the mineral, and the other two to enable farming and provide hydraulic power to drive the bellows and the mills. The topographic map also shows the location of lagoons (Cabemba, Engolome, Tôa, Salacata)—shown in blue letters—, the forests for firewood (Calaquele, Caçalacata, Casanha, Hougo)—in green letters—, and the demarcation of the *sobados* and *banzas* that would supply the workers, all of it described in the caption at the top of the document. In this caption, letters are used on the right, and numbers on the left represent other elements.

Sara Cruz noted that the elements indicated—"villages, lagoons, and wilderness areas"—are connected by roads and rivers, forming a "whole [that] makes up an almost strategic system, a network of communities."[142] However, we must remember that this is a representation of space that serves political purposes, therefore giving the impression of a continuous occupation with precise connections between the settlements. Thus, unknown areas are presumably filled in with the aim of expressing a territorial unit that "does not exist, but is nonetheless portrayed as communicated." The settlements, the *banzas*, the villages, the *sobados*, the *empacaça* are represented on the map in the same manner, without differen-

---

the Nova Oeiras Iron Factory to oversee the construction of the said factory after the death of the masters sent to that effect; and measured and reduced the maps of all the lands, rivers, and forests that serve the said Factory. There is also a certificate of the registration of the people of war in Angola, which states that the said Manuel Antonio Tavares, a native of Lisbon, voluntarily enlisted as a soldier on June 13, 1764; that on the 18th of the same month and year he became a Squad Corporal (...) And having given clear proof of admirable dedication and particular ingenuity for the science of geometry, and given the progress he has made and the virtue with which he has voluntarily practiced it, from the said day continued in the Royal Service as adjutant until August 6, 1768, when he became an Infantry Captain." Carta sem destinatário assinada por Manuel Antonio Tavares, São Paulo de Assunção de Luanda, 1768. AHU_CU_001, Cx. 52, D. 18.
141 Sara Ventura da Cruz, "A construção de uma ideia de território: a cartografia de Angola na segunda metade do século XVIII," *Cabo dos Trabalhos* 12 (2016): 8.
142 Sara Ventura da Cruz, "A construção de uma ideia de território: a cartografia de Angola na segunda metade do século XVIII," 16.

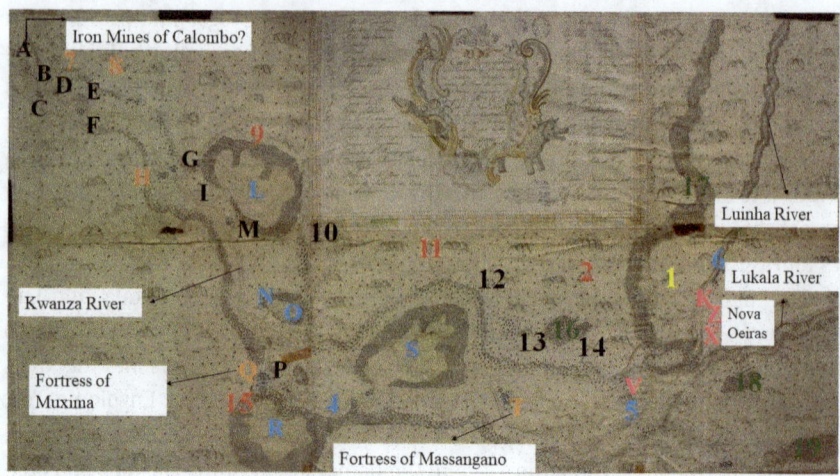

Map 4: Topographic map of the province where Nova Oeiras was located, 1769 c.a.
Source: "Carta Topográfica da Província que fornece Águas, Lenhas, e Serventes à Fabricado Ferro da Nova Oeiras que mandou fazer o Ilmo. Exmo. Senhor D. Francisco Inocêncio de Sousa Coutinho Governador e Capitão General do Reino de Angola, ano 1769". Manuel Antonio Tavares, [Angola], 1769. 1 map ms.: paper, color.: 66x117 cm. (source: AHM). *Apud* Sara Ventura da Cruz, "A construção de uma ideia de território: a cartografia de Angola na segunda metade do século XVIII," 11. Caption on the left: **A.** Sitio de Calumbo; **B.** Sitio de S. José; **C.** Sitio da Kwanza; **D.** Zambela; **E.** Bruto; **F.** Sitio do Guedes; **G.** Molamba; **H.** *Soba* Cacoba; **I.** Catenga; **L.** Cabemba Lagoon; **M.** Cabemba; **N.** Tôa Lagoon; **O.** Salacata Lagoon; **P.** Sitio de Muchacaçoa; **Q.** Fortress of Muxima; **R.** Quizua Lagoon; **S.** Engolome Lagoon; **T.** Fortress of Massangano; **V.** Cacoalâla. Tile and Brick Factory; **X.** Village of Nova Oeiras; **Z.** Building of the Iron Factory; **K.** Weir. Caption on the right: **1.** Iron Hills; **2.** *Soba* Nguengue; **3.** *Soba* Nguindala; **4.** Kwanza River; **5.** Lukala River; **6.** Luinha River; **7.** *Soba* Moene Capexe; **8.** *Soba* Nguinza; **9.** Caculo Cazongo; **10.** Quionzo; **11.** Caculo Cahango; **12.** Empacaça; **13.** Zambiaquela; **14.** Macoche; **15.** *Soba* Quizua; **16.** Mato de Calaquele; **17.** Mato de Caçalacata; **18.** Mato de Casanha; **19.** Mato do Hougo.

tiating which elements were African villages and which were the settlements and fortress founded by the Portuguese in the *sertão*.[143]

---

[143] According to Sara Cruz, all these settlements "present identical roofs and similar patterns of openings, with a clear influence of the colonizer's patterns. Only the fortresses are shaped as forts and some buildings are in different colors, noting that those drawn in red represent public facilities related to the administration and churches, since some of them have crosses on top. In spite of this distinction, the housing types are all the same, with only four types of buildings drawn in black. The homogeneity in the representation of the buildings may be due to a disinterest in individualizing them, since it refers a regional scale, or simply because a representation standard was

The numbers and the letter "H" in red identify the *banzas* and the *sobados*, the Central African settlements in the interior, which are more abundant than colonial settlements. The latter, created in order to defend the territory and colonize the interior, are the fortress, the Nova Oeiras factory and town, and the brick and tile factories. The numbers 1 (iron hills) and 2 (Soba Nguengue) are very close to each other, which leads us to suppose that their political leader was the *soba* Nguengue a Kimbemba, about whom we spoke earlier, who had iron mines and workers at his disposal to exploit them. The map's design reinforces the idea that part of the land in the area belonged to this chieftain and that somehow, through expropriation or sale, it fell into the hands of the Luanda government.

The whole set of occupations linked to work in the iron factory is marked in pink. This space was also occupied by private individuals (the Guedes farm, for example), which demonstrates the political and social complexity of the *sertão*.

As shown in the figures, the town of Nova Oeiras and the iron factory building (letters X and Z) were located at the point where the Luinha and Lukala Rivers meet. In the opinion elaborated by Joaquim de Bessa Teixeira in 1769, he asserted that the supply of wood in the region was endless, that much had already been cut for the construction work, and that there were several qualities of it: "*sorveira* wood [a tree endemic to Madeira Island, probably brought to the region by the Portuguese] measuring 35 to 40 palms in circumference; there are mulberry trees, and among these there are pitch trees, whose logs produce boards measuring three, four, and even five palms wide."[144]

The concern with preserving enough wood to fuel the smelting furnaces meant that all auxiliary factories—the lime, tile, coal, and brick factories, mainly—were built in more distant locations, such as the village of Massangano, which was half a day's walk away. To get an idea of the dimension of the geographical and ecological changes caused by this project, in a single woodcutting incursion in 1769, 800 large

---

employed." Sara Ventura da Cruz, "A construção de uma ideia de território: a cartografia de Angola na segunda metade do século XVIII," 16.

144 Documento que sua Excelência mandou registrar de várias cousas que viu, e observou na Real Fábrica do Ferro da Nova Oeiras o Tenente de Cavalos Joaquim de Bessa Teixeira, São Paulo de Assunção de Luanda February 7, 1769. IEB/USP, Al-083–207. The *soveira* is a tree endemic to the island of Madeira; its wood is white or pinkish, with a fine texture, compact, and very hard. For that reason, it was often used to make parts subjected to constant wear: mill points, spindles, rollers, tool handles. The *tacula* or *takula* is an African tree whose wood is much appreciated and used in dyeing (red dye). According to Adriano Parreira, the *takula* was used in rites among the peoples of West Central Africa in ceremonies and festivities. *Economia e sociedade em Angola na época da Rainha Jinga (século XVII)* (Lisbon: Editorial Estampa, 1997), 55 and 56.

tree trunks were sawed.¹⁴⁵ Not to mention other mining activities, such as the search for gold in the Lombige River, not far from that location. There are no studies on the history of environmental impacts caused by mining in this region of Africa, like Warren Dean's book on Brazil's Atlantic Forest, but there is no doubt that the factory of Nova Oeiras was a factor in changes in ecological cycles. The factory was supplied with ore extracted from the surrounding hills and depended on continuous burning of trees, which contributed greatly to the depletion of natural resources in the region. Of course, this had repercussions on the lives of the people who lived there, as it reduced arable land and could lead to hunger and drought, for example.¹⁴⁶

Regarding the iron hills, Bessa Teixeira counted five, represented in the map by the number 1 ("any of them yields ore forever and without end"). Historiography sometimes relates the factory's failure to the low quality of the iron ore or the poverty of the Nova Oeiras mines, which presumably contained only a few veins. From the government of Antonio Vasconcelos, all the way to the research performed by naturalist José Álvares Maciel, who visited the factory in 1797, samples were sent to Lisbon of both the ferruginous earth and the iron ore found there. Francisco de Sousa Coutinho even sent samples to Dr. Georges-Louis Leclerc, Count of Buffon, in Paris, and Dr. Antonio Ribeiro Sanches, in Lisbon. The amount of iron found in the ore was 65% according to Miguel Franzini, professor of algebra at the University of Coimbra, and 68% according to José Álvares Maciel. The quality of the reduced metal was always considered excellent. Furthermore, iron mining in the locality predates the Portuguese presence, although for lack of archeological studies, we do know much. However, we do know that it was intensely explored during the government of Sousa Coutinho and his successors, who contin-

---

145 Carta de FISC para Francisco de Mendonça, secretário de estado da marinha e ultramar. São Paulo de Assunção de Luanda, May 6, 1769. IEB/USP, Al – 082–156.
146 According to Warren Dean, 600 km² of forest were destroyed in the mining region in Portuguese America in the eighteenth century: "much of this burning also took place in the secondary forest accessible to the towns and gold mines. (...) The exploratory hydraulic and manual removal of the forest floor surface suggests that the seventeenth-century mining enterprise demanded more of the Atlantic Forest than the first two centuries of subsistence farming and wheat and sugar plantations." Warren Dean, *A ferro e fogo: a história e a devastação da Mata Atlântica Brasileira* (São Paulo: Companhia das Letras, 1996), 116. There are studies on the impacts of mining in other regions of Africa. Cf. Josiah Rungano Mhute, "Downcast: Mining, Men, and the Camera in Colonial Zimbabwe, 1890–1930," *Kronos*, no. 27 (2001): 114–132; William Beinart, "Soil Erosion, Conservationism and Ideas about Development: A Southern African Exploration, 1900–1960," *Journal of Southern African Studies* 11, no. 1 (1984): 52–83.

ued to purchase the iron produced by Central Africans. Thus, the iron factory of Nova Oeiras did not fail for lack of an ore with a considerable iron content.[147]

Joaquim de Bessa Teixeira also found many stones to construct the buildings, in addition to "good red clay and *saibro* [coarse sand that also contains larger granules of stone, widely used for construction], which, mixed with lime, is excellent." Also regarding natural resources, it was recorded that "the waters are most excellent, since the village is located between two rivers, the Luinha and the Lukala, and everyone can drink whatever they like."[148]

The letter K of the topographic map "Carta Topográfica da Província que fornece Águas, Lenhas, e Serventes à Fábrica do Ferro da Nova Oeiras" represents the weir "or water dam," created by damming the Luinha River, which took two years to complete (1768–1770) and was destroyed by a great flood on April 3, 1770. For this reason, it was necessary to rebuild "the weir and the channel." The project was sketched and construction started, as can be seen in more detail in Figure 4.[149] The first demarcation of the weir was made by the Biscayan masters who worked there for about three months. For the reconstruction, there was much discussion about how to make it safer. In November 1770, the factory's engineers and master builders declared that the weir measured 269.5 meters (1225 palms) long, six to seven meters wide, and 9.46 meters high. The flume connecting the weir to the factory, the aqueduct, was supported by 22 arches measuring 2.2 meters wide and 3.08 meters high, with a total length of 115.5 meters.[150]

According to the documentation, the work of rebuilding the weir was never completed. In 1772, Sousa Coutinho still insisted to the work inspectors that the weir should be built with the greatest care to prevent it from being destroyed

---

147 Carta de FISC sobre a utilidade da fábrica de ferro. Lisbon, September 16, 1773. BNP, C 8553, F6362.
148 Documento que sua Excelência mandou registrar de várias cousas que viu, e observou na Real Fábrica do Ferro da Nova Oeiras o Tenente de Cavalos Joaquim de Bessa Teixeira, São Paulo de Assunção de Luanda, February 7, 1769. IEB/USP, Al-083–207.
149 As cheias haviam destruído parte da fábrica, foram tão fortes que arrancaram árvores pelas raízes. Joaquim de Bessa Teixeira. São Paulo de Assunção de Luanda, April 25, 1770. BNP, Reservados C 8743, F6377.
150 The measurements are shown in *palmos*, whereby 1 *palmo* = 0.22 m, according to "Quadro geral das principais medidas e moedas utilizadas nos últimos tempos do Brasil colonial," elaborated by Roberto Simonsen, *História Econômica do Brasil*, seventh ed. (S. Paulo: Cia. Ed. Nacional, 1977), 462–463. Termo de juramento feito pelo provedor da Fazenda Real Manuel Cunha e Sousa, José Francisco Pacheco, Antonio de Bessa Teixeira, Antonio Ribeiro Cardoso. São Paulo de Assunção de Luanda, November 17, 1770. ANTT, Condes de Linhares, mç. 51, doc. 1, fl. 198.

by another flood.[151] In 1798, the Secretary of the government of Angola, José da Silva Costa, visited the factory and found the weir destroyed.[152] After this, the factory was abandoned by subsequent governments. In 1830, the weir and the canal through which the water flowed to the factory were still completely destroyed.[153]

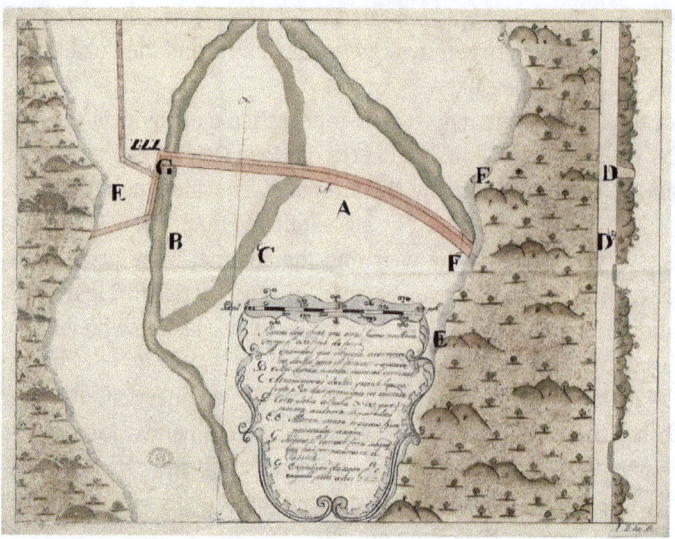

Figure 4: The walls planned to dam the river, 1770 c.a.
Captions: **A**. Wall to block the river's flow to create the weir; **B**. The Luinha River with its natural course; **C**. Redirection of the River carried out to begin building the weir; **D**. Cross-section over line xx showing the wall's height; **E**. Hills between which the water is dammed; **F**. Spillway to release the water not required by the Factory; **G**. Water conduction to the factory through arches **zzz**.
Source: "Planta das obras que estão feitas na Nova Oeiras para a fábrica do ferro." AHU_CARTm_001, D.272.

---

[151] Carta de FISC para Joaquim de Bessa Teixeira, Intendente geral da Real Fábrica do Ferro da Nova Oeiras. São Paulo de Assunção de Luanda, March 19, 1772. SGL, *Arquivos de Angola* 3, no. 30–33 (1958–1963): 423.

[152] "I went to Oeiras, and the factory and everything that has to do with it is in a state of great ruin. The large wall that sustained the channel to the Luinha River fell partly toward the river due to the weight of accumulated water; this River flows very close to the said Factory, and further ahead is next to the channel." Carta de José da Silva Costa para Miguel Antonio de Melo, governador de Angola. São Paulo de Assunção de Luanda, April 30, 1798. AHU_CU_001, Cx. 87, Doc. 71.

[153] Carta de José Maria de Sousa Macedo Almeida e Vasconcelos, governador do Reino de Angola, para Nuno Caetano Álvares Pereira de Melo, ministro assistente do despacho. N.p., December 6, 1830. IHGB, PADAB DL76, 02.35.

The map of the town of Nova Oeiras (Figure 5), was also drawn by Manuel Antonio Tavares and, given its similarity to other maps of the time, we believe it was elaborated around 1770. In it, we can see the two rivers that surround the town: vertically, on the right, is the Lukala River, and horizontally on the bottom is the Luinha River. There are no details regarding the buildings, but 124 of them are carefully drawn, one of them being the church, identified with a cross. There are a few buildings marked in red. Based on descriptions of the time, it is likely that the one located near the point where the rivers meet held the factory's warehouses and furnace. We are unable to identify the two other buildings marked in red.

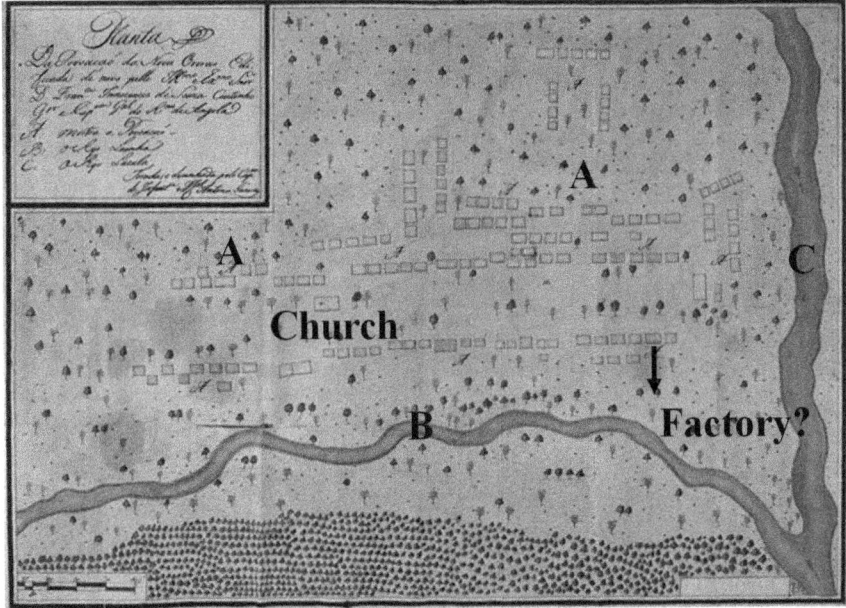

Figure 5: Map of the town of Nova Oeiras, 1770 c.a.
Source: "Planta da povoação de Nova Oeiras edificada pelo Ilustríssimo Excelentíssimo Senhor Doutor Francisco Inocêncio de Sousa Coutinho Governador e Capitão General do Reino de Angola. Feita e desenhada pelo Capitão da Infantaria Manuel Antonio Tavares." Map captions: **A** – the town; **B** – the Luinha River; **C** – the Lukala River. Online catalog of the National Library of Portugal. Available at: http://www.bnportugal.pt/index.php?option=com_content&view=article&id=373%3Aaquisicao-de-quatro-valiosos-manuscritos&catid=49%3Aaquisicoes&Itemid=427&lang=pt. Accessed: August 30, 2012. The markings are ours.

The map is reminiscent of the ideals of "uniformity and rectilinearity" that were applied in various places of the Portuguese Empire to concentrate local populations in "new settlements with a regulated design." For example, in the interior of Mato Grosso, in 1765, the village of São Miguel was redesigned to house the indigenous workers who lived there, among others. Once again, I call attention to the way in which ordering the space of factories and villages responded to interests of disciplinary control of the workers. The new map provided for "long wings of symmetrically aligned residential units [that] appear to be living quarters for the Indians." The facilities were arranged "on either side of a long plaza, in front of which [stood] the homes of the community's administrator"[154] and the vicar.

The engineers trained by Sousa Coutinho no doubt received the same guidelines as those who designed the towns in Mato Grosso, both seeking to follow the urbanization and Europeization program of the Marquis of Pombal.[155]

In February 1769, the cavalry lieutenant Joaquim de Bessa Teixeira was sent to the factory to elaborate an opinion regarding its buildings, and he made a detailed description of what he found:

> There are in this factory fifty-three well-made houses, which include the administration and two adobe warehouses with tiled roofs, one of them to hold goods and other implements, like the factory's tools, and another one to serve as the smithy where the blacksmiths work; the latter has a room to store some materials. Small houses for both white and black people, more than a hundred: In the place of the Factory there are three houses, one for the superintendent, another one for the Captain José Francisco [Pacheco, construction inspector], and another one for the masters and assistants. In this same place is also a big porch where processed lime and wood are collected; in this closed shed are stored the tools employed in the work as well as lime boards, *quindas* [a cylindrical basket without a lid], bags.[156]

---

154 Roberta Marx Delson, *Novas Vilas para o Brasil colônia. Planejamento espacial e social no século XVIII* (Brasilia: Edições Alva, 1997), 34. The occupation of the *sertão* in Minas Gerais and the creation of urban centers at that time were studied in Cláudia Damasceno da Fonseca, *Des Terres aux Villes de l'or. Pouvoir et territoires urbains au Minas Gerais (Brésil, XVIIIe siècle)* (Paris: Fundação Calouste Gulbenkian, 2003).
155 This period was characterized by a "reinforcement of the monarchy's territorial control." Thanks to the technical training of military engineers, these officers were responsible for a "more rationalized vision of the territory, conceiving it as a manipulable object that could be molded in order to make the intervention of the authority for whom they worked—i.e. the king—more effective." Pedro Cardim adds, "eighteenth-century sensibility saw engineers as those who imposed order on a territory lacking the remedial intervention of the monarch and his governing team, an image that is necessarily associated to the emergence of a more 'technical' exercise of politics." Pedro Cardim, "Centralização política e Estado na recente historiografia sobre o Portugal do Antigo Regime," *Nação e defesa*, 2ª série, no. 87 (n.d.): 129–158. Maria de Lurdes Rodrigues, *Os engenheiros na sociedade portuguesa. Profissionalização e protagonismo*, PhD dissertation (Lisbon: ISCTE, 1996).
156 Documento que sua Excelência mandou registrar de várias cousas que viu, e observou na Real Fábrica do Ferro da Nova Oeiras o Tenente de Cavalos Joaquim de Bessa Teixeira, São Paulo de Assunção de Luanda, February 7, 1769. IEB/USP, Al-083–207.

At the time, the town and the factory were growing, considering that there were more than 150 houses. The 53 "well made" houses were reserved for the families, while white single workers and black workers lived in 100 small homes. For a small town in the interior of the Kingdom of Angola, this is a considerable number of houses. For purposes of comparison, the city of Luanda, divided by José Venâncio into four zones, had 378 homes in the commercial zone and 112 in the administrative zone or Upper City.[157] In 1798, the city of Benguela had 281 residences, half of them simple homes, called *sanzalas* (140), mostly inhabited by enslaved and freed people.[158] The architect Fernando Batalha identified part of the ruins of the town and the old church building. Archeological research could determine the number of houses and the agricultural, food, and religious practices, in short, a multiplicity of aspects of the life and work of the town's inhabitants.[159] But these are yet to be conducted.

The officers who administered the construction, as well as the masters, had their own homes by the smithy, the warehouses, and the shed, separate from the rest of the town, according to a workspace arrangement that allowed them to watch over the workers. Once again, something very similar to what we described earlier about the new towns built in Mato Grosso: the administrators, the intendants, and the vicars lived in a privileged location to facilitate surveilling and inspecting the workers—indigenous people in America, Ambundus in Ilamba.

In 1770, another map of the factory was elaborated by the military engineer Dom Miguel Blasco at the request of Sousa Coutinho. Although we do not know its whereabouts, we found a brief description of its caption: the Factory building and, in it, the ironworks: "furnace to liquefy," "furnace to refine," "arches that carry water to the ironworks," "place through which unneeded water is drained."[160] After the death of the Biscayan masters, the Crown closely supervised

---

[157] José Carlos Venâncio, *A economia de Luanda e hinterland, no século XVIII. Um estudo de Sociologia Histórica* (Lisbon: Editorial Estampa, 1996), 38.

[158] Roberto Guedes recalls that the lists of residents only encompassed the small residential area in the Benguela presidio, not counting the *sanzalas* (African villages) in the city's outskirts. Roberto Guedes, "Casas & Sanzalas (Benguela, 1797–1798)," *Veredas da História* VII (2014): 66.

[159] Fernando A. Novais, *Portugal e Brasil na Crise do Antigo Sistema Colonial* (1777–1808), 105.

[160] Planta da Casa da Fábrica do Ferro e açude que se acha na Nova Oeiras, mandada fazer por FISC no ano de 1770. Dom Miguel de Blasco a delineou. São Paulo de Assunção de Luanda, November 12, 1770. ANTT, Condes de Linhares, mç. 51, doc. 1, fl. 194v. "Miguel Ângelo Blasco was appointed colonel in October 1750, as an engineer, with the obligation to serve in Portugal or Brazil, 'in the ports or any part of the *sertões* of Brazil and Maranhão for five years.' He was one of the engineers recruited for the expedition to America, in charge of demarcating limits. With him, Carlos Ignácio Reverend and João André Schwebel were hired for the same service, and Adam Wentzel Hesteko, Manoel Gotz, and Inácio Hatton as assistant engineers. Ângelo Blasco was Genoese. In recognition

what was done with the resources it invested in the enterprise. To determine whether the factory had been built in accordance to the blueprint requested by the governor, the main provider of the Royal Treasury, Manoel Pinta da Cunha e Sousa, summoned Captain José Francisco Pacheco, inspector of the works at the Nova Oeiras iron factory, the engineer Antonio de Bessa Teixeira ("who also assisted the said works for some time"), and the master builder Antonio Ribeiro Cardoso to elaborate an opinion on the state of the construction at the time. They guaranteed that everything was done as described above—"carried out and finished with the greatest safety and perfection"—with the exception of the bellows, because there was no master who knew how to build them. The engineers saw fit to wait for the arrival of the masters who would build them "to their measurements and satisfaction."[161] Therefore, although all the buildings were completed, the engine room had never been used; without the large bellows, the stone and lime factory would remain waiting for technicians to put it into practice.

This document is quite important because it reveals the magnitude of the building complex and the equipment that made up Nova Oeiras. In addition to the machinery related to iron foundry, "an overseer office, two smithies, a jail, a guard corps, and another house to be used for whatever purpose required" were built.[162] The existence of a jail reinforces the idea of constant surveillance of the work. In Cacualala, a town near the factory, indicated by the letter "V" in the 1769 "topographic map of the province where Nova Oeiras was located" (Map 4), tile and brick factories and two warehouses were built, in addition to a lime factory in Muxima.

---

of the valuable services rendered in Brazil, he was promoted on October 2, 1763 to the rank of field marshal, and on March 21, 1769, he was appointed engineer-general of the kingdom, occupying the vacancy created by the death of the illustrious engineer, Lieutenant-General Manoel Maia. One of his many works is the map of Barra do Rio Grande de São Pedro (Rio Grande do Sul), elaborated with the collaboration of José Custódio de Sá e Faria in 1752, to serve as a basis for technical and military operations to demarcate the limits between Portugal's and Spain's possessions. In Santa Catarina, in 1767, he surveyed and drew the blueprints of the forts Santana do Estreito, Conceição de Arçatuba, and São Francisco Xavier." Aurélio de Lyra Tavares, *A Engenharia militar portuguesa na construção do Brasil* (Rio de Janeiro: Editora Biblioteca do Exército, 2000).

161 Termo de juramento feito pelo provedor da Fazenda Real Manuel Cunha e Sousa, José Francisco Pacheco, Antonio de Bessa Teixeira, Antonio Ribeiro Cardoso. São Paulo de Assunção de Luanda, November 17, 1770. ANTT, Condes de Linhares, mç. 51, doc. 1, fl. 198. "Planta da Casa da Fábrica do Ferro e açude que se acha na Nova Oeiras, mandada fazer por FISC no ano de 1770." Drawn by Dom Miguel de Blasco. São Paulo de Assunção de Luanda, November 12, 1770. ANTT, Condes de Linhares, mç. 51, doc. 1, fl. 194v.

162 Idem.

The smelting furnace in Nova Oeiras was not built like the ones in Biscayan water smithies, which used a Catalan furnace, i.e. the bloomery type. Even its architectural style was quite different from the rest of the complex, which indicates a later construction. The blast furnace built next to the warehouses was the result of new experiments conducted by Sousa Coutinho with the help of the engineers he trained in the Geometry Class, and was inspired in French and German furnaces. The governor came to the conclusion that the performance of a hydraulic ironworks would not be sufficient for the amount of iron he wanted to produce in Nova Oeiras. With the blast furnace, he expected to manufacture from 20 to 70 *quintais* of iron per day. However, the foundry never came into operation with these technical specifications, among other reasons because no crucibles (clay pots used to hold the molten metal) capable of withstanding the blast furnace temperatures were found.[163]

In the mid-1800s, Jacinto de Gouvea Leal requested that vacant lands "on both banks of the Luinha [River], in the place called 'Pedra Catão,' to the confluence of the same river with the Lukala," be leased to him through emphyteusis. The petitioner wanted to grow cotton on the site and received a favorable response with a "perpetual concession for himself and his descendants," free of rent, "including in this concession the mines of the old iron factory of Nova Oeiras." The document contains a clause forbidding the demolition of the architectural complex and determining that the lands of the factory could be requested by the Royal Treasury at any time. After analyzing the ruins, Jacinto considered that "this magnificent building, whose fortress walls are [?] made of pumice stone, was so strongly built that it could withstand the weather for centuries."[164]

Gouveia left us some important images and blueprints that help us understand how this great imagined machine should have worked. Figure 8 shows, drawn in perspective from left to right, the warehouses, the machine house, and lastly, with the stairs, the iron smelting furnace.

The blueprints below, Figures 7 and 8, provide details of the building, the location of the furnace, the bellows, the aqueduct, and other factory facilities.

Analyzing the blueprints gathered during their documentary research and current photographs of these buildings, a team of architects composed of Giovana Gomes Carreira, Katia Sartorelli Verissimo, and Stefane Saraceni Kaller arrived at the conclusion that the furnace building, marked with a letter C, was built after A, the warehouses. As we have seen, the furnace actually took longer to complete and,

---

163 Carta de FISC para Martinho de Melo e Castro, secretário de estado da marinha e do ultramar. São Paulo de Assunção de Luanda, August 12, 1771. AHU_CU_001, Cx. 55, Doc. 52 and 56.
164 Carta de Jacinto Gouvea Leal para o Conselho Ultramarino. N.p., March 8, 1855. AHU, Conselho Ultramarino Angola, Cx. 35, Doc. 1598.

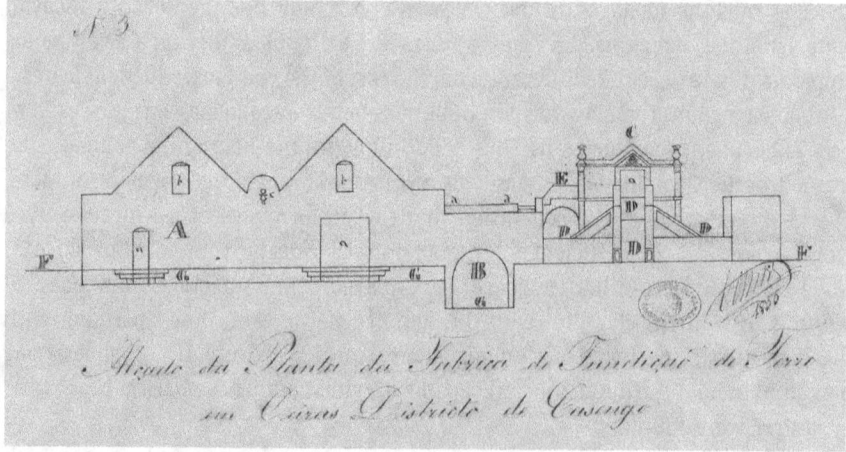

Figure 6: Front view of the iron foundry of the Oeiras Factory, 1855.
Source: Alçado da Planta da Fábrica de Fundição de Ferro em Oeiras, Distrito do Cazengo, 1855. N. 3. Signed by: Jacinto de Gouvea Leal. AHU_CARTm_001, D.1343. Caption: **A**. Warehouse; **B**. Machine Room; **C**. Furnace building; **D**. Stairs to the Furnace Terrace; **E**. Tank; **F**. External surface; **G**. Interior; **a**. Doors; **b**. Windows; **c**. Pipe for Roof water; **d**. Railings for the wall that leads to the Tank. Scale in English feet.

because of the smelting experiments that deteriorated its walls, it may have undergone other changes. The structures, the layouts, the styles, and the thickness of the walls (the warehouse walls are up to two meters thick) indicate that they are very different buildings; the furnace building has architectural details with better workmanship. In the warehouses, iron ore, firewood, coal, European smelting instruments ("furnace complete with an anvil") were stored, and that was where white blacksmiths worked, re-melting the iron bars produced by the Ambundu technicians and making tools and instruments.[165] All iron instruments for the factory were locally produced. By 1772, these buildings were completed. From this and other drawings, the architects prepared the schematic layout below, as well as images of three-dimensional models that allow us to visualize the architectural complex from different perspectives (see Attachment 5).

The machine room—letter B in the previous blueprint—was where the great wooden water wheels were to be located, to propel the bellows and the large ham-

---

[165] "The product of a full smelting is being sent; as soon as possible, white blacksmiths will be sent to reduce the iron bars." Carta de FISC para João Baines *capitão-mor* do Golungo, e intendente da fábrica do Novo Belém. São Paulo de Assunção de Luanda, April 9, 1767. BNP, C 8742, F 6362, fl. 166.

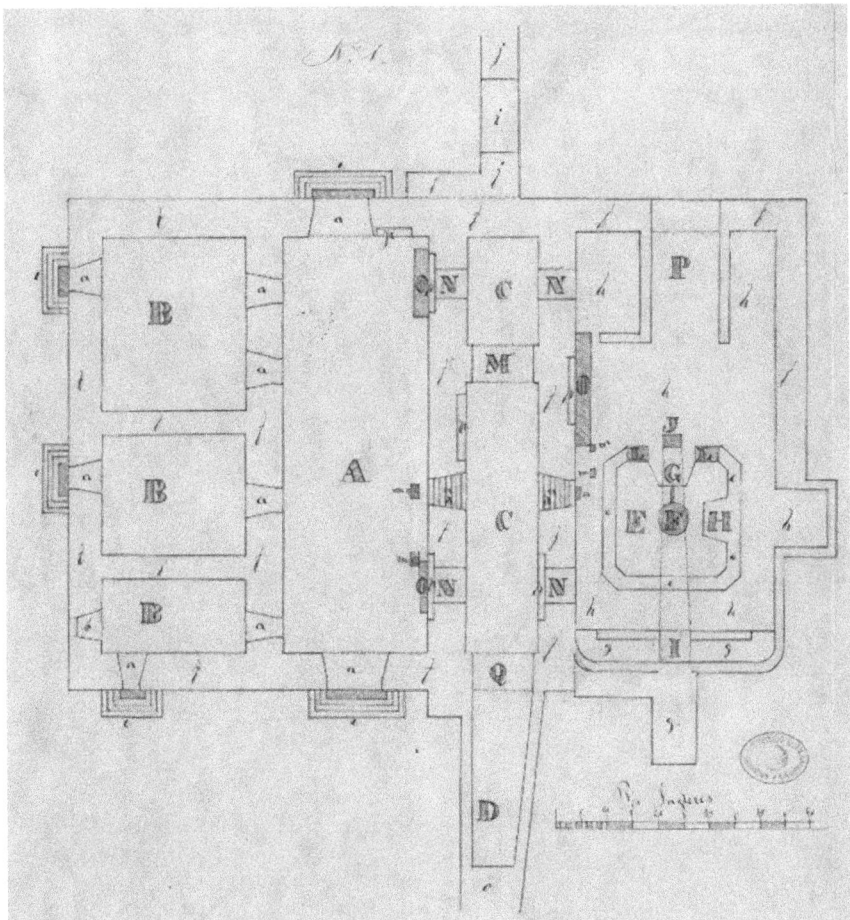

Figures 7 and 8: Blueprints of the iron foundry in Oeiras, 1855.
Source: Planta da Fábrica de Fundição de Ferro em Oeiras, Distrito do Cazengo, 1855. N. 1. Signed by: Jacinto de Gouvea Leal. AHU_CARTm_001, D.1341-42. Scale in English feet. Caption: **A** – Factory; **B** – Warehouses; **C** – Machine Room; **D** – Water Pipe; **E** – Furnace Base; **F** – Furnace; **G** – Location of the Bellows; **H** – Door to the crucible; **I** – Enclosure for the Pipe; **J** – Vent for the Pipe; **L** – Pillars for the Bellows' axes; **M** – Arch of the Tank; **N** – Arches where the wheels operate; **O** – Wheel pads; **P** – Ramp to the furnace; **Q** – Front arch. **a** – doors; **b** – windows; **c** – stairs to the lower level and factory entrance; **d** – stairs to the Machine Room; **e** – *sapata* (sic) of the furnace; **f** – factory walls; **g** – base of the stairs to the upper level of the furnace; **h** – place where the furnace sits; **i** – gutter arch; **j** – aqueduct; **l** – stairs to the tank and aqueduct; **m** – place for the crossbars of the wheel axles; **n** – pipe to drain water from the furnace; **o** – bridge of the drain pipe; **p** – ditches for the wheels.

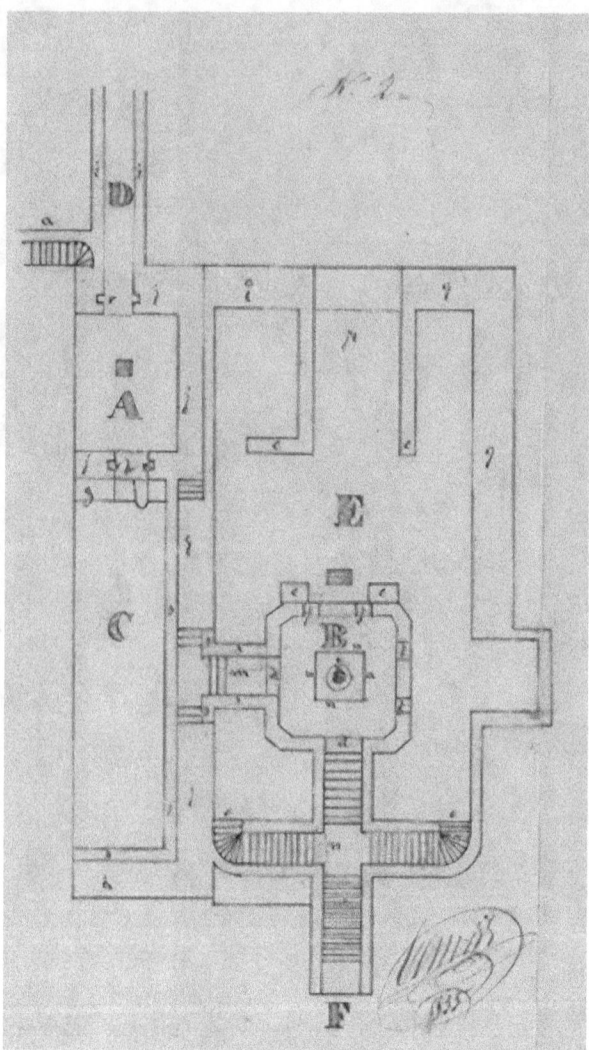

Figure 8: Details of the smelting furnace building:
A – Tank; B – Upper platform of the furnace; C – Machine room; D – Flume on top of the aqueduct; E – Area; F – Front stairs; a – stairs to the flume; b – conduit for the wheel; c – bellows pillars; d – doors; e – upper furnace mouth; f – windows; g – arch sustaining the tank; h – front arch; i – edge of the flume; j – edge of the tank; l – wall and passage to the tank; m – arch leading to the exit to the tank; n – stairs leading to the furnace platform; o – stairs from the area to the furnace platform; p – ramp to the area; q – furnace walls; r – gates; s – wall and corridor guards.
Source: Planta da Fábrica de Fundição de Ferro em Oeiras, Distrito do Cazengo, 1855. N. 1. Assinada por: Jacinto de Gouvea Leal. AHU_CARTm_001,D.1341-42.

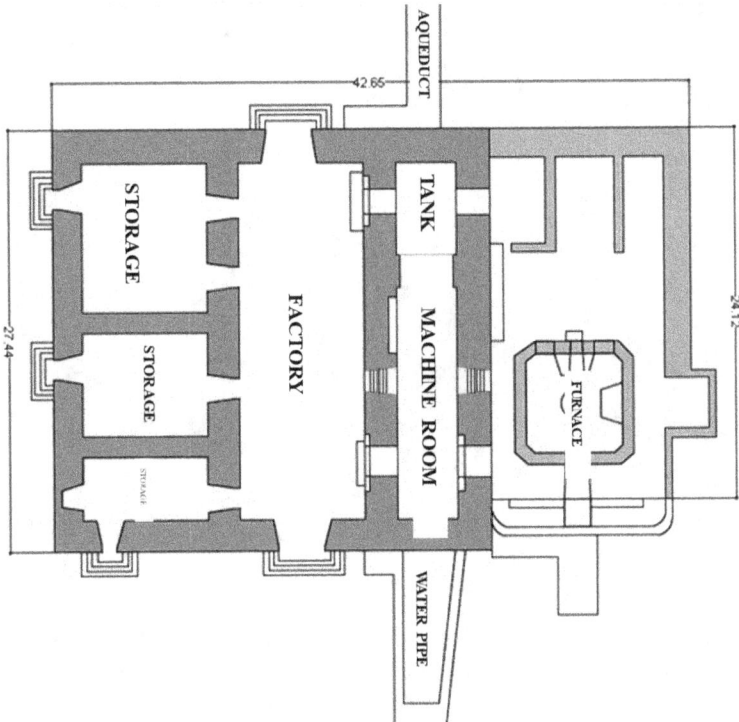

Figure 9: Schematic layout of the iron factory's building.
Source: Giovana Gomes Carreira, Katia Sartorelli Verissimo, and Stefane Saraceni Kaller, schematic layout derived from the 1855 blueprint – Ground Floor. It reproduces the factory as it existed in the eighteenth century and the iron furnace (a more recent construction in a different architectural style). The scale is in meters and was established considering a larger set of blueprints and drawings analyzed during the research.

mer, manufacturing iron according to European methods (an operation that never took place). This machine remained only in the governor's imagination. In his 1779 memoirs, where he celebrated his accomplishments, Sousa Coutinho reminisced about the past: "I imagined the idea of an iron factory, so useful because of its quality, the need we have for it, the different price because it is sold in America, and the ease with which it could be carried in black [slave] ships as ballast with no expense."[166] We find details of the Machine Room in drawings and blueprints from 1769–1770, especially two very similar blueprints, one of them signed by Manuel

---

166 Breve e útil ideia de comércio, navegação e conquistas d'Ásia e da África (n.p., 1779). *Arquivos de Angola*, v. 3 (1935): 140.

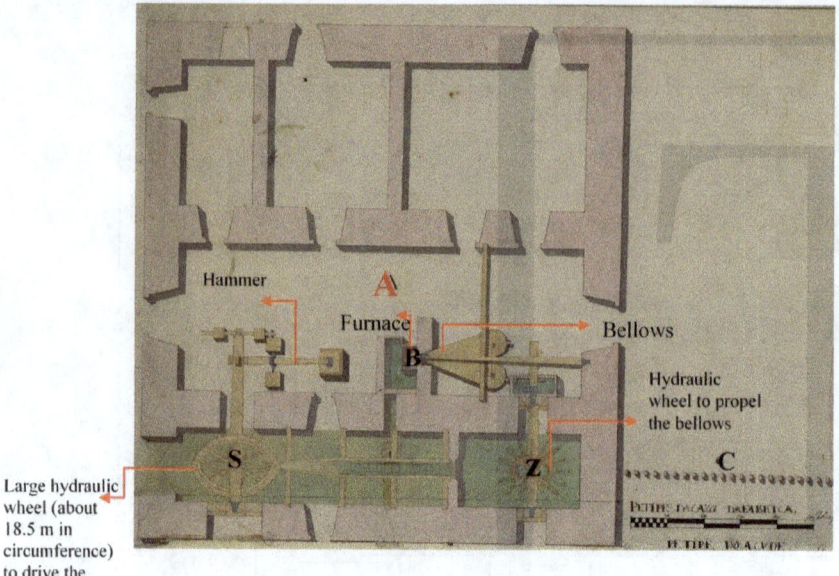

Figures 10 and 11: Interior of the machine room, hydraulic forge, and storeroom. Representation of the weir, 1770. Blueprint of the Iron Factory and weir in Nova Oeiras, elaborated by the Most Excellent Mr. FISC (...) in the year 1770. **A** – Factory building and ironworks in it S, Z. **B** – Furnace where iron is liquefied. **C** – Height of the arches over which flows the water to the ironworks.

Antonio Tavares and the other one by artillery lieutenant João Manoel Lopes. We reproduce the latter below, containing a wealth of details.

Note that there is no mention of the building called the "Furnace Room" by Gouvea in 1855, which houses a blast furnace. The blueprint shows only the machine room and the storerooms; the furnace located in front of the bellows is of a low type, as were those of hydraulic ironworks of the time. This means that the blast furnace had not yet been built. We did not find the letter "F" indicated in the caption, which was the place to which the discarded water was channeled after propelling the big wheel (18.59 m in circumference) that drove the hammer and the smaller wheel (10.56 m in circumference) that drove the bellows.[167] The following drawing gives an idea of the land where the factory was built and the details of the furnace building mentioned above.

---

[167] Measurements described in: Termo de juramento feito pelo provedor da Fazenda Real Manuel Cunha e Sousa, José Francisco Pacheco, Antonio de Bessa Teixeira, Antonio Ribeiro Cardoso. São Paulo de Assunção de Luanda, November 17, 1770. ANTT, Condes de Linhares, mç. 51, doc. 1, fl. 198.

2.3 Nova Oeiras, a "Machine" Conceived in the *Sertão* — 131

Figure 11: D – Weir from where water flows to the factory. E – Cross-section of the Factory Building through line XX of blueprint A. F – Place to drain water not needed by the ironworks.
Source: Planta da Fábrica de Ferro e açude de 1770, assinada pelo Tenente de Artilharia João Manuel Lopes. ANTT, Condes de Linhares, bundle. 103, doc. 1.

In 1769, Sousa Coutinho reported that the town of Nova Oeiras had been established, as well as the "church, administration buildings, smithies, treasuries, prisons, and houses for the masters of all trades and engineers." Next to the machine room and the storerooms shown above, forgotten in a hasty description by the governor, in the shade of the large factory, a "smaller factory was built for the Negroes to work in."[168] It was there that all the iron produced in Nova Oeiras was made. The sources provide little information as to what this building, called "Casa de Fundição dos Pretos," looked like.[169]

To keep Central Africans from interrupting work during the rainy season, "one hundred covered and raised places, or large sheds," were built.[170] This "other" factory occupied a small part of the enormous lime and stone architectural ensemble

---
168 Carta de FISC para Francisco Xavier de Mendonça Furtado, secretário de estado da marinha e ultramar. São Paulo de Assunção de Luanda, September 6, 1769. IEB-USP, Al – 082–175.
169 "The Casa de Fundição dos Pretos was better placed next to the large one, at some proportionate distance, because the same inspector oversaw both works." Carta de FISC para Antonio Anselmo Duarte de Siqueira, intendente da fábrica de ferro de Nova Oeiras. São Paulo de Assunção de Luanda, July 22, 1769. IEB/USP, Al-083–274.
170 Carta de FISC para Antonio Anselmo Duarte, intendente geral da fábrica de ferro. São Paulo de Assunção de Luanda, December 10, 1766. BNP, C 8742, F6364.

Figure 12: View of the iron factory in Oeiras, 1855.
Source: Vista da Fábrica de Fundição de Ferro em Oeiras, 1855. Signed by: Jacinto de Gouvea Leal. AHU_ICONm_001_I, D.470.

and, unlike it, took little time to build. It was not built with well-finished stone like the façades of Nova Oeiras and did not withstand the passage of time like the big factory. However, the "smaller" factory was the only success of this grandiose undertaking, because the only successful iron smelting techniques—the Ambundu techniques—were employed there, a fact overlooked by the historiography that examined the "big factory" and its failures.

In the small foundry, furnaces dug in the earth, bellows covered with goat hair, and stones were the tools employed by the Ambundu blacksmiths and smelters, who exported approximately 60 tons of iron and steel from 1765 to 1800 (see Attachment 1), in addition to 30 to 40 *quintais* (1.8 t to 2.4 t) per month that supplied the Kingdom of Angola. It is worth remembering that Central Africans did not work only in iron smelting and forging. Who built Nova Oeiras, the great and beautiful arches of its aqueduct? In the historiographical production, there is an emphasis on the designer of this great machine, but did Governor Sousa Coutinho, the engineers, the intendants, and the inspectors drag the blocks of stone? Who rebuilt the building that was ravaged by floods and that, at least once, caught fire? Who plowed the land, who cut 800 tree trunks at once, who carried the iron bars, made tiles, sorted, ground, and calcined the lime?[171]

2.4 Civilian Settlements

The factory could only survive with the support of a town capable of producing food and providing the labor force for both the ironworks and the tile, brick, lime, and coal factories. In yet another attempt to follow the Count of Oeiras's decision to transform Angola into a colony of civilian settlements, Sousa Coutinho fostered white settlement in the hinterland near Luanda. As already mentioned, in honor of his intellectual and administrative affiliation, he called the new town at Lumbu "Nova Oeiras." At Ilamba Baixa, the town of Novo Belém was created. The governor often sent Portuguese and Brazilian soldiers to these settlements. In September 1765, for example, nine soldiers from the Kingdom of Portugal were sent to Oeiras, some of them workers and "big farmers." These men were to leave aside the "soldier idea" and refrain from wearing uniforms, since "military ornaments are not befitting of civilian life." Once they had settled and were able to support themselves, the soldiers would be discharged and no longer receive a salary. The newcomers were encouraged "to marry and to work as farmers or as blacksmiths and charcoal burners, in the case of those who are inclined to the latter trades." They were to marry only to white women, "honest girls with some slaves," living in Massangano.[172] If we take into account Miller's hypothesis that the "white women" of Angola were actually local women who benefitted from upward social mobility through marriage relations with white people, grew rich through the trade of enslaved people, and owned many goods and properties in the Kingdom of Angola, we may conclude that these women were in fact the *donas*, whose protagonism has been reconstituted by historiography.[173]

---

[171] Bertold Brecht, "Perguntas de um operário que lê," trans. Haroldo de Campos, in *Breve Antologia de Brecht* (Tempo Brasileiro. Rio de Janeiro, April/June 1966), no. 9–10.

[172] "Instrução que deve guardar Antonio Anselmo Duarte de Siqueira servindo o emprego de intendente geral da Fábrica do Ferro e que executaram também os capitães mores como intendentes particulares na parte que lhes é respectiva." São Paulo de Assunção de Luanda, January 12, 1767. AHU_CU_001, Cx. 52, Doc. 73. Carta de FISC para Antonio Anselmo Duarte, intendente da fábrica de ferro. São Paulo de Assunção de Luanda, January 12, 1768. The governor does not mention who were the white women of the presidio next to Nova Oeiras who possessed enslaved people. One hypothesis is that they were orphans with a dowry awaiting marriage, as we shall see below.

[173] Selma Pantoja, "Gênero e comércio: as traficantes de escravizados na região de Angola," *Travessias*, no. 4–5 (2004): 79–97; Selma Pantoja, "As fontes escritas do século XVII e o estudo da representação do feminino em Luanda," in *Construindo o passado angolano: as fontes e a sua inter-*

The Pombaline directive to colonize the *sertões* of overseas conquests was a reform of the space carried out through the establishment of "proper civilian settlements that are useful to the common good of the Crown and the peoples." The Count of Oeiras employed this phrase in 1752 in a secret letter to his brother, Francisco Xavier de Mendonça Furtado, at the time the newly appointed governor of Grão-Pará and Maranhão. One of the governor's first actions in the Amazon was to send an expedition with Azorean colonists to found the new settlement and fortress of Macapá. The plan was for the town to be inhabited at first by about 600 white people. One of the objectives was for it to serve to attract the Indians who lived deep in the forest, fleeing from the villages until then under missionary control. Pombal wanted to advance into the *sertões*, populating the new settlements and conquering new labor force. Mendonça Furtado also founded other settlements, such as Bragança and Ourém—Portuguese names like Nova Oeiras and Novo Belém, replicating toponyms of important cities in the Kingdom to "reaffirm the fact that these settlements belonged to a space that was unquestionably Portuguese."[174]

In Angola, Sousa Coutinho believed that coexistence with Africans had corrupted the customs of Europeans, especially with regard to the abandonment of the Christian faith. According to the royal official, what caused such a deviation was the excess of luxury, the "vanity of sunny regions," because these families never left home without "an excessive number of black and mulatto women to accompany them," "pieces of gold, silver, and precious stones to adorn them," "expensive dresses," or were transported in "litters or hammocks."[175] These elements were signs of social distinction in that society.

The corruption of the customs of those who were born in Angola—most of them children of Portuguese men with African or Luso-African women—was presumably due to their upbringing, since, in the words of Sousa Coutinho, these chil-

---

pretação. Actas do II Seminário internacional sobre história de Angola (Lisbon: Comissão Nacional para as comemorações dos Descobrimentos Portugueses, 2000), 583–596; Mariana Candido, "Dona Aguida Gonçalves marchange à Benguela à la fin du XVIII siècle," *Brésil(s). Sciences humaines et sociales* 1 (2012): 33–54; Vanessa de Oliveira, "Mulher e comércio: a participação feminina nas redes comerciais em Luanda (século XIX)," in Selma Pantoja, Edvaldo A. Bergamo, Ana Claudia da Silva (org.), *Angola e as angolanas. Memória, sociedade e cultura* (São Paulo: Intermeios, 2016), 134–152.

174 Renata Malcher de Araujo, "A urbanização da Amazónia e do Mato Grosso no século XVIII povoações civis, decorosas e úteis para o bem comum da Coroa e dos povos," *Anais do Museu Paulista: História e Cultura Material* 20, no. 1 (2012): 57.

175 Memórias do Reino de Angola e suas conquistas escritas por D. Francisco Inocêncio de Sousa Coutinho, governador e capitão general do Reino de Angola, escritas entre 1773 a 1775. Torre do Tombo, Condes de Linhares, mç. 44, doc. 2

dren were raised in "a harem of corrupt and filthy black and mulatto women." Thus, Luso-Africans grew up "loosely raised," speaking the local languages, and incapable of the "least work." Mulatto women were considered "second-class" women; Sousa Coutinho claimed that most of them prostituted themselves publicly and, when they became pregnant, they killed their children "suffocating them in secret." Those who survived were poorly raised and, in the governor's opinion, were of little value to carry out his plans to spread European values in the *sertão*. In addition, there was a strong presence of local religions, which led the Portuguese to believe Central African "superstitions." Sousa Coutinho's entire rhetoric was opposed to the "mixture of blood," because this first pollution was presumably the reason for the failure to maintain European customs in Angola.[176]

To remedy this situation, it was necessary to incite the spread of the Catholic religion by means of "religious wise men," who should replace Angola's corrupted clergymen. Secondly, "all pagan customs" should be forbidden, i.e. the *"entambes* (funeral chants in Kimbundu), wedding patrons, and black cures." Finally, in order to prevent miscegenation, it was necessary to limit the number of African women, whether enslaved or free, who lived in Portuguese homes or near them.

In *Fragmentos Setecentistas*, Silva Lara discusses how, throughout the eighteenth century, attempts to eliminate "vagrants" and combat the corruption of enslaved and mulatto women were common.[177] In Angola, Governor Francisco Inocêncio de Sousa Coutinho proposed the creation of a "house of devotion" to teach trades to mulattos, in addition to promoting a marriage policy, something similar to what the Count of Resende suggested for Portuguese America. Silvia Lara comments that the formerly enslaved became targets of constant criticism and punishment. For colonial administrators, it was necessary to control and discipline the multitudes of colored men and women who refused to be submissive. Evidently, this bothered the colonial masters and authorities, since it jeopardized the tense and delicate balance of political and hierarchical relations that structured that society.[178]

The derogatory classification of mulatto women was also perceived on the Brazilian side of the Atlantic Ocean. Colonial authorities associated social condition and skin color, which in the case was related to bastardy, social dereliction, and

---

[176] Idem. The dependence on Kimbundu was such that merchants in the *sertões* could do little without mastering the Ambundu language.
[177] Silvia Hunold Lara, *Fragmentos setecentistas, escravidão, cultura e poder na América portuguesa* (São Paulo: Companhia das Letras, 2007), 273 and ff.
[178] "The massive presence of free black and mulatto men no doubt presented an eminently disruptive political potential." Idem, 279.

"manias of nobility."[179] The word "mulatto" acquired derogatory connotations over time, a disqualification associated to bastard birth and descendance. We should recall that birth criteria were signs of social distinction in the Old Regime. In general, the prohibitions and admonitions regarding black women's behavior had a cause of urgent concern: the conquests and demands of the enslaved and formerly enslaved called into question the traditional policies of seigneurial dominion.

Something that is beyond the scope of this study is to examine the specificities of the Kingdom of Angola with regard to the governor's criticism of miscegenation and coexistence with black men and women. How were the categories of color, origin, and social condition related in eighteenth-century Angola?

For now, suffice it to say that a counter-reading of Sousa Coutinho's opinion reveals the importance of African women and their descendants in raising and educating the children of Portuguese and Luso-African families. How could those people survive in Angola without speaking Kimbundu and/or Kikongo, without knowledge of local foods, plants, and herbs? How could a settlement be sustained without African medical knowledge, when Europeans were massacred by fevers and malaria and lacked enough qualified surgeons? Reflecting briefly on these questions, we know that, at least as far as the language was concerned, the dependence on Kimbundu was such that its use was eventually forbidden. It was African women who were responsible for raising the colonists' children as their mothers or as enslaved women in their homes. Apparently, Ambundu women represented a threat to seigneurial and colonial plans, and were responsible for the socialization of Luso-Africans, who continued to speak the local languages and to dress and behave like Ambundus.[180] That was one more reason for the emphasis on colonization with white women.

The two towns where the iron factories would be built had to follow Sousa Coutinho's guidelines. The towns were founded on high ground to benefit from the winds, which would provide greater hygiene, keep diseases away, and correct the "climate's defects"—one of the causes of the constant death of Europeans in the *sertões*. Agriculture was an *a priori* condition for the establishment and maintenance of the towns, taking advantage of the fact that there were "admirable

---

179 "The discomfort was apparently caused by the luxury and habits of women who were not white, yet boasted rich outfits or went out at night." Idem, 98 and 99.
180 While boys were prepared for public life and therefore learned some Portuguese, girls remained without any instruction. Jan Vansina, "Portuguese vs Kimbundu: Language Use in the Colony of Angola (1575–c. 1845)," *Bulletin des Séances de l'Académie royal e des Sciences d'Outre-Mer* 47, no. 3 (2001): 267–281; Beatrix Heintze, "A lusofonia no interior da África Central na era pré-colonial. Um contributo para a sua história e compreensão na actualidade," *Cadernos de Estudos Africanos* 7/8 (2005): 179–207.

lands" in the surrounding area; in the governor's words, "the more settlements, fields, and flour mills are established, the more iron will be produced." Raising cattle brought from Caconda (Kingdom of Benguela) was encouraged to transport the iron, as was planting *erva tete*[181] to feed the donkeys that would be sent from America, as well as fruit trees; there were even constant shipments of vegetable seeds to the "new colonies." The settlers were to be employed in agriculture, felling trees, and manufacturing charcoal or iron. Taverns were forbidden, as well as any similar establishment that fostered a "colony of bandits."[182]

The documentation on the Novo Belém Factory and its town is not as extensive as that on Nova Oeiras, but settlers and workers were also sent there. The Belém Factory produced iron from 1765 to 1768 under the administration of intendant João Baines. Lacking techniques to "tear up the ground" to explore underground mines, only ironstones from Oeiras were processed in Novo Belém. Since the trips were expensive and no one knew when there would be technicians available who knew how to dig galleries for underground exploration, nor was there any reason to divide the workers between the two factories, in October 1768, the governor ordered both factories to come together in Nova Oeiras, sending all the iron produced and all the new workers to the new location.[183] Note that the colonial administration was unaware of the technology to explore the underground mines held by African elites, as in the case analyzed of the *soba* Kabanga kya Mbangu, in the same region where Novo Belém operated, in Ilamba.

---

181 Might this be *caruru* (*amaranthus viridis*), *ewétètè*? Scholars believe that it was culturally introduced by Africans into Brazilian culture. It is a very good indicator of soil quality. All the parts of *caruru* are edible. It is rich in iron, potassium, calcium, and vitamins A, B1, B2 and C. It has medicinal lactogenic properties, combatting infections, liver problems, hydropsy, among others. The seeds can be consumed toasted or in breads and other recipes.
182 "Instrução que deve guardar Antonio Anselmo Duarte de Siqueira servindo o emprego de intendente geral da Fábrica do Ferro e que executaram também os capitães mores como intendentes particulares na parte que lhes é respectiva." São Paulo de Assunção de Luanda, January 12, 1767. AHU_CU_001, Cx. 52, Doc. 73. There is not much information about the town of Novo Belém, so we will focus on the creation of Nova Oeiras. In 1769, when Joaquim de Bessa Teixeira visited Nova Oeiras, he said that white people had lived there before: "located at a site that had previously been inhabited by many white men, as is evident from the foundations of old houses, of which there are still many remnants, as well as the many thorn trees present, for black people always plant fruit trees." Being close to Massangano, perhaps colonizers lived there in the sixteenth and seventeenth centuries. Documento que sua Excelência mandou registrar de várias cousas que viu, e observou na Real Fábrica do Ferro da Nova Oeiras o Tenente de Cavalos Joaquim de Bessa Teixeira, São Paulo de Assunção de Luanda, February 7, 1769. IEB/USP, Al-083–207.
183 Carta de FISC para São Paulo de Assunção de Luanda, August 7, 1768. IHGB 126, PADAB DVD10, 22 DSC00197.

To create new white families in civilian settlements, the "orphans and maidens" of the town of Massangano were encouraged to marry the soldiers, workers, and other white men sent to Nova Oeiras. Those women were under the yoke of guardians who controlled their possessions and did not allow them to marry. One of the goals of the Sousa Coutinho administration was to put an end to corruption in the administration of inheritance goods by the Provedoria dos Defuntos e Ausentes (Office for the Provision of Orphans and the Deceased).[184] The governor was in the process of liberating young women from this theft when, in October 1767, he ordered that, within two months, they should all be married. He hoped that, in gratitude for having been thus liberated and having their dowry saved, the ladies from the towns of Massangano, Lembo, and Quisecle (the latter two in the vicinity of Massangano) would choose husbands among the men of Nova Oeiras.[185]

One month later, the governor congratulated the *capitão-mor* of Massangano for having carried out his orders, but reiterated the prohibition of marriage between white and black people, which was common, because it "brought total ruin to this kingdom's interests."[186] Despite the governor's insistence, the measures did not bear the fruits expected. One year after the first orders to promote the town of Nova Oeiras, the few marriages between women from Massangano and men from Nova Oeiras became a problem, as it led to the "transmigration of entire families" together with the brides, as was the local custom, depopulating the town established around the fortress.[187] Even when he successfully achieved his goals, Sousa Coutinho encountered new obstacles.

Families, soldiers, and convicts were also systematically sent to the factories, especially from 1765 to 1772, under the Sousa Coutinho administration. As a result of the attempts to reestablish the iron factory in the late-eighteenth century, from 1765 to 1800, at least 168 people were sent, among specialized workers (85), people to populate the new towns (68)—most of them soldiers—, factory workers (10), and

---

184 Selma Pantoja, "Luanda: relações raciais e de gênero," in *II RIHA* (Rio de Janeiro, 1996), 75–81.
185 Letters and official documents addressed to the regents of the town of Massangano can be found in: BNP, C 8742, F 6364. FISC ordered the iron factories' intendant: "as in Quisecle and Massangano, there must be white women and honest girls with some slaves; your grace shall make every effort to engage them with the said fiancés and to ensure that the latter be pleased with the said ladies, for there are no other means to populate the land." Carta de FISC para Antonio Anselmo Duarte de Siqueira, intendente geral das fábricas de ferro. São Paulo de Assunção de Luanda, September 25, 1767. BNP, C 8742, F 6364, fl, 231 v.
186 Carta de FISC para Pedro Matoso de Andrade, *capitão-mor* de Massangano. São Paulo de Assunção de Luanda, November 14, 1767. BNP, C 8742, F 6364, fl, 240.
187 Carta de FISC para Antonio Anselmo Duarte de Siqueira, intendente geral das fábricas de ferro. São Paulo de Assunção de Luanda, July 10, 1768, IEB/USP, AL-083–084.

engineers (5), in addition to the Ambundu workers sent by the *sobas* every month. In this group, we identified 22 convicts and people who came or were sent from Lisbon, Madeira Islands, Biscay, France, Bahia, Luanda, Muxima, Pedras de Pungo Andongo, Ambaca, Bambambe, Encoge, and Massangano.

Despite all these efforts to develop Nova Oeiras and Novo Belém on the basis of white colonization, the living conditions in the *sertões*, the shortage of supplies, the frequent fevers, crop failures, and the hard life in construction work or as blacksmiths and smelters turned the town into a "drain of people." The factory apothecary was often supplied with the available medicines, the few bottles of quinine available, and "English water." Cattle breeding became unviable because the pastures were what Sousa Coutinho described as "poisonous."[188] This was compounded by the incursions of "barbarians"[189] who robbed the towns, not to mention the harassment and abuse that the residents suffered at the hands of factory officers. The soldiers sent to Nova Oeiras often fled because of hunger, as was the case in 1768, when the soldiers sent from the new settlement of the Encoge fortress returned there, fleeing from the precarious living conditions.[190] Desertion could also happen because, as we have already mentioned, since their wages were paid in goods prized in the trade of captives, the soldiers preferred to abandon their hard work in Nova Oeiras and join the mercantile networks that ventured into the *sertões*.

It is not by chance that there was a prison in the town—those who neither engaged in farming nor were interested in ironwork were to be immediately arrested. The governor had to ask the *soba* Kabuku Kambilu to send his "offspring" to assist in agricultural tasks because the soldiers were not interested, deserted, or were unable to produce.[191] In 1769, to make matters worse for the residents of Nova

---

188 The factory works inspector explained that the plots of land were not suitable for farming, for they were too rocky or too small. Carta de Antonio de Lencastre para Martinho de Melo, secretário de estado da marinha e do ultramar. São Paulo de Assunção de Luanda, March 31, 1773. AHU_CU_001, Cx. 52, D. 28.
189 Because of these incursions, it was necessary to fortify the settlers. Carta de FISC para Salvador de Menezes e Silva *capitão-mor* e juiz da povoação do Novo Belém. São Paulo de Assunção de Luanda, January 14, 1772. SGL, *Arquivos de Angola*, v. 3, n. 29, 1958–1963, p. 377.
190 Carta de FISC para o *capitão-mor* do presídio do Encoge, Paio de Araújo. São Paulo de Assunção de Luanda, April 4, 1768. AHA, Códice 79, fl. 98v. Regarding supplies for the apothecary, see: Portaria para o doutor provedor da Fazenda Real aprontar e remeter para Nova Oeiras, vários remédios de Botica. São Paulo de Assunção de Luanda, April 12, 1769. AHA, Códice 271, fl. 20v.
191 Carta de FISC para Francisco Xavier de Mendonça Furtado, secretário de estado da marinha e do ultramar. São Paulo de Assunção de Luanda, May 16, 1769. AHU_CU_001, Cx. 52, D. 29; Carta de FISC para Antonio Anselmo Duarte de Siqueira, intendente geral das fábricas de ferro. São Paulo de Assunção de Luanda, October 27, 1767. BNP, C 8742, F 6364.

Oeiras, there was a great drought—"with a great lack of water does heaven punish us"—followed by a great flood the following year, which destroyed a large part of the buildings.

Paradoxically, however, three years after he started sending white or "almost white" people to the towns, in August 1769, the governor stated that only 20 white people had died, in addition to the specialized workers who had been sent there.[192] There were at least 153 residents, according to the houses counted by Joaquim de Bessa Teixeira, who described "small houses of white and black people, more than a hundred." There were also "many trees of various fruits, and vegetables, everything most abundant, and beautiful pasture," and yet they were unable to raise "beef cattle."[193] Governor Sousa Coutinho always tried to emphasize that the town could be successful, turning a blind eye to the constant failures of his initiatives.

The number of white people dead in 1773 increased to 77, five of them women, in addition to the "hundreds of black people" who were not recorded. Although the sources often do not cite the African town residents, we know that they were the main labor force employed. We can imagine that not all of them could go to Nova Oeiras and return to their *sobados* every day, since some came from distant villages up to eight days away. They must have lived, at least temporarily, in or around the town, but there is little data in this regard. As we said earlier, there are indications in the documentation that there were houses of both white and black people there.[194]

The complete failure of the plans to create a white colony was acknowledged in 1771, when Sousa Coutinho decided that the best way to establish a settlement was to "introduce 200 married couples of fourteen- [or] sixteen-year-old youths, in order for the males to learn and do the factory work and the females to cultivate the land that would feed them," "the same way that other [lands] in the country used to feed the couple."[195] The only way to cultivate the land and bring in workers was to employ Central African labor—not only their labor power, but also the Am-

---

192 Carta de FISC para Francisco Xavier de Mendonça Furtado, secretário de estado da marinha e do ultramar. São Paulo de Assunção de Luanda, August 1, 1769. IEB/USP, Al – 082–164.

193 Documento que sua Excelência mandou registrar de várias cousas que viu, e observou na Real Fábrica do Ferro da Nova Oeiras o Tenente de Cavalos Joaquim de Bessa Teixeira, São Paulo de Assunção de Luanda, February 7, 1769. IEB/USP, Al-083–207.

194 Certidão de José Francisco Pacheco, inspetor das obras da fábrica, sobre o estado da fábrica de ferro. São Paulo de Assunção de Luanda, March 13, 1773. AHU_CU_001, Cx. 57, D. 28.

195 Carta de FISC para Joaquim de Bessa Teixeira, Intendente geral da Real Fábrica do Ferro da Nova Oeiras. São Paulo de Assunção de Luanda, November 26, 1771. BNP, Reservados, C 8744, F 6443, fl. 181v.

bundu knowledge and techniques for farming, cattle raising, and mining and forging iron. But he was at the end of his government and soon returned to Lisbon.

As soon as he was appointed, the new governor, Dom António de Lancaster (1772–1779), ordered the closure of the iron factory, arguing that it was too costly an enterprise that, once ready, would not be as profitable as expected. Lencastre rescinded Sousa Coutinho's ordinance that determined that workers should be paid wages, which led most of the population living there to leave. Still, the town was not entirely abandoned: when the mineralogist José Álvares Maciel visited the factory around 1795, he met town residents who made a living solely of iron production: "they have lived in that place and its surroundings for many years."[196]

---

[196] Carta de Miguel Antonio de Melo, governador de Angola, para Rodrigo de Sousa Coutinho, secretário de estado da marinha e do ultramar. São Paulo de Assunção de Luanda, March 18, 1800. *Arquivos de Angola*, 2ª serie, v. X, no. 39–42 (n.d.): 195. José Álvares Maciel, "Notícia da Fábrica de ferro da Nova Oeiras do Reino de Angola." São Paulo de Assunção de Luanda, December 15, 1797, [p. 9]. AHTC, Erário Régio, 4196.

Chapter 3
Work and Workers in Nova Oeiras

3.1 Labor Regulations

On July 20, 1767, the Royal Treasury Board of the Kingdom of Angola analyzed a plea by the African chiefs in charge of sending workers to the ironworks that were being built in the colony's hinterlands. The chiefs requested that "their work be rewarded by being exempted from paying the tithe." Their justification was that the exchange would be advantageous to them because it would put an end to the "violence exerted by the collectors."[1]

The chiefs had the duty to send workers to the factories, who received "modest wages"[2] in return, just like those who worked in public works. Apparently, the tribute collection system did not work well from the standpoint of Central African chiefs, and the *sobas* decided to write to the governor requesting that, instead of paying wages to their dependents, the Royal Treasury exempt the chiefs from paying the tithe.

It is impossible to know when and with what exact words the local leaders addressed the president of the Royal Treasury Board, since only a summary of their request remains in the archives. However, the use of the word "plea" in that excerpt can be understood as an indication that these authorities had learned to deal with the bureaucracy of the Portuguese administration—and had a command of the customs, etiquette, and norms that mediated the relations of the vassals subjected to the rule of the king of Portugal.

---

[1] Cópia do Termo da Junta da Fazenda Real do Reino de Angola assinado por Manuel da Cunha e Sousa, ouvidor e provedor da Fazenda Real, João Delgado Xavier, juiz de fora e procurador da Fazenda Real e Francisco Inocêncio de Sousa Coutinho (FISC), governador e presidente da Junta da Fazenda Real. São Paulo de Assunção de Luanda, July 20, 1767. The agreement is attached to Carta de FISC, para Francisco Xavier de Mendonça Furtado, secretário do Conselho Ultramarino. São Paulo de Assunção de Luanda, August 22, 1768. AHU_CU_001, Cx. 52, D. 27. In April 1767, in a letter to the factories' intendants, the governor had made a reference to this request from the *sobas*: "because they tell me that the *sobas* and *imbari* offer to work always in the factories with no other payment than the tithe exemption." Carta de FISC para Antonio Anselmo Duarte de Siqueira e João Baines, intendentes das fábricas de ferro. São Paulo de Assunção de Luanda, April 14, 1767. BNP, C-8742, F-6464.
[2] Carta de FISC para João Baines, tenente general. "Instrução que lhe dou a respeito da fábrica de ferro." São Paulo de Assunção de Luanda, March 8, 1766. BNP, C-8742, F-6464. The instructions specified "prompt modest payments, which can please and attract black people to this service, and others from a different jurisdiction."

This was the result of more than two centuries of contact with the Portuguese, but it was also part of the relations of domination established among African authorities. As we described in the first chapter, when a chief was *undado* by an African sovereign, thus becoming his subject, he had to periodically deliver part of his production—flour, beans, goats, chickens, salt stones—as tribute. With the Portuguese conquest, the *undamento* became part of the vassalage agreements. In general, when African chiefs were defeated, they were forced by Portuguese weapons to sign a mutual agreement through which they submitted to the dominion of the Portuguese king as his vassals. The king provided protection against their enemies in exchange for military aid, payment of tribute (products or enslaved people), and the opening of their territories to Portuguese trade, especially of enslaved people.[3] When *undados*, the *sobas* were subjected to the jurisdiction of a fortress, under the authority of a *capitão-mor.*

Sousa Coutinho was the first governor to elaborate a set of regulations for *capitães-mores*, on February 24, 1765. In them, the governor established "limits" for these officials' authority, with the aim of putting an end to the "iniquitous barbarities" committed "in some of their fortress." Appointing the *capitães-mores* was a prerogative of the king; both residents of Portugal and settlers in Angola could apply for the position on a three-year basis. However, due to the noxious climate, harmful to the Portuguese, Luandans and *sertanejos* or residents of the region were preferred. At first, *capitães-mores* did not receive wages; only in 1772 did they begin receiving a salary of 300,000 réis per year. The main reason to begin paying wages was the fact that these officials made their fortunes with the trade of enslaved people, neglecting their administrative and military responsibilities and taking advantage of their close relationship with the *sobados* to favor their trade. Once paid, the *capitães-mores* were forbidden to participate in the trade. But this prohibition did not change much; in practice, they continued to be key players in the trade routes in the hinterlands of the Kingdom of Angola.[4]

---

[3] Beatrix Heintze, "Luso-African Feudalism in Angola? The Vassal Treaties of the 16th to the 18th Century," *Separata da Revista Portuguesa de História* 18 (1980): 111–131.

[4] Idem, 53–71; Carlos Couto, *Os capitães-mores em Angola no século XVIII. Subsídio para o estudo da sua actuação* (Luanda: Instituto de Investigação Científica de Angola, 1972), 104 and 105. Many historians have called attention to the extensive participation of royal officers in the trade of enslaved people. C.f.: Joseph C. Miller, *Way of Death. Merchant Capitalism and the Angolan Slave Trade, 1730–1830* (Madison: University of Wisconsin Press, 1988), 268; Roquinaldo Ferreira, *Cross-Cultural Exchange in the Atlantic World. Angola and Brazil during the Era of the Slave Trade* (New York: Cambridge University Press, 2012), 44; Mariana P. Candido, *An African Slaving Port and the Atlantic World. Benguela and its Hinterland* (New York: Cambridge University Press, 2013), 175–185; Flávia Maria de Carvalho, *Sobas e homens do rei: interiorização dos portugueses em Angola (séculos XVII e XVIII)* (Maceió: Edufal, 2015), 89 and 90.

One of the duties of the *capitães-mores* that most led to complaints to the government of Luanda by the *sobas* and their subordinates was the collection of tithes. As in other Portuguese overseas colonies, in Angola the tithes were collected by whoever obtained the triennial contract. If the contract holder failed to collect the amount expected by the Royal Treasury, he would be responsible for paying the missing part. The *dizimeiros*, as the contract holders were called, collected the tithes in the districts surrounding the city of Luanda. In the fortress and inland jurisdictions, the *capitães-mores* were to assist in the collection. The *dizimeiros* hired collectors, who effectively visited the *sobados*. Payment was made in products, mostly foodstuffs—flour, corn, oil, animals, cotton, among others.

According to Correa Silva, the difficulties faced to collect the tribute, which contributed to the misallocations committed by the collectors, were the "distance of the fortress and the poor state of the roads, the precariousness of transportation." According to the "law of the *dizimeiros*," as Silva Correa called the abusive procedures of these officials, those who collected the tributes increased their profits in accordance to their "ambition" and not to the capacity of the population. *Capitães-mores* and collectors joined forces to make the business more profitable. One example was the standard measure employed in the collections, which was always heftier than that established by the government—the scales and other instruments of measurement employed to weigh the goods delivered as tribute were often modified to obtain greater profits.[5]

The tithe contract was "envied" in the *sertões* because it enriched the contract holders. Sousa Coutinho investigated the situation and found that the tithes were "payed by whoever wanted to and that the collectors transformed everything that should be a tithe into *telecos*, i.e. lodging, for which they practiced all sorts of violence against the wretched Negroes."[6] We can infer that the *telecos* referred to the

---

[5] Elias Alexandre da Silva Correa, *História de Angola*, v. 1, 37. Agriculture was not ideal for tithe collection, which was equivalent 10% of agricultural production. The tithes collected were very small; between 1730 and 1765, the annual revenue was between 1 and 2.5 *contos* per year. Silva Correa pointed out that some *sobados* were exempted from "the scourge of tithes" because the volume of agricultural production was minute and they were unable to contribute. In return, the exempt *sobas* provided the governor with an annual gift, probably consisting of enslaved people. Even with the tithes paid by the *sobados* that were obliged to do so, the amount was insufficient to ensure the subsistence of Luanda's residents, who often had to import food ("foreign aid") and other basic commodities. Elias Alexandre da Silva Correa, *História de Angola*, v. I, 165. On determining the tithe amounts, see: Maximiliano M. Menz, "Angola, o Império e o Atlântico," in *Anais do XI Congresso Brasileiro de História Econômica* (2015).

[6] Carta de FISC ao secretário do Conselho Ultramarino, Francisco Xavier de Sousa Furtado. São Paulo de Assunção de Luanda, June 30, 1765. ANTT, Ministério do Reino mç. 600, caixa 703, doc. 101. Cadornega also speaks about a seventeenth-century tithe collector, Bartolomeu Nunes,

time the collectors spent in the *sobados* during the tribute collection. The presence of these officials on the *sobas*' lands, at the latter's expense, was not something they were formally bound to, but that the colonial situation imposed on them.[7] For the *sobas* and their dependents, the collection was synonymous with indebtedness, which increased their dependence on the captains. Thus, complaints against the *telecos* were common. For example, João Martins Laraxa, captain of the Dande district, was discharged from his position because he "practiced violence in the collection of tithes," charging an extra *tostão* for each receipt he issued to the *sobas*.[8]

In addition, the military officer Elias Correa mentions the fact that, during their "lodging," the collectors also sought sexual relations.[9] Vansina cited the presence of commercial agents in the *sobados* as the cause of many conflicts involving adultery and theft, which brought insecurity and instability to the Ambundus under the *sobas*' rule. This was so because the penalties for these transgressions were quite high, including the culprits' enslavement.[10]

The governor of Angola mentions the *telecos* in a context that also involves robberies and raids, indicating that the *sobados* suffered attacks and threats: "I know for a fact that in the jurisdiction of Golungo (...) there are still many vagrants from the troops of this capital and the fortress, who go around robbing the people

---

born in Elvas, married and resident of Luanda. Antonio de Oliveira Cadornega, *História das Guerras Angolanas (1680)*, annotated and revised by José Matias Delgado (Lisbon: Agência-geral do Ultramar, 1972), v. I, 316.

7 Carta de FISC ao secretário do Conselho Ultramarino, Francisco Xavier de Sousa Furtado. São Paulo de Assunção, June 30, 1765. ANTT, Ministério do Reino mç. 600, caixa 703, doc. 101. Elias Alexandre da Silva Correa, *História de Angola*, v. 1, 163–167; see also: Carlos Couto, *Os capitães-mores em Angola no século XVIII. Subsídio para o estudo da sua actuação* (Luanda: Instituto de Investigação Científica de Angola, 1972), 124–133.

8 Carta de FISC para o tenente Joaquim de Bessa Teixeira. São Paulo de Assunção de Luanda, August 17, 1768. IEB/USP, AL-083–115. Another consequence of the pressures caused by the payment of tithes to the *sobados* can be observed in the collections made in connection with the fortresses of Ambaca and Cambambe. The residents of the *sobados* bound to these fortresses traded spun cotton and had to deliver this commodity as tithe payment. The tax collectors started to demand that the cotton be delivered in "yarn sticks" the "thickness of a human leg." Reacting to the increased volume of payments, the Africans, "forced to thicken the volumes to a satisfactory size," shredded rags and old clothes and covered them with thread to thicken the bundles." We know that textiles were an important currency, easily transformed into goods and enslaved people. Cotton was also used to make other products, such as hammocks and clothes. The collectors were no doubt interested in its production for this reason. Elias Alexandre da Silva Correa, *História de Angola*, v. I, 164.

9 Elias Alexandre da Silva Correa, *História de Angola*, v. I, 94 and 95.

10 Jan Vansina, "Ambaca Society and the Slave Trade c. 1760–1845," *The Journal of African History* 46, no. 1 (2005): 7; Mariana Candido, *An African Slaving Port and the Atlantic World*, 204–205; Joseph Miller, "Angola Central e Sul por volta de 1840," *Estudos Afro-asiáticos* 32 (1997): 30–32.

and demanding *telecos*."¹¹ There is also a reference that "*teleco* porters or any other gratuitous collections that greed invented"¹² should be avoided—i.e. the collectors and captains demanded other illegitimate payments, such as taking porters by force from the inhabitants or from African chiefs. The relationship between tribute collection by the *capitães-mores*, enslavement, armed violence, and raids was also frequent during the payment of the royal fifths, collected in the form of enslaved people. Moreover, non-payment was one of the "just" reasons, within the concept of the just war,¹³ used by Crown officials to attack the *sobados*; one of the results of these attacks was the enslavement of their "offspring." It is likely that sexual abuse, capture, and enslavement of subjects of the *sobas* were among the conflicts to which African officials referred. And the chiefs strove by all means to protect their dependents from the onslaught of outsiders.¹⁴

Sousa Coutinho fostered a change in tribute collection: he attempted to put an end to *telecos* and, instead of goats, chickens, flour, corn, beans, or cotton, he established that payment should be made in salt stones—one per *fogo* (family), worth 80 réis.¹⁵ Salt stones were a common currency in Angola's *sertão*, and the governor

---

11 Carta de FISC para Antonio Anselmo Duarte de Siqueira. São Paulo de Assunção de Luanda, June 15, 1768.IEB/USP, AL-083–070.
12 Portaria assinada por FISC. São Paulo de Assunção de Luanda, October 29, 1768. IEB/USP, AL-083–138.
13 In short, war against those who resisted converting to Christianity. On the concept of just war, see: Ângela Domingues, "Os conceitos de guerra justa e resgate e os ameríndios do Norte do Brasil," in Maria B. N. Silva (org.), *Brasil: colonização, escravidão* (Rio de Janeiro: Nova Fronteira, 2000). Works that also demonstrate the enslavement of Christians: José C. Curto, "The Story of Nbena, 1817–1820: Unlawful Enslavement and the Concept of 'Original Freedom' in Angola," in Paul E. Lovejoy and David V. Trotman (orgs.), *Trans-Atlantic Dimensions of Ethnicity in the African Diaspora* (London: Continuum, 2003), 44–64; Ferreira, *Cross-Cultural Exchanges in the Atlantic World* (2012), 52–87; Mariana Candido, "O limite tênue entre liberdade e escravidão em Benguela durante a era do comércio transatlântico," *Afro-Ásia* 47 (2013): 239–268.
14 Jan Vansina, "Ambaca Society and the Slave Trade c. 1760–1845," *The Journal of African History* 46, no. 1 (2005): 7.
15 Carta de FISC ao secretário do Conselho Ultramarino, Francisco Xavier de Sousa Furtado. São Paulo de Assunção de Luanda, June 30, 1765. ANTT, Ministério do Reino mç. 600, caixa 703, doc. 101. In Angola, salt was obtained from salt mines in Benguela and in the so-called Cacuaco, near Bengo, sources of sea salt. The salt trade was managed by a hired administrator, but from 1762 onwards, the Administração da Venda do Estanco do Sal was created, which became responsible for purchasing, transporting, and selling salt. Its objective was to reduce the high prices charged by private traders. José Carlos Venâncio, *A economia de Luanda e hinterland no século XVIII. Um estudo de sociologia histórica* (Lisbon: Editorial Estampa, 1996), 55 and 56.

wanted to standardize the collection. The values corresponding to the products could be expressed in their equivalent in réis (see Attachment 4).[16]

Colonial tribute was compatible with the logic of the *sobas*' subjection to a superior authority, which preceded the Portuguese presence in the continent. While in the past they paid tribute to African rulers, with the vassalage agreements, the African political elites were obliged to pay tribute and other taxes on the production of goods to the Portuguese. However, the vassal relationship did not tolerate abuse and vexation.

Father Raphael Bluteau defines abuse as "anything done against good reason, good order." Vexation, on the other hand, was synonymous with "mistreatment" and, furthermore, "refers in particular to the collectors, who with unjust demands and deception mistreat the parties; and to some rulers who mistreat the province with tyranny and persecute the villagers."[17] Thus, the *sobas*, perfectly aware of the Portuguese policies of domination, pointed to the illegitimacy of the actions of the tax collectors and *capitães-mores*.

African rulers attempted to put an end to the abuse and vexation through an exchange: they offered their subjects' labor in the ironworks, accepting as their sole payment the exemption from paying tribute.

The petition made in 1767 by the *sobas* of Ilamba gave rise to a process undertaken by the government of the Kingdom of Angola to review all the ways of employing the vassal *sobas*' labor since the first vassalage agreements. The result was an intense review of the archives, as well as consultations on the matter with historians and other Crown officials. The *sobas*' plea was promptly accepted by the governor and attended to by the Royal Treasury Board of the Kingdom of Angola, and after it was approved by the King of Portugal, it resulted in the ordinance of October 1768, which regulated the wages of workers in the iron factories and the exemption from tribute of vassal *sobados*.[18] The document did not put an end to

---

[16] Starting in 1770, there was an increase in collections by the Royal Treasury, and the tithes from the *sertão* grew likewise. This was perhaps one of the results of Governor Sousa Coutinho's policies to reform Angola's economy. Nonetheless, the collection, when compared to the values from other parts of the Portuguese overseas dominions, was still quite modest. There were fertile lands, workers to till them, a dynamic trade, and the *arimos* had an average of 37.5 captives per unit. One possible explanation is that the structure of Angola's economy was based on the trade of enslaved people, with few sectors devoted to other activities. Maximiliano M. Menz, "Angola, o Império e o Atlântico," 14.

[17] Raphael Bluteau, *Vocabulário portuguez e latino*, 10 v. (Lisbon / Coimbra: Colégio da Cia. de Jesus, 1712–1728), entries "abuso" and "vexação".

[18] "Having the August Majesty Our Lord the King used his generous and royal mercy for the benefit of the miserable blacks employed in the iron factory, it was ordered that the wages they were to receive be established." Portaria assinada por FISC. São Paulo de Assunção de Luanda, October

the discussion about the compensation for African labor. In December 1770, a new ordinance determined that "all services [should be] paid to those who perform them, at the rates common in the land."¹⁹ The debate that started as a discussion of labor compensation for iron factory workers led to an entire investigation into how all forms of services rendered by the *sobas*' dependents in the Kingdom of Angola were performed and paid for. This bureaucratic undertaking was the result of a successful strategy by African leaders to protect their interests and to obtain and guarantee rights. At the same time, these legal decisions demonstrate that Portuguese authorities acknowledged their significant dependence on the local chiefs to carry out any enterprise in the colony. This relationship of dependence resulted from the chiefs' power over their subordinates.

In the 1770 ordinance, the first conclusion reached by royal officials was that the services that the *sobas* rendered free of charge to the Portuguese was not established as an obligation in the first vassalage agreements, as we saw in Chapter 1. We have already examined the normative side of the regulation of the labor of the *sobas*' dependents; we will now analyze its practical side. In other words, we will analyze how Portuguese authorities reached this conclusion and what can be said about the practical origins of co-opting the subjects of the vassal *sobas* for a variety of services.

In the "juridified" culture of the Old Regime, a set of norms guaranteed order, the common good, in short, the smooth operation of the social body, led by a just ruler.²⁰ Breaking the rules threatened the entire corporativist society, so transgressions had to be avoided. In theory, the king and his representatives should be the arbitrators of conflicts, reestablishing social balance through justice.²¹ These are the concepts that oriented Sousa Coutinho's reading when he judged the practice of co-opting the *sobas*' dependents to work free of charge as an abuse.

Catarina Madeira Santos interprets the tribute exemption for those *sobas* who sent workers to the iron factories as a result of Pombaline policies, since enlightened ideas enabled a "reconfiguration of the vassalage agreements." The author

---

29, 1768. IEB/USP, AL-083–138. The governor is referring to this ordinance, but dated November 5, 1768; perhaps there was a second publication.

19 Portaria em que se estabelecem os jornais dos "pretos trabalhadores", assinada por FISC. São Paulo de Assunção de Luanda, December 7, 1770. AHU_CU_001, Cx. 55, doc. 6 and 7.

20 Antonio Manuel Hespanha, *As vésperas do Leviatã. Instituições e poder político. Portugal, século XVII* (Coimbra: Almedina, 1994); Pedro Cardim, *Cortes e cultura política no Portugal do Antigo Regime* (Lisbon: Ed. Cosmos, 1998).

21 "The king exercises a 'trade' whose purpose is the common good, and which consists of justice and governance according to the law, respecting the communities' authority." Armando Luis de Carvalho Homem, "Dionisius et Alfonsus, Dei Gratia Reges et Communis Utulitatis Gratia Legiferi," *Separata da Revista da Faculdade de Letras*, II Série, Vol. XI (1994): 12.

argues that it was thanks to the enlightened gesture of going back to the archives "that a discussion on the type of services owed by the *sobas* to the administration took place."²²

What we have done so far is to demonstrate that the new policy regarding labor and the tribute exemption were actually initiated by the vassal *sobas*' "plea." The process therefore occurred in the opposite direction, determined by local conflicts more than by European ideas. The internal dynamics of African societies and the dependence on Ambundu labor to carry out the colonial plans of iron exploitation were more decisive than the Enlightenment. Broader imperial policies were related to local situations, in a context of claims and negotiations with the African elite in the Kingdom of Angola; the history of Ambundu labor in the iron factory is an example of this.

For the Royal Treasury provider Manuel Cunha e Sousa, the use of free labor of the *sobas*' subjects derived from the imposition of tributes at the "time of the conquest and the foundation of the fortress." He speculated that, at the moment of the *undamento*, the *sobas* promised to voluntarily "fulfill the said obligations, doing so with great satisfaction," so much so that he added, "from what I hear, they are willing to do anything." However, when he analyzed the available documents to draft his opinion—the vassalage agreements we discussed in Chapter 1 and the *undamentos* of the Duke of Wandu and of Ndembu Ambuíla (which he annexed to his opinion)—he did not find a "clear obligation to provide offspring, or vassals, for any services other than protecting the fortress and fortresses with their vassals and weapons."²³ Here, the provider refers to the support expected in times of war. The chiefs, after all, were not "willing to do anything." On the contrary, they were well aware of their obligations and did not tolerate abuses.

The provider expressed his "embarrassment" because, if the *sobas* had indeed been obliged in the vassalage agreements to provide free service to the colonists, the *ilamba* could not have been in the same situation and should therefore be "exempted or at least remunerated."²⁴ There was therefore a difference between the obligations of the *sobas* and those of the *ilamba*. In this respect, there is a disagree-

---

22 Catarina Madeira Santos. *Um governo "polido" para Angola. Reconfigurar dispositivos de domínio (1750– c. 1800)*, dissertation (PhD in History) (Lisbon: Faculdade de Ciências Sociais e Humanas da Universidade Nova de Lisboa, 2005), 322.
23 "Certain services performed by them in the neighboring fortresses, such as repairing the church, the fortress, the *capitão-mors*' homes, providing oil for the guard corps, assisting in the vicinity of the Kwanza [River], canoes and boats to transport the soldiers' uniforms to the fortresses." Informação do provedor da Fazenda Real do Reino de Angola, Manuel Pinto da Cunha e Sousa. São Paulo de Assunção, September 30, 1770. AHU_CU_001, Cx. 55, D. 6 and 7.
24 Idem.

ment between the governor and the provider: while the former said that there were specific services provided by the "*ilamba* and other destined peoples," the latter considered that, since they were allies, these "soldiers of the Crown" should not be obliged to provide further services. According to "Notícias do presídio de Ambaca," the *ilamba* and the *imbari* were engaged "exclusively in royal service, particularly in war."[25] Still, many *ilamba* and *imbari* sent workers to the iron factories, which demonstrates that they were subjected to the same "abuses" as the *sobas*, despite the false impression that, since they were "spies" and "captains in the Black War," they only benefited from the colonizers.

Finally, in 1770, the provider reached the same conclusion as Governor Sousa Coutinho: the cause of the injustices were the actions of the *capitães-mores* in the fortress, who, "degenerating in abuses against the Negroes," even took possession of work tools (hoes, nails) and exploited the *sobas*' subjects as their "slaves." The association with slavery was directly related to the gratuitousness of the service, since the workers provided firewood, coal, and "whatever else was required from them without even receiving food."[26] In fact, there were *sobas* who were appointed to serve the *capitão-mor*, literally, "for the personal service of *capitães-mores*," in their kitchen, or were simply required to "provide offspring for the service of the *capitães-mores*."

What the provider's opinion indicates is that there might have been a local custom that preceded the arrival of the Portuguese, and that the *capitães-mores* took advantage of that to obtain the free labor of the *sobados*' dependents. However, we have no information to prove the existence of such practice. The tribute system of the Kingdom of Ndongo involved the annual delivery of produce from the chiefdoms, which was called *luanda* and consisted of "many oxen and goats, chickens, and everything they have on their land." Beatrix Heintze comments that, in addition to cattle, there is reference in the seventeenth century to palm oil and enslaved people.[27] In the studies that examine the forms of payment of taxes in the Kingdom of Ndongo, there is no reference to the provision of services by the subjects of the *sobados* to the *ngola*. The people delivered to the *ngola*'s ambassadors were enslaved, as the *Livro dos Baculamentos* shows. There is no description of contingents of workers who left their *sobados* for a certain period of time to

---

25 Notícias do presídio de Ambaca, January 1798. IHGB/PADAB, DL 32.4.
26 Informação do provedor da Fazenda Real do Reino de Angola, Manuel Pinto da Cunha e Sousa. São Paulo de Assunção, September 30, 1770. AHU_CU_001, Cx. 55, D. 6 and 7.
27 Beatrix Heintze, *Fontes para a História de Angola do século XVII. Memórias, relações e outros manuscritos da coletânea documental de Fernão Sousa (1622–1635)* (Stuttgart: Steiner-Verlag-Wiesbaden-Gmbh, 1985), 207.

serve the *ngola*, except during war campaigns, but in this case, the purpose was obviously different.

However, in the system of masters derived from the conquest, we can find the first hints of the provision of services by the *sobas*. In addition to tributes in the form of various products, the Portuguese demanded enslaved people, and for "*ad hoc*, made up" reasons, as Beatrix Heintze says, the *sobas* were obliged to perform various tasks, "among them cultivating the fields, building houses, and serving as porters."[28] Thus, the obligation to work for free on the master's land was not established in any legislation. Cadornega also stated that, since the arrival of the first conquerors, the *sobas*' dependents served them "building their homes and in the fields," building fortresses and trenches.[29]

Therefore, based on Heintze's studies and our discussion in Chapter 1, and taking into account the new possibilities of understanding tribute payment based on *Livro dos Baculamentos*, we believe that, in short, the practice of employing the labor of the *sobas*' subjects was not set forth in the treaties established between the Ambundu chiefs and the representatives of the Portuguese Crown. After all, the royal authorities themselves admitted that the regulation of Ambundu labor was not a clause in the political treaties sealed during the Portuguese conquest. Rather, it was "invented" and probably, in the course of time, became seen as an "old custom," conveniently immemorial.[30]

According to the *undamentos* collected by the *capitães-mores*, the obligations of some *sobas* bound to Massangano are generic: they were to provide "offspring" for all services required. The expression "royal service," which indicated, in the vassalage agreements, the obligation to provide services of interest to the Portuguese monarch, meant that many chiefs were forced to send workers for a wide variety of services. In Muxima, the *undamento* agreement of the *soba* Ucusso Dom Manoel Domingos obliged him to make available "all his offspring, *sobetas*, and *imbari* to attend the work of the Royal Service." In this passage, the text refers to the expected support during wartime, which was one of the main clauses of vassalage. However, the passage allows for other interpretations, because it was made explicit that the *soba* should serve with his subjects in "any other task of the serv-

---

28 Beatrix Heintze, *Angola nos séculos XVI e XVII. Estudos sobre Fontes, Métodos e História* (Luanda: Kilombelombe, 2007), 262.
29 Antonio de Oliveira Cadornega, *História das Guerras Angolanas*, v. I, 45; v. II, 67.
30 Carlos Couto examines the issue in the chapter entitled "O trabalho forçado e gratuito, condenação do abuso e sua regularização pelo Reino," in Carlos Couto, *Os capitães-mores em Angola no século XVIII. Subsídio para o estudo da sua actuação* (Luanda: Instituto de Investigação Científica de Angola, 1972), 245–252.

ice."[31] Apparently, colonial authorities of the *sertão*, private individuals (settlers, merchants), missionaries, soldiers, and "travelers, deserters, and fugitives" took advantage of the vagueness of the expression "royal service" to exploit the populations under their dominion. Sousa Coutinho even uses the expression "personal labor"[32] for this category of service provided to private individuals, which was common in the *sertões* and was reproved by him.

It must be emphasized that African authorities were well aware that they were being "abused." For example, in 1732, the *soba* Kabuku Kambilu, Dom André, requested a resolution to put an end to the "abuses" committed by white men, traders of enslaved people, ivory, and wax, who forced him to provide porters and even "kept" some of them, without returning them to the *soba*. This was a reference to the enslavement of porters, which was a constant risk in the *sertões*.[33] The *soba* made this request because he knew that he had no obligation to carry the loads of private individuals, only those of "His Majesty."[34] There is no mention of payment; on the contrary, this was a case of *"teleco* porters," taken by force from the *soba*.

What fell under obligations for royal service? To put an end to confusion, in the ordinance of 1770, the governor legislated two types of service. "Royal services, more or less burdensome to the peoples, which either arose with the foundation of this kingdom or developed with the diversity of times" were the following:

> building churches and supporting missionaries in their various journeys, whether in the functions of their sacred ministries or in the process of regaining their health, because they must pay nothing and have no means to do so; and it is their right that those whom they serve

---

[31] Portaria em que se estabelecem os jornais dos "pretos trabalhadores," assinada por FISC. São Paulo de Assunção de Luanda, December 7, 1770. AHU_CU_001, Cx. 55, doc. 6 and 7.
[32] Idem.
[33] Mariana Candido analyzed the process of enslavement of porters and their vulnerability in the *sertões* in *An African Slaving Port and the Atlantic World*, 216 and 217. In the sources, the *capitão-mor*s are considered the major culprits for the injustices and abuses that the *sobas* complained about in the *sertões*. Silva Corrêa commented on this important labor force and the abuses committed against the porters: "The *sobas*' submission to the *capitão-mor* makes them dependent. The wet and dry goods traded around the continent are deposited on the shoulders of native porters. Each trader requires a certain number of porters. The *capitão-mor* is obliged to provide them for the benefit of commerce, but their ambition is such that they have gone as far as selling them under the guise of an honest transaction; what I mean is that, in the face of a shortage of porters, he is rewarded in advance to obtain them, without whose services the goods would be stalled, without reaching the markets of destination." Elias Alexandre da Silva Correa, *História de Angola*, v. 1, 37.
[34] Requerimento de Kabuku Kambilu, *soba* da jurisdição de Cambambe. Cambambe, June 4, 1732. AHU_CU_001, Cx. 29, D. 2806.

should serve them as well; building fortresses, the homes of overseers and *capitães-mores*, and public prisons; [providing] oil for the guard corps, drivers, or couriers of letters either for this government or for the potentates of the *sertão*; providing the porters necessary for expeditions of the troops and those of justice when the guilty cannot pay for their faults; straw and corn for the horses.[35]

The other category of services were those that "grew arbitrarily" and did not have a "just" origin:

the capital's major works with workers from afar and without the necessary food; new facilities built for free by distant people who had no interest in their beginning or end; the almost free labor in mines; the hoes taken from the *sobas* to be employed in royal works; other unpaid goods taken by force; the plunder committed by the *capitães-mores*; the barbarity of the soldiers and the iniquity of the *sertanejos*.[36]

Among the second type, Sousa Coutinho did not include those services considered "personal labor" mentioned above, because he said that they were already abolished and those who practiced them had been severely punished.

In any case, this description encompasses a wide range of tasks that until then were performed by the "offspring" of African chiefs without any compensation: construction work in the capital, in mines, in royal works, providing tools and "other goods not paid for and taken by force." The ordinance established that all of these services should now be compulsorily remunerated, whether by the Royal Treasury, by private individuals, or by the Reverend Chapter.

Moreover, the royal or military officials who served in the interior enjoyed significant autonomy from the government of Luanda due to the difficulties of the *sertões*, which did not allow frequent inspection. They could act according to their own interests, collecting excessive amounts of tributes, in tithes, for example, and employing the free labor of the *sobas*' subjects. On the other hand, the vassalage relationship ended up being a way of guaranteeing that the local authorities could denounce abuses, even forcing a *capitão-mor* to be tried for his inappropriate conduct. Roquinaldo Ferreira argues that we should think of these alliances between Portuguese and African leaders in the larger context of the "commercial and diplomatic geopolitics" of Luanda's hinterland. For the Portuguese, these ties

---

35 Portaria em que se estabelecem os jornais dos "pretos trabalhadores," assinada por FISC. São Paulo de Assunção de Luanda, December 7, 1770. AHU_CU_001, Cx. 55, doc. 6 and 7. The governor also mentions the Axiluanda, the residents of the island of Luanda, who were employed at sea and on land in return for meager wages. They were sentenced to a sort of "perpetual slavery" for having allied themselves with the Dutch during the Dutch invasion in the seventeenth century.
36 Idem.

were essential to maintain the colony's security and to strengthen trade; for that reason, the treaties had to be respected.[37]

The *sobas* knew that they could claim vassal status even if the reality of vassalage imposed on them abuses and vexations against which they could do little. When, in 1767, the *sobas* who sent their subjects to work in the iron factory requested to be "compensated for their labor with the exemption from paying tithes," they had in mind all of these actions by the *capitães-mores* and *dizimeiros*, who constantly invaded their towns and charged excessive tributes, "a violence done to them by the collectors."[38] So much so, that Africans who worked in other services promptly requested a tax exemption as well.[39]

The demands of the local chiefs led to that investigation in the Luanda and fortress archives, as well as consultations with historians and high-ranking officials in the administrative and political organization. Beyond the ordinance that regulated "black worker" wages, the result of this "investigation" was the acknowledgment by colonial authorities of how little they knew about the history of the Portuguese presence in Angola and the forms of recruitment and control of African labor, which to a large extent was in the hands of private individuals and the less distinguished authorities of the *sertões*, especially the *capitães-mores*. In order to correct this behavior, the governor and other leaders of the Kingdom of Angola devised new mechanisms to exercise greater control over labor relations.

It is worth remembering once again that employing the labor of the subjects of the vassal *sobas* was a general practice. Holding the *capitães-mores* responsible was only a way to distance themselves from the blame that fell upon them.

One example of the attempt to attain greater dominion over the dependents of the vassal *sobas* are the inventories elaborated by the officers of the iron factories, which describe the local leaders who provided workers for the factories; the number of "offspring able to work," i.e. how many people available for work the *sobas*, *ilamba*, and *imbari* claimed to have; how many of those people had been sent per month; the value of the tithes in products or salt stones from which they would be

---

37 Roquinaldo Ferreira, *Cross-Cultural Exchange in the Atlantic World*, 42.
38 Cópia do Termo da Junta da Fazenda Real do Reino de Angola assinado por Manuel da Cunha e Sousa, ouvidor e provedor da Fazenda Real, João Delgado Xavier, juiz de fora e procurador da Fazenda Real e Francisco Inocêncio de Sousa Coutinho (FISC), governador e presidente da Junta da Fazenda Real. São Paulo de Assunção de Luanda, June 20, 1767. The agreement is attached to Carta de FISC, para Francisco Xavier de Mendonça Furtado, secretário do Conselho Ultramarino. São Paulo de Assunção, August 22, 1768. AHU_CU_001, Cx. 52, D. 27.
39 The workers of the "Luz de Teles" *arimos* also wanted a tithe exemption. Carta de FISC para Antonio Anselmo Duarte de Siqueira, intendente da fábrica de ferro. São Paulo de Assunção de Luanda, July 18, 1768. IEB/USP, AL-083–098.

exempted; as well as the value of the tithes in réis (see Attachment 4). This information was needed by the governor in order to calculate the tithe exemption. Thus, for example, it was established that Ngongue a Kamukala Antonio Pedro, having declared that he had 250 "able offspring," would provide 42 of those dependents to work in the factory.

Although some of the inventories are not dated, cross-referencing the sources reveals that they were elaborated between 1768 and 1770.[40] The list with the largest number of vassal authorities and workers shows a total of 3,716 "able" workers, 538 of which were sent per months to work at the factory. This inventory corresponded to only a third of those "able for work" available in the *sobados*, because the factory officers were not to overburden the *sobados*, taking from them the labor necessary for the development of agriculture and, in the case of blacksmiths and smelters, for the production of neck shackles and chains to supply the trade of enslaved people and agricultural tools. This means that, under the rule of 67 chiefdoms in the region—65 from Golungo and two from Ambaca[41]—, there were at least 11,148 subordinates considered "able" to work, as inventoried by the *sobas* themselves. This survey is the most complete because it was probably elaborated by the *capitães-mores* and intendants in response to the governor's orders to inventory what the *sobados* near the factories could provide in terms of labor. Even if initially all of these leaders collaborated with the colonial project, there is evidence that this partnership did not persist over time.

There is no mention of what was meant by "able for work." We know that the "servants who transported materials" in the royal works were women[42]; therefore, it was probably no different in the iron factories, and women carried rocks, perhaps raw iron ore, and performed other services. With the demand for young men for the transatlantic trade, it is possible that any child, old man, or woman able to work was included in the list. It is worth emphasizing the colonial efforts

---

[40] We conclude that the inventories and maps are from this period because there is indication in the letters exchanged between the governor of Angola and the factories' intendants that these documents were sent or received. For example, in July 1768, the intendant Antonio Anselmo Duarte said that, attached to his letter to the governor, was the inventory of the *sobas*: "Attached is the assessment requested by Your Excellency and the letter, which has been recorded, and with it I enclose the inventory of the *sobas*, the number of people they provide (...)." Carta de Antonio Anselmo Duarte, intendente geral das reais fábricas de ferro, para FISC. Nova Oeiras, June 24, 1768. IEB/USP, AL-083–100.

[41] Ambaca was further away from Nova Oeiras, although there were many smelters and blacksmiths working there.

[42] "(...) the servants who transport materials, a service that is usually performed by women." Carta de Antonio de Vasconcelos, governador de Angola, para Sebastião José de Carvalho e Melo, conde de Oeiras. São Paulo de Assunção de Luanda, May 14, 1760. AHU_CU_001, Cx. 46, D. 4261.

to portray as "fair" a practice that until recently had been considered an "abuse." After all, the payment of wages for all services and the tribute exemption only served to legitimize work under the same precarious conditions as usual, but regulated. The working conditions in the iron factory support this argument.

This is very important because, by correcting an abuse in the legal terms of the time, colonial agents created new mechanisms to exploit the labor of free Africans: in this case, "constrained"[43] labor with a tribute exemption. Thus, Ambundu workers in Nova Oeiras were bound by rules of a different type of coercion than slavery. The *sobas*' subjects were "constrained" to work because of the exemption from paying the tithe. They were not considered enslaved; for royal authorities, the counterpart of payment was the guarantee that no enslaved labor was employed. The word *constrangido* (constrained) seems to us a good definition for the period, because it incorporates the idea of hierarchical relations and dependence that structured both societies in the modern era—the European society of the Old Regime and the Ambundu society with its political mechanisms based on kinship. At the same time, the term reinforces the coercion inherent in the process, because it introduces the notion of coercion, the idea that someone was "coerced by force or necessity" into a compulsory labor relationship.[44]

That said, let us return to the analysis of the "inventories of able offspring." In another list from the same period, dated 1768, the general intendant of the iron factories listed only 15 local leaders who served the factories with their subjects —a much smaller number than the 67 *sobas, ilamba,* and *imbari* listed before. The able offspring of these 15 leaders totaled 1,913, 273 of whom were sent per month.[45] There are also authorities listed from other jurisdictions, Cambambe and Massangano. For Golungo, only six *sobas* from the previous survey are listed, but the number of workers, both "able" and sent, decreased for all of them. While

---

[43] FISC distinguished those "constrained" from those who worked at the factory voluntarily: "To the Negroes (...) who work at the said factory voluntarily or constrained." Portaria assinada por FISC. São Paulo de Assunção de Luanda, October 29, 1768. IEB/USP, AL-083–138. Another example, when giving instructions on how to deal with soldiers who did not participate in agriculture as they should: "doing as I have so often told you, constraining those who do not work willingly and gladly." Carta de FISC para Antonio Anselmo Duarte de Siqueira. São Paulo de Assunção de Luanda, February 26, 1769. IEB/USP, AL-083–222.

[44] According to R. Bluteau, *constrangimento* (constraint) is defined as coercion; "to constrain" is to force someone, and being "constrained" is being "obliged by force or necessity." Raphael Bluteau, *Vocabulário portuguez e latino*, 10 v. (Lisbon / Coimbra: Colégio da Cia. de Jesus, 1712–1728).

[45] Carta de FISC para Antônio Anselmo Duarte de Siqueira, intendente geral das reais fábricas do ferro. Anexo: Inventário dos *sobas, ilamba* e *imbari* (São Paulo de Assunção, December 29, 1768). IHGB 126, PADAB DVD10,22 DSC00303.

in the previous list these leaders had 520 able offspring, in the 1768 list they only had 328; the number of subjects that should be sent dropped from 122 to 56. In Ambaca, the number of offspring to be sent was revised because of adjustments in the payment of tithes. As a result, the number increased—able offspring went from 460 to 600, while the number of people sent per month jumped from 120 to 180.

This mismatch between the lists becomes more evident when the numbers are compared with data from an undated document entitled "Mapa dos *sobas* e *ilamba* que se desanexam do serviço da fábrica por serem remissos em aprontarem seus filhos para o serviço dela"[46] (see Attachment 4.4). Thus of the 74 chiefs listed in the two previous lists, 37 from Golungo were "disincorporated" from factory service; with them, 344 able offspring and 80 workers sent per month were removed (according to the first list: 3,716 able offspring, 538 per month). The "disincorporated" *sobas* were again obliged to pay the tithe.

In 1773, José Francisco Pacheco, then work inspector at the Nova Oeiras factory, reported that only nine chiefdoms sent their subjects to the factory. They were chiefs from the district of Golungo (6), Ambaca (2), and Cambambe (1), who sent 310 dependents per month. Among them, only Mwata a Kamba from Golungo was not present in previous lists.[47] It is worth noting that, over time, from an initial list of 67 local leaders who contributed to the work in the factories, only nine remained. The reluctance of the local chiefs in sending workers is evident in that they sometimes collaborated and sometimes rebelled, disobeying royal orders. The factory intendants often complained of a shortage of workers. This attitude was not expected from a vassal, and as a result, the chiefs were punished in various ways. To cite one example, the *sobas* bound to the Massangano fortress were forced to pay a fine in salt stones for the time their subjects were absent from work. The *capitão-mor* charged them excessively, and was reprimanded and forced to return part of the payment.[48]

If we examine the documentation more closely, we can identify the local chiefs with the largest number of able dependents under their control, which indicates those who ruled over a large number of people. Since authority over a large population was what determined the power of an Ambundu leader, this documentation also provides an image of local socioeconomic and hierarchical differences.

---

[46] "Mapa dos *sobas* e *ilamba* que se desanexam do serviço da fábrica por serem remissos em aprontarem seus filhos para o serviço dela e devem de hoje em diante, pagar o dízimo pela nova regulação que se fez," n.d. ANTT, Condes de Linhares mç. 46, doc. 11.

[47] Carta de José Francisco Pacheco. Fábrica da Nova Oeiras, March 5, 1773. AHU_CU_001, Cx. 57, D. 28.

[48] Carta de FISC para Manoel de Abreu Aguiar, *capitão-mor* regente de Muxima. São Paulo de Assunção, January 21, 1772. AHA, Códice 80, fl. 48v-49.

Most of the chiefdoms—41 out of 67—had up to 15 able offspring for work, 14 had up to 50, six had from 50 to 80, and seven had from 150 to 1,000. It is likely that these seven authorities were the main ones in the region among the vassals of the Portuguese Crown at the time. Another conclusion derived from the analysis is that small chiefdoms were the most common in the region. As Vansina observed, this was the result of the political and economic breakdown experienced by the *sobados* over time as a result of colonial occupation and the demands of the transatlantic trade.[49]

The *soba* Mbangu kya Tambwa stands out from the rest, for he was the only one with 1,000 "able" dependents—as we have seen, an important *soba* for the maintenance of colonial domination, a long-time ally of the Portuguese. Mbangu had many artisans under his control—masons, carpenters, blacksmiths. The latter worked mainly on commission; the clients provided the iron and they created the objects, which were easily sold, since the *sobado* was near Luanda on one of the main trade routes. The Carmelite mission in their land may have favored this, since the priests encouraged training in mechanical trades. The governor repeatedly ordered the factory intendant to resort to this *soba* when needed, since he had "more offspring."[50]

After him, Ngola Kimbi and Kabuku Kambilu are reported to have a much smaller number of able offspring—400 each—, followed by Ngongue Embo Francisco Lourenço, Muzenze a Nzenza Felipe Antonio, and Kilombo kya Katubia Antonio, all of them with 300 subjects. Among the chiefdoms with the largest number of able dependents, there is also Kilamba Ngongue a Kamukala Antonio Pedro (owner of the iron mines where Novo Belém was built), with 250 offspring, and Mbumba Ndala Bento de Souza, with 150. With the exception of Ngola Kimbi, from Ambaca, and Kabuku Kambilu, from Cambambe, all the others were vassals of the Golungo district.

Among these names written in a Portuguese manner, Ambundu political titles stand out: *sobas* are identified as *ngola* and *ndala*, while others are titled *nzenza* (which can be read as an association to the Mbangala, as well as *kilombo*). *Kilamba*, as we saw earlier, referred to a military authority associated to the Portuguese.[51] If

---

[49] Jan Vansina, "Ambaca Society and the Slave Trade c. 1760–1845," 3.
[50] Carta de FISC para Antônio Anselmo Duarte de Siqueira, intendente geral das reais fábricas do ferro. São Paulo de Assunção, July 4, 1770. BNP, C 8742, F 6367.
[51] *Ndala* was a *Vunga* title introduced among the Ambundus by the *Hango* from Libolo: "the ancient Mbundu probably used the name Libolo only to refer to the regions south of the Kwanza River, where the Hango kings had their capitals. The Mbundu kingdoms were usually named after the titles of their kings, in this case the Hango. However, Libolo is the name used today by traditional Mbundu historians." There are cases similar to the *Ndala* south of the Kwanza River.

we leave aside the criterion of the chiefs with more able offspring, we see that a significant number of *ilamba* and *imbari*, the military agents of the Black War, strongly connected to the trade of enslaved people, were responsible for a significant number of workers. Therefore, it seems that other chieftaincies competed with the regional power of the *sobas*, as they controlled a considerable number of people in the region.[52]

A letter from the intendent of the Novo Belém factory dated December 1768 offers further insights into how the number of workers sent was related to local political/administrative factors.[53] The document is a response to the governor regarding the standards employed to determine the number of dependents that a *soba* should provide for royal service. For example, the *soba* Mbangu kya Tambwa, who had the largest number of able subjects (1,000), only provided 50 workers per month, while Kilamba Ngongue a Kamukala Antonio Pedro, who had 250 able offspring, provided 42. João Baines replied that the discrepancy between Mbangu kya Tambwa and the other chiefs was because the demand for labor in the Novo Belém factory was much smaller than that of the Nova Oeiras factory. To correct this error, once the two factories were united in Nova Oeiras in 1768, the *soba* would send 100 workers per month.

Actually, Mbangu kya Tambwa did not consider the collection of tithes fair because his ancestors had obtained an exemption from this tribute from Governor

---

In the case of *Nzenza*, Nzenza Ngombe is identified in seventeenth-century military chronicles as a Mbangala leader who was defeated by the Portuguese, subsequently becoming an important ally of colonial conquest. The term *Kilombo* is more complex and polysemic and has changed over time. It refers to a Mbangala association: "the original and primary meaning of the word used to designate a male association open to anyone regardless of lineage, whose members subjected themselves to impressive initiation rituals that removed them from the protective bosom of their native affiliation group and simultaneously created strong bonds among the initiates, as warriors in a regiment of supermen who became invulnerable to their enemies' weapons." Joseph C. Miller, *Poder político e parentesco: os antigos Estados Mbundu em Angola*, trans. Maria da Conceição Neto (Luanda: Arquivo Histórico Nacional de Angola, 1995), 90–94, 159–161, 214.

52 In addition, as Mariana Candido reminds us, the terms that designated the chiefs were used by Portuguese colonization to classify those who were presumably under its dominion: "the Portuguese explorers and administrators classified the leaders in the Central African region as *mani*, *dembo*, or *soba*, regardless of the political organization or linguistic group to which they belonged." Mariana Candido, "Jagas e *sobas* no 'Reino de Benguela': vassalagem e criação de novas categorias políticas e sociais no contexto da expansão portuguesa na África durante os séculos XVI e XVII," in Alexandre Vieira Ribeiro, Alexsander Lemos de Almeida Gebera, and Marina Berthet, *África: histórias conectadas* (Niterói: PPGHISTORIA-UFF, 2014), 66.

53 Carta de João Baines para FISC, intendente da fábrica de ferro de Novo Belém. São Paulo de Assunção, December 17, 1768. IEB/USP, AL-083–203.

Dom Lourenço Almada (1705–1709), because of the "mission they served."[54] The Mbangu resisted sending more workers because their ancestors had presumably been exempted by Governor Almada after performing a mission.

In the case of the two *sobas* of Ambaca, Ngola Kimbi and Kariata Kakavingi, the number of able dependents differed considerably: the former claimed to have 400, while the latter claimed 200. However, the number of workers sent was almost the same, 50 and 40 respectively. Moreover, both paid tributes worth the same amount—30$000 réis. According to Baines, this disparity is the result of a logic of tribute delivery, whereby the *sobas* observed "the method of their ancestors." Let me explain: for some unknown reason, the ascendant chiefs of these *sobados* were granted smaller tribute payments, as was Mbangu, and therefore provided fewer dependents for royal service. Ngola Kimbi and Kariata Kakavingi, as their descendants, demanded the same benefits.[55] Two *sobas* from Golungo— Ngongue Embo Francisco Lourenço and Muzenze a Nzenza Felipe Antonio—also followed to this precept, i.e. they claimed rights earned by their ancestors.

As we can see, the Ambundu political elite kept a careful record of their ancestors' conquests. The diplomatic strategy of following "the method of their ancestors" allowed them to maintain the rights conquered by the previous generations that first came into contact with the Portuguese (through vassalage and military conquest). This memory of conquered agreements and privilege allowed them to achieve greater autonomy.

João Baines did not merely increase the number of workers sent by Mbangu kya Tambwa per month. The intendent suggested that the only way to arrive at a fair number of workers sent per *sobado*, according to the colonizers' "rule of reason," was to count the *fogos* (families) in each of them. This implied that the local authorities should allow the royal officers to enter their villages and count the number of families and people fit for work. Evidently, this was not a desirable procedure for the *sobas*, since it would reveal the *sobados*' resources, how many people were available for work and for war, the number of subjects, and the number of people enslaved—i.e. information that would further subject them to colonial rule. In the case of Mbangu kya Tambwa, for example, the tithe collector Maximo Mathias Raposo Pimental counted the *sobado*'s families and charged 200 réis per family—a total of 300,400 réis (1,502 families). The other African authorities feared

---

54 Carta de João Baines para FISC. Town of Novo Belém, December 17, 1768. IEB/ AL-083–203.
55 "The first ancestors of the current states limited the tithe payment, and their successors continue doing likewise when they provide offspring, and that is the reason for the difference, because even if one has much power over his offspring and another has little, they want to follow their ancestors in terms of the regulations applied to them." Carta que João Baines escreveu para FISC. São Paulo de Assunção, December 17, 1768. IEB/USP, AL-083–203.

the same inventory, which demonstrates that they omitted the real number of able offspring they had.[56]

Baines wanted to replace the "method of the ancestors" that governed diplomatic relations between the *sobas* and royal officials with the "rule of reason." He thus wished to disregard the *sobados*' history and their prerogatives conquered in order to gain greater control over the populations of the *sertão*. This was obviously not well received by the *sobas*.

The measures proposed by João Baines express the interests of expanding and reaffirming the Portuguese presence in the interior of the Kingdom of Angola. In addition to listing the vassal *sobas*, their forms of service, and how many able dependents they had, the colonial administration defined the limits of the territory of the *sobados* that were exempted from paying tithes in exchange for labor in the iron factories. The instructions issued by the Overseas Council determined that the *sobas* chosen to serve in the factories should have a wooden sign in their lands "in which an R is engraved with fire on the top, with the letters N. P. D. below, which mean *Não Paga Dízimo* [Does Not Pay Tribute], and below that, provides so many men per month for factory service."[57] This resolution implied a change in the relationship of Ambundu chiefs to the land, which, as we discussed earlier, neither was fixed nor had easily defined borders. Displacements in search of better lands or because of droughts, wars, or floods, were a common local practice. Delimiting the *sobados* was one more attempt to expand the colonial influence and dominion over the lands and people ruled by Ambundu authorities.

The establishment of the iron factories is an expression of attempts to exert greater control over the *sobados* and their offspring. The royal agents counted the "offspring able to work" and the number of residents of the *sobados*, disregarded privileges obtained by the *sobas*' lineages, and demarcated the lands to prevent the *sobados*' itinerancy, which in turn ensured an uninterrupted supply of workers for colonial enterprises.

However, their dominion extended beyond the vassal *sobas* listed in the inventories. Ambundu workers in the factories did not come only from the *sobados* in the region. There are also records of people sent from nearby *arimos*, for example, from the Luz de Teles *arimo*. In this case, they received wages, but did not benefit

---

[56] "Because they somehow seek relief, which they are doing with Mbangu kya Tambwa in Ambaca and other parts." Idem.

[57] Carta de FISC para Joaquim de Bessa, tenente regente da Real Fábrica de Ferro. São Paulo de Assunção, August 16, 1770. BNP, C 8744, F6443. This description is from 1770, but the order of the Overseas Council to have the *sobados* demarcated is from April 1768. AHU, Códice 472, fl. 150–153.

from a tribute exemption, despite having requested it.[58] Specific tasks, such as brick production, were performed by "Negroes from forlorn *arimos*."[59] It is likely that unemployed people in general were coerced to work in the factories.

There is also evidence that there were "freed Negroes taken from the slave houses of white people."[60] The major captain of Cambambe said that he could only "prepare" from 67 to 100 "Negroes from the *sobas*" to send to Nova Oeiras. Included in these numbers were workers taken from slave houses of white settlers. This information is interesting because, in spite of Sousa Coutinho's many attempts to weaken the *capitães-mores*' authority, they continued to be the ones pressuring African leaders to provide "offspring," obtaining labor in the jurisdiction of their fortress or district, including from settlers.

This citation also reminds us of the enlistment of "people of arms," which settlers, *sobas*, *ilamba*, and *imbari* were obliged to provide in times of war, and once again demonstrates the role of *capitães-mores* as the most important royal authorities in terms of the relations between African chiefdoms and the colonial administration. Apparently, colonial authorities resorted to the same mechanism as military conscription to recruit workers. In war, "each [*capitão-mor*] calculate[d], from the number of *sobados*, what each *soba* should provide, without, however, depleting the forces of their states."[61] As with enlistment, the *capitão-mor* employed to the settlers' dependents as labor force when necessary. The dependents were not paid for participating in war because their cooperation was an obligation as vassals. What did serve as an attraction were the profits from the spoils of war. We believe that the military experience may have contributed to the dependents' free employment, reinforcing the invention of an "immemorial custom."

As we have seen, the main change introduced by the labor regulation ordinances of 1770 was related to wages. For example, when Sousa Coutinho requested that a fortress prison be repaired, he ordered the intendant to send "Negroes (...) be-

---

[58] Carta de FISC para Antonio Anselmo Duarte, intendente geral das reais fábricas de ferro. São Paulo de Assunção, July 18, 1768. IEB, USP, AL-083–098.

[59] Carta de FISC para Antonio Anselmo Duarte, intendente geral das reais fábricas de ferro. São Paulo de Assunção, June 15, 1768. IEB, USP, AL-083–070.

[60] Carta de FISC para Francisco Xavier de Mendonça Furtado, secretário de Estado da Marinha e Ultramar. São Paulo de Assunção, November 15, 1768. AUH_CU_001, Cx. 52, D. 68.

[61] Elias Alexandre da Silva Correa, *História de Angola* (Lisbon: Clássicos da Expansão Portuguesa no Mundo. Império Africano, 1937), v. II, p. 49 and 50. On the recruitment of people for the Black War, see: Roquinaldo Ferreira, *Transforming Atlantic Slaving. Trade, Warfare and Territorial Control in Angola, 1650–1800*, dissertation (PhD) (University of California, Los Angeles, 2003), 174–176; Ariane Carvalho da Cruz, *Militares e militarização no Reino de Angola: patentes, guerra, comércio e vassalagem (segunda metade do século XVIII)*, thesis (Master's) (Universidade Federal Rural do Rio de Janeiro, 2014), 105 and 106.

longing" to that jurisdiction, with the only condition that they should be "promptly paid."[62] The payment of wages and the way in which the *sobados*' dependents should be treated was another element that caused conflicts in Angola's interior. The workers from *sobados* exempt from paying tribute should also receive wages, albeit much more modest than the others—the fact that the *sobas* were exempt from paying the tithe did not imply that their subjects should work for free.[63]

This administrative gesture to better control lands and people, demarcating the tithes, was not devoid of tensions. Since the first experiences with the iron mines in the region, the governor had ordered that Africans be paid modest wages, as long as they did not overburden the Royal Treasury, and that they be calculated in accordance to the wages received by laborers of public works in Luanda. According to him, wages were needed to "attract" Africans to the factories, thus making the settlements in the *sertão* "flourish."[64] The fact is that, without the Ambundus, Sousa Coutinho's audacious plans were impossible. The insistence on paying wages and the idea of employing free people who were not subjected to mistreatment had to do with Sousa Coutinho's experience observing previous attempts to recruit Ambundus forcibly for colonial projects. This concrete fact of the colonial situation was more important than any enlightened ideas.

The governor specifically stated that it was necessary to avoid the "means employed to assist work in Lombige," i.e. the search for gold mines in the region.[65] In Lombige, an impressive total of 170,400 people were recruited in two and a half years to pan in search of gold and to accomplish "other necessary things."[66] The

---

62 Carta de FISC para Joaquim de Bessa Teixeira, intendente da fábrica de ferro. São Paulo de Assunção de Luanda, May 22, 1772. AHA, Códice 80, s. fl.
63 "(...) because if they work every day they cannot be paid with the tithe, and must receive a wage." Carta de FISC para Antonio Anselmo Duarte, intendente geral das fábricas de ferro. São Paulo de Assunção, June 15, 1768. IEB, USP, AL-083–070.
64 In a letter to João Baines, lieutenant general and intendant of the iron factory of Novo Belém, FISC said: "Your Grace must avoid the use of force as much as possible, so that the Negroes who are paid modest wages up the amount paid to workers in this city can not only live happy and satisfied to earn a living in their own place of residence, but that their joy may attract other dispersed Negroes, so that instead of abandoning their villages due to the customary violence in this *sertão*, those villages can be the most flourishing and populated in it." Carta de FISC para João Baines, tenente general. São Paulo de Assunção de Luanda, March 8, 1766. BNP, C – 8742, F – 6364.
65 Idem.
66 The number is surprising, but it is what was recorded by the document's author; remembering that they resorted to a partial recruiting regime, it represents the number of people who worked there for two years, but not necessarily at the same time. Carta de Antonio de Vasconcelos, governador de Angola, para Tomé Joaquim da Costa Corte Real. São Paulo de Assunção, January 6, 1759. SGL, *Arquivo das colônias*, v. V, no. 30 (1930): 148. There is no archive reference to the document in the transcription. But whoever transcribed it noted the following: "This document was in the pos-

number was calculated by the six miners who worked there; the laborers worked in a relay system similar to that in place in the iron mines.

Furthermore, the then governor Antonio de Vasconcelos stated that the "camp" of the expedition that mined the gold "never had less than 500 or 400" workers. The "vexations" against the local populations were so serious that "the hunger they suffered was great, especially among the Negroes, for they only received three sacks of flour and a third of a sack of beans per month per thirty people." With that little food, the workers labored long hours for more than six days. This led to many deaths and escapes, which were punished by the soldiers who persecuted the fugitives, "mistreating and driving everything away." This was the historical experience of labor exploitation in the mines remembered by the royal officials as well as the *sobas* and their dependents. Sousa Coutinho understood that he had to dissociate his great enterprise from any reference to the gold exploitation that took place in a region that was very close to where the iron factories were established, since Lombige was adjacent to the lands of Mbangu kya Tambwa in Golungo. For that reason, according to him, the person responsible for the factory should avoid the violence exerted in that episode and employ a "softer method" of treating workers instead.

To have an idea of how that number of workers was an enormous amount of people, at the height of gold mining in Minas Gerais, the approximate average of enslaved people in the region was 100,000.[67] Obviously, that number does not represent exclusively those captives who worked in mining. Today we know for certain that there was a wide variety of economic activities in that mining region throughout the eighteenth century. Therefore, some of the enslaved performed urban services or engaged in commercial and agricultural activities. Therefore, in comparison, the number of Ambundus working in Lombige is immense.

The *capitães-mores* were ordered to "force" all *ndembu* and *sobas* "of every district they encounter[ed]" to provide the "Negroes they need[ed]."[68] It is hard to know whether those people were enslaved or were there like the workers of the

---

session of the Marquis of Sá da Bandeira for his studies on Angola, perhaps when he was compiling elements for his Map of Angola." I imagine that Sá da Bandeira also used this document to develop his argument on the extinction of forced recruitment of porters.

67 Historians have not reached a definitive number for the enslaved population in Minas Gerais in the eighteenth century, due to difficulties with documentation. It was only after 1776 that colonial authorities started to order inventories of all segments of the population. Therefore, the number 100,000 is only an estimate. Douglas Cole Libby, "As populações escravizadas das Minas Setecentistas: um balanço preliminar," in Maria Efigênia Lage de Resende and Luiz Carlos Villalta (org.), *História de Minas Gerais. As Minas Setecentistas* (Belo Horizonte: Autêntica, 2007), v. 1, 407–439.

68 Carta de Antonio de Vasconcelos, governador de Angola, para Tomé Joaquim da Costa Corte Real. São Paulo de Assunção, January 6, 1759. SGL, *Arquivo das colônias* V, no. 30 (1930): 148.

iron mine—co-opted or coerced with the justification of a presumably "immemorial custom" of employing the free labor or the *sobas*' dependents. It is possible that such a large number of workers was made up of both enslaved people and free Ambundus, coerced "offspring." The governor of Angola said that it became necessary to put an end to gold mining in Lombige both because of the "soldiers' excesses" and the "abandonment of the lands, due to the natives' fear of been forced to work."[69] We can therefore assert that African labor was greatly employed in the mines of the Kingdom of Angola, which was not only a trading post where Africans were enslaved and sent to the gold mines on the other side of the Atlantic Ocean—it was a colony where local workers were greatly exploited.

In the instructions given to the intendant Antonio Anselmo Duarte in January 1767, the governor associated the good treatment of Ambundus to the factory's success, stating that the bases of any work could not be endured if they were "put together with blood and tears." For that reason, he had to do "eradicate all violence and tyranny of which there were such ill-fated examples in times past, ordering that the Negroes be very well paid and treated."[70] From his predecessors' experience, Sousa Coutinho understood that abuse was not the best way to maintain an enterprise such as he intended to carry out—in a place to which people had to be sent to create a settlement, with a climate that "swallowed people," in a conquest where the colonists' access to land was always mediated by the *sobas* and other local authorities.[71]

He believed in indirect means of persuasion: wages, for example, which were not part of the local logics of employment of the labor of the *sobas*' subjects. This made no sense to *capitães-mores*, private individuals, or merchants, who for centuries had taken advantage of the autonomy of the *sertões* to commit abuses, demanding free labor; nor did it make sense to the *sobas* and *makota*, who were served by and received taxes from their subjects because they were owed loyalty and obligations based on the logics of kinship and relations of dependence.

---

69 Idem. These workers also seem to have been remunerated in plantations, but the payment did not compensate the precarious working conditions. In 1756, 300$000 réis were spent in plantations on the "payment of workers in the mines." Carta de Antonio Álvares da Cunha, governador de Angola. São Paulo de Assunção de Luanda, January 22, 1756. AHU_CU_001, Cx. 40, D. 72.
70 "Instrução que deve guardar Antonio Anselmo Duarte de Siqueira, servindo o emprego de intendente geral da fábrica do ferro, e que executarão também os capitães-mores, como intendentes particulares na parte que lhes é respectiva" (FISC). São Paulo de Assunção de Luanda, January 12, 1767. AHU_CU_001, Cx. 52, D. 73.
71 Carta de FISC para João de Meneses, *capitão-mor* de Muxima. São Paulo de Assunção, February 6, 1768. AHA, Códice 79.

The governor believed that it was necessary to change the "Negroes' character," turning them into "active workers," but "without scaring them."[72] For that reason, Sousa Coutinho determined that working conditions should be rigorously observed. The iron bars should not be carried on the backs of the Ambundus, but of donkeys he had sent from Brazil; the punishment for failing to work should be a discount in wages and "not beatings under any circumstance"; they were also allowed "half an hour for lunch and two for dinner," at the most appropriate times to "escape from the sun."[73] In addition, the *sobas* should send a third of the workers they had to ensure that every worker served only four months per year in the factories.[74] This instruction also responded to the concern that there be enough workers in the *sobados* for agriculture.[75]

It was also decided that a sort of "time book" be used, where worker absences were recorded. From this book, "at the end of the month, the clerk" would elaborate lists specifying the monthly wages to be paid to the workers. In addition, the workers were inspected three times a day—"all workers [were] inspected in the morning, during dinner, and in the evening."[76]

As we said in Chapter 2, concentrating the workers in a controlled work environment compromised the technical control over the labor process, the productivity, and the commercialization of products that outside the factory were still determined by the workers.[77] Commenting on the organization of labor in the colonies, Edgar de Decca sheds light on the issue: "discipline, order, and hierarchy were el-

---

[72] "Instrução que deve guardar Antonio Anselmo Duarte de Siqueira, servindo o emprego de intendente geral da fábrica do ferro, e que executarão também os capitães-mores, como intendentes particulares na parte que lhes é respectiva" (FISC). São Paulo de Assunção de Luanda, January 12, 1767. AHU_CU_001, Cx. 52, D. 73.

[73] Carta de FISC para Francisco Xavier de Mendonça Furtado, secretário de Estado da Marinha e Ultramar. São Paulo de Assunção de Luanda, October 29, 1768. AHU_CU_001, Caixa 52, D. 48.

[74] Carta de FISC para Antonio Anselmo Duarte, intendente geral das fábricas de ferro. São Paulo de Assunção, July 29, 1768. IEB, USP, AL-083–090. "(...) I command the establishment of a standard load for distant work and the construction of the corresponding number of roads, whether from the iron mountains or the charcoal works to the factory, which are common to all." Portaria estabelecendo os jornais dos trabalhadores da Fábrica de Ferro de Nova Oeiras. São Paulo de Assunção, October 20, 1768. IEB, USP, AL-083–138.

[75] "(...) always providing the third of the offspring they have to work during those months, so that the other two [thirds] can rest and cultivate the land in the proper seasons." Portaria estabelecendo os jornais dos trabalhadores da Fábrica de Ferro de Nova Oeiras. São Paulo de Assunção, October 20, 1768. IEB, USP, AL-083–138.

[76] Portaria estabelecendo os jornais dos trabalhadores da Fábrica de Ferro de Nova Oeiras. São Paulo de Assunção, October 20, 1768. IEB, USP, AL-083–138.

[77] Edgar Salvadori de Decca, *O nascimento das fábricas* (São Paulo: Editora Brasiliense, 1982), 43 and ff.

ements that were always present during the entire period of colonial production (...)." In other words, the social organization of labor in the factory was necessary not in response to a technological requirement. What was at stake was increasing profits, and to that end, colonial exploitation made use of "disciplinary control" to ensure productivity.[78]

The "time book," the hierarchy in the administration and between specialized and unqualified workers (as well as between Europeans and Africans, free, coerced to work, and enslaved), the discipline, surveillance, the punishments, and the increase in working hours, speed and the pace of work were means to try to exert that control. It was not by chance that this new attempt at establishing a new organization of labor in Angola's *sertões* led to many forms of resistance.

Work oversight and inspections also served to keep records used to pay wages and to avoid the theft of tools or even iron, which was a common currency in the *sertões*. Workers were paid for the days they traveled to the factory and back.[79] The wages were established as follows:

> Negroes from territories exempt from the tithe will be paid according to the days of effective labor at a rate equal to the daily wages paid in this city, 60 réis per day in textiles, salt, and supplies, receiving per month, within the scope of these wages, at least half an *exeque* of flour, *massa mbala* [sorghum], or beans, because otherwise they would starve to death.[80]

Wages were therefore paid in the form of subsistence goods: salt, flour, beans, fish, but also textiles. Among the expenses incurred with worker wages calculated by Antonio de Lencastre from 1766 to 1773,[81] not counting the expenses with the smelters contracted by the Biscayan governor, who received a daily wage of 2$400 réis, the enterprise's greatest expenditures were with common wages, i.e. with unqualified workers, as we can see in the graph bellow:

---

78 Idem, 43 and 53.
79 "(...) Your Grace shall order to count and pay the Negroes called to work at this Factory for the days of effective work and those required to travel back and forth, but not for days spent in laziness, only thus required to travel to the factory and back like any diligent man would, and to that end Your Grace shall make a list of the travel days required for each of the villages that are obliged to provide workers for the factory according to the tithe regulation, in order to fairly and wisely count the travel days in both directions, and pay them accordingly." Carta de FISC para Joaquim de Bessa Teixeira, tenente regente da real fábrica de ferro. São Paulo de Assunção, September 22, 1770. BNP, C 8744, F6443.
80 Carta de FISC para Francisco Xavier de Mendonça Furtado, secretário de estado da marinha e ultramar. São Paulo de Assunção, November 28, 1768. AHU_CU_001, Caixa 52, D. 44.
81 Conta da despesa feita com a construção da fábrica de ferro de Nova Oeiras desde o primeiro de janeiro de 1766 a março de 1773. AHU_CU_001, Cx. 57, Doc. 28.

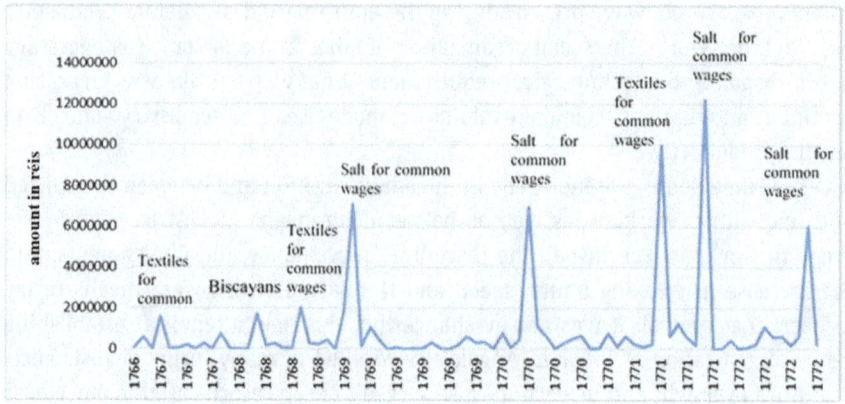

Graph 1: Factory expenses (1766–1772).
Source: Accounts of expenses with the construction of the Nova Oeiras iron factory from January 1, 1766 to March 1773. AHU_CU_001, Cx. 57, Doc. 28.

The highest points in the graph correspond to the period during which rocks were extracted for the construction and the repairs to the Luinha River weir, from 1770 to 1771, which required a great deal of labor. With those expenses, we can calculate approximately how many laborers worked in the factory. For example, in this "peak" in 1771, expenses totaled 12:232$327 réis (in salt) only with common wages. If we consider that the factory remained two months without operating due to accidents, rains, and fires, we have 300 workdays. Each worker received at least $60 réis per day; therefore, about 600 "common" workers may have really worked per day cleaning the area, gathering rocks for construction and ore for the foundry, tilling the land, and constructing all the buildings for the factory and the town.

Carpenters, blacksmiths, and masons were paid in cash. At earlier times, they were sometimes paid in goods or *beirames* (Indian textiles). There is no distinction between Ambundus, Luso-Africans, Europeans (other than the Biscayans), or Brazilians in these lists. However, other documents demonstrate that differences did exist. In Attachment 3, where we list all the mechanical officers sent to Nova Oeiras, exiled convicts were to be paid "according to their merits"; some artisans negotiated their wages beforehand (for example, $600 réis per day); Basques were the best paid. On the other hand, the Ambundu blacksmiths who worked at the "Casa de Fundição dos Pretos" received from $80 réis to a maximum of one *vintém* per day.[82] This demonstrates how "modest" the wages were for Africans in comparison to those of the technicians of other origins.

In addition to the expenses with wages, there were significant expenditures with drivers, caravans, and canoes, which once again proves that nothing was done without porters. In Nova Oeiras, they were apparently paid. The pharmacy also generated expenses (medicines and wages for the pharmacist and the bloodletter), since the workers, especially Europeans, tended to get sick often. There were also expenses purchasing tools (mostly anvils) and unspecified supplies, as well the annual wages of the intendant, the clerk, and the work inspector. The only expense with materials was "making lime" and "wages for making lime," which was produced in a factory in Massangano. Otherwise, the region's natural resources provided everything.

These norms were not entirely consistent; contradictions existed. The factories' intendants and the *capitães-mores* could seek "Negroes from other territories who, voluntarily or coerced, went to work in the said factory and received eighty réis."[83] These voyages in search of workers lasted up to eight days, which demonstrates that people at greater distances were also forced to work there. The passage reveals the contradictions of the enlightened pragmatism that permeated colonial plans. In principle, abuses were combatted, but in practice, those who did not accept going to the factory voluntarily could be "coerced," i.e. forcefully engaged by factory officials. This is more evident in another passage where it is established that worker recruitment should be done "willingly whenever possible, and, in the spirit of profit, forcefully only as a last result, when persuasion bears no fruits."[84] What we are emphasizing here is that coercion in worker recruitment was therefore permitted in the norms of colonial administration, even if only in extreme cases.

3.2 Disputes, Resistance, and Violence in the Sertão

The factory had a minimal hierarchical and fiscal structure: intendant, clerk, treasurer, and inspector or construction superintendent. The positions were mostly held by military officers, *capitães-mores*, and *sertanejos* who had stood out in prior mis-

---

[82] Carta de José Francisco Pacheco. Fábrica da Nova Oeiras, March 5, 1773. AHU_CU_001, Cx. 57, D. 28. At first, before the ordinances to regulate wages, the governor established the amount of 2$400 réis per quintal of iron produced, paid to the blacksmiths and smelters in textiles.
[83] Portaria assinada por FISC. São Paulo de Assunção de Luanda, October 29, 1768. IEB/USP, AL-083–138.
[84] Idem.

sions and demonstrated some experience and knowledge of the territory, the climate, and the local customs, since most royal officials in Angola were Africans and Luso-Africans. These officials were in charge of controlling the factory's internal activities and carrying out the governor's orders, which were issued almost 200 kilometers away from the factories' location.

However, the sources indicate that what happened in the factory buildings differed in many ways from colonial plans. Perhaps for that reason, the governor took a different stance when he suggested that the work be performed by 200 enslaved couples.[85] Sousa Coutinho asserted that it was easier to attain his objectives with enslaved people, for they were "more comfortable and constant." This model is entirely contrary to the ideal of a white settlement with European customs, founded on "well paid and well treated" Ambundu labor.

The governor's reference for the idea of employing enslaved workers in the foundries was a factory established by the French in Mauritius in the same period as Nova Oeiras: the smithies of *Mon Désir* (1752–1772), an undertaking that employed up to 790 enslaved people. The French factory had a blast furnace that produced close to eight tons of iron per week (Nova Oeiras produced around two tons per month). The governor believed that, by employing enslaved workers, Nova Oeiras would obtain large profits, since such workers were available at a lower cost in Angola than the directors of *Mon Désir* paid for them in Mauritius.[86]

The first aspect to be considered was the great instability and dispute over Ambundu labor caused or, rather, made more evident by the factories. Vansina comments on the context of fierce competition between the *sobas*, *ilamba*, *imbari*, and settlers, who were often rich patrons and officials of the Crown, over the wealth and the "peoples," their dependents. For the author, the eighteenth century was a period of great insecurity for Africans in the territory under Portuguese influence. The most humble lineages were continuously exploited by those who managed to become stronger over time. The African elite had survived by accumulating wealth, employing legal mechanisms for enslavement, and making alliances with

---

[85] Portaria em que se estabelecem os jornais dos "pretos trabalhadores," signed by FISC. São Paulo de Assunção de Luanda, December 7, 1770. AHU_CU_001, Cx. 55, doc. 6 and 7. "(...) And it will also be more convenient for His Majesty to purchase enslaved couples to settle in that town, having the men work in them [the factories] and the women in the fields that shall feed them all, and providing them at the end of the year with the fabrics needed by them and their children."

[86] Carta de FISC para Francisco Xavier de Mendonça Furtado, secretário de estado da marinha e ultramar. São Paulo de Assunção de Luanda, December 5, 1769. IEB/USP, AL – 082–198. Huguette Ly-Tio-Fane Pineo, *Ile de France, 1747–1767* (Mauritius: Mahatma Gandhi Institute, 1999), 246–250.

the colonial elite, as well as through marriages, since, after all, "they were all relatives." [87]

On one hand, the *sobas* whose subjects had already been co-opted to work for *capitães-mores*, missionaries, and merchants had to perform yet another function. On the other hand, these people of the *sertão* of the Kingdom of Angola had no interest in losing the customary "aid" from the *sobados*. The workers co-opted to work in the iron factories—carpenters, masons, and blacksmiths—stopped doing construction work in the fortress, repairing churches, and working for private individuals. The disputes were not only over enslaved workers; the labor of "coerced" workers was essential for the colony's maintenance. Sousa Coutinho determined that iron production was a priority and ordered the *capitães-mores* to request the factory's intendant to determine how many "offspring" were available for other tasks in other places.[88] By establishing another authority in the *sertões*— the factory's superintendent—, the governor interfered in the control exerted by the *capitães-mores* when recruiting "offspring" for work, which led to significant opposition from the captains.

In 1772, the iron factory's superintendent denounced the regent of Golungo, Félix da Cunha de Almeida, for employing the *sobas* bound to his jurisdiction in "*mucanos*,[89] collecting the tithes of previous years and other services," instead of sending them to the factories. Actually, almost all the leaders of the Golungo jurisdiction were obliged, due to their tithe exemption, to serve the factory, which resulted in excessive work for the dependents of the region's *sobados*. The factory official complained that months went by without receiving workers from some of the *sobas* of the region, while others sent a much smaller number than was established, which hindered the conclusion of the factory's construction. The *sobas* in turn claimed that, since they had to comply with those other obligations, they were unable to "provide the offspring they promised in the agreement they signed." They also argued that, according to the vassalage agreements, they owed obedience to the *capitães-mores*, and not to factory officials.[90] The *sobas* justified each

---

[87] Jan Vansina, "Ambaca Society and the Slave Trade c. 1760–1845," 11.
[88] Carta de FISC para Francisco Xavier de Andrade, *capitão-mor* do presídio de Ambaca. São Paulo de Assunção, September 15, 1770. BNP, C 8744, F 6443. Carta de FISC para Antonio Anselmo Duarte de Siqueira, intendente geral da fábrica de ferro. São Paulo de Assunção de Luanda, September 18, 1768. IEB/USP, AL-083–133.
[89] From the Kimbundu *mukanu*, conviction, fault, guilt. Beatrix Heintze, *Angola nos séculos XVI e XVII*, 420.
[90] Carta de Joaquim de Bessa Teixeira, intendente geral da fábrica do ferro da Nova Oeiras, para FISC. Nova Oeiras, December 28, 1771. SGL, AA, v. 3, no. 29, 361–393.

disobedience both because they were aware of their rights and because they feared punishment.

Two weeks later, the governor ordered the regent to "promptly send the workers" requested by the intendent of the iron factory, "with no excuses." Cunha de Almeida was to employ the workers in no other activity than finishing Nova Oeiras.[91]

The regent of Golungo is an exemplary case of the internal dynamics of the *capitães-mores*' activities regarding the *sobados*. In addition to collecting tributes, Félix intervened in the *mucano tribunals*, "an African institution incorporated by the Portuguese legal system in the mid-seventeenth century, which synthesized the interlinked nature of customs, power, and the law in Portuguese Angola."[92] In the African context, the *mucanos* were courts where civil conflicts were resolved, and where the "notion of debt was central." Theft or adultery were considered a "violation of property" and were resolved with the payment of hefty fines whose purpose was to restore the social balance. They were therefore seen as compensation.[93] The *capitães-mores* started participating in these tribunals and, from the late-seventeenth century, the Portuguese Crown tried to regulate their participation in the *mucanos* in response to recurrent complaints of abuses committed against the *sobas* and their subjects, especially massive enslavement. In addition to requiring the presence of clerks and witnesses, it was determined that all disputes regarding enslavement should be tried in Luanda, with the governor as judge. However, the *capitães-mores* continued to play a central role because it was they who took the African authority to the court in the capital city. The well-known abuses continued; the captains acted according to their own interests, demanding bribes, which were paid with enslaved people.[94]

At the same time, the situation was unfavorable for merchants, especially in Ambaca. Jan Vansina wrote about that region, the most significant area of the Kingdom of Angola: the largest, most populated, and most important from the standpoint of the trade of enslaved people in the *sertões*, and an obligatory stopover

---

[91] Carta de FISC para Félix da Cunha de Almeida, capitão regente do Golungo. São Paulo de Assunção, January 10, 1772. SGL, AA, v. 3, no. 29, 361–393.

[92] Roquinaldo Ferreira, *Cross-Cultural Exchange in the Atlantic World*, 99.

[93] Jan Vansina, "Ambaca Society and the Slave Trade c. 1760–1845," 11. Regarding the changes in the *mucano courts* established during Sousa Coutinho's administration, see: Catarina Madeira Santos, "Entre deux droits, les Lumières en Angola (1750–v. 1800)," *Annales. Histoire Sciences Sociales*, no. 4 (2005): 817–848.

[94] Roquinaldo Ferreira, *Cross-Cultural Exchange in the Atlantic World*, 105–106. Roquinaldo Ferreira followed the history of illegally enslaved Africans who challenged their condition in these courts.

for the caravans coming from the distant *sertões* on route to Luanda. For that reason, it concentrated a large population attracted by the trade's subsistence activities, and there was significant movement of people and goods.⁹⁵

At first, the large number of blacksmiths and smelters caught the governor's attention, who requested "only half of the aforesaid offspring." Four months later, he decided that only the blacksmiths and smelters from Ilamba should go to the factories, and that the workers from Ambaca should stay there preparing the iron and the "hoes, *libambos*, and other instruments for their agriculture and trade, all of which benefits the trade of people itself."⁹⁶ The region's merchants depended on ironwork more than anyone else did, and the factory's demand started to compete with their need for the metal. Nova Oeiras produced up to 40 *quintais* of iron per month, which was sent to Luanda, Lisbon, Rio de Janeiro, and once to an Indian ship—there is no doubt that the factory destabilized the local market for ironworks. There is a documentary reference that the governor established a small factory in that jurisdiction, probably analogous to the "Casa de Fundição dos Pretos," in an effort to appease the merchants.⁹⁷ Nonetheless, the shortage persisted.

The conflicts continued and Sousa Coutinho accused the merchants from Ambaca of spreading lies about the work performed in the iron foundry, for they attributed the "country's desertion and ruin" to the terrible working conditions in Nova Oeiras.⁹⁸ The governor defended himself arguing that the calamities of the Kingdom of Angola were due to the *pumbeiros*, who practiced *reviro*⁹⁹ and usurped

---

95 In addition, Elias Correa informs us that there were large cotton and agricultural plantations there, as well as the manufacture of lineage textiles (yet another essential item for commerce—"currency," in the military officer's words) and excellent clay vases. Elias Alexandre da Silva Correa, *História de Angola*, v. I, p. 121, 154, 156, 165
96 Cartas de FISC para Francisco Matoso de Andrade, *capitão-mor* de Ambaca. São Paulo de Assunção de Luanda, May 5 and 25, 1767. BNP, C 8742, F 6364.
97 This being only a brief citation, we found no further information on this small "factory." Carta de FISC para José Antunes de Campos, regente de Ambaca. São Paulo de Assunção de Luanda, January 25, 1768. IEB/USP, AL-083–002. "Should the Superintendent find that this Iron Factory, which I established in this District for the Merchants and Negroes, creates the troubles I have been informed of, or is of no advantage nor meets the needs that the said Negroes and Merchants have when they require all the iron they want without constraint or violence, Your Grace shall leave the Black Blacksmiths and Smelters free to do as they please, there being no other way to manage such people."
98 Idem.
99 The *pumbeiros* from Ambaca were known for practicing the *reviro*. The commercial agents were hired by merchants from Luanda to purchase enslaved people in the inland markets, with the goods provided in advance by the merchant. The *reviro* (resale) of the enslaved people obtained

the "government of the *sobas' sanzalas* [villages]." Only in the case of *soba* Ngonga a Mwiza,[100] for example, "a few merchants took forty *sanzalas*."[101] Governors, merchants, captains, and *sobas* fought over the government of the *sanzalas* and their people.

According to the factory's intendant, Joaquim Teixeira, the merchants spread rumors that the workers of Nova Oeiras suffered "ill-treatment" and "beatings" and that labor in the factories implied exhausting work, but the real reason of those rumors was that the merchants wanted to "liberate the Negroes from working" in the factories because they wanted them for their own "conveniences." Addressing the governor, the intendant observed:

> there is no merchant in that province [Ambaca] who does not have two or three *libatas**, or villages bound to them for their own services, whose people they defend and sponsor, as well as their enslaved, for they employ them, and the same is practiced in all jurisdictions, and for that reason they publish their pernicious words, blaming the factory for everything.[102]

It is likely that Joaquim Teixeira used the merchants' intrigues to cover up the physical punishment suffered by the workers of Nova Oeiras. Nonetheless, there was a conspicuous dispute over the work of the dependents of Ambundu villages, who were exploited by all the agents of the *sertões*, as evident in the citation above, which compares their treatment to that applied to the enslaved. Since slavery and enslavement defined social and work relations, how to institute well paid and well treated labor in that context? The result were the abuses.

The merchants and *sobas* from Ambaca also complained of the distances that the workers had to travel to work in the factory. To this, the intendant responded:

> I find it surprising that they forget the time when every month 200 workers were sent from that province to this capital city, led by soldiers on horseback, without complaining of the distance, and now that it is only a three day trip, it seems long to them.[103]

---

in the *sertão* was common—i.e. the *pumbeiros* would sell the captives to another merchant who offered a higher price, disrespecting the deal with the first merchant.

100 B. Heintze studied this *sobado*. It was located between the Lukala and Lutete Rivers, and was made a vassal in the early-seventeenth century. C.f.: Beatrix Heintze, *Angola nos séculos XVI e XVII*, 539–554.

101 Carta de FISC para Francisco Xavier de Andrade, *capitão-mor* do presídio de Ambaca. São Paulo de Assunção, September 15, 1770. BNP, C 8744, F 6443.

102 Carta de Joaquim de Bessa Teixeira, intendente geral da fábrica do ferro da Nova Oeiras, para FISC. Nova Oeiras, December 28, 1771. SGL, *Arquivos de Angola* 3, no. 29 (n.d.): 361–393.

103 Carta de Joaquim de Bessa Teixeira, intendente geral da fábrica do ferro da Nova Oeiras, para FISC. Nova Oeiras, December 28, 1771. SGL, *Arquivos de Angola* 3, no. 29 (n.d.): 361–393. The soldiers on horseback were more intimidating to the group of workers. Roquinaldo Ferreira comments that

This is a reference to the recurrent custom of forcing the *sobas'* "offspring" to serve in royal works. The main issue was that the service in Nova Oeiras took from the merchants of that jurisdiction the labor force that was not only necessary for all services, but especially for two in particular that were most important to them: the porters[104] necessary for the caravans and the blacksmiths and smelters, who made the neck shackles. The merchants of Ambaca were not the only ones displeased, since Sousa Coutinho determined that "in those lands that provide people for iron, no porter should be given to anyone, for any reason."[105]

Finally, in the factory of Nova Oeiras, escapes of Ambundus from Ambaca were so common that, in 1769, the governor ordered that no further workers be requested from that place. Sousa Coutinho claimed not to understand the reason for those "desertions," since the workers were paid and "better treated than they are by merchants."[106] There is no doubt that the workers in Nova Oeiras were subjected to precarious life conditions, which was more than enough reason for escaping. Perhaps the Ambaca escaped more often because near that jurisdiction there was an important market that received enslaved Africans from the Kingdom of Holo, the Bondo. There, the fugitives "lived freely in spite of the complaints by itinerant merchants (*sertanejos* and market vendors) who operated in the region on behalf of merchants from Luanda."[107]

In Cambambe, a very important chiefdom rebelled and stopped serving the iron factory. The first written references to the *soba* Kabuku Kambilu date from

---

with the horses the soldiers could more successfully pursue fleeing populations defeated in war. Roquinaldo Ferreira, *Transforming Atlantic Slaving*, 171.
104 The *capitão-mor* of Ambaca said that he found it difficult to provide porters for the merchants because work in Nova Oeiras still occupied "many Negroes." FISC denounced "the violence they inflict on the porters, giving them exorbitant loads, so that, in order to avoid death on such a long journey, the latter must divide the load, hiring another porter at their own expense." Carta de FISC para Francisco Xavier de Andrade, *capitão-mor* de Ambaca. São Paulo de Assunção, April 15, 1772. AHA, Códice 80.
105 Carta de FISC para Antonio Anselmo Duarte, intendente geral das reais fábricas de ferro. São Paulo de Assunção, June 15, 1768. IEB, USP, AL-083–070.
106 Carta de FISC para Antonio Anselmo Duarte. São Paulo de Assunção, November 7, 1769. BNP, C 8743, F 6367.
107 According to the *capitão-mor* of Ambaca, Bondo was "a land of many runaway communities formed by enslaved people who fled from white people who sometimes were able to capture those fugitives, as long as they were not related to Africans in the country. Often the fugitives took advantage of relations with the local population to create large communities led by fugitives who became their leaders. Some met their former owners on the road, and after repeated entreaties provided the service asked of them, after which they returned freely to their homes." Roquinaldo Ferreira, "Slave Flights and Runaway Communities in Angola (17th–19th Centuries)," *Anos 90* 21, no. 40 (2014): 72.

the late sixteenth century, where it appears as an important chiefdom in the political/military context of the Kingdom of Ndongo. As a vassal of the Portuguese Crown, this *sobado* had a long relationship with the agents of the colonial administration until the late-nineteenth century, when it lost its political supremacy.[108] In the second half of the nineteenth century, Kabuku was one of the main African leaders in the north of Kwanza, possessing religious powers, with a large population and therefore military might. He had expanded his dominion over the lands of the *sobados* along the Kwanza River, which allowed him to control essential trade routes.

The *soba* Kabuku Kambilu Dom André Fernandes, who was one of the main collaborators of the iron factories, sent 400 workers every month. The chief stopped serving the factory for two months, because the *capitão-mor* of the fortress to whom he owed allegiance "notified him to accompany him with all his troops to a mission in the province of Libolo,"[109] probably an incursion with "people of the Black War," like the *soba*'s troops, to chastise vassals from that province. The *soba* explained that he could not "burn in two fires" and that, for that reason, he had not sent to Nova Oeiras the 40 workers he was obliged to. As a result of the conflict, the governor ordered José Tomás Xavier, the *capitão-mor* of Cambambe, to send the workers promptly to Nova Oeiras and to continue sending them every month.[110]

The *soba* Kabuku did not comply with the orders because, in May 1772, four months after the *capitão-mor* notified him, the governor ordered the *soba* to send his subjects to the factories under penalty of losing the rank that the governor had conferred upon him,[111] as well as the "tithe exemption."[112] The threat meant that the *soba* would lose two important achievements: a military rank, a symbol of social distinction in the *sertão*, and the tithe exemption in his lands,

---

108 Jill Dias, "O Kabuku Kambilu (c. 1850–1900). Uma identidade política ambígua." See also Roquinaldo Ferreira, *Cross-Cultural Exchange in the Atlantic World*, 41 and 42.
109 Carta de Joaquim de Bessa Teixeira, intendente geral da fábrica do ferro da Nova Oeiras, para FISC. Nova Oeiras, December 28, 1771. SGL, AA, v. 3, n. 29, p. 361–393.
110 Carta de FISC para José Tomás Vaz Vieira, *capitão-mor* de Cambambe. São Paulo de Assunção, January 10, 1772.SGL, AA, v. 3, n. 29, p. 361–393.
111 No matter how hard anyone tried to put an end to the policy of offering concessions to the *sobas* in the form of ranks, they were common. It was an important strategy to incorporate African chiefs with positions in the Portuguese administration. At the same time, it generated new hierarchies in the *sertões*. C.f.: Ariane Carvalho da Cruz, *Militares e militarização no Reino de Angola: patentes, guerra, comércio e vassalagem (segunda metade do século XVIII)*, thesis (Master's) (Universidade Federal Rural do Rio de Janeiro, 2014).
112 Carta de FISC para D. André Fernandes *Soba* Kabuku Kambilu. São Paulo de Assunção, May 7, 1772. SGL, AA, v. 3, no. 30–33, 401–445.

i.e. the *soba* would have to pay taxes again and deal with the tax collectors. Two months later, the *soba* was summoned to appear before the governor. Dom André Fernandes was to explain why he was still not contributing with the iron factory, within 15 days; otherwise, Sousa Coutinho would order "harsh proceedings" against him because of his disobedience,[113] mentioning military raids on Kabuku's lands as punishment if he did not comply with the order. Those raids resulted in large numbers of people enslaved.[114]

We do not know whether Kabuku was attacked by the *capitão-mor* of his fortress, but apparently he was reprimanded because, in September of that same year, he signed an agreement whereby he promised to "fulfill, observe, and carry out" the orders of the factory's intendant, "under penalty of punishment," not failing to send "a single Negro in the appropriate time" to which he had committed.[115] According to the reports of the *sobas* who sent workers to Nova Oeiras, Kabuku continued to provide this service until 1773 (see Attachment 4, Table 4.5).

It is interesting to note that, even under threats, the *soba* Kabuku repeatedly disregarded the orders of the factory intendant, the *capitão-mor*, and the governor. Apparently, the importance of this African political title was consolidated over time, since, in the eighteenth century, Kabuku had a large number of dependents under his rule. The history of that *sobado*'s political and economic relations with colonial agents reveals a complex plot that goes from "collaboration to resistance," from "adaptation to rejection,"[116] whereby the leaders of the *sobado* managed, with great difficulties and constant reprimands and threats, to maintain sovereignty over time.

These conflicts reveal the tension that permeated relations between the government of Luanda and royal officials in the interior, as well as between the latter and the merchants and vassal *sobas*. On the other hand, with the arrival of the iron factory, the local authorities were under even greater pressure to send their dependents to meet the many demands described above. Even in a situation of multiple tensions, the *sobas* took advantage of the fact that all these demands depended on the labor of their dependents, which gave them some leeway.

In the "map of the *sobas* and *ilamba* that disengage themselves from factory service by failing to provide offspring for it," 37 local authorities are listed who

---

[113] Carta de FISC para D. André Fernandes Soba Kabuku Kambilu. São Paulo de Assunção, July 29, 1772. AHA, Códice 80.
[114] Joseph C. Miller, *Poder político e parentesco: os antigos Estados Mbundu em Angola*, trans. Maria da Conceição Neto (Luanda: Arquivo Histórico Nacional de Angola, 1995), 150.
[115] Carta de FISC para Joaquim de Bessa Teixeira, intendente da fábrica de ferro. São Paulo de Assunção, September 9, 1772. AHA, Códice 80.
[116] Jill Dias, "O Kabuku Kambilu (c. 1850–1900). Uma identidade política ambígua," 15.

also abandoned factory service and were therefore obliged to pay tithes again.[117] Among them, we do not find the *ndembu* Kakulo Kakahenda, who was excluded from factory service by the intendent, apparently because he did not have enough "offspring" to send. The reason for his absence in that list is that, in December 1771, the *ndembu* was readmitted to the Nova Oeiras factory. The governor ordered the intendent to receive him, even though the *ndembu* could only send 16 workers per month.[118]

Sousa Coutinho even determined that the factories' intendant send soldiers to punish those *sobas* who benefitted from the tithe exemption but failed to send workers. In taking this aggressive measure, the governor's conclusion was that the *sobas* themselves, through their disobedience, generated the violence they complained about,[119] a reasoning that was in line with the concept of just war, since the *sobas* owed obedience as vassals and, once they rebelled, they deserved the punishment established in the vassalage agreements.

It seems that, in trying to escape the violence of the tithe collectors, these chiefs ended up experiencing abuses from the Luanda government and its officials in the iron factories. In the case of the *soba* Kabuku, from Cambambe, the justification for his disobedience was his inability to meet multiple demands simultaneously, a situation that other *sobados* surely also experienced. On the other hand, accounts of the reasons for the flight of the subjects of the *sobas* of the Nova Oeiras town are more abundant. In a communication to the governor of Angola, the *soba* Dom Manoel Mendes Kisala specifies the reasons why his dependents abandoned the work in the factory. He complained of the "many punishments, insolence, imprisonment, and theft" his offspring suffered in Nova Oeiras.[120] In addition, contrary to what the 1768 and 1770 ordinances determined, the subjects of

---

117 The *soba* Kabuku does not appear in the list. "Mapa dos *sobas* e *ilamba* que se desanexam do serviço da fábrica por serem remissos em aprontarem seus filhos para o serviço dela e devem de hoje em diante, pagar o dízimo pela nova regulação que se fez," n.d. ANTT, Condes de Linhares mç. 46, doc. 11.
118 Carta de FISC para Joaquim de Bessa Teixeira, intendente geral da fábrica do ferro da Nova Oeiras. São Paulo de Assunção, December 22, 1771. SGL, AA, v. 3, n. 29, 343–351.
119 "First of all, the Negroes should be regulated as I ordered, because it is unfair for some *sobas* to be exempt from paying the Tithe without working at the Factory, and although I said that soldiers should not be sent there to avoid intimidating them, it should be understood that this is so as long as they obey the orders, because otherwise they themselves are causing the wrongs they complain about, and this being a most important matter, I hope Your Grace will not neglect it." Carta de FISC para Antonio Anselmo Duarte de Siqueira. São Paulo de Assunção, November 16, 1769. BNP, 8743, FF 6377.
120 Carta de FISC para Joaquim de Bessa Teixeira, intendente geral da fábrica do ferro da Nova Oeiras. São Paulo de Assunção, February 24, 1772. SGL, AA, v. 3, n. 30–33, 401–445.

soba Kisala did not receive payment for cleaning the town, which the governor considered a "common good" and therefore did not need to be remunerated.[121]

This is not the only evidence of lack of payment. In October 1767, the governor explained to the factory intendent that, as long as the Biscayan masters did not arrive, no payments could be made. The offspring of *soba* Kabuku Kambilu who should be summoned to assist the soldiers in agricultural work for the town would receive no wages. Only at harvest would they receive the portion corresponding to their labor.[122]

In 1770, José Francisco Pacheco, then inspector of the factory's construction work, was admonished by the same governor, already explicitly aware of the reasons for the desertions: "the Negroes at work complain about the beatings they receive and for that reason they desert, your grace must avoid such tyranny."[123]

The verb "to desert" was employed in military circles. According to Bluteau, "to desert" is a "military term, to escape and leave the field, the army, the garrison, the regiment, or the company in which any soldier is."[124] As we have already said, the military experience of recruiting people for war defined the relations established with the *sobas*' subjects who were "coerced" to work. This was so because the governor expected similar obligations from the *sobas*' subordinates to those expected from the soldiers sent to Nova Oeiras under his command. The *sobas*' offspring in turn were not under the direct command of the governor or the factory officials; they were there in obedience to their *makota, sobas*. Even with all these attempts to regulate labor relations, the colonial administration failed in this regard—the local leaders, even subjected to all those pressures, managed to maintain dominion over their people.

The news of beatings, lack of payment, and theft were not new. In a letter to the *capitão-mor* of Muxima, the governor cautioned:

> I must advise Your Grace to pay a fair and moderate wage to the carpenters and to the Negroes who help them because the King does not want the blood of his vassals, and the reality and helplessness of this conquest consists in the general lack of payment for the miserable sweat of those who work, because no one is so barbaric as to refuse to work when they are satisfied, and the Negroes themselves have enough reason to know these principles, if

---

[121] Carta de FISC para Joaquim de Bessa Teixeira, intendente geral da fábrica do ferro da Nova Oeiras. São Paulo de Assunção, March 19, 1772. SGL, AA, v. 3, n. 30–33, 401–445.

[122] Carta de FISC para Antonio Anselmo Duarte de Siqueira, intendente geral das fábricas de ferro. São Paulo de Assunção de Luanda, October 27, 1767. BNP, C 8742, F 6364.

[123] Carta de FISC para José Francisco Pacheco, inspetor das obras de Nova Oeiras. São Paulo de Assunção de Luanda, May 14, 1770. BNP, C 8743, F6377, fl. 189v.

[124] Raphael Bluteau, *Vocabulário portuguez e latino*, 10 v. Lisbon/Coimbra: Colégio da Cia. de Jesus, 1712–1728, entry "desertar."

they run away from work it is because it only brings them beatings and insults; this being the beginning of the country's ruin and decadence, it is impossible for me to act in such a manner, especially since I have taken so many measures to remedy it and have multiplied all works.[125]

The settlers of the towns were forbidden to "employ Negroes for their private service," a reference to the "offspring" paid by the Royal Treasury. They took advantage of the situation to make the *sobados*' subjects assist them "building houses or working [in] agriculture."[126]

As we can see, there was a cycle of abuses: the workers were mistreated in the factories; they pressured the chiefs, who stopped sending them; and they ended up suffering violence in their own towns at the hands of the soldiers sent there to punish them and to make sure they fulfilled their vassal obligations. The *sobas* and their subordinates fought against those abuses, i.e. that which was not established in the agreements signed with the Crown.

Another reason for escaping was the risk of enslavement. All these people in the hands of *capitães-mores*, the intendant, factory officials, and *pumbeiros*—all admittedly connected to the trade—were at risk of being captured or kidnapped. To keep them from trading in enslaved people, factory officials were to be well paid, as were the *capitães-mores*. However, that did not prevent them from enslaving many of the *sobas*' "offspring" sent there—at least we have some evidence to think so. The governor ordered the intendant to return to *soba* Kisala the "offspring unjustly seized from him," as well as everything "stolen from him" by three factory assistants.[127] In addition, the iron factory's superintendent, Antonio de Siqueira, was discharged from factory service because the governor discovered that he participated in the trade networks. This was not really news, since Siqueira was a native of the Kingdom of Angola and had served as cavalry lieutenant and sub-lieutenant, and it had long been known that he "wandered in the *sertão* 'doing business in which he went bad.'"[128]

---

[125] Carta de FISC para Antonio João de Meneses, *capitão-mor* de Muxima. São Paulo de Assunção de Luanda, February 6, 1768. AHA, Códice 79, fl. 78.

[126] "Instrução que deve guardar Antonio Anselmo Duarte de Siqueira, servindo o emprego de intendente geral da fábrica do ferro, e que executarão também os capitães-mores, como intendentes particulares na parte que lhes é respectiva" (FISC). São Paulo de Assunção de Luanda, January 12, 1767. AHU_CU_001, Cx. 52, D. 73.

[127] After this, Sousa Coutinho ordered that Kisala's offspring should be remunerated. Carta de FISC para Joaquim de Bessa Teixeira, intendente geral da fábrica do ferro da Nova Oeiras. São Paulo de Assunção, March 19, 1772. *Arquivos de Angola* 3, no. 30–33 (n.d.): 401–445.

[128] AHU, CCU, Avulsos Angola, March 14, 1756, Caixa 40, documento 119. *Apud* Ariane Carvalho da Cruz, *Militares e militarização no Reino de Angola: patentes, guerra, comércio e vassalagem (segunda metade do século XVIII)*, 132. Sousa Coutinho tells us the following story, which took place at the

Some workers preferred fleeing to the *arimos* in the region than work in the factory. In Bernardo Rabelo's *arimo*, 20 workers were "sheltered." When this became known, Rabelo was ordered to send the workers to Nova Oeiras. He replied that he did not know them and that it would be better to send someone to his *arimo* to identify them, and then his *maculunto* (from the Kikongo *nkuluntu*, the eldest, the superior) "would deliver them punctually."[129]

The reports sent to Antonio de Lencastre show that the factory's construction and maintenance cost the lives of many workers. The 1773 testimony is by Infantry Captain José Francisco Pacheco, who served as inspector of the factory's works and accompanied the four Biscayan masters who were sent there, as well as Portuguese workers and exiled convicts employed as blacksmiths, carpenters, miners, and drivers, in addition to soldiers and other people sent to populate Nova Oeiras. Of this contingent (approximately 168 people, according to our estimate), the captain counted 77 white deaths and hundreds of black deaths, which were not even recorded in his notes because there were so many that he was unable to keep his records up-to-date.[130]

Captain Pacheco made sure that the wages were paid as established, including the trip back and forth. Regarding the working conditions, he stated the following:

> Constantly, a large number of Negroes deserted and abandoned their former villages and others ended their lives miserably in this factory and in the voyages, some from natural diseases and others from a thousand disasters, like being crushed by rocks or rubble, drowned in river crossings in times of floods, and some caught by crocodiles, which is still happening in the said factory, and all of it because of the work, as correctly reported by the *capitães-mores* of the fortress and denounced by the *sobas* and *ilamba*, parents of the deceased and the deserters, whose number it is impossible to know for sure.[131]

---

time of the intendant's appointment: "I understand that this man [Siqueira] was the only one present in these first establishments, and I believe he served them quite well, and was most generous abandoning his commerce, which he began after leaving military service because he had been somewhat mistreated during the two previous administrations." Carta de FISC para Francisco Xavier de Mendonça Furtado, secretário de Estado da Marinha e Ultramar. São Paulo de Assunção de Luanda, February 17, 1767. AHU_CU_001, Cx. 52, D. 73.

129 Carta de FISC para Antonio Anselmo Duarte, intendente das fábricas de ferro. São Paulo de Assunção de Luanda, February 18, 1767. BNP, C 8742, F6364. The military officer Elias da Silva Correa said that most *arimo* owners rarely visited them out of fear of diseases in the *sertões*, leaving production and the work of the enslaved in charge of an overseer. That trusted man, the *maculunto*, could also be enslaved. Elias Alexandre da Silva Correa, *História de Angola*, v. I, 112.

130 "However, I cannot provide the exact number of Negroes who came to serve in those tasks and died in the process, because there were hundreds of them and I had no time to record the number of those wretches." Carta de José Francisco Pacheco. São Paulo de Assunção, March 13, 1773. AHU_CU_001, Cx. 57, D. 28.

131 Carta de José Francisco Pacheco. Nova Oeiras, March 5, 1773. AHU_CU_001, Cx. 57, D. 28.

The quote corroborates what can be found in other documents cited so far: that the experience of the factory reveals the tensions that existed in the *sertões* regarding the employment of the labor of "coerced" workers. These situations led to a "deeply felt hatred" by Ambundus toward factory work, making it necessary to "send for them with violence." Pacheco's account also reveals how the workers were taken to Nova Oeiras: they were led by the *makota*, the *sobas*' advisors, who Ambundu subjects feared and were obliged to respect and obey. The fear of going to Nova Oeiras was so great that the workers fled from their "own" *makota* on the way to the factory.[132]

A literary document of the time, an anonymous letter dealing with the failures of the iron factory, also provides evidence of how the workers were led. One of the characters states that, every month, "hundreds and hundreds of Negroes who lived two, four, and even eight days away" were sent to the factory, led "with guards and jails, as if they were being taken to be tormented." The use of jails and guards were measures employed to prevent the recurrent escapes. This is confirmed by the rest of the account, which is quite similar to that written by the works inspector José Francisco Pacheco:

> Your Honor also knows that these Negroes were always looking for opportunities to desert; and that they often did so on the 29th day of work, even being one [day] away from the end of the month and therefore their payment; losing all of their wages due, quite willingly, only to keep from losing one day to escape. The worst thing is that none of these deserters ever went back to their former village, going into the woods for fear of being sent back to the factory, and for this reason the states of many *sobas* are almost uninhabited.[133]

Regarding everyday work at the factories, the sources—texts written at the time of Sousa Coutinho, his own correspondence, and those written to criticize his government—agree. For example, fleeing before receiving payment was also cited by iron factory officials: the situation was so critical that the workers were not interested in their payment, "they fled before receiving it," even on the 29th day of work.[134]

Resistance to slavery in the Kingdom of Angola, especially in the form of escapes, has been examined in important works by historians committed to asserting

---

132 Idem. The author's astonishment is evident: "they fled from their own *makota*."
133 The similarity between José Pacheco's account and that of the anonymous interlocutor in this document leads us to two hypotheses: either José Francisco is the author of both documents, or whoever wrote the anonymous letter read Pacheco's account. In any case, it was someone who had access to the documents elaborated about the factory. "Resposta que um sujeito do Brasil deu ao outro de Angola, sobre a Fábrica do Ferro". n.p. n.d. BNP, Reservados, MSS Caixa 246, no. 22.
134 Carta de José Francisco Pacheco. Fábrica da Nova Oeiras, March 5, 1773. AHU_CU_001, Cx. 57, D. 28.

that resistance was "constant wherever enslavement became endemic and slavery flourished."[135] Analyses of the formation of runaway communities, such as the aforementioned case of Bondo, and *quilombos* also point in that direction.[136] Those studies help us reconstruct the history of the experiences of the Nova Oeiras workers who, after all, were subjected to working conditions typical of slavery. The difference is that colonial regulations established that "coerced" workers should not be treated in the same manner.[137]

According to Roquinaldo Ferreira, one of the main reasons for the flight of captives in Angola was the exhausting working conditions,[138] which relativizes the thesis that enslaved Africans fled and created runaway communities mostly because they feared being shipped and ending up ensnarled in the transatlantic trade.[139] The iron foundries demonstrate that the local exploitation of labor was a decisive factor for the flight not only of enslaved Africans, but also of free Africans under a compulsory labor regime.

Analyzing this set of documents reveals that the main consequence of the life and working conditions to which the Ambundus were subjected led to the gradual depopulation of the *sobados*. The workers fled from the "customary violence"[140] of

---

135 José C. Curto, "Resistência à escravidão na África: o caso dos escravizados fugitivos recapturados em Angola, 1846–1876," *Afro-Ásia*, no. 33 (2005): 72. Roquinaldo A. Ferreira, "Escravidão e revoltas de escravizados em Angola (1830–1860)," *Afro-Ásia* 21–22 (1998–1999): 9–44.
136 Beatrix Heintze, *Asilo ameaçado: oportunidade e consequências da fuga de escravizados em Angola no século XVII*. In Beatrix Heintze, *Angola nos séculos XVI e XVII*, 507–539; Ainda Freudhental, "Os Quilombos de Angola no Século XIX: A Recusa da Escravidão," *Estudos Afro-Asiáticos*, no. 32 (1997); Roquinaldo Ferreira, "Slave flights and runaway communities in Angola (17th–19th centuries)" (2014).
137 The research demonstrated that there were fewer enslaved people in Nova Oeiras, as we will analyze further in this chapter.
138 Roquinaldo Ferreira, "Slave flights and runaway communities in Angola (17th–19th centuries)," 70.
139 According to Thornton, the local labor regime was less important than the possibility of being sent to the Americas. "Where one can see clear-cut opposition to slavery in Africa is in its runaway communities. In some cases, these are clearly connected to resistance to export in the Atlantic slave trade, as was the case in the slave runaway communities that grew up south of the Kwanza River in Angola [Kisama], and dogged the Portuguese for virtually the whole length of their tenure there. Likewise, the thousands of slaves who were harbored in southern Kongo, similar runaways, were fleeing the deadly prospect of trans-Atlantic transportation and not a labor regime." John Thornton, "Africa and Abolitionism," in Seymour Drescher and Pieter Emmer (eds.), *Who Abolished Slavery? Slave Revolt and Abolitionism: A Debate with João Pedro Marques* (New York: Berghahn Books, 2010).
140 An expression employed by the governor when commenting on the wages for Ambundus: "(...) up to the amount paid to workers in this city, so they can not only live happy and satisfied to earn a living in their own place of residence, but that their joy may attract other dispersed Negroes, so

the *sertão*, from beatings by factory officials, from the heavy work that awaited them, carrying ore and stones for stonework, breaking through mountains, cutting wood to make coal, working in the iron foundry. They did not return to their villages because they feared being sent back to the factory. The continuous desertions depopulated the *sobados*, brought instability and insecurity, reduced autonomy, and threatened the power of the *sobas* and the *makota*, who had to choose who among their dependents would be sent to work each month. It is no wonder that many disengaged themselves from Nova Oeiras or refused to send their people there.

The issue of depopulation is controversial in historiography. Thornton argues that the transatlantic trade had no significant impact on the internal constitution of Central African societies. Demographic losses were recovered through biological reproduction because African women were not the main target of the trade. For Miller, the demographic reconfigurations in West Central Africa were the result of environmental factors such as climate changes, disease, and famine, rather than the impact of the trade of enslaved people.[141] Vansina, Heintze, Candido, and other authors, when addressing specific historical situations in the region, pointed to the Atlantic economy's demand for enslaved people and the expansion of colonial occupation as reasons for the chiefdoms' political breakdown, which led to the depopulation of entire regions.[142] Coerced labor regulated by the colonial initiative was a factor of political and economic instability in the region, leading colonial authorities to acknowledge the depopulation of the *sobados* that were the source of workers for the iron foundries.

3.3 Dominion, Dependence, and Work Relations

The "offspring" who were under the *sobas*' tutelage were called "resident Negroes," "farming Negroes," "worker Negroes," "*soba*'s Negroes," "people," "weaver Negroes," "neighboring peoples" (of the fortress), "tilling Negroes," "helpers,"

---

that instead of abandoning their villages due to the customary violence in this *sertão*, those villages can be the most flourishing and populated in it." Carta de FISC para João Baines, tenente general. São Paulo de Assunção de Luanda, March 8, 1766. BNP, C-8742, F-6364.
141 John Thornton, "The Slave Trade in Eighteenth Century Angola: Effects of Demographic Structure," *Canadian Journal of African Studies* 14, no. 3 (1980): 417–427; Joseph Miller, "The Significance of Drought, Disease, and Famine in the Agriculturally Marginal Zones of West Central Africa," *Journal of African History* 23 (1982): 30.
142 Jan Vansina, "Ambaca Society and the Slave Trade c. 1760–1845"; Beatrix Heintze, *Angola nos séculos XVI e XVII*; Mariana Candido, *An African Slaving Port and the Atlantic World* (2013).

"servants," "naturals," "bush dwellers," "peoples subjected to the *sobas*," "poor Negroes," and "offspring able to work."[143] Their identity is intimately related to work: they farm, they weave, they till the land, they are "able to work," and they produce wealth. They appear in the sources as dependents, subjects, subordinates, and, as Vansina said, "too often, African rural societies are viewed as if they were merely a part of the landscape." [144]

For the governor of Angola, the legal status of the "offspring" sent to work in the iron factories was that of free people. In 1769, he stated that about "400 free Negroes"[145] worked there per month. Sousa Coutinho viewed them as free because they were presumably remunerated and well treated. As we have seen so far, these assumptions in no way correspond to the situation to which the *sobas*' "offspring" were subjected and to the orders that the governor gave to the officials of Nova Oeiras. What the sources demonstrate is that, from the workers' standpoint, the meager wages offered by the factory were of little value in a context of mistreatment and strenuous work.

Sousa Coutinho's ideas of well-paid labor without ill-treatment were the result of a historical experience of failures recruiting local labor, as was the case of the gold mines along the Lombige River, but not only this. The governor participated in the main discussions on how to obtain greater control over the local populations in the various colonies of the Portuguese Empire. A paradigmatic example is the 1755 *Diretório dos Índios*, a Pombaline project that reorganized indigenous labor in Portuguese America. The person who implemented the legal norms of the *Diretório* in Brazilian lands was Francisco Xavier de Mendonça Furtado, brother of the Marquis of Pombal and one of Sousa Coutinho's main interlocutors, since he was secretary of state during his administration. Immediately prior to serving as head of the Navy and Overseas Affairs (1760–1769), Mendonça Furtado was governor of the province of Grão-Pará and Maranhão (1751–1759).

Generally speaking, before the *Diretório*, indigenous people were either free or enslaved. Indians concentrated in villages were free, having been convinced by

---

143 We gathered these terms throughout the research. See: Elias Alexandre da Silva Correa, *História de Angola* (Lisbon: Clássicos da Expansão Portuguesa no Mundo. Império Africano, 1937), v. I and II. Cadornega, *História das Guerras Angolanas (1680)*, annotated and revised by José Matias Delgado (Lisbon: Agência-geral do Ultramar, 1972), v. I, II and III.

144 The only thing I would change is "rural societies" for "societies of the *sertões*," to keep from incurring in the oppositions rural vs. urban and rural populations vs. industrial populations, which did not exist at the time and contribute little to the analysis. Jan Vansina, "Ambaca Society and the Slave Trade c. 1760–1845" (2005), 3.

145 Carta de FISC para Francisco Xavier de Mendonça Furtado, secretário de estado da marinha e ultramar. São Paulo de Assunção, December 29, 1769. AHU_CU_001, Cx. 50, D. 64

missionaries to leave the *sertões* and live in villages near Portuguese settlements. This practice was known as *descimento* and its purpose was "both to civilize the Indians and to employ their services."[146] The villages were inhabited only by the priests who ran them and the Indians. Nearby residents could hire the Indians' services, which were remunerated from the start: "whether the villages are administrated by missionaries or settlers, the laws establish a wage, the modes of payment, and the length of service."[147] The way in which working hours were established was intended to enable Indians to provide for their own sustenance, cultivating the village's fields. The "good treatment of Indians" ("kind and peaceful") was always recommended, although rarely complied with, since the settlers of the *sertões* attempted to maintain village Indians under conditions of enslavement.

In many ways, we can compare the Indians concentrated in villages to the Ambundus who worked in Nova Oeiras: they were free and were supposed to receive wages, be treated well, and encouraged not to work all year in order to promote agriculture. In addition, most importantly, access to their labor was mediated. In Portuguese America, the villages were run by missionaries who negotiated indigenous wages and length of service with the settlers; in the Kingdom of Angola, the settlers' access to *sobado* labor was also mediated by the *sobas* and *makota*, who in a way also negotiated wages, since they offered free service in exchange for an exemption from paying tithes.

With the *Diretório*, this situation changed. In the *sertões* of Portuguese America, all Indians were declared free, and the villages were transformed into towns. They were still forced to work, but under different rules. Mediation by the missionaries was abolished; the Indians were to be "governed by ordinary judges, town councilors, and other officers of justice." According to José Alves de Souza Junior, "the institution of the *Diretório*'s regime meant a complete laicization of the administration of the existing Indian villages in the state of Grão-Pará and Maranhão." [148]

Another piece of information of interest to us is that all Indians over the age of 13 had to be registered annually as "able to work." That is exactly the same expres-

---

[146] Beatriz Perrone-Moisés, "Índios livres e índios escravizados: os princípios da legislação indigenista do período colonial (século XVI a XVIII)," in Manuela Carneiro da Cunha, *História dos Índios no Brasil* (São Paulo: Companhia das Letras, 1992). See also John Monteiro, *Negros da terra. Índios e bandeirantes nas origens de São Paulo* (São Paulo: Companhia das Letras, 1994).
[147] Beatriz Perrone-Moisés, "Índios livres e índios escravizados: os princípios da legislação indigenista do período colonial (século XVI a XVIII)," 129.
[148] José Alves de Souza Júnior, "Negros da terra e/ou negros da Guiné: trabalho, resistência e repressão no Grão-Pará no período do Diretório," *Afro-Ásia* 45 (2013): 173–211.

sion employed in the inventories that listed the *sobas*' "offspring able to work." The comparisons are not limited to what has been said so far. In the *sertões* of Portuguese America, disputes over indigenous labor among settlers, missionaries, and colonial authorities were frequent, as well as abuses and mistreatment in both public works and services provided to private individuals.[149]

The main difference between these historical experiences was the *sobas*' dominion over their "offspring." While the *Diretório* was a successful legal norm in removing control over the labor of village Indians from the missionaries, Sousa Coutinho's ordinances, which regulated the wages of "working Negroes" and ensured that the *sobas*' subjects were well treated (putting an end to "vexations" and "violence in the *sertões*"), were not enough to take control from the *sobas* and *makota* over their dependents.

To do justice to the comparison, Patrícia Sampaio records an event in which Indigenous leaders, the "chiefs of the land," were dissatisfied because "the government over their indigenous subjects was taken from them" and, "offended and displeased," threatened to leave with their subjects and go to Spain's dominions.[150] This is an indication that indigenous leaders also resisted the loss of their dominion over their dependents.

It is important to remember that, among the Ambundus, as in other African societies, a chief's power was measured by the number of dependents under his control. For the *sobas*, their subordinates, whether free or enslaved, and the services rendered by them constituted their main source of wealth. This dominion was based on the norms of matrilineal kinship, whereby the offspring in a *sobado* did not belong to their father or mother, but to the mother's family, namely to the maternal uncle, who was the head of his sister's children and controlled matrimonial alliances, the "transactions implicit to marriage and dowries, arising from the movement of women."[151]

As Paul Lovejoy explained, within a lineage, "elders controlled the means of production and access to women, and thus political power was based on gerontocracy." From the African standpoint, labor relations were permeated by bonds of

---

149 Idem. Ibidem. The competition resulting from the employment of Indians in public and private services bothered the colonists significantly. In 1703, the Maranhão Trading Company presented the Portuguese Crown with a detailed description where they complained of the employment of 400 Indians to work at the Navy Arsenal. Idem, 178.
150 Patrícia Maria Melo Sampaio, "'Vossa Excelência mandará o que for servido...': políticas indígenas e indigenistas na Amazônia Portuguesa do final do século XVIII," *Tempo* 12, no. 23 (2007): 41.
151 On matrilineal societies in Africa, see: Christian Geffray, *Nem pai, nem mãe. Crítica do parentesco: o caso Macua* (Lisbon: Caminho, 2000).

dependence, since "the dependents were mobilized in the lineage's interest as determined by the elders" in hunting expeditions, village defense, and religious ceremonies.[152]

The bonds of dependence in times of trouble could become more precarious precisely for those who relied on them the most: the youngest relatives who had no financial resources or were even too young to fend for themselves. It was therefore necessary to resort to other non-biological connections as a supplement, and one of them was pawning. It was no accident that children were the people most often pledged as collateral for debts.

According to Lovejoy, slavery was also a bond of dependence.[153] From very early on, colonial agents learned to identify who among the Africans was free according to the "law of the *sobas.*" According to Beatrix Heintze, in the Kingdom of Ndongo in the sixteenth century, the Portuguese Jesuits recorded that prisoners of war and enslaved people purchased were called *mobicas* (from the Kimbundu *mubika*, plural *abika*). Enslaved Ambundus, on the other hand, were known as *quisicos* (from the Kimbundu *kijiku*, plural *ijiku*). Enslavement was a penalty imposed on criminals. The term *quisico* was used by the colonizers to designate the "totality of the enslaved population as opposed to the *morinda* (from the Kimbundu *murinda*, plural *arinda*), the free Ambundus." Free Ambundus were organized along matrilineal lines. The term *quisico* was also used to name "the villages of these same slaves" and "a certain type of slave, for example, only the children of slaves." The *ngola* used the *ijiku* as payment of tributes and employed them for military support. The *ijiku* were of great political importance in Ndongo, and "regardless of the fact that the superiors could employ the *ijiku* with greater freedom and decision than others, it is to be assumed that their daily life in these villages was not very different from that of the free population."[154]

Heintze notes that Cavazzi observed that the clothing of the enslaved was poorer. Besides the *ijiku* villages, there were people enslaved for domestic service, probably already called *mukama*, as early as the late-sixteenth century. Over time,

---

[152] Paul E. Lovejoy, *Transformations in Slavery: A History of Slavery in Africa* [1983], second ed. (Cambridge: Cambridge University Press, 2000), 13; Joseph C. Miller, *Poder político e parentesco: os antigos Estados Mbundu em Angola* (1995).

[153] Idem, 14–15.

[154] Beatrix Heintze, *Angola nos séculos XVI e XVII*, p. 486. According to Heintze, "there was a hierarchy among the various types of enslaved people." Prisoners of war were the "least fortunate" and were even used in human sacrifices. The degree of "integration of the enslaved in their own sociopolitical system" was taken into account when incorporating them into the new society; in other words, the hierarchical position they occupied in their community of origin was taken into account when assigning them new functions.

in some villages, the enslaved started being considered property to keep them from being traded for others of lesser value. The main difference between free and enslaved people was their belonging to a lineage. As summarized by Vansina, "a person without a lineage was a slave; a person with one was free."[155] Hence, the power of the *sobas* and the council of elders was central to this relationship of dependency, as they were largely the ones who decided who would continue to belong to a lineage and who would be expelled.

In the episode narrated by José Curto about the 10,000 subjects stolen from the *ngola* in the seventeenth century, even the heiress who claimed ownership of the subjects, disputing ownership with the king of Ndongo, admitted that, among the thousands, there were vassals who had fled from the "violence of tyrants" who were not enslaved.[156] In a different case, Silvia Lara noted that, after the *ngola*'s defeat and the imprisonment of his relatives, his subjects who should have been enslaved according to the laws of war were not, because the members of the Overseas Council understood that they should remain "in the power of the surrounding kings and *sobas*." After all, as Cadornega explained, many were "free by birth."[157] Linda Heywood also found the same pattern of recognition for Kongo: "The terms *gente* [people], *naturaes* [natives] and *naturaes forros* [free natives] referred to a different social group from the term *fidalgo* (nobleman)" and "outsider."[158]

There were also gradations between the conditions of free and enslaved. Pawning is the best example; it was the condition whereby a free person could be pledged in exchange for a loan or as debt payment, but remained free and could be recovered at any time by his relatives. According to Vansina, the big change in relation to the people pledged was that, precisely in the eighteenth century, they started being offered "in exchange for the loan of goods equivalent to the value of an enslaved person," in response to the Atlantic economy's growing demand to "produce slaves." The author argues that the practice became common due to the concentration of power in "corporate matrilineages" governed by the lineage's "elders," who began to employ their dependents as a way to avoid their own enslavement (handing them over or pawning them in their stead) or

---

[155] Jan Vansina, "Ambaca Society and the Slave Trade c. 1760–1845," 6; Joseph Miller, *Poder político e parentesco*, 48.

[156] José C. Curto, "A restituição de 10.000 súditos Ndongo 'roubados' na Angola de meados do século XVII: uma análise preliminar," in Isabel Castro Henriques (ed.), *Escravatura e transformações culturais. África – Brasil – Caraíbas* (Lisbon: Editora Vulgata, 2002), 185–208.

[157] Silvia Hunold Lara, "Depois da Batalha de Pungo Andongo (1671): o destino atlântico dos príncipes do Ndongo," *Revista de História* (USP), no. 175 (2016), 214.

[158] Linda Heywood, "Slavery and its Transformation in the Kingdom of Kongo: 1491–1800," *Journal of African History* 50 (2009), 4.

to pay back debts and obtain goods and wealth, since they were involved in a broad network of indebtedness around the goods that circulated in the context of the transatlantic trade.[159]

Colonial authorities acknowledged that it was common for free and pawned people who worked to pay back their own or someone else's debts to be unjustly enslaved, kidnapped, or stolen.[160] In this case, when a free person was captured and/or sold into slavery, he or she was no longer part of the lineage.

In the eighteenth century in this region, the trade of enslaved people had already become the foundational element of the economic and social order, and it was through the action of its agents (traffickers, colonial officials, among others) that colonization was consolidated: the Portuguese language, the Catholic religion, new patterns of food and consumption, changes in gender relations, everything came into the colonial orbit or was modified by it. The legal and illegal forms of enslavement within the *sobados* also changed with the pressure of the Atlantic economy. Under Portuguese influence, even before the conquest, the ways of enslaving the *arinda*, the free people from the *sobados*, had already undergone changes, especially due to the development of the trade of enslaved people. One example of this was the "commutation of the death penalty handed down in case of rebellion against the sovereign, adultery committed by his wives, or theft, for perpetual slavery" and banishment, including the convict in the networks of the trade of enslaved people.[161]

The situation was undoubtedly one of everyday insecurity in the *sobados*. The residents subordinated to the elders of their lineage felt those tensions and became even more dependent on those authorities, who could protect them from slavery. The danger was real. Recent studies have demonstrated that slavery was a threat mainly to vassals, both those who lived on the Coast, participated in the trade, were part of family networks and mastered the Portuguese language, and those who were under the dominion of the local authorities, even though they were protected by the Portuguese legislation and had recourse to the instruments of justice in the case of unjust enslavement.[162] They were enslaved illegitimately.

---

[159] Jan Vansina, "Ambaca Society and the Slave Trade c. 1760–1845," 18.
[160] Roquinaldo Ferreira, *Cross-Cultural Exchange in the Atlantic World*, 78.
[161] Beatrix Heintze, *Angola nos séculos XVI e XVII*, 206, 486. Regarding Kongo, Duarte Lopes observed, "You can find in São Tomé and Portugal no small number of slaves born in Kongo sold for this necessity among whom were some of royal blood and principal lords." Linda Heywood, "Slavery and its Transformation in the Kingdom of Kongo: 1491–1800," 7.
[162] Roquinaldo Ferreira, *Cross-Cultural Exchange in the Atlantic World. Angola and Brazil during the Era of the Slave Trade* (New York: Cambridge University Press, 2012); Mariana P. Candido, *An*

In a way, this book demonstrates how the history of labor and the forms of control of the *sobas*' dependents were intertwined with the conceptions of slavery promoted by the Atlantic slaveholding society. From this standpoint, we can understand why the residents of Ambaca became patrons of "offspring" who lived in their *libatas* and who, although not enslaved, were sometimes treated as if they were.[163]

When an "offspring" was chosen by the *makota* to go work in Nova Oeiras, this entire complex universe of obligations and ties of dependency came into action. Disobeying the elders who controlled the political and economic life of one's lineage was not only an affront to the spirits of the ancestors; it represented the loss of important connections, which were even more precious when one had to balance on the increasingly fine line that delimited the boundaries of legal or illegal enslavement. It is thus understandable that many of these people, after fleeing from the violence to which they were subjected in the iron factories, did not return to their towns of origin, since there was no guarantee that their act of rebellion would not be used as a reason for enslavement.

Obedience was not an easy way out either. For some, working at the factory meant living in Nova Oeiras. Working and even living away from that network of protection and solidarity could also be dangerous, for it could mean greater vulnerability to enslavement. As we have seen, there are reports of "offspring" effectively enslaved by factory officials. Roquinaldo Ferreira tells a story that contributes to this argument. Cambiza, a pawned woman, was sent to an island to work and thus pay her relatives' debt, who had pawned her to *soba* Axila ya Bangi. It was then that she suffered attempts at enslavement, which, as the author said, was a common situation encountered by pawned people.[164]

African Slaving Port and the Atlantic World. Benguela and its hinterland (New York: Cambridge University Press, 2013).
163 "For there is no merchant in that province [Ambaca] who does not have two or three *libatas*, or villages, bound to them for their own services, which the people defend and sponsor as much as their enslaved, because they employ them as such, and the same is practiced in all jurisdictions, and for that reason they publish pernicious words blaming the factory for everything." Carta de Joaquim de Bessa Teixeira, intendente geral da fábrica do ferro da Nova Oeiras, para FISC. Nova Oeiras, December 28, 1771. SGL, *Arquivos de Angola* 3, no. 29 (n.d.): 361–393.
164 Roquinaldo Ferreira, *Cross-Cultural Exchange in the Atlantic World*, 78.

3.4 "All Those Who Have Some Notion of Ironwork"

Portugal did not have an iron mining tradition. In pursuing the goal of turning the Kingdom of Angola into a major exporter of iron that would supply the demands of the Portuguese empire and conquer new markets, Francisco de Sousa Coutinho (and his successors) called upon the knowledge of every blacksmith, smelter, locksmith, and gunsmith who was or could be sent to Angola, "where all those who have some notion of ironwork are now needed," in his words.[165] Artisans to construct the factory building were also requested. From 1764 to 1790, a total of 85 mechanical officers went through Nova Oeiras: three miners, two stonemasons, 212 carpenters, 14 blacksmiths, nine smelters, one iron smelter and refiner, one plater, two iron refiners, seven tinsmiths, four locksmiths, and 21 masons. However, the most outstanding characters in this history were the four Biscayans who arrived there.

In 1766, Francisco Xavier de Mendonça Furtado was authorized by the king to look for a "foreign foreman" to establish the factory. With each new letter exchanged between the Secretary of State of the Navy and Overseas Affairs and the governor of Angola, the wait for the foremen was a recurring theme. From Lisbon, Furtado attempted to make up for the foremen's absence by sending all the blacksmiths and smelters he could to Angola, including those jailed in Limoeiro.[166] In African territory, Coutinho provided every detail so that, when they arrived, the foremen would find ideal working conditions: houses were built, canoes with canopies were provided for shelter from the sun, a doctor was hired, not to mention the preparation and stockpiling of wood for charcoal and ore for the foundry.[167] It

---

[165] Carta de FISC para Francisco Xavier de Mendonça Furtado, secretário de Estado dos Negócios da Marinha e Domínios Ultramarinos. São Paulo de Assunção de Luanda, August 27, 1768. IEB/USP, AL – 082–087.

[166] "In order to advance as much as possible with the said factory, His Majesty decided to have some blacksmith officers sent, among those imprisoned in this Court's prisons, to be employed in that work, waiting for the arrival of the said master before sending others even more skilled, in order to fully establish the said factory." Carta de Francisco Xavier de Mendonça Furtado, secretário dos Negócios da Marinha e dos Domínios Ultramarinos, para FISC. Palácio de Nossa Senhora da Ajuda, July 21, 1767. AHU, Códice 472 – fl. 124–126v.

[167] In 1768, Sousa Coutinho ordered the intendant to take care of preparations: "Your Grace shall suspend iron manufacturing and employ the blacksmiths only to use the bars I sent you for the Artillery's repairs, employing all the Negroes to gather the raw iron to ensure that everything is ready, and likewise with charcoal, if there is a way to preserve it free of humidity. Your Grace must hurry with the Brick Factory so they can have at least twelve thousand bricks ready to build the furnaces. You should also have more canoes made so the heavy tools can be transported." "Regarding the houses, I hope that Your Grace has built accommodations appropriate for these men, so they are no longer befuddled by this inconvenience surprising." Carta de FISC para Anto-

took almost one year until, in 1767, the Secretary of the Navy and Overseas Affairs received a letter from the Town of Bergara, in the province of Gipuzkoa, informing that the foremen were on their way to Lisbon.[168]

Generally speaking, the Kingdom of Angola was one of the places that was most feared by those sentenced to exile, since the voyage usually meant a death sentence.[169] What reasons would make a Biscayan blacksmith or smelter to embark voluntarily on this adventure? In this case, the wages must have been a factor, since they were significant—2$400 réis per day. Perhaps, as an employee in an ironworks, a Biscayan artisan's income was inferior or varied greatly. Blacksmiths and smelters in northern Spain received the equivalent of the fifth of the iron they produced.[170] If they were apprentices, payment was even less and could be made in the form of clothing and shoes. Spending some time in distant lands would suffice to amass wealth and achieve better living conditions.

We do not know what other reasons may have led the foremen to accept the proposal, although we can imagine that the adventure of establishing an ironworks in Angola's *sertões* and learning other forms of smelting was also relevant. The fact is that, in April 1768, Joseph Manuel de Echevarria[171] and Francisco Xavier de Zu-

---

nio Anselmo Duarte de Siqueira, intendente da fábrica de ferro. São Paulo de Assunção de Luanda, July 3, 1768. IEB/USP, AL-083–079.
168 Carta de Francisco Xavier de Mendonça Furtado, secretário dos Negócios da Marinha e dos Domínios Ultramarinos, para FISC. Palácio de Nossa Senhora da Ajuda, May 1, 1767. BNP, F3315.
169 Angola in particular was seen as "the very residence of death" due to its climate, the fevers, and the wars with Central Africans. FISC, "Memórias do Reino de Angola e suas conquistas, escritas em Lisboa nos anos de 1773 e 1775," BMP, Codices 437, document 10.
170 Pablo Quintana Lopez mentions how much the workers at the Santa Eufemia ironworks in Los Oscos earned in 1679. The *aroza*, the most experienced blacksmith who was in charge of the ironworks, earned $900 réis; the *tirador*, the forger, and the two auxiliary smelters received $400 réis each; the *tazador*, the lowest-ranking officer, who could be an apprentice, received $200 réis. These values are outdated to serve as a parameter in the late-eighteenth century, but they help us get an idea of the low wages received by blacksmiths and smelters. Pablo Quintana Lopes, *La labranza y transformación artesanal del hierro en Taramundi y Los Oscos. Siglos XVI–XVIII. Aportación a su conocimiento* (Taramundi: Associación "Os Castros," 2005), Tomo I, 143.
171 Rafael Ayo cites José Echevarri as an important iron ore trader in Portugalete, Biscay, in 1826–27. Echevarri or Chavarri was one of the four major traders in the region, with the largest number of businesses. I believe that there might be a relation with the master sent to Angola. It is also worth taking into account that the Chavarri family came from a lineage of large owners of land, iron mines, and companies involved in the ore trade. Rafael Uriarte Ayo. "Minería y empresa siderúrgica en la economía vizcaína preindustrial (s. XVI–XVIII)," *XI Congreso Internacional de la AEHE* (Madrid, 2014), 9 and 10. "Some of the old dealers became the main producers in Biscay, so an elite of miners developed, which controlled most of the concessions, among whom were the local owners, especially the Ibarra, Chavarri, and Ustara families, who possessed concessions since

luaga,[172] natives and residents of the Province of Gipuzkoa, Francisco de Echenique,[173] from the Kingdom of Navarra, and Joseph de Retolaza, from the Lordship of Biscay, were hired and convinced to embark for the Kingdom of Angola to "work in ironwork and instruct others in this trade" for a period of three years. Two of them used part of their wages to support their family, which remained in Spain. Manuel de Echevarria sent $600 réis of his daily wages to his wife Maria Josefa de Arana, in the town of Bergara, in Gipuzkoa. His countryman Francisco de Zuloaga stipulated the same amount to be sent to his uncle and aunt, Francisco de Errasti and Ana Batista de Aguirre, who lived in the same town.[174]

On October 24, 1768, the Biscayans disembarked in Luanda. By then, they had survived the "scurvy"[175] epidemic that killed 11 soldiers and a drummer during the trip. They were lodged at Sousa Coutinho's house and, on November 3, they left for Nova Oeiras. More than a year after being hired and after a journey of five and a half months, on November 14, 1768, the foremen arrived in that town. Accompanied by factory officials, the foremen visited the surrounding region to analyze the potential of the rivers, the ore, and the forest, and found everything to be excellent.

On the third day after their arrival, on November 17, two foremen fell ill and the doctor José Serra Botelho prescribed bloodletting and medicines. The town's apothecary was in terrible condition and there was not enough medicine, no stove, no cooking pot, no scales, and no mortar. The governor blamed the doctor for neglecting the pharmacy's continuous supply and, in order to provide some relief, he sent English water, a widely used remedy to combat fevers, both in Portugal

---

the first years of the demarcation of the mines." Eneko Pérez Goikoetxea, *Minería del hierro en los montes de Triano y Galdames* (Bilbao: E. Bilbao, 2003), 65.

172 There are three ironworks named Zuluaga in Guipúzcoa in the survey elaborated by Luis Miguel Díez de Salazar for that place for the sixteenth and seventeenth centuries. Luis Miguel Díez de Salazar, "La industria del hierro en Guipúzcoa (siglos XIII–XVI) (Aportación al estudio de la industria urbana)," *La Ciudad Hispánica*, Editorial de la Universidad Complutense (1985), 251–276.

173 Another possible family relation with the areas related to iron mining. In 1825, José Francisco de Echenique leased the ironworks of Bereau and Biurra because of the unemployment that gravely affected ironworks at the time. Pilar Erdozáin Azpilicueta and Fernando Mikelarena Peña, "Siderurgia tradicional y comunidad campesina. La gestión de las ferrerías municipales de Lesaka y Etxalar en 1750–1850," *Vasconia*, no. 32 (2002): 509.

174 Idem.

175 We found the following description in the glossary published with the commented edition of *Ensaios sobre as enfermidades de Angola*. Scurvy was also called *mal de Luanda* (Luanda's disease): "Contagious disease of the blood (...) one of whose major symptoms is the appearance of pale blotches in various parts of the body, a propensity for passive hemorrhages, especially of the gums, which become soft, swollen, fungous, and with a pale aspect." Valdez: II, 387, in José Pinto de Azeredo, *Ensaios sobre algumas enfermidades de Angola* [1799], ed. Antonio Braz de Oliveira and Manuel Silvério Marques (Lisbon: Edições Colibri, 2003), 99.

and overseas. In his *Ensaios sobre algumas enfermidades de Angola* (Essays on Some Angolan Diseases), the Luso-Brazilian physician José Pinto Azeredo said that he often used this water because it contained considerable amounts of quinine and was more palatable than pure quinine.[176]

Sixteen days after his arrival, Joseph de Retolaza died, according to reports from the governor, a victim of "scurvy" and the region's bad weather conditions. The same causes led to the death of Francisco de Zuluaga on December 8 and Francisco de Echenique on December 29.

The governor lamented these losses in his letter, as he was beginning to realize that his resources to maintain the factory were coming to an end. The fact that Joseph Manuel de Echevarria survived was the argument he used with the Secretary of the Navy and Overseas Affairs to defend the success that his factory was still capable of attaining. His argument was that this blacksmith was "the best in his art": "because if he died and the other three remained, nothing could be done, since he alone masters his art, while among the others, one was only a blacksmith, and the other two, foundry apprentices."[177]

The Portuguese Crown's investment had been too large to accept simple explanations of the causes of these deaths. In a little less than a month, a number of opinions from the factory's officials, the governor, the doctor in charge of the Biscayans' health, and the Secretary of State of the Navy and Overseas Affairs were elaborated. First, Sousa Coutinho reminded the Secretary of Overseas Affairs that the foremen arrived in Angola in the worst season "for new arrivals," in November, during the torrential rains that ruined agriculture and multiplied diseases.[178]

---

[176] José Pinto de Azeredo, *Ensaios sobre algumas enfermidades de Angola*, 50. Quinine was essential for the expansion of the Portuguese empire. "From the Amazon in Brazil, trees were transplanted to São Tomé, where tons of quinine were produced and distributed throughout the colonial domains." Jean Luiz Neves Abreu, "O saber médico e as experiências coloniais nos Ensaios sobre algumas enfermidades de Angola," in José Pinto de Azeredo, *Ensaios sobre algumas enfermidades de Angola* [1799], ed. Antonio Braz de Oliveira and Manuel Silvério Marques, 204.

[177] Carta de FISC para Francisco Xavier de Mendonça Furtado, secretário dos Negócios da Marinha e dos Domínios Ultramarinos. São Paulo de Assunção de Luanda, November 25, 1768. São Paulo de Assunção de Luanda, January 20, 1769, IEB/ AL – 082–142.

[178] So much so that the military officer Elias Alexandre observed, "In the dry years, diseases are fewer and more benign." For example, the disease known as *carneirada* – "an annual disease that leads many people to the grave" –, an intermittent tertian fever, as is described in *Ensaios sobre as enfermidades de Angola* (1799), was common in the rainy seasons. Also in the glossary of *Ensaios sobre algumas enfermidades de Angola*; Carneirada: "intermittent tertian fever. 'Carneiraça or carneirada, illness of the island of São Tomé.' Bluteau, C, 153. 'From this rottenness originate those pestilent fevers called *carneiradas* in the mines of Mato Grosso, Cuiabá, and Guaiazes [Goiás]. Other diseases so common to all of Brazil, such as the most harmful insects and other common diseases,

Manuel de Echevarria begged the governor to let him return to his homeland, to no avail. According to Sousa Coutinho, he would not arrive alive even in Muxima, or perhaps in the town of Bergara in Biscay. To the governor's misfortune, shortly afterwards, on January 23, 1769, Echevarria also died of a violent fever. Despite the shipment of supplies and medicines, measures to avoid being exposed to the sun and "getting their feet wet," and bloodletting, the foremen did not resist. The deaths were attributed to the behavior of the deceased, who disregarded the advice about the climate's noxiousness and overindulged in eating and drinking.[179]

Death was actually the certain fate of most of the workers sent to the factories. According to Jill Dias and Joseph Miller, in the rainy seasons, malaria and smallpox epidemics were more common. Diseases of the intestinal tract, especially those described in the sources as "dysentery" or "diarrhea," in addition to respiratory problems such as bronchitis, pneumonia, and tuberculosis, were also responsible for endemic diseases in Angola.[180]

In addition to the Biscayans, there was at least one initiative of the Portuguese Crown to send large numbers of specialized European workers to Angola in 1771. In that year, a "list of the mechanical officers appointed to embark for the Kingdom of Angola" was elaborated: two master tinsmiths (one of them Castilian), a tinsmith officer, a bell caster, an iron smelter and refiner, an iron refiner and blacksmith, an iron refiner (French), two smelters, and eight carpenters (see Attachment 3). The artisans travelled together with military officers, all of them assigned to serve in the iron mines and factories. The tools and blueprints for the ironworks also travelled with them: boilers, saws, iron rings for the bellows, and models for the blacksmith's equipment.

Some masters stand out in the list. Matheus Pirson Niheul was French, living in Rua do Vale, parish of Nossa Senhora das Mercês, in Lisbon. The "iron refining

---

have the same origin,' Sanches, 1756, 31. Malaria; malaria epidemic; a disease endemic to the banks of the São Francisco River during the ebb tide." José Pinto de Azeredo, *Ensaios sobre algumas enfermidades de Angola*, 94. Elias Alexandre da Silva Correa, *História de Angola* (Lisbon: Clássicos da Expansão Portuguesa no Mundo. Império Africano, 1937), v. I, 80. Carta de FISC para Francisco Xavier de Mendonça Furtado. São Paulo de Assunção de Luanda, August 26, 1768. São Paulo de Assunção de Luanda, January 20, 1769, IEB/ AL – 082–089.

179 Carta de Joaquim de Bessa Teixeira, intendente da fábrica de ferro, para FISC. Nova Oeiras, December 27, 1768. AHU_CU_001, Cx. 53, Doc. 8. Carta de FISC para Francisco Xavier de Mendonça Furtado, secretário de Estado da Marinha e Ultramar. São Paulo de Assunção de Luanda, January 20, 1769. AHU_CU_001, Cx. 53, Doc. 8.

180 Jill Dias, "Famine and Disease in the History of Angola c. 1830–1930," *The Journal of African History* 22, no. 3 (1981): 358; Joseph Miller, "The Significance of Drought, Disease and Famine in the Agriculturally Marginal Zones of West Central Africa," *The Journal of African History* 23, no. 1 (1982): 23.

master" arrived in Angola in 1771. In Africa, he settled in Nova Oeiras with a daily wage of 1$200 réis and got married. His responsibility in the factory was to refine the molten iron, i.e. to remove as much slag as possible. Six years later, in 1777, when the factory was abandoned by Governor Lencastre, the master received a notice ordering him to return to Portugal.[181]

Two metalworkers—whose nationality was not mentioned—who had fled from a French ship were also sent to the factory. Before that, they spent some time repairing weapons at the Luanda arsenal. One of them was an excellent cutler and even made a razor that was later sent to Lisbon, with the iron produced in Nova Oeiras, which was good to make cutting instruments.[182] Unlike an iron refiner, a cutler or metalworker could not be expected to have technical mastery of any step to obtain the metal. Their knowledge was in making valuable objects, such as the razor mentioned above.

Francisco de Sousa Coutinho sought various means to implement his project. There are reports that the governor of Angola corresponded with other authorities of the Portuguese colonial empire in search of blacksmiths and smelters, as well as tools and all sorts of help he could find. In 1767, the then governor of Bahia, Count of Azambuja, sent three blacksmiths in response to Sousa Coutinho's entreaties—a Portuguese man who had learned in the factories of Galicia and two "excellent" officers. When they arrived in Benguela, "trusting in the robustness of Brazil," they decided to go hunting, after which they became seriously ill and did not resist. Still, the governor insisted that the count send one or two additional men "who mastered the craft of smelting iron ore perfectly and skillfully," and he begged to spread the word: "if they master the said craft, they be very well paid." He

---

[181] Matheus left a woman in Lisbon to whom he was engaged, Genoveva Lara. At first, he presented her as his sister, requesting that $240 réis of his daily wages be delivered to her. In 1776, he wrote to the Armazéns Reais of Lisbon requesting the suspension of the pension because Genoveva was not really his sister and he had already married in Angola. In 1779, Genoveva asked to continue receiving the pension, since she had no means to support herself and her siblings, nor could she marry, having been the blacksmith's lover. "Relação dos oficiais militares, oficias mecânicos voluntários e degradados, e mais degradados que devem embarcar na Sumaca que se acha próxima a partir para o Reino de Angola." Palácio de Nossa Senhora da Ajuda, March 22, 1771. BNP, MSS Caixa 250, n. 71, Procuração de Matheus Pirson Niheul, mestre de refinar ferro para que entregassem a sua irmã Genoveva Lara, uma pensão de 240 réis por dia pagos do ordenado de 1200 réis que ele vence. Lisbon, October 12, 1771. AHU_CU_001, Cx. 54, D. 101. Catálogo cronológico de todas as ordens régias que existem na Secretaria do Estado do Reino de Angola. São Paulo de Assunção de Luanda, June 18, 1777. AN (RJ), Códice 543. Carta de Genoveva Lara para a rainha, D. Maria I. Lisbon, May 11, 1779. AHI_CU_001, Cx. 65, D. 35.

[182] Carta de FISC para Francisco Xavier de Mendonça Furtado, secretário de Estado dos Negócios da Marinha e Domínios Ultramarinos. São Paulo de Assunção de Luanda, August 27, 1768. IEB/USP, AL – 082–087.

also requested that any blacksmith who committed a crime in Bahia be sentenced to exile in Angola, with travel expenses paid.[183] Renato Pinto Venâncio found records for that same year of 1767 of several enslaved blacksmiths from Bahia sent to work at a workshop in Angola.[184]

The Morgado of Mateus, governor of São Paulo (1765–1775) and Sousa Coutinho's brother-in-law, was repeatedly consulted about the possibility of sending disciples of the master responsible for iron extraction at the Araçoiaba hill, where the future iron factory of Ipanema would be later established. The request was for at least one or two apprentices. This would suffice to lay the factory's foundations: it was enough to have those "who have obtained from him [the master] the secret not only of the foundry, but of the construction of the building and the mills."[185] The enticement of high wages was reiterated in each letter to these overseas Portuguese authorities.

The practice of sending convicts from various parts of the empire who had a trade related to iron smelting and forging to Nova Oeiras was constant. It was a large contingent that did not necessarily have to be paid. Some of the main masters of Nova Oeiras were convicts, such as the master carpenter Antonio Joaquim de Almeida and Antonio Ribeiro, who built the factory furnace. In fact, this category of convicts constituted an important source of labor for the Kingdom of Angola; they were also subjected to precarious working conditions in Nova Oeiras. One of the masons responsible for the stonework of the smelting furnace, Gregório José, was shackled with a *calceta*[186] while he worked, for despite being an excellent artisan, he was also a "fine thief."[187] The eight convicts sent to Nova Oeiras in 1771 were paid "according to their merits." Others worked only in exchange for food.[188]

A survey of the mechanical officers of Luanda dated 1801 lists 374 workers divided into stonemasons (4), masons (46), painters (2), turners (8), tinsmiths (6), blacksmiths (26), combers (3), caulkers (11), finishing carpenters (52), riverboat car-

---

[183] Carta de FISC para Antonio Rolim de Moura Tavares, conde de Azambuja, govenador da Bahia. São Paulo de Assunção de Luanda, August 6, 1767. BNP, C 8742, F6364, fl. 210.
[184] Renato Pinto Venâncio, *Cativos do Reino: a circulação de escravos entre Portugal e Brasil, séculos 18 e 19* (São Paulo: Alameda, 2012).
[185] Carta de FISC a Luis Antonio de Sousa, morgado de Mateus, governador de São Paulo. São Paulo de Assunção de Luanda, March 6, 1769. IEB/USP, AL-083–210.
[186] *Calceta:* shackle or iron ring attached to the foot of the enslaved person or galley prisoner.
[187] Carta de FISC para Joaquim de Bessa Teixeira, intendente geral das fabricas de ferro. São Paulo de Assunção de Luanda, January 10, 1772. *Arquivos de Angola* III, no. 29 (1937): 361–363.
[188] In 1769, Sousa Coutinho sent to Nova Oeiras "a detained black stonemason" who was to receive "the necessary food." Carta de FISC para Antonio Anselmo Duarte de Siqueira Intendente Geral das Reais Fábricas do Ferro. São Paulo de Assunção de Luanda, January 1, 1769. IEB/USP, AL-083–192.

penters (10), hairdressers (21), tailors (69), shoemakers (28), coopers (44), and goldsmiths (11). They were divided into masters (65), officers (225), and apprentices (84). Of the total of 374 artisans, 168 were enslaved and 206 were free.[189]

There is no mention of freedmen, which does not seem to correspond to the facts, since the caption of the "map" mentions that one of the carpenters was "black, old, and a freedman of the expelled Jesuits," and that one of the master turners was also a former slave of the priests. Perhaps freedmen were lumped together with free men, but we cannot be certain of this because the categorization criteria are not explicit. Miguel Antonio de Melo, the governor at the time who submitted the list, also noted that, among the free workers, many served as soldiers and had been deported from Europe and Brazil. Although most were classified as "officers"—meaning that they had completed their apprenticeship—the governor deemed them "so unskilled that in any other country they would be considered apprentices and even beginners."[190]

It is interesting to note once again that the history of the Nova Oeiras project provides relevant data and topics regarding labor in the Kingdom of Angola. The count of the artisans was made with the iron factory of Ilamba in mind. The document is addressed to Rodrigo de Sousa Coutinho, who in the last years of the eighteenth century revived his father's plans. Attached to the "map" is a list of workers who could be sent to rebuild the factory.

In this context of shortage of skilled labor, convicts became a permanent source of artisans. If this was the case in the city of Luanda, it was even harder to find skilled labor for royal works in the interior. The fear of sending convicts to the *sertões* was that, without constant surveillance, they would flee or "desert," as the sources cite.[191] For this very reason, in an attempt to escape from prison,

---

[189] "Mapa dos oficiais mecânicos que presentemente há nesta cidade, extraído do que se ordenou do estado da sua povoação no mês de janeiro do corrente ano de 1801." São Paulo de Assunção de Luanda, April 2, 1801. AHU_CU_001, Cx. 100, D. 4.

[190] "Mapa dos oficiais mecânicos que presentemente há nesta cidade...." According to the local authorities, most of the exiled metalworkers could only make nails. "We also need two or three good metalworkers, for there are no local ones, and the exiles so named can only make nails, which does a remarkable disservice to Your Majesty's Royal Treasury." Carta de Antonio Álvares da Cunha, governador de Angola, sem destinatário. São Paulo de Assunção de Luanda, February 28, 1756. AHU_CU_001, Cx. 43, Doc. 4027.

[191] The authorities complained that in the fortresses in the *sertões*, it was easier to escape: "His Majesty's Royal Order, issued on November 14, 1761, in which the said lord orders that those artisans be kept locked up in this city's train, for fear that they may flee to the *sertões*; and despite the fact that in the said fortresses there are insufficient measures to avoid similar flights, I always sent them with the necessary recommendations, not daring to take any other measures upon myself." Carta de FISC para Francisco Xavier de Mendonça Furtado, secretário de Estado dos Negócios da

many convicts lied about their experience with a trade. For example, in 1771, five blacksmiths were sent to Nova Oeiras, but only one of them was a blacksmith officer, "the others confessing that, to free themselves from the imprisonment they suffered, they claimed expertise in trades they did not have."[192] This apparent lack of artisans must be nuanced. Africans were carpenters, blacksmiths, weavers, builders, and certainly learned mechanical trades in the Jesuit missions or serving the Portuguese or Brazilians. Many must have even used those trades to save money to purchase their freedom. Undoubtedly, just as the colonial government failed to control the blacksmiths and smelters and to impose on them working conditions that were alien to their own, they failed likewise with other manual workers.

In addition to the convicts, volunteer artisans went to Angola. Like Matheus Pirson, the Portuguese masters who went there received 1$200 réis per day, plus some allowances that included travel and accommodation expenses. Note that the masters and officers of the 1771 commission, who, according to the hierarchy of mechanical trades, were the best prepared among the artisans, received half of what the Biscayan masters who went there in 1768 received (their salary was 2$400 réis). However, the French refiner was mentioned separately, receiving advance payment for four months of work and two months allowance, totaling 108 $000 réis. Thus, Crown officials made greater efforts to convince him.

According to a letter from Frenchman José Le Vache,[193] foundryman and director of the iron foundries of Foz de Alge and Machuca, in Vila de Figueiró dos Vinhos, Conselho de Tomar (Portugal), some Portuguese iron refiners who worked in the mines were sent at "the time of the Marquis of Pombal" to a factory in Angola, where they died. As one might have expected, this was the Nova Oeiras factory. Francisco de Sousa Coutinho cited the arrival of the "smelters from Figueiró" and elaborated a favorable opinion of their behavior, since they were quite devoted to their work.[194] They were part of the 1771 group that included the seven workers from the Tomar mines. Four of them were refiners and iron hammerers, and

---

Marinha e Domínios Ultramarinos. São Paulo de Assunção de Luanda, June 10, 1764. ANTT, Ministério do Reino mç. 600, caixa 703, doc. 25.

192 Carta de FISC para Martinho de Melo e Castro, secretário de Estado dos Negócios da Marinha e Domínios Ultramarinos. São Paulo de Assunção de Luanda, September 20, 1771. BNP, C 8553, F6362.

193 Carta de José Le Vache para Martinho de Melo e Castro, Secretário de Estado dos Negócios da Marinha e Domínios Ultramarinos. Figueiró dos Vinhos, November 8, 1791. AHU, Reino, Cx. 25, D. 31. Le Vache was a French family that settled in Portugal in the mid-eighteenth century and whose members were traditionally bell casters.

194 Carta de FISC para Martinho de Melo e Castro, secretário de Estado dos Negócios da Marinha e Domínios Ultramarinos. São Paulo de Assunção de Luanda, August 12, 1771. AHU_CU_001, Cx. 55, D. 52 and 56.

among the other three there was a master tinsmith, a tinsmith officer, and a bell caster (see Attachment 3).

Before the names of the foundrymen from Figueiró, we read the expression "volunteer but obliged." This phrase refers to the conditions under which these artisans were sent to Angola. The term "volunteer" meant that they were free and were not sentenced to the voyage as a form of punishment, as in the case of exiled convicts. "But obliged" indicates that, although they were not being punished for a crime, they were obliged to go because they were appointed by the king, which forced them to embark. In the books about Foz de Alge, no details are found about the daily work there or how the eight officers were sent to Africa. Some imprecise data is cited by Antonio Costa Simões in "Topografia Médica das Cinco Vilas e Arega" (Medical Topography of the Five Villas and Arega) (1848),[195] without any documentary reference. Costa Simões claims to have collected reports from the local population that, around 1760, the Marquis of Pombal had the foundrymen arrested, without any justification.

The masters were imprisoned in Lisbon while they awaited shipment, "they don't know whether to Goa or to Angola, to teach ironmaking there." The only purpose of the unjust imprisonment was to promote the iron industry overseas, and José Le Vache escaped for one reason only—being a foreigner. Although we cannot verify this narrative by cross-referencing it with other sources, the fact that the foundrymen were identified as "volunteers but obliged" is a clue that they were not hired without some constraint. According to historian Costa Simões, the foundries of Foz de Alge closed due to a lack of technicians. However, some authors maintain that its closure was due to the difficulties in transporting the iron to Lisbon.[196] The two hypotheses complement each other. The problems with the Portuguese factories were a good reason to invest in more promising enterprises in the colonies, as Nova Oeiras seemed to be, at least in the eyes of colonial authorities.

Furthermore, like the Biscayans, these masters suffered from the harsh local climate: Manuel Simões was the first to be struck down by fevers as soon as he arrived, in August 1771. The only one we know to have survived was Francisco Lourenço, who was ordered to return to the Court in 1777, together with the Frenchman Pirson.[197]

---

[195] Antonio Augusto Costa Simões, *Topografia Médica das Cinco Vilas e Arega: ou dos concelhos de Chão de Couce e Maçãs de D. Maria em 1848* [1860]. 2nd ed. (Coimbra: Minerva, 2003).

[196] Jorge Gaspar (dir.), *Monografia do concelho de Figueiró dos Vinhos* (Figueiró dos Vinhos: Câmara Municipal de Figueiró dos Vinhos, 2004), 90.

[197] Catálogo cronológico de todas as ordens régias que existem na Secretaria do Estado do Reino de Angola. São Paulo de Assunção de Luanda, June 18, 1777. AN (RJ), Códice 543.

Despite knowing and benefiting from the metallurgical knowledge of the blacksmiths and smelters from Ilamba, the governor of Angola did not acknowledge the African capacity to produce iron. So he tried by all means to import masters he considered more skilled, without realizing the implications and problems of these procedures. The successive deaths were the first obstacle to building a European-style factory. When this strategy failed, it was necessary to resort to local skilled labor.

Finally, "slaves for hire," as the captives hired to perform tasks for a wage were called, belonging to settlers of nearby towns or even from Luanda, also worked in Nova Oeiras. We found data on at least 12 enslaved carpenters and masons who received wages from 1768 to 1772, among them, four officers and one apprentice. Note that these enslaved artisans did not work in the foundry or as blacksmiths; this work was performed mainly by Ambundu blacksmiths, who depended on the region's *sobados*.

Table 2: Enslaved laborers who worked at Nova Oeiras, 1768–1772.

Name	Trade	Master	Wages and dates of work
Pedro	Mason apprentice	D. Teresa de Barros da Silva (heir of Luis Gouvea, her brother).	Worked from 1768 to 1770 – 18$300 réis
Antonio	Masson officer	Antonio Simões da Silva	Enslaved workers of the same master worked from March 1772 to April 1773 – 194$200 réis
André	Mason officer	Antonio Simões da Silva	Enslaved workers of the same master worked from March 1772 to April 1773 – 194$200 réis
Miguel	Mason officer	Antonio Simões da Silva	Enslaved workers of the same master worked from March 1772 to April 1773 – 194$200 réis
Caetano Miguel	Carpenter	D. Maria da Conceição Simões	Worked in 1771
Antonio Francisco	Carpenter	D. Maria da Conceição Simões	Worked in 1771
Paulo João	Carpenter	D. Maria da Conceição Simões	Worked in 1771
Amaro	Carpenter	Paulo Gabriel Moreira Rangel	Worked in 1771
Ventura José	Carpenter	Luis Prates	Worked in 1771
João Felipe	Carpenter	D. Teresa de Barros	Worked in 1771
Paulo Sebastião	Carpenter	Cônego Gonçalo Cardia	Worked in 1771

Table 2: Enslaved laborers who worked at Nova Oeiras, 1768–1772. *(Continued)*

Name	Trade	Master	Wages and dates of work
Gaspar	Mason officer	Joaquim da Costa Braga	Worked from February to December 1772 – total wages 59$600 réis

Sources: AHTT, Erário Régio 4191; AHA, Códice 271, C-14-4.

Enslaved workers with some specialization have been a recurring topic in Brazilian historiography for various reasons. On one hand, they were worth more than enslaved people without defined skills and yielded more profits to their master through work for hire, for example. On the other hand, for enslaved people, a trade could represent a means to accumulate wealth in order to obtain their freedom.[198] Analyzing a document that deals with the seizure of the Jesuits' possessions in Angola provides a glimpse of what having a trade meant for captives in Luanda. Among the possessions confiscated by the Royal Treasury after the priests were expelled, there were many enslaved mechanical officers. According to the source, these captives could purchase their freedom for a "good price" because they had "acquired the means to do so with their trades." The text also adds that the enslaved relied on this hope for fear of "being sold to be shipped."[199] Therefore, in the Kingdom of Angola, where there was a shortage of artisans, skills in a certain trade were not only a way to accumulate wealth, they could also keep them from being ensnarled in the transatlantic trade.

As can be seen throughout this chapter, the mechanical officers who built the iron factory and worked there had a variety of backgrounds and legal and social conditions. There were those who were serving time—mostly Europeans and Brazilians—; those who went there voluntarily, persuaded by high wages and promises made by colonial administrators; those who were appointed, coerced, and perhaps even imprisoned, such as the foundrymen of Figueiró dos Vinhos; the Central African "able offspring" of the vassal *sobas*, also coerced to work there, but by means of other social ties, kinship relations; the enslaved for hire, with some possibility of autonomy, among other enslaved workers.

---

[198] "The slaves of artisans and shopkeepers also had many opportunities to purchase their freedom (...) Slaves with such talents not only had a higher prize in the slave market than their unskilled counterparts, but were also highly sought after." A. J. R. Russell-Wood, *Escravizados e Libertos no Brasil Colonial*, trans. Maria Beatriz Medina (Rio de Janeiro: Civilização brasileira, 2005), 62.
[199] Carta de Antonio de Vasconcelos, governador de Angola, para o conde de Oeiras. São Paulo de Assunção de Luanda, May 14, 1760. AHU_CU_001, Cx. 46, D. 4261.

It is worth noting the peculiar organization of labor in Nova Oeiras. The hierarchies within the factory, based on qualification and remuneration, guaranteed discipline, just as the hard work also required the imposition of disciplinary control. However, labor relations were permeated by the logic of social hierarchy and, among the Ambundus, of kinship.

Labor relations were subject to specific obligations that varied depending on the place each one occupied in a complex hierarchical fabric, characteristic of Old Regime societies, also found among Central Africans, in spite of their many differences. The Biscayan master smelters had the best houses, received medical attention when ill, and were well treated, well paid and well fed. The Portuguese masters and Matheus Pirson also enjoyed some comfort. The vast majority of convicts had no privileges; some worked in prisons and many deserted. The largest number of workers were the *sobas*' dependents, who were certainly those subjected to the worst living and working conditions. The enslaved for hire apparently had more autonomy and mobility than those "constrained."

Apparently, the more fragile the ties of dependence, the more devoid of prestige and influence, the more vulnerable these people were to domination and abuse by their superiors. Clearly, origin and social and legal status governed the living and working conditions to which the workers of Nova Oeiras were subjected.

Chapter 4
Blacksmiths and Smelters

4.1 Jingangula, Pulungus and Bellows Operators

As has been said a few times, metallurgy was not a traditional economic activity in Portugal. Therefore, Francisco de Sousa Coutinho took every chance he had to obtain skilled labor. If, on one hand, this led to the death of many European and Brazilian artisans, on the other hand, it increased the dependence of colonial plans on other skilled technicians: the blacksmiths and smelters of Ilamba. In the foundries, they were the best paid. In addition, the governor ordered that those who worked

> forging and with such a violent action of fire, which exceeds what is common, shall receive extra pay, from 10 réis to one vintém per day, which will also apply to apprentices after they have demonstrated outstanding skill, with much higher wages ensured once they have perfectly mastered the trade, so that they can substitute the masters.[1]

Those trades depended on knowledge of smelting and forging iron and accessed the unseen world—which endowed the men who performed them with specific powers, which could result in accumulation of wealth and great political influence in the Ambundu social structure. How did these men end up in the iron factories? Was receiving from 10 réis to one vintém more than other workers enough to attract men of wealth and prestige to the brutal work in the factories? To answer these questions, it is first necessary to understand the blacksmith trade in the Central African context.

There are many academic works on the role of blacksmiths in Central Africa that emphasize that the occupation transcends the limits of the exercise of a trade whose purpose is merely economic.[2] In that region, the trades that transformed nature (smelter) and matter (blacksmith) were related to a complex network of cosmological, social, economic, and political meanings. Being a blacksmith or a

---

[1] Carta de FISC para Francisco Xavier de Mendonça Furtado, secretário de Estado da Marinha e Ultramar. São Paulo de Assunção, November 28, 1768. AHU_CU_001, Caixa 52, D. 44.

[2] Specifically on the blacksmith trade in Central Africa, see: Eugenia W. Herbert, *Iron, Gender and Power. Rituals of Transformation in African Societies* (Bloomington and Indianapolis: Indiana University Press, 1993); Colleen E. Kriger, *Pride of Men. Ironworking in 19th Century West Central Africa* (Portsmouth, NH: Heinemann; Oxford: James Currey; Cape Town: David Philip, 1999); and Juliana Ribeiro da Silva, *Homens de ferro. Os ferreiros na África-central no século XIX* (São Paulo: Alameda, 2011).

smelter was therefore more than just a profession—these people had a different status, had to obey rules and prohibitions, but also enjoyed privileges. About this, Colleen Kriger states that iron artisans shared an "identity based on their occupation, gender, and privilege."[3]

The sources employ words such as craft, master, and apprentice, which refer to a conception of work related to European craft guilds, whereby masters, wage-workers, and apprentices labored in a workshop at a pace that responded to economic demands.[4] Performing a traditional trade was very different among the Ambundus, even though it also involved a process of teaching and learning. Even knowing this, we will employ European words to analyze this topic, since we have no access to the terminology used in the Kingdom of Angola.

There are at least two clear divisions of labor among iron and fire artisans: there were those who smelted the metal and those who shaped it by heating and hammering it; both could have several assistants.[5] In the circumstances in which the Nova Oeiras factory was built, we find three different but inseparable specializations: smelting, forging, and operating the bellows.

The bibliography reiterates the blacksmith's prestige described in missionary narratives since the seventeenth century. In many founding mythos of Central African societies, the association between blacksmiths and political power is common. According to Antonio de Oliveira Cadornega, the first king of Ndongo was a blacksmith called *gongolhas* (sic) (in Kimbundu/Kikongo, *ngangula*, plural *jingangula*), which made the occupation highly esteemed and endowed with social and economic prestige.[6] There were also other words for blacksmith: *musuri, kateli, unsugula, muxiri, ungoxilaekete.*[7]

---

[3] Colleen E. Kriger, *Pride of Men: Ironworking in 19th Century West Central Africa*, 13.
[4] For Portugal, the process of learning a trade prepared new artisans based on successive examinations. *Examined officers* had a right to their own tent. *Masters* were in charge of construction work, "being able to employ workers and receive apprentices." *Workers* were officers who, without having been examined, worked for pay. Finally, *apprentices* were under the responsibility of a master to receive training in his trade. José Newton Coelho Meneses, *Artes Fabris e Serviços Banais: ofícios mecânicos e as Câmaras no final do Antigo Regime. Minas Gerais e Lisboa (1750–1808)*, dissertation (PhD) (Universidade Federal Fluminense, Niterói, 2003), 4, 8.
[5] Colleen E. Kriger, *Pride of Men: Ironworking in 19th Century West Central Africa*, 13.
[6] Antonio de Oliveira de Cadornega, *História geral das guerras angolanas (1681)*, annotated by José Matias Delgado (Lisbon: Divisão de Publicações e Biblioteca–Agência Geral das Colónias, 1940), vol. I, 56.
[7] Antonio da Silva Maia, *Dicionário complementar: português–Kimbundu–kikongo*; A. de Assis Júnior, *Dicionário Kimbundu–Português*; K. E. Laman, *Dictionnaire kikongo–français avec une carte phonétique décrivant les dialectes les plus importants de la langue dite Kikongo*.

Historical linguists have found two variations for the word blacksmith in Lower Kongo, *ngangula* and *npangula*, both derived from the Bantu verb pàngʋd, which means "to cut, separate."[8] Therefore, it had no direct connection to the spread of metallurgy in the region. Over time, it is possible that the political title *ngangula* became metaphorically associated to a blacksmith who, as a leader, was also responsible for resolving disputes ("to separate").[9] Metallurgy and royalty shared a common understanding of nature and the sources of power and their control. In Kongo, chiefs and blacksmiths were initiated under similar circumstances, in collective cults of affliction. They could be of the same lineage, respected food taboos, and wore the same jewelry, bracelets. The blacksmiths were also priests and interceded with the *bisimbi*, creator spirits of metallurgy. By the twentieth century, the accounts of the anthropologist Mertens (1942) record the participation of blacksmiths in the rituals during the investiture and burial of chiefs.[10] Even if blacksmiths were not exclusively kings or noblemen, they participated in these societies as respected leaders.

In other seventeenth-century narratives, such as those by Cavazzi or Antonio Gaeta, the lineage of the king of Ndongo was also related to the mastery of blacksmith techniques.[11] The so-called Mubanga, the main *soba* of Ilamba Alta or Lumbu, was the heir of this lineage. For Cavazzi, the "most respectable craftsmen"

---

8 Koen Bostoen, Odjas Ndonda Tshiyayi, Gilles-Maurice de Schryver, "On the Origin of the Royal Kongo Title Ngangula." *Africana Linguistica* 19 (2013), 56 and ff.
9 Idem.
10 Eugenia W. Herbert, *Iron, Gender and Power*, 136–144; J. Mertens, *Les chefs couronnés chez les Ba Kongo orientaux: étude de régime successoral* (Brussels: G. van Campenhout, 1942); Wyatt MacGaffey, *Religion and Society in Central Africa: the Bakongo of Lower Zaire* (Chicago and London: University of Chicago Press, 1986); Robert Slenes, "L'Arbre Nsanda replanté: cultes d'affliction Kongo et identité des esclaves de plantation dans le Brésil du Sud-Est (1810–1888)," *Cahiers du Brésil Contemporain*, Paris, no. 67/68, partie II (2007): 217–313; Jan Vansina, "Linguistic Evidence for the Introduction of Ironworking in Bantu-Speaking Africa," *History in Africa* 33 (2006): 321–361; John Thornton, "The Regalia of the Kingdom of Kongo, 1491–1895," in E. Beumers and P. Koloss (eds.), *Kings of Africa: Art and Authority in Central Africa* (Maastricht: Foundation Kings of Africa, 1992), 56–63.
11 According to the accounts of the missionary Cavazzi, in the Kingdom of Ndongo, the first "chief of the country" was chosen because Ngola-Mussuri, which means "blacksmith king," was "shrewder than others," as he knew "how to prepare iron" and employed his knowledge with "sagacity and helped everyone in public needs, earning the people's love and applause." Giovanni Antonio Cavazzi de Montecúccolo, *Descrição Histórica dos Três Reinos, Congo, Matamba e Angola, Junta de Investigações do Ultramar,* bibliographic introduction by F. Leite Faria, trans. Father Graciano Maria de Leguzzano (Lisbon, 1965), vol. I, 253. Antonio da Gaeta, *La meravigliosa conversione a lla Santa Fede di Cristo d ellaregina Singa e del suo regnodi Matamba* (Naples: Francisco de Maria Gioia, 1669).

were blacksmiths.[12] As we saw in Chapter 2, it was in this region that the iron factory was built in the eighteenth century. In the words of Cadornega, the *ngangula* "is a highly esteemed trade among these people, and with it they acquire slaves and goods, because it is the most necessary for farming (...),"[13] which refers to the necessary material presence of blacksmiths for the development of agriculture, hunting, and warfare.

According to some authors, smelters did not have the political prominence of blacksmiths, although they were ritually important.[14] Cavazzi, for example, when explaining the origin of wrought iron in Angola, said that, near the mines, "during the rainy season, they take a certain soil carried by water to the roads or ditches and, placing it over coal, work on it with bellows until, separating the slag, the iron is well melted and purged."[15]

The missionary did not refer to the smelter when discussing blacksmiths, highlighting their social place and the esteem of their art, only narrating the smelting process. This leads us to the following hypotheses: that the same artisan performed both functions—a smelter-blacksmith—or that iron smelting was not a trade that guaranteed political influence, at least not like that of a blacksmith. Cadornega made no comments about smelting, so we have no further clues for the late-seventeenth century. In any case, these trades must have been interdependent, for the

---

12 The blacksmith's activity was as follows: "The metalworker sits on the floor bent over painfully, which greatly fatigues him, and hammers with one hand while he drives the bellows or handles the iron with the other." At the end of the forging process, the product was "an arrow, an axe, or an *alfanje* [machete]." Giovanni Antonio Cavazzi de Montecúccolo, *Descrição Histórica dos Três Reinos, Congo, Matamba e Angola*, v. I, 164 and 165.

13 Antonio de Oliveira Cadornega, *História das Guerras Angolanas*, v. I, 25 and 26. In "Catálogo dos governadores do Reino de Angola" and "História de Angola," by Elias Alexandre da Silva Correa, there are references to the history of iron smelting in Nova Oeiras, but no specific details on the work process in the blacksmith's or smelter's workshops. "Catálogo dos governadores do Reino de Angola. Com uma prévia notícia dos princípios de sua conquista e do que nela obraram os governadores dignos de memória," in *Coleção de notícias para a História das nações ultramarinas que vivem nos domínios portugueses ou lhe são vizinhas*. Academia Real das Ciências de Lisboa. Lisbon. Tip. da Academia Real das Ciências de Lisboa, 1826. Elias Alexandre da Silva Correa, *História de Angola*, 3 v. (Lisbon: Clássicos da Expansão Portuguesa no Mundo. Império Africano, 1937).

14 Pierre de Maret, "The Smith's Myth and the Origin of Leadership in Central Africa," in P. Shinnie and R. Haaland, (eds.), *African iron working*. Bergen: *Norwegian University Press* (1985), 73–87; Maria das Dores Cruz, "Ritos e ofícios. Algumas notas sobre a metalurgia do ferro em Angola," in M. Conceição Rodrigues, *Homenagem a J. R. dos Santos Júnior* (Lisbon: Instituto de Investigação Científica Tropical, 1993), v. II, 131–143.

15 Giovanni Antonio Cavazzi de Montecúccolo, *Descrição Histórica dos Três Reinos, Congo, Matamba e Angola*, v. I, 164 and 165.

smelter, once he made the iron, needed the blacksmith to transform it into bars or objects. At least in the sources consulted, the two trades were always cited together as complementary occupations.

Rather than reviewing descriptions of the symbolic and ritual relevance of blacksmiths, our goal here is to examine this trade through eighteenth-century sources in that specific historical context. In this respect, we seek to understand how the master blacksmiths and smelters articulated the set of myths surrounding their craft to exercise their dominance over their dependents and communities in the Ilamba occupied by the Nova Oeiras iron factory.

In December 1768, the Kilamba Ngongue a Kamukala, Antonio Pedro, informed the intendant of the Novo Belém iron factory that he had 42 offspring to offer for work. Among them, 12 were smelters—called *pulungu* in the "language of the land"—, two were blacksmiths, and 28 were bellows operators.[16] In the same region, in the place called Cathari (jurisdiction of Golungo Alto), in 1800, the major and adjutant Antonio Salinas de Benevides described the smelters and blacksmiths as *pulungus* and *gangulas*, respectively.[17]

We were unable to find in Bantu language dictionaries a meaning for the word *pulungu* that is related to the work of a smelter.[18] The only hypothesis that seems plausible to us is the one we were able to propose based on Colleen Kriger's studies. Words for "furnace" that share this root (*-lungu*) have bene found in different regions of Central Africa—Lwena, Luba-Shaba, Hemba, Tabwa, Bemba, and Fipa.[19] According to Krieger, this repetition represents the interchange of technical knowledge between smelters and blacksmiths of different origins. *Pulungo* would thus be related to the smelting furnace and therefore to the smelter's work.

---

[16] Carta de João Baines para Francisco Inocêncio de Sousa Coutinho. Novo Belém, December 17, 1768. IEB, USP, AL-083–203.
[17] Carta de Antonio Salinas de Benevides. São Paulo de Assunção de Luanda, November 15, 1800. *Arquivos de Angola*, v. IV, no. 52 (1939), 323. Benavides considered Cathari a more appropriate location for a foundry: "This place is one and a half leagues further away from the Lukala River than Oeiras and is more salubrious because it is also further from the Lembo lagoons, despite the inconvenience of being further from the river through which exports are carried."
[18] *Pulungu* is usually translated as poor, a miserable beggar. Antonio da Silva Maia, *Dicionário complementar: português–Kimbundu–kikongo* (native tongues of central and northern Angola) (1961); A. de Assis Júnior. *Dicionário Kimbundu–Português* (Luanda: Argente, Santos e Comp., Lda., [n.d.]); K. E. Laman, *Dictionnaire kikongo–français avec une carte phonétique décrivant les dialectes les plus importants de la langue dite Kikongo* (Mémoires de la Classe des Sciences Morales et Politiques, IRCB, 1936).
[19] I would like to thank Professor Robert Slenes for pointing out this hypothesis and calling attention to this word in Kriger's studies. Colleen E. Kriger, *Pride of Men*, 84 and ff.

The *sobas* distinguished between smelters and blacksmiths among their workers.[20] In 1767, at the "Casa de Fundição dos Pretos," where Ambundu smelters, blacksmiths, and bellows operators worked, there were 36 forges, each with three workers—"a smelter and two bellows operators" (a total of 108 people). In ten other forges, three men also worked, "a blacksmith and two bellows operators, who beat the pulp produced by the smelters and shaped them into bars" (a total of 30 people).[21] We can therefore conclude that the division between these specializations did exist. However, they were not independent, but complementary trades.

The smelters and blacksmiths who were subjects of African authorities, such as the aforementioned Kilamba Ngongue a Kamukala or the many blacksmiths of Mbangu kya Tambwa, worked in Nova Oeiras because, as "offspring," they were obliged by kinship relations to do so. They could also have been captured in raids or defeated in war. In any case, these artisans must have been coveted targets in the region. The *sobas* were interested in maintaining a labor force that allowed them to accumulate wealth and military power, given the huge market for iron products in the Kingdom of Angola. It was also in their direct interest to have, among their dependents, those who, through magical-religious powers, legitimized their authority, either by participating in specific rituals or by producing emblems of power, besides being essential craftsmen for the art of war, producing knives, spears, and axes, repairing firearms, and making bullets. This political strategy was not exclusive to chieftains in Angola. In Lower Guinea, in the Ashanti Empire, for example, leaders extended their territorial and political dominion while encouraging arts and crafts. With the Ashanti Confederation, specialized centers emerged—Fumesua, for example, brought together blacksmiths and smelters.[22]

It was not only the *sobas* who had an interest in having these workers around. As the demand for neck shackles, manacles, and prisons increased, merchants and settlers also became their patrons or protectors. This happened especially in Ambaca, which, as we have seen, was the place most affected by the shortage of iron

---

20 In Mbangu kya Tambwa, there were news of "quite a few blacksmiths" who produced hoes, hatchets, and other tools. There were only blacksmiths there, since the metal they used was imported from other places or delivered when the tools were ordered. We have already mentioned the two mines in Ilamba, Quituxe and Calombo, of "ferruginous earth," which were exploited by digging galleries, "deep *furnas*." This demonstrates that different towns could specialize their production according to local demands. Carta de Antonio de Vasconcelos, governador de Angola, para Francisco Xavier de Mendonça Furtado, secretário de Estado da Marinha e do Ultramar. São Paulo de Assunção de Luanda, May 9, 1762. BNP, C. 8553, F. 6362.

21 Carta de José Francisco Pacheco. São Paulo de Assunção, March 15, 1773. AHU_CU_001, Cx. 57, D. 28.

22 J. Anquandah, *Rediscovering Ghana's Past* (Harlow: Longman, 1982), 40.

for these and other objects, such as agricultural tools, caused by the demands from Nova Oeiras—which led to many complaints from the merchants.

On the other hand (or for this very reason), the trade gave blacksmiths and smelters greater mobility—they could leave a *sobado*, or even flee, and seek the protection of other leaders. They would surely be welcome.[23]

Specialized workers could be forced to work in Nova Oeiras, as can be inferred from the recruitment strategies analyzed in Chapter 3.

Another factor that cannot be ignored was access to the mines. The craftsmen had the knowhow, but the mines were exploited by powerful *sobas* and *ilamba* who had long guarded them. To gain access to the ore, one had to negotiate with the local authorities. This might be another reason why many impoverished blacksmiths and smelters went to work in Nova Oeiras, to gain access to the ore and somehow steal the iron produced for their own works or even to sell it, since it was a common object currency in Angola. When in 1762 the governor ordered experiments to determine the quality of the iron produced, he stated that he could not ascertain for sure the amounts manufactured because the "Negroes [blacksmiths and smelters] stole some pieces" of the metal they smelted. If we add this information to the constant surveillance to which the workers were subjected in the factory (they were searched three times a day), it seems plausible to believe that having access to ore was not a simple task and that Oeiras was an opportunity to escape the control of the local chiefs.[24]

Finally, these people were paid in Nova Oeiras. As we have seen, they could be paid in textiles, a valuable commodity that could be easily exchanged for foodstuffs or even enslaved people. For those who were in a situation of poverty, this could be a viable opportunity.

The bibliography points to the existence of ethnic groups linked to the blacksmith trade.[25] Evidence of this can be found in documents referring to the Ilamba factories. In 1767, the governor of Angola ordered the *capitão-mor* of Ambaca to enlist blacksmiths and smelters from Ilamba, but without resorting to the Mubires

---

23 In 1803, "black blacksmiths and smelters" of the *sobas* attached to the presidio in Massangano were living as "refugees" in the lands of other *sobas*. Carta ao regente da Vila de Massangano. São Paulo de Assunção de Luanda, July 8, 1808. AHA, Cód. 91, fl. 97v.
24 Carta de Antonio de Vasconcelos, governador de Angola, para Francisco Xavier de Mendonça Furtado, secretário de Estado da Marinha e do Ultramar. São Paulo de Assunção de Luanda, July 10, 1762. AHU_CU_001, Cx. 45, D. 68.
25 Eugenia W. Herbert, *Iron, Gender and Power*; Colleen E. Kriger, *Pride of Men. Ironworking in 19th Century West Central Africa*.

"until further notice."[26] In the seventeenth century, Cadornega referred to the Vili or Mubires as "black rogues" who roamed the Kingdom of Kongo and "all other parts"; they "roamed around" and were feared for being "great sorcerers."[27] These characteristics are related to the blacksmith craft in Central Africa. With their few tools (besides bellows, they could use stones as anvils and hammers to forge the metal), they could travel around the region in search of customers and markets to trade their products.

In 1656, the Mubires were accused of provoking a rebellion among the enslaved people in the *sanzalas* and *arimos*, inciting them to flee to join "a Negro of the King of Kongo who is leading their war against the Count of Sonho."[28]

In his travel notes from the end of the nineteenth century, Alfredo Sarmento recounts around 1759, when the Encoge fortress was founded, "Mubire Negroes," natives of Loango. He said that "those Negroes' customs and traditions" were different; for example, they did not accept slavery among them. The Mubires paid tribute to the Ndembu and considered themselves foreigners, not including themselves in the local lineages. They were "hardworking and intelligent"; among them were blacksmiths and carpenters. Their commercial identity was related to the trade of enslaved people.[29] Among the characteristics attributed to the Mubires, their social isolation stands out, which can also be considered an aspect of blacksmiths. Since their trade was related to weapons, and therefore to death, blacksmiths were both respected and feared. Moreover, they had an interest in protecting their technical knowledge—isolation contributed to maintain them in secret.

If the Mubires were in Encoge, it is possible that they were recruited to work in Nova Oeiras at some point. However, Sousa Coutinho seemed disinclined to approve of the Ambaca captain's initiative to go get them, perhaps due to their reputation as instigators of rebellion, their isolation, and their fame as powerful sorcerers. We can say no more about the Mubires because we found only one reference to them in the documentation. Apparently, they were a craft-oriented people, including or mainly with iron.

---

[26] Carta de FISC para Francisco Matoso de Andrade, *capitão-mor* de Ambaca. São Paulo de Assunção, May 25, 1767. BNP, C 8742, F 6364.

[27] Antonio de Oliveira Cadornega, *História das Guerras Angolanas*, v. I, 271. David Birmingham demonstrates how the Vili became great merchants of enslaved people in the seventeenth century. David Birmingham, *Central Africa to 1870: Zambezia, Zaire and the South Atlantic* (Cambridge: University Press, 1981), 68.

[28] Carta da Câmara de Luanda, January 19, 1656; Consulta do Conselho Ultramarino, August 3, 1656. AHU_CU_001, Cx. 6, D. 61.

[29] Alfredo de Sarmento, *Os sertões d'África. Apontamentos de uma viagem* (Lisbon: Francisco Arthur da Silva, 1880), 153, 159–161.

We found iron artisans with leadership attitudes in accordance to their position in that society, guaranteed both by their dependence on their practical knowledge and by the *bisimbi* spirits that protected them. Opposing the iron factory, in Ambaca, "Negroes and traders" complained of the shortage of metal. Because of this, "black blacksmiths and smelters" were no longer able to meet the demands of their jurisdiction and of Nova Oeiras simultaneously. The governor, fed up with the intrigues and resistance, ordered the regent of Ambaca: "Your Grace shall leave the black blacksmiths and smelters free to do as they please, since there is no other way to lead such people."[30] "Such people" were apparently not as easily co-opted or "led" as the governor expected—neither with "persuasion" nor with "modest wages." As a result of these pressures, in 1769, Sousa Coutinho ordered that the subjects of the chiefdoms of Ambaca no longer be sent to the factory. Therefore, the artisans involved in ironwork and the "violent action of fire" resorted to the material, cultural, and cognitive resources at their disposal to assert their will in an unfavorable situation, negotiating the terms under which they would work in Oeiras and the length of time they would collaborate with the governor's projects. Their importance and capacity for political articulation was such that the governor of Angola ordered the factory's officers to leave them "free to do as they please."

There is a reference that brings together craft, access to spiritual powers, and political prominence and, contrary to what is usually found in historiography, it has to do with a smelter and not a blacksmith. It is one more evidence of the interdependence between the two trades, and of the fact that both were privileged among the Ambundus. The reference is from March 1800, when the mineralogist José Álvares Maciel described his expenses with some iron smelting experiments. One of them was "to the *soba* of this Ilamba, who performed the first smelting according to their rites," with a payment of 2$400 réis,[31] a considerable amount, since it was the same wage that the Biscayans had received years earlier. In this case, the highest authority of a town, the *soba* himself, was the smelter, which leads us to believe that many political chiefs may have been smelters and blacksmiths and controlled both the iron mines and large numbers of subjects of the same trade.

What reasons might have led smelter *sobas* or "black blacksmiths and smelters," who acted "as they pleased," and political chiefs whose sovereignty depended on their association with iron to collaborate with the Nova Oeiras factory? First,

---

30 Carta de FISC para José Antunes de Campos, regente de Ambaca. São Paulo de Assunção de Luanda, January 25, 1768. IEB/USP, AL-083–002.
31 Carta de José Álvares Maciel para Miguel Antonio de Melo, governador de Angola. Trombeta, March 2, 1800. BNP, C 8553, F6362.

they had requested exemption from the tithe, and in return, they promised workers, or they were vassals who owed obedience; therefore, they would be punished if they failed to collaborate. Second, their alliance with the Portuguese and their participation in the construction of a large factory meant social ascension and prestige in the complex local hierarchy. Sousa Coutinho repeatedly promised that those who collaborated with the factory would become rich. If the *sobas*, *ilamba*, and *imbari* frequently requested military ranks, they were no doubt interested in the mechanisms of social distinction offered by the colonizers.

Finally, according to the local logic, the choices made by smelters and blacksmiths regarding specific techniques and rites were not dissociated from their own economic aspirations. On the contrary, maintaining the location of mines a secret, as we saw in Chapter 2, and hindering access to their specific knowledge through rites and secrets were strategies aimed not only at controlling the labor of their apprentices and dependents, but also at guaranteeing the exclusivity of their products. Working in the factory on a daily basis was a way to know everything that happened there, and perhaps a way to sabotage the colonial project from the inside. In the end, the main reason that Nova Oeiras, built with stone and lime, collapsed was the resistance of those who worked in the "Casa de Fundição dos Pretos." The blacksmiths and smelters rejected the pace of the work and the production demands that the Royal Iron Factory attempted to impose. This was so because they followed a different pace that had nothing to do with the discipline of the factory, casting and forging "according to their rites."

What can be said about those rites? Many rituals were recorded by ethnologists throughout the twentieth century. Obviously, we cannot claim that the rites involving smelting in the late-eighteenth century correspond to those observed more than two hundred years later. However, as the historian Hampatê-Bá reminds us, "traditional crafts are the great vectors of oral tradition."[32] The author considers the exercise of a craft as the ultimate example of the oral tradition because it contains more than actions and gestures; by transmitting knowledge to an apprentice, the master is sharing "veritable moral, social, and legal codes that are peculiar to each group, transmitted and faithfully observed by oral tradition."[33]

---

32 Amadou Hampatê Bá, "A tradição viva," in Joseph Ki-Zerbo (org.), *História Geral da África I. Metodologia e pré-história da África* (São Paulo: Ed. Ática/UNESCO, 1980), 202. It is interesting to note that also in the old French Western Africa, in the Bambara tradition of Komo (Mali), which is the region of Hampatê-Ba's research, many of the rituals described in Redinha's transcriptions are also performed by that region's blacksmiths. For example, the use of special outfits, plants, and prayers was also observed there.
33 Idem, 199.

One example of this continuity is the use of *pemba*, a white clay that was cited by Miller as a sacred powder used by some Ambundu lineages to ensure women's fertility.[34] Around 1950, José Redina recorded the rituals of an iron foundry that also used *pemba*, in the village of Tchiungo-Ungo.[35] In the foundries examined by Redina, the furnace was modeled with female characteristics—with breasts, navel, and female genitalia, at the place from which the iron drained. Redina observed that smelting simulated childbirth. In this context, the use of *pemba* seems to be quite allusive because it ensured a good outcome of the work, in the same way that its use in women of Ambundu lineages ensured their fertility.

In this foundry in the 1950s, the entire process took approximately 11 hours because, during the smelting, the master smelter, who was the *soba*'s son, performed a series of rites in addition to the one described above: he dressed in special clothes ("a doe skin"), said prayers "over the place where the air enters," invoking "the grandparents and uncles, who were successive masters of the trade, requesting their blessing to ensure perfect smelting," among other ceremonies.[36]

The documentation consulted for the eighteenth century, basically composed of administrative sources, records that the pace of work of Ambundu blacksmiths was a hindrance to "industry" and an evidence of "laziness." The use of local tools and techniques was seen as "crude" and "barbaric." One example is Governor Antonio de Vasconcelos's 1759 description:

> since they [blacksmiths and smelters] are naturally lazy and of little industry, they perform only what is necessary according to orders, wasting infinite time for lack of instruments, using only a piece of goatskin as bellows and a stone to beat the iron if they do not have something that can be used as a hammer.[37]

---

34 Joseph C. Miller, *Poder político e parentesco*, 47.
35 Among the Cokwe. José Redinha, *Campanha etnográfica ao Tchiboco (Alto-Tchicapa)*, 2 v. (Lisbon: Companhia de Diamantes de Angola; Museu do Dundo, 1953–1955). *Apud* José Bacellar Bebiano, *Museu do Dundo: notas sobre a siderurgia dos indígenas de Angola e de outras regiões africanas* (Lisbon: Publicações culturais da Companhia de Diamantes de Angola, 1960), 36–43.
36 Idem, 37.
37 Carta de Antonio de Vasconcelos, governador de Angola para Francisco Xavier de Mendonça Furtado, secretário de Estado da Marinha e Ultramar. São Paulo de Assunção, January 18, 1759. BNP 8553, F 6362. Another example, referring more specifically to the economic question: "The opposite happens here, where the Negroes' poverty, their laziness, and their lack of industry, with a total contempt for possessing wealth, makes it truly impossible for them to desire, in the spirit of profit, to increase their service and the production of iron." Carta de Francisco Inocêncio de Sousa Coutinho para Francisco Xavier de Mendonça Furtado, secretário de Estado da Marinha e Ultramar. São Paulo de Assunção, November 25, 1768. AHA – Governo. Ofícios para o Reino. Códice n. 3, fls. 287v-288v.

As we learn from the smelter *soba* Cokwe, the pace of work of any traditional craft in Africa was in tune with two rituals necessary to obtain the ancestors' approval and, in this case, to obtain good results in the smelting process. Ambundu techniques were underestimated by colonial authorities. Colleen Kriger demonstrated that, using tools that at first sight seemed rustic, such as those described above, Central African smelters and blacksmiths developed sophisticated techniques to produce iron by delicately controlling the amount of air blown into the furnace by the bellows. In this way, the smelters were able to determine the quality of the iron they produced, its ductibility, fusibility, and malleability.

The "Casa de Fundição dos Pretos" operated according to local iron smelting methods. When the factory intendant received an order from the governor for 150 quintals of iron (nine tons), he enlisted 138 specialized smelters, blacksmiths, and bellows operators. They worked "daily" in groups of three for "more than five months" to reach the goal set by the governor.[38] The smelters' furnaces together produced an average of two and a half arrobas of iron (30 to 45 kg) per day, and ten blacksmiths' forges transformed the mass of molten iron into *"barretas"* (bars).[39]

For this production, the factory official noted that every day 50 loads or ore were consumed in the factory. As the ore[40] was mined at a distance of three leagues (approximately 15 km) from the factory site and carried by 50 workers, only one trip per day was made.[41] For the tasks described here, 188 people were employed daily in iron production alone.

In addition, each of the 46 forges consumed three bags of charcoal per day, for a daily total of 138 bags.[42] There were also those who cut the firewood, made the

---

[38] It is more likely that, in 150 days, 1 quintal per day (60 kg) was produced, with an average for the governor of 30 to 40 quintals per month. Carta de José Francisco Pacheco. Fábrica da Nova Oeiras, March 5, 1773. AHU_CU_001, Cx. 57, D. 28.

[39] Idem.

[40] Several types of iron ore were found in the region. "In general, in Angola, limonite (hydrated iron), known locally to Europeans by the misnomer 'pyrites,' was extracted from swamps. In Massangano, magnetite was extracted from alluvial sands. In the region of Zenza de Itombe, near Dondo, smelters employed the *embassa* ore (magnetite)." Let us recall that Nova Oeiras was located in Ilamba Alta, in what is now the Dondo province. José Bacellar Bebiano, *Museu do Dundo: notas sobre a siderurgia dos indígenas de Angola e de outras regiões africanas*, 23.

[41] Carta de José Francisco Pacheco. Fábrica da Nova Oeiras, March 5, 1773. AHU_CU_001, Cx. 52, D. Carta de FISC para Francisco Xavier de Mendonça Furtado, secretário de Estado da Marinha e Ultramar. São Paulo de Assunção de Luanda, May 6, 1769. IEB/USP, Al – 082–156.

[42] One charcoal maker with six helpers produced 500 *fangas* of coal in 40 days. Considering that the measurement indicates bushels in liters, it would be equivalent to around 645 liters of coal.

charcoal, and carried it to the factory. The number of workers involved in the activities that supported smelting must have been even larger.

We know the names of six "black smelters" who worked in the foundry: Pedro Manoel, Damião Antonio, Sebastião Antonio, Cristóvão João, Ismão Sebastião, and João André. Their names indicate that they were baptized and vassals of the Portuguese Crown. They were summoned to find out how much their method yielded in iron. Pedro Manoel, the smelter with whom we began this book, with his two bellows operator "servants," consumed 60 pounds of "raw ore," that is, an average of 28 kg of ore mined in the hills surrounding the factory. Pedro built his furnace and, with the help of the bellows operators, started smelting the ore. On the first day, after the smelting, 40 pounds remained; on the second, 20 pounds, about 9 kg of iron. Therefore, two smeltings were needed to produce the iron. These 9 kg of iron went to the blacksmith's forge who, "refining" it, removing the slag, with the help of two assistants, reduced the iron to a small bar weighing four and a half pounds (2 kg).[43]

All other smelters employed the same method and arrived at similar results, ranging from four to four and a half pounds of iron. The smelters, the bellows operators, and the blacksmith who made the bars received $80 réis per day, totaling 3 $200 réis. Twelve kg of iron were produced from 168 kg of ore in 48 hours.

For the governor, this amount of iron was too small; he wanted higher yields like the ones the Biscayans achieved in their hydraulic ironworks.[44] The thing is that, in Biscay, they worked day and night for six days a week—the workers even slept in the foundry. One has to wonder: what *ngangula* and *pulungu* would want to do that?

In Ilamba, the blacksmith's trade seems to have been exclusively male. Antonio Salinas Benevides cited in 1800 that blacksmiths in Golungo Alto would leave their wives to cultivate the field and went to smelt iron. Isolation and the exclusion of women were common characteristics of this trade in Central and West Africa. Eugene Herbert considers that the taboos surrounding the female presence at the time of smelting must be understood in terms of social control of sexuality and reproduction.[45] We also have to consider, as Colleen Kriger reminds us, that the rituals, the secrets, and the exclusion of certain groups from iron and fire crafts are

---

[43] Certidão de José Francisco Pacheco, inspetor das obras da fábrica, sobre o estado da fábrica de ferro. São Paulo de Assunção de Luanda Luanda, March 13, 1773. AHU_CU_001, Cx. 57, D. 28.

[44] In the section "From Biscay" in this chapter, we will examine the everyday operation of a hydraulic ironworks.

[45] Carta de Antonio Salinas de Benevides. São Paulo de Assunção de Luanda, November 15, 1800. *Arquivos de Angola* IV, no. 52 (1939): 323; Eugenia W. Herbert, *Iron, Gender and Power. Rituals of Transformation in African Societies*, 96.

related to strategies of the craftsmen themselves to maintain control over an activity that, as we have seen, endowed them with social, economic, and political privileges.[46] Therefore, the pace of work, the discipline, and the idea of a foundry building was an intrusion into a closed and sacred practice.

Kriger points out that, in Central Africa, smelting took place in the dry season (in this case, during the *cacimbo*, from March to August) because the trees and the ore in stone or earth became soaked during the rains, which reduced the quality of the charcoal and thus of the iron that would be smelted. We found two mentions of this in the sources. Governor Sousa Coutinho ordered the construction of the "Casa de Fundição dos Pretos," a covered place, so they could work during all seasons of the year, avoiding "the excuses that the rains give rise to, hindering the blacksmiths' work."[47] Moreover, in one of his letters, he comments that it was impossible to recruit all the blacksmiths and smelters in Ilamba, since some remained at the place where iron was smelted during the "months of the *cacimbo*."[48] Hence, in the villages, the blacksmiths worked in specific seasons, and in the foundry they operated furnaces all year round.

If the foundry created problems for the internal dynamics of the craft, the hydraulic ironworks completely changed the relation of Ambundu blacksmiths and smelters with their practice. Many became superfluous, since in a hydraulic ironworks it took only about six workers, master smelters and blacksmiths to operate the factory and produce from 40 to 50 tons of iron per year. The "Casa de Fundição dos Pretos" produced about 18 tons per year and employed 138 blacksmiths and smelters. If Nova Oeiras were to operate as a waterwheel-driven ironworks, it would threaten the survival of a trade and all the prestige and social significance that surrounded it inside and outside the factory. Pedro Manoel and his fellow craftsmen, the smelter *soba*, as well as the rebellious "black smelters and blacksmiths" from Ambaca perceived the governor's intentions, even if they had no knowledge of Biscay, and they must not have appreciated the idea.

In Biscay, the trade associations of blacksmiths and smelters refused to turn to blast furnace smelting because it threatened their survival as a craft. Why would it be different with the Ambundus, who perceived all these changes and attempts at interference? That said, the hypothesis that they may have tried to sabotage the colonial project from within becomes more plausible.

---

46 Colleen E. Kriger, *Pride of Men. Ironworking in 19th century West Central Africa*, 57.
47 Carta de FISC para Antonio Anselmo Duarte, intendente geral da fábrica de ferro. São Paulo de Assunção de Luanda, December 10, 1766. BNP, C 8742, F6364.
48 Carta de FISC para Francisco Matoso de Andrade, *capitão-mor* de Ambaca. São Paulo de Assunção, May 25, 1767. BNP, C 8742, F 6364.

4.1 Jingangula, Pulungus and Bellows Operators — 219

The factory attempted to impose a pace of work conceived according to European notions of labor, which in the eighteenth century had already led to patterns and paces that required discipline in the work routine. The organization of labor in the Nova Oeiras iron factory required confinement, division of tasks, formation of hierarchies (factory officials, specialized technicians, and those who performed simple tasks), surveillance and discipline enforcement officials (intendents and factory inspectors), in addition to numerous attempts to instill an "economic use of time" for workers to acquire "working habits."[49] The "time book," daily searches, and timed lunch breaks are examples of this.[50]

Obviously, this was not a Manchester factory model. However, it is equally clear that Governor Sousa Coutinho wanted to institute new forms of social organization of labor—discipline, order, hierarchy—to ensure greater productivity. These onslaughts are evident in the following quote: "here, where the poverty of the Negroes, their laziness, and their lack of industry, with a total contempt for possessing riches, makes it truly impossible for them to desire, in a spirit of profit, to increase their service and the utility of iron."[51] In a quote mentioned earlier, another governor complained that the local artisans worked "wasting infinite time."[52]

The factory was therefore a machine conceived to control, discipline, and hierarchize the labor process of iron production. The changes in work times introduced by Nova Oeiras did not correspond to the expectations of productive work and the meaning of labor for the Ambundus. The Ambundu concept of work obeyed different rhythms and logics of labor organization.

---

[49] These expressions are used by Thompson to describe the attacks against English working habits in the late-eighteenth and early-nineteenth centuries. E. P. Thompson, *Costumes em comum* (São Paulo: Companhia das Letras, 1998), 292 and 293.
[50] See Chapter 3.
[51] Carta de Francisco Inocêncio de Sousa Coutinho para Francisco Xavier de Mendonça Furtado, secretário de Estado da Marinha e Ultramar. São Paulo de Assunção, November 25, 1768. AHA – Governo. Ofícios para o Reino. Códice n. 3, fls. 287v-288v.
[52] Carta de Antonio de Vasconcelos, governador de Angola para Francisco Xavier de Mendonça Furtado, secretário de Estado da Marinha e Ultramar. São Paulo de Assunção, January 18, 1759. BNP 8553, F 6362. Another example, referring more specifically to the economic question: "The opposite happens here, where the Negroes' poverty, their laziness, and their lack of industry, with a total contempt for possessing wealth, makes it truly impossible for them to desire, in the spirit of profit, to increase their service and the production of iron." Carta de Francisco Inocêncio de Sousa Coutinho para Francisco Xavier de Mendonça Furtado, secretário de Estado da Marinha e Ultramar. São Paulo de Assunção, November 25, 1768. AHA – Governo. Ofícios para o Reino. Códice n. 3, fls. 287v-288v.

These two different conceptions clashed in Nova Oeiras, not only in terms of opposing worldviews, but also between the people representing these systems of thought. This context allows us to understand the reasons for the constant escapes, the beatings, and the fact that the governors considered the Ambundus lazy and indolent. The factory took away the autonomy of itinerant service, the prestige of the *jingangula*, and the sacredness that made work inseparable from other aspects of life.

The confrontations were also the result of the colonial situation. The enlightened governor included the African "other" in the legal status of "miserable person"—the allusions to "miserable Negroes" and "poor peoples" are frequent—lacking the means to take advantage of the natural and technological resources at their disposal, and therefore requiring colonial tutelage. This type of justification was developed because, to some extent, the Ambundus were not seen as historical subjects possessing the same complexity as Europeans and, therefore, endowed with equally multifaceted knowledge, culture, and language.[53] It was this worldview that did not allow colonial administrators to perceive the contradiction in the fact that these "miserable and artless" people were metallurgical technicians capable of producing "40 and 50 quintals of iron" per month only with their "small bellows."[54]

Sousa Coutinho not only underestimated the Ambundus' ability to subvert the meaning of Nova Oeiras; he did not take into account the techniques and rustic instruments that produced the high-quality iron and steel he so highly praised, because, in his view, this working process produced very small amounts of iron. To understand the governor's misunderstanding, it is necessary to know some details of the metallurgical techniques employed by Central Africans and their potential.

It may not seem so at first glance, but the rites and ceremonies, the use of plants during smelting, and the rhythm of the bellows have much to do with chemical knowledge, although they transcend this technical function.[55] Iron ore, found in nature, needs to be smelted to become metal. The steps to work with iron can be

---

53 Achille Mbembe, *A crítica da razão negra*, trans. Marta Lança (Lisbon: Antígona, 191); Georges Balandier, "A Situação Colonial: Abordagem Teórica" [1951]. *Cadernos Ceru*, série 2, v. 25, n. 1, June 2014.

54 Carta de Francisco Inocêncio de Sousa Coutinho, governador do reino de Angola, a Francisco Xavier de Mendonça Furtado, secretário de Estado da Marinha e Ultramar, informando sobre o estabelecimento da real fábrica do ferro. São Paulo de Assunção de Luanda, December 29, 1766. RJIHGB/ PADAB DVD10,20 DSC00396.

55 Jacob Bronowski had this idea. After analyzing iron foundries in Sub-Saharan Africa, he said, "When you have no written language, when you have nothing that can be called a chemical formula, then you must have a precise ceremonial which fixes the sequence of operations so that they are exact and memorable." Jacob Bronowski, *The Ascent of Man* (London: BBC, 1973), 171.

broadly divided into mining the ore, making fuel (charcoal in this case), building the smelting furnace, smelting the ore, and finally forging the iron ball obtained to produce bars, utensils, and finished objects. During the smelting process in the furnace, the ore undergoes chemical reactions as a result of its heating, which can be at temperatures above or below the metal's melting point (in the case of iron, 1,538 °C).

In industrial blast furnaces, the product of this operation is liquid pig iron with an iron content of about 95%, which can be readily used in different molds. In the African foundries described in the Nova Oeiras documentation, the iron was obtained in a solid state through a method known as direct reduction, that is, by reducing iron oxides into metallic iron at temperatures below the melting point. The fuel employed was mainly charcoal, which provides heat and which, combined with oxygen during combustion, produces carbon monoxide. This in turn reduces the iron oxides, producing metallic iron and carbon dioxide. Carbon monoxide is very important in this process, "as it provides a reducing atmosphere for smelting iron ore, and by limiting the amount of air supplied to the furnace, smelters can create more carbon monoxide and therefore a larger working area in the furnace."[56]

Put another way, the greater or lesser amount of carbon molecules combined with iron results in metals with different properties. Iron with small amounts of carbon is more malleable; "iron with moderate carbon content (steel) is durable and strong; cast iron with high carbon concentration can be brittle and very difficult to forge."[57] Thus, solid-state iron casting "involves a delicate balance of important factors: air supply and temperature,"[58] both of which are controlled by the iron artisans. The final result of smelting is a mass of iron with impurities, called bloom, which can be turned into products, after hand or mechanical hammering on an anvil.

Some of the technical aspects described so far should be put into perspective. As Colleen Kriger rightly points out, the blast furnaces developed in Europe are not more sophisticated and technically developed than the bloomeries used in Africa. It was long believed that high temperatures could not be achieved with a bloomery. The assumption was that the melting temperatures of some metals could only be obtained with blast furnaces. Actually, those small furnaces are capable not only of reaching high temperatures, but also of maintaining them. In experimental bloom-

---

56 Colleen E. Kriger, *Pride of Men. Ironworking in 19th Century West Central Africa*, 7. See also: Anicleide Zequini, *Arqueologia de uma fábrica de ferro: Morro de Araçoiaba, séculos XVI-XVIII*, dissertation (PhD in Archeology) (São Paulo: USP, 2006), 63 and 64.
57 Colleen E. Kriger, *Pride of Men. Ironworking in 19th Century West Central Africa*, 33 and 34.
58 Idem, 88.

eries, temperatures around 1,600 °C have been obtained. The goal of the African smelters was not only to reach high temperatures. Rather, the challenge was to maintain the temperature controlled at around 1,200 °C and 1,300 °C, and thus the furnace's "reduction atmosphere" was sufficient to create cast iron with "great tensile strength and relatively low carbon content." In other words, "a material that could be conveniently transformed by the blacksmith into various types of products."[59]

In addition, the slag contained in bloomery iron enables greater fusibility, so that pieces of iron can be welded together without the need for a fluxing agent. This makes utensils made with this iron easily repaired, reshaped, and sharpened. With this information in mind, it is interesting to reread some of Sousa Coutinho's comments about the iron produced by the Ambundus. The governor considered this metal superior "to all others for cutting instruments," and the tools produced with it resisted a long "duration" and various uses, as he noted.[60]

The minimum requirements for building a bloomery are: a bowl-shaped furnace dug into the ground, which can be made of clay; one or more conductor pipes through which air is blown into the furnace; and the bellows to supply the air. Walls can be built around the furnace that are many meters high; there is a vast variety of furnace shapes. What enables one furnace to produce more iron than another is not its height or its depth—different smeltings in the same furnace can produce very different results. "To assess the potential capacity of a furnace, i.e. the size of the mass of iron produced or the bloom it could produce, one must be able to measure the potential size of the furnace's working area,"[61] the area with carbon monoxide. To make more bloom, one must increase the area of carbon monoxide production, which can be done by allocating air-conducting tubes at different angles to each other.[62]

José Álvares Maciel wrote the most complete account of all the details involved in the iron smelting process in Nova Oeiras. In it, we find all the technical elements described so far. The mineralogist visited the region of Ilamba (then called Trombeta) several times between 1795 and 1800, and made drawings and took notes based on his observations of local smelters and blacksmiths. Maciel was an impor-

---

59 Ibidem.
60 Carta de FISC para Francisco Ferreira Guimarães. São Paulo de Assunção de Luanda, February 13, 1768. AHA, Códice 79, fl. 78v – 80.
61 Colleen E. Kriger, *Pride of Men. Ironworking in 19th Century West Central Africa*, 63.
62 In a furnace with only one tube to supply air, the carbon monoxide is produced near the tube's mouth. By increasing the number of tubes, it is possible to increase the area of carbon monoxide production, thus increasing the resulting spongy mass of iron. Ibidem.

tant naturalist, a graduate of the Faculty of Natural Philosophy at the University of Coimbra, with extensive experience in mineralogical studies.[63]

In "Notícia da Fábrica de Ferro de Nova Oeiras do Reino de Angola," he identified the tools and the entire process to obtain iron.[64] Two pictures describing two smelting processes are shown below.

José Álvares Maciel explained how local smelters made bloomery iron. He began by describing the tools: the furnace was "less than a foot to a foot and a half in diameter" and eight inches high (approximately 20 cm). Its walls were made of small pieces of "tile or pots" and therefore had some openings. Its shape was that of a basin built above ground. The bellows, just above, had the shape of a wooden drum, and at the top, they had a goat or sheep skin tightly tied, forming a small closed balloon. At the top of the drums, rods were inserted by means of which, with a quick back and forth movement, it was possible to control the air supply. The *longa* was a clay tube that had the same length as the furnace's diameter.[65] It was the tube through which the air was blown into the furnace, also called *porta-vento* or *alcaraviz* or *algaraviz*, which could be made of clay or wood. The number of *longas* and their arrangement were important in the smelting process because they resulted in more or less air flow into the furnace (increasing or decreasing the area of carbon monoxide), therefore resulting in a greater production of iron.[66]

The bundle of *mabú*, which they called *tábua*, the length of the diameter of the cylindrical furnace, was laid down in the furnace so that, after it was burned, it would make way for the *longa*, which moved toward the opposite wall of the furnace as the ore melted. The *mabú*, as we explained in the image caption, is the stem of the papyrus, *Cyperus papyrus*,[67] and is rich in silica. Studies on iron smelting

---

63 A Brazilian, he was sentenced for his involvement in the Inconfidência Mineira and was deported to Angola. Robson Jorge de Araújo, *José Álvares Maciel: o químico inconfidente*, available at https://bibliotecaquimicaufmg2010.files.wordpress.com/2012/02/josc3a9-c3a1lvares-maciel.doc, accessed February 2013.
64 José Álvares Maciel, *Notícia da Fábrica de Ferro da Nova Oeiras do Reino de Angola*. São Paulo de Assunção de Luanda, December 15, 1797. AHTC, Erário Régio, 4196.
65 We did not find the word *lunga* in the Kimbundu and Kikongo dictionaries with any references to smelting (*longa* or *lunga*). Once again, we resort to the idea that it is a word related to the root – *lungu*, which might be related to smelting furnaces.
66 "The distribution and placement of the *porta-ventos* aims at avoiding diametrically opposite positions that could lead to conflicting air flows that could counteract their effect." José Bacellar Bebiano, *Museu do Dundo: notas sobre a siderurgia dos indígenas de Angola e de outras regiões africanas*, 28.
67 "Silica bodies in countless shapes and sizes exist in grasses and palms, and an extensive taxonomy is derived from them." "Cyperuspapyrus (Cyperaceae) – Stem: triangular silhouette, parasitic

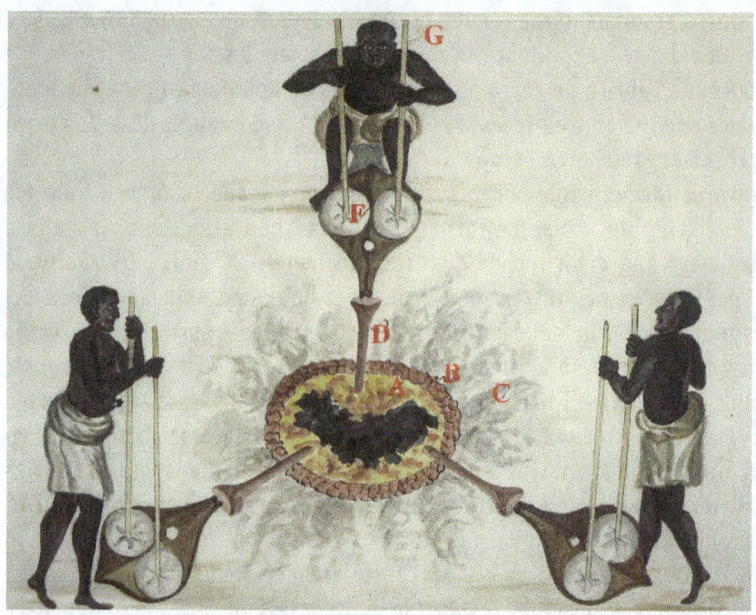

Figures 13 and 14: Iron smelting in Nova Oeiras, 1797.
"A = The smelting furnace, to make iron bars, the ironstone is placed below the coal to be smelted.
B = The furnace wall, built with pieces of tiles.
C = The smoke that comes out from the holes in the wall.
D = The clay pipe through which the bellows blow air.
F = The bellows' leather.
G = Sticks with which they operate the bellows.
This smelting is performed in a short time and it takes little more than an hour."
Source: *Notícia da Fábrica de Ferro da Nova Oeiras do Reino de Angola*. São Paulo de Assunção de Luanda, December 15, 1797, fl. [8]. AHTC [Portugal], Erário Régio, 4196.

processes conducted in Nsukka, Nigeria, demonstrate the use of silica as flux (chemical cleaning or purifying agent) to lower the melting point of the gangue (impurities contained in ores), and thereby extract more iron from the ore.[68]

---

stomata, conical silica bodies in the epidermis cells above the fiber bundles of the hypodermis, parenchyma network with large air spaces, vascular bundles scattered in the parenchyma." David F. Cutler, Ted Botha, and Dennis Wm Stevenson, *Anatomia vegetal: uma abordagem aplicada* (Porto Alegre: Artmed, 2011), 115 and 209.

[68] Edwin Eme Okafor, "Twenty-five Centuries of Bloomery Iron Smelting in Nigeria," in Hamady Bocoum (ed.), *The Origins of Iron Metallurgy in Africa. New light on its antiquity: West and Central Africa* (Paris: UNESCO, 2004), 45–46. Traces of papyri have been found in slag analyzed by arche-

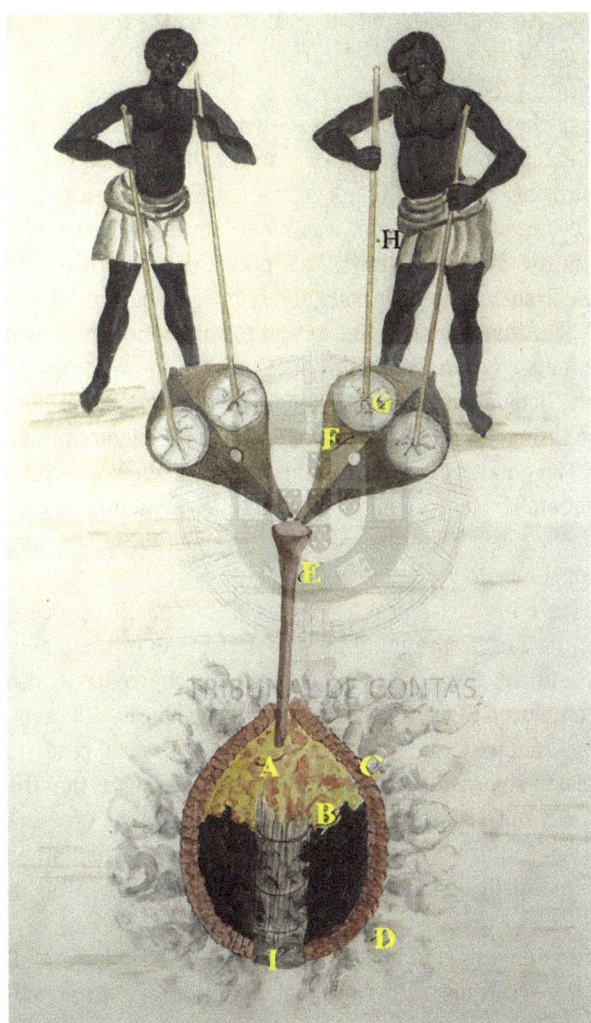

Figure 14: "**A** A bundle of *mabú**, or straw, placed in the middle of the furnace. **B** The iron covered with coal, placed on the sides of the straw, which is also covered with the coal, and as it burns, the clay tube is inserted. **C** Furnace wall with a lattice of pieces of tile. **D** The smoke coming out of the holes in the furnace wall. **E** Clay tube meeting the bellows. **F** The tube reaching the stone. **G** Bellows leather. **H** Stick to move the bellows. **I** the ironstone is smelted.
This smelting is with ironstone, I placed two arrobas and six pounds of ironstone, and in four hours it smelts up to [the manuscript does not provide the amount] pounds of iron."
*Bundle of papyri, its stems. In Antonio de Assis Júnior, *Dicionário kimbundu-português, linguístico, botânico, histórico e corográfico. Seguido de um índice alfabético dos nomes próprios* (Luanda: Argente, Santos e Comp. Lda., [n.d.]), 271. Source: *Notícia da Fábrica de Ferro da Nova Oeiras do Reino de Angola* (São Paulo de Assunção de Luanda, December 15, 1797, fl. [9]. AHTC, Erário Régio, 4196).

The bundle of straw might have been used only to heat the furnace for smelting and open the way for the *longa*; however, we venture that the *mabú* was used to increase and enhance the iron produced.

After placing the coal at the bottom of the furnace, where there was a small opening (into which the molten iron drained), they inserted the crushed ore together with the coarsely broken coal. The "mouth of the *longa*" was then placed at the head of the straw cylinder and the iron was melted in the furnace with the air supply provided by the manual bellows. This operation could take one hour in the first picture, which shows three workers and represents bar iron smelting (a re-melting process), and four hours in the second picture, where only two men are shown and represents iron ore smelting.

Maciel also recorded the body movement of the smelter and bellows operators —the smelter, squatting (or sitting) on the floor, controlled the process, determining the rhythm of the bellows. The other two men, standing, moved the bellows with a repetitive and rhythmic motion. The movement of the bellows was essential to control the quality of the iron. We can presume that specific smelting songs were chanted, setting the pace of the bellows.[69]

Álvares Maciel did not take into account other stages of the smelting process: the time required to build the furnace, to mine the iron-rich stone in the mountains, to grind those stones, to cut down trees and prepare the charcoal. He also did not calculate the time employed after the smelting, when the blacksmith, hammering the iron in his forge, removed most of the slag, leaving the metal ready to make a wide variety of tools. In any case, what Colleen Kriger points out is that the bloomery type of furnace did not require large investments of energy, ore, and fuel, and all the resources needed to use it were abundantly found in the Ilamba region.[70] The bellows were manually operated and the ore was easily accessible in the area.

Colonial officials did not understand why Ambundu smelters produced small amounts of metal and worked according to rhythms that were contrary to the "spi-

---

ologists in the Kingdom of Buganda, current-day Uganda, in the Great Lakes region. Louise Iles, "The Use of Plants in Iron Production," *Archaeology of African Plant Use* 61 (2013): 267.

69 Christopher Roy recorded the iron smelting process in the town of Dablo in Burkina Fasso. In this video, rhythmic songs are sung by the bellows operators during the smelting process. Christopher D. Roy, Jean-Baptiste Kientega, Jacob Bamogo, and Abdoulaye Bamogo, *From Iron Ore to Iron Hoe: Smelting Iron in Africa* (United States: CustomFlix, DVD, 2005). Part of the DVD's content is available online at https://www.youtube.com/watch?v=RuCnZClWwpQ, accessed March 15, 2016.
70 Colleen E. Kriger, *Pride of Men. Ironworking in 19*th *Century West Central Africa*, 59.

rit of profit."⁷¹ What the governor and the officials did not know was that the local artisans possessed an ancient knowledge that allowed them to control the natural resources at their disposal, employing an appropriate technique. They controlled the knowledge of iron and fire; they knew how much air the bellows should supply, when to stop, and when to place crushed ore or coal in the furnace. Such knowledge was related to the artisans' traditional responsibility to preserve the balance between the forces of nature, but not only this. The magical/religious connotation attributed to the trade had practical implications.

For example, to make charcoal, the smelters selected the most appropriate wood to produce better quality charcoal. According to factory officials, Central Africans did not know how to make it from "thick wood," thus wasting what they believed was the "best wood." The Ambundus used only the "branches."⁷² Paradoxically, the previous year, Sousa Coutinho gave instructions to cut the wood "as the Negroes do" because, "with this method, the next year they have access to the same amount of trees and bushes as they did this year."⁷³ Perhaps the charcoal makers employed the *árbol tras mocho* technique, like the Biscayan blacksmiths: they preserved the tree trunks, cutting only the branches, in order to increase the plant's lifespan and the number of cuttings. In addition, the trees suitable for smelting were slow-growing trees in the region; they took about 20 years to reach the stage where they could be used.⁷⁴ Large-scale woodcutting would make this resource scarce, and therefore it had to be used sparingly. In any case, the Portuguese believed that the Ambundus had to be told to refrain from employing this method, which white charcoal makers considered inefficient.

What is most interesting is that the prejudiced colonial view resulted in economic losses for the colonial agents themselves. Let me explain: the factory's work inspector reported that the bars produced by Ambundu smelters and black-

---

71 Carta de Francisco Inocêncio de Sousa Coutinho para Francisco Xavier de Mendonça Furtado, secretário de Estado da Marinha e Ultramar. São Paulo de Assunção, November 25, 1768. AHA – Governo. Ofícios para o Reino. Códice n. 3, fls. 287v-288v.
72 Carta de Antonio Anselmo Duarte de Siqueira, intendente geral das fábricas de ferro, para FISC. São Paulo de Assunção de Luanda, July 24, 1768. IHGB/ PADAB, DVD10,22 DSC00189.
73 "Instrução que deve guardar Antonio Anselmo Duarte de Siqueira, servindo o emprego de intendente geral da fábrica do ferro, e que executarão também os capitães-mores, como intendentes particulares na parte que lhes é respectiva" (FISC). São Paulo de Assunção de Luanda, January 12, 1767. AHU_CU_001, Cx. 52, D. 73.
74 "Of considerable ecological importance is the fact that tree species suitable for charcoal also tend to be slow-growing. For example, replacement of the two *B. africana* trees will require more than twenty years of growth." Candice L. Goucher, "Iron is Iron 'Til it is Rust: Trade and Ecology in the Decline of West African Iron-Smelting," *The Journal of African History* 22, no. 2 (1981): 181. In Angola, this species of tree is known as *Carapingau* or *Pau ferro*.

smiths underwent a second refining process in the forge of the white blacksmiths, in order to "better refine it," because, according to the official, the iron produced had too much slag. This process reduced the daily production by up to one arroba (15 kg).[75] If we recall that African craftsmen purposefully produced iron with more slag to ensure greater fusibility, we realize that the colonial initiative lacked the necessary technical knowledge to take advantage of Ambundu knowledge. Thus, much of what ensured the quality of the local iron was removed and remained in the forge of the white blacksmiths.

Reading the notes of overseas authorities and those of José Álvares Maciel shows that Ambundu ironmaking technology was thoroughly analyzed. In this respect, Nova Oeiras is different from the Mon-Désir factories of Île de France and any others we know of. If in Mauritius the enterprise was the initiative of a private individual who, with European smelting techniques, employed enslaved labor, in Angola, Sousa Coutinho insisted that the enterprise should be managed by the Royal Treasury, drawing on the skills of local blacksmiths and smelters, even if they had to be taught how to increase production.

The "practical Negroes," as the local blacksmiths and smelters were called, and the *sobas* and *makota* to whom they were subjected, interpreted the royal initiatives differently: as an intrusion by *sertanejos* and naturalists in an activity that had sacred elements and as a continuous exploitation of their skills in Nova Oeiras, imposing on them an extenuating pace and work conditions, contrary to the Ambundu ways of being and working. As the sources allow us to perceive, the workers' escapes and the *sobas*' resistance to continue sending their "offspring" indicate that Central Africans did not intend to collaborate with a factory that only harmed them. All of Sousa Coutinho's efforts to demonstrate that his projects could bring prosperity to the region proved ineffective. The process was not linear, but over time, the workers and their chiefs decided that the business was of no interest to them. For the local chiefs, Nova Oeiras meant the loss of specialized workers, of profits from the iron trade, and another source of loss of their dependents, and for the blacksmiths, at the very least, the end of a traditional trade that gave them social prestige and autonomy.

In this complex and violent clash of interests, the quick death of many of the European experts who could have harnessed African knowledge and transformed Nova Oeiras into a hydraulic ironworks first and a blast furnace factory like that in Mauritius later did not allow European techniques to take root in Angola. However, to blame the hostile climate and disease or mismanagement by royal officials for

---

[75] Carta de José Francisco Pacheco. Fábrica da Nova Oeiras, March 5, 1773. AHU_CU_001, Cx. 57, D. 28.

the continued use of African technology would completely overlook the agency of the blacksmiths and the political elite of Ilamba in the historical process. In their own way, Central Africans rejected the Portuguese industrial experiment. Thinking otherwise would reiterate Eurocentric versions of this history, for we would miss the most important argument developed here: that the Ilamba technology continued to be used at the factory because of its excellence. Even using prejudiced expressions to characterize African labor, such as "imperfect" or "defective," and judging the simple tools they employed as an example of "ignorance" and "poverty," the enlightened governor acknowledged their merits. In 1768, in a letter to the Morgado of Mateus, he said: "I have many much better Negroes, who not only have made this kingdom subsist for four years without iron from Europe, but have produced many hundreds of quintals that I have sent to His Majesty."[76]

Reflecting about African scientific contributions such as metallurgy allows us to "decolonize" the history of science of the field of study known as intellectual history or the history of concepts and discourses.[77] We can recognize this today because scholars started to wonder about the potentialities of African iron. All the technical aspects that Colleen Kriger masterfully details were discovered since the 1970s. Before then, the "pyrotechnic model," based on the understanding that metallurgy developed as furnaces reached higher temperatures, held sway. Only when archaeologists started experimenting with bloomeries to test temperatures did they begin to discover the potential of these furnaces and of the iron produced by them.

What I mean by this is that it was not only Sousa Coutinho who was immersed in prejudices that separated the "primitive," "slow," "traditional" world from the "dynamic," "modern," and "civilized" world. The colonial perspective persisted in science and history until very recently, being questioned mainly after the independence of African countries. In the case of the present study, as long as we look only at the stone and lime monument of the Royal Iron Factory of Nova Oeiras, we will continue to repeat the colonial gesture that attempted to conceal[78] the experience and dynamic history of the iron trades among the Ambundus and to neglect

---

[76] Carta de FISC para Luis Antonio de Sousa, Morgado de Mateus, governador de São Paulo. São Paulo de Assunção de Luanda, November 30, 1768. ANTT, Projeto reencontro Morgado Mateus mf. 12.

[77] Nancy Rose Hunt, "The Affective, the Intellectual, and Gender History," *Journal of African History* 55, no. 3 (2014): 331–345. Some studies on the topic: V. Y. Mudimbe, *The Invention of Africa* (Bloomington: Indiana UP, 1988); Ngugiwa Thiong'o, *Something Torn and New: An African Renaissance* (New York: Basic Civitas, 2009); Frederick Cooper, *Africa in the World: Capitalism, Empire, Nation-State* (Cambridge, MA: Harvard UP, 2014).

[78] Enrique Dussel, *1492: el encubrimiento del otro* (La Paz: Plural, 1994).

the existence of the "Casa de Fundição dos Pretos," the mines of Samba-Quiba, Mbangu kya Tambwa and Ngongue a Kamukala, and their protagonism.

It was a common practice for colonizers to incorporate African knowledge and traditions, and some studies have examined the development of knowledge in colonial circuits, especially in regards to therapeutic traditions. Although at first Europeans attempted to treat the diseases they encountered in Africa according to their tradition, with time and after observing local medical treatments, they adopted local knowledge to treat unknown diseases in an unfamiliar environment. Surgeons, physicians, travelers, and naturalists observed the so-called "black bloodletters," the healers, and learned about herbs and "all the elements that are applied in African societies to cure ailments due to scabies, foot worms, wounds, and scurvy."[79]

In Mozambique, African therapeutic practices were added to European and Asian ones, including those of Muslim and Hindu origin. By analyzing the history of the Royal Hospital of the Island of Mozambique, which dates back to the beginning of the sixteenth century, Eugenia Rodrigues demonstrated how these influences were present there. The references to the knowledge of local surgeons and physicians indicate that the "domestic medicine" of Mozambique was practiced there by Goans and enslaved and free Africans. Its apothecary had medicines of European origin, but also Indian drugs from Goa.[80]

The historiography on African influences on American culture and knowledge is more comprehensive. Judith Carney and Richard Rosomoff wrote a book full of information about plants, eating habits, and farming techniques originating in West Africa and brought by Africans and their descendants to America, with a multidisciplinary approach based on archeology, ethnography, and oral history, whereby the authors argue that the enslaved provided their masters not only with manual labor, but especially with intellectual work. Thanks to the beds in which they cultivated the seeds they brought from Africa and their culinary skills, food be-

---

[79] Maria Cristina Cortez Wissenbach, "Ares e azares da aventura ultramarina: matéria médica, saberes endógenos e transmissão nos circuitos do Atlântico luso-afro-americano," in Leila Mezan Algranti and Ana Paula Megiani (orgs.), *O império por escrito: formas de transmissão da cultura letrada no mundo ibérico séculos XVI–XIX* (São Paulo: Alameda, 2009), 375–394. See also Cristiana Bastos and Renilda Barreto (orgs.), *A circulação do conhecimento: medicina, redes e impérios* (Lisbon: ICS, 2011).

[80] Eugénia Rodrigues, "Moçambique e o Índico: a circulação de saberes e práticas de cura," *MÉTIS: História & Cultura* 10, no. 19 (2012): 32.

came a powerful vehicle to preserve and create memories in the diaspora. Moreover, African ingredients became the basis of American food.[81]

For all these reasons, the iron factory in Ilamba and the contribution of the Ambundus could not be excluded from the mineralogical and scientific studies that multiplied in the second half of the eighteenth century, in the context of the Pombaline policies to promote manufacturing.

I think it has become clear here that the construction of the factory is not related to a technical superiority of hydraulic ironworks. The Ambundus smelted excellent iron with their own tools and knowledge. We still need to understand better the reasons for building such a factory.

4.2 From Biscay

Paradoxically, the iron produced by the Ambundu artisans was consistently praised by colonial authorities, but the techniques employed by the local smelters and blacksmiths were considered inefficient because they did not produce large amounts. When Sousa Coutinho requested that Biscayan blacksmiths be employed, he chose them because their technique, which was very close to that of Central Africans, could correct that "defect" of the small local foundries. The big difference between the Biscayan and the African method was the size of the bellows, which were driven by hydraulic force. The ones used in Spain were larger and therefore allowed increasing the production, and consequently the profits.[82]

The Luanda government's comparison of the techniques used by Ilamba smelters and blacksmiths and those employed by the Biscayan workers was not fortuitous. Sousa Coutinho no doubt sought to inform himself about the ironmaking technologies available at the time and the one most suited to local techniques. The Biscayan hydraulic ironworks were famous for producing high-quality iron, which, until the late-eighteenth century, was one of the main Spanish export products, together with wool. It was mainly during this period that Biscayan iron lost market share to iron made in Sweden, Russia, and England, with the spread of cok-

---

81 Judith A. Carney and Richard Nicholas Rosomoff, *In the Shadow of Slavery: Africa's Botanical Legacy in the Atlantic World* (Berkeley, Los Angeles, and London: University of California Press, 2009).
82 "This same method is employed by the country's Negroes, differing only in the quantities, and therefore, as soon as they learn how to make greater quantities with larger bellows than they currently use, the factory's profits will multiply considerably." Carta para Francisco Xavier de Mendonça Furtado. São Paulo de Assunção, January 20, 1769, IEB/ AL – 082–142.

ing coal smelting.⁸³ However, as Chris Evans reminds us, while one should not underestimate African iron production, we should not overestimate European production either. Manufacturing iron in blast furnaces was limited to a small region in the Austrian Alps. Wrought iron, especially "travel iron," tailor-made for West African markets, dominated the market in Europe.⁸⁴

In Biscay, the use of hydraulic power to drive large bellows and hammers made these mechanisms more powerful and efficient, reducing the work of the bellows operators and the blacksmiths who hammered the pasty mass to remove the slag. As we know, "technical progress appears as a response to the imperatives of the disciplinary and hierarchical organization of labor."⁸⁵ At the same time, the new machinery considerably increased production. Other than this, the chemical process was the same as in Central Africa, i.e. the direct reduction of iron oxide using charcoal as fuel.⁸⁶

Since Sousa Coutinho wanted to increase the factory's production, a hydraulic ironworks seemed to him the most adequate alternative. The necessary resources were within reach and the technical process was very similar to that of the local blacksmiths and smelters. According to his plans, the similarities would help Central Africans to learn the new technology that promised greater productivity.⁸⁷ In

---

83 With the introduction of coking coal in northern Europe (1709), iron smelting started to be done in blast furnaces made of brick, using coaking coal as fuel. In 1735, Abraham Derby was the first to operate a blast furnace using only coaking coal. By replacing charcoal, deforestation was no longer an obstacle to the development of the European steel industry. Joaquín de Almunia y de León, *Antigua indústria del hierro en Vizcaya* (Bilbao: Caja de Ahorros Vizcaina, 1975), 3–5.
84 Chris Evans, "'Guinea Rods' and 'Voyage Iron': Metals in the Atlantic Slave Trade, their European Origins and African Impacts," *Economic History Society annual conference* (2015), 1–15.
85 Edgar Salvadori de Decca, *O nascimento das fábricas* (São Paulo: Editora Brasiliense, 1982), 60.
86 Although in Spain blast furnaces using charcoal were created before coking coal-fired blast furnaces, it was only in the nineteenth century that this technology started being used in Spanish factories. Until then, hydraulic ironworks predominated in the region, manufacturing iron with the direct reduction method. The first charcoal-fired blast furnaces (indirect reduction) in Spain were built in Cantabria in 1628–29. The investment in blast furnaces came from the Spanish Crown itself in order to increase the war industry. Pedro Arroyo Valiente and Manuel Cordera Millan, *Ferrerías en Cantabria. Manufacturas de ayer, patrimonio de hoy* (Santander: Asociación de Amigos de la Ferrería de Cades, 1993), 12–19. Joaquín de Almunia y de León, *Antigua industria del hierro en Vizcaya*, 15–35.
87 The governor of Angola demonstrated his knowledge of the techniques to produce iron in the region of Biscay. Francisco Coutinho discusses how widespread the techniques and factories were in that locality: "because in Biscay it suffices for one resident to build one of these factories for his neighbor to want another one, and thus they reproduce throughout the province." Carta de FISC para Francisco Xavier de Mendonça Furtado. São Paulo de Assunção de Luanda, November 25, 1768. IEB/ AI – 082–109.

December 1768, for the governor, "the most important business" in the factory was to "teach the black smelters to produce larger quantities working with large bellows, and therefore the masters must teach them promptly."[88] The masters he was referring to were the unfortunate Biscayans who met their death quickly. Part of the project of the enlightened administrator was to turn Nova Oeiras into a great workshop where local workers would be trained to operate hydraulic machinery. This would reduce expenses with foreign skilled labor and control the technical process of the local blacksmiths.

The Nova Oeiras iron factory was therefore planned according to the models of the Biscayan ironworks. As discussed in Chapter 2, the site was chosen because of its proximity to the Luinha River (which was dammed) and the Lukala River, to woods, and to iron ore, all of which were necessary to establish the ironworks.

The governor wanted to build a factory not because of a presumed technological superiority of hydraulic ironworks. On the contrary, the Ambundus smelted iron and steel that was in no way inferior to that produced in Biscay. It must be emphasized that his goal was to increase production. Stephen Marglin elucidated something similar: "The factory's origin and success are not explained by technological superiority, but by the fact that it takes all control from the workers" and gives, in this case to the governor/Royal Treasury, "the power to prescribe the nature of the work" and the "amount to be produced."[89] Confining the Ambundu smelters in the factory allowed seizing from them their control over the work process, the secrets they so protected, and imposing the necessary work pace to increase productivity. The *jingangula* certainly understood this.

The migration of skilled workers from Biscay to guide the operation of foundries and to teach their technique was not new to the Portuguese. Smelters from northern Spain had been working in the ironworks and mines of the Pyrenees since the Late Middle Ages.[90]

In Biscay, it was in the Somorrostro mines that iron ore extraction developed most intensely and continuously. The ore was traded by sea along the Cantabrian coast and by land to the interior of Biscay, north of Álava and Burgos. Work in the mines was seasonal: it began in the spring, reached its highest productivity in the summer, and ended in the fall. In the eighteenth century, during these six months with an average of 140 workdays, 420 people were employed, mining four hours a

---

[88] Carta de Francisco Inocêncio de Sousa Coutinho para o capitão José Francisco Pacheco. São Paulo de Assunção de Luanda, December 3, 1768. IEB/USP – Col. ML, 83.
[89] Stephen Marglin, "Origens e funções da parcealização das tarefas. Para que servem os patrões," in André Gortz, *Crítica da Divisão do Trabalho* (São Paulo: Martins Fontes, 1980), 24.
[90] Rafael Uriarte Ayo, "Minería y empresa siderúrgica en la economía vizcaína pre-industrial (s. XVI-XVIII)," *XI Congreso Internacional de la AEHE* (Madrid, 2014), note 3, p. 2.

day, not counting the travel time to the mines (an average of six hours). In addition, from 400 to 500 workers carried the ore from the mounds to the shipping place, using mules and ox carts. About 1,000 sailors were employed on the ships that carried the ore by sea. Therefore, about 2,000 workers, mostly peasants, were involved in extracting and transporting the ore.[91]

Another important step for iron smelting was cutting trees and preparing the charcoal. To prevent a shortage of fuel, a specific cutting method (*árbol trasmocho*) was adopted, which, as we saw, allowed the regular extraction of wood without having to fell the trees. The central trunk of the young tree was cut at a height of about two meters from the ground, favoring the development of side branches, which were used to manufacture charcoal. This was also a seasonal activity—the cutting was done in the winter and charcoal was manufactured during spring and summer. In this period, the days were longer and there was less risk of storms. Rafael Ayo observes that, although it cannot be quantified, charcoal making was probably the fastest growing forest activity in Biscay and the one that employed the largest number of workers, mostly peasants.[92]

Starting in the second half of the seventeenth century and throughout the eighteenth century, the difference between a larger ironworks, where raw iron was obtained or transformed into bars, and a smaller one where the iron was further elaborated or transformed into products disappeared. The new ironworks, which integrated both stages, was called *ferrería tiradera*, i.e. marketable iron was obtained from the ore (in Spanish, *se tiraba el hierro*, hence the name *tiradera*). The Biscayan ironworks employed four to five workers, a master forger (a blacksmith specializing in "pulling" the iron and giving the piece the first forged finish),[93] two smelters, and one apprentice. One administrator who lived near

---

91 Idem, 8.
92 Idem, 12.
93 In the ironworks of Taramundi and Los Oscos (Asturias), for example, the technical organization of work was divided between five officers: one *aroza*, one *tirador*, two smelters, and one *trazador*. The team leader was the *aroza*, a term that in Basque means person in charge or foreman of an ironworks, "a blacksmith with ample knowledge in the matter, which he acquired directly from another *aroza* and which he broadened with experience—a knowledge he guarded jealously until it was time to pass it on to his successor." He was the highest-paid officer in the factory. He was followed in the hierarchical structure by the smelters, who controlled the ore's reduction in the furnace, the loads of ore and coal, distributing them correctly to ensure a greater yield, as well as the work of the bellows. "At the same work and economic level was the *tirador*, a specialized blacksmith in charge of 'pulling' the iron" and giving the piece its first forged finish. This was the most strenuous job, for he worked near the furnace's heat, beating the masses of iron that came out of the furnace every four hours. The lowest-ranking officer was the *tazador*, who crushed the ore until it was the size of a hazelnut before it was placed in the furnace, and helped other

the ironworks was responsible for the factory's operation, its financing, hiring officers, acquiring ore and fuel, solving conflicts, disciplinary tasks, and other duties.

In this space, people worked day and night for six days a week. The artisans ate and slept in the ironworks. Remuneration varied according to the amount of iron produced, with a bonus for each quintal. The master iron maker was paid more than the smelters, and the smelters were paid more than the apprentices, who received a pair of shoes and some cash. Different demands resulted in considerable variations in the machinery, which in turn resulted in different production outcomes. The process depended on the amount of water in the rivers (which varied during the dry seasons), the availability of raw materials, the capacity to maintain and repair the machines, and market conditions. Precisely for this reason, the ironworks rarely operated uninterruptedly the whole year. In the late-eighteenth century, an iron factory produced about 40 to 50 tons per year. In 1784, there were about 140 such factories in Biscay.[94]

The factory had a stone building that housed the machinery and the reduction furnace. Outside, the main infrastructure was the hydraulic structure, destined to capture and distribute the water needed for the factory's operation: the weir that intercepted the water from a river and diverted it through a channel to the factory's reservoir (the *banzado*), which was below the hydraulic wheels. The weirs were built far from the factory in order to ensure the necessary slope for the plant's dimensions. The Nova Oeiras factory was built according to this model. The weir was built with stone, which provided a better seal. The canal was made with arches that, according to Villarreal, were a technical improvement, since they saved construction material and ensured greater safety for the building.[95]

There could be many internal divisions, but they all composed a single ensemble: one of the facilities housed the hammer and the bloomery (called *la fragua*); the bellows and their infrastructure were on the other side of the wall where the furnace was located (the *bergamazo* wall, also known as the forge wall). Other

---

officers with a variety of tasks; for this reason, it was usually a young apprentice. Pablo Quintana Lopes, *La labranza y transformación artesanal del hierro en Taramundi y Los Oscos. Siglos XVI-XVIII. Aportación a su conocimiento* (Taramundi: Asociación "Os Castros," 2005), vol. I, 142 and 143.
94 Idem, 23. "According to data estimated for different areas of the territory (1827), the weekly product varied from a minimum of 2,562 kg in the Marquina ironworks to a maximum of 3,345 kg in Valmaseda and Trucíos."
95 P. B. Villarreal de Berriz, *Máquinas hidráulicos de molinos y herrerías y govierno de los árboles y montes de Vizcaya* (San Sebastián: Sociedade Guipuzcoana de Ediciones y Publicaciones de la Real Sociedade Vascongadas de Amigos del País y Caja de Ahorros Municipal de San Sebastián, 1973), n.p.

spaces in the same building were used to store the coal and the ore, as well as serving as dormitories for the workers.

The following figures show detailed interior blueprints of the ironworks and the foundry, where smelters and blacksmiths used levers to control the operation of the hydraulic wheels that propelled the large bellows and the hammer, in addition to working in the forge transforming the iron obtained into bars (as we see in Figure 10).

The bellows were usually made of leather and wood, and as time went by, models only in wood appeared, consisting of interconnected compartments that allowed capturing and expelling the compressed air between them. In Nova Oeiras, the bellows designed by the Biscayan blacksmiths were supposed to be made of leather and wood.[96]

The hammer was driven by cams[97]; the one shown in the figure above and in the Nova Oeiras blueprints[98] is the *martillo de cola* (tail hammer). This was the most commonly used hammer in the north of Spain. The expression "tail hammer" derives from the fact that the cams acted on the rear end of the hammer's axle or shaft. The movement lifted the hammerhead, which fell due to its weight on the anvil, where the iron was forged. The hammerheads weighed from 50 to 350 kg, striking the mass of iron with a frequency ranging from 120 blows per minute —when the lifting height was 48 cm— to 300 blows per minute, with a height of 15 cm.[99]

The model described so far is the one found in the Nova Oeiras blueprints designed by the military engineers Manuel Antonio Tavares, João Manoel de Lopes, and Miguel Blasco, as shown in Chapter 2. According to the ideal plan, those responsible for the factory's design and construction were the four Biscayan masters

---

96 In January 1769, the intendant received an order to maintain in good condition "all of the Factory's instruments, keeping them from rusting and preventing the hides used for the large bellows from rotting." Carta de FISC para Antonio Anselmo Duarte de Siqueira, intendente da fábrica de ferro. São Paulo de Assunção de Luanda, January 29, 1769. IEB/ USP, AL-083–214.
97 A cam (*came* or *camo*) is a mechanical element employed to drive another one, called *seguidor* (follower) through direct contact.
98 In Nova Oeiras, the hammer was built as follows: "the block that holds the hammer's handle measures three palms [0.66 m] thick, and under the ground the same number of palms, with the platform and the walls equally secured; the hammer's handle measures 24 palms long (5.28 m) and four palms thick (0.88 m) on the side of the axle, ending with six palms (1.32 m) in circumference." Termo de juramento feito pelo provedor da Fazenda Real Manuel Cunha e Sousa, José Francisco Pacheco, Antonio de Bessa Teixeira, Antonio Ribeiro Cardoso. São Paulo de Assunção de Luanda, November 17, 1770. ANTT, Condes de Linhares, mç. 51, doc. 1, fl. 198. Considering 1 palm = 0.22 m.
99 Pedro Arroyo Valiente and Manuel Cordera Millan, *Ferrerías en Cantabria. Manufacturas de ayer, patrimonio de hoy*, 34.

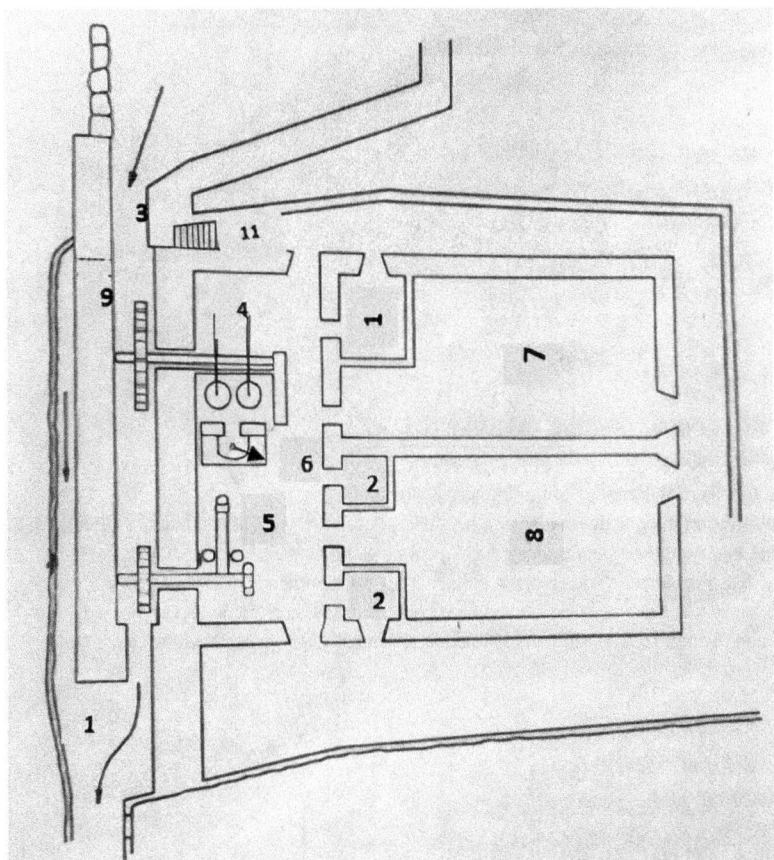

Figure 15: Interior of a hydraulic ironworks.
1. Iron storage.
2. Officials' dormitory.
3. *Banzado* (water reservoir below the wheels).
4. *Barquinera* (mechanism of the large water-propelled bellows).
5. Hammer propelled by the waterwheel.
6. Furnace.
7. Wood storage and *tazadera* (where the ore is broken into smaller pieces to put them in the furnace).
8. Coal yard.
9. *Banzado* overflow.
10. Disposal/drain.
11. Stairs to access the *banzado*.
Source: Ferrería de Sargadelos. Distribución en planta de una ferrería de finales del siglo XVIII y comienzos del XIX. Dibujo de J. Pena tomado de Clodio Gonzáles Pérez. *A produción tradicional do ferro em Galicia. As grandes ferrerías da província de Lugo* (Lugo: Diputación Provincial de Lugo, 1992). Apud Pablo Quintana Lopes, *La labranza y transformación artesanal del hierro en Taramundi y Los Oscos*, 146.

Chapter 4 Blacksmiths and Smelters

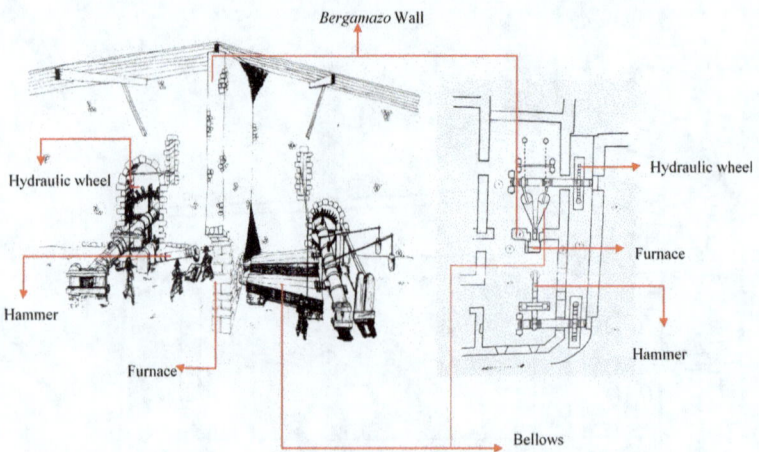

Figure 16: Details of the interior of the foundry building.
Sources: Disposición interior de una ferraría hidráulica. Pedro Arroyo Valiente, Manuel Cordera Millan, *Ferrerías en Cantabria. Manufacturas de ayer, patrimonio de hoy*, 13.
Parte de la "Casa de Ferrería" que aloja la maquinaria. Carlos Fernández García, *Ferrerías y mazos entre el río Xunco y el Navia* (Escuela Universitaria de Arquitectos técnicos de La Coruña, n.d.). *Apud* Pablo Quintana López, *La labranza y transformación artesanal del hierro en Taramundi y Los Oscos*, 148.

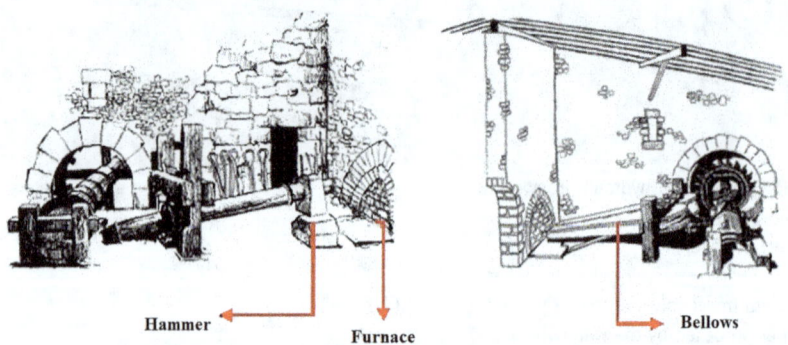

Figure 17: Water wheels that propelled the hammer (left) and the bellows (right).
Source: C. Ceballos Cuerno, *Las grandes familias de ferrones de Cantabria en el Antiguo Régimen*. In *De peñas al mar* (Santander: Sociedad e instituciones en la Cantabria Moderna, 1999).

hired for that purpose. In the contract they signed with Portugal's Secretary of State of the Navy and Overseas Affairs, the Biscayans committed themselves to provide the "necessary instructions for the laboratory building, the factory, and the ironworks."[100]

The use of water as the driving force changed the working process in the ironworks. It required more skilled labor, larger architectural dimensions, and new divisions between tasks considered skilled and unskilled. As a result, it required new forms of discipline and control of the labor process.

The high cost of wages and sustenance for the masters was justified by the fact that, once the factory was built and new masters were trained, the Biscayans would no longer be needed. Sousa Coutinho's idea was that Central Africans trained in the new techniques would be a cheap source of skilled labor force. The organization of the work process he proposed would allow exploiting the Ambundu labor force, offsetting the initial investments.

The governor actually planned to train both white people of Nova Oeiras and the "country's Negroes" in all mechanical trades—masons, carpenters, blacksmiths, smelters—because there was a shortage of such artisans in Angola and the few that existed were in Luanda. In addition, it was necessary to better control the local populations, changing their way of life, making them more productive. Regarding smelting techniques, the foreign masters were to instruct the "black smelters," since they already had accumulated knowledge on the subject. The *jingangula* and *pulungus* were presumably more apt to learn the new method, so that "with different forges and bigger bellows," iron production could be increased.[101] The idea of turning Nova Oeiras into a workshop is also established in the Spaniards' terms of employment, since in the negotiations they committed themselves to teach "with all diligence and without hiding anything of our art from those apprentices who come to us." In exchange, they requested coal, firewood, ore, and all "opportune materials," a bigger hammer, and other tools.[102] The plan was to "successively train many able men, not only to comfortably substitute the current ones, but so that many factories can be reproduced over time."[103]

---

100 Condições do contrato firmado entre Francisco Xavier de Mendonça Furtado, secretário de Estado dos Negócios da Marinha e Domínios do Ultramar, e Joseph Manuel de Echevarria, Francisco Xavier de Zuluaga, Francisco de Echenique e Joseph de Retolaza. Lisbon, April 30, 1768. AHU_CU_001, Cx. 52, D. 15.
101 Carta de FISC para Antonio Anselmo Duarte de Siqueira, intendente da fábrica de ferro. São Paulo de Assunção de Luanda, October 31, 1768. AHU_CU_001, Cx. 52, Doc. 15.
102 Idem.
103 Portaria sobre os jornais pagos aos trabalhadores de Nova Oeiras. São Paulo de Assunção de Luanda, October 29, 1769. AHU_CU_001, Cx. 52, Doc. 15.

The Biscayan masters prepared all the necessary materials for the facilities they would build in Nova Oeiras and insisted on taking tools, including some iron bars imported from Sweden and Biscay itself. The list of tools sent on José da Silveira's ship Nossa Senhora das Merês in 1768[104] is interesting:

1 anvil
1 bellows
1 mallet
1 hammer
1 furnace
1 iron ring
1 iron handle
1 shaft for the axle
2 pipes for the bellows
2 cramps for the bellows
4 clamps for the bellows
1 board for the bellows
8 arched (sic) iron plates
3 planks for the forge's drain
2 thick planks with notches
3 long, straight planks
1 sledge
2 copper plates for the forge's *algaraviz* weighing 3 arrobas and six *arráteis*.
10 boxes with ironware
1 box for the steel
new bellows

The list contains several tools related only to the bellows, such as wooden boards, pipes, clamps, and cramps. The large bellows of hydraulic ironworks required specific parts that the masters would find it harder to manufacture in Angola. They also took copper plates to build the forge's *algaraviz*, i.e. the pipe that connected the end of the bellows to the forge. The tools give the impression that the Biscayan masters had some prior knowledge of African techniques. It is likely that, just as Sousa Coutinho was aware of the techniques and the value of Biscayan iron, news about African smelters arrived in northern Spain.

---

[104] Relação das ferramentas conduzidas por José da Silveira, mestre da charrua Nossa Senhora das Mercês, para a fábrica de ferro no Reino de Angola. Lisbon, April 29, 1768. AHU_CU_001, Cx. 52, Doc. 15.

After inspecting Nova Oeiras, the Biscayans decided to build a weir on the Luinha River, cleared the road, and marked the river with stakes, which served to guide the weir's construction. Regarding the wood supply for charcoal, they said that, for as long as "the world was the world," there would be woods to explore in that area, especially along the Engolome lagoon. They also examined the five iron mines and marveled at the iron-rich rock hills.[105]

In the first iron smelting experiment, the masters smelted three pounds in three hours, consuming "a fourth of the rock that each Negro spends in the furnaces they make" and a third of the coal. The intendant asked the masters to perform the experiment in front of the local blacksmiths and smelters to convince them that the new methods were more productive. Considering that Central African smelters smelted approximately two pounds of iron in four hours, the difference was not as great as the factory official claimed.[106] But the efforts of the Biscayans seemed enormous in the eyes of the colonizers.

Despite successive orders to the Biscayans to dedicate themselves to teaching their technique with large bellows to the local smelters, the time they survived was not enough for the teaching/learning process to bear fruit. From then on, the hopes for the factory's success rested on the knowledge of the few "white blacksmiths" with the little they were able to learn from watching the only smelting made by the Biscayans.[107] Another issue that hindered the circulation of knowledge was the division of tasks and the multiple hierarchies that developed in the factory —between masters, technicians, "common" workers, Europeans, Africans, exiled convicts.

Even so, somehow their knowledge bore fruit. The descriptions and blueprints of the factory facilities drawn up by the Biscayans were the starting point for the construction of Nova Oeiras. The engineers trained at the Geometry and Fortification Course in Luanda completed the blueprints. In addition, the engineers Manuel Antonio Tavares, Luís Candido Cordeiro, João Pedro Miguéis, Antonio de Bessa

---

[105] Carta de Antonio Anselmo Duarte de Siqueira, intendente da fábrica de ferro, para FISC. Nova Oeiras, November 15, 1768. AHU_CU_001, Cx. 52, Doc. 38. Carta de Feliciano Pinto da Costa para FISC. Nova Oeiras, November 20, 1768. AHU_CU_001, Cx. 52, Doc. 15. Carta de FISC para Francisco Xavier Mendonça Furtado, secretário de Estado da Marinha e Domínios Ultramarinos. São Paulo de Assunção de Luanda, December 3, 1768. AHU_CU_001, Cx. 52, Doc. 15. Certidão do escrivão da Real Fábrica do Ferro de Nova Oeiras Hipólito Fernandes Pinto. Real Fábrica do Ferro da Nova Oeiras, November 21, 1768. IEB/USP, AL-083–206.
[106] Carta de Antonio Anselmo Duarte de Siqueira, intendente da fábrica de ferro, para FISC. Nova Oeiras, November 21, 1768. AHU_CU_001, Cx. 52, Doc. 38.
[107] Carta de FISC para Francisco Xavier de Mendonça Furtado, secretário de Estado dos Negócios da Marinha e Domínios Ultramarinos. São Paulo de Assunção de Luanda, March 6, 1769. AHU_CU_001, Cx. 53, Doc. 18.

Teixeira, and his brother Joaquim de Bessa Teixeira, who was also the inspector of royal works for the factory, also worked in Nova Oeiras.

4.3 Figueiró dos Vinhos

As we saw, after the Biscayans' death, the masters from the Portuguese ironworks of Foz de Alge, from the parish of Figueiró dos Vinhos, went to Angola. As soon as they arrived in Luanda, they were put to their first test: to smelt the local iron ore. They had to build a furnace that could accommodate the hand bellows used by Central Africans, "whose blowing was always uncertain." In spite of the difficulties, they succeeded in reducing the iron, which "liquefied perfectly."[108] From their second experiment, the governor concluded that the masters from Figueiró did not succeed in smelting the iron with the hand bellows, since in the ironworks of Tomar the bellows were immense and propelled by water wheels. When the Portuguese tried to imitate the Africans, they failed entirely, for they did not know how to use the local tools. Sousa Coutinho also feared sending them to Nova Oeiras, where they could build a hydraulic ironworks, out of fear that they could die like the Biscayans.[109]

Even though he acknowledged that each ore required specific knowledge, Sousa Coutinho believed that a more experienced master could live up to the challenge and achieve his goals through experimentation. The governor's goal was for the Figueiró smelters to teach the locals to smelt larger quantities; he wanted a technique that would allow them to do so with hand bellows—"adapting the furnace to small bellows." According to the technical precepts we have described here, increasing production without increasing the facilities, in particular the size of the bellows, was no easy task. One has to consider that the Portuguese refiners and tinsmiths knew little about a factory's facilities, a knowledge that their director, José Le Vache, certainly mastered, but he had remained in Portugal. In addition, the Figueiró smelters liquefied iron. That means that they used a different technology than that employed in Biscayan hydraulic ironworks and Central African bloomeries. In the ironworks of Foz de Alge, one blast furnace was employed to obtain iron in liquid state, and another one to refine it.

The history of the ironworks at Foz de Alge, located along the Alge river, can be divided into two stages: the first one goes back to the early-seventeenth century

---

108 Idem.
109 Carta de FISC para Martinho de Melo e Castro, secretário de Estado dos Negócios da Marinha e Domínios Ultramarinos. São Paulo de Assunção de Luanda, September 20, 1771. BNP, C 8553, F6362.

and lasts until 1761, when it was closed by Pombal; the second one encompasses the reign of D. Maria I, when it was reopened under the direction of José Bonifácio de Andrade e Silva, and operated until 1834. The model for its construction in the seventeenth century was the Biscayan ironworks; so much so that one of the blueprints of the ironworks bears the following phrase as the title of the figure below: "Drawing depicting the arrangement of the ironworks and mills in the form employed in the Kingdom of Biscay, showing what is to be done and the arrangement necessary for the ironworks that His Majesty intends to build in this kingdom near Vila de Tomar." The difference between the hydraulic ironworks blueprints already analyzed and the one built in Figueiró is that a blast furnace was employed there, which used charcoal as fuel and, precisely because of this, the iron needed to be re-melted in a refining furnace. This explains why, in the figure below, we see two furnaces into which air is blown by large bellows driven by hydraulic power.

It was not just the factories of Foz de Alge and Machuca that were inspired by Biscayan technology. The partnership between the Portuguese and the Biscayans regarding metallurgical technology goes back a long way. The oldest Portuguese enterprise of this kind, the Ferrarias del Rey in Barbacena, in 1487, was based on the Biscayan ironworks. Furthermore, they were managed by Spaniards. Biscayan masters prevailed in Barbacena throughout the entire sixteenth century, successively taking over the ironworks' production management: Rodrigo Manhoz, Baltazar Manhoz (or Manhorca), and Cristóvão de Manhorca.[110]

Still, the Biscayan influence was not the only one in Foz de Alge, since the ironworks was run by the French father and son Francisco and Pedro Dufour in the late-seventeenth century. Since then, many French artisans were hired. Joseph Le Vache is just one example in a long list: Estêvão Levoim, master smelter; Martim Vernete, master refiner; Clodo Miguel, master forger; Estêvão Matheus, all of them French and hired in 1670.[111] Therefore, the techniques in that factory came from a variety of sources of knowledge, in addition to the refinement and development of the craftsmen's own methods there. In Foz de Alge, the interest in importing French technicians can be explained by the use of the blast furnace, which was much more common in Sweden and England than in Biscay until the end of the eighteenth century.

---

110 José Luís Gomes e João Luís Cardoso, "As Ferrarias Del Rey, Fábrica da Pólvora de Barcarena. Resultados da Intervenção Arqueológica Realizada em 2009," *Estudos Arqueológicos De Oeiras* 18 (2010/2011): 147–173.
111 Miguel Ângelo Portela, "A superintendência dos tenentes de artilharia Francisco Dufour e Pedro Dufour nas Reais Ferrarias da Foz de Alge e Machuca," in *Anais do XXI Colóquio de História Militar* (Lisbon, 2012), 517.

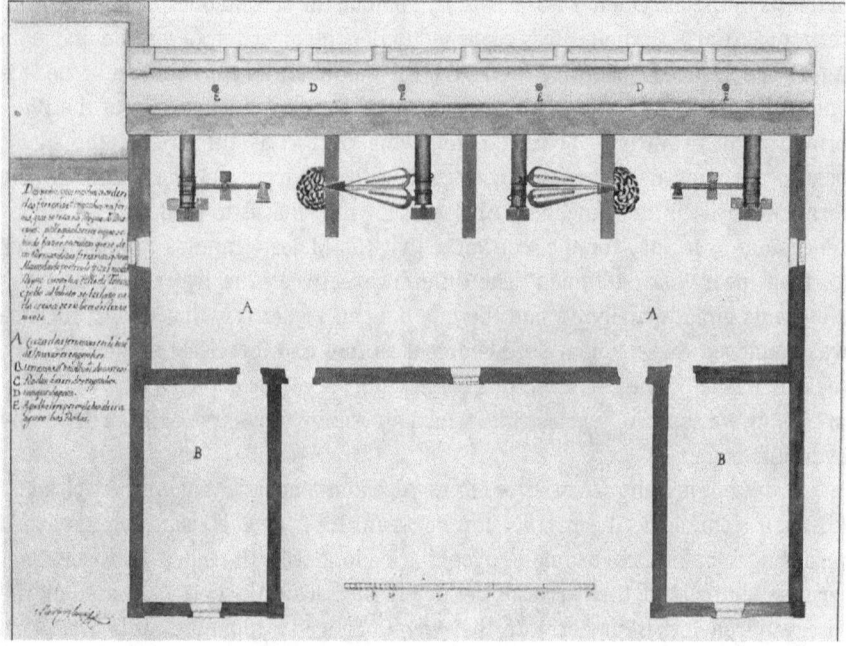

Figure 18: Blueprint of the Figueiró ironworks (circa 1624).
Source: "Desenho que mostra a ordem das ferrarias e engenhos na forma que se usa no Reino da Biscaia: pelo qual se vê o que se há de fazer e a ordem que se deve ter nas ditas ferrarias que sua majestade pretende fazer neste reino junto a Vila de Tomar e pelo alfabeto se declara cada coisa per si bem distintamente." "**A** – Ironworks building where the mills shall be built; **B** – Coal storage area; **C** – Mill wheels and axles; **D** – Water tank; **E** – Water outlet for the wheels." Signed by the architect Diogo Marques Lucas.
Source: "Desenho que mostra a ordem das ferrarias...". [Reino] [s.n.], [ca. 1624]. - 1 planta: papel, color., ms.; 42,4 x 56,3 cm. AHU_CARTm_076_D.1. *Apud*: Luiza da Fonseca, "As ferrarias de Tomar." In *Quarto Congress* (1940), 351.

The blast furnace operating with charcoal was a consequence of the use of larger bellows in hydraulic mills. The increased efficiency of the bellows made it possible to build larger furnaces that completely melted the iron, liquefying it, and to increase production. However, a large amount of impurities was added to the liquid iron, making it brittle. In order to use this iron, it had to undergo a second smelting operation to refine it—hence the refining furnace. The refining process yielded a liquid iron adequate to build molded objects such as weapons, cannonballs, church bells, railings, and other tools that could not always be made using the mass of wrought iron produced by bloomeries. Even so, the blast furnaces did not substitute the smithies because the iron obtained in them was competitive due to some of its properties, such as greater malleability.

In northern Spain, this technology arrived around 1628–29; however, the hydraulic ironworks that used bloomeries were the most common, both because the Spanish blacksmith associations resisted the introduction of the new system and because the mills required more coal, and therefore more woods, and the Iberia Peninsula had few tree reserves.[112] It is worth noting that, like the Ambundus in Angola, Spanish blacksmiths resisted technological innovations because, although they appear to increase productivity and efficiency, the technology is a response to the need for discipline, hierarchical control, and to prevent the artisans from controlling their own work process.

Furthermore, when thinking about French artisans in Foz de Alge, it is worth recalling that the importance of a craftsman's skill is not limited to having the necessary knowledge to operate a blast furnace. Metalworking involved a wide variety of skills, and the divisions between blacksmith, smelter, refiner, cutler, and tinsmith were not fortuitous. With time, technological advancement went hand in hand with a diversification of trades, giving rise to new professional divisions, which required specialized workers to shape liquid iron or use clay molds, for example. The hierarchization of work also made it possible to exercise more rigorous surveillance and control over workers.

Undoubtedly, Pedro Simões, Manuel Simões, Manuel Nunes, Julião Miguel, Francisco Lourenço, Manuel dos Santos, and Manuel José Ferraz were indispensable professionals in Figueiró dos Vinhos and made efforts to learn how to smelt the iron ore from the Ilamba region. They were unsuccessful mainly because each ore, due to its different chemical composition, requires special knowledge, acquired over time through experiments; besides, they had probably worked for many years in the hydraulic ironworks of Foz de Alge, which did not require any knowledge of bloomery smelting methods.[113]

4.4 Knowledge Mismatch

In the face of the failed attempts to establish a technique that allowed greater iron production in Ilamba, Sousa Coutinho brought together the engineers trained by him at the Geometry Course in Luanda and all bibliographic materials he had com-

---

[112] Pedro Arroyo Valiente and Manuel Cordera Millan, *Ferrerías en Cantabria. Manufacturas de ayer, patrimonio de hoy*, 17.
[113] Catálogo cronológico de todas as ordens régias que existem na Secretaria do Estado do Reino de Angola. São Paulo de Assunção de Luanda, June 18, 1777. AN (RJ), Códice 543.

piled, and studied the best way to build a smelting furnace. In October 1771, an experimental furnace was built near Fortaleza de Penedo, in Luanda. In it, Sousa Coutinho managed to melt iron completely: "the iron flowed," in his words.[114] One of the books he consulted was volume seven of the "Encyclopedia," which contained the entries "forge – mechanical arts." The copy was sent together with the tools and the workers in 1771, and among its contents there were guidelines for the charcoal makers, the smelters, and the hammer operators; instructions on how to "organize and search the mines"; and discussions on "water reserves and water usage," firewood, bellows, and furnaces.[115]

At that point, the only remaining obstacle was finding a crucible stone capable of withstanding the high temperatures of the furnace. Following the advice of the Figueiró smelters, Coutinho had stones brought from Figueiró and from Belas, Portugal. He also sought them in Angola and experimented with some "red" stones found in Cambambe, without success. There is no evidence that the blast furnace built in Nova Oeiras ever smelted a single gram of iron.[116] Archaeological research will be able to fill in the gaps in the written sources.

In 1770, when the engineers and the master builder wrote their opinion on the state of the factory when they left, they warned that, although they had prepared

---

114 In a letter to the Morgado of Mateus, the governor said, "Because when eight very rustic and very ignorant smelters arrived here, since I wanted not only to try them in this city, but to have their skill communicated to natives and residents, and since to that end a smaller furnace adequate for hand bellows had to be built, this visible defect was not corrected the first time nor the second, and clearly because of its difficulty it did not enter those heads, which attributed it to the iron's poor quality, which is actually the best. Imagine, Your Excellency, that afflicted as I was with the expenses and labor invested in the factory's construction, I rejected those men and went back to the books, and immediately Providence decided that the smelting should succeed with a wonderful effect, demonstrating the iron's generosity, and confounding the presumed Masters." Carta de FISC a Luis Antonio de Sousa, morgado de Mateus, governador de São Paulo. São Paulo de Assunção de Luanda, October 9, 1771. BNP, C 8744, F 6443, fl. 156v.

115 Carta de Martinho de Melo e Castro, secretário de Estado dos Negócios da Marinha e dos Domínios Ultramarinos, para FISC. Palácio de Nossa Senhora da Ajuda, March 25, 1771. AHU, Códice 472 – fl. 160–283.

116 Carta de FISC para Martinho de Melo e Castro, secretário de Estado dos Negócios da Marinha e Domínios Ultramarinos. São Paulo de Assunção de Luanda, November 29, 1771. AHU_CU_001, Cx. 55, D. 84. Carta de FISC para José Tomás Vieira, *capitão-mor* de Cambambe. São Paulo de Assunção de Luanda, November 25, 1771. BNP, C 8744, F6443. In 1772, Pedro Schiappa Pietra, Genoese master who worked at the Fábrica de Serralheria in Lisbon, sent the stones to Angola. Carta de Pedro Schiappa Pietra, Mestre da Fábrica de Serralheria de Lisboa, para FISC. Lisbon, April 24, 1772. AHU_CU_001, Cx. 56, D. 32.

all the necessary materials, the bellows were not built because there were no masters who knew how to make them.[117]

In 1773, when he was already far from Luanda, but continued to defend the idea of the iron factory, Sousa Coutinho considered that both the Portuguese masters and Pirson, the French master, should be fired for not being fit for service. He insisted that it was necessary to find a skilled master who was able to invent a mechanism to increase the amount of iron produced with the Central African method. Once that was done, according to the governor's plans, the Ilamba blacksmiths and smelters would learn the new technique and would work in their smithies and sell the iron at the Royal Factory. According to his calculations, this would give rise to around 400 small factories. Nova Oeiras, the Royal Factory, should only operate using the French method that liquefied the iron. This would provide the Portuguese with iron of both qualities: wrought or beaten iron from the small factories and molten iron, obtained in a liquid state from the Royal Factory.[118]

What is common to the artisans discussed in this chapter is their specific knowledge, both in terms of construction techniques, as in the case of stonemasonry, and of what was of more immediate interest to an iron factory, metallurgical experiments. The workers from the town and iron factory of Nova Oeiras knew the secrets of working with iron—everyone, Brazilians, Africans, Portuguese, Spanish, French, knew some stage of the smelting and forging process. They possessed knowledge acquired in a teaching/learning process related to the traditional practice of a trade—years of experience and contact with the knowledge of other masters. Representatives of several cultural matrices, the craftsmen were cherished because they knew the secret of how to transform ore into iron, which was unknown to the most enlightened noblemen in Angola, among them governor

---

117 "They have not been built because it was deemed better and more convenient to wait until the masters came, so they could be built according to their measurements and satisfaction; however, in the building where they are to work, everything they may need is ready, such as: eight planks, four of them measuring five palms wide and twenty-six palms long and almost one palm thick, and four of them with the same thickness and length, but three and a half palms wide, ready leathers, nails, strings. And as soon as the said masters arrive, they will be built to their satisfaction in eight days. The iron next to the bellows' mouth has not been built either for the same reason, considering it more convenient to wait for it to be made as the masters who will work with it see fit; however, this can also be made at the same time as the bellows, and be finished long before them." Termo de juramento feito pelo provedor da Fazenda Real Manuel Cunha e Sousa, José Francisco Pacheco, Antonio de Bessa Teixeira, Antonio Ribeiro Cardoso. São Paulo de Assunção de Luanda, November 17, 1770. ANTT, Condes de Linhares, mç. 51, doc. 1, fl. 198.
118 Carta de FISC sem destinatário. São Paulo de Assunção de Luanda, September 16, 1773. BNP, C 8553, F6362.

Sousa Coutinho. Even when the governor, as a member of the liberal arts, turned to books and managed to liquefy the iron, his feat was short-lived, for he lacked a crucible made of appropriate stone, carved by a stonemason. The stone was sent from Portugal, and yet the iron factory never operated because there were no skilled masters who knew how to put the mills and the furnace into operation.

My argument is simple: more than manual workers, these artisans were the chemists and mineralogists of Nova Oeiras and, in many ways, employing the resources provided by their sociocultural environment and especially oriented by their trade's secrets, they resisted the loss of control of their own work process.

Until the mid-eighteenth century, the trade masters, in their workshops and in their daily practice, controlled the knowledge necessary for metallurgy. It is worth highlighting their intellectual contribution, even if for the eighteenth century this is an anachronistic idea, because the mechanical arts were far from the liberal arts, and practical knowledge was not considered indispensable for scholars. So much so that it was only during the Enlightenment that laboratories became places of academic practice and chemistry subjects were associated with the teaching of metallurgy, technology, and cameralism, and with mining schools. Before that, the study of chemistry was much more closely related to medicine, pharmaceutics, and botany than mineralogy.[119]

According to Elena Faus, "an anonymous multitude of talented individuals" was responsible for the knowledge of iron smelting until the nineteenth century. Craftsmen like the many artisans discussed in these pages are the protagonists of the history of the technique (some of them no longer so anonymous to history). Their method was that of praxis—trial and error.[120] They kept their knowledge under lock and key. Religiosity and secrecy were not exclusive to Central Africans. When the mineralogist Maciel took over the direction of mineralogical studies in Angola, he noted, "Among European masters who have no studies, these things are of the greatest secrecy, passed as a heritage from fathers to sons."[121]

---

[119] Juergen Heinrich Maar, "Aspectos históricos do ensino superior de química," *Scientiæ Studia* 2, no. 1 (2004): 33–84. "Cameralistics was a discipline introduced in German universities in 1727 (Halle and Frankfurt/Oder), created for those who were destined to public service, teaching everything from aspects of administration and economics to arts and trades and other matters of interest to the future administrator." Juergen Heinrich Maar, "Glauber, Thurneisser e outros. Tecnologia química e química fina, conceitos não tão novos assim," *Química Nova* 23, no. 5 (2000): 710.

[120] Elena Faus, *La labranza del hierro en el País Vasco* (Bilbao: Servicio Editorial Universidad del País Vasco, 2000), 51.

[121] Carta de José Álvares Maciel e Miguel Antonio de Melo, governador de Angola. São Paulo de Assunção de Luanda, March 31, 1800. *Arquivos de Angola* IV, no. 52–54 (1939): 300–306.

In the factory, the hierarchy among artisans, the division of tasks, and the working conditions made the circulation of knowledge and techniques impossible in many ways. The secrecy surrounding the craft may also have been one of the reasons why we have not been able to identify any interaction, especially in the exchange of technical knowledge, between craftsmen of different origins, even though Nova Oeiras was the scene of great transit of people. As already mentioned, the intention was to transform Nova Oeiras into a workshop to prepare and train local blacksmiths and smelters in European smelting techniques. Although not all the Europeans died, it does not seem to us that they effectively devoted themselves to teaching the local workers. Teaching necessarily involved changing the ways the craftsmen worked. I do not believe they were inclined to that.

Due to illness and in the face of refusals of their requests to return to Spain, the Biscayans were unwilling to train technicians to operate the hydraulic mills in their place. When asked why they did not at least teach the white blacksmiths, they answered that they "wore cuff shirts that were unsuitable for such a workshop." Indeed, the Biscayans wore special clothing to work at the forge; however, their explanation was a blunt response to those who did not allow them to return to Biscay.[122] Once again, I believe that what was at stake here was the trade's secrecy and the control of the work process.

As Juliana da Silva reminds us, the Central African blacksmiths incorporated European tools over time. In an 1884 account, the merchant Antonio Silva Porto (1817–1890) noted that blacksmiths from Bié used imported files. We have no similar information for Nova Oeiras. Between 1768 and 1804, mallets, anvils, bellows, hammers, and many other types of European tools related to blacksmithing were sent to the factory. It is possible to hypothesize that these tools were manipulated by the *jingangula* and *pulungus* both to facilitate the manufacture of specific objects and optimize the work process and to incorporate a symbol of social distinction, as happened with other European tools.[123] An account by the naturalist Maciel may help us think about the rejection of foreign tools, at least as far as the larger bellows are concerned. The chemist noted that it was necessary to use large hammers proportional to the bellows, because the small mallets used by Ambundu blacksmiths were not appropriate to forge large amounts of iron. If the local

---

[122] Carta de Joaquim de Bessa Teixeira, intendente geral da fábrica de ferro, para FISC. São Paulo de Assunção de Luanda, December 27, 1768. *Arquivos de Angola*, 2ª serie, X, no. 39–42 (1953). Blacksmiths and smelters in Biscayan ironworks wore a long robe that went down to their heels, called *obreras*, and a wide-brimmed hat to protect their head from the heat. Joaquín de Almunia y de León, *Antigua industria del hierro en Vizcaya*, 10.

[123] Juliana Ribeiro da Silva, *Homens de ferro. Os ferreiros na África-central no século XIX*, 155. "Espólio de Silva Porto," July 10, 1884. SGL, Cx. 1, Cad. 4, 6.

blacksmiths attempted to use their mallets on larger amounts of metal, they would burn their hands.[124] These heavy tools were an added risk of accident and a hindrance to the trade's nomadic nature. The blacksmiths did not want to give up their autonomy.

Outside the factory, what we observe is the emergence of more specialized trades among Africans and their descendants: cutlers, riflemen, and tinsmiths. The coexistence with Portuguese nationals, exiled convicts, and Brazilians of various trades led them to learn other functions. For example, the constant shortage and decay of the militia's armament made it necessary to seek someone who knew how to fix weapons. This was the case of one of Ndembu Kabuku's dependents[125]; his "nephew" Antonio Francisco da Silva was an "excellent metalworker and rifleman," who could do repairs.[126] European weapons were also a symbol of prestige among the Africans, who invented new ways to repair and use them, even producing iron bullets, which were lighter than lead bullets.[127]

In general, in the factory, the special division of labor itself, separating the "Machine Building" with the mills and water wheels from the "Casa de Fundição dos Pretos," did not contribute to an exchange of knowledge. Both the Biscayans and the Figueiró blacksmiths observed at least one smelting by the Ambundus, who in turn were also to observe the European methods in order to learn them. Apart from these observations, the impacts of the knowledge exchange escape us. What is clear is that, for most workers in Nova Oeiras, it was an experience marked by punishment, "insolence," "imprisonment," "theft," and death—for Europeans, the threat was the climate and tropical diseases; for Africans, the terrible living and working conditions.

For the Ambundus, the appropriation of knowledge was also synonymous of persecution and enslavement, in addition to the beatings they suffered in the factory. In "Resposta que um sujeito do Brasil deu ao outro de Angola, sobre a Fábrica de Ferro" (Answer that a subject from Brazil gave to another from Angola, regarding the Iron Factory), we find a quote that shows that the number of blacksmiths and smelters decreased after the establishment of the iron factories: "The many Negro blacksmiths are no longer so plentiful because the governor [Sousa Coutin-

---

[124] Carta de José Álvares Maciel para Miguel Antonio de Melo, governador de Angola. São Paulo de Assunção de Luanda, November 1, 1799. AHU_CU_001, Cx. 93 A, D. 1.
[125] This might be a mistake by the governor; he is probably referring to *soba* Kabuku Kambilu.
[126] Carta de Luiz da Motta Feo Torres, governador de Angola, para Joaquim Germano de Andrade, *capitão-mor* de Ambaca. São Paulo de Assunção de Luanda, December 3, 1818. AHA, Códice 93, A – 20 – 3.
[127] Juliana Ribeiro da Silva, *Homens de ferro*, 181.

ho] consumed a large number of them between deaths and escapes."[128] However, that labor force had been exploited before Sousa Coutinho's government. Many of the skilled workers who lived in Ambaca were actually natives of Ilamba who had migrated there due to famines in their homeland.[129]

The demand for these skilled workers during the Portuguese occupation must have driven them to the interior. This because, in 1762, blacksmiths and smelters from Ilamba were captured and sent to Lisbon so that their iron mining technology could be studied in the metropolis.[130] In July of the same year, Governor Vasconcelos said that he would not send "more practical Negroes (...) because, after seeing the first ones embark, everyone was alarmed."[131] The workers were sent to Lisbon together with samples of the iron they produced, as if the workers themselves were samples of a knowledge to be explored.[132]

As Mariana Candido pertinently observed, famines, droughts, and other natural disasters that appear in Portuguese sources must be analyzed as a consequence of human actions and not merely as ecological cycles.[133] In this case, the famine that made the blacksmiths flee from Ilamba seems to have been related to the imprisonment of these workers to be sent to Lisbon. After all, the expansion of control and exploitation of the colonial territory and people involved the appropriation of knowledge, techniques, and traditions, as demonstrated by the analysis of the sources above.

---

128 "Resposta que um sujeito do Brasil deu ao outro de Angola, sobre a Fábrica do Ferro," n.p., n.d. BNP, Reservados, MSS Caixa 246, no. 22.
129 "Likewise, I know for a fact that throughout this jurisdiction there are many blacksmiths and smelters from Ilamba, who, because of famines, left their lands and came to these ones." Carta de FISC para Francisco Matoso de Andrade, *capitão-mor* de Ambaca. São Paulo de Assunção de Luanda, January 4, 1767. BNP, C – 8742, F – 6364.
130 Carta de Antonio de Vasconcelos, governador de Angola, para Francisco Xavier de Mendonça Furtado, secretário de Estado da Marinha e do Ultramar. São Paulo de Assunção de Luanda, May 9, 1762. BNP, C 8553, F6362.
131 Carta de Antonio de Vasconcelos, governador de Angola, para Francisco Xavier de Mendonça Furtado, secretário de Estado da Marinha e do Ultramar. São Paulo de Assunção de Luanda, July 10, 1762. AHU_CU_001, Cx. 45, D. 68.
132 Ângela Barreto synthesizes well this interest in inventorying techniques and minerals: "the desire to have an empire ruling over the world required understanding that world over which one wanted to exercise the *imperium*." Ângela Barreto Xavier, "O orientalismo católico. Rotinas do saber na Goa da época moderna," in *Conferência no Simpósio Internacional Novos Mundos – Neue Welten. Portugal e a época dos Descobrimentos* (Berlin: Deutsches Historisches Museum, 2006), 4.
133 Mariana P. Candido, *An African Slaving Port and the Atlantic World. Benguela and its Hinterland* (New York: Cambridge University Press, 2013), 275.

When they arrived in Lisbon, the Central African blacksmiths who survived the trip did not smelt the iron samples from Ilamba. At the Court, the experiment did not result in the highly praised Central African metal, even though the Portuguese attempted to reproduce exactly the same scenario in Angola: ore from Ilamba, local blacksmiths, and their everyday tools.[134] We can imagine that the African artisans were unsuccessful because they had no access to the materials needed to build a furnace and for a smooth smelting process (the clay, the *mabú* itself, the charcoal produced in Angola), or that they were just apprentices, or even that they were unwilling to collaborate with the Europeans—after all, they had been captured and enslaved. What is certain is that, in spite of their prejudices regarding Central African tools and techniques, the royal authorities attempted to extract from the craftsmen their methods and metallurgical secrets. If the *soba* Mbangu kya Tambwa remained three years in prison without revealing the way to the gold mines, the Ilamba smelters might have employed the same strategy, since secrecy was one of the obligations of their trade. In the end, the Europeans tried to make use of the science of those they intended to conquer, in this case to explore the mineral wealth and human resources of the Kingdom of Angola, and to do so they could imprison an Ambundu blacksmith, who could end up in the very shackles he produced.

---

134 Carta de FISC para Francisco Xavier de Mendonça Furtado, secretário de Estado da Marinha e Ultramar. São Paulo de Assunção de Luanda, December 18, 1765. AHU_CU_001, Cx. 49, D. 71.

Chapter 5
Successes and Failures

5.1 "Dry Thunderstorms": The Factory after Sousa Coutinho

When Sousa Coutinho left the government of Angola, the Nova Oeiras factory became the responsibility of his successor, Antonio de Lencastre (1772–1776). After consulting with factory officials, master smelters, and engineers who attempted to establish the foundry using a blast furnace, the new governor did not consider the iron factory a prosperous venture, suitable for the Ilamba landscapes. The main reason for Lencastre's rejection was the cost of iron production, which could reach 45$000 réis per quintal, overburdening the Royal Treasury. According to Lencastre's accounts, what made iron more expensive were the wages of workers employed in the most varied services at the factory, however small they might be: together, they represented too high a sum for the public coffers. For this reason, he suspended all work at the factory and did not send to Nova Oeiras the stones and equipment that had been shipped to Lisbon to give continuity to Francisco de Sousa Coutinho's plans.[1]

To substantiate his opinion about Nova Oeiras, in early 1773, Lencastre commissioned many opinions, accounting reports, and smelting experiments. First, he used the furnace built by his predecessor, which was located near the Penedo Fortress and was of the French type. Two unsuccessful attempts cost the Royal Treasury 171$330 réis. That amount was spent on stonemasons, masons, master smelters, white and "black" blacksmiths, miners, servants who assisted in the work, and firewood and charcoal for the furnace. The blacksmiths and smelters, engineers and factory employees were unable to operate it, "reducing all the ore to slag, without obtaining from them [the ironstones] any liquefied iron."[2]

He then went on to build bloomeries to employ the Biscayan method. Wages for workers and technicians was also the factor that made production more expensive; in this case, the expense was 91$500 réis, of which 67$200 réis went to the smelters alone. The cost of the iron produced was 28$900 réis per *arrátel* (450 g), obtaining only slightly more than three pounds.

The experiments with European furnaces were unsuccessful, but he wagered on the practice of Central African artisans. He summoned six local smelters. The

---

[1] Carta de Antonio de Lencastre para Martinho de Melo, secretário de Estado da Marinha e do Ultramar. São Paulo de Assunção de Luanda, March 31, 1773. AHU_CU_001, Cx. 52, D. 28.
[2] Idem.

average expense at each smelting was $533 réis, a much smaller amount than the previous experiments, because the African workers' wages were smaller. But since the production itself, in terms of amount, was not significant—only from four to four and a half pounds per smelting—, Lencastre did not consider the Ambundu technique profitable.

To build the French furnace mentioned above, at the end of his government, Sousa Coutinho requested the help of the military engineers he trained in the Geometry Course in Luanda: Luis Candido Cordeiro and João Pedro Miguéis. Lencastre summoned them to give their opinion. The engineers said that they did not have sufficient specific knowledge to evaluate the causes of the successes or failures of each smelting, so they limited themselves to giving a succinct account of the experiences they had witnessed.

In regards to profits, Lencastre failed to observe simple matters. As evidenced by the graph of factory expenses in Chapter 3, the largest expenses during all the years of operation of Nova Oeiras were spent on common wages, i.e. for the workers who built the factory building. The stone and lime factory was the loss, besides being unproductive; in contrast, the "Casa de Fundição dos Pretos" was inexpensive and profitable because it employed local skilled labor, which manufactured excellent iron.

Manoel Antonio Tavares and José Francisco Pacheco, former plant administrators, were also summoned to elaborate opinions on the quality of the iron mines. Lencastre wanted to know whether they agreed with the explanations given by the white master smelters that those mines contained only limited iron particles, which made it impossible to extract larger amounts of metal from the ore. The factory's works inspector, José Pacheco, described what he witnessed in Nova Oeiras's daily operation: mistreatment, frequent deaths, terrible conditions for agricultural development—parcels with too many rocks or too small—, and the little amount of iron produced there.[3]

The then Sergeant Major Manoel Tavares replied that the many metallurgical experiments did not produce enough metal to make the enterprise profitable, and that the coal spent was worth more than the iron that was extracted. For that reason, he agreed with the masters' opinion, who in turn blamed the poverty of the mines and the invisible iron particles. Manoel Tavares was therefore the only person to state explicitly that he considered the factory unfeasible; the others merely presented descriptions of the services provided.

With these assessments, Lencastre formed his own opinion. The effort to produce documents demonstrating the failure of Nova Oeiras was not only an admin-

---

3 Idem.

istrative initiative seeking to optimize the revenues and expenses of the Royal Treasury of the Kingdom of Angola. The reports were also a political strategy to legitimize a decision made for reasons that had little to do with the kingdom's finances, as we can see from the repercussion of this news in Angola and at the Court.

In February 1773, José Plácido Correia de Brito, clerk of the Royal Treasury, wrote to Francisco de Sousa Coutinho explaining the reasons that led Manoel Antonio Tavares, whose career had been consolidated under the protection of the former governor, to turn against him.[4] According to Correia de Brito, Manoel Tavares was pressured by the new governor to confirm the opinion of the master smelters. He even said, "Your Excellency [Francisco de Sousa Coutinho] is over there and he [Manoel Antonio Tavares] is here under the orders of one who can destroy him in a few days." Another threat was imprisonment—the "lord general" would "send him to a prison loaded with irons."[5]

There was a conflict between diverging interests during the elaboration of the reports on the factory, which included controversies about who wrote them, whether it was the colonial officials or the highest royal authority in Angola at the time, the governor, who commissioned the documents. Tavares's first assessment, transcribed by José Plácido, was merely descriptive, like the others, and like the engineers, he said he was not a smelter and therefore could not speak conclusively about the techniques employed in Oeiras. Correia Brito explained how the governor pressured and forced the former factory administrator to change his opinion. In fact, in the attachments to Lencastre's letter, Manoel Tavares modified the text, ratifying the version of the factory's failure.

To ease Sousa Coutinho's fury, who was indignant with Tavares' treason, José Plácido sent him what was presumably Manoel Tavares's first response to the new governor's ordinance, which, as we said, was very different from the version attached to Antonio de Lencastre's correspondence. In the original, Tavares reiterated that neither the master smelters who were in Nova Oeiras, nor he and the other military engineers, were practical metallurgists. The masters who remained after the desertions and successive deaths "never worked smelting iron, and the craft of some is to refine, and that of others is to cast bells." For that reason, he was unable to ratify their opinions, as they were produced by non-experts.

The experiments conducted by the engineers and by Tavares were based on the French notebooks on forges and furnaces left behind by Sousa Coutinho. To jus-

---

4 Carta de José Plácido Correia de Brito, escrivão da Fazenda Real, para FISC, ex-governador de Angola. São Paulo de Assunção de Luanda, February 11, 1773. ANTT, Condes de Linhares, mç. 44, doc. 100.
5 Idem.

tify his inability to solve the problem and to argue that only practical smelters knew the secrets of smelting, Tavares resorted to these books and paraphrased a passage:

> It should not be deemed strange that a rich mine produces little iron; this happens if the facility is not built according to the rules of the Art, if the wind blows too obliquely or horizontally; if the chimney or inner cavity does not have the necessary dimensions; *if the smelter does not master his Art* and pay the necessary attention that significantly contributes to obtain larger or smaller amounts of the product. I read further down that, although in 24 hours a furnace can produce 7,500, 6,000, 4,000, and even 3,500 pounds, if the smelter is ignorant, with the same amount of coal with which in the said time he would have smelted the said amounts, he will not obtain more than 1,500 or 2,000 pounds" [emphasis in the original].[6]

Manoel Tavares attested to what we have repeatedly stated: the main reason that Nova Oeiras did not become a large iron export factory was the lack of smelters who, mastering the techniques to transform the ore, were willing to collaborate with the colonial plans. The Central Africans had enough knowledge of the smelting processes, but they continued to use their own mining and manufacturing techniques, at most adopting some foreign tools. That was a successful tactic to maintain control over the iron trade and a very important craft for those societies. The Europeans who were also master smelters had died, and those who remained alive were not sufficiently skilled to found the factory. The death of the European technicians was one of the decisive factors for the Portuguese dependence on Central African metallurgical knowledge.

The narrative of personal and political relations surrounding the elaboration of Lencastre's reports on the factory demonstrates how fragile his explanations are and how much he tried to confer an appearance of impartiality and administrative suitability for a simple issue: there was no skilled labor among the Portuguese public agents and masters in Angola to carry out the plans of the administrative elite. On the other hand, while this could be resolved by sending new masters, Lencastre was explicitly stating that he would not embark on this adventure like his predecessor. To understand the new governor's position, it is necessary to revisit some of the information analyzed in Chapter 3, especially with regard to how the iron factory was not positively viewed by other subjects of the Portuguese Crown.

As we have seen, the *sertão* merchants, the *capitães-mores,* and the traders of enslaved people saw the labor force that had previously served them in various forms diverted to Nova Oeiras. The many conflicts caused by Nova Oeiras shed light on the extent to which the *sobas*' "able offspring" were exploited by these col-

---

6 Idem.

onial agents and how much they missed the endless supply of workers that was abruptly interrupted. The Ambaca traders even complained that the concentration of blacksmiths in Nova Oeiras resulted in fewer neck shackles available for trafficking. It was therefore not only the scarcity of people at their disposal that bothered them, but also the scarcity of iron. Thus, the main players representing colonial power in Luanda's hinterland did not support the Angolan government's initiative.[7]

When Sousa Coutinho, the great promoter of the project, left the government, Nova Oeiras lost its pillar of support. The plan for the Royal Factory of Nova Oeiras was abandoned and was never again consolidated. The factory had no place in the political engineering of Lencastre's government. It is quite likely that he yielded to pressure from the *capitães-mores*, the merchants, and other public officials.

One example of the weight of political decisions for the iron factory's success or failure is precisely the document "Resposta que un sujeito do Brasil deu ao outro de Angola, sobre a Fábrica do Ferro."[8] It is an anonymous letter found in Antonio de Lencastre's correspondence, with no date or place of writing. A later note indicates a probable author: the colonel of the infantry regiment João Monteiro de Moraes, head of one of the main Luso-African families in Luanda, who was part of an interim government after the death of Governor José Gonçalo da Câmara (1779–1782).[9] Elias Alexandre da Silva Correia describes him as "quite instructed in the belles-lettres."[10] In short, the colonel was one of the emblematic figures of Luanda's elite and, given his education and literary tendencies, he might have been indeed the author of the aforementioned "Resposta."

---

[7] In 1801, the governor of Angola, Miguel Antonio de Melo, reached the same conclusion regarding Nova Oeiras: "The merchants and settlers of this kingdom are usually such that they never contribute to the public cause; rather, they strive to prevent and ruin everything that is of public interest, as has been confirmed by endless events that have occurred at different times." Carta de Miguel Antonio de Melo para Rodrigo de Sousa Coutinho, secretário de Estado da Marinha e do Ultramar. São Paulo de Assunção de Luanda, April 3, 1801. *Arquivos de Angola* IV, no. 52–54 (1939): 253.
[8] "Resposta que um sujeito do Brasil deu ao outro de Angola, sobre a Fábrica do Ferro," n.p., n.d. BNP, MSS, Cx. 246, no. 22. I would like to thank Rodrigo Ricupero for indicating this source.
[9] According to Antonio Brásio, he was the author of one of the versions of "Catálogo dos Governadores do Reino de Angola," chronicles that were common in this part of the Portuguese Empire. Antonio Brásio (org.), *Monumenta Missionária Africana* (Lisbon: Agência Geral do Ultramar, 1973), 576. *Catálogo dos Governadores do Reino de Angola; com huma previa noticia do principio da sua conquista, e do que nella obrarão os governadores dignos de memória* (Lisbon: Academia Real das Sciencias, 1826). Another version of the governors' catalogue was written by Manoel Antonio Tavares. John K. Thornton, Joseph C. Miller, "A crónica como fonte, história e hagiografia; o Catálogo dos Governadores de Angola," *Revista Internacional de Estudos Africanos*, no. 12–13 (1990): 9–55.
[10] Catarina Madeira Santos, *Um governo "polido" para Angola*, 318.

However, the manuscript makes harsh criticism of Governor Francisco de Sousa Coutinho—which apparently is not consistent with the history of relations between the latter and Colonel Moraes's family. His son, Joaquim Monteiro de Moraes, was one of the engineers trained at the Geometry and Fortification Course, was later a professor in that course, and was responsible for a number of administrative tasks under Sousa Coutinho's leadership, being one of the governor's trusted men. For Francisco de Sousa Coutinho, Colonel Monteiro Moraes was the "only support of truth and zeal in the real service of this land."[11]

Nevertheless, it is very likely that João Monteiro was the author of the manuscript in question. This can be inferred from a private letter from José Plácido Correia de Brito to Sousa Coutinho. Without mentioning Monteiro de Moraes's name, referring only to the "colonel," to the "lieutenant colonel," or to "your beloved colonel," the clerk of the Royal Treasury held him responsible for the abandonment of Nova Oeiras. According to Brito, the colonel, "depraved in the tongue," was "the most ungrateful" of all, for he had convinced the new governor that the factory should be abandoned and that he had never been in favor of the project.[12]

It is not difficult to conclude that an anonymous and defamatory manuscript that was widely disseminated could contribute to dissuade any initiative to revive the factory. Correia de Brito did not explain why Monteiro de Moraes turned against the enterprise that had been the apple of Sousa Coutinho's eye. One hypothesis is that Moraes waited for Sousa Coutinho to leave the government to express his criticisms without fear of reprisal. In the "Resposta," the person who writes it claims to have waited five years before producing the text. It is also likely that, just as Nova Oeiras disrupted the business of other public agents for the reasons already mentioned, it also harmed the colonel. As soon as he could, he used his influence and prestige to ruin the industrial enterprise permanently.

"Resposta que um sujeito do Brasil deu ao outro de Angola sobre a fábrica do ferro" is a *pasquim*, i.e., an anonymous manuscript with satirical or eulogistic purposes, very common at the time. The *pasquins* followed a "discursive tradition of insulting and criticizing authorities,"[13] typical of eighteenth-century rhetorical re-

---

11 Ofício de FISC. São Paulo de Assunção Luanda, January 25, 1764. Filmoteca Ultramarina Portuguesa, R-5–3–17, AL, M-99, Papéis vários sobre Angola, fl. 90. *Apud* Catarina Madeira Santos, *Um governo "polido" para Angola*, p. 318.

12 Carta de José Plácido Correia de Brito, escrivão da Fazenda Real, para FISC, ex-governador de Angola. São Paulo de Assunção de Luanda, February 11, 1773. ANTT, Condes de Linhares, mç. 44, doc. 100.

13 Luiz Carlos Villalta, "As origens intelectuais e políticas da Inconfidência Mineira," in M. E. L. de Resende and L. C. Villalta (orgs.), *As Minas Setecentistas 2* (Belo Horizonte: Autêntica; Companhia do Tempo, 2007), 579–580.

sources. The purpose of these texts was to defend what was thought to be correct in a good political order, for the "common good," since in colonial literature in general, satire is "charitable warfare: it wounds in order to heal."[14]

In this case, Monteiro de Moraes wanted to show that Nova Oeiras was a work contrary to the common good, "from its very beginning repugnant and dubious," the result of daydreams of a "famous hero of rascals," and that it should be closed down. The "subject of Brazil" argued that, with Sousa Coutinho's government, "all the good order with which government was exercised was altered imprudently."[15] The literary text simulates a response from a "subject of Brazil" to a letter he presumably received five years earlier from someone in Angola about the iron factory. The letter is a dialogue in which the former quotes, comments, and criticizes excerpts written by his interlocutor, who was a defender of Francisco de Sousa Coutinho's ideas and the iron factory. Without mentioning the governor's name, Moraes chose him as the satirized authority, a caricature character, exaggerating the description of his traits: "your grace has now painted the governor's nature with all its colors: much promise, much pretense, much fantastic appearance."[16]

Based as it was on a series of eighteenth-century rhetorical conventions, the satire had no commitment to portraying reality. However, reading this text allows us to understand important elements of the politics, economy, and society of the Kingdom of Angola. The colonial authors appropriated colonial references and "transform[ed] them, quote[d] them, and parody[ed] them."[17] Without those references, the rhetorical games would not be understandable. Moreover, it is quite evident that the author of the document was aware of the events that followed the construction and maintenance of Nova Oeiras, since he describes very specific situations in detail.[18] In this regard, the strong connection with Brazil is also worth

---

14 João Adolfo Hansen, *A sátira e o engenho: Gregório de Matos e a Bahia do século XVII*, second edition (São Paulo: Ateliê Editorial; Campinas: Editora da Unicamp, 2004), 48.
15 "Resposta que um sujeito do Brasil deu ao outro de Angola, sobre a Fábrica do Ferro."
16 "Resposta que um sujeito do Brasil deu ao outro de Angola, sobre a Fábrica do Ferro." About the rhetorical codes of satire that condition the construction of caricatural characters like that of the governor, the "exaggerations of the typifying traits of the satirized person must be pleasurable to the public, which finds in them, in addition to the pleasure of recognizing the deformity in the caricature, also the pleasure of recognizing an adequate performance of the technique of poetic fantasy." Idem, 54.
17 João Adolfo Hansen, "Letras coloniais e historiografia literária," *Matraga*, Rio de Janeiro, v. 18 (2006), 24.
18 He says, for example, that the cost of iron from Nova Oeiras was 45,000 or 46,000 réis. Only someone very close to the correspondence between governors and the Court could have this information.

noting, since the sender is from Brazilian lands and was intimately aware of facts that took place in Angola's hinterlands.

The letter is divided into chapters that address topics related to the feasibility and the impacts of establishing Nova Oeiras in the Ilamba region. Among the many laudatory texts about Sousa Coutinho, who called himself the "philosopher administrator," this source stands out from the rest, providing a new perspective on how his government was viewed by some of his contemporaries. The criticism reveals the daily exploitation of the Ambundus' labor in the factory; the high expenses of the Royal Treasury with wages, equipment, and supplies; the illnesses, deaths, and difficulties of living in Ilamba. These are topics we have discussed in this book based on other sources, but the critical interpretation of the "Resposta" synthesizes a view of everyday life in Nova Oeiras: "This governor of yours, not content with exhausting the Royal Treasury of Angola, also intended to exhaust the kingdom of vassals; it is enraging to the point of killing!"[19]

A recurrent point in the text is the analysis of the quality of the mines and ore hills. The governor's opponent believed that the ore could not yield larger amounts of iron, and that that was the cause of the successive failures in the smelting experiments. Nonetheless, since he was unable to make a more precise assessment, he concluded that the samples sent to Lisbon should be retested. The central focus of the criticisms is the governor's behavior, which is seen as hyperbolic: his promises regarding the factory were "dry thunderstorms" that only frightened the ears.

Finally, one last aspect deserves to be highlighted: the discussion about whether Angola was a country for factories or not. The opinion of Sousa Coutinho's detractor was the following: "Angola is not a country for factories, and certainly not for iron factories, for in no way can the qualities of Nature and Art that your grace insinuates contribute to it." The "Resposta" makes it clear that, for its author, it was impossible to establish profitable iron factories in Angola because the mines were unproductive and no technical effort was able to overcome that natural obstacle. Besides, the factory was leading the kingdom to ruin, because it concentrated a labor force that could be employed in other activities such as commerce. In this regard, the main commercial activity of the Kingdom of Angola was the trade of enslaved people.

The Pombaline project for Angola was to transform this kingdom into more than a trading post—a colony with civilian settlements, to use the expression of the Count of Oeiras himself—whose main function was not the export of enslaved people, but a diversified economy, promoting agriculture, establishing factories, and exploiting nature for commercial ends. These guidelines were to be followed

---

19 "Resposta que um sujeito do Brasil deu ao outro de Angola, sobre a Fábrica do Ferro."

by Angola's governors, who, although they enjoyed a certain autonomy, were obliged to follow a frame of reference and a program. This more general picture of colonial administration is important because, in the sources analyzed, we can see that the ideas of Portuguese enlightened reformism depended on the support of a broad political network. They began in the offices of the metropolis, continued with the local elites in the colonies, especially personalities such as João Monteiro de Moraes, and ended with the *capitães-mores* of the fortress in the distant interior of the Kingdom of Angola.

It seems to us that Nova Oeiras did not find the necessary support from key people to enable the plans to be effective in the Kingdom of Angola: the merchants, the *capitães-mores*, and the local political elite. This was also an important factor in its downfall. The refusal to continue the project is evident in Monteiro Moraes's *pasquim*; as the opponent of the "philosopher administrator" said, "Angola is no country for factories."

Can it be said the rejection of Nova Oeiras was a repudiation of the entire Pombaline program to promote manufacturing in Angola? The iron factory cannot be analyzed in isolation, since other enterprises were planned to operate like it, such as the lime factories and the incentive to exploit saltpeter and sulfur in Benguela. None of them achieved the expected results. This issue deserves a detailed examination, highlighting the private initiatives and the eventual conflicts with the Royal Treasury. For now, we have no elements for a deeper analysis, but there is evidence that points to the resistances to the changes introduced by Sousa Coutinho. This leads us to a central question: to what extent were the subjects of the Portuguese Crown willing to turn Angola into a colony of civilian settlements and to invest in areas other than the trade of enslaved people, a business in which they were directly or indirectly involved and was the source of their fortunes? Apparently, the illustrious residents of Luanda were unconvinced by the rhetoric of the "philosopher administrator." In Monteiro Moraes's satire, these contradictions and tensions become clear: his text is constructed by the opposition between the defender of enlightened reforms, on one hand, and a head that does not understand the need for such changes, on another. Let us look at an example.

The apologist for Nova Oeiras considered an iron factory in Angola "an extraordinary event" because, at last, a "skillful and vigilant governor" had paid attention to the "treasures that nature offers in the form of iron hills," something the conquest had never considered until then, because it was wrongly believed that "the forces of that vast and useful region" were limited to supplying "the necessary Negroes" for the "deceitful gold mines and sugar mills in Brazil." According to this reasoning, Sousa Coutinho was the shrewd administrator who would elevate Angola to the same status as Brazil, overcoming its function as a mere trading post that supplied enslaved people to the other side of the Atlantic Ocean.

This logic made no sense to the "subject of Brazil." In his opinion, furnishing enslaved people was a function to be praised, along with the export of ivory. The conquests in Africa already yielded what they could yield; there was nothing more to exploit:

> What man, no matter how senseless, has dared say until now that the productions of the conquests of Africa should prevail over the gold and sugar mills of Brazil? And what man, no matter how mediocre, fails to understand that West Africa provides all it can provide, in addition to its valuable ivory, by supplying the necessary slaves for the most useful services of the mines, mills, and farms of Brazil?[20]

In a way, Sousa Coutinho tried to negotiate with those conflicting political forces and used strategies to convince the African authorities. So much so that he often emphasized the need not to subtract labor force and iron from agriculture, nor to divert porters from activities that were indispensable for any expeditions in the *sertões* and, in particular, for the trade of enslaved people. There could be no shortage of iron and blacksmiths to make agricultural tools and neck shackles.[21] Such measures were intended to avoid confrontation with important people in the *sertões* of the Kingdom of Angola, whose support he sought. The local elites, such as the Monteiro family, were strongly connected to the trade of enslaved people, as Thornton and Miller remind us:

> these Angolan or Luso-African 'Portuguese' were traders of enslaved people, smugglers, held middle and low positions in the civil, military, and ecclesiastical bureaucracy of the colony, and constituted the closest equivalent of a local agrarian aristocracy.[22]

Finally, the "Resposta" is an interesting document that allows us to reflect on the reinvention or subversion of ideas and projects conceived at the center of the Empire as they arrive in colonial areas. Analyzing it enables us to reconstruct the circumstances under which administrative decisions were made in the Kingdom of Angola. When historiography cites Governor Antonio de Lencastre's decision to close Nova Oeiras, it does so as if that choice stemmed solely from his political will or from a rigorous examination of the financial losses caused by the factory.[23]

---

20 "Resposta que um sujeito do Brasil deu ao outro de Angola, sobre a Fábrica do Ferro."
21 Carta de FISC para Francisco Matoso de Andrade, *capitão-mor* de Ambaca. São Paulo de Assunção de Luanda, May 25, 1767.BNP, C – 8742, F – 6364, fl. 182v.
22 John K. Thornton and Joseph C. Miller, "A crônica como fonte, história e hagiografia; o Catálogo dos Governadores de Angola," *Revista Internacional de Estudos Africanos*, no. 12–13 (1990): 15.
23 Ana Madalena Trigo de Sousa, *D. Francisco de Sousa Coutinho em Angola: Reinterpretação de um Governo 1764–1772*, thesis (Master's in History) (Funchal/ Lisbon: Universidade de Nova Lisboa, 1996), 102. Catarina Madeira Santos, *Um governo "polido" para Angola*, 533.

João Monteiro de Moraes and his efforts to influence the governor in his satirical *pasquim* are not taken into account. However, they document a dynamic internal to the colonial universe that cannot be ignored in the analysis.

Our brief exercise to try to understand the local logics that oriented political agreements reveals the complexity of the motivations to abandon the plans to develop the iron industry in Angola and the extent to which governors' actions were limited, conditioned as they were by the interests of other subjects of the Portuguese Crown. The effectiveness of colonial plans depended largely on them. At the end of his government, Sousa Coutinho considered that this type of undertaking was "extravagant," since it depended on many arms and was beyond his ability considering the colonial structure in place in Angola and the little time he spent there: "such works are not for governors whose term ends, they are for the king, who lives on, and who can tame the laziness, ignorance, and concerns of the people and the governors."[24]

Since this did not happen, at the end of his government, he was substituted by an administrator who was opposed to his ideas. With the support of the forces contrary to Sousa Coutinho, and unable to face Central Africans' resistance and their resolve to maintain their "secrets," Antonio de Lencastre closed the iron factory in Nova Oeiras: he suspended the wages, ordered the deportation of the European masters present there, and abandoned the building.

5.2 Other Landscapes, Same Issues

In June 1767, the governor of Angola asked his brother-in-law, Luis Antonio de Sousa Botelho de Mourão, Morgado of Mateus, governor of the captaincy of São Paulo (1765–1775),[25] to send him a detailed description of the iron factory that "was being built in São Paulo": "whether it is far from the ocean, what masters it has, the number of people who work there, how much iron it produces per day, and

---

24 Carta de FISC para Luis Antonio de Sousa, governador de São Paulo. São Paulo de Assunção de Luanda, May 4, 1770. BNP, C – 8743, F – 6377.
25 Like Sousa Coutinho, the Morgado of Mateus received instructions from the Count of Oeiras on how he should administer the captaincy. The instructions are the same: "These were (...) the coordinates of his administration during the ten years it lasted: territorial exploration, settlement and urbanization, economic development, military strengthening, and bureaucratic/administrative organization." Heloísa Liberalli Bellotto, *Autoridade e conflito no Brasil colonial: o governo do morgado de Mateus em São Paulo (1765–1775)*, second ed. (São Paulo: Alameda, 2007), 88.

how much it costs."²⁶ The buildings of the Ipanema Iron Factory were built only in 1811. However, the information and research on iron mining in the hill of Araçoiaba (Iperó, São Paulo) dates back to the sixteenth century and an iron factory operated there in the mid-eighteenth century, during the administration of Luis Antonio de Sousa, who considered iron smelting one of the main concerns of his government.

On that occasion, the Morgado of Mateus requested the blueprints for Nova Oeiras in order to establish the factory on Araçoiaba Hill based on them.²⁷ The blood-related royal officials shared experiences in order to observe the guidelines promoted by the Count of Oeiras to establish factories in colonial areas. In the correspondence between the two governors, the subject appears frequently. They discuss technical information on smelting and even the possibility of jointly hiring and exchanging skilled workers, master smelters, blacksmiths, and forgers.

These were not the only cases involving the development of manufactured products, especially iron, by administrators of the Portuguese Empire. In Portuguese America, the promotion of this type of industry was also a relevant topic for Governor D. Rodrigo José de Menezes, who governed Minas Gerais from 1780 to 1783. To solve the issue of the waning of gold production, Menezes proposed "a new establishment that at first might [seem] contrary to the spirit and the administration system" of the captaincy, "but whose thorough examination reveals reasons (...), most solid and convenient, its usefulness." This new "remedy [was] the establishment of an iron factory."²⁸

We must remember that promoting iron production in the colony was acknowledged by Rodrigo de Menezes, "at first sight," as diverging from metropolitan policies, since it was contrary to royal monopolies and would decrease the collection of tributes derived from the rights of the Entries Contract²⁹ on imported iron.

---

26 Carta de FISC para Luis Antonio de Sousa, govenador da capitania de São Paulo. São Paulo de Assunção de Luanda, May 4, 1770. ANTT, Projeto Reencontro Morgado Mateus, mf. 12.
27 Carta de FISC para Luis Antonio de Sousa, govenador da capitania de São Paulo. São Paulo de Assunção de Luanda, May 4, 1770. BNP, C – 8743, F – 6377.
28 Exposição do Governador D. Rodrigo José de Menezes sobre o estado de decadência da Capitania de Minas – Gerais e meios de remedia-lo, 04/08/1780. In Livro Primeiro de registro dos ofícios dirigidos à Corte Pelo Ilmo. e Exmo. Senhor D. Rodrigo José de Menezes, Governador e Capitão General desta Capitania de Minas Gerais, APM – Seção Colonial, Códice 224, fl. 314.
29 The right of Entries was collected in fiscal stations and imposed taxes on the products that entered the Mines. It was also one of the main ways of monitoring the circulation of merchandise, including gold. This tribute had been collected through contracts since 1715, and it was a way to pay the royal fifth owed to the Crown. The system of collection through contracts was in place until 1789, when the Royal Treasury started to collect the tribute. Cláudia Maria das Graças Chaves, *Perfeitos negociantes: mercadores das Minas Setecentistas* (São Paulo: Annablume, 1999), 85.

Besides, it seemed contradictory to promote the development of an economic activity that favored the colony's autonomy. The governor's position confirms the difficulties encountered by an enlightened Portuguese when faced by the need to respond pragmatically to the complex reality of Minas Gerais, since "the norm would be not to stimulate such industries in the colony; yet circumstances imposed it."[30] This applied especially to iron—a most needed metal that Portugal did not produce, thus having to bear the burden of large imports. In Minas Gerais, it was Manoel Ferreira da Câmara Bethencourt e Sá, the General Intendant of Mines and Diamonds, who was in charge of building the Royal Iron Factory of Morro do Pilar (1812).

Since there is a more direct connection between Nova Oeiras and Ipanema thanks to the extensive correspondence exchanged between its creators, we will only propose a few reflections on the problems faced by Luis Antonio de Sousa in Brazilian lands, for comparative purposes.

In 1763, it was the Portuguese Domingos Pereira Ferreira who resumed iron ore extraction activities in Araçoiaba, receiving a concession of *sesmarias* to gain access to the wood necessary for the foundry.[31] As soon as he arrived at the town of Sorocaba, Domingos Pereira began the first experiments in a small forge, with the help of ironmaster João de Oliveira Figueiredo. In December 1765, the governor of São Paulo sent samples of the iron extracted by Ferreira to the Count of Oeiras. After a little over a year, with the help of the Morgado of Mateus, Domingos Ferreira obtained financing of 10,000 cruzados to lay the factory's foundations, through a partnership established with entrepreneurs trusted by the governor. At that time, that amount was used to conduct further experiments on the "stone's productivity" and to find out if the "master's art" would be able to melt large amounts of iron. In addition, the partners committed themselves "to erect all other factories thought to be necessary to provide abundant iron, not only for this entire captaincy [of São Paulo], but also the others in Brazil, with the whole society contributing to all expenses."[32]

In the captaincy of São Paulo, the Morgado of Mateus relied on the resources of private enterprise, since ore exploitation had been previously granted to the Portuguese Domingos Pereira. In Angola, until 1770, when the idea of establishing

---

30 Fernando A. Novais, *Portugal e Brasil na Crise do Antigo Sistema Colonial (1777–1808)* (São Paulo: Hucitec, 1995), 285.
31 Domingos Ferreira Pereira also received a concession to mine lead.
32 Carta de Luis Antonio de Sousa, governador da capitania de São Paulo, para Sebastião José Carvalho de Melo, conde de Oeiras. São Paulo, January 3, 1768. In *Publicação Oficial de documentos interessantes para a história e costumes de São Paulo*, v. XIX (São Paulo: Arquivo do Estado de São Paulo, Typographia da Companhia Industrial de São Paulo, 1896), 39–41.

a factory driven by a blast furnace still seemed feasible, Sousa Coutinho advocated that the Royal Treasury assume all the factory's financial costs, because it would be much more advantageous for "its profits to strengthen the garrisons needed by these kingdoms."[33]

In August 1770, Luis Cantofer, a merchant from Madras, India, son of a Portuguese mother and a German father, who was passing through Angola, became interested in purchasing the iron factory of Nova Oeiras, promising to pay all expenses incurred with the factory until then.[34] The merchant's interest was justified by the many advantages that Nova Oeiras would bring to his business in India, which he extended to Portugal's trade with Indian products:

> Nothing could (...) be more interesting to the Kingdom of Portugal than the commerce with India that I intend to establish, His Most Loyal Majesty permitting, than this Factory, because by sending to India shipments of iron, of which there is so much need in those parts, all sorts of products can come without having to take from the Kingdom the large amounts of gold that are sent there every year.[35]

The merchant arrived in Luanda by chance; the ship on which he was a passenger experienced technical problems and had to make a forced stop in the city's port. The crewmembers were in a hurry to leave for Salvador, their original destination,

---

33 In 1765, Sousa Coutinho argued, "I know well that only with the Royal Treasury will [the factory] last and grow, while everything will be lost if it were handed over to private individuals." Carta de FISC para Francisco Xavier de Mendonça Furtado, secretário de Estado da Marinha e do Ultramar. São Paulo de Assunção de Luanda, December 29, 1766. AHU_CU_001, Cx. 50, D. 64. In 1770, the governor explained that before that year he thought it best to keep the initiative away from private individuals. "If I did not believe that there were such important and large businesses interested in it and able to help the factory significantly and continuously, I would vote as I have already done, that it be kept under the royal administration to ensure that its profits strengthen the garrisons." Carta de FISC para Martinho de Melo e Castro, secretário de Estado da Marinha e do Ultramar. São Paulo de Assunção de Luanda, August 23, 1770. AHU_CU_001, Cx. 57, D. 45.
34 Roquinaldo Ferreira commented on Luis Cantofer's trajectory in the commercial context. Roquinaldo Ferreira, "Dinâmica do comércio intracolonial: jeribitas, panos asiáticos e guerra no tráfico angolano de escravizados (século XVIII)." In João Fragoso, Maria Fernanda Bicalho, and Maria de Fátima Gouvêa, *Antigo Regime nos trópicos. A dinâmica imperial portuguesa (séculos XVI–XVIII)* (Rio de Janeiro: Civilização Brasileira, 2001), 358 and ff.
35 Carta de Luis Cantofer para FISC. São Paulo de Assunção de Luanda, August 18, 1770. BNP, C – 8743, F – 6377. Luis Cantofer also participated in the trade of enslaved people in River Plate Basin. In 1782, he was authorized by the Spanish Crown to take 1,000 enslaved people to Buenos Aires in Portuguese ships. Fábio Pesavento, "Para além do império ultramarino português: as redes trans, extraimperiais, no século XVIII," in Roberto Guedes (org.), *Dinâmica Imperial no Antigo Regime Português. Escravidão, governos, fronteiras, poderes e legados: séc. XVII–XIX* (Rio de Janeiro: Mauad X, 2011).

and the merchant intended to live in Lisbon and promised to become a Portuguese citizen as soon as possible. Cantofer could speak, read, and write Portuguese, and had the support of the Royal Treasury's administrator and Luanda's merchants. Before heading to Portugal, he wanted to sell the goods he had brought from Goa, shipping 316 pieces of crockery to Brazil.

This time, the governor of Angola was in favor of surrendering the privileges over the factory to Luis Cantofer for "a certain number of years." For a period to be determined, the Crown would give up the income from the factory, but after that, the factory would return to the Royal Treasury. Sousa Coutinho made this decision because he feared that his successors would not be interested in his project, which required "continuous assistance."[36]

Luis Cantofer was unable to fulfill both his commercial plans and his intention to take over Nova Oeiras. Because he owned a large number of estates (the equivalent of 200,000 cruzados), was a foreigner, and had only been married a short time, Cantofer was considered suspicious by the Crown, which at the time was seeking to regain control of the routes to the Orient. Thus, the deal was not approved.

A few months later, however, early in the following year (1771), the governor of Angola wrote to the Count of Oeiras reversing his opinion. Sousa Coutinho explained that he had believed Cantofer and would never hand the factory over to a foreigner.[37]

Iron factories were not new as one of the colonial economic activities that were left to private enterprise. After all, during the entire colonization process, the Portuguese Crown relied on the resources of private initiative, seeking its support while trying to control it.[38] The fear of losing command of the Nova Oeiras factory and the large profits it promised was no doubt a decisive factor in maintaining it under the Royal Treasury's administration.

---

36 Carta de FISC para Martinho de Melo e Castro, secretário de Estado da Marinha e do Ultramar. São Paulo de Assunção de Luanda, August 23, 1770. AHU_CU_001, Cx. 57, D. 45.
37 Carta de FISC para Sebastião Carvalho de Melo, marquês de Pombal. São Paulo de Assunção de Luanda, February 13, 1771. IEB/ USP, AL – 082–302. Another reason for the governor's change in position could be the fact that Cantofer was not Portuguese; he would have to "naturalize" in order to be entitled to lease the factory.
38 Rodrigo Ricupero, "Governo-geral e a formação da elite colonial baiana no século XVI," in Maria Fernanda Bicalho e Vera Lúcia Amaral Ferlini (orgs.), *Modos de Governar. Ideias e práticas políticas no Império Português, séculos XVI a XIX* (São Paulo: Alameda, 2005), 119.

In his efforts to establish an ironworks in the town of Sorocaba, Luis Antonio de Sousa communicated often with Angola, which influenced the fate of that enterprise. Precisely when they obtained the financing to build the factory, the entrepreneurs from São Paulo found themselves with their hands tied because João de Oliveira Figueiredo, the master smelter who had been hired by Domingos Ferreira, decided to remain in Rio de Janeiro, for he intended to embark to Angola. As soon as the Morgado de Mateus found out, he wrote to the viceroy to have him arrested and sent to São Paulo, which was promptly done. The master returned arrested to Sorocaba in February 1767.[39]

Master João de Oliveira no doubt heard the news that the governor of Angola had disseminated in Brazilian lands that he was looking for experienced foundrymen for Nova Oeiras and that the candidates would be generously rewarded.[40]

From the time of João de Oliveira's return to Sorocaba to the end of 1768, the efforts focused on exploring the land where the factory would be located: "the ironstone mine extends over an area of two *léguas em quadra*,[41] with plenty of firewood and water to sustain the factories." Afterwards, expenses began with the structure of the furnaces and the smelting experiments: "large and small furnaces of different types, anvils, hammers, mallets, wheels and engines to move them." Even though the governor sent "ingenious and experienced people" to assist the works, it was not "possible to smelt the iron well, nor to obtain the same result as in the first sample" that was sent to the Count of Oeiras.[42]

The Morgado of Mateus suspected that the master was unskilled, "because he had never worked in a factory, nor seen those of Biscay." He also suspected that "ill-intentioned people" had bribed the master ("in order for him to pretend ignorance") to keep the factory from prospering.[43] The governor's suspicion about the lack of support from the local elite to develop the project is evident here. In 1769, he said that the vast extensions of forest and the great availability of water to move the mills and to transport the iron to distant regions were of no use because the

---

39 Carta de Luis Antonio de Sousa, governador da capitania de São Paulo, para Sebastião José Carvalho de Melo, conde de Oeiras. São Paulo, January 3, 1768. In *Publicação Oficial de documentos interessantes para a história e costumes de São Paulo*, v. XIX, 41.
40 See Chapter 4.
41 *Léguas em quadra* usually referred to the number of leagues on each side of a square. Therefore two *léguas em quadra* was equal to four square leagues (T.N.).
42 Carta de Luis Antonio de Sousa, governador da capitania de São Paulo, para Sebastião José Carvalho de Melo, conde de Oeiras. São Paulo, January 3, 1768. In *Publicação Oficial de documentos interessantes para a história e costumes de São Paulo*, v. XIX, 41.
43 Ibidem.

master responsible had "little experience" and no "skillful and curious people" were found who, with dedication, "could uncover the secret."[44]

As we can see, the secret of metal casting was an unsolvable problem for the Portuguese authorities. Luis Antonio de Sousa proposed to his brother-in-law in Angola that they both request "once again other masters from Biscay" for both factories. In Brazilian lands, which were "healthier" and enjoyed a better climate than those of the Kingdom of Angola, it would not be difficult to train enough smelters to reestablish both factories.[45] From Angola, Sousa Coutinho replied declining the offer, for he no longer had the strength or the resources to have masters from Biscay sent.[46]

The big possible difference between Nova Oeiras and the factory in Sorocaba was that, in Angola, Sousa Coutinho resorted to the knowledge of practical Central African smelters. In Morro de Araçoiaba, as we shall see, they were far away, but resorting to that knowledge was not a remote possibility.

Throughout the eighteenth century, indigenous labor was widely employed in the captaincy of São Paulo. What came to be known as the substitution of indigenous slavery for African slavery took place gradually and was only consolidated at the end of the eighteenth century.[47] In the second half of the eighteenth century, there was a decline in the capture of Indians, due, among other reasons, to the difficulties encountered to penetrate the *sertões*. Importing enslaved Africans was one of the alternatives to the Indian slavery crisis, first adopted by the wealthier masters. We must remember that enslaved Africans had been introduced in São Paulo since the beginning of colonization, albeit in much smaller numbers than indigenous slave labor, which predominated since the sixteenth century.[48]

---

44 Carta de Luis Antonio de Sousa, governador da capitania de São Paulo, para FISC. São Paulo, October 30, 1769. In *Publicação Oficial de documentos interessantes para a história e costumes de São Paulo*, v. XIX, 406–408.
45 Ibidem.
46 Carta de FISC para Luis Antonio de Sousa, governador de São Paulo. São Paulo de Assunção de Luanda, May 4, 1770. BNP, C – 8743, F – 6377.
47 "But to speak of a transition, at least in the sense of the replacement of indigenous captives in agricultural tasks, would be hasty: this process remained incomplete in this period and was only consummated in the late-eighteenth century, when the growth in sugar production revitalized the São Paulo economy." John Manuel Monteiro, *Negros da Terra: índios e bandeirantes nas origens de São Paulo* (São Paulo: Companhia das Letras, 1994), 220.
48 Idem, 221.

According to Maria Marcílio, "the city [of São Paulo] saw an increase, after 1740–1750, in the number of enslaved people of African origin."[49] In the late-1760s, the population of the captaincy of São Paulo reached 83,880 people; of these, 23,333 were enslaved Africans and 2,736 were subjugated Indians—not counting the thousands of Indians who lived in the *sertões*, outside the Portuguese domain.[50] During the eighteenth century, the captive population in the captaincy remained at 24.2%. According to Fabiana Schleumer, based on the 3,398 death records located at the Cúria Metropolitana of São Paulo, most of the enslaved (489) in São Paulo and its surroundings came from Guinea. The author also highlights other places of origin: Congo, Cape Verde, Mozambique, and Rebolo.[51]

Between 1801 and 1805, according to data collected by Regiane Matos in "Maços de população da cidade de São Paulo," two Central African ethnic groups predominate: 1,427 captives from Benguela and 609 from Angola. The third group is from Mina, with 243 captives.[52] Thus, in the late-eighteenth and early-nineteenth century, we can say that in São Paulo there were enslaved Africans from the West Coast and West Central Africa.[53]

At the Sorocaba factory, Luis Antonio de Sousa recounted in one of his letters that the little iron that was produced was due to the "crude intelligence of a Negro who, having started working with the master, obtain[ed] better castings when he

---

49 Maria Luíza Marcílio, "A população paulistana ao longo dos 450 anos da Cidade," in Paula Porta (org.), *História da Cidade de São Paulo. A cidade colonial (1554–1822)* (São Paulo: Paz e Terra, 2004), 254.
50 Francisco Vidal Luna and Herbert S. Klein, *Evolução da sociedade e economia escravista de São Paulo, de 1750 e 1850*, trans. Laura Teixeira Motta (São Paulo: EDUSP, 2005), 45.
51 Fabiana Schleumer, "Recriando Áfricas: presença negra na São Paulo colonial," *Histórica – Revista Eletrônica do Arquivo Público do Estado de São Paulo*, no. 46 (February 2011): 2.
52 Regiane Augusto de Mattos, *De cassange, mina benguela a gentio da Guiné. Grupos étnicos e formação de identidade africanas na cidade de São Paulo (1800–1850)*, thesis (Master's in Social History) (Universidade de São Paulo, 2006), 89.
53 It is important to consider that we only know the places of origin of enslaved Africans taken to Portuguese America through specific ethnic designations called "nations." These classifications present in colonial sources—especially in baptism, marriage, and death certificates—had more to do with to the trade or to the construction of an identity by colonizers than with specific African ethnicities. According to Mariza Soares, "there is no homogeneity in the names of origin, [which] go from the names of islands, the ports of departure, villages, and kingdoms, to small ethnic groups." The term Angola, for example, is very generic, for it corresponds to several ethnic groups from West Central Africa embarked at the port of Luanda. Mariza de Carvalho Soares, *Devotos da cor: identidade étnica, religiosidade e escravidão no Rio de Janeiro, século XVIII* (Rio de Janeiro: Civilização Brasileira, 2000), 109.

[was] in command."⁵⁴ We do not know the origin of this skillful enslaved smelter who surpassed the Portuguese master, or even if he was African. However, this quote can bring together the two shores of the Portuguese Atlantic in terms of the exploitation of African metallurgical knowledge. The Africans brought to the captaincy of São Paulo, "in spite of the radical separation from their societies of origin, struggled (...) to organize"⁵⁵ their lives based on Bantu sociocultural elements. An ancient wisdom from West and Central Africa, metallurgy, like other intellectual contributions such as medical and culinary practices, was part of a set of African traditions reinvented in the colonial context as a form of resistance and struggle for survival.⁵⁶

Archeological research in Sorocaba also provides clues of the presence of African techniques in smelting furnaces. The furnaces found are the bloomery type laid on the ground: the furnace's circular wall is "laid directly on the ground and consists of bricks and pieces of tiles and mortar with clay from the original soil itself."⁵⁷ The soil analysis also identified an opening in the furnace that was responsible for draining the slag, typical of these direct iron ore reduction structures. The archeologists' hypothesis is that the bellows employed were "hand-operated." All these features are found in African furnaces, and they may be another indication of the presence of African smelters in that iron factory.⁵⁸

---

54 Carta de Luis Antonio de Sousa, governador da capitania de São Paulo, para FISC. São Paulo, October 30, 1769. In *Publicação Oficial de documentos interessantes para a história e costumes de São Paulo*, v. XIX, 406–408.
55 Robert W. Slenes, *Na Senzala, uma Flor. Esperanças e recordações na formação da família escravista*, second ed. (Campinas: Editora da Unicamp, 2014), 155.
56 Robert Slenes analyzed some aspects of blacksmiths based on studies focusing on the Congo region in Central Africa, and demonstrated that the work of smelters and blacksmiths was related to ritual ceremonies. In addition, Slenes calls attention to the importance of blacksmiths as leaders of revolts, like the *quilombola* insurrection of 1848 in Vassouras, led by a freed mulatto who was a blacksmith. Robert Slenes, "L'Arbre Nsanda replanté: cultes d'affliction Kongo et identité des esclaves de plantation dans le Brésil du Sud-Et (1810–1888)," *Cahiers du Brésil Contemporain*, no. 67/68, partie II (2007) : 217–313.
57 Anicleide Zequini, *Arqueologia de uma fábrica de ferro: Morro de Araçoiaba, séculos XVI–XVIII*, dissertation (PhD) (São Paulo: Universidade de São Paulo, 2006), 193.
58 Flávio Gomes and Luís Symanski studied archeological remains found on two coffee plantations in the Paraíba Valley in the nineteenth century. In Santa Clara, they found iron smelting slag, white clay, and quartz flakes. The authors demonstrated that these elements are related to Central African cosmology regarding the supernatural powers surrounding blacksmiths. The persistence of these ideas demonstrates the presence of African technologies in Brazil. Luís Cláudio P. Symanski e Flávio dos Santos Gomes, "Iron Cosmology, Slavery, and Social Control: The Materiality of Rebellion in the Coffee Plantations of the Paraiba Valley, Southeastern Brazil," *Journal of African Diaspora Archaeology and Heritage* 5, no. 2 (2016): 174–197. Regarding the transfer and cultural con-

There is little information about the workers present at the Sorocaba factory in the eighteenth century. In 1815, there are reports that 16 Indians brought from the villages of Itapecirica, M'Boy, Carapicuíba, Barueri, and Itapevi worked at the then Royal Iron Factory of Ipanema.[59] It is possible that Indians worked in the factory in the eighteenth century; however, for now, there is no evidence that the many and diverse indigenous societies of Portuguese America knew about smelting and forging metals.[60] It is possible, however, that the native populations learned it from Europeans or Africans, since there are accounts of Indian attacks against plantations using "many barbed arrows made of iron and copper."[61]

There is evidence that the factory that was under construction during the government of the Morgado of Mateus lacked sufficient workers. The shareholders complained that they could no longer "continue building the said factory for lack of enslaved people to serve them." They suggested seeking captives in the "Arassariguama" plantation, where there were many "without paid employment." They also offered to pay the wages of the enslaved until a solution was found for the lack of workers: "to obtain up to twelve enslaved workers (...) to be paid the wages offered, which are of forty réis, and food for three months."[62] We do not

---

tinuity of African metallurgical techniques in America, in this case in the Caribbean, see also: Candice Goucher, "African Metallurgy in the Atlantic World," in Akinwumi Ogundiran and Toyin Falola (eds.), *Archaeology of Atlantic Africa and the African Diaspora* (Bloomington: Indiana University Press, 2007).

59 The explorers of the mines were responsible for labor costs, so it is likely that they took indigenous people in their excursions. Among them: Afonso Sardinha and Francisco de Sousa (sixteenth and seventeenth centuries), Luis Lopes de Carvalho (seventeenth century), and Domingos Pereira Ferreira (eighteenth century). During the attempts to build the factory in the seventeenth century, one of the private individuals who began exploring the mines suggested that the São Paulo Council send, from "the villages that have free Indians, one hundred couples of Indians to create a Village at the place where the factory is to be built." However, there is no evidence that this actually happened. Anicleide Zequini, *Arqueologia de uma fábrica de ferro*, 125. Anicleide Zequini, "Técnicos e Práticos fundidores: a produção de ferro no Brasil nos séculos XVI e XVIII," in *ANPUH – XXV SIMPÓSIO NACIONAL DE HISTÓRIA* (Fortaleza, 2009), 1–13.

60 "Unlike in the Spanish colonies in America, the indigenous people found here [in Brazil] had no metallurgical knowledge, and therefore did not use any smelting techniques that could be adapted to the interests of the colonizer," Anicleide Zequini, *Arqueologia de uma fábrica de ferro*, 125.

61 Carta de Luis Antonio de Sousa, governador da capitania de São Paulo, para Sebastião Carvalho de Melo, conde de Oeiras. São Paulo, May 19, 1769. In *Documentos interessantes para a história e costumes de São Paulo*. v. XIX (São Paulo: Arquivo do Estado de São Paulo, Typographia da Companhia Industrial de São Paulo, 1896), 346–348.

62 Carta de Luis Antonio de Sousa, governador da capitania de São Paulo. Sem destinatário. São Paulo, June 3, 1769, in *Publicação Oficial de documentos interessantes para a história e costumes de São Paulo*, v. 65 (São Paulo: Arquivo do Estado de São Paulo, Typographia da Companhia Industrial de São Paulo, 1896), 346–348.

know whether this idea actually came to fruition. What is certain is that it constitutes evidence that enslaved Africans and their descendants mined, smelted, and forged iron in the captaincy of São Paulo.

According to Azevedo Marques, from 1766 to 1770, the factory run by Domingos Ferreira produced about four arrobas of iron per day,[63] an amount that was made possible by the "crude intelligence of a Negro." As was the case in Angola, African knowledge and skill, although negatively perceived, was very useful for the production of iron and, in a way, to increase the Crown's wealth.

Another similarity with Nova Oeiras was the limit on productivity, as Sorocaba was unable to produce more than a few arrobas per day. In both factories, the lack of European masters capable of increasing production through the use of blast furnaces or Biscayan hydraulic ironworks was one of the main reasons why both initiatives were abandoned.

The late-eighteenth century projects for the Sorocaba mines fell short of expectations. In the first decade of the nineteenth century, the Sorocaba factory was reopened and enjoyed a period of high productivity. There are relevant studies on the labor of enslaved and free Africans employed in the factory in the nineteenth century.[64] The records for this period describe the ethnonyms that identified the Africans who worked in the foundry, which point to a more direct link between the place of origin and the possession of metallurgical knowledge. Francisco Angola, for example, worked "in the ironworks with blast furnaces."[65]

Francisco de Sousa Coutinho and the Morgado of Mateus, two enlightened administrators, repeatedly failed to promote the iron factories. However, this enterprise, which promised to enrich the Portuguese colonial empire, was not forgotten

---

[63] It is not known how this amount was used or how it was sold or traded. Manoel Eufrasio de Azevedo Marques, *Apontamentos históricos, geográficos, biográficos, estatísticos e noticiosos da província de São Paulo. São Paulo* São Paulo: Martins, 1954), v. 1, p. 248. Apud Heloísa Liberalli Bellotto, *Autoridade e conflito no Brasil colonial*, 181.

[64] Og Natal Menon, *A Real Fábrica de Ferro de São João do Ipanema e seu mundo (1811–1835)*, thesis (Master's) (São Paulo: PUC, 1992; Afonso Bandeira Florence, "Resistência escravizada em São Paulo: a luta dos escravizados da fábrica de ferro São João Ipanema, 1828–1842," *Afro-Ásia*, no. 18 (1996): 7–32; Jaime Rodrigues, "Ferro, trabalho e conflito: os africanos livres na Fábrica de Ipanema," *História Social*, no. 4/5 (1997/1998): 29–42; Mario Danieli Neto, *Escravidão e indústria: um estudo sobre a Fábrica de Ferro São João de Ipanema, Sorocaba (SP), 1765–1895*, dissertation (PhD) (Unicamp, Instituto de Economia, 2006); Mariana Alice Pereira Schatzer Ribeiro, *Entre a fábrica e a senzala: um estudo sobre o cotidiano dos africanos livres na Real Fábrica de Ferro São João do Ipanema – Sorocaba – SP (1840–1870)*, thesis (Master's) (Unesp, Faculdade de Ciências e Letras de Assis, 2014).

[65] Jaime Rodrigues, "Ferro, trabalho e conflito: os africanos livres na Fábrica de Ipanema," 37.

by the governors and ministers who succeeded them on both shores of the South Atlantic.

In 1795, Luis Pinto de Sousa Coutinho, then Secretary of State of Foreign Affairs and War, wrote to the Viceroy of Brazil advocating for the development of the iron industry in Brazil. The first justification was the "defective tariffs that regulate the entry of iron, paying for it the same amount per weight that fine textiles paid in customs."[66] The minister investigated whether there were quality mines near the capital city. As soon as the first sample of the "ferruginous stones" appeared, he sent them to João Manso Pereira,[67] "a person of considerable knowledge of chemistry and mineralogy," to conduct the first experiments. Lacking crucibles and other instruments to set up a "more decisive" laboratory, the minister sent the stones to Lisbon, where they could be better analyzed. Pinto e Sousa had "high hopes" that he would find abundant mines to establish a good factory. He already asserted that European masters "with solid knowledge and recognized experience" were needed. The factory should be well managed to guarantee that the investments made to build and maintain it were not "rendered useless." At this point, Pinto e Sousa cited Nova Oeiras and Ipanema as models of what should not be done: "following the example of what took place in the Captaincy of São Paulo and in the Kingdom of Angola; where having very wealthy mines, little was produced, turning everything into a regrettable loss."[68] Important changes were necessary to make iron mining profitable.

---

[66] Luis Pinto de Sousa, secretário de Estado dos Negócios Estrangeiros e da Guerra, para José Luís de Castro, Conde de Resende, vice-rei do Brasil. AN (RJ), Códice 68, v. 12.
[67] João Manso Pereira was an important naturalist hired in 1796 by Rodrigo de Sousa Coutinho to study the mines of São Paulo together with other researchers. These studies oriented the new phase of the Ipanema factory. Born in 1750, with no specific reference to his birthplace, Manso Pereira studied at the Lapa seminary in Rio de Janeiro. He was professor of Latin grammar, and spoke Greek, Hebrew, and French. He did not study abroad like the other naturalists of his generation, but remained in Portuguese America and was self-taught, as many of his biographers describe him. He was a member of the Literary Society of Rio de Janeiro, where he elaborated a memoir that, according to Alexandre Varela, united two chemical traditions: pre-Lavoisier and modern chemistry. The manuscript that resulted from his experiments with the minerals, cited by Luis Pinto de Sousa, was entitled "De alguns fenômenos que se apresentam intentando-se a análise do mineral descoberto pelas diligências do Ilmo. Sr. conde vice-rei," dated 1795. Alex Gonçalves Varela, *Atividades científicas na "bela e bárbara" capitania de São Paulo (1796–1823)*, dissertation (PhD) (Instituto de Geociências da Universidade Estadual de Campinas, Campinas, 2005), 115–120.
[68] Luis Pinto de Sousa, secretário de Estado dos Negócios Estrangeiros e da Guerra, para José Luís de Castro, Conde de Resende, vice-rei do Brasil. AN (RJ), Códice 68, v. 12.

5.3 Administration and Science

Natural History was on the rise in the eighteenth century, and it was especially thanks to Pombal that this cultural and scientific movement was consolidated. The process began and became effective with the reforms in Coimbra, with the creation of the museums and botanical gardens of Coimbra and Ajuda and the Royal Academy of Sciences in Lisbon.[69]

According to Kenneth Maxwell, in Portugal, in the second half of the eighteenth century, a generation of scholars was concerned with issues related to philosophy and education, seeking with this knowledge to promote social and economic changes. According to the author, it was a diverse and contradictory period.[70] The paradox of the reformism of Minister D. José I can be understood as a confluence of initially opposed knowledges that come together and end up expressing a political effort to associate conflicting social forces. This paradox was perceived not only by historians who have analyzed this past, but especially by Pombal and the generation of intellectuals that surrounded him. This situation acquired new contours with the manufacturing projects of Rodrigo de Sousa Coutinho,[71] the son of the governor of Angola, Francisco de Sousa Coutinho, who also promoted the production of studies and memoirs resulting from travels, expeditions, and explorations, in order to intervene directly in Portugal's economic growth. These studies reflected the Crown's main concerns in the late-eighteenth century: the "advancement of National Instruction, [the] perfection of the Sciences and the Arts, and [the] development of popular industry."[72]

---

[69] Silvia F. de M. Figuerôa, Clarete Paranhos da Silva, and Ermelinda Moutinho Pataca, "Aspectos mineralógicos das 'Viagens Filosóficas' pelo território brasileiro na transição do século XVIII para o século XIX," *História, Ciências, Saúde* 11, no, 3 (2004): 715.

[70] Kenneth Maxwell, *Marquês de Pombal: paradoxo do Iluminismo* (Rio de Janeiro: Paz e Terra, 1996), 2.

[71] On the life and political trajectory of Rodrigo de Sousa Coutinho, see: Andrée Mansuy-Diniz Silva, *Portrait d'un homme d'État: D. Rodrigo de Souza Coutinho, Comte de Linhares 1755– 1812*, vol. I and II (Lisbon, Paris: Centre Culturel Calouste Gulbenkian – Comissão Nacional para as Comemorações dos Descobrimentos Portugueses, 2002).

[72] Planos do Estatuto da Academia, in José Silvestre Ribeiro, *História dos estabelecimentos científicos, literários e artístico de Portugal nos sucessivos reinados da monarquia*, T. II (Lisbon: Tipografia da Academia Real das Ciências de Lisboa, 1872), 39. Apud Alex Gonçalves Varela, *"Juro-lhe pela honra de bom vassalo e bom português": Filosofo Natural e Homem Público – Uma análise das Memórias Científicas do Ilustrado José Bonifácio de Andrada e Silva (1780–1819)*, thesis (Master's in History) (Campinas: Universidade Estadual de, Campinas, 2001), 98. The Academy consisted of three courses: two in Sciences (Observation Sciences—Meteorology, Chemistry, Anatomy, Botanics, and Natural History—and Calculation Sciences—Arithmetic, Algebra, Geometry, Mechanics, and Astronomy) and a Literature course.

To have an idea of how these issues are related to the history of Nova Oeiras, it is worth citing an example. As early as the 1770s, the information network composed of various members of the world of eighteenth-century Enlightenment (colonial authorities, naturalists, Coimbra University professors, scientists of the time) reached an international level. This enabled the French naturalist Georges-Louis Leclerc, Count of Buffon, to come in contact with Antonio Ribeiro Sanches and the governor of Angola, through a communication channel between Luanda and Paris, passing through Lisbon, to discuss the quality of Angolan iron and the ways to make use of it in the Nova Oeiras iron factory. To determine the quality of the iron ore from Ilamba, Sousa Coutinho had sent samples first to Miguel Franzini, professor of Algebra at the University of Coimbra, who responded that the ore offered "a benefit of 65 per 100." After that, the governor sent other samples to his brother, Vicente de Sousa Coutinho, then ambassador in Paris. That is how Monsieur Buffon, together with Antonio Ribeiro Sanches, had access to the sample from the mine in Angola.

The naturalists' assessment was: "Everyone praises the excellent quality of iron from Angola, which can be [compared] to that of the Mongolians, which is sold at the price of silver for cutting instruments, so the convenience of the Portuguese working these mines is quite evident."[73]

At this meeting, Buffon and Sanches sent, through Vicente Coutinho, "Uns Quesitos de História Natural" (Some Matters of Natural History), a booklet sent to Angola to help advance with the iron factory.[74] These were "the French notebooks" used by Sousa Coutinho to guide his last attempt to build a blast furnace. The exchange between Paris and Luanda demonstrates the "administrator-philosopher's" compromise with his most prestigious project, while revealing the new possibilities of pragmatic studies on the riches of overseas possessions.

Throughout the eighteenth century, European naturalists "planned to make a great inventory of nature and peoples, for which purpose they traveled the seas and lands with teams of gardeners and artists." The wise men who participated in philosophical voyages "as economists and ethnographers" also aimed to record "the native techniques to transform nature."[75] They were also seen as explorers, a

---

[73] Carta de FISC sobre a utilidade da fábrica de ferro. Lisboa, September 16, 1773. BNP, C 8553, F6362.
[74] Idem.
[75] Ronald Raminelli, *Viagens Ultramarinas: Monarcas, vassalos e governo a distância* (São Paulo: Alameda, 2008), 97.

notion that was related to different objectives, "but which always combined geostrategic and naturalist functions."[76]

William Joel Simon's detailed description of the procedures adopted by naturalists to catalogue nature, techniques, and peoples allows us to understand how in Portugal these voyages were planned by Paduan naturalist Domingos Vandelli (1735–1816), one of the first professors recruited by the Crown to teach at the University of Coimbra and the Colégio dos Nobres, with an important role at the Academy of Sciences in Lisbon. In addition, the professor had a considerable impact on generations of Portuguese and Brazilian naturalists. Among the students who stood out are Alexandre Rodrigues Ferreira and Manuel Galvão da Silva (both of them born in Bahia), Joaquim José da Silva and João da Silva Feijó (both from Rio de Janeiro), and Joaquim Veloso de Miranda (from Vila Rica).[77]

To promote his plans to explore the colony's natural wealth, Vandelli resorted to the "Portugal's protector of Sciences at the time,"[78] Martinho de Melo e Castro (1761–1765), then Portugal's Secretary of the Navy and Overseas Affairs, who held important positions during the reign of D. José I and was a key figure in the continuity of Pombaline policies to encourage philosophical voyages during the reign of Queen D. Maria I. Thus, a Natural History of Portuguese colonies developed, which made the plans to colonize the overseas domains and exploit their natural resources feasible, as these studies were eminently utilitarian in nature.

A striking fact about the objectives of colonial exploration in philosophical voyages is that they were proposed in conjunction with the expeditions of the border demarcation commissions. The planning for the first naturalist voyages to the colonies dates back to 1778, the year when the Treaty of San Ildefonso was signed, which resulted in a new geographical delimitation of Brazilian lands. According to historiographical studies on the subject, there is no way to understand those voyages independently of the demarcation commissions.[79]

---

76 Ermelinda Pataca, *Terra, Água e Ar nas viagens científicas portuguesas (1755–1808)*, dissertation (PhD in Geoscience) (Campinas: Unicamp, 2006), 11.
77 William Joel Simon, *Scientific Expeditions in the Portuguese Overseas Territories* (1783–1808) (Lisbon: Instituto de Investigação Científica Tropical, 1983), 9.
78 Ibidem.
79 Silvia F. de M. Figuerôa, Clarete Paranhos da Silva, and Ermelinda Moutinho Pataca, "Aspectos mineralógicos das 'Viagens Filosóficas' pelo território brasileiro na transição do século XVIII para o século XIX," 717. See also: Ângela Domingues, *Viagens de exploração geográfica na Amazônia em finais do século XVIII: política, ciência e aventura* (Coimbra: Imprensa de Coimbra, 1991); Artur C. Ferreira Reis, "Limites e demarcações na Amazônia Brasileira," *Revista Trimensal do Instituto Histórico e Geográfico Brasileiro* 244, no. 3 (n.d.): 3–103. Magnus Pereira's works on the reform of the University of Coimbra and the role played by João da Silva Feijó and Elias Alexandre e Silva, among other naturalists and travelers, are also important. Magnus Roberto de Mello Pereira and Ana

According to Vandelli, the voyages were a means to inventory economic resources. The collection and study of ores preceded planning for their extraction.[80] Vandelli advised naturalists to always carry a "small laboratory" to analyze the chemical composition of the ores *in loco*:

> It is impossible to know what a mine contains without resorting to chemical means; in a voyage there are no conditions for a large laboratory to conduct the tests, so it is enough for us to take wherever we travel the small laboratories employed in England, with the necessary tools for small-scale smelting.[81]

However, there was no consensus among the Portuguese authorities regarding the incentives to mineral extraction, at a time when Portugal's economic problems deepened with the gold mining crisis in Minas Gerais. Some administrators considered mining harmful and one of the causes of the empire's stagnation. On the other hand, other scientists who studied mining techniques and were connected to the University of Coimbra and the Royal Academy of Sciences believed that "the decline, not only of gold production, but of the mining sector in general, is the result of technical and scientific problems." They therefore advocated for the "introduction of modern mineral extraction techniques."[82] The lack of technical resources and tools on the part of the Portuguese to perform the underground extraction of ores, for example, was highlighted several times in this book when discussing iron mining in Angola.

In any case, mineralogical studies were eventually consolidated as vital for the maintenance of Portugal and its overseas domains. In the late-eighteenth century, proposals and memoirs were written on the various regions of the empire. Opin-

---

Lúcia Rocha Barbalho da Cruz, "Ciência, identidade e quotidiano: alguns aspectos da presença de estudantes brasileiros na Universidade de Coimbra, na conjuntura final do período colonial," *Revista de História da Sociedade e da Cultura* 9 (2009): 205–23; Magnus Roberto de Mello Pereira, "Rede de mercês e carreira: o 'desterro d'Angola' de um militar luso-brasileiro (1782–1789)," *História. Questões e Debates* 45 (2007): 97–128; Magnus Roberto de Mello Pereira, "Um jovem naturalista num ninho de cobras: a trajetória de João da Silva Feijó em Cabo Verde, em finais do século XVIII," *História. Questões e Debates* 19, no. 36 (2002): 29–60; Magnus Roberto de Mello Pereira (org.), *João da Silva Feijó; Um homem de ciência no Antigo Regime português*, first ed. (Curitiba: Editora da UFPR, 2012), v. 1, 19, no. 36 (2003): 29–60.

80 Ermelinda Pataca, *Terra, Água e Ar nas viagens científicas portuguesas (1755–1808)*, 30.
81 Domingos Vandelli, *Viagens filosóficas ou dissertação sobre as importantes regras que o filósofo naturalista nas suas peregrinações deve principalmente observar* (Lisbon, 1779). Academia Real das Ciências de Lisboa, Manuscritos Vermelhos, 405.
82 Silvia F. de M. Figuerôa, Clarete Paranhos da Silva, and Ermelinda Moutinho Pataca, "Aspectos mineralógicos das 'Viagens Filosóficas' pelo território brasileiro na transição do século XVIII para o século XIX," 715.

ions were elaborated regarding the alum factories on São Miguel Island and lead extraction in the Pisco River region, activities in the iron factories of Figueiró resumed, etc.[83]

Ermelinda Pataca specifically researched the narratives produced by naturalists and travelers in Africa, providing an opportunity to know not only the universe of colonial writings, but also the methodological strategies to analyze them. The author divides the voyages between the administrations of the Ministries of the Navy and Overseas Affairs, Martinho de Melo and Castro (1777–1795) and D. Rodrigo de Sousa Coutinho (1796–1802), focusing more on the first period given the amount of information available. She developed a general picture by analyzing voyages, instructions, correspondence, routes, maps, drawings, memoirs, and diaries. She thus elaborated a detailed description of "the geographical areas explored, the natural products researched, the technical/scientific composition, the correspondence during the voyages, the scientific command carried out by naturalists such as Júlio Mattiazzi, Domingos Vandelli, Félix de A. Brotero, and Frei Veloso."[84]

There were many scholars who held administrative positions and who were also naturalists. Many authors point to this relationship between state policy and the enlightened mentality.[85] Such is the case of one of Vandelli's students, Manuel Galvão da Silva, who was appointed Secretary of the Government of the General Captaincy of Mozambique on November 23, 1782.[86] In one of the letters sent to Martinho de Melo e Castro, in August 1785, Manuel Galvão briefly discusses the iron mines he discovered: "The iron mine found in the Mutipa Mountains has veins of the same stones, of which I am sending a sample."[87]

Joaquim José da Silva had a similar trajectory to that of Manuel Galvão; he was appointed Secretary of Angola in December 1782. The naturalist went on five expeditions between Angola and Benguela: Luanda-Cabinda-Luanda (1783–1784); Luanda-Massangano–Luanda (1784); Luanda-Benguela-Cabo Negro-Benguela (1785–

---

[83] Fernando A. Novais, *Portugal e Brasil na Crise do Antigo Sistema Colonial (1777–1808)*, 283.
[84] Ermelinda Pataca, *Terra, Água e Ar nas viagens científicas portuguesas (1755–1808)*, vii.
[85] Idem, 79. See also: Maria Odila da Silva Dias, "Aspectos da Ilustração no Brasil," *Revista do Instituto Histórico e Geográfico Brasileiro* 278 (1968): 105–170; Maria de Fátima Gouvêa, "Poder político e administração na formação do complexo atlântico português (1645–1808)," in Maria Fernando Bicalho, João Fragoso, and Maria de Fátima Gouvêa (orgs.), *O Antigo Regime nos trópicos: A dinâmica Imperial Portuguesa (séculos XVI–XVIII)* (Rio de Janeiro: Civilização Brasileira, 2001): 285–315.
[86] William Joel Simon, *Scientific expeditions in the Portuguese overseas territories (1783–1808)*, 60.
[87] Carta de Manoel Galvão Silva para Martino de Melo e Castro. Moçambique, August 21, 1785. AHU, Moçambique, Caixa 22. *Apud* William Joel Simon, *Scientific Expeditions in the Portuguese Overseas Territories (1783–1808)*, 153.

1787); Benguela-Luanda (1787), and Luanda-Fortress of Ambaca–Luanda (1794–1796).

On his first voyage to Cabinda, he found, among other discoveries, "some stones (...) that indicated the existence of a good iron mine."[88] In addition, he found a mountain range rich in minerals. He also collected oil, prepared some plants, and participated in lime manufacturing.[89]

When he arrived in Massangano together with the draftsman José Antonio, both fell ill. Their objective was to fish a "woman fish" and a "sea horse" (hippopotamus) in the lakes near the fortress in the same jurisdiction. The draftsman died and the naturalist was forced to anticipate his return to Luanda because of the fevers. Commenting the same expedition, Silva said that he was sent there as a "spy" with the pretext of "Natural History" to observe "the army that was then in Kisama." He also added, "As before, I was sent to Cabinda to observe what was happening there for certain purposes, quite different from Royal service."[90] The passages are revealing in terms of the conjunction between philosophical voyages and the colonial administration's political and military objectives of expansion and dominion.

From Benguela, Joaquim da Silva sent a copper sample to the Ajuda Botanical Garden, which was highly praised after being analyzed by the museum's director, Julio Mattiazzi. It was in the south of this region that the naturalist remained the longest (two years and two months). Most of the time he traveled to the *sertões* in

---

[88] Carta de Joaquim José da Silva para Martinho de Melo Castro. Luanda, March 17, 1784. AHU, Angola, Caixa 39. *Apud* William Joel Simon, *Scientific Expeditions in the Portuguese Overseas Territories (1783–1808)*, 158.

[89] Joaquim José da Silva was born in Rio de Janeiro around 1755. He studied Mathematics and Medicine at the University of Coimbra and afterwards he worked at the Botanical Garden and the Museum of Ajuda in Lisbon, as Vandelli's assistant. He went on philosophical voyages to the kingdom, in Serra da Estrela and Serra do Gerês, before traveling to Angola in the early 1780s. Ermelinda Pataca, *Terra, Água e Ar nas viagens científicas portuguesas (1755–1808)*, 382–389. See also: William Joel Simon, *Scientific Expeditions in the Portuguese Overseas Territories (1783–1808)*; Maria Emília Madeira Santos, *Viagens de exploração terrestre dos portugueses em África*, second edition (Lisbon: Centro de Estudos de História e Cartografia Antiga, 1988); Henrique Coutinho Gouveia, "Aspectos das relações entre Portugal e Angola no Domínio Museológico – As viagens de exploração científica setecentistas," in *III Encontro de Museus de países e comunidades de língua portuguesa* (Bissau, 1991), 77–118; Marcio Mota Pereira, "As luzes se ascendem em África: viagens filosóficas de um naturalista luso-brasileiro em Angola (1783–1808)," *E-hum* 8, no. 2 (2015): 103, notes 13 and 14.

[90] Carta de Joaquim José da Silva para Julio Mattiazzi, n.p. *Apud* Marcio Mota Pereira, "As luzes se ascendem em África: viagens filosóficas de um naturalista luso-brasileiro em Angola (1783–1808)," 103, notes 13 and 14.

the company of military retinues. Joaquim da Silva often complained of the limited personnel available to him—his draftsman had died and there were not enough porters to carry the boxes with his collections—and the lack of instruments to prepare and transport animals. The expedition's records are in a diary known as "Extrato da viagem, que fez ao sertão da Benguela no ano de 1785 por ordem do Governador e Capitão General do Reino de Angola."[91]

In Luanda, he divided his time between his activities as Secretary of State of Angola and the collection and envoy of natural products to Lisbon. The envoys demonstrate his incursions into the regions near the city, such as the visit to the vicinity of the Ndande River. In one of the reports sent to Lisbon, there is:

> One herbarium with 37 skeletons
> One collection of eleven prints
> One small bottle of Oil from the Ndande [River]
> One piece of *Tales Rubrica* from the Ndande [River]
> Three pieces of flint (Silex Marmoreis) from Cabinda
> Two of the same from the Ndande [River]
> One piece of rock from the Ndande [River] from which lime is made for the royal works
> Two pieces of rough marble from Angola
> One small wooden box with insects
> Two pieces of sulfur from Benguela
> One piece of copper ore from Benguela (from the *sertão*)
> One tip of a mountain goat from Benguela
> Two tips from another animal not yet observed by me
> Eight teeth from a sea horse from the Kwanza [River]
> Seven ribs of the so-called Woman Fish, which is the Triceclus Manatus
> Two swordfish tips
> Four salt crystals from the Kisama [River].
> List of loose samples not included in the aforementioned box.
>
> One tin cylinder with fish from the open sea and from this Coast
> Two hides of wild ox.[92]

The list is indicative of the potential for exploiting the products from the three kingdoms of nature through the scientific method of observation and experimentation. Such information could precede the elaboration of economic policies for ag-

---

91 "Extrato da viagem, que fez ao sertão da Benguela no ano de 1785 por ordem do governador e capitão general do Reino de Angola o Bacharel Joaquim José da Silva, enviado a aquele Reino como naturalista, e depois secretário do governo. De Luanda para Benguela," *O Patriota* 1 (1813): 86–100.
92 "Relação das peças que vão na caixa pertencente a História Natural, remetida pelo naturalista de Angola," Joaquim José da Silva. São Paulo de Assunção de Luanda, March 20, 1784. AHU_CU_001, Cx. 68, D. 47.

riculture, mining, and commerce. As for observation, the naturalists not only described plants, animals, and minerals; they were interested in recording the customs and practices of local societies. The text "Breves instruções aos correspondentes da Academia das Ciências de Lisboa sobre as remessas dos produtos e notícias pertencentes à História da Natureza, para formar um Museu Nacional" (Brief Instructions to the Correspondents of the Academy of Sciences of Lisbon on the Shipments of Products and News Relative to the Natural History to Create a National Museum),[93] in addition to being a guide on the practice of collecting and shipping artifacts, was also a manual on how to observe and record lifestyles, customary practices, and "peoples' morals."

In Benguela, Joaquim da Silva described the construction of *bimbas* and rafts, as well as the manufacture of palm oil by Africans near the fortress of Novo Redondo. In addition to documenting the techniques, he portrayed the dwellings, clothing, ornaments, and political structure of the societies he found. He also noted the characteristics of the workers: "the natives are well built and, as in other parts, those who are employed in royal works earn a wage, and all of them are vassals of the two closest and most important *sobas* in that territory."[94]

The labor relations observed by the naturalist are similar to those found at the Ilamba iron factory. In both, the Africans who worked in "royal works" were vassals of the *sobas* whose villages were close to the work site. "As in other parts" under the Portuguese administration, the workers received a "wage." We therefore have an example of another place where the labor of the subjects of the local *sobas* was exploited.

The Secretary of Angola kept in touch with another of Vandelli's disciples, José Álvares Maciel, then exiled to Angola for having participated in the Inconfidência Mineira. On the voyage to Ambaca in search of gold mines, Silva was accompanied by Maciel. They found no evidence of the presence of precious metals there, only "poor quality emery." After this expedition, the secretary focused on his administrative career, relegating his role as a naturalist to a secondary position.[95]

---

[93] "Breves instruções aos correspondentes da Academia das Ciências de Lisboa sobre as remessas dos produtos e notícias pertencentes a História da Natureza, para formar um Museu Nacional. Dedicado à sua alteza real o sereníssimo príncipe do Brasil. Pelo doutor José Antonio de Sá. Opositor as cadeiras de leis da Universidade de Coimbra e correspondente da Academia das Ciências de Lisboa" (Lisbon: Oficina de Francisco Borges de Sousa, 1783). *Apud* Ermelinda Pataca, *Terra, Água e Ar nas viagens científicas portuguesas (1755–1808)*, 92.
[94] "Extrato da viagem, que fez ao sertão da Benguela no ano de 1785 por ordem do governador e capitão general do Reino de Angola," 100.
[95] Marcio Mota Pereira, "As luzes se acendem em África: viagens filosóficas de um naturalista luso-brasileiro em Angola (1783–1808)," 109.

In 1784, José Maciel had traveled to research minerals in Serra da Estrela in northern Portugal, and had conducted a series of mineralogical studies in Minas Gerais.[96] A native of Vila Rica and a descendant of a family of rich plantation owners, Maciel graduated in Natural Philosophy from the University of Coimbra in 1785 and spent some time in England, where he perfected his knowledge of chemistry and "studied the theory and practice of various branches of the manufacturing industry." He returned to Rio de Janeiro in 1788, where he met with Joaquim José da Silva Xavier before returning to Vila Rica.[97]

In the Inconfidência Mineira proceedings, Maciel said that he traveled to the *sertão* of Minas Gerais to "examine the productions of nature he found." It was on the outskirts of Vila Rica that he conducted mineralogical analyses and discovered "copper vitriol on the foothills of the Saramenha [hill] next to the river that flows there, in the district of the parish of Antonio Dias."[98] He also found "a micaceous clay similar to mica and green in color." On the Lages hill, there was an abundance of "arsenic, gold, pepper, and iron." His expeditions in the captaincy of Minas Gerais were interrupted due to the 1789 conspiracy, when he was imprisoned for his involvement in the movement. Maciel managed to escape the death penalty in exchange for being deported to the fortress of Massangano in 1792.

In the Kingdom of Angola, José Álvares Maciel survived as a merchant, selling "textiles that the traders elaborated for him." The mineralogist once again put his knowledge as a naturalist in practice and was appointed director of the Nova Oeiras iron factory thanks to the insistence of then Minister of State of the Navy and Overseas Affairs, Rodrigo de Sousa Coutinho, to further promote iron manufacturing in that kingdom.

Having inherited many memories from his father, Rodrigo Coutinho, one of the most important references of Enlightened Reformism in Portugal, presented stud-

---

96 "Memória analítica sobre a memória escrita e enviada do degredo de Angola pelo inconfidente Dr. José Álvares Maciel sobre a fábrica de ferro de Nova Oeiras," in Marcos Carneiro de Mendonça, *O Intendente Câmara* (São Paulo: Companhia Editora Nacional, 1958).

97 Ermelinda Pataca, *Terra, Água e Ar nas viagens científicas portuguesas (1755–1808)*, 330–332. See also: Francisco Antonio Lopes, *Alvares Maciel no degredo de Angola* (Rio de Janeiro: Ministério de Educação e Cultura, 1958); Robson Jorge de Araújo, "José Alvares Maciel: o químico inconfidente," available at www.fafich.ufmg.br/~scientia/art_araujo.htm, accessed on April 5, 2013. It is interesting to note that one of the interests of the *inconfidentes* was precisely the promotion of iron ore and that Maciel had all the necessary requirements to develop it—a knowledge that would be used to execute the opposite project: the development of iron factories under the administration of the metropolis.

98 Ofício de Miguel Antonio de Melo, governador de Angola, para Rodrigo de Sousa Coutinho, secretário de Estado da Marinha e do Ultramar. São Paulo de Luanda, September 19, 1799. *Apud* Francisco Antonio Lopes, *Alvares Maciel no degredo de Angola*, 41–42.

ies and opinions favorable to mining explorations several times.[99] His idea was to train a cadre of technicians capable of developing mining activities, especially iron extraction, an industry that would contribute to the weapons industry and other manufacturing branches of Portugal. According to Nívia Cirne Santos, the most original feature of Rodrigo de Sousa Coutinho's presence among the administrators at the time was "his conception of balance of power, based on the assumption that the existence of the Portuguese empire was directly related to the maintenance of colonial territories."[100] Regarding the Kingdom of Angola, he returned to the idea of transforming that possession into more than a trading post or a reservoir of enslaved labor for Portuguese America, encouraging the development of other economic activities and the settlement of the *sertões*, as Francisco de Sousa Coutinho had desired. The then governor of Angola, Miguel Antonio de Melo (1797–1802), provided the necessary support for Rodrigo Coutinho to implement plans in line with the Enlightenment, revitalizing his father's projects.

One of those plans was to reconstruct the iron factory of Nova Oeiras. In the time between the complete abandonment of the factory by Antonio de Lencastre (1772–1779) and its resumption by Miguel de Melo, Angola was governed by José Gonçalo da Câmara (1779–1782), governing councils after his death (1782–1784), José de Almeida e Vasconcelos de Soveral (1784–1790), and Manuel de Almeida e Vasconcelos (1790–1797). José Gonçalo da Câmara received instructions from the then Secretary of State of the Navy and Overseas Affairs, Martinho de Melo e Castro, to forget the iron mines, for resuming their operation would be "reckless," especially "in such an unsanitary place, where rarely someone who went there escaped alive."[101]

Apparently, the factory was left abandoned during those years, since in 1796 Manuel de Almeida and Vasconcelos ordered the regent of the town of Massangano to go to Nova Oeiras from time to time to make sure that the factory was maintained and the grass was cut, "in order to prevent a fire, also digging a ditch to

---

99 Rodrigo de Sousa Coutinho wrote "Discurso sobre a verdadeira influência das minas e dos metais preciosos na indústria das nações que as possuem e especialmente da portuguesa" in 1789, and "Memória sobre o melhoramento dos domínios de Sua Majestade na América" in 1797. In Andrée Mansuy-Diniz Silva (dir.), *D. Rodrigo de Sousa Coutinho. Textos políticos, econômicos e financeiros (1783–1811)* (Lisbon: Banco de Portugal, 1993), v. I and II.

100 Nívia Pombo Cirne dos Santos, *O Palácio de Queluz e o mundo ultramarino: circuitos Ilustrados. (Portugal, Brasil e Angola, 1796–1803)*, dissertation (PhD) (Instituto de Ciências Humanas e Filosofia, Universidade Federal Fluminense, 2013), 13.

101 Carta de Martinho de Melo e Castro, secretário de Estado da Marinha e Ultramar, para José Gonçalo da Câmara, governador de Angola. Palácio de Nossa Senhora da Ajuda, June 22, 1779. AHU_CU_001, Cx. 62, D. 58.

protect the walls." In the same letter, the governor commented that Dr. Maciel could "advance with the factories, but since he did not wish to do so, he should comply with his deportation sentence, an obligation imposed on him."[102] The comment reveals a possible conflict, indicating the naturalist's possible resistance to collaborate with the metropolis's decisions. This behavior may be related to his stance in the 1789 conspiracy, when he advocated for political emancipation and the development of industries in the colony.

Perhaps his hard life as an exile at the Massangano fortress and the meager resources obtained from trading in the *sertões* mitigated the doctor's resistance, because one year later, in 1797, he decided to advise the Angolan government on research on the Ilamba iron ore. Rodrigo de Sousa Coutinho requested information from the governor of Angola on the situation of Nova Oeiras. José Álvares Maciel again emerged as the ideal person for the job, much better versed in mineralogical and chemical studies than any other person who had ever been in Ilamba. His visit to the factory resulted in a brief report. In it, the Brazilian naturalist mentioned the terrible condition of the buildings and the tools and said that the furnace was built following the "Nuremberg design." The result of his examination of the mines could not have been better: the "amount of mineral is immense" and "in my latest test I obtained 68 per quintal, even though I used black flux, which is not the best for iron testing."[103] The ease of transportation, the proximity of rivers and forests, all the circumstances investigated by Francisco de Sousa Coutinho and his team of military engineers, *sertanejos*, and master smelters were approved by the naturalist, as was the skill of the smiths of Ilamba, sustained by the "great and continuous use" they made of the mines.

In tune with the enlightened ideas of the former governor, the naturalist suggested that the apprentices be chosen among those whose "trade was to smelt the iron from the same place" where they sold their "iron bars weighing two pounds, for a knife that costs us thirty réis." He pondered "that it would be most useful to teach the natives to employ themselves in the mine for their own benefit"! In these lines, the naturalist reiterates Sous Coutinho's idea of turning Nova Oeiras into a

---

102 Carta de Manuel de Almeida e Vasconcelos, governador de Angola, para Miguel Jesus e Abreu, regente da Vila de Massangano. São Paulo de Assunção de Luanda, August 20, 1796. AHA, Códice 89, A-19 – 3.
103 "(...) The hill's entire surface is covered with it [iron], the configuration is pebbly, the outer color is black and lustrous, and others are rusty brown, inside a bluish brown, its *fisso* (?) is composed of small grains similar to those presented by steel in its fracture." Memória de José Álvares Maciel sobre a fábrica de ferro de Nova Oeiras. São Paulo de Assunção de Luanda, November 1797. BNP, C 8553, F6362.

large workshop where Ambundu smelters, already initiated in working with iron, would learn techniques to increase their production.

In spite of the high cost of rebuilding the weir, obtaining new wood, and having tools and masters sent from Europe, since there was no skilled labor available locally to coordinate the construction of a building of such dimensions, Maciel maintained that "the wealth of the mine and all other advantages" would result in "greater profits than those obtained in all other known mines." The essential element was changing the factory's location, because the "evil climate" of Nova Oeiras was an "insurmountable obstacle." Maciel himself, on a previous trip to the region, fell ill as soon as he arrived, and the fevers haunted him for months.

Governor Miguel Antonio de Melo only disagreed with a key point of the naturalist's discourse. The administrator, perhaps aware of the difficulties entailed in rebuilding Nova Oeiras, said that, considering the current state of the factory, it was not worthwhile burdening the Royal Treasury with new expenses. It would be better to begin iron mining at a new site, Calumbo, quite close to Luanda, free of the "evil climate" of Ilamba and with the same ease of access to firewood and the Kwanza River. In Nova Oeiras, the workers would only mine the "ore stone." The governor said that it was time to take steps to establish a new business: to trade Ambundu iron, just like they traded ivory and wax. To follow up on the idea, new samples, "a few iron bars smelted by the Negroes, some of their musical instruments, household implements, and weapons" were sent to Lisbon.[104]

Ten months later, D. Rodrigo replied that the "iron bars" provided "the best possible iron, docile and easy to work with either cold or hot."[105] Immediately, the secretary obtained the queen's approval to send the necessary tools and crucibles to Angola. The idea of obtaining iron from Central Africans pleased the Court, since the metal could be exported to Brazil, where it was needed and was imported from abroad. To "encourage" the new trade, His Majesty decreed a tax exemption for the shipment of iron from Angola to Brazil. He also authorized Sousa Coutinho to appoint José Álvares Maciel as director of the new factory.[106] To prepare as much as possible in advance, Maciel was in charge of teaching the Ambundus

---

104 Carta de Miguel Antonio de Melo, governador de Angola, para Rodrigo de Sousa Coutinho, secretário de Estado da Marinha e do Ultramar. São Paulo de Luanda, December 19, 1797. *Arquivos de Angola* IV, no. 52–54 (1939): 259–262.
105 Carta de Rodrigo de Sousa Coutinho, secretário de Estado da Marinha e do Ultramar, para Miguel Antonio de Melo, governador de Angola. Palácio de Queluz, October 7, 1798. *Arquivos de Angola* IV, no. 52–54 (1939): 263.
106 Carta de Rodrigo de Sousa Coutinho, secretário de Estado da Marinha e do Ultramar, para Miguel Antonio de Melo, governador de Angola. Palácio de Queluz, October 11, 1798. *Arquivos de Angola* IV, no. 52–54 (1939): 263 and 264.

how to "work the mine on a large scale." Calumbo would become a "school for Negroes" who later could even carry out Francisco de Sousa Coutinho's plans for Nova Oeiras: "transporting that new industry to the establishment in Nova Oeiras, where they live and we cannot live."[107]

D. João VI's decision when he assumed the regency in 1799 was no different. In addition to obtaining Central African iron, he ordered the reestablishment of the iron factory, giving it a "great extension."[108] The sovereigns were once again convinced of the enterprise's potential benefits for the colonial Empire.

Two years after writing his first impressions of the iron mines in the Kingdom of Angola, José Maciel wrote a new document in which he changed his initial opinion about establishing a factory in Calumbo. With better information about the terrain, the means of transportation from the mine down rivers, and the way of life of Ilamba blacksmiths, the naturalist reached the conclusion that a place called Trombeta (where the Novo Belém factory was located) would be the most appropriate. A mission to Kasanje at the governor's service allowed him to get to know the region better, leading him to choose a new place for iron extraction: "four days away from this city, I discovered that the same mountain range in Ilamba where the iron is mined for Nova Oeiras goes all the way to a place called 'Trombeta' in the Golungo jurisdiction, and that there is plenty of wood there, high waters, air as pure and healthy as that of Luanda, at a short distance from the Nzenza River." The new location had an important attraction, as it was where most of the "black blacksmiths" lived exclusively from their trade, providing "all instruments for agriculture, prisons, and some nails used in the *sertão*." The idea of establishing a new enterprise near the blacksmiths' homes had the purpose of preventing the "repugnance" they felt for work when they had to leave their homes and families.[109]

However, this was not the only change proposed by Maciel, who also gave up on building a blast furnace. That was the first point on which he diverged from Francisco de Sousa Coutinho's proposals. Living in the *sertão*, which no governor would ever do, the naturalist realized that working with a blast furnace would deprive Ilamba blacksmiths "of their freedom, which disgusts them and leads them to flee." In addition, as it was already known, there was a lack of crucible stones,

---

[107] Carta de Rodrigo de Sousa Coutinho, secretário de Estado da Marinha e do Ultramar, para o marquês Ponte de Lima, mordomo-mor. Palácio de Queluz, October 28, 1798. ANTT, Projeto reencontro, MF0027.

[108] Carta de Rodrigo de Sousa Coutinho, secretário de Estado da Marinha e do Ultramar, para Miguel Antonio de Melo, governador de Angola. Palácio de Queluz, September 22, 1799. *Arquivos de Angola* IV, no. 52–54 (1939): 265–269.

[109] Carta de José Álvares Maciel para Miguel Antonio de Melo, governador de Angola. São Paulo de Assunção de Luanda, November 1, 1799. AHU_CU_001, Cx. 93 A, D. 1.

wooden bellows not made in Angola, and wheels to propel the machine. Once again, the colonial administration's dependence on the knowledge of Ambundu blacksmiths is evident. The only way to gain access to that knowledge was with their collaboration; violence only resulted in flight: "to attract the Negroes of their own free will and for their own profit, against which the slightest shadow of force or violence must be avoided to keep them from abandoning their homes and fleeing, as they commonly do."[110] The experience of the workers in the factory in the 1760s had already proved this—Maciel had certainly heard about it, as he frequently mentioned data from the factory's history.

The naturalist proposed a different solution. With sand from Massangano, he would build small furnaces suitable for the leather bellows used by the Ambundus. However, he would do so in such a way that production could be increased by making some changes in the way those tools were made. He would also teach them "the use of hammers" so they could pound a larger portion of iron "without getting burned with the small mallets they use." Maciel's method promised to produce up to six times as much iron in the same time. The costs would be negligible, and once they were accustomed to a new work rhythm, it would be easier to convince them to work in a large factory.

In order to organize this team of blacksmiths, Maciel proposed creating a "Village of black blacksmiths." The naturalist's reference to the village was derived from what he observed in Portuguese America: "in Brazil, each indigenous village has a director, thus avoiding the dependence on the *capitão-mor.*" He therefore proposed that the village, or the *quilombo*, as was expressed in the documents, should have its own regiment and the director should be the factory inspector.

In Portuguese America, since the *Diretório dos índios* implemented in the second half of the eighteenth century, indigenous settlements had been raised to the status of towns or villages administrated by a director. As mentioned in Chapter 3, the *Diretório* was key to take control of indigenous labor from the hands of the missionaries, replacing the clergy with officials at the service of the Crown. Álvares Maciel seemed to want to do likewise in this situation: to eliminate the Crown's dependence on the *sobas* and the *capitães-mores* to gain access to the labor force. The workers would now be controlled directly by the colonial administration, without intermediaries.

This passage illustrates possible transformations that the establishment of the Nova Oeiras factory may have caused in the region. This is so because at no time does Maciel cite *sobas, ilamba, imbari,* or any other African authorities to whom the blacksmiths might be subjected. The mediator who could cause some conflict

---

110 Idem.

was the *capitão-mor*. It is quite likely that, even after the factory closed, the blacksmiths who gathered there during the years of its operation continued to work independently in the vicinity. Those who were residents of neighboring *sobados* did not return to their homes, as was common after the escapes or "desertions" recorded in the documents.

As this source allows us to see, some of the problems faced by the "philosopher administrator" in previous years were still present during Maciel's time. So much so that the naturalist requested that the *capitães-mores* be kept off the administration of the "village," that they refrain from forcing blacksmiths to work in other services, and that they keep from taking supplies and other items from them, complaints that were common when Nova Oeiras was being built. Apparently, Sousa Coutinho's measures to reduce the power and autonomy of the *capitães-mores* in the *sertão* did not have the expected results over time.

José Álvares Maciel also requested that one of the rules of the "villages" be a tithe exemption for blacksmiths who produced a certain amount of iron. The naturalist noted that this was a "privilege they appreciated over all things and that it had been granted earlier to the Oeiras Factory."[111] Preserving the memory of their conquests was very important to the Ambundus, for it was a way to negotiate their condition as vassals with the sovereign and the representatives of the Portuguese Crown. The blacksmiths of Ilamba did not forget the tithe exemption that their ancestors had conquered and continued to demand it.

One example of the above is that, when organizing Maciel's expedition to Trombeta, the governor wrote to the *capitão-mor* of Massangano with all the recommendations made by the naturalist in terms of avoiding mistreating the blacksmiths and taking by force whatever iron they did not want to hand over or sell. At no point did Miguel de Melo refer to African authorities; he only mentioned the independently hired "Negroes from Ilamba" who were supposed to help the naturalist in exchange for a weekly wage.[112]

The lack of references to the local Central African elite does not mean that there were no influential *sobas*. One evidence of this is the fact that, in Maciel's expeditions, the workers who served cutting wood or in the lime factory or the quarries were called "offspring" of the region's *sobas* (see Annex 4); only the blacksmiths do not appear with that "filiation." The Portuguese presence hardly changed in the little more than 20 years between the two events examined

---

111 Carta de José Álvares Maciel para Miguel Antonio de Melo, governador de Angola. São Paulo de Assunção de Luanda, November 1, 1799. AHU_CU_001, Cx. 93 A, D. 1.
112 Carta de Miguel Antonio de Melo, governador de Angola, para Pedro Muzzi de Barros, tenente do regimento de infantaria e regente do Golungo. São Paulo de Assunção de Luanda, November 4, 1799. *Arquivos de Angola* v. IV, no. 52–54 (1939): 274–276.

here. In fact, until at least 1880, colonial agents depended heavily on the alliances they established with local leaders during the centuries of occupation.

In sum, in 1800 and 1801, Maciel traveled through Ilamba, living in the region and conducting experiments in several smelting furnaces, making charcoal and tiles. He even built a "test house," another one for the masons and blacksmiths, and another one for himself. About 134 workers participated in these voyages, "offspring" of the region's 32 *sobas* and *ilamba*.[113] All were remunerated or were paid in goods common to the *sertão*, in *jeribita* (spirits) or *cré* (fine textiles). Maciel faced great difficulties controlling the workers, because while he was watching the quarry workers, those who were in charge of making charcoal had already gone back their villages or were sitting idly with no interest in their work. For that reason, he counted only 70 people actually employed in the daily chores of iron extraction.[114] Here we learn a bit more about the tactics employed by the Ambundus to escape the colonial imposition of new working conditions. While in theory it was easier to found a "Village of black blacksmiths," in practice, Maciel found it very difficult to deal with Ambundu workers and their leaders in his exploration voyages.

Unlike Governor Francisco de Sousa Coutinho, José Álvares Maciel gave up on the lime and stone building, the blast furnace, and the daily production of large amounts of iron. Finally, a royal official understood that the only successful way of obtaining iron from the Ambundus was to elaborate a proposal that took into account the labor process, the Ambundu way of producing iron, making only small changes. It was necessary to respect their tools, their techniques, their work rhythm, their relationship with their family and dependents. For the first time, a colonial agent analyzed the history of Nova Oeiras and discovered that the only thing that had been successful there was the "Casa de Fundição dos Pretos." After all, that was precisely the project he wanted to resume with the "Village of black blacksmiths." The difference was the working conditions: for the naturalist, it was obvious that the mistreatment had to end in order for the Ambundus to gradually get used to a new work rhythm, so that in the future they could be employed in a large factory, as Nova Oeiras was supposed to be. It must be emphasized that even with all these adjustments, the Ambundu workers resisted Maciel's plans. They resisted the new attempts to control their work process.

---

113 José Álvares Maciel, "Relação dos *sobas* e *ilamba* que dão presentemente filhos para este trabalho." Trombeta, March 2, 1800. BNP, C 8553, F6362.
114 Carta de José Álvares Maciel e Miguel Antonio de Melo, governador de Angola. Trombeta, March 2, 1800. *Arquivos de Angola* IV, no. 52–54 (1939): 283–290.

The naturalist identified several "tide mines," which were quickly exhausted, and others of greater longevity: those of Canzengo, Gariabaile, Valereo, Sambaquiba, and Quiabala. The mines around Nova Oeiras were very rich: "it is found on the surface of the earth and contains no sulfur or zinc, only some quartz mixed in, and very little of it."[115] Maciel discovered the flux employed, an agent that reduced the slag during smelting, in other words, that removed impurities from the metal. The substance was *castina*, or limestone, which is widely used in iron smelting. These experiments allowed Maciel to discover how to perfect the ore extraction methods in Ilamba. He also left a list with everything that would be necessary for the new iron factory, from specialized mechanical officers to farmers and miners (four enslaved workers who should be brought from Minas Gerais), tools, boats, books, laboratory supplies, to the factory's administrative and fiscal structure—treasurer, clerk, director, inspector, surgeon.[116]

Dr. Maciel's research of the mines in Ilamba and the techniques employed by the blacksmiths who lived there resulted in a considerable documentation that demonstrated the great advantages of developing iron extraction in Angola.[117] Nonetheless, despite his efforts and those of the governor of Angola and Rodrigo de Sousa Coutinho, the funding was denied. In a last attempt, Miguel Antonio de Melo suggested that the factory be handed over to private entrepreneurs. The Frenchman Francisco Agostinho Guilhebel became interested in the proposal.[118]

---

115 Carta de José Álvares Maciel e Miguel Antonio de Melo, governador de Angola. Trombeta, dois de março de 1800. *Arquivos de Angola* IV, no. 52–54 (1939): 283–290.

116 "Relação do que se necessita e neste reino falta absolutamente para se poder dar princípio à fundição de uma fábrica de ferro." José Álvares Maciel, São Paulo de Assunção de Luanda, April 2, 1801. *Arquivos de Angola* IV, no. 52–54 (1939): 339–345.

117 A new voyage was undertaken to ascertain Maciel's information. The major and assistant major, Antonio Salinas de Benavides, visited the Ilamba region soon afterwards and concluded that Cathari, also in Golungo, was a more appropriate place to establish a foundry: "this place, which is one league and a half further away from the Lukala River than Oeiras, is more salubrious, since it is farther from the Lembo lagoons, although it is also farther from the river through which exports will be carried." Carta de Antonio Salinas de Benavides para Miguel Antonio de Melo, governador de Angola. São Paulo de Assunção de Luanda, November 15, 1800. *Arquivos de Angola* IV, no. 52 (1939): 323.

118 "Francisco Agostinho Guilhebel, a Frenchman by origin and birth but married to a Portuguese woman and established in Tornegal, who had owned a Button Factory earlier and, in 1796, engaged in farming and trade, assisting the Old Treasury at the Casa de Parte do Izodoro, requested information on the site, the wealth of the mines, and the conditions present to establish a factory there. The said sergeant major answered those questions in detail, after performing the duty I entrusted to him, providing the said Francisco Agostinho Guilhebel a sample from the mine and taking charge of delivering the letter sent to you by the division chief Joaquim José Monteiro Torres when at the end of last year the Medusa ship sailed for this Kingdom with a stopover in Rio de

Nívia Cirne attributed the disagreements between D. Rodrigo and the president of the Royal Treasury, Ponte de Lima, representative of the nobility, directly affected by the Pombaline policies carried out by the minister, as one of the causes for the lack of response regarding the requested investments.[119]

As a result of his voyages and the exhausting work at the foundries, José Maciel fell seriously ill in 1800. In March 1804, when the required tools and stones finally arrived in Luanda, Maciel had already died and the new governor, Fernando Antonio de Noronha, had not yet found a replacement for the naturalist, since he was the only one capable of directing those plans in Angola.[120] During his government, he was unable to find a new director or to rebuild the factory.

After that, the next governor to deal with the issue was Antonio Saldanha de Gama, in a letter to the *capitão-mor* of Golungo. He discussed the importance of the discovery of iron in the area and the "desired factory" that never materialized. This governor continued to purchase iron from the Ambundus and to promise shipments to Lisbon.[121]

Once again, Nova Oeiras became the subject of proposals and memoirs on mining in the colonies. Nonetheless, no new project to revitalize the factory was put in practice. In spite of its promises of becoming one of the symbols of the alliance between science and government that characterized the pragmatism of the Enlightenment in Portugal, it became yet another example of its contradictions.

For the colonial administration, the Nova Oeiras Royal Factory failed and the blast furnace with a Nuremberg design, as identified by the Luso-Brazilian naturalist, remained "virgin," in his own words. The European project to import Biscayan, German, and French techniques did not come to fruition, and the building complex was abandoned, remaining as an emblem of Francisco de Sousa Coutinho's bold vision.

Janeiro." Carta de Miguel Antonio de Melo, governador de Angola, para Rodrigo de Sousa Coutinho, secretário de Estado da Marinha e do Ultramar. São Paulo de Luanda, January 31, 1801. AHU_CU_001, Cx. 98, D. 50.

119 Nívia Pombo Cirne dos Santos, *O Palácio de Queluz e o mundo ultramarino: circuitos Ilustrados. (Portugal, Brasil e Angola, 1796–1803)*, 340.

120 Carta de Fernando Antonio de Noronha, governador de Angola, para João Rodrigues de Sá e Mello de Menezes e Sottomayor, Visconde de Anadia, secretário de Estado da Marinha e do Ultramar. São Paulo de Assunção de Luanda, March 15, 1804. *Arquivos de Angola* IV, no. 52–54 (1939): 347 and 348.

121 Carta de Antonio Saldanha da Gama, governador de Angola, para o capitão do Golungo. São Paulo de Assunção de Luanda, September 14, 1807. AHA, Códice 322, D – 2–5. Carta de Antonio Saldanha da Gama, governador de Angola, para João Rodrigues de Sá e Mello de Menezes e Sottomayor, Visconde de Anadia, secretário de Estado da Marinha e do Ultramar. São Paulo de Assunção de Luanda, January 14, 1801. AHU_CU_001, Cx. 119, D. 1.

5.4 An Inside-Out Project

The comings and goings in the history of Nova Oeiras reveal the complex mosaic of interests that conditioned the fate of that enterprise. For some, it was merely a chimera with no practical foundation; for others, it represented a threat to their lifestyle and the privileges acquired until then. The main conflict involved those interested in the trade of enslaved people and those who did not want to lose the labor force employed to maintain the trade (porters, farmers, soldiers, and blacksmiths to make shackles). There were also those who, allied to the representatives of a new form of government, saw the potential of studying Natural History and intended to turn Angola into a large colony with diversified economic activities.

In a way, the assessment made by Antonio de Lencastre served as the basis for a narrative of the undertaking's failure, which predominated in the way its history has been told over time.

During the Estado Novo, a period of Portuguese history in which celebrating colonialism was key to maintaining its overseas possessions, Francisco de Sousa Coutinho was repeatedly described as the great Pombaline administrator. Among these authors are Gastão de Sousa Dias, Jofre Nogueira, and Ralph Delgado, who describe Sousa Coutinho as a governor "as firm as he was conscientious," and call him "the unforgettable reformer of Angola," among other epithets.[122]

In these studies, Nova Oeiras is seen as a prime example of the governor's enlightened efforts, which were misunderstood by his contemporaries, who were unable to keep up with the "bold vision" of an "irreproachable and enlightened man," "tirelessly devoted to the progress of the province." In this context, the impressive stone and lime buildings of the factory were examples of the "grandeur of national work in Africa."[123] According to these authors' interpretation, the factory failed, and the great culprit was Antonio de Lencastre, who abandoned the project.

---

[122] Jofre Amaral Nogueira, *Angola na época pombalina: o governo de Sousa* Coutinho (Lisbon: n.p., 1960); Ralph Delgado, "O Governo de Sousa Coutinho em Angola," *Stvdia*, no. 6 (1960): 19–56; no. 7 (1961): 49–86; no. 1 (1962); Gastão de Sousa Dias, D. Francisco Inocêncio de Sousa Coutinho, *Administração Pombalina em Angola* (Lisbon: Editorial Cosmos, Cadernos Coloniais), no. 27. See also: Maria Teresa Amado Neves, "D. Francisco Inocêncio de Sousa Coutinho: Aspecto moral da sua acção em Angola," in *I Congresso de História da Expansão Portuguesa no Mundo* (Lisbon: Sociedade Nacional de Tipografia, 1938), 120–150; A. Fuentes, "Dom Francisco Inocêncio de Souza Coutinho. Esboço de uma obra que se perdeu," *Boletim do Instituto de Angola*, no. 4 (1954): 35–40; Marques do Funchal, *O Conde Linhares* (Lisbon: n.p., 1950).

[123] Gastão de Sousa Dias and D. Francisco Inocêncio de Sousa Coutinho, *Administração Pombalina em Angola* (Lisbon: Editorial Cosmos, Cadernos Coloniais), no. 27; Jofre Amaral Nogueira, *Angola na época pombalina: o governo de Sousa* Coutinho (Lisbon: n.p., 1960), 165.

In *História de Angola*, published by the People's Movement for the Liberation of Angola (MPLA) in 1965, the factory was "a very advanced capitalist experience" that attracted many Africans "who, realizing that the factory was an experience against slavery," went there to live and work. This reading is based on the fact that there was "wage labor in a land where only enslaved labor was known. In short, it was like a well in the middle of the desert."[124] The text's political aspirations are evident, creating an anachronistic opposition for the Modern Age between colonialism and slavery versus independence and freedom. The presumed freedom that emerged with liberalism and its association with capitalist, free, and remunerated labor are senseless concepts in the universe where Nova Oeiras was created, since they did not exist in that historical context.

Moreover, or for that very reason, by advocating that the Ambundus be remunerated in the factory, Sousa Coutinho in no way intended to put an end to the trade of enslaved people or slavery in general. On the contrary, as we have repeatedly emphasized throughout the book, when recruiting workers, Sousa Coutinho determined that sufficient blacksmiths should be available to manufacture shackles for the trade of enslaved people. Well-paid labor without violence was a new way to control the workers because the governor depended on them.

We may perhaps consider it an "advanced capitalist experience," if we insist on the anachronism, because a form of organization of labor based on discipline, surveillance, order, and hierarchy was created there, for the purpose of increasing the colonial enterprise's productivity through the exploitation of workers.

What is surprising is that, even this book, first published in Algiers, which aimed at arming the revolutionaries against a colonizing reading of the History of Angola, perceived the factory only from the point of view of the colonial administration and, from that standpoint, only noted its failure.

This reading persists in other texts, to the point of suggesting, in 1984, that Sousa Coutinho was a "precursor of the abolition of slavery" thanks to the labor regulations he inaugurated. According to Mimoso Barreto, the governor undertook "a plan aimed squarely at rehabilitating the colored man" and in favor of the peaceful coexistence "among black people and between them and white people." The history we have narrated here is diametrically opposed to those ideas; the factory was an exploitation strategy that inaugurated new ways of exercising colonial domination. Violence is the defining characteristic of the workers' condition there. Barreto's short article had a completely different objective than the book published

---

[124] *História de Angola*. Centro de Estudos Angolanos. 2nd ed. (Porto: Edições Afrontamento, 1975). Published initially in Algiers in July 1965 by the Centro de Estudos Angolanos, Grupo de Trabalho História e Etnologia, 107–109.

by the MPLA, since the author clearly defended colonialism.[125] Nonetheless, the conclusion is the same: Lencastre turned Sousa Coutinho's proposals "inside out," imposing failure on Nova Oeiras.

David Birmingham offered a critical view of colonialism, and his studies aimed to combat the idea that Portuguese colonization was peaceful and devoid of conflicts; for that reason, he focused on the history of the trade of enslaved people and the wars to conquer Ndongo. When citing iron smelting, Birmingham included the enterprise among the other manufactures promoted at the time. "All of these efforts led nowhere," concluded the historian. He observed that the factory's impacts on Mbundu society were an increase in the labor force available to the Portuguese and a more effective collection of tithes.[126] We have already dealt with these issues above. Although from a completely different perspective, the thesis of failure also persists in this historian's approach.

In 1972, an event marked the two hundredth anniversary of Nova Oeiras's existence. On the occasion of the II Centennial of the Nova Oeiras Iron Factory, Antonio da Silva Rego wrote a small text celebrating the conservation of the factory's ruins, which, "as eloquent as those of a church, a fortress, or a Misericórdia," proclaimed "loud and clear the uniqueness of the Portuguese presence in Africa." Even celebrating the stone and lime building as a landmark of colonial occupation, the author admits that it had been "swallowed up by time," and lists the same aforementioned reasons for its failure.[127]

The bibliography on Sousa Coutinho's government inevitably devotes part of its analyses to Nova Oeiras, since it is the project that, after a certain moment, occupies most of the documentation. I highlight here Ana Madalena Trigo e Sousa's 1996 thesis, which aims to reinterpret this period in the history of the Kingdom of Angola, precisely because she believes that, until then, there was no literature on the contradictions between the enlightened discourse and the effective practice of Sousa Coutinho's government. This work breaks with the colonial perspective. The author invites us to reflect on the "real dimension and scope of Sousa Coutinho,"

---

125 J. Mimoso Barreto, "Sousa Coutinho, percursor da abolição da escravatura," in *Boletim da Sociedade de Geografia de Lisboa*, Série 102, no. 1–6 (1984): 69–77. "Before the stain of slavery we must not harbor a guilt complex, for the system already existed in the world before we adopted it, and continued to exist elsewhere after we abolished it. Only a part of this guilt belongs to us, the least painful part in fact, which does not overshadow the many-sided progress brought to humanity by the Discoveries." Idem, 76.

126 David Birmingham, *Trade and Conflict in Angola. The Mbundu and their Neighbours under the Influence of the Portuguese 1483–1790* (Oxford: Clarendon Press, 1966), 157 and 158.

127 António da Silva Rego, "A Academia Portuguesa da História e o II Centenário da Fábrica do Ferro de Nova Oeiras, Angola," in *Colectânea de Estudos em Honra do Prof. Doutor Damião Peres* (Lisbon: Academia Portuguesa da História, 1974), 387–398.

refraining from viewing his government "as a glorious time of the Imperial past in Africa." In fact, Trigo e Sousa's text, although more descriptive than interpretative, points to the contradictions of this enlightened man's ideas in his attempt to put them in practice in Angola. In the same vein as this study, Monica Tovo Machado Soares sought to analyze "aspects of the colonialist ideology" of previous studies, emphasizing "native resistance in the period." In both theses, there are many observations on the importance of African labor in the context of the iron factory, but the analysis tends to reiterate the narrative of failure. The authors attribute such failure to the lack of materials, skilled European technicians, and the failure to mobilize African labor.[128]

Catarina Madeira Santos wrote a dense analysis of the period in question. As for the factory, analyzed by her as a case study, the author also revisits its brief history and affirms the relevance of blacksmiths and smelters as traditional trades, without which Nova Oeiras could not subsist. According to Santos, the factory is "a 'rough' contrast between a scientific and a ritual and political reading" of the impact of the Enlightenment in Angola. Since her perspective is the cultural history of the encounter between "technique and magic, Enlightenment scientism and traditional African knowledge," she ends up reiterating the version of the "failure of this first industrialization in Angola."[129] The author explains that the failure is directly related to the successive deaths of the master smelters.

As much as the most recent historiography reiterates the importance of the blacksmiths and smelters of Ilamba, their participation in the factory is related to a trade that, being traditional, belongs to different economic patterns, and is therefore always seen as external to the factory. For example, these studies do not examine the systematic, organized, rhythmic, and concrete dimension of the "Casa de Fundição dos Pretos" or the "Village of black blacksmiths." Perhaps this is why they take up the narrative of failure, albeit from different perspectives.

Recently, in an Angolan publication about the city of Dondo, failure, abandonment, and "desertion" once again set the tone of the narrative. Something important is highlighted in this book, but it gets lost in the development of the argument:

---

[128] Ana Madalena Trigo de Sousa, *D. Francisco de Sousa Coutinho em Angola: Reinterpretação de um Governo 1764–1772*, thesis (Master's in History) (Funchal/ Lisbon: Universidade de Nova Lisboa, 1996). See also: Ana Madalena Trigo de Sousa, "Uma tentativa de fomento industrial na Angola setecentista: a 'Fábrica do Ferro' de Nova Oeiras (1766–1772)," *Africana Studia*, no. 10 (2007): 291–308. Mônica Tovo Soares Machado, *Angola No Período Pombalino: O Governo De Dom Francisco Inocêncio De Sousa Coutinho – 1764–1772*, thesis (Master's) (Faculdade de Filosofia, Letras e Ciências Humanas da Universidade de São Paulo, 1998).

[129] Catarina Madeira Santos, *Um governo "polido" para Angola*, 547.

> The factory of Nova Oeiras remains silent, waiting for the day when the effort of the miners from Massangano and Ilamba, the Brazilians, the Biscayans, and all those who contributed to make the ironworks produce iron that was exported to Brazil and Portugal, albeit for a short time, may be resumed.[130]

The authors discuss how players who are essential to understand this history ended up being forgotten. Their relevance, however, is understood as something able to foster the resumption of iron mining today. Thus, Nova Oeiras is seen as a "good lesson" for the development of national industry—an example of how to exploit "the country's raw materials, in this case minerals, instead of exporting them raw." The true value of the history of the workers who went through the factory is once again overlooked.

In this book, there are also remnants of the idea that the factory was a stronghold of free labor in the midst of slave practices—an alternative of freedom where the transatlantic trade was the only option. Sousa Coutinho is celebrated for this achievement. This analysis is strongly based on the notion that, in Angola, the Portuguese engaged only in the trade of enslaved people and that this trade was the only form of exploitation of local labor. As we saw in Chapter 3, this narrative does not hold up. Even though the trade of enslaved people was deeply rooted in the structure of Ambundu society, Africans were employed in various compulsory services, under precarious working conditions, in Luanda and its hinterland, from the beginning of the conquest.

Thus, the version of failure widely disseminated by Governor Antonio de Lencastre and in "Resposta que um sujeito do Brasil deu ao outro de Angola, sobre a Fábrica do Ferro" is reiterated by historiography, with a wide variety of approaches. The notion that Ambundu techniques—belonging as they did to a traditional trade related to magic—were less efficient or profitable than European ones is also reiterated, with various nuances, in the bibliography. According to this interpretation, the *sobas*' "offspring" continue to be seen as belonging to an archaic, rural, traditional, and completely stagnant world. On the other hand, there were societies that were more complex—urban, industrial, and dynamic. Such dichotomies of the present, imposed on the past, end up completely erasing the multifaceted action of the blacksmiths and smelters of Ilamba.

In addition, the problem of the Nova Oeiras factory's operation was not technical. Neither Sousa Coutinho nor Maciel were able to perceive this in the late-eighteenth century, but we can. A careful examination of African iron production

---

[130] Alexandra Aparício, Rosa Cruz e Silva, and Honoré Mbunga, *A cidade do Dondo e o seu desenvolvimento econômico: aportes para a sua história* (Luanda: Arquivo Nacional de Angola, Ministério da Cultura, 2015), 32.

based on Colleen Kriger's studies demonstrates that this conception is entirely wrong. The iron produced in Ilamba was of high quality and as useful, and sometimes more, than the iron imported from Europe.

Iron production in Ilamba did not fail, and by saying this, in no way are we celebrating Francisco de Sousa Coutinho's actions. First, how can a factory that produced 40 quintals per month for seven consecutive years, supplying the arsenals in Luanda, providing the tools needed in the *sertão*, and sending iron to Lisbon (only the shipments added up to more than 60 tons), India (at least once), and Brazil can be considered a failure? Novo Belém, which because of its short life has been overlooked by historiography, and Nova Oeiras were productive: many quintals of iron and steel were manufactured there and many tools were forged. The enlightened governor returned to Lisbon and the production of iron and tools continued.

There is therefore a double issue to be explained: we need to understand the reason for those successful initiatives and the reason for their denial by historiography.

If, on one hand, some authors we have cited considered the importance of blacksmiths and smelters from Ilamba for colonial plans, on the other hand, they did not propose a different interpretation. It is true that the stone and lime factory was abandoned and never came into operation. The smaller one, however, the "Casa de Fundição dos Pretos," operated for years, and the "Village of the black blacksmiths" never stopped, since the *jingangula* and the *pulungus* continued to smelt and forge iron their own way. The blacksmiths, smelters, and *sobas* deliberately rejected the stone and lime factory as much as they could.

You see, the factory was not built because local techniques were inferior to European ones. The Ambundu foundry produced excellent iron and steel, which were often praised (even the Count of Buffon acknowledged their quality). In Chapter 4, I pointed out that the factory's construction had a single objective: to increase productivity. The purpose of building Nova Oeiras was to deprive the *jingangula* and *pulungus* of their autonomy and control over the production process. In the factory, the power to determine the working conditions and the amounts produced passed into the hands of the governor and the Royal Treasury.

That being so, what did the stone and lime factory mean and why was it synonymous of so many tensions? For the colonial administration, the factory represented an increase in iron production and therefore income. How could such increases be obtained? The first step was to ensure the availability of land and natural resources through the purchase or expropriation of land and mines. It was then necessary to ensure a continuous supply of labor force, delimiting the boundaries the *sobados* that sent the workers in the outskirts of Nova Oeiras. The subjects' labor force became concentrated in the factory. In order to maintain the work pace, it was essential to create a new way of organizing labor relations in Angola's *sertões*. The ordinances regarding "black worker wages" regulated daily work and established measures in an attempt to exert greater control over the workers: forced recruitment; the "time book"; wages; consecutive searches during the day; punishments; imprisonment (given the presence of a jail next to the factory); surveillance by intendants and inspectors; work and meal times; and moving the workers' lodgings to the outskirts of the town of Nova Oeiras.

An iron factory touched a neuralgic point in the Portuguese colonization of Angola. To maximize profits, it was necessary to gain full control over the working process of the blacksmiths and smelters of Ilamba, to make them abandon their tools, and to work with the large stone machine with its immense hydraulic wheels. There were many efforts made in this regard: the payment of wages and, at least according to the norms, a working regime devoid of ill-treatment. In order for the "machine imagined" in the *sertões* to attain its maximum efficiency, the artisans had to abandon their itinerant lifestyle, their proximity to their families, their tools, their rites, their work times. More than anything, they had to separate life from work. How could a *ngangula* or a *pulungu* separate the act of smelting and forging iron from the sacred, the political, and the ties of kinship that were reaffirmed with each smelting?

In order for the factory to work, the Inconfidência revolutionary Maciel asserted that the "black blacksmiths" of Ilamba should not be deprived of "their freedom [because] they would take offense and flee."[131] They had an "entrenched hatred" and a "repugnance" for work in the factories and mines, which kept them away from their homes and families. The recurring reference to the need to be with the "family," as royal officials translate, is indicative of the value of kinship relations among the Ambundus, of how important it was for them to "belong" to the lineages. The "freedom" they desired was not only related to autonomy in the sense we have been discussing here, or to the defense of their lifestyles. On the other hand, it is not a concept of freedom close to the liberal notion of inalienable individual rights, which is anachronistic for the period. The Ambundus seemed to value, above all, the networks of protection and solidarity that real or symbolic kinship provided for them. As Vansina said, what differentiated a slave from a free person was belonging to those lineages, according to the "law of the

---

131 Carta de José Álvares Maciel para Miguel Antonio de Melo, governador de Angola. São Paulo de Assunção de Luanda, November 1, 1799. AHU_CU_001, Cx. 93 A, D. 1. Thompson called attention to this: "There was another non-industrial institution that could be used to instill the 'economic-use-of-time': the school." E. P. Thompson, *Costumes em comum* (São Paulo: Companhia das Letras, 1998), 292.

sobas." The factory also interfered with this larger network of meanings of "freedom."[132]

The artisans were indispensable for all activities that required iron tools, especially the trade of enslaved people. How to count on their collaboration? Dr. Maciel and Rodrigo de Sousa Coutinho had an idea: to instill new work habits gradually in a "school."[133] The method aimed at adapting the local blacksmiths gradually to the factory's rhythms, techniques, and tools, without "scaring" them.

In the end, the secretaries of overseas territories, the governors of Angola, their officials, and José Álvares Maciel failed to convince or force the Ambundus to abandon their old ways.

In fact, the *sobas*, the "offspring," and the Ambundu blacksmiths and smelters defended the autonomy of their way of life. Their strategies of resistance and survival have been described at length in this book: they disobeyed the royal agents' orders, they escaped, they procrastinated (let us recall that Maciel complained that, as he watched the quarry workers, those engaged in charcoal production had already left for their villages or were sitting idly with no interest in their tasks),[134] and rejected the pace of the blast furnace. However, they also developed a complex relation within the colonial plan, working at the factory, sometimes collaborating in iron production and sometimes sabotaging Nova Oeiras.

The blacksmiths and smelters of Ilamba continued to do what they had been doing for generations. Actually, they did more than that; they invented new trades, they adapted to the new commercial routes and demands inaugurated by the growth of the trade of enslaved people.

In general, since historiography did not put blacksmiths and smelters at the center of the narrative as subjects of their own history, the version of the colonial initiative's failure prevailed. I have attempted to invert that perspective of analysis in this book: the success of the Ambundus, their technical knowledge, and their tactics of resistance led the great stone and lime machine to failure. The "Casa de Fundição dos Pretos" worked because by meeting the Ambundus' demands, by negotiating with the smelters, it created a new form of organization of labor that is the expression of this clash of political projects: 138 blacksmiths and smelters together in one workplace under the watchful eye of the intendants—as the enlightened

---

[132] "A person without a lineage was a slave; a person with one was free." Jan Vansina, "Ambaca Society and the Slave Trade c. 1760–1845," 6; Joseph Miller, *Poder politico e parentesco*, 48.

[133] Carta de Rodrigo de Sousa Coutinho, secretário de Estado da Marinha e do Ultramar, para o marquês Ponte de Lima, mordomo-mor. Palácio de Queluz, October 28, 1798. ANTT, Projeto reencontro, MF0027.

[134] José Álvares Maciel, "Relação dos *sobas* e *ilamba* que dão presentemente filhos para este trabalho." Trombeta, March 2, 1800. BNP, C 8553, F6362.

governor desired—but using local techniques and tools and receiving in return the tithe exemption, as the *sobas* and smelters demanded.

Still, the changes in the social organization of labor led to many conflicts. The governor started to realize that the only way to obtain the continuous collaboration of the local smelters was to let them produce iron according to "their rites." At the end of his government, he proposed that the stone and lime factory employ enslaved labor because that way it would achieve the discipline and obedience necessary for the factory's operation, which he was unable to impose on the rebellious local smelters. The latter in turn defended a different project: smelting the iron in their communities and selling the bars to the Royal Treasury or delivering them in lieu of paying tithes. The one person who actually presented a new proposal to earn the cooperation of the *jingangula* and the *pulungus* was José Álvares Maciel.

Maciel's idea of establishing a "Village of black blacksmiths" emerged after his incursion into the *sertões*, where he was able to observe firsthand the Ambundus' desires and demands regarding the factory's construction. The blacksmiths of Ilamba imposed one condition to work there: that the tithe exemption conquered years before by the *sobas* who sent their dependents to Nova Oeiras also applied to them. The logic is once again inverted: it was not the "polite government" which proposed the tithe exemption in exchange for the labor of the *sobas* who served the factory; it was the African authorities who elaborated the proposal and negotiated with the governor on their terms. Maciel makes it clear that the request for the tithe exemption came from the blacksmiths.

The same claim can be found years later. Since 1808, the *sobas* of Massangano promised to deliver six pounds of iron per *fogo* (family, residence) of their *sobados*, with the condition of being exempted from paying the tithe.[135] The episode generated conflicts with their blacksmith and smelter dependents, because a few years later, in 1813, the "black blacksmiths and smelters" of the *sobas* bound to the fortress of Massangano had sought "refuge" in the lands of other *sobas*, having "fled from the work to which they should apply themselves."[136] Skilled laborers continued to find ways to protect their craft, their product, and their trade. The obligation of delivering the stipulated amounts may have weighed heavily on the blacksmiths. The colonial initiative insisted on increasing productivity. The six pounds per *fogo* (2.76 kg) could be an excessive amount, if we recall that each smelting resulted on average in two to four pounds. For a *sobado* with 100 *fogos*, at least 150

---

[135] Carta ao regente da Vila de Massangano. São Paulo de Assunção de Luanda, July 8, 1808. AHA, Cód. 91, fl. 97v.
[136] Carta de José de Oliveira Barbosa, governador de Angola, para Manuel Antonio da Silva, *capitão-mor* de Ambaca. São Paulo de Assunção de Luanda, November 16, 1813. AHA, Códice 92, A-20–2.

smeltings per month would be necessary to meet the *sobado*'s basic needs—for agriculture, war, rituals, and ornaments.

In 1830, José Almeida e Vasconcelos, then governor, recalled the large expenses made with the iron factory, which was in complete ruin: "the building and the machines, everything is reduced to nothing; the weir and the channel through which water flowed to the factory are destroyed." He reported that, at that time, there was in Trombeta (Golungo) a *coberto*, a simple building, where "the Negroes (...) are obliged by contract to pay the tithe in [iron] bars, which have been sent to the Royal Navy Arsenal in this city, for the price of 25 réis per arratel [or pound]."[137]

Everything indicates that, in the end, Maciel's idea was partially put in practice. According to Almeida e Vasconcelos, the iron was manufactured "with the greatest ignorance and a poorly conceived routine," with very simple tools, as was done in the "Casa de Fundição dos Pretos":

> with underground pits instead of furnaces, with a jaguar skin full of air instead of bellows, using a clay beak to expel the air, applied at the place of the fire in order to extract the iron, employing coal made by them with the same type of knowledge.[138]

Behind this narrative permeated by a demeaning discourse, we can identify the same tools described in the notes of the naturalist Maciel. The persistence of a trade, working "according to their rites," maintaining their "routine," after all those attempts to destroy their techniques, their work rhythm, and their way of life... that is what we find in these excerpts. This continuity was an achievement of the Ambundus of Ilamba.

The reports on the "Village of black blacksmiths" and the like continue in the nineteenth century. In his memoirs (1838), the military officer Fortunato de Melo (1797–1853) noted that, in the Golungo district, there was "a small factory where eight iron bars measuring 9 inches long are made per day."[139] In 1840, there was an unsuccessful initiative by merchants in Lisbon to attempt to explore those mines again.[140] In 1866, ten iron bars of "native extraction" were sent to the gov-

---

[137] Carta de José Maria de Sousa Macedo Almeida e Vasconcelos, governador de Angola, para Nuno Caetano Álvares Pereira de Melo, ministro assistente ao despacho. Luanda, December 6, 1830. IHGB – PADAB, DL76,02.35.

[138] Idem.

[139] Fortunato de Melo, *Memória sobre Angola*, published in *Periódico dos pobres de Lisboa*, August 17, 1838. *Apud* José Joaquim Lopes de Lima, *Ensaios sobre as possessões portuguezas na África Ocidental e Oriental, Ásia Ocidental, China e Oceania* (Lisbon: Imprensa Nacional, 1844), 23.

[140] Idem.

ernment of Luanda from the mines of Trombeta and Zenza in Golungo Alto.[141] However, these were other times, other ways of organizing the work process, other challenges, other blacksmiths and smelters with new demands, new knowledges and techniques, always reinventing the traditions bequeathed by the proud "black blacksmiths and smelters" of Ilamba; so I stop here.

---

[141] Boletim Oficial do Governo Geral da Província d'Angola, no. 28, July 9, 1866, Luanda, Imprensa do governo.

Final Words

In the kingdom and colony of Angola, the Portuguese employed intermediaries to exercise their dominion over autonomous political units controlled by the *sobas* and *ilamba*. The fortress, their garrison, the towns around them, the commercial routes, the markets, the ecclesiastical missions, the civilian towns, the iron factory, and the vassal *sobados* composed a dynamic interior in the vicinity of Luanda, a discontinuous triangle, threatened from within and from without by African potentates and by trade with other European nations. In the second half of the eighteenth century, the colonial power was interested in demarcating land, occupying the *sertão*, optimizing fiscal systems, investing in the development of militias and military hierarchies. A goal less considered by historiography was to exert greater control over the work of the Ambundus, directly related to the land issue, as we saw in the case of the demarcation of lands of the *sobados* exempt from paying tithes, which sent workers to Oeiras.

Analyzing the vassalage deeds allows us to understand how labor relations were regulated and how they changed over time. In the first political treaties with African leaders and in the *baculamentos*, there is no indication that the dependents of the *sobados* were obliged to work for the colonists or to serve them for free. Nor is there any evidence that the *sobas*, when under *ngola* rule, sent their subjects to work for them. The obligation to work was a tradition invented during colonial rule and perpetuated over time as an "immemorial custom."[1]

This subject deserves a more thorough examination than we have undertaken here. The field of studies on free, compulsory, penal, or forced labor in Angola between the sixteenth and the eighteenth centuries has been only cursorily examined by historiography, which usually addresses those topics in the nineteenth and twentieth centuries. This is justified by the scarcity of sources; however, this book intends to serve as an example of how to reread official documentation and search between the lines, in its subtexts and ambiguities, and how to reconstruct the workers' history. An analysis is yet to be made that scrutinizes, as early as the conquest, the political agreements, the conflicts involving the "off-

---

[1] "The term 'invented tradition' is employed in a broad, but not imprecise sense. It includes both 'traditions' actually invented, constructed and formally instituted, and those emerging in a less easily traceable manner within a brief and dateable period." They are a "set of practices normally governed by overtly or tacitly accepted rules and of a ritual or symbolic nature, which seek to inculcate certain values and norms of behavior by repetition, which automatically implies continuity with the past." Eric Hobsbawm and Terence Ranger (orgs.). *A invenção das tradições* (Rio de Janeiro: Paz e Terra, 1984), 9.

spring" of the vassal *sobas*, the forms of enslavement, the work performed at the missions and the fortress, and the recruitment of workers for the royal works, in addition to the status of the *Axiluanda* described by the governor, i.e. the punishment that consisted of working for modest wages for having aided the Dutch during the Dutch invasion of the Kingdom of Angola, which is another story yet to be told.

The issues addressed in Chapter 2 outline a history of transformations involving a clash between the colonial gesture and the interests of residents, *sobas* and *ilamba*, literally on the ground. The colonial initiative occupied a part of the region of Ilamba, creating the towns of Novo Belém and Nova Oeiras, and established new towns in Portuguese America such as Bragança, Oeiras, and Ourém. The names were Portuguese, in accordance with the "civilizing" project to transform villages, *banzas*, *libatas*, and *palhoças* into colonization centers. The historiography on civilian settlements rarely examines the planned towns north of the Kwanza River; it mostly focuses on those founded in the Kingdom of Benguela.[2] It is true that the towns where the iron foundries were built had a short life—few accounts remain of Belém. Nonetheless, 168 people, among Europeans, Brazilians, and locals, were sent to form the towns, not to mention the families from Massangano that migrated to Oeiras. In addition to the iron factory's physical structure, 153 homes composed the nucleus of residents made up of soldiers, exiled convicts, "white" women, "white" or "almost white" men, and a multitude of Ambundus who were not even counted.

The iron factory's architectural design was developed with the collaboration of engineers trained in the Geometry Course that Sousa Coutinho relaunched in Luanda and with the skill of the local, Portuguese, Brazilian, and African stonemasons. The Engine House and the Weir were planned by the Biscayan masters, who left some sketches in Oeiras. Manoel Antonio Tavares and other engineers elaborated a new blueprint based on those sketches. The quick death of the Spanish technicians hindered even the factory's construction. There are aspects of the architecture of Oeiras, the materials used, and stylistic details that deserve the attention of heritage history. The complex is relatively small, but similar to those of fac-

---

[2] Catarina Madeira Santos mentions and briefly describes the towns of Novo Belém and Nova Oeiras, but like other authors, she discusses at much greater length the towns south of the Kwanza River in her dissertation. Catarina Madeira Santos, *Um governo "polido" para Angola. Reconfigurar dispositivos de domínio (1750–c. 1800)*, dissertation (PhD in History) (Lisbon: Faculdade de Ciências Sociais e Humanas da Universidade Nova de Lisboa, 2005); Mariana P. Candido, *An African Slaving Port and the Atlantic World. Benguela and its Hinterland* (New York: Cambridge University Press, 2013), 175–185; Flávia Maria de Carvalho, *Sobas e homens do rei: interiorização dos portugueses em Angola (séculos XVII e XVIII)* (Maceió: Edufal, 2015).

tories in other locations, with a solid stone and lime structure. The blast furnace built later has more details, such as the coat of arms of Portugal and the ornamental stairs. No advances have been made by research studies on the subject of whether African construction and ornamentation techniques were employed.[3]

The political leaders of Ilamba, owners of the land where the foundries were built, maintained their sovereignty in the region at least since the early-seventeenth century. The *sobas* Kabanga kya Mbangu, Nguengue a Kimbemba, Mbangu kya Tambwa, Ngombeya Nambwa, and the *kilamba* Ngongue a Kamukala are examples of leaders who had become vassals of the Portuguese Crown since the seventeenth century and were established in lands surrounding the iron factories and mines. These leaders requested a tithe exemption in exchange for collaborating by sending workers to the factories. The *sobas* pleaded and demanded the compliance with what had been agreed upon in the vassalage agreements, requested benefits granted to their ancestors, and managed to safeguard the "method of the ancestors" as a way to ensure the tax exemption. The African political elite was acquainted with European codes of conduct of a vassal and knew their rights, even if they were few in comparison with their obligations and duties to the king of Portugal.

Faced with the appropriation of lineage lands by the Crown, missionaries, and settlers, African chiefs reinvented the formulas of European wills in land titles, which also served to legitimize the history of the lineages. While devising ways to resist the advancement of colonial occupation, the chiefs concentrated power in their hands, legitimizing lineages and land ownership.

What made this exchange of legal and cultural practices possible was the phenomenon of transculturation. Mary Louise Pratt makes use of this concept to "describe processes whereby members of subordinated or marginal groups select and invent from materials transmitted by a dominant or metropolitan culture."[4] The

---

[3] Kristen Windmuller analyzes how, in Ethiopia, Ethiopians, Indians, and Egyptians designed and built Catholic temples, mixing European standards with Ethiopian architecture. Kristen D. Windmuller-Luna, *Building Faith: Ethiopian Art and Architecture during the Jesuit Interlude, 1557–1632*, dissertation (PhD) (Princeton University, 2016). For eighteenth-century Vila Rica and Mariana, Fabiano Gomes da Silva manages to map African techniques and stylistic themes in the way they are used to make *carrancas*, which incorporate traces and symbols of the cultures of West Central Africa. Fabiano Gomes da Silva, *Pedra e Cal, os construtores em Vila Rica no século XVIII (1730–1800)*, thesis (Master's) (Belo Horizonte: Universidade Federal de Minas Gerais, 2007).

[4] Mary Louise Pratt, *Imperial Eyes: Travel Writing and Transculturation* (Nova York: Routledge, 2008), 7 and 8. I followed Robert Slenes's reading list in his review of Roquinaldo Ferreira's *Cross-Cultural Exchange in the Atlantic World. Angola and Brazil during the Era of the Slave Trade*. Robert Slenes, "Trocas culturais no 'rio Atlântico': Angola no auge do trato de escravizados," *Afro-Ásia* 49 (2014): 365–378. Transculturation is a term coined by Fernando Ortiz to describe Afro-

notion presupposes subordination and resistance, but leaves room for the invention of new practices and the elaboration of solutions to conflicts. This is evident in the case of the request made by the *sobas* to the president of the Council of the Royal Treasury of Angola, asking for an exemption from paying the tithes in exchange for their dependents' labor. The request was presented by the *sobas* to solve a situation that had long been vexing them: the collection of taxes, the tithe, more specifically the violence of the collectors, *dizimeiros*, and *capitães-mores*. This request paved the way for a revision of the ways to recruit the labor of the *sobas*' dependents, the conditions under which workers were sent, and the payment for their service, which became mandatory with the ordinances enacted by Sousa Coutinho's government. The foundation and operation of the ironworks are a good moment in the history of Angola to understand these issues.

The lists we gathered of the "offspring able to work" contain the names of many eighteenth-century chiefs. This documentation can be useful to reconstruct the region's micropolitical history, besides providing data on the tithes and their collection that we have not explored here.

After Sousa Coutinho's ordinances, all services became compulsorily remunerated: in the royal works, in the limekilns, in the Axiluandas' island, delivering mail, working for *capitães-mores*, private individuals or missionaries, transporting goods. This demonstrates that, before that, the wages were insignificant or nonexistent. The royal authorities themselves admitted that the *sobas* and *ilamba* were obliged to serve "for free," and that this was an abuse. Especially in the iron factories, the governor determined that, in addition to wages, the workers should be well treated. Operating with the precepts of decent wages and good treatment, Sousa Coutinho sought to attract workers, persuading them of the benefits that the factories would bring to the region.

In daily practice, permeated by the usual violence in the *sertões*, the workers suffered ill-treatment and fatal accidents in the grandiose construction work for the Nova Oeiras aqueduct and weir. In addition, they were abused by the *capitães-mores*, factory employees, and settlers, being robbed, persecuted, forced to serve private individuals, and led to work in chains. Such oppressions were perpetuated over time as an immemorial custom. The *sobas*, *ilamba*, and *imbari*, for their part, continually denounced these violations and refused to send workers to the best of their ability, since they feared further punishment.

The institution of the *Diretório dos Índios* (1755) in Portuguese America was not an entirely colonial decision either; on the contrary, "the restauration of guard-

---

Cuban culture. Fernando Ortiz, *Contrapunteo cubano* [1947, 1963] (Caracas: Biblioteca Ayacucho, 1978).

ianship was a response to the question raised by the mass defection of Indians from colonial villages."[5] Payment for indigenous service rarely occurred, as the colonists found ways to circumvent the legislation, seeking to enslave the Indians.

The result of these politics to control labor in the *sertões* of the Amazon and Angola was the mass escape and death of Indians and Africans. Among the reasons for the flights and deaths of indigenous people are the ill-treatment, lack of payment, sexual harassment, meals provided with spoiled food, and malnutrition, among others. The Ambundus also fled for the same reasons, in addition to the imminent danger of enslavement. Like indigenous people in the Americas, they created runaway communities, took refuge in the residents' *arimos* and *sobados*, and did not return to their villages. When they did, they could flee again when threatened with recruitment for labor, living a cycle of violence that resulted in the depopulation of the *sertões*.

The *Diretório* and the "good treatment and good wages" of Sousa Coutinho's ordinances legitimized compulsory obligations different from slave labor, perpetuating violence and precarious living conditions that were legally accepted under the mask of work performed by free indigenous and black people, considered far from slavery, since they were paid and "well treated." Therefore, the Pombaline reforms that focused on labor relations failed on both sides of the Atlantic.

While the *Diretório* was effective in removing control from the missionaries over the Indians concentrated in *aldeamentos*, Sousa Coutinho's ordinances regulating the wages of "black workers" were not enough to take control from the *sobas* over their "offspring." However, the pressures to serve in different undertakings—by the king, the *capitão-mor*, the settlers, the missionaries—destabilized the *sobados* demographically and socially. The "offspring" lived in permanent insecurity, especially those in more fragile positions such as those who had been pawned, youths, and children.

In recent years, historians have focused on scrutinizing the forms of enslavement in the Kingdom of Angola and the Kingdom of Benguela.[6] In this book, I have attempted to show that, at the same time as the mechanisms to enslave vassals intensified, new ways of legitimizing and justifying the compulsory labor of free Africans, which we call here constrained labor, were created. In Nova Oeiras, this category of compulsion was legitimized by the tithe exemption. However, it is possible to assert that even the "voluntary" workers were constrained: when persuasion

---

5 José Alves de Souza Júnior, "Negros da terra e/ou negros da Guiné: trabalho, resistência e repressão no Grão-Pará no período do Diretório," *Afro-Ásia* 45 (2013): 173.
6 Roquinaldo Ferreira, *Cross-Cultural Exchange in the Atlantic World. Angola and Brazil during the Era of the Slave Trade* (New York: Cambridge University Press, 2012); Mariana P. Candido, *An African Slaving Port and the Atlantic World* (2013).

was not enough to convince them to work, factory officials had the governor's approval to use force. Other people of different origins and social conditions worked in the factories and also suffered the experience of compulsory work: many exiled convicts, serving their sentences as artisans; enslaved people; "obliged volunteers." There were also volunteers and hired workers such as the Biscayans, who also had their mobility curtailed. This diversity was reflected in the way people were treated. In general, Europeans were not mistreated, they received wages, the necessary food, and were assisted by apothecaries and a doctor when they fell ill; convicts and Ambundu workers suffered all sorts of violence.

The blacksmiths and smelters with their bellows operators appear as a different category of "offspring." Those who worked in the factories received better wages because they suffered the hardships of the "violent exercise of fire"—a strenuous work with bellows, mallets, and anvils, enduring high temperatures.[7] These "practical Negroes" remained in the "Casa de Fundição dos Pretos," separate from other workers who received "common" wages and mechanical officers and from the white blacksmiths who worked in the factory buildings. Like the other workers, they were searched three times a day to ensure that they did not steal any tools or the iron they made.

The hydraulic ironworks did not meet technical needs. The Ambundu technology produced high-quality iron and steel. Nova Oeiras was built to ensure control over the social organization of labor and the level of production.

The rhythm of work in the factories, imposed by a system that aimed to discipline workers, was in many ways rejected, above all by the iron artisans. Above all, they rejected the hydraulic foundry, the blast furnace, and everything that those "innovations" implied: a smaller number of master blacksmiths and smelters, uninterrupted production (without stopping during the months after the *cacimbo*), the greater time spent in the factories away from their families, the desecration of their craft, and the end of their exclusivity and secrecy—since the governor's plan was to create a large apprentice workshop. They resisted as a way of defending a traditional trade that conferred social, economic, and religious prestige to those who exercised it, as well as a lifestyle. In addition, the rituals performed by the blacksmiths in ceremonies and the insignias they produced were structural elements in Ambundu society.

Frederick Cooper describes how, in the post-emancipation period, Europeans had to somehow respect the local work rhythms in order to continue to exploit

---

[7] Perhaps these men suffered from what we know today as occupational lung diseases, caused by inhalation of inorganic dust and manifest as interstitial lung diseases. Eduardo Algranti, "Poluição e doenças ocupacionais pulmonares," *Jornal de Pneumologia* 25, no. 5 (1999): 241–244.

local labor. They did so by adhering to African labor practices and by maintaining culturally established authorities. This set of characteristics made up the idea of "Africans' peculiarity," developed in the late-eighteenth and early-twentieth centuries, i.e. the work habits that were peculiar to them.[8] The "Casa de Fundição dos Pretos" is an example of an earlier period of this same clash of forces. To continue to have access to iron at a cheaper price than the European product, the colonial authorities had to accept its production according to Central African customs, and started to obtain iron from the Ambundus as they did ivory. The blacksmiths and smelters delivered the iron bars produced in exchange for payment without external interference in the work process and its organization. This was how the Nova Oeiras factory produced iron in the second half of the eighteenth century. Even so, the project was only possible thanks to the establishment of the tithe exemption for the nomadic blacksmiths and smelters as well as the *sobas*, who delivered the iron instead of the tax.

The trade of enslaved people was a fundamental element in the changes that the blacksmith and smelter trades underwent over time. The high demand for shackles, nails, knives, and cold weapons of all sorts changed the organization of work related to the production of those instruments. Some objects, such as the double bell or the *malunga*, lost much of their sacredness once they were employed in the colonial context. The same may have happened to the sacredness of the craft. This might have led many apprentices, less powerful masters, and blacksmiths captured in raids to work for the *sobas* who had access to the mines. One can imagine that the Portuguese and the Brazilians who worked as blacksmiths in Luanda and its hinterland also contributed to the trade's expansion outside the realm of the "sacred," occupying the place of more traditional blacksmiths and smelters, who had access to the *bisimbi* spirits.

Pedro Manoel, the Ambundu smelter with whom we began this book, lived in this context. Like other smelters and blacksmiths of the region of Ilamba, he produced excellent iron, as good as or better than any European metal. The big problem was that the governor and other royal officials, while praising Ambundu iron, despised their techniques and tools because of their limited productivity.

Faced with the threat of losing the iron mines, the control over iron production, and the trade in the products they made, the chiefs, blacksmiths, and smelters engaged in strategies to preserve the secret of smelting.

---

[8] Frederick Cooper, Thomas C. Holt, and Rebecca Scott. *Além da escravidão: investigações sobre raça, trabalho e cidadania em sociedades pós-emancipação* (Rio de Janeiro: Civilização Brasileira, 2005).

The foreigners did not record the secret rituals that metallurgical techniques involved because they did not understand their usefulness. Not even José Maciel, the revolutionary chemist, was able to recognize in those rites chemical procedures that ensured the quality of the metal manufactured. When attempting to reproduce Ambundu-style smelting, the Portuguese masters failed, probably because they were unaware of the rites and therefore the technical details. The blacksmiths captured and sent to perform a smelting experiment in Lisbon did not smelt the metal under the watchful eyes of scientists, royal authorities, and colonial administrators. The narratives of the secret were sacred, and therefore impervious to the colonial gaze.

European master smelters and blacksmiths also conceived the trade as a hermetic craft passed down from father to son as a family heritage. Europeans and Ambundus recognized each other as smelters—after all, they watched each other. They were even encouraged by the governor to analyze each other's techniques. However, the rhythm of the factory, the hierarchy of work, and the premature death of the Europeans made it difficult to exchange knowledge.

Governor Sousa Coutinho himself tried to study to build a blast furnace. To that end, he received help from the Count of Buffon and from Antonio Ribeiro Sanches. With the thread of philosophical voyages and naturalist knowledge, the history of Nova Oeiras connected Luanda to Lisbon and Paris.

When Lencastre shut down the iron foundry in Nova Oeiras, the smelter Pedro Manoel continued exercising his trade. Every *cacimbo*, he would retreat to the mines with his apprentices, who were called by the spirits of the ancestors and who worked the bellows together with other masters. According to their secret rites, they invoked protective spirits with prayers and girded the furnace with *pemba* [clay] to ensure a good smelting. They knew the how to identify the rocks, selecting the ones with greater iron content, and the trees suitable for charcoal, pruning them to stimulate the renewal of branches. The smelting process took days. Pedro Manoel made excellent iron that was worked in the blacksmith's forge. What was the secret? After tiring the reader with these hundreds of pages and having barely glimpsed what happened in the smelting furnace of a *pulungu* in the eighteenth century, I must admit: much of Pedro's practice remains secret knowledge, impervious to this researcher's onslaughts. But this should not be surprising; after all, it seems that this is precisely what he wanted.

* * *

The first time I read, in an article by Frederick Cooper, the phrase "in Africa, the conflicts of the past are an active part of the present,"[9] I could not have imagined how much these words would mark my own research. After all, I am dealing with a subject of the modern era, centuries removed from the wars of independence, not involving mainly the traffic of enslaved people or even local slavery, topics whose debates tend to be more politicized among Africanists. When I had the opportunity to visit the factory in Nova Oeiras, near the town of Dondo, the words above took on a different meaning. I was with friends, and when we requested permission to enter the region and asked an "elder" in which direction Nova Oeiras was located (referring to the factory), he answered, "Everything here is Nova Oeiras."

It may seem quite common for the toponyms of a settlement founded in the eighteenth century to survive today. However, in this case, that Portuguese name in the midst of so many African names—Cazengo, Golungo, Dondo—became ingrained in the land and in memory because of the building of the Royal Iron Factory, which still stands imposing amidst the vegetation.

In the last chapter, I dealt with how Francisco de Sousa Coutinho and the iron factory, the ultimate symbol of his enlightened government, persisted in history as signs that celebrated Portuguese colonialism. Recent historiography has criticized the bricolage whereby works and characters from the past were used to justify the colonial actions of the Estado Novo. Symptomatic of this memory is one of the plaques that today identify the architectural ensemble of the iron factory as part of the "Heritage of Portuguese Influence."[10]

In the text engraved in stone, the phrase "tribute to the genius and will of the Portuguese people" stands out. Thus, the genius and strength of Sousa Coutinho's will are confounded with the colonialist vocation of the "Portuguese people"; it is a temporal bridge that joins the second half of the eighteenth century to the twentieth century, justifying and celebrating different stages of the history of colonialism. The fact that the stone and lime factory never operated as it was intended, or that it was the target of various criticisms during and after its construction, was overlooked. Those who visit what remains of Nova Oeiras today and see the grandiose presence of the building, with its two-meter-wide walls, the result of solid construction, cannot imagine that the smelting furnace was never used there. Nothing in this perspective allows us to glimpse the stories of exploitation

---

[9] Frederick Cooper, "Conflito e conexão: repensando a História Colonial da África," *Anos 90*, v. 15, n. 27 (2008): 56.
[10] Project and website to catalogue the heritage of Portuguese origin around the world: http://www.hpip.org/def/pt/AcercaDoHPIP/ApresentacaodoPortal.

Figure 19: Plaque identifying the architectural ensemble of the iron factory, 1973.
Source: Plaque near the Nova Oeiras Iron Factory in Dondo. Author's collection, October 2015.
"On the Bicentennial of the foundation of the Royal Iron Factory of Nova Oeiras, built by orders of Governor Sousa Coutinho, the nation, represented by the His Excellency the Governor General of the State of Angola, the Engineer Fernando Augusto Santos e Castro, pays tribute to the genius and will of the Portuguese people. 1772–1972. Nova Oeiras, September 29, 1973."

of Ambundu labor or the fierce determination of the Ilamba blacksmiths to maintain control over their ancestral craft.

Another plaque, which appears to be newer and to have replaced the old sign, is indicative of a dispute over this memory. After all, to whom does the memory of Nova Oeiras belong? In it, we read "National History Cultural Heritage." Apparently, with independence, the factory was nationalized and ceased to be a symbol of Portuguese colonization and became an expression of the young nation's culture.

Not only in plaques is the significance of the Royal Iron Factory disputed. As we have seen, many historians analyzed the factory as a prime example of enlightened administration in Angola. It marks the apex of the Pombaline plans to promote manufacturing and its policy of taking advantage of Central Africa's natural

Figure 20: Plaque identifying the architectural ensemble of the iron factory (?).
Source: Plaque on the wall of one of the warehouses of the Nova Oeiras Iron Factory in Dondo. Author's collection, October 2015.
Note: The plaque does not contain the date when it was placed. May 28, 1923 is the date of the ordinance that establishes Nova Oeiras as a historical heritage. Note that the description mistakenly asserts that the buildings were built in the seventeenth century.

potential and the knowledge of its people, implementing colonization centers. Without a doubt, Nova Oeiras represented the commitment that befitted an administrator during the Enlightenment.

However, in the concrete colonial context, faced with the difficulties of implementing the Pombaline plans, the iron factory revealed the contradiction of that government project. After all, the supply of enslaved people to America continued to be Angola's main economic function in the Portuguese Empire. The colonial project of extending colonial domination to the interior, which the authorities attempted to put in practice in the second half of the eighteenth century, tried to consolidate political treaties with African authorities, to conquer new chieftaincies, to guarantee the vassal's protection—*sobas*, *ilamba*, and *imbari* and their dependents—, and to safeguard the interests of traders of enslaved people. Those interests, however, were irreconcilable.[11] Iron production in Nova Oeiras is an emblem of that fact: when the "Casa de Fundição dos Pretos" produced iron for export, the traders complained about the lack of labor force and metal to produce the shackles, handcuffs, prisons, and agricultural tools they so desperately needed.

The pressures of the transatlantic trade and its agents imposed barriers to the establishment of an iron factory. The slaveholding colonial elite set the tone: "An-

---

11 Mariana Candido, *An African Slaving Port*, Chapter 3.

gola is no country for factories."[12] This does not mean that Angola was only a trading post in the sense that all enslaved Africans were sent to the Atlantic. The very maintenance of colonial power required establishing policies to control the labor of Central Africans in the region. In addition to the workers provided by the *sobas*, other forms of exploitation of Central African labor force developed; the work of the "constrained" emerged in this context. This is an important part of the history of the iron factory that had to be told.

This research, by seeking the voices of Central Africans, allowed us to tell the factory's history from a different standpoint. To that end, we had to "strip the documents of their Luso-centric and prejudiced attire, resulting from readings marked by Portuguese ideologies and cultural systems," and to "highlight the creative and dynamic Angolan presences."[13] The sources do not allow us to know what the smelter Pedro Manuel thought about all these topics. But they open the way to tell the version of the history of iron exploitation in Angola from the Ambundu perspective, especially that of the Ilamba blacksmiths.

We must place the Ilamba blacksmiths at the center of the story to understand how iron mining and manufacturing, and therefore colonial exploitation, the development of Natural History, and the implementation of enlightened ideas, took place in Angola. What we can say is that, at least until the mid-nineteenth century, Central Africans successfully continued to mine iron in their own way, without submitting to colonial plans and knowledge.

Something essential for us is that blacksmiths and smelters were simultaneously subverting the colonial legal and cultural project and subsidizing the colonizers' economic project, since iron was essential to maintain and extend their dominion over the colony.[14] This is indicative of the intrinsic ambiguities of colonial relations. The authorities were unable to train disciples according to European techniques and to establish a hydraulic ironworks, but by obtaining iron through the tithe exemption in exchange for the delivery of specialized workers and iron

---

[12] João Monteiro de Moraes, "Resposta que um sujeito do Brasil deu ao outro de Angola, sobre a Fábrica do Ferro," n.p., n.d. BNP, MSS, Cx. 246, no. 22.

[13] Isabel de Castro Henriques, "Presenças angolanas nos documentos escritos portugueses," in *Actas do II Seminário Internacional sobre a História de Angola. Construindo o passado angolano: as fontes e a sua interpretação* (Lisbon: Comissão Nacional para as Comemorações dos Descobrimentos Portugueses, 2000), 31.

[14] Frederick Cooper observed the same dynamics in the prostitution circuits analyzed by Luise White in Nairobi. Frederick Cooper, "Conflito e conexão: repensando a história colonial da África," *Anos 90*, v. 15, n. 27 (n.d.): 43; Luise White, *The Comforts of Home: Prostitution in Colonial Nairobi* (Chicago: University of Chicago Press, 1990).

bars, they had access to the necessary metal for shackles, handcuffs, tools, and knifes.

We make an appeal for archeological excavations—to the extent that such an enterprise is possible, given the existence of landmines left over from wars in the region—to rescue from oblivion whatever the ruins of Nova Oeiras are still able to tell us; to bring to light the "Casa de Fundição dos Pretos," which is probably to the right of the blast furnace of the architectural ensemble, and the "Village of black blacksmiths" in Trombeta, where Novo Belém used to be, which have disappeared from the land and from memory.

Attachments

Attachment 1: Iron shipments to Luanda and Lisbon, 1762–1814 ——
Attachment 2: Soldiers, farmers, cooks, and practical workers from the *sertão* sent to Nova Oeiras (1766–1771) ——
Attachment 3: Mechanical officers sent to work at the iron factories of Nova Oeiras and Novo Belém, 1767–1800 ——
Attachment 4: Workers from *sobados* provided to the iron factories, 1768–1800 ——
Attachment 5: Models and images of the iron factory ——

Attachment 1: Iron shipments to Luanda and Lisbon, 1762–1814

Year	Description of the shipment	Amount in kilos
1762	Shipment of iron extracted in Angola	
1765	82 quintals, 2 arrobas, and 28 lb of iron from Ilamba	4 t, 962 kg 880 g
1767	16 boxes with 32 quintals of iron, marked with and R and a P to indicate that it is from ironstone, onboard Boa Fortuna Corvette owned by Companhia de Pernambuco	1 t, 920 kg
1767	Iron shipment: 27 bars of steel	
1767	47 boxes of iron containing 95 quintals, 2 arrobas, and 6 lb as ballast for the corvette. The iron is from the Royal Factory of Ilamba	5 t, 732 kg, 760 g
1767	40 quintals and 8 lb of iron from the Novo Belém Factory	2 t, 403 kg, 680 g
1767	16 quintals, 1 arroba and 17.5 lb of iron and 4 quintals, 2 arrobas, and 27 lb of cabo de alicondo e gife (sic)	1 t, 265 kg, 470 g
1767	55 quintals and 5 lb of iron as ballast onboard the Boa Fortuna Corvette	3 t, 302 kg, 300 g
1767	35 quintals (10 from Nova Oeiras).	2 t, 100 kg
1767	891 bars of iron with 93 quintals, 2 arrobas, and 2 lb from the two factories of Novo Belém and Nova Oeiras	5 t, 640 kg, 920 g
1767	117 bars of iron, 10 quintals, 3 arrobas, and 27 lb from the new factories	667 kg, 420 g
1767	1,520 large stone iron bars weighing 156 quintals, 2 arrobas, and 8 lb; 3 boxes with earth iron bars "marked with a cross, with the same weight"	9 t, 393 kg, 680 g
1767	Reception of iron and pitch from the ship from India	
1768	2,480 iron bars weighing 163 quintals, 3 arrobas, and 29 lb, divided as follows: 1,633 large bars of stone iron weighing 140 quintals, 2 arrobas, and 27 lb, freestanding, and as ballast for the Santa Rosa ship: 9 boxes with 220 bars of earth iron marked with a cross, weighing 19 quintals and 2 arrobas: two boxes with 627 bars of poorly manufactured steel weighing 3 quintals, 2 arrobas, and 14 lb	Stone iron: 8 t, 42 kg, 420 g; Soil iron: 1 t, 170 kg;

Continued

Year	Description of the shipment	Amount in kilos
1768	Letter from Francisco Xavier Mendonça Furtado, Secretary of the Navy and Overseas Affairs, confirming receipt of the iron shipments	Steel: 216 kg, 440 g
1768	Letter confirming the receipt of 50 quintals and 5 lb of iron divided in 30 boxes	3 t, 2 kg, 300 g
1768	Reception of 55 quintals and 5 lb of iron sent in 30 boxes on the Boa Fortuna Ship	2 t, 2 kg, 300 g
1768	Shipment of iron as ballast for a ship: 40 quintals – 423 bars in 10 boxes	2 t, 400 kg
1768	556 iron bars weighing 42 quintals, plus 3 quintals, 2 arrobas, and 14 lb of steel in 627 bars, "all of it from the Novo Belém Royal Factory, requesting an additional shipment of 40 iron bars weighing 6 quintals and 6 lb, as well as 280 bars [illegible]"	2 t, 565 kg of iron and 36 kg, 440 g of steel
1768	405 bars of iron	
1770	12 quintals, 17 lb of iron from Nova Oeiras	727 kg, 820 g
1770	70 bars of iron weighing 15 quintals, 2 arrobas, and 15 lb from Nova Oeiras	936 kg, 900 g
1770	57 of iron weighing 12 quintals and 7 lb from Nova Oeiras	723 kg, 220 g
1771	Shipment to Benguela of 4 quintals and 20 lb of iron from Nova Oeiras	249 kg, 200 g
1800	1579 bars of iron "extracted from the Mines of this Kingdom and smelted by the Negroes in their barbaric ways"	
1807	Receipt of iron shipment	
1808	The governor sends a shipment of iron he was preparing: "although it is still not much, I believe that this time it might be of service; and as soon as possible I will continue sending everything I consider convenient to the establishment of the Navy in this Port"	
1808	743 bars of iron weighing 95 arrobas and 22 lb	1 t, 435 kg, 120 g
1813	Shipped one iron bar	
1814	Iron bars received by the Royal Council	

Continued

Year	Description of the shipment	Amount in kilos
	Total	60 t, 641 kg, 390 g of iron and 252 kg, 880 g of steel.

Obs.: 1 quintal = 60 kg, 1 arroba = 15 kg, 1 lb = 460 g. According to "Quadro geral das principais medidas e moedas utilizadas nos últimos tempos do Brasil colonial," elaborated by Roberto Simonsen, *História Econômica do Brasil*, 462–463. 7th ed. S. Paulo: Cia. Ed. Nacional, 1977. These measures are close to those established by Adriano Parreira: 1 lb or arrátel = 450 g; 1 quintal = 4 arrobas = 60 kg. Table 4, in Adriano Parreira, *Economia e Sociedade em Angola na época da Rainha Jinga, século XVII*, 97. Lisbon: Editorial Estampa, 1997.
Sources: AHU_CU_001, Cx. 45, D. 68; AHU_CU_001, Cx. 51, D. 1; AHU_CU_001, Cx. 51, D. 44; AHU_CU_001, Cx. 52, D. 15; AHU_CU_001, Cx. 52, D. 73; AHU_CU_001, Cx. 119, D. 15; AHU_CU_001, Cx. 119, D. 16; AHA, C – 14–3; AHA, C – 14–4; AHA, A-2–2, fl. 166; AHA, D – 2–5; AHA, A – 20–2; IHGB – PADAB, DVD9,19 DSC00153; IHGB – PADAB, DVD9,19 DSC00198; IHGB – PADAB, DVD10,20 DSC00415; BNP,C 8742, F6364; BNP, F3315; IEB/USP, Al-082–024.

Attachment 2: Soldiers, farmers, cooks, and practical workers from the *sertão* sent to Nova Oeiras (1766–1771)

From	To	Worker / Number	Trade	Sent from	Origin	Obs.	Remuneration
1766		Lourenço Lopes	Cattle worker in the *sertão*	Luanda			
1767		Francisco José Leitão	Soldier		Islander	Farmer	
1767		João Pereira	Soldier		Islander	Farmer	
1767		7	Soldier				
1767		10	Soldier	Muxima, Pedras, Ambaca, Kambambe.		"Married and poor to settle in Nova Oeiras."	
1767		Antonio dos Santos e família	Cook	Luanda		Volunteer; "cook who was the bishop's and is a mulatto, is in-	

Continued

From	To	Worker / Number	Trade	Sent from	Origin	Obs.	Remuneration
						dustrious and hard-working, and serves to make bread and feed the masters, and also their family; to that end, Your Grace shall have an oven made and shall have him established with land to grow his food, since being from Portugal and having good fortune, he shall easily find it."	
1767		Tomé Tomaz	Soldier			He shall be discharged after marrying.	
1767		José Xavier	Soldier			He was discharged; his wife was to be sent to Nova Oeiras, as he had requested.	
1767		José Gouvea	Soldier			He was discharged; he was ill and wanted to return to the capital. He was ordered to remain in Nova Oeiras.	
1767		José Gonçalves Vila Poca	Soldier			He was discharged; he was ill and wanted to return to the capital. He was ordered to re-	

Continued

From	To	Worker / Number	Trade	Sent from	Origin	Obs.	Remuneration
1768		José Correia Dias	Soldier	Luanda		main in Nova Oeiras. He was sentenced to work two months in the factory's public works.	
1768		15	Soldier		Vila Real	"A young man from the outskirts of Vila Real, who is an excellent Stonemason, a great Farmer, and a good charcoal maker, I believe he is a good match for those lands, and if Your Grace treats him well, he will make an excellent settler in those lands."	
1768			Soldier				
1768		Domingos Correa	Soldier				
1768		15	Soldier		Europe	"Europeans and farmers as new settlers in that town [Nova Oeiras]."	
1771		Albano de Caldas e Araujo	Captain	Lisbon			Wages paid until February 1771.
1771		Luís da Silva	Squadron corporal	Lisbon		In front of his name is written: "Escaped."	Wages paid until February 1771.
1771		Manoel Ferreira de Sousa	Soldier	Lisbon			Wages paid until February 1771.

Continued

From	To	Worker / Number	Trade	Sent from	Origin	Obs.	Remuneration
1771		José Nunes	Soldier	Lisbon			Wages paid until February 1771.
1771		Cipriano José da Silva	Lieutenant	Lisbon			Received an advance of four months' wages, to be deducted in Angola.
1771		Manoel do Nascimento	Lieutenant	Lisbon			Received an advance of four months' wages, to be deducted in Angola.
1771		Domingos Valente	Soldier	Lisbon		Exiled	
1771		Baltazar Tinoco	Soldier	Lisbon		Exiled	
1771		Felipe Tinoco	Soldier	Lisbon		Exiled	
1771		Joaquim Marques Lagoa	Soldier	Lisbon			
1771		Joaquim Pedro de Lacerda	Soldier	Luanda			

Note: A total of 68 persons.
Source: BNP, MSS Caixa 250, n. 71; AHU_CU_001, Cx. 54, D. 101; IEB/USP, AL- 083–070; IEB/ USP, Al-83–037; IHGB-PADAB, DVD9,19 DSC00394; BNP, C 8742, F6364; IHGB-PADAB, DVD10,22 DSC00044; IHGB-PADAB, DVD10,22 DSC00209; IHGB – PADAB, DVD10,22 DSC00230

Attachment 3: Mechanical officers sent to work in the iron factories of Nova Oeiras and Novo Belém, 1767–1800

Miner

From	To	Name (or number)	Trade	Sent from	Origin	Notes	Remuneration
1769			Miner		France	"I made another one with excellent charcoal, employing a French soldier who possessed that Art."	
1772	1773	Francisco Furtado de Mendonça	Master miner				Paid daily wages, he worked from June 1772 to February 1773 in Nova Oeiras, for a total of 56$550 réis.
1773		Diogo Espinado	Charcoal works master			For the price of 537 *tangas* of charcoal he made in January 1773 at 40 *réis*, for a total of 21$480 réis.	

Stonemason

From	To	Name (or number)	Trade	Sent from	Origin	Notes	Remuneration
1770		Joaquim Freire	Stonemason				Wages of 1$600 réis
1770		Luiz José	Stonemason				Wages of 1$600 réis

Carpenters

From	To	Name (or number)	Trade	Sent from	Origin	Notes	Remuneration
1768		4	Carpenters				
1769		Domingos Viegas	Carpenter			"Should return [to Luanda] to be trained on the factory's model."	
1769		Antonio Ribeiro	Master carpenter				
1770		João dos Santos	Carpenter	Lisbon			Wages of 1$600 réis
1770		José Antonio	Carpenter				Wages of 1$600 réis
1770		Manoel dos Santos Tarouca	Carpenter of houses and wells			Exiled; he was detained at the Inspectorate of the Chamber of Commerce.	
1770		Manoel José da Cunha	Carpenter of houses and wells			Exiled; he was detained at the Inspectorate of the Chamber of Commerce.	
1771		Antonio Joaquim de Almeida	Carpenter	Lisbon		Exiled	"They must be paid in Angola according to their merits at work."
1771		José Joaquim Sabido	Carpenter	Lisbon		Exiled	"They must be paid in Angola according to their merits at work."
1771		João Bento	Carpenter	Lisbon		Exiled	"They must be paid in Angola according to their merits at work."
1771		Antonio Rodrigues	Carpenter	Lisbon	Castilian	Exiled	"They must be paid in Angola according to their merits at work."

Attachment 3: Workers sent to Nova Oeiras e Novo Belém (1767-1800) — **325**

Carpenters *(Continued)*

From	To	Name (or number)	Trade	Sent from	Origin	Notes	Remuneration
1771		Manoel de Oliveira	Carpenter	Lisbon		Exiled	"They must be paid in Angola according to their merits at work."
1771		Caetano Miguel	Carpenter			Enslaved at the service of D. Maria da Conceição Simões	
1771		Antonio Francisco	Carpenter			Enslaved at the service of D. Maria da Conceição Simões	
1771		Paulo João	Carpenter			Enslaved at the service of D. Maria da Conceição Simões	
1771		Amaro	Carpenter			Enslaved at the service of Paulo Gabriel Moreira Rangel	
1771		Ventura José	Carpenter			Enslaved at the service of Luis Prates	
1771		João Felipe	Carpenter			Enslaved at the service of D. Teresa de Barros	
1771		Paulo Sebastião	Carpenter			Enslaved at the service of Canon Gonçalo Cardia	
1790		Estanislao Cosme	Ship carpenter	Lisbon		He appears in the list of artisans approved to go to the Kingdom of Angola; he was a carpenter at the Arsenal of the Royal Navy.	
1790		Antonio José Fernandes	Home carpenter	Lisbon		He appears in the list of artisans approved to	

Carpenters *(Continued)*

From	To	Name (or number)	Trade	Sent from	Origin	Notes	Remuneration
						go to the Kingdom of Angola; he was a home carpenter at the Arsenal of the Royal Navy.	
1800		"Carpenters of the land"	Carpenters				

Blacksmiths

From	To	Name (or number)	Trade	Sent from	Origin	Notes	Remuneration
1767		2	Blacksmith	Luanda		"Here goes another blacksmith to help the former reduce the iron in large bars."	
1767		1	Blacksmith			"I sent Your Grace a white blacksmith with bellows."	
1767		3	Blacksmiths	Bahia, Brazil		They never reached the factory. They died after going hunting in Benguela.	
1769		Feliciano Pinto	Blacksmith			Fugitive	
1769		Francisco Antonio	Blacksmith				
1770		Carlos Firpo	Blacksmith	Lisbon			Salary: 1$600 réis
1770		José da Silva Castelhano	Blacksmith	Lisbon		Exiled; he was detained at the Inspectorate of	

Blacksmiths *(Continued)*

From	To	Name (or number)	Trade	Sent from	Origin	Notes	Remuneration
1770		Roque Soares Lima	Blacksmith	Lisbon		the Chamber of Commerce. Exiled; he was detained at the Inspectorate of the Chamber of Commerce.	
1770		Francisco Fernandes	Blacksmith	Lisbon		Exiled; he was detained at the Inspectorate of the Chamber of Commerce.	
1770		João Bento	Blacksmith	Lisbon		Exiled; he was detained at the Inspectorate of the Chamber of Commerce.	
1772	1772	José de Freitas Santos	Ironworks master				Paid per day, he worked from May to November 1772, total of 75$900 réis.

Smelters

From	To	Name (or number)	Trade	Sent from	Origin	Notes	Remuneration
1768	1768	Francisco Xavier de Zuloaga	Master smelter	Lisbon	Province of Guipozcoa	Arrived on 11/14/1768 in Nova Oeiras, died on 12/08/1768.	He was supposed to work for 3 years with a salary of 2$400 réis per day, with travel costs covered by the Royal Treasury.
1768	1768	Francisco de Echenique	Master smelter	Lisbon	Kingdom of Navarra	Arrived on 11/14/1768 in Nova	He was supposed to work for 3 years with

Smelters *(Continued)*

From	To	Name (or number)	Trade	Sent from	Origin	Notes	Remuneration
						Oeiras, died on 12/29/1768.	a salary of 2$400 réis per day, with travel costs covered by the Royal Treasury.
1768	1769	Joseph Manoel de Echevarria	Master smelter	Lisbon	Province of Guipozcoa	Arrived on 11/14/1768 in Nova Oeiras, died on 01/23/1769.	He was supposed to work for 3 years with a salary of 2$400 réis per day, with travel costs covered by the Royal Treasury.
1768	1768	Joseph de Erretoloaza	Master smelter	Lisbon	Biscay	Arrived on 11/14/1768 in Nova Oeiras, died on 12/06/1768.	He was supposed to work for 3 years with a salary of 2$400 réis per day, with travel costs covered by the Royal Treasury.
1769		Inácio				"Should work continuously smelting iron to attempt to smelt 16 lb at a time."	
1769		José de Freitas				"Should work continuously smelting iron to attempt to smelt 16 lb at a time"; blacksmith, factory officer.	
1771		Manoel Nunes	Bell caster	Lisbon		Voluntary officer, died in 1772 in Nova Oeiras. In a list dated	Wages: $600 réis, once he started to work, according to his

Attachment 3: Workers sent to Nova Oeiras e Novo Belém (1767-1800) — **329**

Smelters *(Continued)*

From	To	Name (or number)	Trade	Sent from	Origin	Notes	Remuneration
						1770, among the mechanics appointed to sail to Angola, he appears as "volunteer, but obliged." Married to Casimira Josefa, resident of Douro in the Town of Figueiró dos Vinhos, District of Tomar.	trade, he should receive 1$200 réis per day; he left his daily wages of 300 réis to his wife and children.
1771		Manoel Simões	Iron smelter and refiner	Lisbon		Voluntary officer. In a list dated 1770, among the mechanics appointed to sail to Angola, he appears as "volunteer, but obliged." Married to Rosa Maria, resident of Moinhos Fundeiro in the Town of Avelar, District of Cinco Vilas. Died in 1771, in Nova Oeiras.	Wages: $600 réis, once he started to work, according to his trade, he should receive 1$200 réis per day; he left his daily wages of 300 réis to his wife and children.
1771		Francisco Lourenço	Iron smelter	Lisbon		Voluntary officer. In a list dated 1770, among the mechanics appointed to sail to Angola, he appears as "volunteer, but ob-	Wages: $600 réis, once he started to work, according to his trade, he should receive 1$200 réis per day; he left his daily wages of 300

Smelters *(Continued)*

From	To	Name (or number)	Trade	Sent from	Origin	Notes	Remuneration
						liged." In 1774, he was ordered to return to Portugal. Married to Domingas de Jesus, resident of Casal Velho in the Town of Avelar, District of Cinco Vilas.	réis to his wife and children.
1771		Matheus Pisson Nihoul	Smelter	Lisbob	France	Iron refining master: in 1774, he was ordered to return to Portugal.	He received an advance of 108$000 réis for months and 2 months and 2 months allowance.

Plater

From	To	Name / Number	Trade	Sent from	Origin	Notes	Remuneration
1790		José Candido	Plater officer	**Lisbon**		Appears in the list or artisans approved to sail to the Kingdom of Angola; he was a plater officer at the Army's Royal Arsenal.	

Attachment 3: Workers sent to Nova Oeiras e Novo Belém (1767-1800) —— 331

Tinsmiths

From	To	Name / Number	Trade	Sent from	Origin	Notes	Remuneration
1771		Manoel dos Santos	Master tinsmith	Lisbon		Voluntary officer; in a list dated 1770, he appears among the mechanics appointed to sail to Angola as "volunteer, but obliged."	Wages of $600 réis, when he started to work, according to his trade, he should receive 1$200 réis per day; he left his daily wages of $200 réis to his daughter; resident of Forte da Junqueira, Parish of N. S. da Ajuda. He requested that his wife, Maria Jacinta Rosa, go with him.
1771		Manoel José Ferraz	Tinsmith officer	Lisbon		Voluntary officer; in 1774, he was ordered to return to Portugal. In a list dated 1770, he appears among the mechanics appointed to sail to Angola as "volunteer, but obliged" who was "at home."	Wages of $600 réis, when he started to work, according to his trade, he should receive 1$200 réis per day; he left his daily wages of $200 réis to his wife; married to Isabel Genovesa, resident of the city of Lisbon, on Rua da Paz, Parish of N. S. das Mercês.
1771		Manoel do Nascimento	Master tinsmith	Lisbon		Voluntary officer.	Wages of $600 réis, when he started to work, according to his trade, he should

Tinsmiths *(Continued)*

From	To	Name / Number	Trade	Sent from	Origin	Notes	Remuneration
							receive 1$200 réis per day
1790		Manoel dos Reis	Foundry tinsmith	Lisbon		He appears on the list of artisans approved to sail to the Kingdom of Angola; he was a foundry tinsmith at the Army's Royal Arsenal.	
1790		André Maria	Tinsmith officer	Lisbon		He appears on the list of artisans approved to sail to the Kingdom of Angola; he was a foundry tinsmith at the Army's Royal Arsenal: "he knows how to work with clay and casting bells."	
1790		José da Costa Rosado	Tinsmith	Lisbon		He appears on the list of artisans approved to sail to the Kingdom of Angola; he was a foundry tinsmith at the Army's Royal Arsenal. His master, João Monteiro Nazaré, said: "where he learned and has demonstrated	

Tinsmiths *(Continued)*

From	To	Name / Number	Trade	Sent from	Origin	Notes	Remuneration
1790		Ambrósio Ferreira	Tinsmith officer	Lisbon		to be skillful and has hope of great dexterity, for he is unhindered making anything asked of him, whether on the forge, soldering, or molding." He appears on the list of artisans approved to sail to the Kingdom of Angola; he was a tinsmith officer at the Army's Royal Arsenal.	

Masons

From	To	Name / Number	Trade	Sent from	Origin	Notes	Remuneration
1768		4	Masons				
1768	1770	Pedro	Mason apprentice			Enslaved to D. Teresa de Barros da Silva (heir of Luis Gouvea, her brother)	Paid daily wages, he worked from 1768 to 1770, 18$300 réis
1769			Mason	Luanda		Imprisoned black man "who shall work in exchange for food."	Worked for his food.
1770			Masons	Massangano			
1770		Manoel Teixeira	Mason				Wages: 1$600 réis

Masons *(Continued)*

From	To	Name / Number	Trade	Sent from	Origin	Notes	Remuneration
1770		João Martins	Mason			Wages: 1$600 réis	
1770		Pedro Bogarim Castelhano	Mason			Exiled; he was detained at the Inspectorate of the Chamber of Commerce.	
1770		José Inácio	Mason			Exiled; he was detained at the Inspectorate of the Chamber of Commerce.	
1771		José Inácio	Mason	Lisbon		Exiled	"Must be paid in Angola according to his merits at work."
1771		Manoel de Oliveira	Mason	Lisbon		Exiled; forced labor onboard	"Must be paid in Angola according to his merits at work."
1771		Francisco da Rocha	Mason	Lisbon		Exiled; forced labor onboard	"Must be paid in Angola according to his merits at work."
1771	1773	Antonio	Mason officer			Enslaved to Antonio Simões da Silva	Daily wages, the three of them worked from March 1772 to April 1773, total 194$200 réis
1771	1773	André	Mason officer			Enslaved to Antonio Simões da Silva	Daily wages, the three of them worked from March 1772 to April 1773, total 194$200 réis

Masons (Continued)

From	To	Name / Number	Trade	Sent from	Origin	Notes	Remuneration
1771	1773	Miguel	Mason officer			Enslaved to Antonio Simões da Silva	Daily wages, the three of them worked from March 1772 to April 1773, total 194$200 réis
1772		Gregório José	Mason officer			"A good mason officer and very skillful, and also a fine thief"; he was to "prepare the rocks needed for the furnace."	
1772	1772	Gaspar	Mason officer			Enslaved to Joaquim da Costa Braga	Daily wages, worked from February to December 1772, total 59$600 réis
1772	1773	João Miguel	Mason officer				Daily wages, worked from February 1772 to February 1773
1772	1773	Protázio Inácio	Mason officer				Daily wages, worked from June 1772 to April 1773, total 39$150 réis
1790		Pedro José	Mason officer	Lisbon		Appears on the list of artisans approved to sail to the Kingdom of Angola; he was a mason officer at the Royal Arsenal.	

Iron refiners

From	To	Name / Number	Trade	Sent from	Origin	Notes	Remuneration
1771		Julião Miguel	Iron refiner	Lisbon		Voluntary officer; in a 1770 list of the mechanics appointed to sail to Angola, he appears as a "volunteer, but obliged."	Wages of $600 réis, when beginning to work, according to his trade, he should receive 1$200 réis per day; he left $300 réis of his daily wages to his wife and children; married with Rosa Maria, resident of Casal Velho.
1771		Pedro Simões	Iron refiner refinador e martelador de ferro	Lisboa		Voluntary officer, died in 1772 in Nova Oeiras. In a 1770 list of the mechanics appointed to sail to Angola, he appears as a "volunteer, but obliged."	Wages of $600 réis, when beginning to work, according to his trade, he should receive 1$200 réis per day; he reserved $300 réis of his daily wages "for food for his four sons and three daughters"; widow of Serafina Ramos, resident of Chimpeles.

Metalworkers

From	To	Name / Number	Trade	Sent from	Origin	Notes	Remuneration
1764			Metalworker	Lisbon		Exiled	

Metalworkers *(Continued)*

From	To	Name / Number	Trade	Sent from	Origin	Notes	Remuneration
1768		2	Metal-worker		Luanda	They presumably fled from a French ship, one of them was an "admirable cutler."	
1768		Cristovão Pegado	Metal-worker			Fixing weapons	
1790		Ambrósio José	Metal-worker officer		Lisbon	Appears on the list of artisans approved to sail to the Kingdom of Angola; he was a metal-worker officer at the Army's Royal Arsenal.	

Note: Total: 85 mechanical officers, among them three miners, two stonemasons, 21 carpenters, 14 blacksmiths, nine smelters, one iron smelter and refiner, one plater, two iron refiners, seven tinsmiths, four metalworkers, 21 masons. Workers who appear with generic information, such as "carpenters of the land," without specifying the number of carpenters, were not included.

Sources: ANTT, Ministério do Reino mç. 600, caixa 703, doc. 25; ANTT, Condes de Linhares mç. 47, doc. 20; ANTT, Condes de Linhares mç. 52, doc. 74; ANTT, Projeto reencontro, BN(RJ), MF0027; BNP, C 8742, F6364; IHGB-PADAB, DVD 9,18 DSC00174; IHGB-PADAB, DVD9,19 DSC00394; IHGB-PADAB, DVD10,22 DSC00087, IHGB-PADAB, DVD10,22 DSC00044; IHGB-PADAB, DVD10,22 DSC00209; IHGB – PADAB, DVD10,22 DSC00212; IHGB – PADAB, DVD10,22 DSC00230; IHGB – PADAB, DVD10,22 DSC00251; IHGB-PADAB, DVD 9,18 DSC00301; AHA, A-17–2; AUH_CU_001, Cx. 52, D. 68; AHU_CU_001, Cx. 52, D. 73; AHU_CU_001, Cx. 53, D. 8; AHU_CU_001, Cx. 54, D. 101; AHU_CU_001, Cx. 75, D. 77; AHU_CU_001, Cx. 96, D. 54; IEB/USP – Col. AL- 83–070; IEB/USP – Col. AL- 82–087; IEB/ USP, Al-83–037; IEB/USP, AL-83–098; IEB/USP – AL-83–192; IEB/USP – AL-83–252; AHTT, Erário Régio 4191; AHA, A-17–2; AHA, C-14–4; BNP, C 8743, F6377; BNP, MSS Caixa 250, n. 71; SGL, AA, v.3, n. 29, p. 361–393; AN (RJ), Códice 543, Negócios de Portugal.

Attachment 4: The "offspring," workers from the *sobados* sent to the iron factories, 1768–1800

The following tables contain information from the "inventories of able offspring" of the *sobados* exempt from paying the tithe, which were obliged to send workers to the factory from 1768 to 1800. The values of the tithes each authority paid were calculated in products and in réis.

Table 4.1: Workers provided by the *sobas* of Golungo 1768(?).
"Inventário dos *Sobas, Ilamba e Imbari* do Distrito do Golungo que servem no serviço das Fábricas do Ferro de Novo Belém e Nova Oeiras donde se mandaram anexar todos por ordem do Ilmo. e Exmo. Snr. General e sobre os dízimos que pagavam antes de serem isentos e pelo que regularam na regulação que se fez e o número de filhos capazes que cada um tem e os que dão por mês."

Soba	"Able offspring"	Workers provided per month	Tithe	Tithe value
Quitala Quazumba Andre Fernandes	60	15	12 *exeques* of flour, 2 piglets, 2 goats, and 2 chickens	12$000 réis
Quitendele Quiacababa Antonio João	3	1	2 *exeques* of flour, 1 piglet, and 1 chicken	2$000 réis
Kilamba Cangondo Caquilvangi Francisco da Costa	4	1	2 *exeques* of flour, 1 piglet, and 1 chicken	2$000 réis
Bango Aquitamba Jeronimo de Gregorio	1000	50	338 *exeques*: 100 of flour, 100 of beans, and 138 of corn	310$400 réis
Quimbar Cabombe Manuel Antonio	3	1	2.5 *exeques*: 1.5 of flour, 1 of corn, 1 chicken	2$300 réis
Kilamba Gongue Acamucala Antonio Pedro	250	42	40 *exeques*: 20 beans, and 20 of flour	40$000 réis
Kilamba Calunga Cagombe Domingos Antonio	15	3	4 *exeques* of corn and 3 chickens	3$200 réis
Kilamba Bango Bango Pascoal Pedro	80	24	20 *exeques*: 10 of beans, 10 of flour	20$000 réis
Gola Bumba Antonio Matheus	20	4	3.5 *exeques* of corn and 6 chickens	2$800 réis
Dala Hui Antonio Gaspar	10	3	2.5 *exeques* of corn and 2 chickens	2$000 réis
Zombo andala Alexandre Francisco	4	1	4 *exeques* of corn and 3 chickens	3$200 réis
Quilombo Quiacatubia Antonio Jeronimo	300	30	9.5 *exeques* of corn and 6 chickens	7$600 réis
Muquixi Aquhuano Antonio Garcia	4	1	2 *exeques* of flour and 3 chickens	2$000 réis

Table 4.1: Workers provided by the *sobas* of Golungo 1768(?).
"Inventário dos *Sobas, Ilamba e Imbari* do Distrito do Golungo que servem no serviço das Fábricas do Ferro de Novo Belém e Nova Oeiras donde se mandaram anexar todos por ordem do Ilmo. e Exmo. Snr. General e sobre os dízimos que pagavam antes de serem isentos e pelo que regularam na regulação que se fez e o número de filhos capazes que cada um tem e os que dão por mês." *(Continued)*

Soba	"Able offspring"	Workers provided per month	Tithe	Tithe value
Kilamba Quiapangi Antonio Pedro	4	1	3.5 *exeques* of corn and 2 chickens	2$800 réis
Bumba Andala Bento de Souza	150	20	9 *exeques* of corn and 6 chickens	7$600 réis
Cahondo Cacatua Bernardo Pedro	10	2	5 *exeques* of flour and 3 chickens	5$000 réis
Bango a Musungu Cristóvão Salvador	24	6	5 *exeques* of flour and 3 chickens	5$000 réis
Cabanga Cacalunga Domingos Jorge	10	2	3.5 *exeques* of corn and 4 chickens	2$800 réis
Bango Azongo Diogo Matheus	25	5	3.5 *exeques* of corn and 4 chickens	2$800 réis
Bumba Ndonda Domingos Simão	6	1	3.5 *exeques* of corn and 4 chickens	2$800 réis
Kilamba Maluvo Aluango Domingos Pereira	12	3	4 *exeques* of corn and 3 chickens	3$200 réis
Quiluangi Quiadonda Diogo Ventura	8	2	4.5 *exeques* of corn and 4 chickens	3$600 réis
Angabambi Domingos Manoel	3	1	2 *exeques* of flour	2$000 réis
Golungo Aquicuim Francisco Matheus	20	3	3 *exeques* of corn and 4 chickens	2$400 réis
Kilamba Luangariamalolo Fernando Antonio	30	6	4 *exeques* and 3 measures of corn and 4 chickens	3$800 réis
Quiabale Quia Caboco Gregorio Bernardo	10	3	3.5 *exeques* of flour and 4 chickens	3$500 réis
Captain of the *Imbari* Francisco Bernardo	8	2	3.5 *exeques* of flour	3$500 réis
Caculocahogi Francisco Antonio	8	2	4.5 *exeques* of corn and 4 chickens	3$600 réis
Gonguembo Francisco Lourenço	300	40	9.5 *exeques* of corn and 6 chickens	7$600 réis
Gandoacabuto Gabriel Antonio	12	3	3 *exeques* of corn and 3 chickens	2$400 réis
Quibembe Quiamatue Gaspar João	8	2	4.5 *exeques* of corn and 4 chickens	2$800 réis

Table 4.1: Workers provided by the *sobas* of Golungo 1768(?).
"Inventário dos *Sobas, Ilamba e Imbari* do Distrito do Golungo que servem no serviço das Fábricas do Ferro de Novo Belém e Nova Oeiras donde se mandaram anexar todos por ordem do Ilmo. e Exmo. Snr. General e sobre os dízimos que pagavam antes de serem isentos e pelo que regularam na regulação que se fez e o número de filhos capazes que cada um tem e os que dão por mês." *(Continued)*

Soba	"Able offspring"	Workers provided per month	Tithe	Tithe value
Nambua Quisanga Garcia João Domingos	23	6	4.5 *exeques* of corn and 4 chickens	2$800 réis
Kilamba Antonio Felicia João Domingos	24	6	4 *exeques* of corn and 3 chickens	3$200 réis
Quiluangi Quiamuende José Manoel	16	3	4 *exeques* of corn and 4 chickens	3$200 réis
Bango Namboa José Domingos	10	2	4.5 *exeques* of corn and 4 chickens	3$600 réis
Quibila Quiaquisuto João Luiz	6	1	3.5 *exeques* of corn and 4 chickens	2$800 réis
Cabangi Casamba João Gaspar	10	2	3 *exeques* of corn and 3 chickens	2$400 réis
Kilamba Cabrito Catonhi João Agostinho	4	1	2.5 *exeques* of corn and 2 chickens	2$000 réis
Ilhutaucamba Joannes Sebastiam	40	8	5 *exeques*, 1 measure of corn, and 6 chickens	4$200 réis
Casaqui Candala Lourenço Domingos	4	1	3.5 *exeques* of corn and 2 chickens	3$200 réis
Cavungi Camona Lourenço Luiz	4	1	3.5 *exeques* of flour	3$500 réis
Kilamba Lourenço Riavondo Matheus Manoel	3	1	1 *exeque* of corn and 1 chicken	$800 réis
Kilamba Diogo André Miguel Fernandes	10	3	10 *exeques* of flour and 5 chickens	10$000 réis
Cala Canambua Manoel Luiz	10	3	3.5 *exeques* of corn and 3 chickens	2$800 réis
Sala Cabanga Miguel João	9	3	3.5 *exeques* of corn and 4 chickens	2$800 réis
Golapapo Paulo Antonio	6	1	6 *exeques* of corn and 3 chickens	4$800 réis
Kilamba Simão riaganga Pedro Jacinto	40	9	4.5 *exeques* of corn and 2 chickens	3$600 réis
Cabanga Caposse Pedro Alexandre	24	6	5 *exeques* of flour and 3 chickens	5$000 réis
Canzele Caquisuto Paulo João	8	2	2 *exeques* of flour and 4 chickens	2$000 réis

Table 4.1: Workers provided by the *sobas* of Golungo 1768(?).
"Inventário dos *Sobas, Ilamba e Imbari* do Distrito do Golungo que servem no serviço das Fábricas do Ferro de Novo Belém e Nova Oeiras donde se mandaram anexar todos por ordem do Ilmo. e Exmo. Snr. General e sobre os dízimos que pagavam antes de serem isentos e pelo que regularam na regulação que se fez e o número de filhos capazes que cada um tem e os que dão por mês." *(Continued)*

Soba	"Able off-spring"	Workers provided per month	Tithe	Tithe value
Cabanga Cabango Salvador Agostinho	4	1	2 *exeques* of flour and 3 chickens	2$000 réis
Kilamba Quixinga Quiagonga Salvador Manoel	3	1	1 *exeque* of corn and 1 chicken	$800 réis
Quiluangi Quiabanza Sebastião João	6	1	3.5 *exeques* of flour and 2 chickens	3$500 réis
Mucungo aposse Sebastião Francisco	12	1	4.5 *exeques* of corn and 3 chickens	3$600 réis
Gola Cabangi Vicente Bernardo	30	6	3.5 *exeques* of corn and 4 chickens	2$800 réis
Kilamba Quiseele Quiaquitexi Alexandre Salvador	8	2	2 *exeques* of flour and 1 chicken	2$000 réis
Kilamba Alexandre Maria Benedito Lopo	12	3	3 *exeques* of flour	3$000 réis
Quimbar Zombayango Lourenço Dias	4	1	2 *exeques* of flour and 1 chicken	2$000 réis
Kilamba Zumba Quiluangi Simão Pedro	8	2	2 *exeques* of flour and 1 chicken	2$000 réis
Quimbar Mauricio Antonio Sebastiam	3	1	2 *exeques* of flour and 1 chicken	2$000 réis
Quimbar Cossoria Mucutu Sebastiam Francisco	4	1	2 *exeques* of flour and 1 chicken	2$000 réis
Kilamba Zamba Riasungui Sebastiam Miguel	50	21	3.5 *exeques* of flour and 6 chickens	3$500 réis
Musengue azenza Felipe Antonio	300	40	7 *exeques* of flour and 5 chickens	7$000 réis
Kilamba Pedro Ambaxi Lourenço Agostinho	60	27	10.5 *exeques* of corn and 6 chickens	8$400 réis
Musuço Embo João Manoel	40	10	9 *exeques* of corn and 6 chickens	7$200 réis
Quiambata Quiagota Paulo Alexandre	60	21	7 *exeques* of flour and 4 chickens	7$000 réis
Total	3264	480	651.5 *exeques*, 4 piglets, 3 goats, and 193 chickens	

Table 4.2: *Sobas* from Ambaca who provided workers for Novo Belém.
"Declaração dos dois *Sobas* da Jurisdição de Ambaca que estavam anexos ao Novo Belém e passarão para a Fábrica de Nova Oeiras adonde trabalham desde o princípio da dita Fábrica até o presente e são os seguintes."

Soba	Able offspring	Provided for service per month	Paid in tithes	Valued at
Soba Gola Quimbi Antonio da Silva	400	40	300 salt stones	30$000 réis
Soba Cariata Cacavingi	60	20	300 salt stones	30$000 réis
Total	460	60	600 salt stones	60$000 réis

Source: IHGB-PADAB, DL81, 02.19, n.p., possibly elaborated between 1768 and 1770.

Table 4.3: Workers provided by the *sobas* of Golungo, Cambambe, Ambaca, Massangano – 1768.
"Inventário dos *Sobas, Ilamba e Imbari* anexos ao serviço desta Fábrica do Ferro de Nova Oeiras respectivos os dízimos que pagavam antes da isenção que lhes concedeu o Exmo. Snr. e pelo que regulando de próximo, número de Filhos, que cada um em e os que dão por mês para o serviço da mesma Fábrica." São Paulo de Assunção, December 29, 1768.

Soba	Location	"Able offspring"	Workers provided per month	Paid in tithes per month	Total
Soba D. Andre Fernandes Kabuku Kambilu	Fortress of Cambambe	400	50	129 textiles 1 metal plate worth 600 réis	90$650 réis
Soba Gola Guimbi	Ambaca	380	40	300 salt stones worth 100 réis	30$000 réis
Soba Cariata	Ambaca	200	20	300 salt stones worth 100 réis	30$000 réis
Soba Itombe	Massangano	100	20	15 textiles worth 700 réis	10$500 réis
Soba Zambi Aqueta	Massangano	120	25	25 textiles worth 700 réis	17$500 réis
Soba Guengue	Massangano	50	15	12 textiles worth 700 réis	8$400 réis

Table 4.3: Workers provided by the *sobas* of Golungo, Cambambe, Ambaca, Massangano – 1768. "Inventário dos *Sobas, Ilamba e Imbari* anexos ao serviço desta Fábrica do Ferro de Nova Oeiras respectivos os dízimos que pagavam antes da isenção que lhes concedeu o Exmo. Snr. e pelo que regulando de próximo, número de Filhos, que cada um em e os que dão por mês para o serviço da mesma Fábrica." São Paulo de Assunção, December 29, 1768. *(Continued)*

Soba	Location	"Able offspring"	Workers provided per month	Paid in tithes per month	Total
Soba Gola Quiato with his 3 *macotas* and his *sobeta* [Magoxi?]	Massangano	300	40	40 textiles worth 700 réis	28$000 réis
Soba Zumba a Quizunde	Massangano	20	4	9 textiles worth 700 réis	4$900 réis
Soba Cabuto	Massangano	15	3	8 textiles worth 700 réis	5$600 réis
Soba Mussengue Azenza	Golungo	200	30	3 *exeques* of flour worth 10 réis	3$000 réis
Soba Mussuso	Golungo	30	8	3 *exeques* of flour worth 10 réis	3$000 réis
Soba Quiambata	Golungo	20	5	2 *exeques* of flour worth 10 réis	2$000 réis
Kilamba Pedro Ambaxi	Golungo	40	6	2 *exeques* of flour worth 10 réis	2$000 réis
Soba Zamba Riasungui	Golungo	30	5	2 *exeques* of flour worth 10 réis	2$000 réis
Soba Dala Huy	Golungo	8	2	1 *exeques* of flour	1$000 réis
Total		4	1913	273	238$550 réis

Source: Carta de D. Francisco Inocêncio de Sousa Coutinho para Antônio Anselmo Duarte de Siqueira, intendente geral das reais fábricas do ferro. Attachment: Inventário dos *sobas, ilamba* e *imbari*. São Paulo de Assunção, December 29, 1768. IHGB 126, PADAB DVD10,22 DSC00303.

Table 4.4: Local authorities detached from factory service for being remiss. N.d.
This is the inventory of the *sobas* and *ilamba* who stopped sending workers to the factories and therefore had to pay the tithes again, in the amounts shown in réis.
"Mapa dos *sobas* e *ilamba* que se desanexam do serviço da fábrica por serem remissos em aprontarem seus filhos para o serviço dela e devem de hoje em diante, pagar o dízimo pela nova regulação que se fez," n.d.

Sobas, ilamba, and *imbari*	Amount
Soba Quitala quia Zumba Andre Fernandes	12$000 réis
Soba Quitendele quia Cabana Antonio João	2$000 réis
Kilamba Cagondoca Quiluangi Francisco da costa	2$000 réis
Soba Zombo Andala Alexandre Francisco	3$200 réis
Soba Muquixi Aquihuano Antonio Garcia	2$000 réis
Soba Kilamba Quiapangi Antonio Pedro	2$800 réis
Soba Cahondo Caatua Bernardo Pedro	5$000 réis
Soba Cabanga Cacalunga Dom Jorge	2$800 réis
Soba Bango Azongo Diogo Matheus	2$800 réis
Soba Quiluangi Quiadonda Diogo Ventura	3$600 réis
Soba Hanga Bambi Domingos Manoel	2$000 réis
Soba Quiabale quia Caboco Gregório Bernardo	3$500 réis
Captain of the *imbari* Francisco Bernardo	3$500 réis
Soba Gandu Acabuto Gabriel Antonio	2$400 réis
Soba Quibembe quia Matue Gaspar João	2$800 réis
Soba Quiluangi quia Muende José Manoel	3$200 réis
Soba Bangoa Anamboa José Domingos	3$600 réis
Soba Quibela quia Quisuto João Luiz	2$800 réis
Kilamba Cabangi Cassamba João Gaspar	2$400 réis
Kilamba Cabrito Catonhi João Agostinho	2$000 réis
Soba Cassaqui Candala Lourenço Domingos	3$500 réis
Soba Cavungi Camona Lourenço Luis	3$500 réis
Kilamba Lourenço Riavondo Matheus Manoel	$800 réis
Soba Sala Cabanga Miguel João	2$800 réis
Soba Canzele Caquisuto Paulo João	2$800 réis
Soba Cabanga Cabango Salvador Agostinho	2$000 réis
Kilamba Quixinga quia Gonga Salvador Manoel	$800 réis
Soba Quiluangi quia Bunza Sebastiam João	3$500 réis
Soba Mussungo a posse Sebastião Francisco	3$600 réis
Soba Gola Cabangi Vicente Bernardo	2$800 réis
Kilamba Quisegle quia Quitexi Alexandre Salvador	2$000 réis
Kilamba Alexandre Maria Benedito Lopo	3$000 réis
Quimbar Zomba ya Ango Lourenço Dias	2$000 réis
Quimbar Cabombe Manuel Antonio	2$300 réis
Kilamba Zumba Quiluangi Simão Pedro	2$000 réis
Quimbar Maurício Antonio Sebastião	2$000 réis
Quimbar Cosso Riamucutu Sebastião Francisco	2$000 réis

Attachment 4: Workers from the *sobados* sent to the iron factories

Table 4.4: Local authorities detached from factory service for being remiss. N.d.
This is the inventory of the *sobas* and *ilamba* who stopped sending workers to the factories and therefore had to pay the tithes again, in the amounts shown in réis.
"Mapa dos *sobas* e *ilamba* que se desanexam do serviço da fábrica por serem remissos em aprontarem seus filhos para o serviço dela e devem de hoje em diante, pagar o dízimo pela nova regulação que se fez," n.d. *(Continued)*

Sobas, ilamba, and imbari	Amount
Total	107$000 réis

Source: ANTT, Condes de Linhares mç. 46, doc. 11.

Table 4.5: List of authorities who sent workers to the factory in 1773, cited by José Francisco de Pacheco, factory works inspector.

Soba	Jurisdiction	Number of offspring
Kabuku Kambilu	Kambambe	40
Bango Aquitamba	Golungo	60
Ngola Anguimbi	Golungo	40
Gonguembo	Golungo	40
Cariata	Golungo	20
Musengue Anzenza	Golungo	40
Bumba Andal	Golungo	30
Quilombo Quiacatubra	Golungo	30
Muta Acamba	Golungo	10
Total		**310**

Source: Carta de José Francisco Pacheco. Fábrica da Nova Oeiras, March 5, 1773. AHU_CU_001, Cx. 52, D. 28. "A total of 310 workers who must be actively employed, even after the construction work is completed, to maintain and work in the factory while at the same time smelting iron; these *sobas* are exempted from paying tithes, as established in the signs posted in their *banzas* or properties. The signs consist of a stake secured on the ground with a small board nailed on top engraved with the words: 'Does not pay tithes because he provides so many offspring per month to the factory.'"

Table 4.6: *Sobas and ilamba* who served in the factory in 1800.
These are the *sobas* and *ilamba* who worked with the naturalist José Álvares Maciel.
"Relação dos *sobas* e *ilamba* que dão presentemente filhos para este trabalho," March 2, 1800.

Sobas, ilamba, and *imbari*	Offspring
Soba Cabanga	25
Cassange Candala	2
Hango Agueto	1
Ngola Caiuxi	1
Ngola Bumba Capacala	1
Pedro Ambaxi	4
Bango Anzongo	3
Bumba Andondo	2
Ndala Cabange	6
Zamba riafunge	4
Quiluange Quiaebo	4
Quixinga Quia Ngonga	1
Mussungo Aposse	6
Cabanga Caposse	3
Cabanga Cambango	3
Ngola Bumba	4
Caculo Cahogi	2
Bango a Namboa	2
Quiluangi Quiandonda	2
Sala Cabanga	6
Cambuta Cassamba	3
Caculo Camuiza	6
Hoco Acasambi	4
Guito Cacabaca	2
Quiabale	2
Quilombo Quia Catuia	12
Quita quia Macongo	1
Kabuku Cahundo Angombe	1
Captain of the *Imbari*	1
Quizanga Quia Mussunga	1
Catumbo Canguanga	1

Table 4.6: *Sobas* and *ilamba* who served in the factory in 1800.
These are the *sobas* and *ilamba* who worked with the naturalist José Álvares Maciel.
"Relação dos *sobas* e *ilamba* que dão presentemente filhos para este trabalho," March 2, 1800. *(Continued)*

Sobas, *ilamba*, and *imbari*	Offspring
Guanga Angombe	1

Note: *The source states that the total is 134 workers, but the sum above equals 117. "Of these, only 70 actually work, some of the others pretend to be ill, others claim that a relative died and want to be excused to go home (...) Ten are cutting wood, in addition to six carpenters of the land who I have sometimes paid according to the work done and not the days worked, because since there is no one to assist them, they start making benches to sell them for 23 réis and tables that those Negroes buy from them. Ten others work in the quarry with a master to extract stone, they knead clay for bricks and tiles, and the masters are also paid according to the work performed. The others transport the stone and the charcoal."
** This list was sent to José da Silva Costa.
Source: Carta de José Álvares Maciel informando sobre os andamentos de suas experiências. São Paulo de assunção, March 2, 1800. BNP, C 8553, F6362.

Attachment 5: Models and images of the iron factory

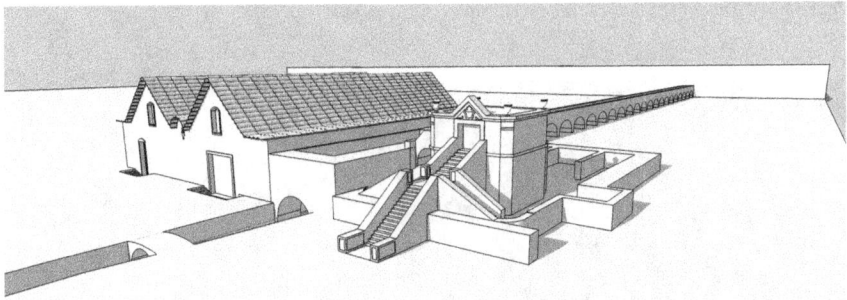

Figure 21: View of the Royal Iron Factory of Nova Oeiras. Model produced from 18th and 19th century documentation and photos (2015). Giovana Gomes Carreira, Katia Sartorelli Verissimo and Stefane Saraceni Kaller formed the team of architects responsible for the models.

Figure 22: View of the Lukala River, by Jacinto de Gouvea Leal (1855).

Figure 23: View of the smelting furnace.

Attachment 5: Models and images of the iron factory — **349**

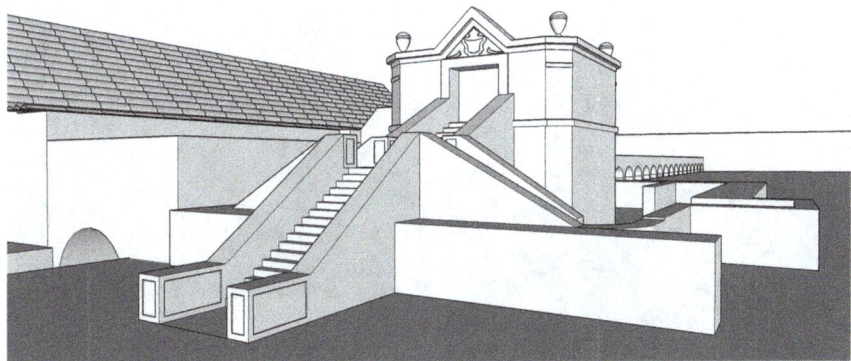

Figure 24: Model of the smelting furnace.

Figure 25: Detail of the smelting furnace.

Figure 26: Aqueduct that conducted river water to the factory (2015).

Figure 27: Detail aqueduct (2015).

Attachment 5: Models and images of the iron factory — **351**

Figure 28: View of the front of the factory and the aqueduct.

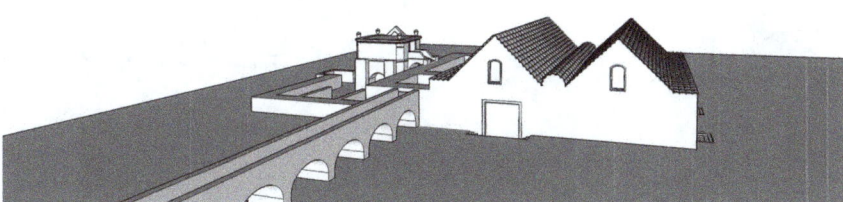

Figure 29: View of the back of the factory and the aqueduct.

Figure 30: View of the back of the factory and the aqueduct (2015).

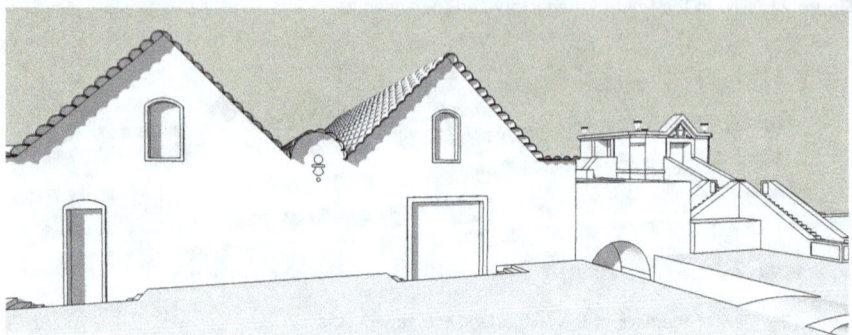

Figure 31: Details of the front of the factory, highlighting the warehouses.

Figure 32: Inside of a warehouse (2015).

Figure 33: View of the factory.

Figure 34: View of the factory and aqueduct.

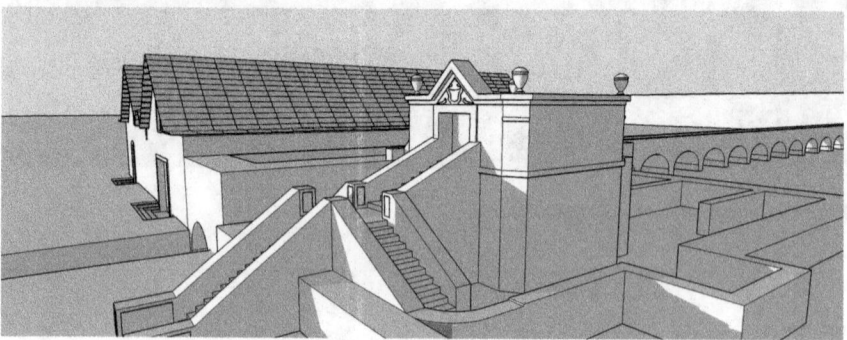

Figure 35: Side view furnace and aqueduct.

Attachment 5: Models and images of the iron factory — 355

Figure 36: Colorful model of the factory and aqueduct.

Figure 37: Colorful factory front model.

Sources and Bibliography

Manuscript Sources

1 Arquivo Histórico Ultramarino (AHU)

Avulsos – Angola (AHU_CU_001): Cx. 35, Doc. 1598; Cx. 35, Doc. 1598; Cx. 41, Doc. 3906; Cx. 43, Doc. 4027; Cx. 45, Doc. 4176; Cx. 45, Doc. 4189; Cx. 46, Doc. 4261; Cx. 45, Doc. 68; Cx. 45, Doc. 94; Cx. 49, doc. 71; Cx. 50, Doc. 64; Cx. 50, Doc. 64; Cx. 51, Doc. 1; Cx. 51, Doc. 8; Cx. 52, Doc. 73; Cx. 51, Doc. 36; Cx. 51, Doc. 39; Cx. 51, Doc. 44; Cx. 51, Doc. 54; Cx. 51, Doc. 58; Cx. 52, Doc. 15; Cx. 52, Doc. 6, 73; Cx. 52, Doc. 15; Cx. 52, Doc. 15; Cx. 52, Doc. 15; Cx. 52, Doc. 15; Cx. 52, Doc. 15; Cx. 52, Doc. 15; Cx. 52, Doc. 15; Cx. 52, Doc. 27; Cx. 52, Doc. 73; Cx. 52, Doc. 73; Cx. 52, Doc. 68,38,47,72; Cx. 52, Doc. 44; Cx. 52, Doc. 48, 64; Cx. 52, Doc. 50; Cx. 52, Doc. 59; Cx. 52, Doc. 69; Cx. 52, Doc. 18; Cx. 53, Doc. 8; Cx. 53, Doc. 12; Cx. 53, Doc. 13; Cx. 53, Doc. 11; Cx. 53, Doc. 17; Cx. 53, Doc. 18; Cx. 53, Doc. 21; Cx. 53, Doc. 23; Cx. 53, Doc. 29; Cx. 53, Doc. 3; Cx. 53, Doc. 40–43 A; Cx. 53, Doc. 49; Cx. 53, Doc. 50; Cx. 53, Doc. 53; Cx. 53, Doc. 62, 63; Cx. 53, Doc. 65, 66, 67; Cx. 53, Doc. 68; Cx. 53, Doc. 72; Cx. 53, Doc. 83; Cx. 53, Doc. 86; Cx. 53, Doc. 44; Cx. 54, Doc. 17; Cx. 54, Doc. 47; Cx. 57, Doc. 45; Cx. 54, Doc. 91; Cx. 54, Doc. 101; Cx. 54, Doc. 113,115; Cx. 54, Doc. 18; Cx. 55, Doc. 6 e 7; Cx. 55, Doc. 21; Cx. 55, Doc. 32; Cx. 55, Doc. 43; Cx. 55, Doc. 52 e 56; Cx. 55, Doc. 61; Cx. 55, Doc. 68; Cx. 55, Doc. 71; Cx. 55, Doc. 76; Cx. 55, Doc. 78; Cx. 55, Doc. 79; Cx. 55, Doc. 83; Cx. 55, Doc. 84; Cx. 55, Doc. 85; Cx. 55, Doc. 88; Cx. 56, Doc. Cx. 56, Doc. 5; Cx. 56, Doc. 14 e 15; Cx. 56, Doc. 32; Cx. 56, Doc. 37; Cx. 56, Doc. 52; Cx. 56, Doc. 54; Cx. 56, Doc. 75; Cx. 56, Doc. 79; Cx. 57, Doc. 1; Cx. 57, Doc. 16; Cx. 57, Doc. 37; Cx. 52, Doc. 28; Cx. 61, Doc. 51; Cx. 61, Doc. 57; Cx. 61, Doc. 107; Cx. 62, Doc. 35; Cx. 62, Doc. 54; Cx. 62, Doc. 57; Cx. 62, Doc. 58; Cx. 65, Doc. 17; Cx. 63, Doc. 34; Cx. 63, Doc. 41; Cx. 64, Doc. 22; Cx. 68, Doc. 46; Cx. 68, Doc. 47; Cx. 71, Doc. 4 B; Cx. 71, Doc. 60; Cx. 68, Doc. 45; Cx. 74, Doc. 23; Cx. 77, Doc. 2; Cx. 75, Doc. 77; Cx. 76, Doc. 16; Cx. 76, Doc. 23; Cx. 77, Doc. 14; Cx. 79, Doc. 66; Cx. 79, Doc. 67; Cx. 80, Doc. 1; Cx. 80. Doc. 66; Cx. 84, Doc. 10; Cx. 86, Doc. 7; Cx. 87, Doc. 71; Cx. 89, Doc. 59; Cx. 90, Doc. 18; Cx. 90, Doc. 50 Cx. 91, Doc. 13; Cx. 92, Doc. 54; Cx. 93, Doc. 38; Cx. 93 A, Doc. 1; Cx. 93 A, Doc. 13; Cx. 93 A, Doc. 14; Cx. 93 A, Doc. 39; Cx. 93, Doc. 18; Cx. 95, Doc. 43; Cx. 96, Doc. 28; Cx. 96, Doc. 73; Cx. 96, Doc. 54; Cx. 97, Doc. 25; Cx. 97, Doc. 32; Cx. 98, Doc. 50; Cx. 100, Doc. 3 e 5; Cx. 100, Doc. 4; Cx. 102, Doc. 26; Cx. 102, Doc. 28; Cx. 102, Doc. 35; Cx. 100, Doc. 4; Cx. 102, Doc. 33; Cx. 99, Doc. 3; Cx. 111, Doc. 28; Cx. 113, Doc. 26; Cx. 117, Doc. 19; Cx. 117, Cx. 117, Doc. 54; Cx. 118, Doc. 17; Cx. 118, Doc. 18; Cx. 118, Doc. 21; Cx. 119, Doc. 1; Cx. 119, Doc. 15; Cx. 119, Doc. 16; Cx. 119, Doc. 17; Cx. 119, Doc. 29; Cx. 119, Doc. 45; Cx. 120, Doc. 1; Cx. 120, Doc. 8; Cx. 120, Doc. 10; Cx. 120, Doc. 37; Cx. 120, Doc. 63; Cx. 120, Doc. 72; Cx. 121 A, Doc. 27; Cx. 121 A, Doc. 35; Cx. 121, Doc. 6; Cx. 121, Doc. 20; Cx. 121, Doc. 34; Cx. 121, Doc. 48; Cx. 121, Doc. 79; Cx. 121 A, Doc. 17.

Note: Research in AHU's *avulso* collection on Angola was conducted from February to June 2015. The *avulsos* have undergone a reorganization, so it is quite likely that the codes for the boxes and documents recorded is already outdated, making it necessary to consult the conversion tables.

Avulsos – Reino (AHU_CU_Reino): Cx. 4 A, Doc. 51; Cx. 8 A, Doc. 35; Cx. 25, Doc. 31; Cx. 19-A, Doc. 32; Cx. 19-A, Doc. 34; Cx. 19-A, Doc. 8; Cx. 27, Doc. 27; Cx. 220, Doc. 61
Codices: 472, 544, 555, 574.
Cartography:
    Blueprint of the Iron Factory in Oeiras, District of Cazengo, 1855. N. 3. Signed by: Jacinto de Gouvea Leal, n. 1, 2 and 3. AHU_CARTm_001,D.1341–42 and AHU_CARTm_001, D.1343
    "Planta das obras que estão feitas na Nova Oeiras para a fábrica do ferro," 1770 c.a. AHU_CARTm_001, D. 272
Iconography:
    "Vista do rio Lukala tirada do sítio de Xiquina na foz do rio Luinha." 1855. Signed by Jacinto de Gouvea Leal. AHU_ICONm_001_I, D.469.
    Alçado da Planta da Fábrica de Fundição de Ferro em Oeiras, Distrito do Cazengo. 1855. Signed by Jacinto de Gouvea Leal. AHU_ICONm_001_I, D.470.
    "Vista da Fábrica de Fundição de Ferro em Oeiras." 1855. Signed by Jacinto de Gouvea Leal. AHU_ICONm_001_I, D.470.
    "Ritare Tambungo ou Pedras de Bungo. Fim da navegação do rio Lukala." 1855. Signed by Jacinto de Gouvea Leal. AHU_ICONm_001_I, D.471.

2 Arquivo Nacional da Torre do Tombo

Coleção Condes de Linhares:
    Livro 50, v. I, caixa 25; Livro 50, v. II, caixa 25.
    Maços: mç. 5, doc. 37; mç. 23, doc. 61; mç. 44, doc. 2; mç. 44, doc. 100; mç. 46, doc. 5; mç. 46, doc. 11; mç. 47, doc. 20; mç. 48, doc. 44; mç. 52, doc. 74; mç. 52, doc. 117; mç. 103, doc. 1.
Arquivo do Arquivo, Avisos e Ordens: maço 4, n. 108.
Manuscritos da Livraria: n. 1116, doc. 58.
Ministério do Reino: Maço 600, caixa 703, doc. 25; doc. 101; doc. 106.
Projeto Reencontro Morgado Mateus: microfilms 12 and 18.
Fundação Biblioteca Nacional (RJ): microfilms MF0027; MF0035.
Projeto Reencontro: microfilm 131.

3 Biblioteca Nacional de Portugal

Reserves: Códices 8742 (Filme 6364), 8743 (F 6377), 8744 (6443).
Manuscripts:
    Coleção Pombalina: PBA 122.
    Avulsos: Caixa 246, n. 22, Caixa 250, n. 71, Caixa 261, n 25.
Noticia e mappa da nova villa de Oeiras no Reino de Angola, e noticia, e planta da casa, e engenhos para a fabrica de ferro do mesmo Reino. – Feita em o anno de 1776. – [1], [4] f., 2 mapas il. desdobr., enc.; 34 cm. Code of the digital version: cod-13424 (available in full at: http://purl.pt/24075).

4 Arquivo Histórico do Tribunal de Contas

Fundo – Erário Régio
Codices 4189, 4191, 4192.
"Notícia da fábrica do ferro de Nova Oeiras do Reino de Angola." São Paulo de Assunção de Luanda, December 15, 1797 [p. 8]. ER, 4196.

5 Arquivo Histórico Militar

Fotografia da antiga fábrica da fundição de ferro das minas da Foz do Alge. PT/AHM/110/F1/PQ/8.
Correspondência de José Bonifácio de Andrade e silva para D. Miguel Pereira Forjaz, Ministro e Secretário de Estado dos Negócios da Guerra, pedindo uma isenção de "aboletamentos" em virtude da sua casa ter sido saqueada pelos franceses, fornecimento de artigos ao corpo militar académico, arsenais, munições e fundições de ferro. PT/AHM/DIV/1/14/177/10.
Nova Teoria fundada em um grande número de experiências por Monsieur Bellidor que ao Ilmo. e Exmo. Snr. Conde de Oeiras do Concelho de Estado de Sua Majestade Fidelíssima, e seu secretário de Estado. PT/AHM/DIV/4/1/07/22.
Deddução dos factos do Bispo de Malaca e do Barão de Moçamedes, Governador de Angola, December 18, 1788, Divisão 2, Secção 2, Caixa 194, n. 1.
Diário de Guerra, na campanha contra o Marquês do Mossulo, em 1790–1791, 2ª Divisão, 2ª secção, Cx. 1, n. 7.
Viagem que eu Sargento-mor dos moradores do Destrito do Dande diz às remotas partes de Cassange, no ano de 1755 thé o seguinte de 1756, 2ª Divisão, 2ª secção, Cx. 1, n. 6.
"Carta Topográfica da Província que fornece Águas, Lenhas, e Serventes à Fabricado Ferro da Nova Oeiras que mandou fazer o Ilmo. Exmo. Senhor D. Francisco Inocêncio de Sousa Coutinho Governador e Capitão General do Reino de Angola, ano 1769". Manuel Antonio Tavares, [Angola], 1769." 1 mapa ms.: papel, color.: 66x117 cm.

6 Academia das Ciências de Lisboa

"Breve e útil Ideia do Comércio, Navegação e Conquista da Ásia e da África, escrita por meu pai. D. Francisco Inocêncio de Sousa Coutinho." 1779. Manuscritos Azuis, 1028.
"Diário ou relação das viagens filosóficas que por Ordem de Sua Majestade Fidelíssima tem feito nas Terras da Jurisdição da Vila de Tete, e em algumas dos Maraves." Manuel Galvão da Silva, 1788. Manuscritos Azuis, 1011.
"Viagens filosóficas ou Dissertação sobre as importantes regras que o Filósofo Naturalista nas suas peregrinações deve principalmente observar." 1779. Manuscritos Vermelhos, 405.

7 Gabinete de Estudos Arqueológicos de Engenharia Militar

Mapas e Cartas geográficas: 10000–1–5 A-93; 1207–2 A-111; 1209–2 A-24 A-111; 4163–1 A-9–13; 4165–1 A-9–13; 4172–1 A-9–13; 3213–2 A-27–39; 3845/III-2–23–32; 3845/IV-2–23–32; 3845/V-2–23–32; 4218–3–41–56.

8 Biblioteca Municipal do Porto

Francisco Inocêncio de Sousa Coutinho, "Memórias do Reino de Angola e suas conquistas, escritas em Lisboa nos anos de 1773 e 1775." Códice 437, documento 10.

Minas do Brasil (1751–1800). Os custos do ferro e a vantagem de explorá-lo nas colônias. 1804. Ms. 464.

"Tratado das queixas endêmicas e fatais nesta conquista." "Direção para prevenir e remediar as doenças destes vastíssimos países de Angola e Benguela sujeitos à grande Monarquia portuguesa e famosíssimo Teatro das Hérvicas ações e incomparável Governo do Ilmo. Exmo. Snr. Dr. Francisco Inocêncio de Sousa Coutinho, seu atual governador e Capitão General." 1770. Ms. 1369.

Maps:

The Western Coast of Africa; from Cape Blanco to Cape Virga; Exhibiting Senegambia proper by T. Jefferys. 1730. BPMP_C-M&A-Pasta25(42)_01.

Mapa Hidro-Geográfico da Costa Ocidental da África. Desenhado pelo Tenente Coronel Luís Candido Cordeiro Pinheiro. 1791. BPMP_C-M&A-Pasta 24(16)_01.

Mapa Hidro-Geográfico da Costa Ocidental da África. Desenhado pelo Tenente Coronel Luís Candido Cordeiro Pinheiro. Cópia posterior. 1791. BPMP_C-M&A-Pasta 24(17).

Mapa Hidro-Geográfico da Costa Ocidental da África. Desenhado pelo Tenente Coronel Luís Candido Cordeiro Pinheiro. Cópia posterior. 1791. BPMP_C-M&A-Pasta 24(17)_a e b.

Mapa Geográfico da Costa Ocidental da África. Desenhado por Justino José de Andrade. 1796. BPMP_C-M&A-Pasta24(18)_01.

9 Instituto de Estudos Brasileiros Universidade de São Paulo

Coleção Alberto Lamego

Livro copiador da correspondência de d. Francisco Inocêncio de Sousa Coutinho, governador de Angola, June 1767 to August 1771. Cod. 82.

Livro copiador da correspondência de d. Francisco Inocêncio de Sousa Coutinho, governador de Angola, January 1768 to July 1769. Cod. 83.

10 Instituto Histórico e Geográfico Brasileiro – Projeto Acervo Digital Angola-Brasil (PADAB)

Letters, petitions, notes of the correspondence of Governador Francisco de Sousa Coutinho: IHGB 126 PADAB DVD09, pasta 18; PADAB DVD10, pasta 20; PADAB DVD10, pasta 22; IHGB DL 76, 02.39; IHGB DL 81, 02.17; IHGB DL 98,02; IHGB DL83, 02.04; IHGB DL 33,02; IHGB DL76, 02.38.14; IHGB DL76,02.35; IHGB DL81, 02.19.

11 Arquivo Histórico de Angola (AHA)

Códice 3 (A – 1–3); Códice 4 (A – 1–4); Códice 6 (A-2–2); Códice 9 (A – 2–5); Códice 85 (A – 18–3); Códice 89 (A – 19–3); Códice 79 (A – 17–2); Códice 80 (A-17–3); Códice 90 (A – 19–4);

Códice 91 (A – 20–1); Códice 92 (A – 20–2); Códice 93 (A- 20–3); Códice 270 (C – 14–3); Códice 271(C – 14–4); Códice 288 (C – 18–1); Códice 322 (D – 2–5); Códice 2512 (8–5–47).

Printed Sources

1 Sociedade de Geografia de Lisboa

Manuscript sources published in periodical series:

Arquivos de Angola (AA): AA, v. I, no. 6, March (1936): 317; AA II (1933–1936): 113; AA III, no. 28 (1937): 321–337; AA III, no. 29 (1937): 361–393; AA III, no. 30–33 (1937): 401–445; AA IV, no. 50 and 51 (1939); AA IV, no. 52–54 (1939).
Boletim da Sociedade de Geografia de Lisboa 56, no. 1 and 2 (1938).
Arquivo das colônias V, no. 30, 148.

2 *Publicação Oficial de documentos interessantes para a história e costumes de São Paulo.* v. 65. São Paulo: Arquivo do Estado de São Paulo, Typographia da Companhia Industrial de São Paulo, 1896

3 Chroniclers, Travelers, and Memorialists

"Extrato da viagem que fez ao sertão de Benguela no ano de 1785 o bacharel Joaquim José da Silva, enviado àquele reino como naturalista e depois secretário do governo." *O Patriota* no. 1 (1813).
"Catálogo dos governadores do Reino de Angola. Com uma prévia notícia dos princípios de sua conquista e do que nela obraram os governadores dignos de memória." In *Coleção de notícias para a História das nações ultramarinas que vivem nos domínios portugueses ou lhe são vizinhas.* Academia Real das Ciências de Lisboa. Lisbon: Tip. da Academia Real das Ciências de Lisboa, 1826.
Livro dos Baculamentos: que os sobas deste Reino de Angola pagam a Sua Majestade (1630). Aida Freudenthal and Selma Pantoja (ed.). Luanda: Ministério da Cultura e Arquivo Nacional de Angola, 2013.
Boletim Oficial do Governo Geral da Província d'Angola. n. 28, July 8, 1866, Luanda, Imprensa do governo.
Azeredo, José Pinto de. *Ensaios sobre algumas enfermidades de Angola* [1799]. Edited by Antonio Braz de Oliveira and Manuel Silvério Marques. Lisbon: Edições Colibri, 2003.
Boletim Oficial do Governo Geral da Província d'Angola, no. 28, July 8, 1866. Luanda, Imprensa do governo.
Bovet, Armand. "A indústria Mineral na Província de Minas Gerais." In *Annaes da Escola de Minas de Ouro Preto: coleções de memórias e de notícias sobre a mineralogia, a geologia e as explorações das minas no Brasil,* 24–40. Ouro Preto: Escola de Minas de Ouro Preto, 1883.

Cadornega, Antonio de Oliveira. *História das Guerras Angolanas* [1680]. Annotated and revised by José Matias Delgado. Lisbon: Agência-geral do Ultramar, 1972.

Cavazzi De Montecúccolo, Giovanni Antonio. *Descrição histórica dos três reinos do Congo, Matamba e Angola*. Translation, notes and index by Father Graciano Maria de Leguzzano. 2 v. Lisbon: Junta de Investigações do Ultramar, 1965.

Eschwege, Wilhelm Ludwig von. *Pluto Brasiliensis*. Translation by Domício de Figueiredo Murta. Belo Horizonte: Itatiaia/ São Paulo: Editora da Universidade de São Paulo, 1979.

Gaeta, Antonio da. *La meravigliosa conversione alla Santa Fede di Cristo della regina Singa e del suo regno di Matamba*. Naples: Francisco de Maria Gioia, 1669.

Gamito, Antonio Candido Pereira. *O Muata Cazembe e os Povos Maraves, Chevas, Muizas, Muenbas, Lundas e outros da África Austral*. Lisbon: Agência Geral das Colônias, 1937.

Gorceix, Henri. "Estudo químico e mineralógico das rochas dos arredores de Ouro Preto." In *Annaes da Escola de Minas de Ouro Preto: coleções de memórias e de notícias sobre a mineralogia, a geologia e as explorações das minas no Brasil*, 5–23. Ouro Preto: Escola de Minas de Ouro Preto, 1883.

Lacerda, Paulo Martins Pinheiro de. "Notícias das regiões e povos de Quisama e do Mussulo – 1798." *Annaes Marítimos e Coloniaes* 4, no. 6 (1846): 119–133. Transcribed by Arlindo Correa. Available at http://arlindo-correia.com/080109.html. Accessed April 30, 2016.

Leitão, Manuel Correa. "Uma viagem a Cassange nos meados do século XVIII [1755]." Edited by Gatão de Sousa Dias. *Boletim da Sociedade de Geografia de Lisboa* 56, no. 1 and 2 (1938).

Lima, José Joaquim Lopes de. *Ensaios sobre as possessões portuguezas na África Ocidental e Oriental, Ásia Ocidental, China e Oceania*. Lisbon: Imprensa Nacional, 1844.

Sarmento, Alfredo de. *Os sertões d'África. Apontamentos de uma viagem*. Lisbon: Francisco Arthur da Silva, 1880.

Silva Correa, Elias Alexandre da. *História de Angola*. 2 v. Lisbon: Clássicos da Expansão Portuguesa no Mundo. Império Africano, 1937.

4 Dictionaries

Assis Júnior, Antonio de. *Dicionário Kimbundu–português, linguístico, botânico, histórico e corográfico. Seguido de um índice alfabético dos nomes próprios*. Luanda: Argente, Santos e Comp. Lda., n.d.

Bluteau, Raphael. *Vocabulário portuguez e latino*, 10 v. Lisbon/ Coimbra: Colégio da Cia. de Jesus, 1712–1728.

Maia, António da Silva. *Dicionário complementar português-kimbundo-kikongo (línguas nativas do centro e norte de Angola)*. n.p.: author's ed., 1964.

Laman, K. *Dictionnaire kikongo-français. Avec une étude phonétique décrivant les dialectes les plus importants de la langue dite kikongo*. Brussels: n.p., 1936.

5 Legislation

Código Filipino, ou, Ordenações e Leis do Reino de Portugal: recompiladas por mandado d'el-Rei D. Filipe I. Facsimile version of the 1821 14th edition by Cândido Mendes de Almeida. Brasilia: Senado Federal, Conselho Editorial, 2004.

Ordenações e leis do reino de Portugal confirmadas e estabelecidas pelo senhor rei D. João IV, novamente impressas e confirmadas com três coleções; a primeira de Leis Extravagantes; a segunda de Decretos e Cartas; e a terceira de Assentos da Casa da Suplicação e relação do Porto, por mandado do muito alto e poderoso rei D. João V nosso Senhor. Livro Quinto. Lisbon: No Mosteiro de S. Vicente de Fora, Câmara Real de Sua Majestade, 1747.

Bibliography

1 Reference Works

Catálogo das publicações da Academia das Ciências de Lisboa. Lisbon: Oficinas Gráficas de Barbosa e Xavier, LDA, 1983.

Dicionário dos mais ilustres Trasmontanos e Alto Durienses. Guimarães: Editora Cidade Berço, 2001. Available at http://www.dodouropress.pt/index.asp?idedicao=66&idseccao=571&id=4137&action=noticia. Accessed April 23, 2016.

Nogueira, Arlinda Rocha, Heloísa Liberalli Bellotto, and Lucy Maffei Hutter. *Catálogo dos manuscritos: Coleção Alberto Lamego.* São Paulo: Instituto de Estudos Brasileiros/USP, 2002.

Parreira, Adriano. *Dicionário glossográfico e toponímico da documentação sobre Angola. Séculos XV-XVIII.* Lisbon: Editorial Stampa, 1990.

Pina, Luís da Câmara (coord.). *A Engenharia Militar no Brasil e no Ultramar Português Antigo e Moderno.* Lisbon: Escolas Profissionais Salesianas, Oficinas de São José, 1960.

2 Books, Articles, Theses, and Dissertations Cited

Adichie, Chimamanda Ngozi. *O perigo de uma história única.* Conference at the event Technology, Entertainment and Design (TED), in 2009. Available at https://youtu.be/qDovHZVdyVQ. Accessed August 19, 2017.

Alfagali, Crislayne Gloss Marão. *Em casa de ferreiro, pior apeiro: as trajetórias dos artesãos do ferro, Vila Rica e Mariana (século XVIII).* Thesis (Master's in History). Campinas: Unicamp, 2012.

Algranti, Eduardo. "Poluição e doenças ocupacionais pulmonares." *Jornal de Pneumologia* 25, no. 5 (1999): 241–244.

Almeida, Suely Creusa Cordeiro de. "O feminino ao leste do Atlântico. Vendeiras, regateiras, peixeiras e quitandeiras: mulheres e trabalho nas ruas de Lisboa e Luanda (séculos XVI-XVIII)." In Roberto Guedes (org.), *África. Brasileiros e portugueses, século XVI-XIX*, 207–227. Rio de Janeiro: Mauad X, 2013.

Alpern, S. B. "Did They or Didn't They Invent It? Iron in Sub-Saharan Africa." *History in Africa* 32 (2005): 41–94.

Amaral, Ilídio do. "Descrição de Luanda oitocentista, vista através de uma planta do ano de 1755." *Garcia de Orta* 9, no. 3 (1961): 409–420.

Amaral, Ilídio do. *O Reino do Congo, os Mbundu (ou Ambundos), o Reino dos "Ngola" (ou de Angola) e a presença portuguesa, de finais do século XV a meados do século XVI.* Lisbon: Instituto de Investigação Científica Tropical, 1996.

Amaral, Ilídio do. *O Rio Cuanza (Angola), da Barra a Kambambe: reconstituição de aspectos geográficos e acontecimentos históricos dos séculos XVI e XVII*. Lisbon: Ministério da Ciência e da tecnologia/ Instituto de Investigação Científica Tropical, 2000.

Amorim, Maria Adelina de Figueiredo Batista. "A Real Fábrica de Ferro de Nova Oeiras. Angola, Séc. XVIII." *CLIO – Revista do Centro de História da Universidade de Lisboa* 9 (2003): 189–216.

Anquandah, J. *Rediscovering Ghana's Past*. Harlow: Longman, 1982.

Aparício, Alexandra, Rosa Cruz Silva, and Honoré Mbunga. *A cidade do Dondo e o seu desenvolvimento econômico: aportes para a sua história*. Luanda: Arquivo Nacional de Angola, Ministério da Cultura, 2015.

Appadurai, Arjun. "Number in the Colonial Imagination." In *Orientalism and the Postcolonial Predicament. Perspectives on South Asia*, by Carol A. Breckenridge and Peter van der Veer, 314–339. Philadelphia: University of Pennsylvania Press, 1993.

Araújo, Renata Malcher de. "A urbanização da Amazónia e do Mato Grosso no século XVIII povoações civis, decorosas e úteis para o bem comum da Coroa e dos povos." *Anais do Museu Paulista: História e Cultura Material* 20, no. 1 (2012): 41–76.

Araújo, Robson Jorge de. *José Álvares Maciel: o químico inconfidente*. Available at https://bib liotecaquimicaufmg2010.files.wordpress.com/2012/02/josc3a9-c3a1lvares-maciel.doc. Accessed February 1, 2013.

Ayo, Rafael Uriarte. "Minería y empresa siderúrgica em la economia vizcaína pré-industrial (s. XVI–XVIII)." *XI Congreso Internacional de la AEHE*. Madrid, 2014.

Azpilicueta, Pilar Erdozáin, and Fernando Mikelarena Peña. "Siderurgia tradicional y comunidad campesina. La gestión de las ferrerías municipales de Lesaka y Etxalar en 1750–1850." *Vasconia*, no. 32 (2002).

Ball, Jeremy. "Relatos de investigação sobre o trabalho forçado em Angola na era colonial." In *Actas do II Encontro Internacional de História de Angola*, 79–110. II vol. Luanda: Arquivo Nacional de Angola; Ministério da Cultura, 2015.

Barros, P. de. "Societal Repercussions of the Rise of Traditional Iron Production: A West African Example." *African Archaeological Review*, no. 6 (1988): 91–115.

Barreto, Mimoso J. "Sousa Coutinho, percursor da abolição da escravatura." *Boletim da Sociedade de Geografia de Lisboa* 102, no. 1–6 (1984): 69–77.

Barreto, Renilda, and Cristiana Bastos (orgs.). *A circulação do conhecimento: medicina, redes e impérios*. Lisbon: ICS, 2011.

Batalha, Fernando. *Povoações históricas de Angola*, Lisbon: Livros Horizonte, 2008.

Bebiano, José Bacellar. *Museu do Dundo: notas sobre a siderurgia dos indígenas de Angola e de outras regiões africanas*. Lisbon: Publicações Culturais da Companhia de Diamantes de Angola, 1960.

Beek, Walter E. A. van. "The Iron Bride: Blacksmith, Iron and Femininity among the Kapsiki/ Higi." In *Metals in Mandara Mountains' Society and Culture* by David Nichols. New Jersey: Africa World Press, 2012.

Beinart, William. "African History and Environmental History." *African Affairs* 99, no. 395 (2000): 269–302.

Beinart, William. "Soil Erosion, Conservationism and Ideas about Development: A Southern African Exploration, 1900–1960." *Journal of Southern African Studies* 11, no. 1 (1984): 52–83.

Bellotto, Heloísa Liberalli. *Autoridade e conflito no Brasil colonial: o governo do morgado de Mateus em São Paulo (1765–1775)*. Second ed. São Paulo: Alameda, 2007.

Benjamin, Walter, "Sobre o conceito de História." In *Obras Escolhidas*. vol. I, São Paulo: Brasiliense, 1985.

Berriz, P. B. Villarreal de. *Máquinas hidráulicas de molinos y herrerías y gobierno de los árboles y montes de Vizcaya.* San Sebastián: Sociedad Guipuzcoana de Ediciones y Publicaciones de la Real Sociedad Vascongadas de Amigos del País y Caja de Ahorros Municipal de San Sebastián, 1973.

Birmingham, David. *A África Central até 1870. Zambézia–Zaire e o Atlântico Sul.* ENDIPU/UEE, n.d.

Birmingham, David. *Trade and Conflict in Angola: The Mbundu and their Neighbours under the influence of the Portuguese, 1483–1790.* Oxford: Clarendon Press, 1966.

Birmingham, David. *Alianças e conflitos. Os primórdios da ocupação estrangeira em Angola (1483–1790).* Luanda: Arquivo Histórico de Angola, 2004.

Bocoum, Hamady (ed.). *The Origins of Iron Metallurgy in Africa. New Light on its Antiquity. West and Central Africa.* Barcelona: Unesco, 2004.

Botha, Ted, David F. Cutler, and Dennis Wm Stevenson. *Anatomia vegetal: uma abordagem aplicada.* Porto Alegre: Artmed, 2011.

Bostoen, Koen, Odjas Ndonda Tshiyay, and Gilles-Maurice de Schryver. "On the Origin of the Royal Kongo Title Ngangula." *Africana Linguistica* 19 (2013).

Brecht, Bertold. "Perguntas de um operário que lê." Translation by Haroldo de Campos. In "Breve Antologia de Brecht." *Tempo Brasileiro*, no. 9–10 (1966).

Bronowski, Jacob. *The Ascent of Man.* London: BBC, 1973.

Brown, Michael F. "On Resisting Resistance." *American Anthropologist, New Series* 98, no. 4 (1996).

Caldeira, Arlindo Manuel. "Formação de uma cidade afro-atlântica: Luanda no século XVII." *Revista TEL, Revista Tempo, Espaço e Linguagem* 5, no. 3 (2014).

Candido, Mariana. "African Freedom Suits and Portuguese Vassal Status: Legal Mechanisms for Fighting Enslavement in Benguela, Angola, 1800–1850." *Slavery and Abolition* 32, no. 3 (2011): 447–458.

Candido, Mariana. "Benguela et l'espace atlantique sud au dix-huitième siècle." *Cahiers des Anneux de la Mémoire* 14 (2011): 223–244.

Candido, Mariana. *Fronteras de esclavización: esclavitud, comercio e identidad en Benguela, 1780–1850.* Mexico City: El Colegio de México Press, 2011.

Candido, Mariana . "Los lazos que unen Centroamérica a un puerto africano del Atlántico Sur. Benguela y la Trata de esclavos, 1617–1800." *Boletín AFEHC*, 55 (2012). Available at http://www.afehc-historia-centroamericana.org/?action=fi_aff&id=3229. Accessed May 3, 2013.

Candido, Mariana. "Dona Aguida Gonçalves marchange à Benguela à la fin du XVIII siècle." *Brésil(s). Sciences humaines et sociales* 1 (2012): 33–54.

Candido, Mariana. "Marriage, Concubinage and Slavery in Benguela, ca. 1750–1850." In *Slavery in Africa and the Caribbean: A History of Enslavement and Identity since the 18th Century*, edited by Nadine Hunt and Olatunji Ojo, 66–84. London/New York: I. B. Tauris, 2012.

Candido, Mariana. *An African Slaving Port and the Atlantic World. Benguela and Its Hinterland.* New York: Cambridge University Press, 2013.

Candido, Mariana. "Jagas e *sobas* no 'Reino de Benguela': vassalagem e criação de novas categorias políticas e sociais no contexto da expansão portuguesa na África durante os séculos XVI e XVII." In *África: histórias conectadas* by Alexandre Vieira Ribeiro, Alexsander Lemos de Almeida Gebera, and Marina Berthet. Niterói: PPGHISTORIA-UFF, 2014.

Candido, Mariana. "Conquest, Occupation, Colonialism and Exclusion: Land Disputes in Angola." In José Vicente Serrão, Bárbara Direito, Eugénia Rodrigues, and Susana Münch Miranda (org.), *Property Rights, Land and Territory in the European Overseas Empires*, 223–235. Lisbon: CEHC, ISCTE-IUL, 2015.

Candido, Mariana, and Eugénia Rodrigues. "African Women's Access and Rights to Property in the Portuguese Empire." *African Economic History* 43 (2015): 1–16.

Carney, Judith A., and Richard Nicholas Rosomoff. *In the Shadow of Slavery: Africa's Botanical Legacy in the Atlantic World.* Berkeley; Los Angeles; London: University of California Press, 2009.

Carvalho, Flávia Maria de. *Sobas e Homens do Rei: relações de poder e escravidão em Angola (séculos XVII e XVIII).* Maceió: EDUFAL, 2015.

Carvalho, Flávia Maria de. "*Sobas* rebeldes de Angola." *Impressões Rebeldes*, UFF – Rio de Janeiro, 2016. Available at http://www.historia.uff.br/impressoesrebeldes/?temas=*sobas*-rebeldes-nos-sertoes-do-ndongo-seculo-xvi. Accessed September 20, 2016.

Carvalho, Romulo de. *A História Natural em Portugal no século XVII.* Lisbon: Minsitério da Educação, 1987.

Chaves, Cláudia Maria das Graças. *Perfeitos negociantes: mercadores das Minas Setecentistas*, São Paulo: Annablume, 1999.

Childs, G. "The Peoples of Angola in the Seventeenth Century According to Cadornega." *The Journal of African History* 1, no. 2 (1960): 271–279.

Childs, S. T., and E. Herbert. "Metallurgy and its Consequences." In *African Archaeology: A Critical Introduction*, edited by A. Stahl, 276–301. London: Blackwell, 2005.

Cline, Walter. *Mining and Metallurgy in Negro Africa.* Menasha: George Banta Publishing Company Agent, 1937.

Clist, B. "Vers une réduction des préjugés et la fonte des antagonismes: Un bilan de l'expansion de la métallurgie du fer en Afrique sudsaharienne." *Journal of African Archaeology* 10, no. 1 (2012): 71–84.

Clover, J., and S. Eriksen. "The Effects of Land Tenure Change on Sustainability: Human Security and Environmental Change in Southern African Savannas." *Environmental Science & Policy* 12 (2009): 53–70.

Coates, Timothy J. *Degredados e órfãs: colonização dirigida pela Coroa no Império português, 1550–1755.* Lisbon: Comissão Nacional para as Comemorações dos Descobrimentos Portugueses, 1998.

Coelho, Marcos Vinícuis Santos Dias. *Maphisa & Sportsmen. A caça e os caçadores no sul de Moçambique sob domínio do colonialismo c. 1895–c. 1930.* Dissertation (PhD). Universidade Estadual de Campinas, 2015.

Coelho, Virgílio. "A data de fundação do 'Reino Ndongo.'" In *Actas do II Seminário Internacional sobre a história de Angola. Construindo o passado angolano: as fontes e a sua interpretação*, 477–544. Lisbon: Comissão Nacional para as comemorações dos descobrimentos portugueses, 2000.

Coelho, Virgílio. *Em busca de Kàbàsà. Uma tentativa de explicação da estrutura político-administrativa do reino de Ndòngò.* Luanda: Kilombelombe, 2010.

Cooper, Frederick. "Work, Class and Empire: An African Historian's Retrospective on E. P. Thompson." *Social History* 20, no. 2 (1995): 235–241.

Cooper, Frederick. *Plantation Slavery on the East Coast of Africa.* Portsmouth: Heinemann, 1997.

Cooper, Frederick. *Colonialism in Question: Theory, Knowledge, History.* Berkeley: University of California Press, 2005.

Cooper, Frederick. "Conflito e conexão: repensando a História Colonial da África." *Anos 90* 15, no. 27 (2008): 21–73.

Cooper, Frederick. *Africa in the World: Capitalism, Empire, Nation-State.* Cambridge, MA: Harvard UP, 2014.

Cooper, Frederick, Thomas C. Holt, and Rebecca Scott. *Além da escravidão: investigações sobre raça, trabalho e cidadania em sociedades pós-emancipação*. Rio de Janeiro: Civilização Brasileira, 2005.
Costa, Célio Juvenal. "O Marquês de Pombal e a Companhia de Jesus." In S. L. Menezes, L. A Pereira, and C. M. M. Mendes (orgs.), *A expansão e consolidação da colonização portuguesa na América*. Maringá: EDUEM, 2011.
Couto, Carlos. *Os Capitães-mores em Angola no Século XVIII*. Luanda: Instituto de Investigação Científica de Luanda, 1972.
Cruz, Ariane Carvalho da. "Cor e hierarquia social no reino de Angola: os casos de Novo Redondo e Massangano (finais do século XVIII)." *XIV Encontro Regional ANPUH-Rio de Janeiro*. 2010. Available at http://www.encontro2010.rj.anpuh.org/resources/anais/8/1276742727_ARQUIVO_ArtigoAnpuhAriane.pdf. Accessed May 27, 2016.
Cruz, Ariane Carvalho da. *Militares e militarização no Reino de Angola: patentes, guerra, comércio e vassalagem (segunda metade do século XVIII)*. Thesis (Master's). Rio de Janeiro: UFRRJ, 2014.
Cruz, Maria das Dores. "Ritos e ofícios. Algumas notas sobre a metalurgia do ferro em Angola." In *Homenagem a J. R. dos Santos Júnior* by M. Conceição Rodrigues. Lisbon: Instituto de Investigação Científica Tropical, v. II, 1993, 131–143.
Cruz, Sara Ventura da. "A construção de uma ideia de território: a cartografia de Angola na segunda metade do século XVIII." *Cabo dos Trabalhos* 12 (2016).
Cuerno, C. Ceballos *Las grandes familias de ferrones de Cantabria en De peñas al mar*. Santander: Sociedad e institucionesen la Cantabria Moderna, 1999.
Curtin, Philip. *Economic Change in Precolonial Africa: Senegambia in the Era of Slave Trade*. 2 v. Madison: University of Wisconsin Press, 1975.
Curto, José C. "Demografia histórica e efeitos do tráfico de escravizados em África: uma análise dos principais estudos quantitativos." *Revista Internacional de Estudos Africanos* 14–15 (1991).
Curto, José C. "A Quantitative Reassessment of the Legal Slave Trade from Luanda, Angola, 1710–1830." *African Economic History* 20 (1992): 1–25.
Curto, José C. "Sources for the Population History of Sub-Saharan Africa: The Case of Angola, 1773–1845." In *Annales de démographie historique*, 320–38. Paris: E.H.E.S.S., 1994.
Curto, José C. "The Legal Portuguese Slave Trade from Benguela, Angola, 1730–1828: A Quantitative Re-appraisal." *Africa (Revista do Centro de Estudos Africanos, Universidade de São Paulo)* 16–17, no. 1 (1993–94): 101–16.
Curto, José C. *Alcohol and Slaves: The Luso-Brazilian Alcohol Commerce at Mpinda, Luanda, and Benguela during the Atlantic Slave Trade c. 1480–1830 and its Impact on the Societies of West Central Africa*. Dissertation (PhD). Los Angeles: University of California, 1996.
Curto, José C., and Raymond R. Gervais. "A dinâmica demográfica de Luanda no contexto do tráfico de escravizados do Atlântico Sul, 1781–1844." *Topoi* 4 (2002): 85–138.
Curto, José C. "Un butin illégitime: razzias d'esclaves et relations luso-africaines dans la région des fleuves Kwanza et Kwango en 1850." In *Déraison, Esclavage, et Droit: les fondements idéologiques et juridiques de la Traite Négrière et de l'Esclavage*, edited by Isabel de Castro Henriques and Louis Sala-Mollins. Paris: Unesco, 2002.
Curto, José C. "A restituição de 10.000 súditos Ndongo 'roubados' na Angola de meados do século XVII: uma análise preliminar." In *Escravizadatura e transformações culturais. África–Brasil–Caraíbas*, edited by Isabel Castro Henriques, 185–208. Lisbon: Editora Vulgata, 2002.
Curto, José C. "The Story of Nbena, 1817–1820: Unlawful Enslavement and the Concept of 'Original Freedom' in Angola." In Paul E. Lovejoy and David V. Trotman (orgs.), *Trans-Atlantic Dimensions of Ethnicity in the African Diaspora*, 44–64. London: Continuum, 2003.

Curto, José C. *Enslaving Spirits: The Portuguese-Brazilian Alcohol Trade at Luanda and Its Hinterland, c. 1550–1830.* Leiden: Brill, 2004.

Curto, José C. "Resistência à escravidão na África: o caso dos escravizados fugitivos recapturados em Angola, 1846–1876." *Afro-Ásia*, no. 33 (2005).

Danieli Neto, Mario. *Escravidão e indústria: um estudo sobre a Fábrica de Ferro São João de Ipanema, Sorocaba (SP), 1765–1895.* Dissertation (PhD). Unicamp: Instituto de Economia, 2006.

Davis, Natalie Zemon. "Las formas de la Historia Social." *História Social*, no. 10 (1991): 177–182.

Dean, Warren. *A ferro e fogo: a história e a devastação da Mata Atlântica Brasileira.* São Paulo: Companhia das Letras, 1996.

Decca, Edgar Salvadori de. *O nascimento das fábricas.* São Paulo: Editora Brasiliense, 1982.

Delgado, Ralph. "O Governo de Sousa Coutinho em Angola." *Stvdia*, no. 6 (1960): 19–56; no. 7 (1961): 49–86, no. 10 (1962).

Delson, Roberta Marx. *Novas Vilas para o Brasil colônia. Planejamento espacial e social no século XVIII.* Brasilia: Edições Alva, 1997.

Dias, Gastão de Sousa. *D. Francisco Inocêncio de Sousa Coutinho. Administração Pombalina em Angola.* Lisbon: Editorial Cosmos, 1936.

Dias, Jill. "Famine and Disease in the History of Angola c. 1830–1930." *The Journal of African History* 22, no. 3 (1981): 349–378.

Dias, Jill. "Changing Patterns on Power in the Luanda Hinterland, The Impact of Trade and Colonization on the Mbundu ca. 1845–1920." *Paudema* 32 (1986): 285–318.

Dias, Jill. "Relações econômicas e de poder no interior de Luanda ca. 1850–1875." *I Reunião Internacional de História de África.* Lisbon: Instituto de Investigação Científica, 1989.

Dias, Jill. "As primeiras penetrações portuguesas em África." In Luis Albuquerque (dir.), *Portugal no Mundo*, 281–298, v. I. Lisbon: Alfa, 1989.

Dias, Jill. *África: Nas vésperas do mundo moderno.* Lisbon: Comissão Nacional para as Comemorações dos Descobrimentos Portugueses, 1992.

Dias, Jill. "O Kabuku Kambilu (c. 1850–1900). Uma identidade política ambígua." In *Actas do Seminário Encontro de povos e culturas em Angola.* Lisboa: Comissão Nacional para as Comemorações dos Descobrimentos Portugueses, 15–52. 1997.

Dias, Maria Odila da Silva. "Aspectos da Ilustração no Brasil." *Revista do Instituto Histórico e Geográfico Brasileiro* 278 (1968).

Diop, Cheikh Anta. *The African Origin of Civilisation: Myth or Reality.* Chicago: Chicago Review Press, 1989.

Domingues, Ângela. *Quando os índios eram vassalos. Colonização e relações de poder no norte do Brasil na segunda metade do século XVIII.* Lisbon: CNCDP, 2000.

Dussel, Enrique. *1492: El encubrimiento del otro.* La Paz: Plural, 1994.

Eggert, Manfred K. H. "Early Iron in West and Central Africa." In *Nok: African sculpture in archaeological context*, edited by Peter Breunig, 50–59. Frankfurt: Africa Magna Verlag, 2014.

Eltis, David. *Economic Growth and the Ending of the Transatlantic Slave Trade.* New York: Oxford University Press, 1987.

Ervedosa, Carlos. *Arqueologia angolana.* Lisbon: Edições 70, 1980.

Evans, Chris. "'Guinea Rods' and 'Voyage Iron': Metals in the Atlantic Slave Trade, their European Origins and African Impacts." *Economic History Society Annual Conference* (2015): 1–15.

Fage, John D. "Slavery and the Slave Trade in the Context of West African History." *The Journal of African History* 10, no. 3 (1969): 393–404.

Fage, John D. *História da África.* Lisbon: Edições 70, 1997.

Faria, Paulo Fernando Moraes de. "Afrocentrismo: entre uma contranarrativa histórica universalista e o relativismo cultural." *Afro-Ásia*, no. 29/30 (2003): 317–343.
Farré, Albert. "Regime de terras e cultivo de algodão em dois contextos coloniais: Uganda e Moçambique (1895–1930)." In José Vicente Serrão, Bárbara Direito, Eugénia Rodrigues, and Susana Münch Miranda (org.), *Property Rights, Land and Territory in the European Overseas Empires*, 245–254. Lisbon: CEHC, ISCTE-IUL, 2015.
Faus, Elena. *La labranza del hierro en el País Vasco*. Bilbao: Servicio Editorial Universidad del País Vasco, 2000.
Feierman, Steven. "African Histories and the Dissolution of World History." In *Africa and the Disciplines: The Contributions of Research in Africa to the Social Sciences and Humanities*, edited by R. H Bates, V. Y. Mudimbe, and J. O'Barr. Chicago: University of Chicago Press, 1993.
Ferreira, Aurora da Fonseca. "A questão das terras na política colonial portuguesa em Angola nos anos de 1880: o caso de um conflito em torno da Kisanga." In Maria Emília Madeira Santos (dir.), *A África e a instalação do sistema colonial – c.1885–c.1930*, 261–272. Lisbon: Centro de Estudos de História e Cartografia Antiga, 2001.
Ferreira, Aurora da Fonseca. *A Kisama em Angola do século XVI ao início do século XX: autonomia, ocupação e resistência*. Luanda, República de Angola: Kilombelombe, 2012.
Ferreira, Roquinaldo. "Escravidão e revoltas de escravizados em Angola (1830–1860)." *Afro-Ásia* 21–22 (1998–1999): 9–44.
Ferreira, Roquinaldo. "Dinâmica do comércio intracolonial: jeribitas, panos asiáticos e guerra no tráfico angolano de escravizados (século XVIII)." In *Antigo Regime nos trópicos. A dinâmica imperial portuguesa (séculos XVI–XVIII)* by João Fragoso, Maria Fernanda Bicalho, and Maria de Fátima Gouvêa, 339–78. Rio de Janeiro: Civilização Brasileira, 2001.
Ferreira, Roquinaldo. "'Ilhas Crioulas': o significado plural da mestiçagem cultural na África Atlântica." *História* 155, no. 2 (2006): 17–41.
Ferreira, Roquinaldo. *Transforming Atlantic Slaving. Trade, Warfare and Territorial Control in Angola, 1650–1800*. Dissertation (PhD). Los Angeles: University of California, 2003.
Ferreira, Roquinaldo. "Slaving and Resistance to Slaving in West Central Africa." In David Eltis and Stanley L. Engerman (orgs.), *The Cambridge World History of Slavery, AD 1420–AD 1804*, v. 3. New York: Cambridge University Press, 2011.
Ferreira, Roquinaldo. *Cross-Cultural Exchange in the Atlantic World. Angola and Brazil during the Era of the Slave Trade*. New York: Cambridge University Press, 2012.
Ferreira, Roquinaldo. "Slave Flights and Runaway Communities in Angola (17th–19th Centuries)." *Anos 90* 21, no. 40 (2014).
Figuerôa, Silvia F. de M., Clarete Paranhos da Silva, and Ermelinda Moutinho Pataca. "Aspectos mineralógicos das 'Viagens Filosóficas' pelo território brasileiro na transição do século XVIII para o século XIX." *História, Ciências, Saúde* 11, no. 3 (2004).
Florence, Afonso Bandeira. "Resistência escravizada em São Paulo: a luta dos escravizados da fábrica de ferro São João Ipanema, 1828–1842." *Afro-Ásia*, no. 18 (1996): 7–32.
Fonseca, Cláudia Damasceno da. *Des Terres aux Villes de l'or. Pouvoir et territoires urbains au Minas Gerais (Brésil, XVIIIe siécle)*. Paris: Fundação Calouste Gulbenkian, 2003.
Fragoso, João, and Nuno Gonçalo Monteiro (orgs.). *Um reino e suas repúblicas no atlântico. Comunicações políticas entre Portugal, Brasil e Angola nos séculos XVII e XVIII*. Rio de Janeiro: Civilização Brasileira, 2017.
Freudenthal, Aida. "Os Quilombos de Angola no Século XIX: A Recusa da Escravidão." *Estudos Afro-Asiáticos*, no. 32, 1997.

Freudenthal, Aida. *Arimos e fazendas: a transição agrária em Angola, 1850–1880*. Luanda: Chá de Caxinde, 2005.

Freudenthal, Aida. "Real Fábrica do Ferro." In *HPIP Website*, Heritage of Portuguese Influence/Patrimônio de Influência Portuguesa. Available at http://www.hpip.org/def/pt/Homepage/Obra?a=2061.

Fromont, Cecile. *The Art of Conversion: Christian Visual Culture in the Kingdom of Kongo*. University of North Carolina Press, 2014.

Fuentes, A. "Dom Francisco Inocêncio de Souza Coutinho. Esboço de uma obra que se perdeu." *Boletim do Instituto de Angola*, no. 4 (1954): 35–40; Marques do Funchal, *O Conde Linhares*. Lisbon: n.p., 1950.

Furtado, Júnia Ferreira. *O livro da capa verde: o regimento diamantino de 1771 e a vida no Distrito Diamantino no período da Real Extração*. São Paulo: Annablume, 1996.

Gaspar, Jorge (dir.), *Monografia do concelho de Figueiró dos Vinhos*. Figueiró dos Vinhos: Câmara Municipal de Figueiró dos Vinhos, 2004.

Geffray, Christian. *Nem pai, nem mãe. Crítica do parentesco: o caso Macua*. Lisbon: Caminho, 2000.

Ginzburg, Carlo. "O inquisidor como antropólogo." *Revista Brasileira de História* 1, no. 21, 1991, 9–20.

Goikoetxea, Eneko Pérez. *Minería del hierro en los montes de Triano y Galdames*. Bilbao: E. Bilbao, 2003.

Gomes, Flávio dos Santos, and Luís Cláudio P. Symanski. "Iron Cosmology, Slavery, and Social Control: The Materiality of Rebellion in the Coffee Plantations of the Paraiba Valley, Southeastern Brazil." *Journal of African Diaspora Archaeology and Heritage* 5, no. 2 (2016): 174–197.

Gomes, Heitor. *Monografia do concelho de Figueiró dos Vinhos*. Figueiró dos Vinhos (Portugal): Câmara Municipal, 2004.

Goucher, Candice L. "Iron Is Iron 'Til It Is Rust: Trade and Ecology in the Decline of West African Iron-Smelting." *The Journal of African History* 22, no. 2 (1981).

Goucher, Candice L. "African Metallurgy in the Atlantic World." In *Archaeology of Atlantic Africa and the African Diaspora*, edited by Akinwumi Ogundiran and Toyin Falola. Bloomington: Indiana University Press, 2007.

Gouvêa, Maria de Fátima. "Poder político e administração na formação do complexo atlântico português (1645–1808)." In Maria Fernando Bicalho, João Fragoso, and Maria de Fátima Gouvêa (orgs.), *O Antigo Regime nos trópicos: A dinâmica Imperial Portuguesa (séculos XVI–XVIII)*, 285–315. Rio de Janeiro: Civilização Brasileira, 2001.

Gouveia, Henrique Coutinho. "Aspectos das relações entre Portugal e Angola no Domínio Museológico – As viagens de exploração científica setecentistas." In *III Encontro de Museus de países e comunidades de língua portuguesa*, 77–118. Bissau, 1991.

Graden, Dale T., and Adriano Parreira. "África em debate: uma herança identitária – o trabalho forçado." *Africana Studia*, no. 5 (2010).

Guedes, Roberto. "Branco africano: notas de pesquisa sobre escravidão tráfico de cativos e qualidades de cor no Reino de Angola (Ambaca e Novo Redondo, finais do século XVIII)." In Roberto Guedes (org.), *Dinâmica Imperial no Antigo Regime Português: escravidão, governos, fronteiras, poderes, legados. Séculos XVII–XIX*. Rio de Janeiro: Mauad X, 2011.

Guedes, Roberto. "Casas & Sanzalas (Benguela, 1797–1798)." *Veredas da História* VII (2014).

Hampatê Bá, Amadou. "A tradição viva." In Joseph Ki-Zerbo (org.), *História Geral da África I. Metodologia e pré-história da África*. São Paulo: Ed. Ática/UNESCO, 1980.

Hansen, João Adolfo. *A sátira e o engenho: Gregório de Matos e a Bahia do século XVII*. Second edition. São Paulo: Ateliê Editorial; Campinas: Editora da Unicamp, 2004.

Hansen, João Adolfo. "Letras coloniais e historiografia literária." *Matraga* 18 (2006).

Hanson, Holly. *Landed Obligation: The Practice of Power in Buganda*. Portsmouth: Heinemann, 2003.

Harkot-De-La-Taille, Elizabeth, and Adriano Rodrigues dos Santos. "Sobre Escravos e Escravizados: Percursos Discursivos da Conquista da Liberdade." In *III Simpósio Nacional Discurso, Identidade e Sociedade (III SIDIS)*, 8–9. Campinas: Unicamp, IEL, 2012.

Hartmann, Tekla. "Perfil de um naturalista." In *Memória da Amazônia. Alexandre Rodrigues Ferreira e a Viagem Filosófica*. Coimbra: Museu e Laboratório Antropológico/Universidade de Coimbra, 1991.

Heintze, Beatrix. "Luso-African Feudalism in Angola? The Vassal Treaties of the 16th to the 18th Century." Separata da *Revista Portuguesa de História* 18 (1980).

Heintze, Beatrix. *Fontes para a História de Angola do século XVII. Memórias, relações e outros manuscritos da coletânea documental de Fernão Sousa (1622–1635)*. Stuttgart: Steiner-Verlag-Wiesbaden-Gmbh, 1985.

Heintze, Beatrix. "Written Sources, Oral Traditions and Oral Traditions as Written Sources: The Steep and Thorny Way to Early Angolan History." *Paideuma* 33 (1987): 263–287.

Heintze, Beatrix. "A lusofonia no interior da África Central na era pré-colonial. Um contributo para a sua história e compreensão na atualidade." *Cadernos de Estudos Africanos*, no. 7 and 8 (2005).

Heintze, Beatrix. *Angola nos séculos XVI e XVII. Estudos sobre Fontes, Métodos e História*. Luanda: Kilombelombe, 2007.

Heintze, Beatrix, and Achim von Oppen, eds. *Angola em Movimento. Vias de Transporte, Comunicação e História*. Frankfurt am Main: Lembeck, 2008.

Henriques, Isabel de Castro. *Percursos da modernidade em Angola. Dinâmicas e transformações sociais no século XIX*. Lisbon: Instituto de Investigação Científica Tropical; Instituto da Cooperação Portuguesa, 1997.

Henriques, Isabel de Castro. "A materialidade do simbólico: marcadores territoriais, marcadores identitários angolanos (1880–1950)." *Textos de História* 12, no. 1/2 (2004).

Herbert, Eugenia W. *Iron, Gender and Power. Rituals of Transformation in African Societies*, Bloomington and Indianapolis: Indiana University Press, 1993.

Herbert, Eugenia W. "African Metallurgy: The Historian's Dilemma." *Mediterranean Archaeology* 14 (1999): 41–48.

Herzog, Tamar. *Frontiers of Possession: Spain and Portugal in Europe and the Americas*. Cambridge, Massachusetts: Harvard University Press, 2015.

Hespanha, Antonio Manuel, and Catarina Madeira Santos. "Os poderes num império oceânico." In José Mattoso (dir.), *O Antigo Regime (1620–1807)*. Vol. IV de História de Portugal, 395–413. Lisbon: C. Leitores, 1993.

Heywood, Linda, and John Thornton. *Central Africans, Atlantic Creoles, and the Foundation of the Americas, 1585–1660*. New York: Cambridge University Press, 2007.

Heywood, Linda. "Slavery and its Transformation in the Kingdom of Kongo: 1491–1800." *The Journal of African History* 50, no. 1 (2009): 1–22.

Heywood, Linda. "Descoberta de memória, construção de histórias: o rei do Kongo e a rainha Njinga em Angola e no Brasil." In *Actas do II Encontro Internacional de História de Angola*. Luanda: Arquivo Histórico Nacional de Angola/ Ministério da Cultura, 2014.

Heywood, Linda. *Njinga of Angola. Africa's Warrior Queen*. Cambridge: Harvard University Press, 2017.

História de Angola. Centro de Estudos Angolanos. Second ed. Porto: Edições Afrontamento, 1975.

Hobsbawm, Eric, and Terence Ranger (orgs.). *A invenção das tradições*. Rio de Janeiro: Paz e Terra, 1984.

Hobsbawm, Eric. "A história de baixo para cima." In *Sobre história: ensaios*, 215–232. São Paulo: Companhia das Letras, 1998.

Hunt, Nancy Rose. "The Affective, the Intellectual, and Gender History." *Journal of African History* 55, no. 3 (2014): 331–345.

Iles, Louise. "The Use of Plants in Iron Production." *Archaeology of African Plant Use* 61 (2013).

Inikori, Joseph. *Forced Migrations: The Impact of the Export Slave Trade on African Societies*. London: Holmes and Meier, 1982.

Ito, Alec Ichiro. *Uma "tão pesada cruz": o governo da Angola portuguesa nos séculos XVI e XVII na perspectiva de Fernão de Sousa (1624–1630)*. Thesis (Master's). USP, 2016.

Kantor, Iris. "Cartografia e diplomacia: usos geopolíticos da informação toponímica (1750–1850)." *Anais do Museu Paulista* 17, no. 2 (2009).

Ki-Zerbo, Joseph. "Introdução." In *História geral da África I: metodologia e pré-história da África*. Second revised ed. Brasilia: UNESCO, 2010.

Klein, Herbert. "The Portuguese Slave Trade: From Angola in the Eighteenth Century." *Journal of Economic History* 32 (1972): 894–918.

Klein, Herbert, and Francisco Vidal Luna. *Evolução da sociedade e economia escravista de São Paulo, de 1750 e 1850*. Translated by Laura Teixeira Motta. São Paulo: EDUSP, 2005.

Kreike, Emmanuel. *Deforestation and Reforestation in Namibia: The Global Consequences of Local Contradictions*. Leiden: Brill, 2010.

Kriger, Colleen E. *Pride of Men: Ironworking in 19th Century, West Central Africa*. Portsmouth: N. H: Heinemann, 1999.

Kopytoff, Igor, and Suzanne Miers, eds. *Slavery in Africa: Historical and Anthropological Perspectives*. Madison: The University of Wisconsin Press, 1977.

Lara, Silvia Hunold. *Campos da Violência. Escravizados e senhores na Capitania do Rio de Janeiro (1750–1808)*. Rio de Janeiro: Paz e Terra, 1988.

Lara, Silvia Hunold. *Fragmentos setecentistas, escravidão, cultura e poder na América portuguesa*. São Paulo: Companhia das Letras, 2007.

Lara, Silvia Hunold. "Depois da Batalha de Pungo Andongo (1671): o destino atlântico dos príncipes do Ndongo." *Revista de História* (USP), no. 175 (2016): 205–225.

León, Joaquín de Almunia y de. *Antigua industria del hierro en Vizcaya*. Bilbao: Caja de Ahorros Vizcaina, 1975.

Lopes, Andréa Rollof. *Alexandre Rodrigues Ferreira e a Viagem Filosófica: economia e ciência na Amazônia Colonial*. Thesis (Master's). Curitiba: Graduate Program in History, UFPR, 1998.

Lopes, Pablo Quintana. *La labranza y transformación artesanal del hierro en Taramundi y Los Oscos. Siglos XVI–XVIII. Aportación a su conocimiento*. Taramundi: Asociación "Os Castros," 2005.

Lovejoy, Paul (org.). *Identity in the Shadow of Slavery*. London: Cassell Academic, 2000.

Lovejoy, Paul. *A escravidão na África. Uma história de suas transformações*. Rio de Janeiro: Civilização Brasileira, 2002.

Luís, João Baptista Gime. *O comércio do marfim e o poder nos territórios do Kongo, Kakongo, Ngoyo e Loango: 1796–1825*. Thesis (Master's). Universidade de Lisboa, 2016.

M'Bokolo, Elikia. *África negra. História e Civilizações até ao século XVIII*. Second ed. Lisbon: Edições Colibri, 2012.

Maar, Juergen Heinrich. "Aspectos históricos do ensino superior de química." *Scientiæ Studia* 2, no. 1 (2004): 33–84.

Maar, Juergen Heinrich, and Thurneisser Glauber, et al. "Tecnologia química e química fina, conceitos não tão novos assim." *Química Nova* 23, no. 5 (2000).
MacGaffey, Wyatt. "Dialogues of the Deaf: Europeans on the Atlantic Coast of Africa." In *Implicit Understandings. Observing, Reporting, and Reflecting on the Encounters between Europeans and Other Peoples in the Early Modern Era* by Stuart Schwartz. Cambridge: Cambridge University Press, 1994.
MacGaffey, Wyatt. *Religion and Society in Central Africa: The Bakongo of Lower Zaire*. Chicago and London: University of Chicago Press, 1986.
Machado, Mônica Tovo Soares. *Angola No Período Pombalino: O Governo De Dom Francisco Inocêncio De Sousa Coutinho – 1764 – 1772*. Thesis (Master's). Faculdade de Filosofia, Letras e Ciências Humanas da Universidade de São Paulo, 1998.
Manning, Patrick. "The Enslavement of Africans: A Demographic Model." *Canadian Journal of African Studies* 15 (1981).
Manning, Patrick. "Contours of Slavery and Social Change in Africa." *The American Historical Review* 88, no. 4 (1983): 835–857.
Marcílio, Maria Luíza. "A população paulistana ao longo dos 450 anos da Cidade." In Paula Porta (org.), *História da Cidade de São Paulo. A cidade colonial (1554-1822)*. São Paulo: Paz e Terra, 2004.
Marcussi, Alexandre Almeida. *Cativeiro e cura. Experiências religiosas da escravidão atlântica nos calundus de Luiza Pinta, séculos XVII-XVIII*. Dissertation (PhD). Universidade de São Paulo, 2015.
Maret, Pierre de. "The Smith's Myth and the Origin of Leadership in Central Africa." In *African Iron Working*, edited by P. Shinnie and R. Haaland, 73–87. Bergen: Norwegian University Press, 1985.
Margarido, Alfredo. "Les Porteurs: forme de domination et agents de changement en Angola (XVIIe-XIXe siècles)." In *Revue française d'histoire d'outre-mer*, tome 65, no. 240 (1978): 377–400.
Martim, Luísa F. Guerreiro. *Francisco José de Lacerda e Almeida, travessias científicas e povos da África Central*. Thesis (Master's). Faculdade de Letras da Universidade de Lisboa – Departamento de História, 1996.
Mata, Inocência, and Laura C. Padilha. *A mulher em África: vozes de uma margem sempre presente*. Lisbon: Edições Colibri, 2007.
Mattos, Regiane Augusto de. *De cassange, mina benguela a gentio da Guiné. Grupos étnicos e formação de identidade africanas na cidade de São Paulo (1800 – 1850)*. Thesis (Master's). História Social, Universidade de São Paulo, 2006.
Maxwell, Kenneth. *Marquês de Pombal: paradoxo do Iluminismo*. Translated by Antonio de Pádua Danesi. Rio de Janeiro: Paz e Terra, 1996.
Mbembe, Achille. *A crítica da razão negra*. Translated by Marta Lança. Lisbon: Antígona, 2014.
Mbodj, Mohamed. "Le point de vue de Mohamed Mbodj." *Politique Africaine*, no. 79 (2000).
Mbunga, Honoré. "A problemática da periodização da História de Angola: o período colonial." In *Actas do II Encontro Internacional de História de Angola*. Luanda: Arquivo Histórico Nacional de Angola/ Ministério da Cultura, 2014.
Mendonça, Marcos Carneiro de Mendonça. *O Intendente Câmara*. São Paulo: Companhia Editora Nacional, 1958.
Meneses, José Newton Coelho. "Apresentação." *Varia História* 27, no. 46 (2001): 397–399.
Meneses, José Newton Coelho. *Artes Fabris e Serviços Banais: ofícios mecânicos e as Câmaras no final do Antigo Regime. Minas Gerais e Lisboa (1750 – 1808)*. Dissertation (PhD). Niterói: Universidade Federal Fluminense, 2003.

Menon, Og Natal. *A Real Fábrica de Ferro de São João do Ipanema e seu mundo (1811–1835)*. Thesis (Master's). São Paulo: PUC, 1992.

Menz, Maximiliano M. "Angola, o Império e o Atlântico." In *Anais do XI Congresso Brasileiro de História Econômica*. 2015.

Mertens, J. *Les chefs couronnés chez les Ba Kongo orientaux: étude de régime successoral*. Brussels: G. van Campenhout, 1942.

Mhute, Josiah Rungano. "Downcast: Mining, Men, and the Camera in Colonial Zimbabwe, 1890–1930." *Kronos*, no. 27 (2001): 114–132.

Millan, Manuel Cordera, and Pedro Arroyo Valiente. *Ferrerías en Cantabria. Manufacturas de ayer, patrimonio de hoy*. Santander: Asociación de Amigos de la Ferrería de Cades, 1993.

Miller, Joseph. "The Imbangala and the Chronology of Early Central African History." *The Journal of African History* 13, no. 4 (1972): 549–574.

Miller, Joseph. "Njinga of Matamba in a New Perspective." *The Journal of African History* 13, no. 2 (1975): 201–216.

Miller, Joseph. "The Significance of Drought, Disease and Famine in the Agriculturally Marginal Zones of West Central Africa." *The Journal of African History* 23, no. 1 (1982): 17–61.

Miller, Joseph. *Way of Death: Merchant Capitalism and the Angolan Slave Trade, 1730–1830*. Wisconsin: University of Wisconsin Press, 1988.

Miller, Joseph. *Poder político e parentesco: os antigos estados Mbundu em Angola*. Luanda: Arquivo Histórico Nacional, 1995.

Miller, Joseph, and John K. Thornton. "A crónica como fonte, história e hagiografia; o Catálogo dos Governadores de Angola." *Revista Internacional de Estudos Africanos*, no. 12–13 (1990): 9–55.

Monteiro, Joaquim Rebelo Vaz. *Uma viagem redonda da carreira da Índia (1597–1598)*. Coimbra: Gráfica de Coimbra, 1985.

Monteiro, John Manuel. *Negros da Terra: índios e bandeirantes nas origens de São Paulo*. São Paulo: Companhia das Letras, 1994.

Mota, Maria Sarita. "Apropriação econômica da natureza em uma fronteira do império atlântico português: o Rio de Janeiro (século XVII)." In José Vicente Serrão, Bárbara Direito, Eugénia Rodrigues, and Susana Münch Miranda (orgs.), *Property Rights, Land and Territory in the European Overseas Empires*, 43–53. Lisbon: CEHC, ISCTE-IUL, 2015.

Motta, Márcia M. M. *Direito à Terra no Brasil. A gestação do conflito (1795–1824)*. São Paulo: Alameda, 2009.

Neves, Maria Teresa Amado. "D. Francisco Inocêncio de Sousa Coutinho: Aspecto moral da sua acção em Angola." In *I Congresso de História da Expansão Portuguesa no Mundo*. Lisboa: Sociedade Nacional de Tipografia, 1938.

Nogueira, Jofre Amaral. *Angola na época pombalina. O governo de Sousa Coutinho*. Lisbon: n.p., 1960.

Novais, Fernando A. *Portugal e Brasil na crise do Antigo Sistema Colonial (1777–1808)*. São Paulo: HUCITEC, 1986.

Okafor, Edwin Eme. "Twenty-five Centuries of Bloomery Iron Smelting in Nigeria." In *The Origins of Iron Metallurgy in Africa. New Light on its Antiquity: West and Central Africa*, edited by Hamady Bocoum. Paris: UNESCO, 2004.

Oliveira, Ingrid de. *Textos militares e mercês numa Angola que se pretendia reformada: Um estudo de caso dos autores Elias Alexandre da Silva Correa e Paulo Martins Pinheiro de Lacerda*. Dissertation (PhD in History). Niterói: Instituto de Ciências Humanas e Filosofia, Universidade Federal Fluminense, 2015.

Oliveira, Vanessa. "Gender, Foodstuff Production and Trade in Late-Eighteenth Century Luanda." *African Economic History* 43 (2015): 57–61.

Oliveira, Vanessa. "Mulher e comércio: a participação feminina nas redes comerciais em Luanda (século XIX)." In Selma Pantoja, Edvaldo A. Bergamo, and Ana Claudia da Silva (orgs.), *Angola e as angolanas. Memória, sociedade e cultura*, 134–152. São Paulo: Intermeios, 2016.

Ortiz, Fernando. *Contrapunteo Cubano* [1947, 1963]. Caracas: Biblioteca Ayacucho, 1978.

Palmerim, Manuela. "Identidade e heróis civilizadores: 'l'Empirelunda' e os aruwund do Congo." In *1ª Jornada de Antropologia intitulada "Modernidades, etnicidades, identidades*. Universidade do Minho, 1998. Available at http://repositorium.sdum.uminho.pt/bitstream/1822/5319/3/Identidade%20e%20heróis.pdf. Accessed February 8, 2016.

Pantoja, Selma. *Njinga Mbandi: mulher, guerra e escravidão*. Brasilia: Editora Thesaurus, 2000.

Pantoja, Selma. "As fontes escritas do século XVII e o estudo da representação do feminino em Luanda." In *Construindo o passado angolano: as fontes e a sua interpretação. Actas do II Seminário internacional sobre história de Angola*, 583–596. Lisbon: Comissão Nacional para as comemorações dos Descobrimentos Portugueses, 2000.

Pantoja, Selma. "Donas de arimos: um negócio feminino no abastecimento de gênero alimentício em Luanda nos séculos XVIII e XIX." In *Entre Áfricas e Brasis*. Brasília: Paralelo 15, 2001.

Pantoja, Selma. "Inquisição, degredo e mestiçagem em Angola no século XVII." *Revista Lusófona de Ciência das Religiões* 3, no. 5/6 (2004): 117–36.

Pantoja, Selma. "Gênero e comércio: as traficantes de escravizados na região de Angola." *Travessias*, no. 4–5 (2004): 79–97.

Pantoja, Selma. "Women's Work in the Fairs and Markets of Luanda." In *Women in the Portuguese Colonial Empire: The Theater of Shadows*, edited by Clara Sarmento, 81–93. Newcastle-upon-Tyne: Cambridge Scholars Publishing, 2008.

Parreira, Adriano. *Economia e sociedade em Angola na época da Rainha Jinga (século XVII)*. Lisbon: Editorial Estampa, 1997.

Pataca, Ermelinda Moutinho. *Terra, Água e ar nas viagens científicas portuguesas (1755–1808)*. Dissertation (PhD in Geoscience). Campinas: Unicamp, 2006.

Pena, Eduardo Spiller. "Notas sobre a historiografia da arte do ferro nas Áfricas Central e Ocidental (séculos XVIII e XIX)." In *XVII Encontro Regional de História – O Lugar da História*, Campinas: 2004.

Pereira, Magnus Roberto de Mello. "Um jovem naturalista num ninho de cobras: a trajetória de João da Silva Feijó em Cabo Verde, em finais do século XVIII." *História: questões e debates* 19, no. 36 (2003): 29–60.

Pereira, Magnus Roberto de Mello. "Rede de mercês e carreira: o 'desterro d'Angola' de um militar luso-brasileira (1782–1789)." *História: Questões & Debates*, no. 45 (2006): 97–127.

Pereira, Marcio Mota. "As luzes se ascendem em África: viagens filosóficas de um naturalista luso-brasileiro em Angola (1783–1808)." *E-hum* 8, no. 2 (2015).

Perrone-Moisés, Beatriz. "Índios livres e índios escravizados: os princípios da legislação indigenista do período colonial (século XVI a XVIII)." In *História dos Índios no Brasil* by Manuela Carneiro da Cunha. São Paulo: Companhia das Letras, 1992.

Pesavento, Fábio. "Para além do império ultramarino português: as redes trans, extraimperiais, no século XVIII." In Roberto Guedes (org.), *Dinâmica Imperial no Antigo Regime Português. Escravidão, governos, fronteiras, poderes e legados: séc. XVII–XIX*. Rio de Janeiro: Mauad X, 2011.

Portela, Miguel Ângelo. "A superintendência dos tenentes de artilharia Francisco Dufour e Pedro Dufour nas Reais Ferrarias da Foz de Alge e Machuca." In *Anais do XXI Colóquio de História Militar.* Lisbon, 2012.

Pratt, Mary Louise. *Imperial Eyes: Travel Writing and Transculturation.* Nova York: Routledge, 2008.

Raminelli, Ronald. *Viagens Ultramarinas: Monarcas, vassalos e governo a distância.* São Paulo: Alameda, 2008.

Redinha, José. *Campanha etnográfica ao Tchiboco (Alto–Tchicapa),* 2 v. Lisbon: Companhia de Diamantes de Angola; Museu do Dundo, 1953–1955.

Reefe, Thomas Q. *The Rainbow and the Kings: A History of the Luba Empire to 1891.* Berkeley: University of California Press, 1981.

Rego, Antonio da Silva. "A Academia Portuguesa da História e o II centenário da Fábrica de Ferro em Nova Oeiras, Angola." In *Coletânea de Estudos em honra do prof. Dr. Damião Peres,* 385–398. Lisbon: Academia Portuguesa da História, 1974.

Reid, Richard. "Past and Presentism: The 'Precolonial' and the Foreshortening of African History." *Journal of African History* 52 (2011): 135–155.

Ribeiro, Mariana, and Alice Pereira Schatzer. *Entre a fábrica e a senzala: um estudo sobre o cotidiano dos africanos livres na Real Fábrica de Ferro São João do Ipanema – Sorocaba – SP (1840–1870).* Thesis (Master's). Unesp, Faculdade de Ciências e Letras de Assis, 2014.

Ricupero, Rodrigo. "Governo-geral e a formação da elite colonial baiana no século XVI." In Maria Fernanda Bicalho and Vera Lúcia Amaral Ferlini (orgs.), *Modos de Governar. Ideias e práticas políticas no Império Português, séculos XVI a XIX.* São Paulo: Alameda, 2005.

Ringquist, John. "Kongo Iron: Symbolic Power, Superior Technology and Slave Wisdom." *African Diaspora Archaeology Newsletter,* v. 11, issue 3, article 3 (n.d.). Available at http://scholarworks.umass.edu/adan/vol11/iss3/3/. Accessed August 4, 2016.

Rodney, Walter. *History of the Upper Guinea Coast, 1545–1800.* New York: Oxford University Press, 1970.

Rodney, Walter. *How Europe Underdeveloped Africa.* London: Bogle–L'Ouverture Publications, 1972.

Rodrigues, Eugénia. *Portugueses e Africanos nos rios de Sena. Os prazos da Coroa em Moçambique nos séculos XVII e XVIII.* Lisbon: Imprensa Nacional-Casa da Moeda, 2013.

Rodrigues, Eugénia. "Moçambique e o Índico: a circulação de saberes e práticas de cura." *MÉTIS: história & cultura* 10, no. 19 (2012).

Rodrigues, Jaime. "Ferro, trabalho e conflito: os africanos livres na Fábrica de Ipanema." *História Social,* no. 4/5 (1997/1998): 29–42.

Rosental, Paul-André. "Construir o 'macro' pelo 'micro': Fredrik Barth e a 'microhistória.'" In Jacques Revel (org.), *Jogos de escalas,* 151–172. 1998.

Roy, Christopher, Jean-Baptiste Kientega, Jacob Bamogo, and Abdoulaye Bamogo. *From Iron Ore to Iron Hoe: Smelting Iron in Africa.* United States: CustomFlix, DVD, 2005. Part of the DVD's content is available online: https://www.youtube.com/watch?v=RuCnZClWwpQ. Accessed March 15, 2016.

Rudé, George. *A multidão na história: estudo dos movimentos populares na França e Inglaterra, 1730–1748.* Translated by Waltensir Dutra. Rio de Janeiro: Campus, 1991.

Russell-Wood, A. J. R. "Através de um prisma africano: uma nova abordagem ao estudo da diáspora africana no Brasil colonial," *Tempo,* no. 12 (2001).

Russell-Wood, A. J. R. *Escravizados e Libertos no Brasil Colonial.* Translated by Maria Beatriz Medina. Rio de Janeiro: Civilização Brasileira, 2005.

Salazar, Luis Miguel Díez de. "La industria del hierro en Guipúzcoa (siglos XIII–XVI) (Aportación al estudio de la industria urbana)." In *La Ciudad Hispánica*, Editorial de la Universidad Complutense, 251–276. 1985.

Saldanha, Antonio de Vasconcelos. *As capitanias. O regime senhorial na expansão ultramarina portuguesa*. Funchal: Centro de Estudos de História do Atlântico, 1992.

Santos, Antonio Cesar de Almeida. "O 'mecanismo político' pombalino e o povoamento da América portuguesa na segunda metade do século XVIII." *Revista de História Regional* 15, no. 1 (2010).

Santos, Catarina Madeira. *Um governo "polido" para Angola. Reconfigurar dispositivos de domínio (1750–c.1800)*. Dissertation (PhD in History). Lisbon: Faculdade de Ciências Sociais e Humanas da Universidade Nova de Lisboa, 2005.

Santos, Catarina Madeira. "Entre deux droits, les Lumières en Angola (1750–v. 1800)." *Annales. Histoire Sciences Sociales*, no. 4 (2005): 817–848.

Santos, Catarina Madeira. "Escrever o poder os autos de vassalagem e a vulgarização da escrita entre as elites africanas Ndembu." *Revista de História*, no. 155 (2006).

Santos, Catarina Madeira. "Luanda: A Colonial City between Africa and the Atlantic, Seventeenth and Eighteenth Centuries." In Liam M. Brockey (coord.), *Portuguese Colonial Cities in the Early Modern World, Empires and the Making of the Modern World, 1650–2000*. Farnham, England: Ashgate, 2008.

Santos, Catarina Madeira, and Ana Paula Tavares. *Africae Monumenta: a apropriação da escrita pelos Africanos: volume I – Arquivo Caculo Cacahenda*. Lisbon: Instituto de Investigação Científica Tropical, 2002.

Santos, Elaine Ribeiro dos. *Barganhando sobrevivências: os trabalhadores centro-africanos na expedição de Henrique de Carvalho (1884–1888)*. Thesis (Master's in History). São Paulo: Universidade de São Paulo, 2010.

Santos, Maria Emília Madeira. *Viagens de exploração terrestre dos portugueses em África*. Second ed. Lisbon: Centro de Estudos de História e Cartografia Antiga, 1988.

Santos, Nívia Pombo Cirne dos. *O Palácio de Queluz e o mundo ultramarino: circuitos Ilustrados. (Portugal, Brasil e Angola, 1796–1803)*. Dissertation (PhD). Instituto de Ciências Humanas e Filosofia, Universidade Federal Fluminense, 2013.

Santos, Telma Gonçalves. *Comércio de tecidos europeus e asiáticos na África Centro-Ocidental: fraudes e contrabando no terceiro quartel do século XVIII*. Thesis (Master's). Universidade de Lisboa, 2014.

Schwartz, Stuart. *Implicit Understandings. Observing, Reporting, and Reflecting on the Encounters between Europeans and Other Peoples in the Early Modern Era*. Cambridge: Cambridge University Press, 1994.

Sebestyén, Eva. "Legitimation through Landcharters in Ambundu Villages, Angola." In *Perspektiven afrikanistischer Forschung. Beiträge zur Linguistik, Ethnologie, Geschichte, Philosophie und Literatur. X. Afrikanistentag*, edited by Thomas Bearth, Wilhelm J.G. Möhlig, Beat Sottas, and Edgar Suter, 363–378. n.p., 1993.

Sebestyén, Eva. "Os 'arquivos' de *sobas* Ambundo: um caso transcultural dos testamentos em Angola." In *Actas do IV Curso de Verão da Ericeira. População: encontros e desencontros no espaço português*, 51–74. n.p., 2003.

Sebestyén, Eva. "O contexto cultural dos marcos de terrenos nas aldeias Ambundu/ Angola." *Africana Studia*, no. 24 (2015): 91–106.

Sharpe, Jim. "History from Below." In *New Perspectives on Historical Writing*, edited by Peter Burke. The Pennsylvania State University Press, 1992.

Schimidt, P. R., ed. *The Culture and Technology of African Iron Production*. Gainesville: University Press of Florida, 1996.

Schleumer, Fabiana. "Recriando Áfricas: presença negra na São Paulo colonial." *Histórica – Revista Eletrônica do Arquivo Público do Estado de São Paulo*, no. 46 (2011).

Schoenbrun, D. L. *A Green Place, A Good Place: Agrarian Change, Gender, and Social Identity in the Great Lakes Region to the 15th Century*. Portsmouth: Heinemann, 1998.

Simões, Antonio Augusto Costa. *Topografia Médica das Cinco Vilas e Arega: ou dos concelhos de Chão de Couce e Maçãs de D. Maria em 1848* [1860]. Second ed. Coimbra: Minerva, 2003.

Silva, Alberto da Costa e. "Apresentação à segunda edição." *Revista do IHGB*, no. 427 (2005).

Silva, Alberto da Costa e. *A manilha e o libambo. A África e a escravidão, de 1500 a 1700*. Second ed. Rio de Janeiro: Nova Fronteira, 2011.

Silva, Andrée Mansuy-Diniz (dir.), and D. Rodrigo de Sousa Coutinho. *Textos políticos, econômicos e financeiros, 1783–1811*. Lisbon: Banco de Portugal, 1993, t. I and II.

Silva, Andrée Mansuy-Diniz. *Portrait d'un homme d'État: D. Rodrigo de Souza Coutinho, Comte de Linhares 1755–1812*, vol. I and II. Lisbon; Paris: Centre Culturel Calouste Gulbenkian – Comissão Nacional para as Comemorações dos Descobrimentos Portugueses, 2002.

Silva, Daniel Domingues da. *Crossroads: Slave Frontiers of Angola, c. 1780–1867*. Dissertation (PhD). Emory University, 2011.

Silva, Fabiano Gomes da. *Pedra e Cal, os construtores em Vila Rica no século XVIII (1730–1800)*. Thesis (Master's). Belo Horizonte: Universidade Federal de Minas Gerais, 2007.

Silva, José Gentil. "En Afrique portugaise : L'Angola au XVIIIe siècle." *Annales. Histoire, Sciences Sociales*, 14ème année, no. 3 (1959): 571–580.

Silva, Juliana Ribeiro da. *Homens de ferro. Os ferreiros na África-central no século XIX*. São Paulo: Alameda, 2011.

Simon, William Joel. *Scientific Expeditions in the Portuguese Overseas Territories (1783–1808)*. Lisbon: Instituto de Investigação Científica Tropical, 1983.

Slenes, Robert. *Na Senzala, uma Flor. Esperanças e recordações na formação da família escravista*. Second ed. Campinas: Editora da Unicamp, 2014.

Slenes, Robert. "L'Arbre Nsanda replanté: cultes d'affliction Kongo et identité des esclaves de plantation dans le Brésil du Sud-Est (1810–1888)." *Cahiers du Brésil Contemporain*, no. 67/68 (2007, partie II): 217–313.

Slenes, Robert. "Trocas culturais no 'rio Atlântico': Angola no auge do trato de escravizados." *Afro-Ásia* 49 (2014): 365–378.

Soares, Mariza de Carvalho. *Devotos da cor: identidade étnica, religiosidade e escravidão no Rio de Janeiro, século XVIII*. Rio de Janeiro: Civilização Brasileira, 2000.

Soares, Mariza de Carvalho. "Trocando Galanteria: A diplomacia do comércio de escravizados, Brasil-Daomé, 1810–1812." *Afro-Ásia* 49 (2014): 229–271.

Sousa, Ana Madalena Trigo de. "Uma tentativa de fomento industrial na Angola setecentista: a 'Fábrica do Ferro' de Nova Oeiras (1766–1772)." *Africana Studia*, no. 10 (2007): 291–308.

Sousa, Ana Madalena Trigo de. *D. Francisco de Sousa Coutinho em Angola: Reinterpretação de um Governo 1764–1772*. Thesis (Master's in History). Funchal/ Lisbon: Universidade de Nova Lisboa, 1996.

Souza Júnior, José Alves de. "Negros da terra e/ou negros da Guiné: trabalho, resistência e repressão no Grão-Pará no período do Diretório." *Afro-Ásia* 45 (2013): 173–211.

Souza, Marina de Mello e. *Além do Visível. Poder, catolicismo e comércio no Congo e Angola, séculos XVI e XVII*. São Paulo: Edusp, 2018.

Tavares, Aurélio de Lyra. *A Engenharia militar portuguesa na construção do Brasil*. Rio de Janeiro: Editora Biblioteca do Exército, 2000.
Thompson, E. P. *A miséria da teoria ou um planetário de erros. Uma crítica ao pensamento de Althusser.* Translated by Waltensir Dutra. Rio de Janeiro: Zahar, 1981.
Thompson, E. P. *Costumes em comum*. São Paulo: Companhia das Letras, 1998.
Thornton, John K. "The Slave Trade in Eighteenth-Century Angola: Effects of Demographic Structure." *Canadian Journal of African Studies* 14, no. 3 (1980): 417–427.
Thornton, John K. *The Kingdom of Kongo: Civil War and Transition, 1641–1718*. Madison: The University of Wisconsin, 1983.
Thornton, John K. "The Development of an African Catholic Church in the Kingdom of Kongo, 1491–1750." *The Journal of African History*. Cambridge University Press, 1985.
Thornton, John K. "Art of War in Angola, 1575–1686." *Comparative Studies in Society and History* 30, no. 2 (1988).
Thornton, John K. "Legitimacy and Political Power: Queen Njinga. 1624–1663." *The Journal of African History* 32, no. 1 (1991): 25–40.
Thornton, John K. *Africa and the Africans in the Making of the Atlantic World 1400–1680*. Cambridge: Cambridge University Press, 1992.
Thornton, John K. "The Regalia of the Kingdom of Kongo, 1491–1895." In *Kings of Africa: Art and Authority in Central Africa*, edited by E. Beumers and P. Koloss, 56–63. Maastricht: Foundation Kings of Africa, 1992.
Thornton, John K. "As guerras civis no Congo e o tráfico de escravizados: a história e a demografia de 1718 a 1844 revisitadas." *Estudos Afro-Asiáticos*, no. 32 (1997): 55–74.
Thornton, John K. *The Kongolese Saint Anthony. Dona Beatriz Kimpa Vita and the Anthonian Movement, 1684–1706*. Cambridge University Press, 1998.
Thornton, John K. "Portuguese-African Relations, 1500–1750." In Jay A. Levenson (org.), *Encompassing the Globe. Portugal and the World in the 16th and 17th Centuries. Essays*, 57–65. Washington, DC: Smithsonian Institution, 2007.
Thornton, John K. "Africa and Abolitionism." In *Who Abolished Slavery? Slave Revolt and Abolitionism: A Debate with João Pedro Marques*, edited by Seymour Drescher and Pieter Emmer. New York: Berghahn Books, 2010.
Thiong'o, Ngugiwa. *Something Torn and New: An African Renaissance*. New York: Basic Civitas, 2009.
Thomaz, Luís Filipe. *De Ceuta a Timor.* Lisbon: Difel, 1994.
Vansina, Jan. "Long-Distance Trade-Routes in Central Africa." *The Journal of African History* 3, no. 3 (1962): 375–390.
Vansina, Jan. *Kingdoms of the Savanna*. Madison: Wisconsin University Press, 1966.
Vansina, Jan. "Portuguese vs Kimbundu: Language Use in the Colony of Angola (1575–c. 1845)." *Bulletin des Séances de l'Académie Royal e des Sciences d'Outre-Mer* 47, no. 3 (2001): 267–281.
Vansina, Jan. *How Societies are Born: Governance in West Central Africa Before 1600*. Charlottesville: University of Virginia Press, 2004.
Vansina, Jan. "Ambaca Society and the Slave Trade c. 1760–1845." *The Journal of African History* 46, no. 1 (2005): 1–27.
Vansina, Jan. "Linguistic Evidence for the Introduction of Ironworking in Bantu-Speaking Africa." *History in Africa* 33 (2006): 321–361.
Varela, Alex Gonçalves Varela. *"Juro-lhe pela honra de bom vassalo e bom português": Filosofo Natural e Homem Público – Uma análise das Memórias Científicas do Ilustrado José Bonifácio de Andrada e

Silva (1780–1819). Thesis (Master's in History). Campinas: Universidade Estadual de, Campinas, 2001.

Vansina, Jan. *Atividades científicas na "bela e bárbara" capitania de São Paulo (1796–1823)*. Dissertation (PhD). Campinas: Instituto de Geociências da Universidade Estadual de Campinas, 2005.

Vaz, Francisco A. L. *Instrução e Economia: as ideias econômicas no discurso da Ilustração portuguesa (1746–1820)*. Lisbon: Colibri, 2002.

Venâncio, José Carlos. *A Economia de Luanda e hinterland no século XVIII. Um estudo de sociologia histórica*. Lisbon: Editorial Estampa, 1996.

Viana, Larissa Moreira. *O Idioma da Mestiçagem: as irmandades de pardos na América Portuguesa*. Campinas, SP: Editora da UNICAMP, 2007.

Villalta, Luiz Carlos. "As origens intelectuais e políticas da Inconfidência Mineira." In M. E. L. de Resende and L. C. Villalta (orgs.), *As Minas Setecentistas 2*, 579–580. Belo Horizonte: Autêntica; Companhia do Tempo, 2007.

Vogel, J. O. (ed.). *Ancient African Metallurgy: The Sociocultural Context*. Walnut Creek: Aka Mira Press, 2000.

Volavka, Zdenka. *Crown and Ritual. The Royal Insignia of Ngoyo*. Toronto; Buffalo; London: University of Toronto Press Incorporated, 1998.

White, Luise. *The Comforts of Home: Prostitution in Colonial Nairobi*. Chicago: University of Chicago Press, 1990.

Windmuller-Luna, Kristen D. *Building Faith: Ethiopian Art and Architecture during the Jesuit Interlude, 1557–1632*. Dissertation (PhD). Princeton University, 2016.

Wissenbach, Maria Cristina Cortez. "Ares e azares da aventura ultramarina: matéria médica, saberes endógenos e transmissão nos circuitos do Atlântico luso-afro-americano." In Leila Mezan Algranti and Ana Paula Megiani (org.), *O império por escrito: formas de transmissão da cultura letrada no mundo ibérico séculos XVI–XIX*, 375–394. São Paulo: Alameda, 2009.

Xavier, Ângela Barreto. "O orientalismo católico. Rotinas do saber na Goa da época moderna." In *Conferência no Simpósio Internacional Novos Mundos – Neue Welten. Portugal e a época dos Descobrimentos*. Berlin: Deutsches Historisches Museum, 2006.

Zequini, Anicleide. *Arqueologia de uma fábrica de ferro: Morro de Araçoiaba, séculos XVI–XVIII*. Dissertation (PhD in Archeology). São Paulo: USP, 2006.

Zeron, Carlos Alberto. *Pombeiros e tangomaos, intermediários do tráfico de escravizados na África – século XVI*. São Paulo: Centro Virtual de Estudos Históricos/USP, n.d.

Glossary

Banza: According to Vansina, *mbanza* "or 'capitals' were the homes of the main territorial chiefs, but also included several leaders of kinship groups and their followers." Jan Vansina, "Ambaca Society and the Slave Trade c. 1760–1845." *The Journal of African History* 46, no. 1 (2005): 8.

Cubata: In Kimbundu, *kubhata* means at home. According to Governor Miguel de Melo, *cubatas* were "huts made of straw." Carta de Miguel Antonio de Melo, governador do Reino de Angola, para Rodrigo de Sousa Coutinho, secretário de Estado da Marinha e do Ultramar. São Paulo de Assunção de Luanda, April 30, 1798. *Arquivos de Angola* 1, no. 6: 325.

Enseque: *Enzeque* was a "sack made of bark fiber from the baobab tree." Beatrix Heintze, *Fontes para a História de Angola do século XVII. Estudos sobre Fontes, Métodos e História.* Luanda: Kilombelombe, 2007.

Futa: From the Kimbundo *mfuta*, to pay. "In Kikongo, *nfuta* is a gift, an offering that inferior people give to their superiors as a demonstration of their recognition of their superiority, in the manner of a caretaker to the landlord; a gift voluntarily offered to a superior as an expression of devotion." Beatrix Heintze, *Fontes para a História de Angola do século XVII. Memórias, relações e outros manuscritos da coletânea documental de Fernão Sousa (1622–1635)*, 426 and 437. Stuttgart: Steiner-Verlag-Wiesbaden-Gmbh, 1985.

Kilamba: From the Kimbundo, a person with certain responsibilities. Pl. *ilamba*. According to Virgílio Coelho, it was a priest "in charge of placating the fury of nature's genii." Virgílio Coelho, *Em busca de Kàbàsà. Uma tentativa de explicação da estrutura político-administrativa do reino de Ndòngò*, 161. Luanda: Kilombelombe, 2010. The *kilamba* is described by Cadornega as a "captain of the Black War." The military officer also associated this chieftainship to a foreign origin and its continuous political and economic growth in the region to their military skills. They were "hated" by the *sobas* because, when they settled in their lands, they became spies who reported everything to the Portuguese. Antonio de Oliveira Cadornega, *História das Guerras Angolanas (1680)*. Annotated and revised by José Matias Delgado, 246. Lisbon: Agência-Geral do Ultramar, 1972, v. I. In *Notícias do fortress de Ambaca*, we find something to that effect: the *kilamba* and the *kimbar*, both of them agents of the Black War, owned no land, they only lived in "part of the *sobas*' lands." *Notícias do presídio de Ambaca*, January 1798. IHGB/PADAB, DL 32.4. In his glossary, Heintze defines *Kilamba* as "an African officer in the Black War who was particularly trusted by the Portuguese." Beatrix Heintze,

Fontes para a História de Angola do século XVII, 126. In *Livro dos Baculamentos*, the *ilamba* appear as tax collectors from the *sobas*. Aida Freudenthal and Selma Pantoja (eds.), *Livro dos Baculamentos: que os sobas deste Reino de Angola pagam a Sua Majestade (1630)*. Luanda: Ministério da Cultura e Arquivo Nacional de Angola, 2013, 32. Jan Vansina and Roquinaldo Ferreira identified these chiefs as important agents of the trade of enslaved people. Jan Vansina, "Ambaca Society and the Slave Trade c. 1760 – 1845," 8; Roquinaldo Ferreira, *Cross-Cultural Exchange in the Atlantic World. Angola and Brazil during the Era of the Slave Trade*, 59. New York: Cambridge University Press, 2012.

Kimbanda: *Kimbanda* or *nganga* was "the supreme or principal priest of the cult of nature's spirits." Virgílio Coelho, *Em busca de Kàbàsà*, 2010, 161 and 162; 284 – 287.

Kimbari: The *imbari* were Africans under obligation, "through a vassalage agreement with their *soba*, to do military service for the Portuguese. They made up the African auxiliary army, the Black War, and were under the orders of the captains of Massangano, Cambambe, or Ambaca." Beatrix Heintze, *Fontes para a História de Angola do século XVII*, 126. In 1798, Governor Miguel Antonio de Melo, defined the *imbari* as "free or freed Negros who were bound to white people." Carta do governador Miguel Antonio de Melo para Rodrigo de Sousa Coutinho. São Paulo de Assunção de Luanda, April 30, 1798. *Arquivos de Angola* I, no. 6 (Mar. 1936): 325.

Kitombe ou **Kitome:** A great priest. Virgílio Coelho, *Em busca de Kàbàsà*, 161 and 162; 284 – 287.

Libata: "small settlements belonging to a chief and inhabited only by relatives or dependents of a single leader, who was often also the head or *lemba* of his matrilineage." Jan Vansina, "Ambaca Society and the Slave Trade c. 1760 – 1845," 8.

Luanda: From the Kimbundo, tax. It was paid at first to the *ngola*, and during the Portuguese domination, to the representatives of the king of Portugal, the governors and *capitães-mores*. Aida Freudenthal and Selma Pantoja (eds.), *Livro dos Baculamentos*, 36.

Makota: Plural of *kota*. By analyzing seventeenth-century sources, Beatrix Heintze defines *kota* as "the oldest person of a lineage, a counselor of the *sobas* of the Mbundu and the king of Ndongo." Beatrix Heintze, *Fontes para a História de Angola do século XVII*, 120.

Ndembu: "A set of small African political formations, the *dembo* or *ndembu* were located in northern Angola, along the Kwanza River, probably before the seventeenth century." Catarina Madeira Santos, "Escrever o poder: os autos de vassalagem e a vulgarização da escrita entre as elites africanas *Ndembu*," *Revista de História*, n. 155, 2nd sem. (2006): 82.

Nganga: see Kimbanda.

Ngolambole: *Ngólà à Mbòle*, the commander of the *ngola*'s guards. Virgílio Coelho, *Em busca de Kàbàsà*, 284–287.

Pumbeiro: "The Portuguese of Angola called *pumbo* (*mpumbu*) the markets of some importance in Kongo, where they purchased goods and enslaved people. (...) In the time of Fernão de Sousa, *pombeiro* designated an African merchant in the hinterlands, who acquired for the Portuguese, in the official markets of Southwest Central Africa, mostly enslaved people, but also ivory, in exchange for textiles that their Portuguese employer on the coast gave them on credit. Apparently, the *pombeiros* were often trusted enslaved men. Some of them might have been mestizos. But the term *pombeiro* also referred to any merchant in the hinterlands. Beatrix Heintze, *Fontes para a História de Angola do século XVII*, 124. In West Africa, the terms *tangomaos* and *lançados* were also used to designate intermediaries in the trade of enslaved people. According to Zeron, the difference with the *pumbeiros* was that the *tangomaos* did not have permission from the Crown to trade in the interior. Carlos Alberto Zeron, *Pombeiros e tangomaos, intermediários do tráfico de escravizados na África – século XVI*. São Paulo: Centro Virtual de Estudos Históricos/USP, n.d.

Quipaca: "Fortifications built with stakes," "wattle and daub ramparts." And also, "large enclosures of thick, high stakes forming thick walls, a kind of fortification with which they protect their villages." Elias Alexandre da Silva Correa, *História de Angola*, v. I, 307, 318. Henrique Dias de Carvalho, *O Jagado de Cassange. Província de Angola*, 98. Lisbon: Typographia de Christóvão Augusto Rodrigues, 1898.

Soba: The local chiefs under the dominion of African kings or the king of Portugal when they became vassals of the Portuguese Crown. Beatrix Heintze, *Fontes para a História de Angola do século XVII. Memórias, relações e outros manuscritos da coletânea documental de Fernão Sousa (1622–1635)*, 127. Stuttgart: Steiner-Verlag-Wiesbaden-Gmbh, 1985. According to Vansina, they occupied leadership positions in the "monocephalic chiefdoms," which were the *sobados*. Jan Vansina, *How Societies Are Born: Governance in West Central Africa before 1600*, 196. Charlottesville: University of Virginia Press, 2004.

Sanzala: "*Sanzala*, or *sanza*, of intermediate size, contained relatives and dependents of its leader, who was a small *soba* or a wealthy patron (*mwadi*) whom the Portuguese called *morador* [resident]." Jan Vansina, "Ambaca Society and the Slave Trade c. 1760–1845," 8.

Tandala: The *tándàla* was the third most important authority after the *ngola* and the *ngólàmbòle* (*Ngólà à Mbòle*), the guards' commander. The *tandala* was the "rearguard commander," highly revered during peacetime, and "during war his powers are greatly increased." The *tandala* is also considered the *sobas*' leader. Virgílio Coelho, *Em busca de Kàbàsà*, 284–287. Cadornega assigns one more function to the *tandala:* "he is the interpreter and it was a matter of great authority to see one of these men, whom the gentiles considered an idol, kneeling at the governor's feet in the Dossel room, when a *soba* came to be with him as an interpreter." Antonio de Oliveira Cadornega, *História das Guerras Angolanas (1680)*, v. I, p. 185.

Vestir: A way to impose a forced exchange, introduced by the Portuguese to obtain enslaved people from the *sobas*. Aida Freudenthal, Selma Pantoja (ed.), *Livro dos Baculamentos: que os sobas deste Reino de Angola pagam a Sua Majestade (1630)*. Luanda: Ministério da Cultura e Arquivo Nacional de Angola, 2013.

Index

Ambundu   1–3, 6, 8–10, 15–17, 19 f., 22, 25, 27–30, 33, 41, 44 f., 55, 57, 59, 61, 70–72, 83, 88–92, 101, 105, 109, 126, 132, 135 f., 139, 141, 205, 210, 215 f., 218 f., 226–228, 231, 233, 239, 249, 252, 254, 286, 288, 290, 297 f., 300, 309–311, 313, 315

Black War   9, 18, 21, 28, 35, 68, 82, 91 f., 97, 104, 341 f.
blacksmith   10, 12, 17, 28 f., 51 f., 54–57, 59, 97 f., 113, 205–208, 210 f., 213, 217, 222, 226, 234, 245, 252, 271, 301, 310 f.
blacksmiths   3 f., 14, 17 f., 21, 27 f., 30, 32, 34, 40, 49, 51 f., 54, 56 f., 59, 61, 77 f., 96, 98, 102, 104, 107 f., 122, 126, 132 f., 139, 205–218, 222, 227–229, 231 f., 236, 239, 241, 245, 247, 249–253, 257, 262, 264, 271, 287–291, 293 f., 296–302, 309–311, 313, 315 f.
blacksmiths of Ilamba   96, 289, 301
Biscayan blacksmiths   231–241

Cadornega, Antonio de Oliveira   1, 3, 10, 39, 44, 48, 61, 68–70, 72 f., 78, 92, 99 f., 206, 208, 212, 341, 344
Cavazzi   28, 32, 47, 74, 76, 99 f., 207 f.

Elias Alexandre da Silva Correa   3 f., 10 f., 21, 27, 32, 34, 36–38, 40, 44, 54, 82, 100 f., 208, 257, 277, 343
enslaved   2–7, 9–11, 14 f., 17–19, 21–23, 25–40, 42–63, 47, 69, 71–73, 81, 88, 94, 96 f., 100–103, 106–109, 123, 133, 135 f., 211 f., 228, 230, 252, 256, 260–262, 266, 269–273, 284, 291, 293–295, 297, 300 f., 309 f., 312, 314 f., 342–344

forced labor 142–169
fortress   2–4, 8 f., 13, 16, 21, 30, 33, 35–37, 40 f., 43, 49–51, 53, 59–61, 63 f., 68–70, 72 f., 75–77, 83 f., 87 f., 90, 93, 104, 116 f., 125, 134, 138 f., 212, 261, 280, 282 f., 285, 295, 301, 304 f., 341

fortresses   4, 8, 10, 12, 41, 49, 58, 65, 104, 109, 116
Francisco Inocêncio de Sousa Coutinho   1, 3–7, 9, 11 f., 16, 13, 15, 18, 20, 21–25, 27, 29–32, 34, 36–41, 43 f., 46, 49, 27, 51–59, 60, 64, 66 f., 69, 72, 77 f., 82 f., 87 f., 91, 93, 96, 104–106, 109, 111, 113 f., 116, 118, 118 f., 121, 122 f., 125, 129, 131–134, 134 f, 136, 138–141, 205, 209, 212–214, 218–220, 222, 227–229, 231 f., 233, 239 f., 242, 245, 247 f., 251, 253–255, 257–263, 266 f., 269, 273–276, 284 f., 283–287, 290–298, 300, 305, 307 f., 311–313, 341 f.

imbari   1, 6, 9 f., 13, 15, 17 f., 21, 27–29, 30 f, 65 f., 68, 70, 72, 91 f., 214, 288, 307, 314, 342
insignia   26, 56, 61, 68, 99, 101
iron objects   97 f., 101

José Alvares Maciel   118, 141, 213, 222, 223, 226, 228, 248, 249, 282–287, 289–291, 299–302

kimbari   1, 28

land conflict   74–94

Mbangu kya Tambwa   17–20, 23, 38, 41, 68, 78–80, 82, 98, 109, 210, 252, 306

Natural History 275-283
Ndembu   8, 22, 22 f., 26, 36–38, 43, 46, 47, 60, 63, 89, 91, 100, 100 f., 106, 212, 250, 342
Ndongo   1, 6 f., 9, 16, 22, 25, 27–31, 35, 37, 44, 47 f., 51, 56, 62–64, 68, 70, 74 f., 81, 96, 98, 206 f., 295, 342
ngola   9, 17, 25, 27 f., 31, 44, 47 f., 56, 61, 63, 66, 70, 74 f., 98 f., 101, 304, 342–344
Novo Belém   4, 72, 73, 76, 83, 92, 133, 134, 137, 139, 158, 159, 209, 287, 298, 305, 316
Nova Oeiras   1–5, 7, 9–18, 20–22, 24–45, 49–51, 53, 55–61, 63, 65 f., 68 f., 72–74, 76 f.,

82, 84, 90, 92 f., 102, 109–125, 131–134, 137–141, 206, 208–214, 216, 218–224, 228 f., 233, 235 f., 239–242, 246–250, 253–269, 273 f., 276, 283–298, 300 f., 305, 307–314, 316

São Paulo (Colonial Brazil) 263-274
slavery 187-191
smelter 3, 11–13, 21, 51 f., 55, 205, 208–210, 213, 215–218, 226, 243, 245, 255 f., 268, 271, 301, 310 f., 315
smelters 3 f., 13 f., 18, 21, 26, 28, 32, 34, 51 f., 55 f., 59, 61, 63, 77 f., 80, 102, 104, 108, 132, 139, 205, 208–211, 213–218, 221–223, 226–228, 231–236, 239–242, 246 f., 249–256, 264, 269, 271, 285 f., 296–301, 303, 309–311, 315
soba 1, 10 f., 17 f., 21, 27 f., 33–39, 41, 43, 50, 59, 61 f., 64, 66, 68, 70, 76–79, 81, 83 f., 90–92, 98 f., 117, 137, 139, 207, 213, 215 f., 218, 250, 252, 342–344
sobas 1–31, 33–41, 43-48, 50, 54, 56–70, 72–74, 76–78, 80, 82–93, 99, 109, 139, 210 f., 213, 228, 256, 282, 288–290, 297 f., 300 f., 304–308, 310, 314 f., 341 f., 344

sobado 17, 19, 33, 35 f., 38, 45 f., 68, 70, 72, 79, 89 f., 211, 301
sobados 1–4, 6, 9, 14, 17, 19–22, 25 f., 30 f., 35, 37, 39–44, 49, 53, 56 f., 60 f., 64–67, 72, 74, 90, 97, 113, 115, 117, 140, 289, 298, 301, 304, 308, 343

technique 95, 227, 231, 233, 241 f., 245, 247 f., 254, 259, 296
techniques 16–18, 25, 78, 80, 96, 98, 111, 132, 137, 141, 207, 214–216, 220, 228, 230–232, 239 f., 243, 247, 249, 251 f., 255 f., 271 f., 276–278, 282, 286, 290–292, 297 f., 300–303, 306, 310 f., 315

Vassalagem 56-73

weapon 52, 104, 108
weapons 2, 8, 18, 21, 29, 39, 54, 56, 82, 96 f., 103–105, 107–109, 111, 212, 244, 250, 284, 286, 310
women 26, 27, 29, 47-49, 51, 54, 70, 71, 79, 94, 101, 133, 134-136, 138, 140, 155, 184, 187, 215, 217, 305

www.ingramcontent.com/pod-product-compliance
Lightning Source LLC
Chambersburg PA
CBHW061927220426
43662CB00012B/1831